Infants
and Toddlers
Development and Program Planning

Penny Low Deiner

University of Delaware

Harcourt Brace College Publishers

Fort Worth   Philadelphia   San Diego   New York   Orlando   Austin   San Antonio
Toronto   Montreal   London   Sydney   Tokyo

Publisher	Christopher P. Klein
Senior Acquisitions Editor	Jo-Anne Weaver
Developmental Editor	Tracy Napper
Senior Project Editor	Charles J. Dierker
Assistant Manager of Production	Annette Dudley Wiggins
Assistant Manager of Art and Design	Linda Wooton
Cover Photography	Annette Coolidge, Diane Watts Photography
Cover Collage	Phil Henslee

ISBN: 0-15-502064-1

Library of Congress Catalog Card Number: 96-75659

Address for Editorial Correspondence:
Harcourt Brace College Publishers, 301 Commerce Street, Suite 3700, Fort Worth, TX 76102.

Address for Orders:
Harcourt Brace & Company, 6277 Sea Harbor Drive, Orlando, FL 32887-6777. 1-800-782-4479, or 1-800-433-0001 (in Florida).

Harcourt Brace College Publishers may provide complimentary instructional aids and supplements or supplement packages to those adopters qualified under our adoption policy. Please contact your sales representative for more information. If as an adopter or potential user you receive supplements you do not need, please return them to your sales representative or send them to:

Attn: Returns Department
Troy Warehouse
465 South Lincoln Drive
Troy, MO 63379

Photo credits: Pat Childs—p. 10, 45, 87, 98, 121, 148, 166, 173, 197, 203, 216, 238, 259, 272, 287, 307, 352, 367, 373, 390, 400, 417, 431, 438, 444. Penny Deiner—p. 124, 187, 226, 228, 279, 317, 335, 348, 441, 465, 472, 481, 501. Jane Davidson—p. 254, 340, 456, 503. Helen Capadonno—p. 23. Harcourt Brace, p. 145.

Printed in the United States of America

6 7 8 9 0 1 2 3 4 5   039   10 9 8 7 6 5 4 3 2 1

To Pat Childs

My student, my teacher, my friend

This textbook was written for undergraduate courses on infant and toddler development and program planning. The goal of the book is to integrate a variety of knowledge bases in order to present a more holistic view of infants, toddlers, and two-year-olds. The book draws upon the fields of child development, early childhood education, early childhood special education, and family studies to provide information and theories about how infants and toddlers grow and develop. It also prepares students to use this knowledge to plan programs for infants and toddlers in a developmentally appropriate way, to increase their awareness of the joys and concerns that families have as they raise infants and toddlers, and to support their understanding of and communication with these families. All textbooks are greatly influenced by the author's beliefs and values and this book is no exception.

Application of Knowledge

The inclusion of both developmental theory and program planning reflects my belief that these two areas are inextricably linked. Although some individuals reading this book may actually have no expectations of working in early care and education, I believe that the application of knowledge is a necessary part of learning regardless of whether they choose such a career.

Viewing Infants and Toddlers in the Context of their Environments

Because infants and toddlers cannot be studied in a vacuum, this book has more information on infants and toddlers in the context of families and society than is normally provided. Current research emphasizes the systems approach and the transactional aspects of development. Working with families and understanding them is important because early-care and education professionals must learn to work with families and to view infants and toddlers as actors and reactors within their families.

Inclusion

The movement to include children with disabilities, especially infants and toddlers, in regular early-care and education settings requires that all developmentalists have some knowledge of atypical growth and development and some techniques for including these infants and toddlers in care settings. Information about infants and toddlers with disabilities and about those at risk provide students with the knowledge and skill to include these infants and toddlers in their program planning.

Knowledge about delayed and atypical patterns of development is also helpful in the identification of children with disabilities. Early identification provides the best hope for the future welfare of many of these children.

Cultural Context and Competence

As we view infants in the context of their families and communities, we need to be aware of, acknowledge, and appreciate ethnic and cultural differences. More than older children, infants are dependent upon the communication of relevant adults for their well being. It is important that people who work with infants and toddlers have some awareness of differences and some competence in working with adults and families from various ethnic and cultural groups.

Changing Demographics and Social Issues

The ever-changing demographics of the United States affects the well-being of infants and toddlers, and it is difficult to understand a child's growth and development without knowledge of broader societal contexts. Issues such as child care, child abuse and neglect, the use of drugs and alcohol, poverty, poor nutrition, and the lack of prenatal care influence the well-being of infants. Many young children who live in environments that place them at risk spend a major portion of their day in early-care and education settings. And early-care and education professionals must be prepared to understand and work with these infants and toddlers and their families. The potential for positive intervention is high if students are prepared to work with this population.

Advocacy

The first thing that advocates for young children need is a strong knowledge base. I hope that this textbook provides students with that base and that it nudges them to utilize the experience in their own lives if they choose to have children, but also to help them see infants and toddlers as our nation's most valuable resource.

About the Book

One major issue that all authors face is how to organize a textbook. Books designed for parents are almost always organized around the age/stage concept, whereas textbooks generally look at processes such as motor, cognitive, and language development. This book utilizes both organizational structures. Part I—Developmental Processes—the major portion of the book, is organized by developmental areas. Part II—From Theory to Practice: Planning Programs and Activities for Infants and Toddlers—is organized by age.

Part I—Developmental Processes

Part I contains 12 chapters. The first chapter is an introduction to the field of infants and toddlers and it is followed by three chapters that focus on prenatal development, birth and the birthing process, and the newborn. The next six chapters focus on developmental domains: physical and motor development, sensation and perception, cognitive development, early communication and language development, social development, and emotional development. The two concluding chapters look at infants and toddlers in the context of their families. Chapter 11 looks at the family unit within the larger ecological system, and Chapter 12 focuses on techniques for collaborating with families.

Part II—From Theory to Practice: Planning Programs and Activities for Infants, Toddlers, and Twos

Part II links the developmental-theory base contained in the first part of the book with information on program planning and prototype activities. Chapter 13 looks at early-care and education settings: different types of settings, issues related to quality and cost, and the impact of child care on young children. The next six chapters are specifically devoted to planning for infants and toddlers and have been written in three pairs (a chapter on planning followed by a chapter on prototypical activities). They are divided by major developmental milestones: the nonmobile infants (birth through 8 months), crawlers and walkers (8 to 18 months), and toddlers and two-year-olds (18 to 36 months).

Although I am the sole author of this textbook, it could not have been completed without a strong support system. My family was a solid support for me: My husband remains my most critical editor, and our marriage has again survived the writing and editing process, and Paige, now sweet sixteen, provided anecdotes about the children she was babysitting and even allowed me to come and take pictures. Her "How's it going, Mom?" also provided much needed encouragement. And, Jamie and Michael, who are now living in San Francisco, faithfully inquired about my progress. I also want to acknowledge Harriet Ferguson and Lorna Wells for the unconditional support. I also want to thank Theresa Ford at Kid's Ketch for allowing me to loiter at her store to observe young children and their families, and for showing me the new "in" toys for infants and toddlers.

The University of Delaware Laboratory school, directed by Alice P. Eyman, was a valuable resource—particularly its teachers, Nadine Heim, Jane Davidson, and Nancy Edwards. Nadine allowed me to come into her classroom of toddlers and take pictures, and shared some of the trials and tribulations of teaching very young children. Jane willingly shared photographs with me and traded "author" stories. I also want to acknowledge two graduate students, Shawn Christianson and Joe O'Roark, for providing me with feedback on chapters in progress.

I particularly want to acknowledge Patricia A. Childs, whose progressive ideas continue to influence my thinking and awareness of the challenges that people with disabilities face and the skills that such children need to meet these challenges. In addition, she contributed many photographs and helped me select from the more than 1,500 negatives that we considered.

I owe special thanks to the reviewers of this manuscript, Alice Sterling Honig of Syracuse University, Anne Dorsey of the University of Cincinnati, and David Anderson of Bethel College. They not only provided valuable criticism, but also encouragement that the book was a worthy investment of both their time and mine. They made an extremely positive contribution to the final version of this book. I especially want to thank Jo-Anne Weaver, acquisitions editor, who initially piqued my interest in writing this book. The editors with whom I worked most closely at Harcourt Brace, Tracy Napper and Charlie Dierker, were both competent and interesting. They shared their editorial expertise while providing a parental perspective.

Table of Contents

Infants
and Toddlers

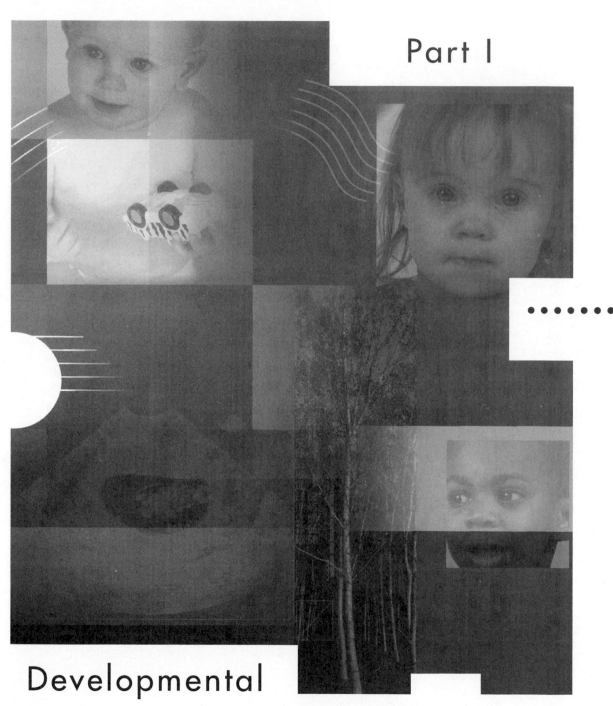

Part I

Developmental
Processes

Part I contains 12 chapters. The first chapter is an introduction to the field of infants and toddlers, which is followed by three chapters that focus on prenatal development, birth and the birthing process, and the newborn. These chapters focus on the study of infants and toddlers and the importance of the first three years of life in and of itself and as related to development throughout life. The impact of heredity and the environment on development before birth and the impact of the birthing process itself are presented in detail. Chapter 4, describing the newborn, highlights the infant and the reflexes and skills he brings to the world, as well as the transition to parenthood for both men and women.

The next six chapters focus on developmental domains: physical and motor development, sensation and perception, cognitive development, early communication and language development, social development, and emotional development.

Although different, Chapters 5 through 10 have a similar format. The first part of each chapter presents relevant theories and how they have guided research in each domain. The chapters then examine issues related to research in a particular domain. This is followed by a segment on developmental perspective, including atypical development. Finally, the chapters illustrate the domain in the context of the family and environment.

The last two chapters in Part I look at infants and toddlers in the context of their families. Chapter 11 examines the family as a unit with the particular tasks that all families must perform. The family is viewed as part of a larger ecological system. Vulnerable families are also discussed. The final chapter in Part I concentrates on techniques for collaborating with families.

Chapter 1

Why Study Infants and Toddlers?

This book brings together current research and theories about how infants and toddlers grow and develop, and applies that information to their early care and education settings. Although focusing on infant and toddler development, it views very young children in the context of their families and caregivers, and the society in which these families live. It looks at the challenges vulnerable families face as they raise infants and toddlers and the challenges society itself faces in helping all infants and toddlers attain their potential.

Why and How We Study Infant and Toddler Development

Think about yourself and why you are the way you are today and why others are different from you. When did this all begin? Last year? In elementary school? At birth? Or perhaps even before? Studying infants and how they grow and develop, we must start at the beginning—before birth. Studying infants in itself is a challenge! How do we know what infants know? They can't tell us with words, they can't bring what we request, they can't even point to a picture we show them.

Most of you have had some experience with infants, in addition to having been one yourself. You have watched them in grocery stores and shopping malls, perhaps you even baby-sat for one, you may want to have children or may already have one of your own. Most parents have infants without having taken a course on "infants and toddlers." These infants have survived and grown into adulthood. What is the difference then between caring for and loving infants and studying about them in a course? Don't women (and perhaps even men) intuitively just "know" what to do? Doesn't it come naturally?

3

Some of your friends may be astounded that you are actually taking a course on "BABIES." Much of what most people know about infants and toddlers is based on everyday knowledge, insight, and intuition. When parents need additional information, they consult with their friends or ask their parents. Some parents read books about child rearing, what toys are good for young children at specific ages, and even books on how to discipline their children. Others feel it is obvious: If a baby cries, see if she is wet or hungry. If you give a baby a toy that he does not play with, give him another. If the baby seems tired, put her to sleep. Above all else, just love them. All these ideas have some validity, but they are not really part of the scientific study of infants and toddlers. It clearly is important to love babies. However, love is not enough. You need knowledge and the ability to use and communicate that knowledge.

The term *infant* derives from a Latin word meaning "without speech." Some see infancy as the first year of life; others see it extending until 18 or even 24 months. This period is followed by toddlerhood, which again has broad definitions. Some view the toddler as the child from one to three years; others see "twos" as a distinctive age beyond toddlerhood. There are no agreed-on age-based definitions. Some scholars opt for a more functional definition, distinguishing between non-mobile infants (birth to approximately 8 months), crawlers and walkers (8 to 18 months), and toddlers and twos (18 to 36 months) as age groups (Bredekamp, 1987). In defining infancy, this text also takes a functional approach.

Prenatal development occurs during the nine months from conception to birth. Although not technically part of infancy, the impact of those months on later development is so great that it is generally considered part of the field. Increasingly, we are aware of the effect of the environment during the prenatal period of growth and development.

During the past three decades, the study of infancy has become a discipline of its own, as much as the study of adolescence has. Infants and toddlers are studied in many disciplines. Physicians and nurses are concerned with medical aspects of infants' health. Child development specialists focus on how the developing infant interacts with his world. Early-childhood educators are interested in developmentally appropriate practices for very young children; early-childhood special educators are interested in identifying infants and toddlers with developmental delays and in designing early intervention programs for them. Developmental psychologists are interested in discovering how infants perceive their world, and child psychologists and psychiatrists are concerned about infant mental health. Increasingly, individuals in advocacy groups, such as the Children's Defense Fund and foundations such as the Annie E. Casey Foundation and the Carnegie Corporation of New York, are advocating social policy changes that affect infants and toddlers. The study of infants and toddlers is many-faceted.

Historic Views of Infants and Toddlers

Childhood has not always been seen as a distinct period of development in the West. In medieval times, there were no separate child labor laws to protect children from working too hard, nor was there a juvenile justice system that viewed children differently from adults when they committed crimes. Early childhood was considered a "waiting" period. Young children had to grow and develop so they could take their place in the work force or be accepted into society. This happened at an early age, since there was no concept of adolescence. Viewed in the light of European society before the 1800s, the lack of interest in childhood in general is understandable. Infants and toddlers as a specific group of children received virtually no scholarly attention because of the following reasons:

- There was little knowledge of birth control, and women frequently had many children. Young children, especially for poor women, were often viewed as a burden.
- Infants frequently died, to the extent that some parents did not even name their infants until they were several months old and tried not to become attached to them.
- In wealthy families wet nurses (women with a young child or a child who had died, and hence had breast milk) were hired to feed and care for the infant until weaning or beyond.
- Unwanted, malformed, or disabled infants were frequently abandoned or killed.

Studies of early childhood were also affected by society's prevailing philosophies. In the Middle Ages, the most prevalent view was that of "original sin." Infants were born as sinners and the role of child rearing was to turn the sinful infant into a god-fearing, competent adult. The means of accomplishing this were often harsh. In the late 1800s, the English philosopher John Locke proposed another view. He felt that children were born like a "blank tablet," a *tabula rasa*. He believed that the experiences of young children influenced how they grew up and he encouraged parents to raise their children with the values they wanted them to have as adults. In the early 1900s, Jean-Jacques Rousseau moved the pendulum to the other side and proposed that infants were born inherently good. The role of child rearing, therefore, was to nurture the child and allow the "innate goodness" to grow.

As economic conditions in Europe improved and knowledge about health and disease increased in the nineteenth century, interest in infancy also increased. Although there were some isolated studies of infants in the late 1700s, it was not until the late 1800s that there was any sustained interest in studying infancy. That developing interest is documented in the form of detailed baby biographies, which were daily records of the activities of infants. These records were usually made by men about their infant sons. Some of the most famous were by Charles Darwin, the originator of the theory of evolution, and Wilhelm Preyer, a German physiologist.

Baby biographers recorded observations about an infant over time (much as one might keep a focused diary). It is partially through these observations that we first learned about the predictable stages infants go through as they master activities such as sitting, walking, or fine-motor activities (for example, modifying how they reach and grasp objects). However, these baby biographies did not solve the problem of generalizing information about any one infant to all infants. What if the observed infant's behavior was unusual in some way?

The need for more generalizable information was solved by the addition of descriptive studies of groups of children. Rather than study only one infant over time, this approach used groups of infants and focused on particular behaviors, or sequences of behavior, in an effort to both describe the developmental process and to establish when particular behaviors happened and in what order they occurred. Researchers wanted to know when the average baby sat alone, walked, and talked. They wanted to know how large average infants were at birth and how their height and weight changed as they grew and developed.

Early Studies of Infants and Toddlers

Most of the early descriptive studies focused on the physical and motor development of infants; there was little concern with social and emotional development. Many of the important studies in motor development were done in the 1920s, 1930s, and 1940s. Although we now know that infants acquire skills slightly earlier than researchers first thought, the patterns of development they found are still used as guidelines today.

Notable researchers included Mary Shirley (1933) who followed the motor development of 25 infants over the first two years of their lives. She was interested in seeing whether or not motor skills developed in the same order for all children and if some skills were prerequisites for others. She found that the sequence of motor development was invariant.

Arnold Gesell (1934) and his associates at Yale University used motion pictures, a new tool at that time, to analyze the components of early motor behavior. He divided the first year of infant motor behavior into four parts, each with a different emphasis: control over eye movements; control over head and arms; control over trunk and hands; and control over legs and feet as well as the thumb and forefinger (Barclay, 1985). He also emphasized the principle that developmental milestones build on each other. Both Gesell and Shirley concluded that motor development was primarily a matter of maturation rather than environment. Investigations of whether or not practice influenced the acquisition of motor skills was a logical follow-up to their studies.

During the 1930s and 1940s, Wayne Dennis (1941) and Myrtle McGraw (1943) studied the relationship between practice and maturation. Separately, both reached similar conclusions. Dennis studied infants who were not given the opportunity to practice skills such as sitting and standing. These infants were not able to perform these skills at the expected ages. However, with the opportunity to practice, they did develop these skills relatively quickly. McGraw tried to train children to master certain skills such as controlling their bladder or riding a tricycle earlier than expected. She concluded that practice was not effective until the child had sufficient maturation.

Descriptive studies served important practical purposes in the past and are still valued today. They also set the stage for one of the recurring issues in the field: the relative contribution of "nature versus nurture."

Exceptions to the early work on physical and motor development were found in the studies of Margaret Ribble, Rene Spitz, and John Bowlby. These researchers focused their attention on emotional aspects of development of infants in institutions. Children living in institutions had previously had a high mortality rate. Of 10,272 children admitted to a Dublin foundling home between 1775 and 1800, only 45 survived (Kessen, 1965). By the 1930s, more infants in institutions were living but were displaying an alarmingly high level of psychological disturbances.

Spitz (1945) undertook a large-scale study to compare infants at two institutions who experienced good medical care but very different conditions in the visiting patterns of their mothers, availability of toys, and visual stimulation. The "Nursery" was an institution for infants of delinquent females who were in a penal institution. Infants in the Nursery were fed and cared for by their mothers or had full-time mother substitutes. They had toys and could see what was going on around them from their cribs. These infants had IQ scores within the normal range and comparable to two control groups of noninstitutionalized infants. Follow-up studies found development to be within the normal range and after three and a half years all children were alive (Thompson & Grusec, 1970).

The "Foundling Home" was an institution for infants whose mothers could not support them. Infants in the Foundling Home had few toys, and, because sheets were hung over the crib rails to control germs, they could see little of what was going on around them. They were interacted with only at feeding time by busy nurses.

> They lay supine in their cots for so many months that hollows were worn into their mattresses and, by the time they were physically able to turn themselves in their cots (about 7 months of age), these hollows prevented them from doing so. Thus, at the age of 10 or 12 months, there were observed lying only on their backs and playing with the only toys they had—their hands and feet. (Thompson & Grusec, 1970)

Deprived of their mothers, toys, and visual stimulation, their IQs dropped dramatically by the end of their first year, and they displayed unusual reactions to strangers, ranging from extreme friendliness to blood-curdling screams. Despite impeccable hygiene, the infants were very susceptible to disease; many succumbed to a measles epidemic.

Conditions for infants at the "Foundling Home" improved. However, in a two-year follow-up study, Spitz (1946) found only a small proportion of the original infants alive. Those located displayed retarded physical development, toilet training, speech and self-help skills. The conditions experienced during the first year of life seemed to have produced irreversible effects. Spitz (1945) attributed the infants' condition to lack of human contact—a mother or mother substitute. Others felt the results could be attributed to lack of environmental stimulation, inherent differences in the two groups, respiratory problems based on inactivity, poor genetic background, poor prenatal care, and other causes (Pinneau, 1950).

Ribble (1944) studied 600 infants who were deprived of adequate "mothering" and described the undesirable and often fatal symptoms she described as "marasmus" or a wasting away of the body. Ribble, too, attributed the effects of institutionalization to maternal deprivation. Her data and theoretical treatment were also criticized.

Bowlby (1940, 1944) concluded that maternal deprivation before the age of 6 months was less detrimental than that occurring later. But if an infant lacked the opportunity to form attachments to a mother-figure during the first three years of life, if he was deprived of a mother-figure for a limited period of time, or if there were changes from one mother figure to another, the result would be an affectionless and psychopathic character (Thompson & Grusec, 1970).

These studies by Spitz, Ribble, and Bowlby caught the attention of other psychologists and the public, and laid the groundwork for an important line of research as well as some public policy changes.

From that point on, the study of infants continued to evolve. More recent studies use direct, systematic, controlled observation and experimentation as a way of answering questions about what infants and toddlers do, as opposed to using casual observation and intuition. Innovative research techniques and technological breakthroughs in the 1960s and 1970s revealed that infants are far more competent and capable than we had previously thought.

The pioneering work of researchers such as Robert Fantz (1963) and his "looking chamber," which involved a wooden structure that allowed the experimenter to present two visual displays on the ceiling above the infant's head ushered in a new phase. To determine the visual preference of infants the experimenter looked through a peephole at the infant's eyes. If the infant was fixating on one of the displays, the experimenter could see the reflection in the infant's eye and time how long the infant looked at each display. That is how we learned that very young infants prefer to look at vertical patterns of black and white stripes.

By today's standards, experiments such as the looking chamber may not seem very sophisticated, but they increased our knowledge about infants, and they paved the way for more experimental work in the field. Once it was determined that very young infants had preferences and were capable of learning, we began to wonder when they started to learn.

Current Research Trends and Issues

Current research helps us understand some of the issues in the field and the direction in which the field is moving. Some issues, such as concerns about heredity and environment and continuity and discontinuity, have been around a long time. Others have appeared more recently. Overall, there seems to be a movement toward applied research that focuses on prevention of adverse developmental outcomes, whether related to early care and education or to at-risk conditions. There is concern for optimizing conditions to help children realize their developmental potential (Ricciuti, 1992). The biological basis of behavior is being probed as a way of learning more about both normal and atypical development (Cicchetti & Tucker, 1994). Increasingly, research turns to family-centered models and seeks approaches that are sensitive to cultural diversity. There also is a great emphasis on the impact of social reform policies, and particular concern about the impact of poverty and violence on infants and toddlers.

✳ Nature Versus Nurture

When we think about infants, we come back to the age-old question of "which is more important, heredity or environment?" Probably the only "pure genetic moment" is at conception. From that moment on there is an interaction between the organism and the environment. The more we learn, the more we think that the interaction is complex and cannot be sorted out into percentages. The nature-nurture model is no longer adequate to describe development (Cicchetti & Tucker, 1994).

Our information about "nature" has vastly increased since the nature-nurture model was proposed. Scientists have found that "the brain development that takes place before age one is more rapid and extensive than we previously realized" (Carnegie Task Force on Meeting the Needs of Young Children, 1994, 7). We know that brain cell formation is almost complete at birth. However, knowledge of the amount of brain maturation that occurs during the first year is relatively new information. Brain cells must form connections or synapses to allow learning to occur. During the first year "the number of synapses increases twenty-fold, from 50 trillion to 1,000 trillion" (Carnegie Task Force on Meeting the Needs of Young Children, 1994, 7). Although professionals agree that there is a genetic component to this growth of the brain, the environment also has a great impact. The development of the brain is more susceptible to environmental influences than had been previously thought. The influence of nutrition on the development of the brain, both prenatally and in early childhood, was previously known, but the role of an early stimulating environment on the brain had been less clear.

The brain has more nerve cells (neurons) and synapses than it needs. This overabundance holds the potential for development that responds to vastly different lifestyles as well as individual personality and temperament. During prenatal development neurons are pruned, whereas in infancy it is the synapses that are pruned (Cicchetti & Tucker, 1994). Pruning, or technically, parcellation, is the process by which the brain eliminates general neurons and synapses as part of the process in achieving the specificity of the mature brain (Brown, 1994). The pruning process appears to be use dependent, that is, synapses that are used stay; those that are not used are eliminated. Early visual deprivation of animals has shown permanent visual impairment, despite earlier functional vision, as a result of this process (Brown, 1994).

Nature provides the structure, the brain, but nurture provides the early experiences necessary to shape the brain into a functionally adaptive network. Who decides what is functional? It appears that the brain is unique and self-regulatory. This process results in increasing complexity of the brain itself, and, because of the self-regulatory mechanism, over time it increases the uniqueness of each child's personality (Cicchetti & Tucker, 1994).

✳ Continuity Versus Discontinuity

There has been a debate over whether development is continuous or discontinuous, or whether in fact it is both. Some feel that development is continuous and that knowledge about a child as a young infant can predict what the infant will do in particular areas in later childhood. (For example, we could predict that a young infant with a high intelligence quotient would do well on the SATs in high school). Others focus on the continuity or consistency of the environment and its effect on the developing infant. There seems to be an assumption that continuity is good and discontinuity in the environment is bad. However, this is unsubstantiated (Peters & Kontos, 1987). If a toddler were in an unstimulating environment and then placed in a developmentally appropriate early care and education setting, this discontinuity might have a very positive effect. Along the same lines in this debate, some ponder whether particular aspects of development, such as cognitive development or attachment behavior, show continuity across time and other behaviors do not. Again, other researchers contend that because development means change, it is by definition discontinuous.

Stage-based theories such as Piaget's opt for discontinuous development. Likewise the concept of a critical period—a fixed time period typically early in development during which certain behaviors optimally appear—supports discontinuity. Research, however, has not substantiated the critical-period concept in humans. It

Infants who live in warm, stimulating environments profit from continuity between their homes and early care and education settings.

does, however, support the idea of more broadly conceived sensitive periods and cycles that are more susceptible to change; that is intervals in development where the impact of events is more pervasive than other times (Thatcher, 1994).

Whether development is continuous or discontinuous or both is still up for debate. The issue is an important one and touches on whether one can compensate for a "less good environment" by spending some time in an optimal environment, or whether infants who are optimally raised become striving adolescents, and those who have had a very difficult early childhood will become juvenile delinquents.

As we focus on questions about nature and nurture and continuity and discontinuity, some of the potential answers are coming from outside the fields that we traditionally consider infant and toddler development. Neurobiology, genetics, and biological advances in psychopathology are providing new information that must be integrated into the system.

Biological Basis for Behavior

As more data become available, we are increasingly made aware of the importance of the early years for future development. Research in the field of infancy is becoming increasingly complex as researchers begin to look at the biological consequences of prenatal risk conditions, brain chemistry, and failure to thrive (Riccuti, 1992). We are finding biological explanations for what was previously just observational data. However, it is clear that the biological conditions can only be understood in the context of social and environmental circumstances.

Researchers today are trying to identify more precisely the causes of risk in both the infant herself and her environment. The Human Genome Project has as its goal "to find the location of the 100,000 or so human genes and to read the entire genetic script, all 3 billion bits of information by the year 2005" (U.S. Department of Health and Human Services, 1995). In 1996, the project was ahead of schedule. Genes influence not only what we look like but also what diseases we may be susceptible to. Errors in genes are responsible for an estimated 3,000 to 4,000 hereditary diseases, and altered genes play a part in many more diseases including cancer, diabetes, and heart disease. Once the molecular base of a disease is discovered, scientists have a better chance of designing highly targeted drugs to defeat the disease or perhaps even correct or replace the altered gene through gene therapy (U.S. Department of Health and Human Services, 1995).

However, in addition to the positive side of genetic research, there is controversy as well. Do you really want to know if you, or your child, has a fatal genetic disease? What if the results are inaccurate? What if you are denied medical insurance because of the results of the genetic testing? There are many ethical and legal considerations in learning about the human genome.

Researchers are also focusing on early experience as a sensitive period in development. A major issue is whether or not early family-centered intervention can in fact increase the likelihood of positive outcomes for at-risk children.

Early studies (1950s) focused on the prevention of mental retardation in cultural-familial retardation (Garber, Hodge, Rynders, Dever, & Velu, 1991). Later research has focused on families in poverty while looking more broadly at the concept of early enrichment. In the vast majority of cases, when infants and toddlers in unstimulating environments were placed in more stimulating environments, positive changes occurred in their behavior. The question was whether or not the gains would remain. Evidence now demonstrates that there are both short- and long-term gains from early intervention in these situations (Consortium for Longitudinal Studies, 1983; Honig, 1979, 1983; Ramey et al., 1992; Seitz, Rosenbaum, & Apfel, 1985). These gains are measured by a variety of indices: better cognitive achievement, higher IQ scores, positive social behaviors, fewer years in special education, less delinquency, fewer repetition of grades, better school attendance, and others. By necessity, these are longitudinal studies and results of studies begun in the 1980s are just beginning to appear. There is some indication that over time the benefits of early intervention are cumulative (Carnegie Task Force on Meeting the Needs of Young Children, 1994). It is expected that neurobiologists will confirm these results in the near future. The hope is that more precise identification of these risk conditions will lead to specific interventions designed to permit better outcomes for children.

Mental Health for Infants and Toddlers

There is increasing concern about the emotional and social functioning of infants and toddlers. Because they themselves lack the language to express their feelings and organize their experiences, it is up to professionals in the field to comprehend the meaning of experiences for infants and toddlers. There is concern that some very young children are the victims of violence and that they can become so accustomed to violence that they readily take the aggressor role and do not empathize with the victim (Osofsky, 1993/1994).

We have known for many years that children who experience chronic stress during early childhood are at risk for negative behavioral outcomes, and for developing a variety of cognitive, behavioral, and emotional problems (Rutter, 1979; Trickett & Kucznski, 1986). Naturally children differ in their resilience, but there are no invulnerable children (Honig, 1986). We are beginning to understand why. Although we can identify both risk and protective factors, researchers are concluding that chronically stressful environments can activate hormones that adversely affect the functioning of the brain, and there is concern that these effects may be permanent (Carnegie Task Force on Meeting the Needs of Young Children, 1994).

Some researchers believe that early environmental stressors may not only shape the brain's representation of those experiences but sensitize the development of the neural network and influence future development. Young children who experience maltreatment may have more permanent and lasting problems than we had previously thought: "The psychiatric consequences of early maltreatment may not be exclusively psychological in nature, but may also emerge due to the effects of traumatic experience on the developing brain" (Cicchetti & Tucker, 1994, 546). That is, as early experience interacts with the self-regulatory system of the brain, it may be that some of the synapses that are pruned are related to traumatic experiences.

Changing Demographics of Infants and Toddlers

The population of infants and toddlers in the United States is rapidly changing, forcing us to investigate the roles of nature, nurture, culture, and the complex intersections of these dimensions in diverse ways (Zahn-Waxler, 1995). The Children's Defense Fund predicts that by 2030 "There will be 5.5 million more Hispanic children; 2.6 million more African American children; 1.5 million more children of other races; and 6.2 million fewer white, non-Hispanic children" (1989, 116). These changes are attributed to higher birth rates among nonwhite, non-Anglo women, increased immigration, and more women of child-bearing age in the nonwhite group (Hanson, Lynch, & Wayman, 1990). Consequently, there will be an increasing need for researchers and early care and education professionals to develop cross-cultural competence (Hanson, 1992).

Gender and Work-Family Issues

Changes in gender roles have had a major impact on the child development and early education fields. Traditional family theory that divided men and women into two different cultures, with males being instrumental (hard, cold, and practical) and females being expressive (emotional, personal, down-to-earth, as well as uninterested in achievements and abstract ideas) has been found wanting (Collins & Coltrane, 1995). Women can and have succeeded in positions of political power, economic control, and scientific investigation. Likewise, when men take on the role of fathering, they are sensitive and caring, not aggressive, with their young children. In actuality, men and women have a mix of instrumental and expressive qualities.

In addition to reevaluation of gender roles, there has been an economic impetus for many women, including those with infants and toddlers, to enter the work force (Gibbs & Teti, 1990). This meant that infants and toddlers who had previously been reared at home by their mothers were now in child care settings. It also brings very different demands to the work place. Work-family issues pose a whole new set of challenges to both families and industry.

Social Policy as It Impacts Infants and Toddlers

Social policy is the government's plan of action that influences the welfare of its citizens. The United States has no comprehensive social policy that relates to families or infants and toddlers; however, it has many individual policies that both directly and indirectly affect infants and toddlers and their families, including programs that relate to child care, nutrition, aid to families of dependent children, welfare programs, medicaid, and many more.

Policymakers not only determine what programs are going to be available, but also what the eligibility criteria for recipients will be. We have acknowledged that the well-being of infants and toddlers is inextricably tied to their families. Some social policies support family integrity and the health, care, and welfare of the infants and toddlers in these families; other policies do not. Increasingly, professionals concerned about infants and toddlers must take their expertise into the political arena in neighborhoods, communities, states, and the nation and become advocates for the needs of the youngest citizens (Annie E. Casey Foundation, 1994, Carnegie Task Force on Meeting the Needs of Young Children, 1994; Children's Defense Fund Reports, 1995).

These trends and issues have focused attention on the early childhood years and stressed the need for information about how infants and toddlers grow and develop and the need to disseminate what we do know. Changing circumstances place different and more complex demands on those working with infants and toddlers and stress the need for collaboration in both planning and delivering a broad base of services. There is a need for skills in interacting among professionals from child care, education, health, and social services, as well as parents and other family members (NAEYC, 1994). New specializations have been created for individuals who concentrate their professional lives on infants and toddlers. There is a need to become a wise consumer of the research that is being generated about infants and toddlers.

Becoming a Critical Consumer of Research

One concern you might have as you read this book is that research findings do not always agree, or that the findings do agree but that researchers have different interpretations of those findings. It may be that what you read in this book is different from what is said in the popular media. What is sensational gets the attention and is often better press than some of the painstaking research that is less volatile. Sometimes good research is reported, but without the cautions or qualifications the researcher stated.

Sometimes there truly is disagreement about findings; an example is the data related to the impact of child care on infants. At other times the differences are more apparent than real. So how do you decide who is "right?" Consider something as seemingly simple as deciding when a child walks. Researcher A claims that the average child walks at 11 months, whereas Researcher B claims that this does not occur until 14 months. You have a child who is 14 months old and not walking. If you believe Researcher A, you might be concerned that your child's development is slow. If you believe Researcher B, you would expect him to walk soon but not be disturbed. Who is right? It is important to become a critical consumer of research. To do that you need to know something about how research is carried out and about some of the variables that influence research.

Operational Definitions

The first thing you might want to find out are the researcher's operational definitions. How do they determine age and how do they decide whether or not a child is "walking?" You discover that they have the following definitions:

Researcher A's definition: Age: A child is a given month until the month ends. That is, a child who is 10 months and 27 days is still considered 10 months old. Walking: A child has to take one or two steps independently. Researcher A believes that parents are good observers of their children and asks that they call in when their child first "walks." Researcher A notes the date on the child's card along with other relevant information.

Researcher B's definition: Age: A child is a given month until 15 days into the next month. Then he becomes the next month's age. That is, a child who is 10 months and 27 days is considered 11 months old. Walking: A child must walk 6 feet independently and Researcher B himself must see it to record it on the child's chart. When parents think the child can walk 6 feet, they notify the researcher. Researcher B then observes the child and decides whether or not he has met the criteria for walking.

Knowing this information, it is not difficult to believe that children in Researcher A's study "walked" earlier than those in Researcher B's study. Obviously, the differences in operational definitions influenced the data. Such differences, then, were more a matter of definition than related to differences in the ages at which children walk.

Generalizability

Another important variable, regardless of research method, is the number of infants you need to study to be sure that the information obtained is representative or can be generalized to other infants. The *universe* is all infants. The *sample* is the part of the universe that is tested. All infants may be the total population we are interested in, but we cannot study all infants. We might decide to concentrate on infants of a particular age, such as infants between 9 and 12 months. Although this eliminates some infants, there are still too many to study. Therefore, we choose a sample of infants to study and then generalize to the larger population. The research concern is whether or not the sample is representative of the population we want to generalize to, and whether the sample is large enough to allow analysis of the information.

The issue becomes more complex when you ask "Can we assume that age of talking is not influenced by such variables as gender, race, ethnicity, geographic location, and socioeconomic status?" In general, you cannot make such an assumption, therefore, the *sample* of infants you choose must be representative of the population of infants you wish to generalize to. If the population you want to generalize to is all infants in the United States, you must choose a sample that is representative of that population. It should include both boys and girls, including at least white, African American, Hispanic, Asian American, and Native American children; the infants must come from cities, suburbs, and rural areas, and they must come from families that have a variety of educational, occupational, and income levels. Obviously, it will be extremely expensive and time consuming to obtain a representative sample for such a large and diverse population.

Overgeneralization is a concern, especially when the results are used to make decisions beyond the group studies. For example, suppose researchers interested in the impact of child care on infants and toddlers only sampled early care and education sites connected to colleges and universities, and then concluded that child care had no negative impact on infant and toddler cognitive and social/emotional development. Could one then conclude that all child care has no negative effects on infants and toddlers? No! That would be an overgeneralization.

In general, researchers qualify who the information can be generalized to. If, for example, they only used African American middle-class suburban boys, then they would qualify their findings saying that the information could only be generalized to this population. Likewise, gathering data only at college-connected child care sites would include a caveat regarding "high quality" child care in their findings. In both cases mentioned, the results might be accurate for the infants and settings studied, but would not be accurate for the total population of infants and early care and education settings. A concern when findings make their way to the popular press is that these qualifications may be lost.

Group Data Versus Individual Needs

Most research is conducted on groups of children, and the focus is on determining how a particular group reacted, for example, to the impact of child care on a group of infants. The data may say that, overall, boys adjusted more quickly than girls. Even though, on the extreme ends of the scale, participant Marco may have a very difficult adjustment and participant Madeline an excellent adjustment. The study typically focuses on the group as a whole, not the individual differences of children within the group. This is *nomothetic* research. The problem often is that you want to know how your child will do in child care. This is an *idiographic* need. You want to know about an individual child, not a group of children. We rarely have this kind of individual data. Conclusions derived from group data may not apply to the child in whom we are interested. That does not mean that the data itself is not accurate, but is a misuse of the information.

Correlation and Causation

Correlational research looks at how two or more events are related. For example, researchers might be interested in comparing the amount of aggressive play a toddler displays in an early care and education setting with the number of hours the toddler spends watching "violent" television programs. It may be that toddlers who watch more violence on television are in fact more aggressive in the classroom. However, this does not mean that watching violence on television causes aggressive behavior in the classroom. Correlation is not causation.

The correlation between screen violence and aggressive behavior in young children that began in the 1960s sparked interest in doing experimental studies that would be able to look more clearly at causation. Experimental studies such as those designed by Aletha Huston showed young children television shows with differing amounts of violence, including highly charged commercials, and then observed their behavior in the classroom. She and her colleagues concluded that viewing screen violence does cause aggressive behavior (Huston, 1992; Huston, Watkins, & Kunkel, 1989; Greer, Potts, Wright, & Huston, 1982).

Sometimes information gets overgeneralized or misinterpreted. There is currently much information about infants and toddlers in the popular literature, in the media, and in texts such as this one. Individuals must become wise consumers of this research to know how to accurately evaluate the information given. People who don't understand some of the principles of research may make mistakes in interpretation. It is important to learn to interpret research findings accurately. Critical consumers of research focus on clear definitions and specificity as opposed to ambiguous meanings of terms. They are concerned that measures are accurate and precise, and hold a critical skepticism about popular generalizations regarding infants and toddlers.

Why study infants and toddlers? The importance of these years as a unique period has been established. Further, we are increasingly aware of the lifelong implications of these years. If individuals working with very young children, and even those who have young children, recognize the importance of these years and plan appropriate environments and experiences for these young children, there are likely to be more positive outcomes for our nation's youngest citizens and the nation itself.

Summary

This chapter has briefly looked at infants and toddlers as the beginning stage of child development. It mentioned an historical, philosophical view of infants and toddlers. It traced the development of scholarly studies of infants and toddlers, covering early studies that focused on establishing norms for physical and motor development, and studies concerned with the effects of institutionalization on infants and toddlers; it also described more recent studies demonstrating the ingenuity of researchers. It further looked at continuing research trends and issues such as nature versus nurture and continuity versus discontinuity. Some newer trends and issues were also discussed: the identification of at-risk conditions, both pre- and postnatally, concerns about infant mental health, the changing demographics relating to infants and toddlers, changing gender roles and work-family issues, and finally the impact of social policy on infants and toddlers and their families.

The role of the individual as a critical consumer of research about infants and toddlers was highlighted, along with some of the important variables necessary to evaluate research. These include operational definitions, generalizability, group data versus individual needs, and the differences between correlation and causation.

Application Activities

1. Talk with your parents about how they made decisions about rearing you. Find out how they decided whether to breast- or bottle-feed you, when you were toilet-trained, and how you were disciplined when you were very young. Find out who they consulted, what books they read (if any), and what their concerns were when you were very young. Ask them how important they thought the first three years were in your development.

2. Justify to a friend why studying infants and toddlers is important.

3. Find an article in the popular press about children between birth and age 3 and critique it.

4. Identify a current social policy that relates to infants and toddlers. Evaluate the policy for both short- and long-term consequences for infants and toddlers, decide what you might change about the policy, and how you would go about advocating that change.

Chapter 2

Development Before Birth

"**I**'m pregnant!" This realization can be greeted with joy for a planned, wanted pregnancy, with surprise and disbelief when it is unexpected and, perhaps, with grief and concern when it is unwanted. Understanding the growth patterns of the fetus and the impact of environmental factors can influence prenatal maternal behavior and birth outcomes. When pregnancies are planned, the prospective mother and father who consciously decide to have a child can make positive changes in their life-style to prepare the environment before conception and during pregnancy. Such conscious decisions may be crucial because prenatal development can dramatically impact the infant. Some prenatal risks can be prevented, others monitored and managed.

Prepregnancy Planning

The United States does little in the way of educating its young women to think about the life skills and healthy living habits they will need in pregnancy. A healthy lifestyle does not guarantee a successful pregnancy outcome, but it should be a goal. Thinking about pregnancy may make a woman more aware of risk areas, and, ideally, she can begin a healthy life when pregnancy is thought about, not after it has already begun.

Prepregnancy and pregnancy planning is more than a nine-month process. Before a woman becomes pregnant, she should make sure she has had the appropriate inoculations such as for rubella. Sexually transmitted diseases, including AIDS and syphilis, need to be acknowledged and decisions made. Planning also gives a woman time to ensure that her diet is adequate for the nutritional demands of pregnancy. Prepregnancy planning also provides time to stop using tobacco, alcohol, drugs, and caffeine, and to avoid harmful environmental exposure (Turner, 1994). These decisions are designed to increase the probability of having a normal, healthy, happy baby.

When pregnancy is unplanned, changes can occur only after the women knows she is pregnant, which may be two to six weeks after conception or more. In the United States, 56 percent of pregnancies are unplanned—this is one of the highest rates in the industrialized world (Williams & Pratt, 1990). When pregnancies are unintended, women are less likely to care adequately for themselves and their unborn child during pregnancy.

There are many factors that influence the development of the fetus before birth. These factors come from the genetic matter that forms the fetus, the environment in which the fetus grows and develops for the first nine months, and the developing fetus himself. The factors are not mutually exclusive; they interact and influence each other and shape the developing organism.

Fertilization and Implantation

The human body is composed of cells and each of us starts out as a single cell, the ovum, or egg. All cells are composed of two basic parts, an outer, jellylike cytoplasm and an inner nucleus. To develop from this single cell to the individual you are today, several processes had to take place: First the egg had to be fertilized by a sperm, the cells had to increase in number through cell division, begin to differentiate to make up different body parts (skin, bones, heart, and so on), and then begin the systemic function of metabolism. All human beings develop in this way. If all humans develop the same way, how do we account for the unique qualities of individuals? Why do some have blond hair and others black, and why are some short and others tall, and some female and others male? The study of growth before birth is a complex, scientific field called embryology, a branch of biology. Infant specialists do not need extensive embryological knowledge, but do need a basic understanding of conception and prenatal development.

Women are born with all their reproductive cells. About 2 million eggs, or immature ova, are present in a female's ovaries at birth; however, only about 500 to 600 are used during the approximately 40 years a woman is capable of child bearing. The mature unfertilized egg, or ovum, is the largest cell in the female's body. It is about the size of the period that ends this sentence. Approximately once a month during a female's reproductive years, an egg ripens, is pushed from the ovary, drops into one of the fallopian tubes, and is available for fertilization. This is called ovulation. If the egg is not fertilized, in approximately 10 to 14 days, the woman's menstrual flow begins, washing away the egg and the lining of the uterine wall. This cycle repeats itself on a regular basis (approximately monthly), unless fertilization takes place (Batshaw & Perret, 1992).

Whereas females are born with immature eggs, males only begin producing sperm at puberty and continue into old age. Each sperm is composed primarily of a large head and a long tail. The head contains the cell nucleus, and the tail is used for propulsion. In the process of intercourse, hundreds of millions of sperm cells are mixed with seminal fluid and deposited in the female vagina. (An ejaculation contains about 300 to 500 million sperm mixed with about 1 tablespoon of fluid.)

Sperm must travel the remaining length of the vagina and push through the cervix into the uterus. Midway in the menstrual cycle, mucus secretions of the vagina and the thinning of the cervix make it easier to penetrate, so fertilization is more likely. The uterine contractions that occur during a female's orgasm help to move the sperm toward the fallopian tubes. Recent research has shown that the ovum may play a more active role in conception than previously thought. The egg itself may give off a series of molecular signals that guide the sperm and may even play a role in the selection of sperm to fertilize the egg (Freedman, 1992). Once in the uterus, the sperm cells must make their way to the correct fallopian tube and then swim up the fallopian tube to meet the egg. Only a few thousand reach the fallopian tube and a few hundred reach the egg. Sperm must travel about 7 inches to reach the egg, a journey of about an hour. Once a sperm penetrates the outer layer of the egg, other sperm cannot penetrate it. The remaining sperm die within 24 hours (Batshaw & Perret, 1992).

From a biological perspective, conception, or fertilization, occurs when a sperm enters the ovum. Fertilization usually occurs in the fallopian tubes. The ovum must be fertilized within approximately 6 to 12 hours after ovulation or it is no longer fertilizable. Once inside the egg, the sperm's tail, or flagellum, detaches, and the nucleus from the sperm and ovum migrate toward each other and join. See Figure 2.1.

| **Figure 2.1** | **Ovulation, Fertilization, and Implantation** |

The ovary discharges an egg into the fallopian tube, where it is penetrated by a sperm. The zygote begins to divide as it moves through the fallopian tube toward the uterus, where it eventually implants and receives nourishment and support from the mother.

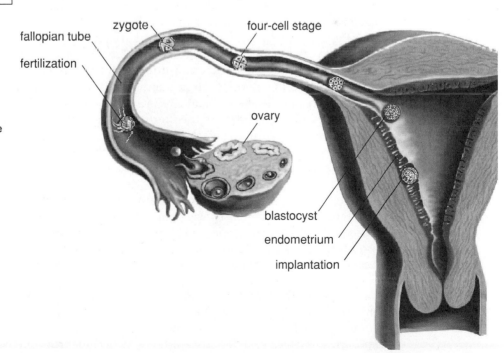

Gestation

The time from conception to birth is called gestation and usually lasts nine calendar months. We arbitrarily divide these nine months into three trimesters. However, there are other periods that are more significant to the developing organism. Each of these has a name: Germinal Period, Embryonic Period, and Fetal Period.

Germinal Period

The first two weeks of prenatal development are referred to as the germinal period. A fertilized egg, called a **zygote,** maintains its initial size, that of the unfertilized egg. However, the fertilized cell makes a replica of itself through a process of cell division called *clevage* or segmentation. After 40 hours the zygote technically becomes a **morula.** It takes about four days for the morula to pass through the narrow uterine tube and reach the uterus. Now the egg mass contains from 16 to 64 cells; its size, however, has not changed.

By about the fourth or fifth day after fertilization, the morula begins to change in size and shape and is called a **blastocyst.** This stage is characterized by cell differentiation. Some cells form the support structure for the developing blastocyst (placenta, umbilical cord, and amniotic sac), while others are part of the developing organism. The embryonic membranes that begin to develop are the ectoderm which evolves into skin, the spinal cord, and teeth; the mesoderm which becomes blood vessels, muscles and bones; and the endoderm which develops into the digestive system, lungs, and urinary tract (Batshaw & Perret, 1992).

Of fertilized eggs, only about half survive to reach the uterus; the others are reabsorbed by the body. Although it is possible for the blastocyst to implant, or attach, itself to the uterine wall in many places, it normally does so in the upper back portion of the uterus. The site of implantation is critical. If the blastocyst attaches itself to the bottom of the uterus, it may cause complications in the delivery, or the placenta may detach too early *(placenta previa).* Sometimes implantation takes place outside the uterus, usually in the fallopian tube. This is called an **ectopic pregnancy** and results in a miscarriage.

Until implantation is complete, the developing organism absorbs nutrients directly from the mother's cells. Implantation is complete at about 12 to 13 days after conception. The blastocyst is then known as an **embryo.** The embryo produces a hormone, chorionic gonadotropin, that prevents the mother from menstruating. During the time leading up to implantation, a woman may not even begin to suspect that she might be pregnant. Her suspicions begin once her menstrual flow is due but does not come.

The sex of the individual is determined when the sperm and the egg join. At this point, the 23 maternal chromosomes pair up with the 23 paternal chromosomes to make up the 46 chromosomes, or 23 pairs of chromosomes, of our species. The chromosomes contain the genetic blueprint for the individual. One of each of the pairs of chromosomes come from the mother and the other from the father. The sex of the infant is determined by the sperm. The ovum always contributes an X chromosome. The sperm carries either an X or Y chromosome. If a sperm carrying an X chromosome fertilizes the egg, the child will be female (XX); if the sperm carries the Y chromosome, the result will be a male (XY). In addition to the sex chromosome, there are over 16,000,000 possible combinations of chromosomes (Gray, 1973). This may partially explain why children with the same parents can be very different.

Multiple Pregnancies

Generally only one ovum at a time is released by the female. If by chance two eggs are released and they are both fertilized, there will be fraternal, or dizygotic, twins. Genetically, fraternal twins are no more alike than other siblings. They are the result of different eggs and different sperm, yet share the uterine environment. Fraternal twinning tends to run in families. Not surprisingly, the trait is carried by the mother. On some occasions two or more eggs are simultaneously released from the ovary. If they are both fertilized, the result is fraternal twins. The rate of dizygotic twinning varies worldwide with Japan having one of the lowest rates (6.7 per 1,000 deliveries) and areas in Africa, particularly Nigeria, some of the highest (40 per 1,000 deliveries) as Crowther (1994) reports. Incidence of dizygotic twins varies with the age of the mother, whether or not there were previous births, racial background, and the use of assisted reproductive techniques. Fertility drugs may cause more than one egg to be released, and in *in vitro* fertilization more than one embryo is typically implanted.

Although fraternal twins share the same environment, they do not have the same genetic makeup.

Identical, or monozygotic, twins come from a single fertilized ovum that at some early point splits into two or more distinct cell groups. Why this occurs is still the subject of speculation. Monozygotic twinning is not a family trait and seems to be the same for all racial groups. Overall, the incidence of fraternal twins is about 1 per 100 deliveries, whereas identical twins occur in only 3.5 to 5 per 1,000 births (Batshaw & Perret, 1992; Crowther, 1994). Multiple births beyond twins can be either monozygotic, dizygotic, or some combination of the two. That is, in a set of quadruplets it is possible that two of the children would be monozygotic twins and the remaining two dizygotic.

Although children from the same parents are different, there are some basic genetic rules that provide guidelines for patterns of inheritance. New developments in the field are making our knowledge of these genetic patterns more precise.

Embryonic Period

The embryonic period begins when implantation occurs and lasts from week 2 to week 8. For the embryo to survive, a complex infrastructure of supports must be further developed to protect and feed the growing organism. These changes are all generated through the differentiation of cells of the developing embryo.

The embryo is attached to the uterine wall by the **placenta.** The placenta is a highly specialized, disk-shaped organ through which the fetus makes functional contact with the wall of the uterus. The embryo is connected to the placenta by the umbilical cord. The umbilical cord is hoselike and contains blood vessels. The amnion, a saclike membrane filled with a clear liquid called amniotic fluid, provides a watery environment which protects the embryo from mechanical injury and allows free movement.

The mature placenta develops rapidly after implantation and covers about 20 percent of the uterus. There is a fetal and a maternal portion of the placenta. Although these intertwine, they do not intermingle. A placental barrier called the **trophoblast** keeps the blood supplies separate. Whereas small molecules can pass through this barrier, large molecules cannot. The exact exchange of substances is very complex. However, in general, nutritive materials, oxygen, water, and salts from maternal blood can cross the placental barrier. Similarly, digestive waste products and carbon dioxide from the developing infant can cross back. Large molecules like red blood cells, most bacteria, maternal wastes, and many dangerous toxins and hormones cannot pass. Once implantation is completed, there is a period of rapid growth because the embryo is getting nourishment from the mother's blood through the placenta. This is far more efficient than absorbing nutrients from the mother's cells.

The direction or pattern of fetal development is predictable: It is both cephalo-caudal and proximo-distal. It follows a **cephalo-caudal** direction—that is, development occurs from the head to the "tail." Earliest development occurs in the head, brain, and sense organs, followed by the trunk area, then the arms and legs. At two months' gestation, the head accounts for about half of the total body length; at birth, the head comprises only about one-quarter of the newborn's

Figure 2.2 | Body Changes from Five Weeks' Gestation to Adult Age

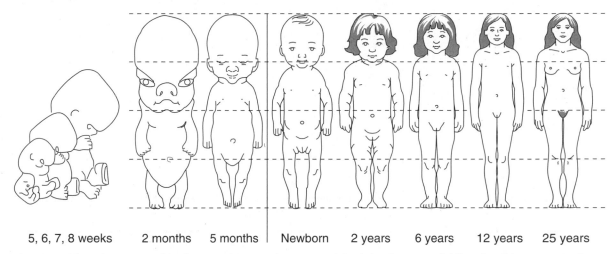

| 5, 6, 7, 8 weeks | 2 months | 5 months | Newborn | 2 years | 6 years | 12 years | 25 years |

Changes in the relative size of body parts during embryonic and fetal development, childhood, adolescence, and adulthood.

body length. In adults, the head is only about 10 percent of a person's height (see Figure 2.2.).

The other predictable pattern of growth is **proximal-distal,** which means, growth proceeds from the middle outward. Structures that are near the midline of the body, such as the spinal cord and the heart, develop before the arms and legs, which develop before the fingers and toes. This pattern of development is also apparent after birth as the infant masters controlling his head before his arms, and his arms before his fingers.

The rate of growth is faster during the embryonic period than at any other time. During the embryonic period, all body tissues, organs, and systems are developing. While all this is happening, a woman still may not even realize that she is pregnant. It is also during this time that the embryo is most susceptible to the influences of disease, drugs, radiation, and other substances. Changes during this time are precise and predictable. Research has shown that "if a child is born with a cleft palate, the defect occurred between days 35 and 37 of gestation, when the palatal arches normally close" (Batshaw & Perret, 1992, 39).

By the fourth week after conception, a primitive head with the beginning of a brain and spinal cord, as well as eye and ear formations, begins to develop. The heart has increased in size, and blood vessels have begun to form. There are limb buds for both arms and legs. In general, the embryo is taking on a more distinctive form.

During the next month, the embryo becomes less markedly curved. The head increases in size; there is a face with a primitive nose, eyes and ears, and upper lip; and the neck has lengthened. The tail-like projection has almost disappeared. There are fully formed arms and legs, hands and feet, and even fingers and toes,

---

| **Figure 2.3** | **The Embryo at 1, 1½ and 2 Months** |

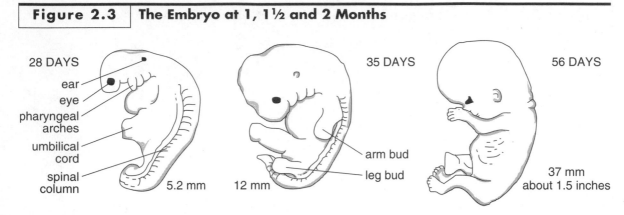

By the end of the embryonic period, all the essential systems are formed and the embryo takes on a very human look.

---

although these are extremely small. The heart and circulatory system are beginning to work, and by the end of the second month the kidneys take over the function of concentrating and excreting urine. Although not functional, there are digestive and respiratory systems. The reproductive system is also forming. There is a skeleton made of cartilage. Even such fine points as eyelids are developed. By the end of the second month of development, the embryo is recognizable as a human being, although a somewhat strange looking one (England, 1990; see Figure 2.3).

Fetal Period

By the end of the first two months, the developing organism is called a *fetus*. The early part of the fetal period is characterized by the development and growth of true bone. Growth of the head has begun to slow; it is about half of the fetus. The remainder of the body now grows more. Nerve-muscle connections have increased; motion is more precise; and the thumb moves into its characteristic position. The reproductive system becomes more differentiated, and by week 12 it is possible to tell visually if the fetus is male or female (England, 1990).

During the third month, the main organ systems (cardiovascular, neurological, digestive, and so on) are further differentiated and established. The fetus is about 3.5 inches long and weighs about 1 ounce. Although he is active, the mother cannot yet feel him. More amniotic fluid is being produced, for a total of approximately 8 ounces. The fluid is recirculated as the fetus swallows it and then excretes it as urine.

Growth continues during the fourth month, with the fetus weighing about 6 ounces and measuring 10 inches. Now, when the fetus moves, mothers can detect movement; this movement is called **quickening.** Tissues and organs continue to develop. The heart can be heard with a stethoscope, or even by placing an ear on

| Figure 2.4 | The Fetus at 4 Months with His Support System |

chorion
placenta
umbilical cord
embryo
amniotic fluid
amnion
maternal blood circulation

The fetal blood circulates through the placenta, picking up oxygen and nutrients and discharging waste into the mother's blood. Amniotic fluid protects the fetus from shock and helps regulate its temperature.

the mother's abdomen. The fetus develops a downy coat of hair called **lanugo** over its body as well as hair on the head. **Vernix caseosa** is excreted. This is a creamy white substance which covers the fetal skin and helps to protect it from the amniotic fluid.

The placenta plays an increasingly important role. It still acts as a barrier against harmful substances that may be in the mother's blood and as the source of nutrients. It is also functionally the fetal lungs, kidneys, intestine, and liver. Additionally, it produces hormones that aid in the continuation of the pregnancy and later production of maternal milk (see Figure 2.4).

During the fifth and sixth months, there are refinements in development (fingernails) and continued growth. By the end of the sixth month, the fetus is about 12 to 14 inches long and weighs about 1.5 to 2 pounds. With the support of neonatal intensive care nurseries, infants born at 22 weeks or later are considered viable.

The major function of the third trimester is to increase fetal weight. The fetus starts storing fat, and life support functions are more fully developed. The brain continues to develop rapidly. The lungs begin to take over some limited exchange of gases. The eyelids open. The skin assumes a pink color, and the lanugo begins to disappear. The fetus becomes plumper. By the end of the ninth month, the fetus is about 20 inches long, usually weighs between 6.5 and 8 pounds and is ready to be born.

Fetal Experiences

The previous sections have described growth and development from the perspective of an outsider looking in. The view is probably very different from the inside looking out. Have you thought about the fetal environment? For a fetus the womb presents a varied environment. Although it offers little visual variety, the environment constantly changes as the mother walks, talks, eats, drinks, laughs, or cries. This might not be your idea of a stimulating environment, but it is most satisfactory for the developing fetus.

The fetus moves very early in pregnancy, but it is only when he is large enough to be sensed beyond the uterus to the abdominal wall that he can be felt by the mother. He turns somersaults and moves his whole body around while there is space. These movements resemble "slow motion" because of the amniotic fluid. Later in the pregnancy, he no longer has enough room to move his whole body and is limited to kicking his legs and flinging his arms and, ultimately, to just fidgeting with his arms and legs, playing with his fingers, and sucking his thumb. He is constantly bumping into the walls of the uterus, the umbilical cord, and himself. He feels all this. It appears his sense of touch and balance are excellent (Maurer & Maurer, 1988).

If one thinks about the location of the uterus, one would anticipate a relatively noisy environment. In addition to the constant beating of the heart, the mother's voice travels into the lungs as part of the speaking process, and the stomach and intestines are noisily breaking down food products. This is all happening while the mother is quiet. If she walks on a hard floor in heels, the skeletal vibrations cause noise. There is evidence that the fetus hears not only sounds from inside the mother's body during the last three months of pregnancy but also some sounds from outside (Maurer & Maurer, 1988).

The fetus seems more likely to respond to sporadic noise than constant noises like the beating of the heart. Just as your voice sounds different when you hear it on a tape recording than it does when you listen to yourself speaking, the mother's voice heard through the amniotic fluid is very different from how it sounds in the air. This makes it seem unlikely that a newborn would recognize his mother's voice. However, he may recognize her vocal rhythms and patterns and does, in fact, recognize his mother's voice before his father's (DeCasper & Prescott, 1984).

Although we do not know a lot about the uterine environment from the fetal point of view, it appears that it is not a stimulus-free environment and that the fetus does act and react to his environment. Because of all the changes that occur during prenatal development and their long term importance, monitoring both the mother and fetus during this time is particularly important.

Prenatal Care

Prenatal care involves systematic monitoring of both the mother and developing fetus. More specifically the first three aims are

- To provide advice, reassurance, education, and support for the woman and her family
- To deal with the minor ailments of pregnancy
- To provide an on-going screening program to confirm that the woman continues to be at low risk.

For those women who are high risk at pregnancy, or move into that category for some reason, a further aim is

- The prevention, detection, and management of those problems and factors that adversely affect the health of the mother and/or infant. (James, 1994a, 21)

Sources of prenatal care vary both within and between countries. In some countries, such as Denmark, midwives have the pivotal responsibility with family doctors playing only a supportive role. In other countries, such as the United Kingdom, the responsibility is shared, with midwives taking major responsibility for normal pregnancies and obstetricians managing high-risk pregnancies. In the United States, most prenatal care is provided by family physicians or obstetricians, although some is also rendered by nurse practitioners. There is no agreement on the number of prenatal visits a woman should make. Recommendations vary from 5 to 15 (James, 1994a). There does appear to be agreement about clinical and laboratory-based screening. This generally includes demographic information (age, ethnicity, socioeconomic and marital status); past obstetric, gynecological, medical, and family history; and a physical examination.

Part of prenatal care involves screening and monitoring both hereditary conditions that may place the fetus at risk as well as infectious diseases that may affect the mother or the fetus. Traditionally in the first trimester, serological screening is done for rubella antibodies, syphilis, hepatitis, and HIV. Physicians also do a Papanicolaou (PAP) smear, urinalysis, full blood count, and a group and antibody screen (James, 1994a). Some conditions, such as high blood pressure, diabetes, and hypoglycemia, cannot be cured but need to be monitored during the pregnancy. Additional information about appropriate exercise, fetal movement, and prenatal classes is given later in pregnancy. During the third trimester a birth plan is developed.

For low-risk women the goal of a birth plan is to offer choices. Women should be able to choose their birth attendant, the place of birth, and the mode of birth. She should be able to choose whether or not she wants electronic fetal monitoring and whether or not she wishes to have pain relief. These decisions should be made before labor begins and be part of the woman's records. The labor experience itself, of course, may change some of these decisions from either the woman's perspective or for medical reasons.

Heredity and Genetics: How It Works

Heredity has a role in how we develop and exerts specific influences on the growth and development of human beings. It was once believed that hereditary factors were the only influences on development. Research has since indicated that this is not true (Brown, 1994; Cicchetti & Tucker, 1994). The genetic makeup within each individual does, however, play a strong role in dictating specific developmental outcomes. The color of our eyes, our height, the size of our feet, the color of our skin, and even the diseases we are susceptible to are all dictated by the genes we inherit from our biological parents. Most biological factors are controlled by our genetic makeup.

For a trait to be inherited, it must be transmitted from one generation to another. To facilitate this transmission, the body has genetic codes for things such as eye color or hair color. These codes are contained in DNA (deoxyribonucleic acid). DNA is found in the center (nucleus) of almost every cell except red blood cells. DNA carries the code for inherited traits. The DNA is packaged into 23 pairs called chromosomes. This package is part of each of the cells in the human body.

Chromosomes are long strands of a chemical substance called DNA that are shaped like a double helix. This is something like a spiral staircase, with the railings composed of sugar and phosphate molecules and the stairs made up of four amino acids: adenine "A," thymine "T," cytosine "C," and guanine "G." What distinguishes one gene from the other is the order in which these amino acids are arranged on the chromosomes.

The body has only 23 pairs of chromosomes; however, there are estimated to be 100,000 genes. A gene is a tiny portion of DNA that carries a code for an inherited trait (U.S. Department of Health and Human Services, 1995). Genes are identified by their unique sequence of DNA.

There are basically two types of problems that can occur in the transmission of the genetic code from one generation to the other. The genetic code itself could be wrong. For example if the code on a gene should read

ATCATCTTTGGTGTT

but instead it reads

ATCATTGGTGTT,

three letters of the code (CTT) have been omitted. Some chemical the body should make does not get made. In this case, the omission of these three DNA bases results in cystic fibrosis. This is a genetic problem and it can be discovered by analyzing a person's DNA.

In other cases the problem is not with the DNA itself but how it was divided up into chromosomes. For example, sometimes genetic material which should be on one chromosome ends up on a different chromosome or there are too many chromosomes. If an individual has three number-21 chromosomes as opposed to the usual pair, it changes the way the body functions. Children born with trisomy 21 have Down syndrome. Chromosomal abnormalities affect about 6.6 percent of births and approximately 60 percent of miscarriages in the first 12 weeks of pregnancy (James, 1994b).

The remainder of this chapter focuses on the general principles and patterns of hereditary and genetic influences and some of the more prevalent birth anomalies.

Hereditary and Genetic Influences

Genetics is a complex field. Most traits that humans are interested in are not located on a single gene, but rather are the result of several genes or the interaction between genes and the environment or both. Personality and intelligence certainly fall into the category of traits caused by multiple genes interacting with the environment.

Our knowledge about particular genetic disorders varies. We have empirical information about probabilities for some genetic disorders. For example, we know that the risk of having a child with Down syndrome varies with maternal age and that the probability is 1:1,528 at age 20 and 1:6 at age 50 (James, 1994b).

We know about other conditions because of inheritance patterns. The basic genetic makeup of an individual is transmitted from the parents and is called a person's **genotype.** The observable characteristics of an individual, both biological and behavioral, are a person's **phenotype.** The phenotype is a result of the interaction of the genetic potential with the environment.

Some traits follow a **Mendelian pattern.** This pattern was discovered by the Austrian botanist Gregor Johann Mendel. His findings were first published in the late 1800s. He did not study animals, but the laws of inheritance he formulated while working with plants provided the groundwork for understanding inheritance patterns.

There is a predictable pattern for determining genetic expressions, if one knows the dominant and recessive genes of the parents. Typically, we use capital letters to indicate dominant genes and small letters to indicate recessive genes. The simplest situation is where both parents contribute either dominant or recessive genes (see Figure 2.5). In situations where the child inherits either dominant or recessive genes from both parents, the child is *homozygous* for that trait (DD or dd). In situations where the child inherits a dominant gene from one parent and a recessive gene from the other, he is *heterozygous* for that trait. A dominant gene is expressed, that is, the child has the trait whether it is paired with another dominant gene or with a recessive gene.

In each of these situations, the child has a 100 percent chance of inheriting whatever the characteristic is. Thus both parents and the child have whatever this characteristic is (Figure 2.5 a and b). Another way of saying this is that the genotype and phenotype are the same. If only one parent has two dominant genes for a characteristic, the child will still display the characteristic; however, the genetic configuration is different (Figure 2.5 c). In this situation the child is heterozygous (Dr) for the particular trait. His genotype and phenotype are different.

The most complicated inheritance pattern to understand occurs when both parents are heterozygous for a trait (Dr). In this situation both parents have the

Figure 2.5 | Mendelian Inheritance Patterns

Mendelian inheritance patterns are based on the predictable relationship between dominant and recessive genes that determines patterns and whether or not a trait will be expressed in an offspring. The sex of the offspring does not influence this pattern.

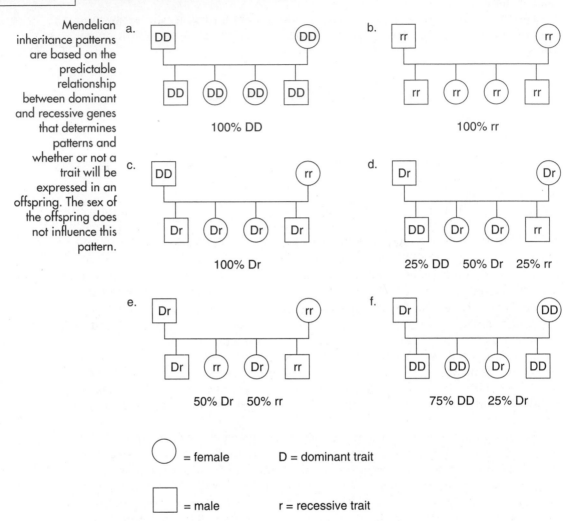

trait but they both have a recessive gene. There is a 75 percent chance the child will have the dominant trait and a 25 percent chance that the child will have the recessive trait (see Figure 2.5 d). It is only in the last pairing that the offspring will be observably different from her parents. In two of the situations (rr and DD) the phenotype and genotype are the same; in the other two they are different. These probabilities are the same for each child. That is, the odds for each child of having the recessive trait are 1 in 4.

Some aspects of development are controlled almost totally by genetics, such as the major motor milestones in infancy (sitting independently, crawling, even tricycle riding). However, in most aspects of development an individual's genotype establishes the upper and lower limits of development, or the reaction range.

This is true in such traits as height and intelligence. A child might inherit the genetic potential to be tall, but as a result of poor nutrition may not reach that potential. Likewise, a child might inherit the potential for having an intelligence quotient of between 100 and 130. If this child is raised in an unstimulating environment, her IQ will be close to average, whereas if she is raised in a very stimulating environment where she is read to, talked to, and encouraged to ask questions, taken on trips, and so on, the expression of this genotype will be a very bright child. As a rule, genes and the environment tend to work together. That is, bright parents are likely to have bright children, they are likely to provide a stimulating environment for these children, and they often encourage the child to take an active part in her environment.

Genetic Disorders

Genetic disorders are related to the hereditary material that is carried on the genes. Genetic disorders can be passed from one generation to another. Some of these abnormalities are relatively unimportant, whereas others can cause disabilities or even be fatal. More than 2,000 single-gene anomalies have been identified. In general, there are more disorders associated with recessive genes than with dominant genes. That is, neither parent has the disorder (for example, cystic fibrosis), but each carries the recessive gene for it. In situations where a dominant gene is identified as causing the problem, the child always has at least one parent who has the same condition, unless the disorder in that child is due to a gene mutation.

Genetic disorders are divided into two broad categories: autosomal disorders and X-linked disorders. Autosomal disorders refer to disorders of the genes in the 22 pairs of autosomal chromosomes. X-linked disorders are those carried on the sex chromosome.

Autosomal Inheritance Patterns

If a disorder is caused by a single autosomal dominant gene, at least one parent will have the same disorder. This parent is most likely heterozygous for that trait. It is very rare to be homozygous (James, 1994b). If one parent has the disorder, the child will have a 50 percent chance of inheriting the dominant gene and hence the disorder (see Figure 2.5 e). Either mothers or fathers can pass the disorder on to the child. An example of a single-dominant gene disorder is achondroplasia. Individuals with this condition are disproportionately short with a large head.

Single-gene recessive traits are the most frequent causes of disorders. In this case both parents carry the same recessive gene. However, neither parent has the disorder. To be affected, the child must receive the recessive gene from both parents (Figure 2.5 d). There is a 25 percent chance that this will happen. There is also a 50 percent possibility that the child will inherit the recessive gene from only one parent. In this case the child will not have the disorder, however, he will become a carrier of the disorder. The probability of disorders from single recessive genes increases when people who are closely related marry or when individuals continually marry within the same group. Hence, many of these disabilities affect some populations and not others.

Sickle cell anemia is an abnormality of the red blood cells that affects all bodily systems and is painful. It primarily occurs in African Americans. Tay-Sachs is a progressive neurological disorder that causes blindness and early death. It occurs primarily in children of eastern European Jewish decent. Cystic fibrosis is another disorder caused by an autosomal recessive gene. It affects the lungs and pancreas; the individual lacks some necessary enzymes and produces excessive amounts of phlegm which is difficult to expel. Phenylketonuria (PKU) is a metabolic disorder that causes mental retardation. Because of the high incidence of carriers of this recessive gene in the population (1 to 2 per 100 persons), infants are screened at birth for this particular disorder. If dietary treatment is started within the first month or two of life, the child is likely to have normal intelligence. The later the treatment is begun, the greater the retardation.

X-Linked Inheritance Patterns

X-linked traits are carried by the X chromosome. The pattern of inheritability of these traits is different from the autosomal chromosomes. The autosomal chromosomes are matched pairs. However, the sex chromosomes in males are not a matching pair. Where females have two X chromosomes (XX), the male configuration is (XY). At this point, no harmful genes have been found on the Y chromosome. As a male has only one X chromosome, any abnormal gene on that chromosome, even if it is recessive, will produce the trait. (With X-linked traits there is greater variability of expression and dominant, recessive, and intermediate expression may occur in the heterozygous female)

The possibilities of this inheritance pattern are shown in Figure 2.6.

Fathers

- If unaffected he can give it to neither sons or daughters (2.6 a).
- If affected, he cannot give it to his sons—the father gives his son his Y chromosome, these disorders are inherited through the X chromosome (2.6 b).
- If affected, he will give it to all his daughters (2.6 b). Whether they display the trait or are carriers will depend on dominance.

Mothers

- If a carrier, she will pass the gene to her son 50 percent of the time and he will display the trait (2.6 c).
- If a carrier, half of the daughters will be carriers (or if dominant, display the condition). (adapted from James, 1994b, 16)

These X-linked traits are far more common in males than in females. Male pattern baldness is an example. The gene for this trait is carried on the X chromosome. A female must inherit this recessive trait from both her mother and father to have the characteristic thinning hair (2.6 d). This is far less common. Males can have this recessive gene on their X chromosome and pass it to their daughters. These daughters will be carriers and not display the trait unless they also receive the recessive gene from their mother. Other examples of X-linked recessive disor-

Figure 2.6 | X-Linked Inheritance Patterns

Traits carried on the X sex chromosome follow a different pattern of inheritance that is influenced by sex of the offspring.

a. Unaffected male and female

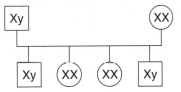

No males or females will be affected

b. Unaffected male, female carrier

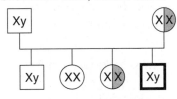

50% of the females will be carriers
50% of the males will have the disorder

c. Affected male, unaffected female

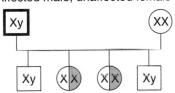

No males will be affected
100% of females will be carriers

d. Affected male, carrier female

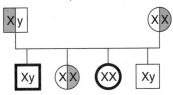

50% of males will be affected
50% of males will not be affected
50% of females will be affected
50% of females will be carriers

○ = female

□ = male

▨ ◑ = carrier

■ ● = has condition, disorder, or trait

ders are color blindness and hemophilia A. Hemophilia is caused by a deficiency in the substances of the blood that lead to clotting.

In addition to traits related to single genes, some disorders are multifactorial, that is, predisposing genes interact in addition to unknown environmental factors but they do not follow the patterns of Mendelian inheritance. These disorders run in families, and close relatives of a person with this trait are more likely to inherit it than the general public (James, 1994b). Examples of these disorders include cleft lip, with or without cleft palate, club foot, and neural tube defects such as spina bifida. Neural tube defects relate to defects in the spinal column where some of the spinal cord is outside the body in a cyst. A cleft lip is the failure of the two sides of the upper lip to grow together, a cleft palate is a split or opening in the roof of the mouth. Both cleft lips and cleft palates can be surgically corrected. A club foot is an awkward, twisted position of one or both feet that cannot be turned back to normal placement.

Chromosome Disorders

Chromosomal disorders involve abnormality in either the number or structure of the chromosomes. Abnormalities in number include either missing or extra chromosomes. Abnormalities in structure include material that is missing, duplicated, in the wrong place on a chromosome, or information that belongs on one chromosome that is located on a different chromosome.

We have learned a great deal about chromosomes and defects related to chromosomal disorders though a procedure called *karyotyping*. To the trained eye each of the 23 pairs of chromosomes is slightly different. In karyotyping, cells are taken from a person, grown in a culture, stopped in the middle of a cell division, treated, and stained. These are then photographed and studied. It is possible to detect chromosomal abnormalities in this way. However, individual genes are too small to be seen with this method (see Figure 2.7).

Disorders of chromosomes occur frequently, and about half of these result in spontaneous abortions. This is particularly true if there are major defects in chromosomes 1 to 12. When the defect occurs in later pairs of chromosomes, the fetus may be carried to term. Down syndrome is the most frequent chromosomal disorder, occurring in 1 in 700 live births. The most common form of Down syndrome (95 to 98 percent) is trisomy 21 (James, 1994b). In this disorder, there is a rearrangement of the 21st chromosome, resulting in three parts instead of two. This rearrangement results in mental retardation, cardiac problems, and some skeletal abnormalities.

Routine Screening

Many screening techniques are used routinely for detecting genetic anomalies and other problems in the fetus. If the screening techniques do indicate an abnormality, other, more complicated, precise, and expensive procedures are used as a

Figure 2.7 | Karyotype

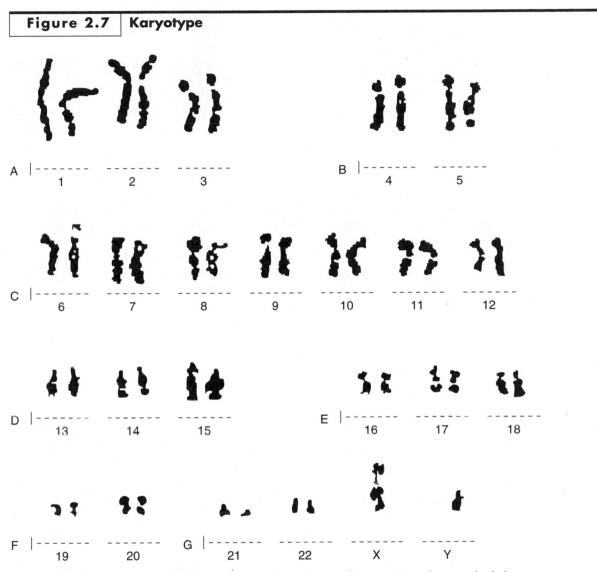

A karyotype is a photograph of all chromosomes contained in a cell. Once micro-photographed, the individual chromosomes are cut apart to form pairs. The last two chromosomes are an XY pair, indicating a male.

follow-up. There are a variety of diagnostic techniques used in genetic screening. They are typically used in combination.

Maternal serum alpha-fetoprotein procedures use blood samples from the mother to determine the level of alpha-fetoprotein in the fetus. Many doctors do this test routinely on pregnant women as there are no risks associated with the test. Alpha-fetoprotein is a substance produced by the liver of the fetus that passes into the mother's blood stream by diffusion through the placenta and amnion. High levels of alpha-fetoprotein between 15 and 20 weeks are associated with neural tube defects, spinal cord, and abdominal wall defects. These malformations allow too much alpha fetoprotein to leak into the amniotic fluid and hence the maternal blood. If high levels are found, doctors typically recommend additional testing and ultrasound examinations (Williamson, 1994). When the levels are found to be out of the expected range, the test is repeated. Reliability is a problem with this procedure. False positive readings are not uncommon and are frequently associated with miscalculations of gestational age.

Levels of alpha-fetoprotein are also associated with chromosomal abnormalities such as Down syndrome. Approximately 45 percent of fetuses with Down syndrome could be detected using maternal serum alpha-fetoprotein levels (Williamson, 1994).

Ultrasonography (ultrasound) uses the echoes from low-energy, high-frequency sound waves to produce a computer video image of the fetus and its internal organs. Some physicians feel that a midtrimester (18 to 20 weeks) obstetric ultrasound examination should be part of routine practice; others do not (Harman, 1994). Information from the ultrasound can confirm the viability of the pregnancy, certify pregnancy dating, identify multiple gestation, and view fetal anatomy for abnormalities. Advocates feel that it demystifies fetal life and stimulates bonding. They have found that it is useful in getting the family involved and in getting compliance from teenage mothers (Harman, 1994).

Ultrasound is also used to confirm or disconfirm fetal malformations such as neural tube defects and Down syndrome initially suspected because of alpha-fetoprotein testing. Ultrasound is used later in pregnancy when there is concern about the relationship between the size of the fetal head relative to the mother's pelvis. When ultrasound examinations are done, follow-up counseling should be immediately available when risks are found.

Amniocentesis involves the removal of fluid which contains cells and biochemical products of the fetus from the amniotic cavity. It should only be done under continuous ultrasound guidance to avoid hurting the fetus and umbilical cord (Ramsey & Fisk, 1994). Amniocentesis was the first technique that allowed access to the intrauterine environment and is the most common invasive procedure for prenatal diagnosis. It involves withdrawing a small amount of amniotic fluid from the mother between the 14th and 19th week of pregnancy. The fetal cells are grown in cultures and analyzed for chromosomal abnormalities and byproducts of inborn errors of metabolism, and the presence of alpha-fetoprotein. The performance of a fetal karyotype is the most common reason for amniocentesis. Prenatal diagnosis can be made of over half the 200 inborn errors of metabolism. Infections such as fetal cytomegalovirus (CMV) can also be detected. Although difficult to quantify exactly, the risk of miscarriage because of amniocentesis is about 1 percent (Ramsey & Fisk, 1994). Again, counseling should be available to couples when results show fetal abnormalities.

Chorionic villus sampling (CVS) is one of the newest procedures of genetic diagnosis. The procedure involves sampling cells from the hairlike villi on the embryonic sac during the 8th to 12th weeks of gestation. This can be done with a needle inserted through the abdominal wall or the cervix under ultrasound. One advantage of this over amniocentesis is that it is done earlier in the pregnancy. It also collects enough DNA for testing, and karyotyping is faster. It is used for the diagnosis of monogenetic disorders, chromosomal breakage syndromes, sex typing in X-linked diseases, and fragile X. It can also be used for detecting most of the metabolic diseases that can be diagnosed with amniotic fluid. However, it is not effective in diagnosing neural tube defects (Holzgreve & Miny, 1994). Medical risks are higher as gestational age advances and before nine weeks gestation. Contamination of chorionic cell cultures with maternal cells can cause false negative diagnosis. However, with more experience with this procedure this risk has decreased. Again, counseling needs to be available to help prospective parents understand the risks to the fetus and provide other relevant information.

DNA technology methods are relatively new tests for determining structural changes in a gene or in DNA. DNA analysis is typically done on cells from the chorion or fetal blood. It can be done from the amniotic fluid, but it takes time to grow sufficient cells to analyze. New methods that do not require a culture (which takes about 6 to 10 days) may mean that results are known sooner. The blood is purified to separate the DNA from other parts of the blood that are not needed for the test. The laboratory then processes the blood by precisely cutting the DNA into small pieces. These pieces are labeled so the DNA fragment of importance can be recognized. A genetic specialist evaluates the results of the testing and explains them (National Center for Education in Maternal and Child Health, 1991). About 50 genetic disorders can be identified in this way, including cystic fibrosis, Duchenne muscular dystrophy, fragile X, hemophilia A and B, and others (Holzgreve & Miny, 1994).

Although these various screening tests have been discussed individually, they are typically done in a series. For example, suppose 1,000 women had a maternal serum alpha-fetoprotein test done. This might be elevated for 50, and the test would be repeated for those 50. After retesting, approximately 25 would have normal alpha-fetoprotein levels. The other 25 would be given an ultrasound examination. The ultrasound might find eight cases of multiple gestation, fetal death, or other problems that do not need follow-up testing. The remaining 17 women would then have some combination of amniocentesis, chorionic villus sampling, DNA analysis, or high-resolution ultrasound. It is likely that these 17 women would be classified as having high-risk pregnancies and therefore would need special monitoring and care as well as counseling, as would perhaps the eight with unusual ultrasound readings. The other 983 would receive routine prenatal care (Williamson, 1994).

When results of diagnostic tests show that the developing fetus has a major abnormality, parents must make a decision about whether the infant will be carried to term or the pregnancy will be terminated. If parents have already made a decision to carry an infant to term, the screening may not be done for diagnostic purposes, but rather to determine the members of the interdisciplinary team who will be needed during the birthing process.

Genetic Counseling

Genetic counseling is the process of advising individuals of the consequence of a disorder, the probability of developing it and transmitting it, and ways in which the disorder can be prevented or ameliorated (James, 1994b). A range of individuals offer genetic counseling, depending on the complexity of the situation. Most obstetricians and other health practitioners, such as family doctors, nurses, midwives, and social workers, feel comfortable providing information about chromosomal abnormalities and common conditions that follow the Mendelian pattern. Beyond this, they may refer individuals to a clinical geneticist.

Genetic counseling before conception can often identify genetic disorders within a family and the risk of occurrence. The goal is to reduce the probability of serious life-threatening disorders occurring or reoccurring in the same family. Parents who have, or who have had, a child with an inherited disease might decide to seek genetic counseling before deciding whether or not to have more children. Genetic counseling might be particularly appropriate for couples from groups with a high incidence of an inherited trait, women over 35, individuals who have had excessive exposure to drugs, chemicals or radiation, and close relatives (first cousins) who plan to marry (Miller, 1990).

Often genetics counseling begins with a family tree, genogram, or pedigree that carefully identifies people in the family who may have the disease or be carriers of the disease. This pedigree includes close family relatives and is done over several generations. For genetic counseling to be effective, all hereditary information needs to be accurate and comprehensive enough to make an accurate diagnosis or estimate of risk. Then this information must be imparted accurately and in a way that the individual understands (James, 1994b). Decision making lies with the individual receiving the information. Genetic counseling should be nondirective and supportive.

In addition to heredity, there are many other factors that affect the developing fetus during the prenatal period. Many of these factors can affect the eventual growth and development of the child after birth. In general, exposure to risk factors during the first three months of pregnancy poses the greatest risk to the developing fetus.

Maternal Diseases, Disorders, and Conditions

There are many different maternal diseases, disorders, and conditions that affect the unborn infant. These can be infectious diseases such as viruses, and even urinary tract infections that contribute to maternal and perinatal morbidity and mortality. Infectious diseases work somewhat differently in pregnant women. During pregnancy, maternal immuno-suppression alters the natural course of many infectious diseases. Some, such as Group B streptococci, are rarely associated with infection in nonpregnant women but are causes of infectious morbidity during pregnancy. Additionally, some noninfectious chronic diseases of the mother, such as diabetes, may need different management techniques because of the demands of pregnancy. Only the most common conditions will be discussed. Negative effects of all of these risk factors can be avoided, cured, or birth outcomes improved, with good prenatal care.

There is a group of infections called TORCH infections that all cause similar malformations. TORCH is an acronym that includes toxoplasmosis, rubella, syphilis, cytomegalovirus, and herpes simplex virus.

Rubella

We have learned a tremendous amount about critical periods in development from children of mothers who contracted rubella (German measles) during pregnancy. We initially thought that the only effect of maternal rubella was congenital hearing impairment. Over time it became clearer that the exact timing of the disease had a tremendous influence on the birth outcome. If the exposure was after 26 weeks gestational age, the infant did not develop congenital rubella syndrome (CRS). This was unrelated to the severity of the mother's case of rubella.

The most profound effects occur if the rubella coincides with the first trimester of pregnancy, when the congenital rubella syndrome produces not only deafness, but stunted growth, cataracts, heart defects, and other problems. Affected children are also likely to be born prematurely. Now, rubella vaccine, which became available in the United States in 1969, is routinely given to children between the ages of 1 and 2 and rates of congenital rubella syndrome have dropped precipitously. Serological testing for immunity is routinely done for all pregnant women. If they are not immune, they should receive the rubella vaccine at least three months before they plan to become pregnant (Pastorek II, 1994). It is the best protection against this syndrome.

Syphilis

Syphilis is a venereal disease that once appeared to be virtually eradicated with the advent of antibiotics. However, it is increasingly becoming a problem again. If it is detected and cured with antibiotics before the 16th week of pregnancy, there are likely to be few adverse effects. Syphilis is challenging to diagnose in the mother and is based on patient history, and a physical examination. (Primary syphilis is typically characterized by a painless chancre or ulcer, secondary syphilis by skin rashes.) Suspicion of syphilis is followed by a variety of specific tests which are confounded by both false positive and false negative results (Giovangrandi et al., 1994).

Although most bacteria cannot cross the placental barrier, the bacterium that produces syphilis is an exception. That particular spirochete can cross the placenta. Whereas some researchers feel the fetus is not at risk until about 18 weeks gestation, and then only during the early stages of the maternal infection (Barron & Lindheimer, 1995), others are not as confident of the time line (Giovangrandi et al., 1994). The risk to the fetus is influenced by the severity of the infection. Many affected infants die before birth or shortly after birth. Those who live have a variety of problems, including blindness, growth retardation, central nervous system problems, anemia, peritonitis, and other effects.

Cytomegalovirus and Herpes Simplex Virus

Cytomegalovirus (CMV) and herpes simplex virus, are DNA viruses and members of the herpes family of viruses. They produce both chronic and recurrent infections in humans that are frequently activated by pregnancy.

CMV is a frequent infection in humans and is found in about 1 percent of all newborns (Pastorek II, 1994). CMV is in many ways a silent or dormant disease that can affect the mother's genitalia, breasts, urinary tract, or cervix, yet it rarely produces symptoms that cause distress, so that women do not know that they have the disease. When symptoms are present, they are indistinguishable from mononucleosis. Identification is challenging. Although CMV can be passed on to the fetus through the placenta at any time, it is most likely to happen when the infant is passing through the cervix during birth. The virus is also excreted in breast milk. There is no accepted therapy for either acute maternal or neonatal infection (Pastorek II, 1994).

CMV causes mental retardation and congenital deafness. It can also cause either small or large head circumference, damage to the retina of the eye, blindness, an enlarged liver and spleen, and psychomotor delay, as well as other symptoms. CMV seems especially prevalent among the sexually active, the young, and the poor. It can be transmitted through sexual activity. Pregnant women are advised to avoid contact with people who are infected. Women working in child-care settings are more at risk for developing CMV because infected infants and toddlers shed the virus from their urine and respiratory tract. Good hygiene measures prevent transmission of the virus. However, as both adults and children who are affected show no symptoms, this is difficult. A vaccine is being researched but is not yet available.

Herpes simplex virus causes a variety of diseases in humans from "fever blisters" to genital infections. Orolabial herpes is primarily a disease of childhood. Adult herpes is transmitted through sexual contact. It is not clear whether or not the fetus is affected before birth. If it is, the current belief is that the disease is fatal to the fetus and causes a spontaneous abortion. Maternal herpes that is serious enough to cause illness may stimulate premature uterine contractions and hence premature delivery. The infection is definitely transmitted when the fetus passes through a birth canal with active lesions. (If there are active lesions, a cesarean delivery is recommended.) About half of the infants are infected. Outcomes vary with the type of infection. There is not a clear syndrome associated with herpes. A few infants will have localized infections, but many infected infants will die. Those that live will probably have some combination of mental retardation, underdeveloped brains, seizures, paralysis, deafness, or blindness.

Like CMV, herpes is difficult to diagnose because a woman may have no active lesions. There is no cure for these infectious diseases. However, if it is known that a woman has CMV or herpes, the pregnancy can be managed in such a way as to reduce the probability of neonatal infection. Without proper management the outcomes are much less positive.

Toxoplasmosis

Toxoplasmosis is one of the most common protozoan parasites in humans. It is contracted through the fecal matter of cats, raw or poorly cooked meat, or raw goat's milk. Most people with toxoplasmosis are asymptomatic. Prevention is the best strategy. If affected, the infant's central nervous system is impacted, which results in *hydrocephalus* (excess cerebrospinal fluid backs up into ventricles of the brain and head size expands), or *microcephalus* (the brain is too small, malformed, or has missing pieces), mental retardation, seizures, and other problems.

Chlamydia

Some sexually transmitted diseases pose serious risks to the fetus. One of the most common, yet least well-known, is chlamydia. This bacterial disease affects between 3 and 10 million people in the United States. If a pregnant woman has chlamydia, the fetus is most likely to be affected during the birthing process. Outcomes range from conjunctivitis (eye inflammation) to pneumonia. It also increases the risk of prematurity and stillbirths. Chlamydia is responsive to antibiotics (Wallis, 1985).

Human Immunodeficiency Virus and AIDS

The first cases of AIDS in adults were reported in 1981, followed a year later by a similar discovery in children (Conlon, 1992). The human immunodeficiency virus (HIV) has caused massive concern in the entire health-care and social system. Adult cases of clinical AIDS have increased exponentially, moved into the general population, and, are paralleled (although at a lower level) with a rise in pediatric cases (Pastorek II, 1994). Initially, the HIV pediatric cases were children with hemophilia. Today over 80 percent of children acquire HIV from their mother. By 1990 the Centers for Disease Control had identified 2,789 cases of pediatric AIDS (Centers for Disease Control, 1991). It is believed that for each case of AIDS there are at least ten others infected with HIV (Conlon, 1992). Even this may be a conservative estimate.

HIV can be transmitted from the mother to the fetus in utero, during delivery, or through breast milk. Women who have no symptoms, but have HIV, can transmit the virus. From 30 to 65 percent of children born to HIV infected mothers actually develop AIDS. Many infants born to these mothers are preterm. It is not known whether this is caused by the HIV or whether it is related to other risk factors such as drug abuse. A number of centers are studying HIV in pregnant women, but the results so far are inconclusive. Studies focus on antiviral therapy to interrupt the transmission of HIV and the efficacy of cesarean delivery to protect against neonatal infection.

Screening tests are 99 percent effective in identifying HIV in adults. Neonates are more difficult to screen as they may retain maternal antibodies for up to 15 months. Initially, infants are screened through blood drawn from their heel. The blood is tested using the enzyme-linked immunosorbent assay (ELISA) (Olson, Huszti, Mason, & Seibert, 1989). ELISA tests for antibodies to HIV in the blood. If positive, it is followed by the Western Blot procedure for confirmation. To better differentiate maternal and child antibodies, a further assay has been developed called polymerase chain reaction (PCR). Using this new procedure, approximately 50 percent of infants at risk for AIDS can be diagnosed at birth and 95 percent by three months (Ammann, 1994). AIDS is also diagnosed based on clinical symptoms and is a concern when young children regress in motor or cognitive functioning when their parents are at risk for the disease (Bale, 1990). It is important that diagnosis is made early so that treatment can begin immediately.

Pediatric AIDS can begin any time between two months and five years after the infant is born. AIDS develops much more quickly in children than adults because of their immature immune system. Many infants who are infected perinatally die before their second birthday (Anderson, 1990). After initial infection, about 25 percent of children develop AIDS within the year, 45 percent within two years, and 80 percent by the end of four years (Gustavasson & Segal, 1994). Infants with AIDS are typically given antibiotics as prophylactic therapy against infection, and medication such as azidothymidine (AZT) to hinder growth of the HIV virus (Bale, 1990).

Children with pediatric AIDS show progressive neurological complications, including impaired brain growth, as well as the viral and bacterial infections that typically accompany AIDS (Pueschel, Scola, & McConnel, 1990). They typically lose developmental and intellectual milestones that they have obtained. Their situation is complicated by parents who may be unable to care for the infant because of their own health-related problems.

Group B Streptococcus

Group B streptococcus was recognized in the 1930s and 1940s as a cause of postpartum infection, but it was not until the 1960s that the scope of the perinatal and neonatal infections was recognized. Neonates who have invasive Group B streptococcal infections have an estimated mortality rate of 20 percent (Gravett & Sampson, 1994). There is no evidence that identification or treatment of women with streptococcal B infections before pregnancy had any benefit. It is recommended that women be routinely screened between 26 and 28 weeks for this infection, and, where the infection is found, treated with antibiotics. There is also concern for infection for women whose membranes rupture 18 hours or more before delivery (Gravett & Sampson, 1994). Group B streptococcus can cause premature rupture of the membranes and preterm labor. In the fetus, it is a leading cause of septicemia and meningitis during the first two months of neonatal life. About 20 percent of affected infants die and others have neurological complications (Gravett & Sampson, 1994).

Women are routinely screened for Group B streptococcal infections between 26 and 28 weeks.

Fetal Hemolytic Disease

All women should have their blood typed and an antibody screen at their first prenatal visit and after delivery. Hemolytic diseases are a result of incompatible blood factors in the mother and fetus. All individuals have one of four major blood types: A, AB, B, and O. In addition to these different types, there are other factors in the blood called antigens which must also be compatible. The problem arises when the mother's body reacts to the antigen in the fetus as a foreign substance and attacks it. There are a variety of different types of blood group incompatibilities that might be discovered. The most common antigens are the Rhesus (Rh) family (D, C, E, c, e). Individuals who have the D antigen are Rh-positive; those who lack the antigen are Rh-negative. In the United States, about 85 percent of the Caucasian population and 92 to 93 percent of the African American population have the D antigen and are Rh-positive (Weiner, 1994).

Rh incompatibility occurs only when a mother is Rh-negative and the fetus is Rh-positive; an Rh-positive mother and an Rh-negative fetus is not a problem. The only way a fetus can be Rh-positive, is to inherit the D antigen from his father. Until an exchange of blood between the fetus and the Rh-negative mother occurs, there are no problems. However, once this exchange has happened and the mother has become sensitized, her body reacts to the infant's Rh-positive blood cells as a foreign substance and develops antibodies to attack the fetus' blood cells causing them to break apart. This can result in brain damage or death for the fetus. Rh incompatibility with a first child is rare because the blood of the fetus must mix with the mother's for the antibodies to be produced. This frequently happens during delivery but rarely before, unless the mother has had a mismatched blood transfusion. Earlier in an initial pregnancy there is some risk of the blood mixing through vaginal bleeding and a 2 percent risk with an amniocentesis (Weiner, 1994).

Initial attempts at controlling this problem were through fetal blood transfusions (both directly after birth and *in utero*). They were increasingly successful and are still used for infants with fetal hemolytic anemia. The development of an immunoprophylaxis, Rhogam, solved the problem in a different way. Rhogam is an anti-D immunoglobulin that prevents the development of the mother's antibodies; hence, preventing the problem in the mother rather than controlling it in the fetus. Nonsensitized mothers must receive Rhogam no later than 72 hours after delivering an Rh-positive infant and are given it for prophylaxis at 28 weeks gestation. This must be done after every possible exposure to Rh-positive blood, for example, after a miscarriage, abortion, or vaginal bleeding of unknown origin.

Diabetes Mellitus

Many women become pregnant already possessing conditions that may affect the fetus; in other situations, pregnancy itself can precipitate risk conditions. Pregnancy causes a number of complex metabolic changes in a woman that can alter previously controlled conditions such as diabetes. Women with diabetes do not produce enough insulin. Before the discovery of insulin in 1921, diabetic women seldom became pregnant; if they did, maternal and fetal mortality rates were high (Landon & Gabbe, 1994). Insulin has resulted in more women with diabetes becoming pregnant, but insulin management is challenging during pregnancy.

Pregnancy influences the amount of synthetic insulin women need in a variety of ways at different times. Early in pregnancy, insulin-requiring diabetic women may have periods of hypoglycemia because of the heightened demands of the fetus for glucose (sugar). Other factors, such as hormones that are produced by the placenta, alter the mother's metabolism and, in general, increase her need for insulin. This produces periods of maternal hyperglycemia resulting in fetal hyperglycemia. Too much glucose results in excessive fetal growth. Diabetic women who receive optimal prenatal care do well; those who do not are more likely to experience sudden and unexplained stillbirths. However, even with optimal care there is still an increased risk for major birth anomalies that occur in about 5 to 10 percent of live births to diabetic women (Landon & Gabbe, 1994).

Women who are not diabetic may become so during pregnancy, particularly if they are obese, because of increased needs for insulin and an underutilization of the available insulin. This occurs later in pregnancy. Diabetes is diagnosed though urine and blood samples taken from pregnant women (Landon & Gabbe, 1994).

Maternal Weight and Weight Gain

Prepregnancy weight is a given and is not amenable to change. However, there are really no standards by which to evaluate weight as a risk factor. In general, the function of evaluating weight is to determine if a pregnant women is under-nourished or obese. The goal for underweight women is to increase caloric intake. Women who are anorexic or bulimic are advised to wait for the eating dis-order to be in remission before becoming pregnant. Underweight women are likely to have infants who are small for gestational age and may experience ane-mia and preterm delivery (Wildschut, 1994).

Women who are overweight are more likely to have hypertensive disorders, gestational diabetes, and urinary tract infections. They are also likely to have infants that are large for their gestational age. Dietary manipulation is not advo-cated during pregnancy as it is viewed as having no benefit to the mother at this time and may be harmful to the fetus (Wildschut, 1994).

Weight gain during pregnancy is a concern for many women. Expectations are that women will gain about 27 pounds. Obviously there are differences that are dependent on weight, age, dietary habits, and other variables. It is perhaps better expressed as an increase of about 17 to 20 percent in body weight (Wildschut, 1994). Mean weight gain is not linear in pregnancy. Little weight is gained in the first trimester, in the second trimester about a pound a week is gained, and this decreases to slightly under a pound per week for the third trimester.

Other Diseases and Conditions

A host of other diseases and conditions can also put the fetus at risk if not known and well monitored during pregnancy. These include infectious diseases such as urinary tract infections, vaginitis, influenza, sexually transmitted diseases, chicken pox, and hepatitis. If possible, these these conditions should be avoided and, if acquired, they need to be treated. Auto immune diseases such as lupus and rheumatoid arthritis affect pregnancy. Obviously, preexisting conditions such as cardiac, respiratory, renal, thyroid, pituitary, and adrenal disorders impact pregnancy. These need to be monitored during pregnancy.

Environmental Factors

There are many factors found within the environment of the pregnant mother that can greatly affect the developing fetus. Radiation is one such commonly occurring factor. Low doses of radiation have not been found to cause harm. However, a mother's excessive or repeated exposure to high levels of radiation has been shown to result in damage to the central nervous system of the fetus. This is why pregnant women should avoid X-rays when possible or wear lead capes to protect the fetus. Females of all ages should wear lead capes when exposed to X-rays to protect their supply of eggs from radiation. Other influences include hyperthermia or exposure to high temperatures, especially during the first trimester, which is why spas and hot baths are not recommended for pregnant women. Maternal exposure to mercury can lead to severe disabling conditions in the infant. Lead has also been shown to cause brain damage in infants in situations where the mother had a high ingestion of lead during pregnancy. Finally, exposure to many environmental pesticides, cleaners, paints, and other toxic substances places the fetus at a great risk for later problems. It is difficult for women to avoid environmental teratogens that come from industrial pollution. The most common of these are polychlorinated biphenyls, or PCBs. These teratogens were banned in the 1970s but can still be transmitted through the food chain. Infants with higher than usual amounts of PCBs in their blood show depressed responsiveness and, later, cognitive problems (Jacobson, Jacobson, Padgett, Brumitt & Billings, 1992).

Substance Abuse During Pregnancy

Substance abuse during pregnancy has become a major health issue. Although there are numerous studies about substance abuse during pregnancy, it should be noted that it is difficult to obtain reliable data on particular substances as they are frequently used in combination and are confounded by other variables. For example, a pregnant woman might use a variety of drugs of various levels of purity which might be smoked or taken intravenously. She might additionally drink alcohol and smoke. Her risk situation may be further compounded by poor nutrition, lack of prenatal care, and poverty. In general, it is difficult to isolate the effects of any one of these variables as a single entity. It is also difficult without accurate knowledge of the quantity, timing, and duration of exposure to make accurate statements about the effects of drugs, alcohol, and nicotine. An additional problem is that pharmaceutical and other lobbies have apparently discouraged or delayed the publication of studies documenting the harmful effects of certain substances (Mason & Lee, 1995).

Teratogens are substances that can adversely affect the development of the fetus. They can cause death, malformations, growth deficiency, and functional deficits. Some common teratogens include alcohol, nicotine, and prescription and illegal drug substances. Many of the effects of specific teratogens are known. For example, thalidomide, a drug used primarily in Europe in the 1960s, caused physical anomalies in children, such as missing or malformed limbs. The most pervasive effects occurred when the drug was used during the first two months of pregnancy.

Because substances such as nicotine, alcohol, and drugs, are widely used and because their negative effects on the fetus are preventable, they are reviewed in more detail here.

Fetal Tobacco Syndrome

Approximately 25 to 30 percent of pregnant women smoke (Gilbert & Harmon, 1993). Smoking is the number-one preventable cause of infants with low birth weights. The degree of low birth weight is directly proportional to the number of cigarettes smoked per day or the length of time a woman is exposed to passive smoke (Gilbert and Harmon, 1993). **Fetal tobacco syndrome** is defined in terms of a mother smoking five or more cigarettes per day, a growth retardation— weighing less than 2,500 grams at 37 weeks—and no history of hypertension or other causes for the growth retardation (Schubert & Savage, 1994).

When a woman smokes, the carbon monoxide from her blood stream crosses the placenta and reduces the amount of oxygen available to the fetus. The nicotine causes the blood vessels to constrict. In response to this, both maternal and fetal heart rate increase and fetal movement is decreased. Cigarette smoke also interferes with the assimilation of essential vitamins and minerals by the fetus. Nicotine has been found in breast milk, although the impact on the infant has not been well documented (Schubert & Savage, 1994). Long-term follow-up has shown impaired intellectual and emotional development. Children of fathers who smoked were twice as likely to develop cancer in adulthood when compared with children whose fathers did not smoke (Sandler, Everson, Wilcox & Browder, 1985).

Prevention involves explaining the risks of maternal smoking, and women are advised to stop or at least reduce the number of cigarettes they smoke and to avoid passive smoke. It is not clear what information techniques are most useful in assisting women to quit smoking.

Fetal Alcohol Syndrome and Fetal Alcohol Effects

Alcohol is abused more than any other drug in the United States today. There are approximately 6 million people in the United States classified as dependent on alcohol and another 10 million who drink enough to be considered problem drinkers (Pietrantoni & Knuppel, 1991). Estimates vary on the number of women who are heavy drinkers. Some estimate as low as 1 to 3 percent (Schubert & Savage, 1994), whereas others estimate that between 8 and 11 percent of women of child-bearing age are either problem drinkers or alcoholics. Approximately 59 to 65 percent of embryo-fetuses are exposed to alcohol in utero (Mason & Lee, 1995; Pietrantoni & Knuppel, 1991). Alcohol intake tends to decrease during pregnancy, but the incidence of binge drinking remains constant or increases (Conlon, 1992).

When a pregnant woman drinks alcohol, both her own blood alcohol content and that of her fetus increase. They increase at the same rate, but the fetus' blood alcohol level remains higher longer because the mother's liver must remove the alcohol from her own blood before removing the alcohol from the fetus. The ethanol in alcohol crosses the placental barrier and goes into both the fetus and the amniotic fluid. The ethanol may impair the placental function of getting essential nutrients to the fetus and interfere with carbohydrate metabolism, resulting in growth retardation. Alcohol causes fetal malformations through chemical imbalances which affect the cells and the DNA. Alcohol also affects fetal breathing and, consequently, levels of oxygen in the blood (Pietrantoni & Knuppel, 1991).

Although alcohol was known as a teratogen that could cause irreversible damage to the fetus, **fetal alcohol syndrome** (FAS) was not formally identified until the early 1970s (Spohr, Williams, & Steinhausen, 1993). Fetal alcohol syndrome results in three characteristic anomalies: interuterine and postnatal growth deficiency, including low birth weight and poor muscle tone; facial anomalies (thin upper lip, flat mid-face, short nose, low nasal bridge, small head, droopy eyes); and central nervous system dysfunction, including irritability, hyperactivity, attention deficit, and mental retardation (Bert, Greene, & Bert, 1992).

Prenatal alcohol use increases the probability of spontaneous abortion and stillbirth. The teratogenic effect of alcohol depends on the amount consumed. Mild FAS, which is characterized by low birth weight, occurs when the daily consumption of alcohol is 1 ounce of absolute alcohol, or two standard drinks. The complete syndrome, which affects 30 to 40 percent of the children of alcoholic mothers, is seen when 2 to 2.5 ounces of absolute alcohol are consumed per day during the first trimester (Pietrantoni & Knuppel, 1991). A safe level of alcohol consumption has not been established, and therefore abstinence is recommended.

In the United States, and in many parts of Europe, FAS is now the leading cause of mental retardation. It is more frequent than Down syndrome, spina bifida, or fragile-X syndrome (Batshaw & Perret, 1992). Although prevalence varies among different populations, estimates are that FAS occurs in 1:300 to 1:2,000 live births in the United States (Pietrantoni & Knuppel, 1991; Schubert & Savage, 1994). It is estimated that FAS among Native Americans may be as high as 1 in 100 births (Johnson, 1991).

Fetal alcohol syndrome can be diagnosed on the basis of a clinical examination of the child. Knowledge of maternal drinking behavior is not essential. When not all of the symptoms are present, an accurate diagnosis cannot be made; this situation is sometimes called fetal alcohol effects (FAE) or alcohol-related birth defects (ARBD). The frequency of ARBD is estimated at 3 to 5 per 1,000 live births (Pietrantoni & Knuppel, 1991). Together, then, FAS and FAE combined affect approximately 6 to 8 infants for each 1,000 live births. Fetal alcohol effects has a milder impact developmentally and is characterized by such things as growth retardation, low muscle tone, and poor sucking. FAE is probably far more prevalent than FAS, yet more difficult to isolate and attribute to alcohol consumption, since low birth weight, for example, could be caused by alcohol consumption or by other factors (Warren, 1985). In many cases it is difficult to determine the cause of congenital anomalies; however, some researchers feel that excessive prenatal alcohol exposure (FAS and FAE together) may account for about 5 percent of all congenital anomalies and 10 to 20 percent of all cases of mild mental retardation (Conlon, 1992).

If alcohol abuse occurs during the first trimester of pregnancy, in addition to an increased probability of miscarriage, the physical signs of fetal alcohol syndrome are likely to be present. Alcohol abuse during the second trimester affects physical and intellectual growth, but there are no physical malformations. If abuse occurs in the third trimester, cognitive development alone is impaired.

Drugs

Drugs are another commonly abused substance. Some pregnant women will use no drugs, others will use only those prescribed. However, some women will be recreational drug users (those who use narcotics sporadically), and others will be addicted (they have a tolerance to the narcotic and show signs of withdrawal when they stop using it). In the United States, the Food and Drug Administration (FDA) is considering methods of testing drugs to collect information about their effects on pregnant women to provide new information about safety. The FDA uses potential fetal risk as its criteria for establishing guidelines for prescribing drugs to pregnant women. Category A drugs have been well studied and have shown no fetal risk. Category B drugs have not shown adverse effects, but the studies have either been done on animals or were not well controlled. Category C drugs have shown adverse effects on animal fetuses, but human studies are not available. Category D drugs show definite human fetal risk, but benefits to the mother may make the risk acceptable (mother's life is threatened). Category X drugs are contraindicated because the fetal risk clearly outweighs any human benefit. Most do not view drugs in Category C, D, or X as safe (Barron & Lindheimer, 1995).

The overall general prevalence of maternal illicit drug use around the time of delivery has been estimated at about 10 to 11 percent (Curet, 1995). The actual incidence of use sometime during pregnancy is much higher than this. It ranges from 3 to 32 percent depending on whether one uses self-report or urine testing (Mason & Lee, 1995). If a woman uses illicit drugs, the specific drugs and the magnitude of use must be determined. Women are routinely asked about their drug use. About one-fourth to one-half deny using drugs even when they know they have just given a urine sample that will show their drug use (Mason & Lee, 1995).

General concerns related to drug use during pregnancy are birth defects, spontaneous abortion, preterm labor, low birth weight, and fetal death. Drugs taken by the mother pass through her system to the infant via the placenta. Commonly used nonprescription drugs such as aspirin and ibuprofen can cause problems for the fetus, especially during the last three months of pregnancy. Prescription medications indicated as sources of possible problems include the anticoagulant Warfarin, certain anticonvulsant medications (especially Dilantin), the drug Valium, and some antipsychotic medications. For most of these drugs, no safe amounts are indicated, and women using them should consult with their doctors before considering becoming pregnant.

Abused substances such as heroin and cocaine affect the central nervous system as stimulants and cause the blood vessels to constrict. The fetus receives less oxygen and nutrients, which interferes with development. These drugs are slow to be metabolized and excreted, remaining in the fetus longer than in the mother (Schneider & Chasnoff, 1987). They can also cause contractions of the uterus and a premature birth or spontaneous abortion.

It is estimated by the National Association for Perinatal Addiction Research and Education that in the United States 375,000 newborns each year are born to mothers who abuse drugs (Curet, 1995). It is also estimated that a single drug-exposed child with significant impairments will consume up to $750,000 in health and education services by age 18 (Mason & Lee, 1995). About 250,000 women in the United States are believed to be intravenous drug users. Most of these abuse opioids, which are available in a variety of forms. Opioids include fentanyl (Inno-var and Sublimaze); heroin; hydromorphone (Dilaudid); meperidone (Demerol); methadone, oxycodone (present in Percodan, Percocet, Tylox, and Vicodon); and propoxyphene (Darvon), as listed by Hoegerman and Schnoll (1991). Approximately 90 percent of these women are of child-bearing age. Opioids are associated with fetal loss and growth retardation and a propensity toward prematurity. Neonatal abstinence syndrome, or withdrawal, occurs in about 30 to 90 percent of infants exposed to either heroin or methadone. Up to 50 percent of pregnant street addicts are first seen when in labor (Schubert & Savage, 1994).

Marijuana

Marijuana is the most commonly used illicit drug among women of child-bearing age and, after alcohol and tobacco, is the most commonly used drug during pregnancy (Day & Richardson, 1991). It is difficult to ascertain accurate rates of use during pregnancy. It is estimated that approximately 20 to 30 percent of pregnant women use marijuana (Gilbert & Harmon, 1993). These rates vary in the population. Most women decrease their use of marijuana early in pregnancy. Marijuana users also tend to use alcohol, tobacco, and sometimes other illicit drugs. Frequency and duration of marijuana use, as well as the concentration of substances in the marijuana itself, are all factors which affect the impact of marijuana.

Marijuana increases the carbon monoxide level in the blood and increases maternal blood pressure and heart rate. There is some indication that infants of marijuana users might be born preterm and have low birth weights; however, this is not conclusive. Effects after birth are that the infants cry more and are difficult to console. However, there is disagreement on the effects of marijuana on the development of the fetus. When confounding variables of race, education, income, marital status, alcohol, and tobacco were controlled, many findings about the detrimental effects of marijuana did not hold up (Day & Richardson, 1991).

Cocaine

Although its use is not as prevalent as alcohol and marijuana, cocaine is another drug that can affect the fetus and infant. Like other drugs, it is rarely used in isolation. Additionally, although labeled as "cocaine," it may take many forms and may be used in different ways: inhaled, smoked, free-based, or injected; also, the concentration may vary. These complexities make it difficult to make conclusive statements. The use of cocaine during pregnancy is increasing dramatically. It is estimated that between 11 and 20 percent of pregnant women in the United States use cocaine (Gilbert & Harmon, 1993). If the male uses cocaine before intercourse, the offspring has an increased risk of abnormality as the cocaine binds to the sperm (Gilbert & Harmon, 1993).

Between 1985 and 1987, a highly crystalline form of cocaine known as "crack" was introduced into the urban areas of the United States. This form of cocaine could be mixed with other drugs or smoked. These methods of using cocaine were far more acceptable to women, and the use of crack cocaine, especially among women of child-bearing age, increased rapidly. Cocaine is highly addictive. About 5 to 10 minutes after using cocaine, an intense state of euphoria begins and lasts about 45 minutes (Conlon, 1992). Cocaine enhances energy, self-esteem, and the pleasure experienced in many activities, including sexual intercourse. These feelings are followed by prolonged periods of anxiety, exhaustion, and depression. The biphasic effects increase the probability of addiction as there is a compulsion to re-experience the "highs" (Conlon, 1992).

Cocaine can affect the unborn child at various stages throughout gestation. The effects of cocaine are both direct and indirect. The major problem appears to be decreased blood flow to the placenta and fetus. Structural defects associated with cocaine use are ascribed to the interruption of the blood flow to developing structures or previously developed structures (Mason & Lee, 1995). Cocaine also stimulates the uterus to contract. This results in a high rate of premature births. The vasoconstriction also results in growth retardation, intracranial hemorrhage, malnutrition, intrauterine hypoxia, and microcephaly (Chasnoff, 1991). Given a quiet, nurturing environment free from overstimulation, cocaine-exposed infants can "catch up" to some extent. But 30 to 40 percent may show some neurodevelopmental abnormalities, often in the language area. Some abnormalities are not apparent until school age (Chasnoff, 1991).

Narcotics

According to estimates there are 9,000 births each year to women who are addicted to narcotics (Hoegerman & Schnoll, 1991). Narcotics include opium and its derivatives such as heroin, morphine, and codeine. All opioids readily cross the placenta. The time during pregnancy when a drug is taken is critical. The first eight weeks of pregnancy are the most critical in causing structural malformations, whereas exposure later in pregnancy could have more profound behavioral effects (Hoegerman & Schnoll, 1991). Fetal drug exposure can have profound effects on the newborn and throughout life. Almost half of all pregnant drug addicts do not receive prenatal care and come to the hospital only for delivery of the baby. Problems with the neonate may be the first clue to addiction (Hoegerman & Schnoll, 1991).

The only drug available to treat pregnant opioid addicted women is methadone. This can be taken orally, is long acting, and a woman can maintain fairly consistent blood levels. The use of other opioids tends to produce rapid swings from intoxication to withdrawal and this adversely effects the fetus. Of babies born to opioid-dependent mothers, more than two-thirds will exhibit signs of neonatal abstinence syndrome (NAS). This is a nonspecific disorder that appears within about three to five days after birth, often after the mother has been discharged. The severity, timing of onset, and duration of NAS is related to total drug intake over the last trimester as well as daily intake and levels at delivery (Hoegerman & Schnoll, 1991). The most common signs of NAS are central nervous system irritability (including irritability, restlessness, sleep disturbances, high-pitched cry, tremors, seizures, and hypertonia). Other common symptoms are gastrointestinal and respiratory abnormalities including poor feeding, vomiting, diarrhea, failure to thrive, and apnea. The most common treatment is a daily methadone dose that is reduced by 10 to 20 percent each day (Hoegerman & Schnoll, 1991).

Heroin

Since menstrual abnormalities and lower fertility are frequent by-products of heroin use, you hear less about infants born to pregnant women addicted to heroin. As with other drugs, it is difficult to attribute specific problems to heroin, as 75 percent of women who use heroin use other drugs as well (Gilbert & Harmon, 1993). Early symptoms of pregnancy (nausea, vomiting, and fatigue) may feel like withdrawal symptoms causing the woman to increase drug consumption rather than seek medical treatment (Mason & Lee, 1995). Heroin reduces blood flow and depresses the respiratory center in the brain stem. General problems that affect the fetus are prematurity and growth retardation. Many of the infants show signs of withdrawal. These signs can occur any time during the first two weeks and may last two to four months (Gilbert & Harmon, 1993).

Summary

This chapter has looked at the process of development before birth and the factors that affect that development. It began with a discussion of decisions that needed to be made before conception and the need for good prenatal care. The biological processes of fertilization and implantation were discussed. Characteristic developmental patterns were highlighted, as well as growth and development that occurs during the embryonic and fetal periods.

General hereditary and genetic patterns were reviewed. Major genetic disorders, both those with autosomal and X-linked patterns, were detailed. Chromosomal disorders were discussed. Routine prenatal screening and the tests that are currently being used for this screening were illustrated. Genetic counseling was discussed. This chapter included a discussion of maternal diseases that can negatively affect pregnancy; infectious diseases including rubella, AIDS, syphilis, CMV and herpes; and other maternal conditions such as diabetes. Environmental factors that affect prenatal development were introduced. Societal and medical concerns about abusing substances such as nicotine, drugs, and alcohol were also described, as well as the developmental problem associated with abuse of various substances.

Application Activities

1. Talk with a pregnant mother about her feelings of being pregnant, the advice she has received from her doctor, and the type of lifestyle changes she has made, if any.

2. Talk with your mother about her experiences being pregnant with you. Ask about the advice her doctor gave her, her concerns at the time, and the lifestyle changes she made. Share with her the differences between when she was pregnant with you and the concerns today.

3. Discuss with your friends their feelings about pregnancy and find out what they know about prenatal development. Share with them some of the concerns in the field today. Then develop a plan to educate young women about pregnancy and lifestyle that improve birth outcomes.

Chapter 3

Birth and the Birthing Process

The process of giving birth to a baby, although one that has occurred for centuries, is a very personal one. In the past women often learned about birthing from their mothers or by helping in the birthing process themselves. Today obstetricians are the most likely people to discuss the birthing process. This is part of prenatal care. During the third trimester, obstetricians talk with pregnant women about warning signs such as bleeding, pain, swelling, and other indicators; make preparations for labor and delivery; and develop a birth plan based on the family's needs and desires and the medical circumstances. Additionally, some postpartum issues are dealt with, including the choice of a physician for the infant and whether or not the mother intends to breast-feed the infant (Stenchever & Sorenson, 1993).

When will the infant come? Although it is difficult to predict the actual day of birth, about 85 percent of women deliver within 7 days (before or after) of their due date. The due date is approximately 266 days after conception and is calculated by counting back three months from the first day of the last menstrual period and adding seven days. Thus, if the mother's last period began on July 4, the baby should be due April 11. We are not clear how the body knows when it is time for the child to be born. However, it predictably happens between 38 and 42 weeks gestation when the fetus is still small enough to fit through the birth canal and mature enough to cope with the extrauterine environment.

Onset of Labor

There are many factors that lead to the onset of labor. Most of these factors are chemical in nature, and the expectant mother is unaware of them. The level of oxytocin increases. Postaglandins, the hormones that keep the cervix and the uterine contents intact, stop circulating and the uterine walls then begin to randomly contract. Catecholamines (primarily epinephrine) and relaxin cause uterine relaxation. Other hormones, including estrogens, play a part. Uterine contractions involve the interaction of the proteins actin and myosin (Wheeler, 1995). This knowledge of chemicals allows us to inhibit labor or induce it, but we are not certain about the role each chemical plays or the interaction of these roles.

Labor and Birthing

How does a mother know that labor is about to begin? An early sign that labor is coming soon is **engagement** or **lightening**: the movement of the fetus into position for birth with the head low in the abdomen, close to the mother's cervix. Other signs include the **bloody show** which is blood-tinged mucus. This mucus was part of the mucus plug that formed the seal of the cervix. As the cervix thins and dilates, tiny blood vessels break and give the mucus a bloody appearance which may be seen on underwear. The **"water"** may break. The water is the amniotic fluid that has surrounded and protected the fetus. The rupture of the fetal membranes is accompanied by a gush of clear, colorless liquid, the amniotic fluid. Sometimes the membranes are artifically ruptured to permit fetal monitoring. When the membranes rupture more than 24 hours before delivery, there is an increased risk of infection. Additionally, there are **contractions.** These are movements of the muscular walls of the uterus that push the fetus through the birth canal and out of the mother's body. Initial contractions may be cramp-like and come at irregular intervals. With time, these contractions become more intense, regular, and closer together.

The process of bringing an infant into the world is called **labor.** Most women who have gone through the process would say that it is an appropriate name. Labor is defined as regular uterine contractions leading to progressive cervical changes. These contractions are different from the Braxton-Hicks contractions (commonly referred to as false labor) that can occur throughout pregnancy, which are painless and do not lead to changes in the cervix. Three changes occur in the cervix during labor: It softens, shortens, and dilates. While these changes are taking place, the fetus begins to descend through the birth canal (Wheeler, 1995).

Labor is a very dynamic personal experience. Technically, it involves discharging the fetus, placenta, and umbilical cord from the uterus. Labor is divided into three stages.

First Stage of Labor

The first stage of labor begins with the onset of regular contractions and continues until the cervix is completely dilated (about 10 centimeters). Over a matter of hours, these initial mild contractions become stronger, last longer, and are more frequent. The first stage is the longest stage of labor and typically lasts from 12 to 30 hours. It is further divided into two phases—a latent phase and an active phase.

The latent phase averages 8 to 12 hours in a woman's first pregnancy (primigravida or primipara) but may last up to 20 hours. It averages about 6 to 8 hours in women birthing later children (multigravida or multipara), but may last as long as 14 hours. Many factors affect the length of this phase, including whether or not the mother has been given any drugs for pain. The expectant mother is usually still at home during the early part of this phase waiting for a pattern of regular contractions to occur about 5 to 6 minutes apart. The latent phase moves into the active phase when the cervix is dilated approximately 3 centimeters.

The active phase of labor normally takes about 5 hours for a primigravida, but only a little over 2 hours for a multigravida (Stenchever & Sorenson, 1993). The active phase is characterized by regular and stronger contractions that occur every 2 to 3 minutes and last for about 1 minute each. The cervix dilates at least 1 centimeter per hour during this phase to about 10 centimeters (about 4 inches), and the fetus descends into the birth canal.

The last portion of this active stage is **transition.** It is the shortest, most intense, and most painful. It typically lasts about an hour although it may seem like forever. Contractions are frequent and strong, the cervix is dilating to 10 centimeters, and women often feel the urge to push, yet this is counterproductive as it makes the cervix swell and delays the birth. Many women become uncomfortable, irritable, and may reassess their need for pain killers. Fathers often decide never to impregnate their wives again.

The descent of the fetus is monitored and measured. The station of the fetal head is measured from 0, which is at the level of the spines of the pelvic inlet, to +5, which is at the perineum (Wheeler, 1995). See Figure 3.1. Examinations of the mother during labor check on the dilation of the cervix and the station of the fetal head.

Second Stage of Labor

The second stage of labor begins when the cervix has fully dilated. The first stage of labor allowed the fetal head to get into position for delivery by gradually molding it to fit the birth canal. The mother's pelvic bones spread, and the cervix dilates. During the second stage of labor, the constriction of the abdominal muscles and the straightening of the fetal body push the fetus into the birth canal. When the fetal head encounters the pelvic floor, the fetal chin flexes or tucks, presenting a smaller diameter for the descent. The fetus then rotates, and the head extends to permit passage through the vulva. This is called crowning. When the fetal head is crowning about 3 to 4 centimeters, a decision will be made about whether or not an **episiotomy** is necessary. An episiotomy is a surgical incision into the perineum to enlarge the vaginal orifice (Afriat & Coustan, 1995). The incision is typically made under a local anesthesia. As with many other areas, there are pros and cons to episiotomies. On the pro side, the reasons for doing an episiotomy are that a clean surgical incision is easier to repair than a spontaneous tear; it shortens the second stage of labor; it spares the fetal head from excessive pressure; and it may spare the pelvic floor musculature. Those who oppose it say that it is unnecessary; it is a discomfort for the woman; and that the depth of the episiotomy is greater than most tears would be (Afriat & Coustan, 1995).

With or without an episiotomy, first the crowning head, then face and chin are delivered. The mouth and nose of the newborn are suctioned to remove fluid

| **Figure 3.1** | **Stations of the Fetal Head** |

The descent of the fetal head is monitored during labor.

while waiting for the next contraction. Following the delivery of the head, there is an external rotation allowing the shoulders to pass through the birth canal, and, finally, the rest of the fetus is expelled. The length of this stage is determined by the mother's ability to push to the point that the infant is deliverable. This may be 30 minutes for a multigravida to 90 minutes for a primigravida. It ends with the birth of the newborn. The umbilical cord is then clamped and cut (Stenchever & Sorenson, 1993). See Figure 3.2.

Third Stage of Labor

The final stage of labor is the expulsion of the placenta or afterbirth. The uterus, cervix, and vagina are inspected for injuries that might have occurred. This stage takes about 20 minutes.

Factors Influencing Labor

Many factors determine the ease with which the birthing process takes place and the birth outcome.

The general physical and emotional condition of the mother plays an important role in the birthing process. If the mother has had good prenatal care, abstained from drugs and alcohol, had a nutritional diet, and developed a good rapport with the obstetrician, the outlook is positive.

Figure 3.2 | **The Fetus, Engagement, and the Three Stages of Labor**

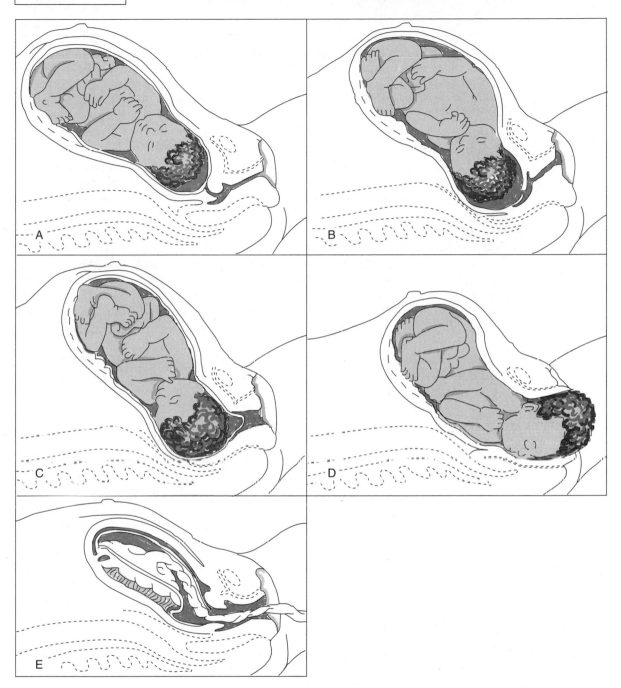

(A) Engagement: The fetus and uterus in position for birth before labor begins. Note the length of the birth canal and the width of the cervix. (B) The first stage of labor: Note the descent of the fetal head, the effacement of and slight dilation of the cervix. (C) The second stage of labor: The cervix is completely dilated and the fetal head is in the birth canal. (D) Crowning: Note the appearance of the fetal head, and how the head has internally rotated toward the mother's back. (E) The third stage of labor: expulsion of the placenta.

Attendance at childbirth education classes provides intellectual preparation for the birth process. However, it also serves other important functions such as drawing the pregnant woman's partner into increased participation in the birthing process, developing a heightened awareness of the impending transition to parenthood, providing a wider network of couples who share many of the same concerns and experiences, giving information about the process involved in labor and birth, and teaching breathing techniques and other practices that are useful during the birthing process (Davis-Floyd, 1992).

The size of the fetus influences the birthing process. There is no accurate way to determine the exact size of the fetus *in utero*. An experienced physician can make a good guess, and ultrasound can provide added information as well. However, the size of the fetus is only one factor; in reality it is the size of the fetal head in relation to the size and structure of the mother's pelvis that is the important variable. A larger pelvis can deliver a larger fetus.

The presentation and position of the fetus are important. The most common presentation is head first, or *vertex*. Although there are a variety of vertex presentations, the most common one is with the chin tucked and the fetus facing the mother's back. This position allows the most efficient descent. In situations where the fetus is malpositioned with his face, brow, or top of the head presented first, vaginal delivery may be difficult or impossible (Stenchever & Sorenson, 1993). When the buttocks or feet are presenting, it is called a **breech** presentation. In that situation, unless the fetus turns spontaneously, he will have to be externally turned or a cesarean section performed.

The quality and type of uterine contractions also influence the birthing process. Uterine muscles are no different from other body tissue. The force and efficiency of uterine contractions are important because it is these contractions that move the fetus through the birth canal. If a mother becomes exhausted or dehydrated, she cannot use these muscles effectively.

The condition of the cervix changes during labor. In the early stages, it is thick and uneffaced. As labor progresses, the cervix becomes softened, thinner, and dilated. The condition of the cervix is used to determine labor readiness (Stanchever & Sorenson, 1993).

The structure of the uterus and pelvis influence delivery. The anatomy and volume of the uterus influence uterine contractions. An overdistended uterus, whether caused by a large fetus, edema (excessive fluids), or other factors, makes labor difficult. Obstetricians identify four basic types of pelvic structures and their useable volume to determine the implication for labor and delivery (Stanchever & Sorenson, 1993).

Although a vast majority of deliveries happen as described above, there are factors that influence labor that require additional measures for a vaginal delivery to be possible. Sometimes a cesarean delivery is necessary.

Operative Delivery

There are two types of operative deliveries: vaginal and abdominal or caesarean. Each is used for a variety of different reasons when a vaginal delivery seems unadvisable.

Operative Vaginal Delivery

For an operative vaginal delivery to be an option, several variables must be in place: The mother's cervix must be fully dilated, the membranes must have ruptured, the position of the fetal head must be known, and there must be adequate analgesia and an experienced operator (Afriat & Coustan, 1995). These are the conditions necessary to use either forceps or a vacuum extractor.

Forceps are tonglike instruments that are placed on either side of the fetus's head, and when the mother pushes, the physician also pulls. Forceps come in over 600 shapes and sizes. However, most are molded to fit around the fetal head. The use of obstetrical forceps is classified by the station of the fetal head when the instruments are applied. A high forceps delivery is when the head is not in the maternal pelvis and is above station 0. This is contraindicated, as it is not possible to tell if the fetal head will fit through the pelvic opening and the chance of fetal or maternal injury is high (Afriat & Coustan, 1995). A cesarean delivery should be done instead. A mid-forceps delivery is above station +2 centimeters, and is done only when there is sudden severe fetal or maternal compromise; simultaneously, arrangements should be made for a cesarean section if the forceps are not successful.

A low-forceps delivery is performed when the forehead has descended to at least +2 centimeters but not down to the pelvic floor. There are general guidelines for using low forceps. One is the expectation of fetal distress; another is when labor has slowed too much. Outlet forceps are used when the fetal head is crowning but not emerging. In general, outlet and low forceps are used to shorten the second stage of labor. Complications with forceps deliveries are similar to vaginal deliveries. However, forceps deliveries are frequently associated with birth injury and neurological damage. A fair assessment of the safety of the forceps method is problematic because it is only used in births where a host of complications influence the outcome. Maternal complications include soft tissue trauma and hemorrhage (Dennen, 1994).

In many parts of the world, a **vacuum extractor** has taken the place of forceps. The vacuum extractor consists of either a metal or plastic cup that fits over the back of the fetal head. The cup is also attached to a pump. Once the cup is in place, a vacuum is generated and the fetus is helped to descend the birth canal. The variables for using vacuum extraction are the same as forceps deliveries.

Cesarean Section Delivery

A **cesarean section** is the removal of the fetus through an incision in the abdominal wall and uterus. The usual incision is very low and horizontal and is used in the vast majority of cesarean sections. The advantage is that the stitched incision will be part of the cervix and lower uterus until very late in future gestations, and thus unlikely to rupture (Afriat & Coustan, 1995). It also means that in future pregnancies the mother can have the option of a vaginal delivery (Dickinson, 1994). In a cesarean section, after the incision is made the head is delivered by **fundal pressure** (pressing on the part of body opposite the head to force the head out) or, if the fetal head is too low, either forceps or a vacuum extractor are used. When the head is out, it is suctioned and the body is gently delivered, again with the support of fundal pressure.

Most cesarean sections are performed for one of four reasons: The fetus is in a breech position; fetopelvic disproportion, that is, the fetal head is too large to fit through the mother's pelvis; fetal distress; or a women has had a previous cesarean section. The mother can be awake under an epidural anesthesia during a cesarean section delivery.

Although relatively safe, a cesarean section is still a surgical procedure and twice as risky as a vaginal delivery (Batshaw & Perret, 1992). The risk to the fetus is premature delivery because of a miscalculation of gestational age. Also, during the first stage of labor, when the infant passes through the birth canal, most of the fluid is squeezed from the fetal lungs. Babies delivered by cesarean section tend to have "wet lungs" that may cause some respiratory distress (Batshaw & Perret, 1992).

For mothers the risks are greater. Although child birth is very safe, with only six maternal deaths for every 100,000 live births, those who deliver via cesarean section are four times as likely to die in childbirth (VanTuinen & Wolfe, 1992). There is an increased possibility of infection, abnormal blood clotting, and injuries to the bowel and bladder. There is typically a longer hospitalization and recovery time as well.

There is concern that too many babies in the United States are delivered unnecessarily by cesarean section. The national rate for cesarean sections was 5.5 percent in 1970 and rose to 24.7 percent in 1988 (VanTuinen & Wolfe, 1992). Beginning in 1990, this rate began to show a slow decline. Using comparative data from other countries, it is estimated that the optimal national cesarean section rate would be between 12 and 14 percent (VanTuinen & Wolfe, 1992). The typical reasons given for the increase are the improved safety of abdominal surgery, concerns about forceps deliveries, and breech births. Other reasons focus on professional liability for birth outcomes and the amount of professional time that vaginal deliveries take (Afriat & Coustan, 1995). There is genuine concern about the number of cesarean sections performed.

Birthing Process from the Fetal Perspective

While the mother's body is being stretched to accommodate the fetus' passage through the birth canal, the fetus is being squeezed. Stretching hurts more than squeezing, and the fetal sense of pain is not well developed. The fetus feels the pressure of uterine contractions, the squeeze of the passage through the birth canal, and the hands that catch him. Each maternal contraction flattens the placenta and compresses the umbilical cord, cutting off the supply of oxygen momentarily. The lull between contractions and the expectant mother's deep breathing restore the oxygen level. The heart rate increases in response to these stresses. The uneven supply of oxygen might make him a bit light headed, perhaps even cause him a pounding headache. In addition to the normal sounds in the womb, labor is a noisy process because the uterine muscles squeeze repeatedly against his ears. Added to this, the newborn abruptly enters a cold world full of bright lights, moving objects, and strange noises. After an initial period of alertness, the infant is likely to sleep for a relatively long time (Maurer & Maurer, 1988).

If painkillers are used during the delivery process, the effect on the infant varies depending on the drugs used. If narcotics are used during the delivery, the baby is likely to act drugged, to be less alert, and to sleep more. Such behavior may last for several days, as the baby has gotten a disproportionate amount of the drug taken by the mother. The drug is likely to reduce the amount of oxygen the infant receives during the delivery process and increase the headache and the consequent depression he feels. Local anesthesia, too, affects the infant and he will not act normally until the drug dissipates. "When he feels high, he will be jumpy and irritable and will cry a lot. When he feels low, he will feel floppy and may be hard to wake up, even to feed" (Maurer & Maurer, 1988, 42).

Changes at Birth

While the transition to parenthood is an abrupt one for adults, leaving the uterine environment and entering a world of air is an equally abrupt change for the infant. It requires not only psychological adjustment, but physiological adjustments as well. The most important changes involve the respiratory and circulatory systems, ability to regulate temperature, and the ability to ingest and absorb nutrients.

The newborn's first breath is a long and difficult one because the lungs are collapsed and full of liquid. Once filled with air, typically from the first cry, they remain open because of a chemical called **surfactant** that coats the alveoli and prevents them from closing. During fetal life the circulation system was different than it is in adults. Since the lungs did not oxygenate the blood and the liver did not eliminate wastes, the circulatory system took shortcuts around these organs. However, the infant's body must now begin to assume these tasks. The first breath, in addition to inflating the lungs, provides the impetus for a series of muscle contractions that close off these "short cuts" and circulate the infant's blood through the lungs and liver (Batshaw & Perret, 1992). Temperature regulation is a challenge because the newborn has a large surface area and little fatty tissue for protection against temperature loss.

Screening Newborns

When infants come into the world, the effectiveness of their transition is rated on the **Apgar scale** at 1 and 5 minutes after birth. If initial Apgar scores were low at 5 minutes, this is often repeated at 10 or 15 minutes after birth (Cashore, 1995). The Apgar scale was developed by Dr. Virginia Apgar and named after her. Her goal was to develop a fast, systematic way to assess the infant's condition after labor and delivery so necessary supports, if any, could be immediate. The scale consists of five measures that are scored 0, 1, or 2. The areas are: heart rate, re-

Table 3.1	The Apgar Scale		
Points	**0**	**1**	**2**
Appearance (body color)	Pale, blue all over	Body pink, blue extremities	Pink all over
Pulse (heart rate)	Absent	Less than 100	More than 100
Grimace (gag reflex)	No response	Grimace	Sneeze, cough
Activity Level (muscle tone)	Limp, floppy	Some flexion of extremities	Active motion
Respiration (respiratory effort)	Absent	Slow, irregular	Normal respiration, strong cry

spiratory effort, muscle tone, gag reflex, and body color. Some find using APGAR as an acronym makes it easier to remember: **A**ppearance, **P**ulse, **G**rimace, **A**ctivity level, and **R**espiration.

Although the use of the Apgar is relatively standard in hospitals, the timing is often more irregular than prescribed, and doctors and nurses may disagree on the scores to be given. Nevertheless, infants with lower Apgar scores are more at-risk. It is rare for an infant to get a 10 on the 1-minute Apgar, and scores of 0 usually indicate a stillborn. In general, a low Apgar indicates that the child is more likely to have a developmental disability. This is particularly true if the score is low at 5 minutes or later, or if the score goes down rather than up. However, a majority of the children with low initial Apgar scores will develop normally (Batshaw & Perret, 1992).

Many factors influence the course of labor, birthing, and the condition of the newborn. Some are known and planned for, whereas others complicate the process.

Complications of Labor and Delivery

Complications can affect the fetus during the birthing process. Labor can be complicated for a variety of reasons. Some complications, such as prematurity or the premature rupture of the membranes, are related to the timing of delivery; others relate to the delivery itself, as in the case of a breech birth or the delivery of multiple babies; and still others relate to the condition of the mother, such as infection and high blood pressure (pre-eclampsia). Some conditions, such as fetal distress, are related to the condition of the fetus.

Timing of Delivery

Sometimes infants are born too early or too long after they were due. Approximately 4 to 5 percent of newborns are delivered before 37 weeks (James, 1994b). Although some causes of premature labor are known, for the most part researchers do not know why labor starts too early in some situations, nor are we successful in stopping labor once it has started. Increased knowledge relates mainly to our ability to help the **neonate**, or newborn, rather than to our skill in prolonging pregnancy. Some drugs have been used to manage premature labor, but have had only limited success.

Most problems of infants born too soon relate to their lack of maturity. Temperature regulation is a problem, and there may be respiratory, neurological, and renal problems. Feeding problems are common as are metabolic problems. There is some threat from infection and jaundice. There is also concern about attachment and social problems, as the mother and infant are separated after birth.

Some infants are born too late. Approximately 90 percent of pregnancies are delivered by 40 weeks after conception (Coustan, 1995). Actually, some findings suggest that this percentage may be low because the time of conception was miscalculated, and that actually only about 3 percent of pregnancies are prolonged. Some women may have longer pregnancies as part of the normal variation in nature. Concerns about postmature pregnancy revolve around placental dysfunction. Typically, labor is induced using a hormone such as oxytocin, commonly called pitocin. Oxytocin is a normal body hormone that promotes smooth muscle contraction of the uterus. It can be administered in synthetic forms to stimulate labor. Opinions on the appropriate dosage vary. These disagreements are compounded by the fact that uterine responses to oxytocin are individualized and that sensitivity to oxytocin increases as labor advances (Gilbert & Harmon, 1993). If induced labor is not deemed appropriate, a cesarean section is performed by 41 or 42 weeks (Coustan, 1995).

Size-for-Dates

There is a predictable relationship between gestational age and weight regardless of when an infant is born. There are concerns when an infant is either too small or too large for dates. Infants who are small-for-dates typically have low fat stores, probably because of hypoglycemia. Because they lack fat, they are susceptible to cold temperatures and need to be kept warm. They may have other birth complications because of lack of tolerance for the periodic decreased supply of oxygen during the birthing process.

Some infants who are large-for-dates may just have large parents; others may be infants of diabetic mothers, where this is an expected problem. However, infants who are large-for-dates risk birth injury because of their large size. When born, they may experience hypoglycemia and need to be fed frequently. If their large size is known, they were probably delivered by cesarean section to prevent birthing problems and may have some respiratory distress. They may experience jaundice and have problems with the sucking and swallowing reflexes initially (James, 1994b).

Bleeding Late in Pregnancy

Bleeding after 22 weeks' gestation is regarded as late bleeding. This age was chosen because there is the expectation that the fetus could live after 22 weeks. (Previously 28 weeks was used, but the improvement of neonatal care has caused the change.) Late bleeding complicates 2 to 5 percent of pregnancies (Konje & Walley, 1994). The most common causes of heavy bleeding late in pregnancy are **placenta previa** and **abruptio placenta.** In placenta previa the placenta is attached so low that it is between the fetus and the birth canal, and the birthing process produces heavy bleeding. This hemorrhaging is life threatening for both the mother and fetus. Maternal mortality has dropped from 5 percent to less than 0.1 percent (Konje & Walley, 1994). Risks to the fetus include prematurity, intrauterine growth retardation, and congenital malformations. It occurs in less than 1 percent of pregnancies. It can be managed if ultrasound has diagnosed the condition. This typically requires a planned caesarean delivery or a number-one emergency after the mother's condition has been stabilized.

In abruptio placenta, which occurs in about 1 in 100 pregnancies, the placenta, although attached in the normal place, detaches early (Batshaw & Perret, 1992). For women who have had this happen on one occasion, the risk is far greater for reoccurrence, in about 5 to 17 percent of women with this predisposition (Konje & Walley, 1994). This condition is associated with smoking, low socioeconomic status, intrauterine growth deficiency, congenital malformations, and increasing parity, that is, numbers of childbirths (Maresh & Neals, 1994). See Figure 3.3.

Premature Rupture of Membranes

Sometimes membranes rupture and are followed by a latent period that shows no contractions. This occurs in approximately 10 percent of pregnancies. When this happens before the 37th week of pregnancy, it is called preterm premature rupture of the membranes and happens in about 5 percent of all pregnancies (Svigos, Robinson, & Vigneswaran, 1994). There is no agreed-upon time when this latent period becomes too long. Concern focuses around infection and whether or not the placenta and umbilical cord are still functioning. The mother and fetus are closely monitored. Concern is greatest when the fetus is preterm and strategies are dependent on fetal gestational age. Strategies are most unclear when the infant is less than 22 weeks' gestation. In this instance, the mother is typically hospitalized and given antibiotics to prevent infection and corticosteroids to enhance fetal lung maturity. Options are then explained to families. When delivery is viewed as the best option, there is controversy whether labor should be induced or a cesarean delivery performed (Svigos, Robinson, & Vigneswaran, 1994). There are also concerns related to maternal–infant bonding.

| **Figure 3.3** | **Placenta: Normal, Previa, and Abruptio** |

Normally the placenta attaches in the upper third of the uterus, allowing it to stay intact during the birthing process and thus providing the fetus a source of oxygen. In placenta previa, the placenta is attached so low that it is between the fetus and the birth canal. In abruptio placenta, the placenta is attached in the appropriate place, but it detaches too early. In the latter two cases, a cesarean delivery is indicated.

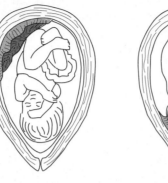

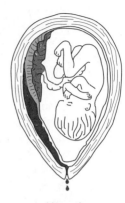

Normal placenta

Placenta previa

Abruptio placenta

Postpartum Hemorrhage

Hemorrhaging during the third stage of labor causes excessive blood loss and is a major contributor to maternal morbidity and mortality. It occurs in about 4 to 6 percent of pregnancies (Still, 1994a). Although what constitutes hemorrhaging versus a normal amount of blood is agreed upon (500 milliliters of blood in the first 24 hours postpartum), it is extremely difficult to accurately measure the amount of blood lost. The most common cause of hemorrhaging is uterine atony or lack of muscle tone in the uterus. It is associated with a previous history of hemorrhaging, overdistension (multiple births), prolonged labor, as well as other variables. Hemorrhaging can also be a result of trauma due to an episiotomy, lacerations, or a cesarean section. The mother should be observed carefully during the hours following childbirth. In some cases after a difficult labor, oxytocics are used prophylactically to reduce the incidence of hemorrhaging.

Delivery of Multiple Births

Women who carry multiple fetuses have increased levels of pregnancy hormones in their blood. They may experience an exaggeration of the usual early pregnancy symptoms of nausea and vomiting. These symptoms may arouse the first suspicion that it is a multiple pregnancy. Miscarriage is more frequent in multiple births than in singletons. There is also greater risk for anemia and hypertension because of increased fetal demands made on the maternal body. The probability of complications increases with multiple births. It is likely that the infants will be premature, small, and the risk of birth anomaly is greater. Any of these conditions could influence delivery.

Preterm delivery occurs in almost half of all twin pregnancies as opposed to about 6 percent of singletons (Crowther, 1994). Preterm delivery is the main risk in multiple births complicated by intrauterine growth restriction. With twins, if there are no problems, vaginal delivery is the choice. Labor proceeds as if there were only one child; however, the level of monitoring is far more intense. There is typically a team available so that an emergency cesarean delivery could be performed should it be necessary. Ultrasound is frequently used to determine the position of the second fetus. After the first infant is delivered, the cord is clamped and cut, and the position of the second fetus is determined. The fetal heart is monitored continually. The second twin usually follows rapidly. Despite the support for delivering twins vaginally, they are more frequently delivered by cesarean section, either as an elective procedure or an emergency before or after the delivery of the first twin (Crowther, 1994). Triplets and other higher multiple births are delivered through cesarean section.

Pre-eclampsia

Pre-eclampsia is hypertension brought on by pregnancy and affects between 0.5 and 7 percent of pregnancies (Maresh & Neales, 1994; Stanchever & Sorenson, 1993). It is diagnosed by persistent blood pressure readings greater than 140/90 during the first trimester of pregnancy. If not treated, seizures (eclampsia) are likely to develop. There are also complications relating to the blood and liver. As with hemorrhaging, the mother's condition must be stabilized before delivery is attempted. Pre-eclampsia is associated with intrauterine growth deficiency. As the condition is life threatening to the mother, it is probable that the maternal condition will be treated by termination of the pregnancy resulting in a premature fetus (Maresh & Neales, 1994).

Speed of Delivery

As with most events, there is an optimal length of time for delivery. Although a short labor sounds enticing, it may create problems. In the first stage of labor, concern focuses on the molding of the fetal head to pass through the birth canal. The different bones of the fetal skull meet smoothly except for a soft spot at the top of the head called the **fontanelle.** The joints between the bones of the skull are soft. Because of this flexibility, the head of the fetus can make some adjustment to fit through the pelvis if this is a gradual process. When this passage occurs too quickly, it often produces small or even large hemorrhages that can injure the brain. There is concern if the second stage of labor is 10 minutes or less. If the contractions are very strong and very close together, they may prevent the normal blood flow from reaching the fetus and hence interrupt the flow of oxygen.

Dystocia is the technical term currently used for labor that is not progressing as expected. In the past it was used to describe a condition where the fetal head was too large for the maternal pelvis. The incidence of dystocia is rising. Some contend that this diagnosis is really a way for physicians, who are impatient with long labors, to justify a cesarean section.

With prolonged labor there is concern about maternal infection, uterine rupture, and postpartum hemorrhaging (Arulkumaran, 1994). As labor is different for all women, there are no universally agreed-upon definitions of poor progress. In the first stage of labor, poor progress is usually determined by assessment of the cervical state rather than contractions. In the latent phase of this stage, women may just be given reassurance, encouraged to walk around, and be given something to drink so they do not become dehydrated. In the active phase, they are often given oxytocin in small amounts to encourage regular contractions.

During the second stage of labor, when the cervix is fully dilated, management may be different. Malpresentation, such as a breech position, is checked for, as is the possibility of malposition that usually is caused by the lack of flexion and rotation of the head. Oxytocin is usually administered. This hormone makes contractions longer and stronger and shortens the relaxation periods in between. Without careful administration, there is concern that these contractions may become so strong that they can rupture the uterus and cut off oxygen to the fetus or injure the fetus (Cunningham, MacDonald, & Grant, 1989). If the fetus is low enough, a vaginally assisted delivery is used; in other cases a cesarean section would be performed (Arulkumaran, 1994). In long deliveries the concern is for **anoxia**, or lack of oxygen for the fetus. This can be caused by the length of time the umbilical cord is squeezed during delivery or by low maternal blood pressure. When there is such a concern, steps are taken to speed up the delivery.

Breech Deliveries

In a small number of instances (3 to 4 percent), the infant is not in the traditional head-down position, but rather the backside or buttocks are first. This is referred to as a **breech** presentation. It is more frequent in preterm infants, on the average 14 percent (Penn & Steer, 1994). There are several different breech presentations. In a frank breech, which accounts for 60 to 70 percent of breech presentations, the buttocks are presenting and the legs are extended. Although more difficult than a head presentation, this fetus could be delivered vaginally if the pelvis permits. In a complete breech, both the feet and the buttocks are presenting, and in a footling breach one or both feet are presenting (Stanchever & Sorenson, 1993). Management of breech presentation is an area of controversy. There is a growing interest in techniques that spontaneously promote the postural change in the fetus—these techniques vary from having a full bladder to assuming positions so the woman's buttocks are higher than her torso.

Breech births are further complicated by the association of this presentation with birth anomalies both full- and preterm. The decision to continue a vaginal delivery in the breech position, to externally turn the fetus, or to use a cesarean section is determined by an obstetrician. If the infant is delivered in the breech position, there is concern that the infant's supply of oxygen will be cut off during the birth process and that the bones of the infant's head and mother's pelvis will have had less time to mold to each other. The infant's head is the widest part of the body. When the head is delivered first, it is gradually molded during the first and second stage of labor to fit the pelvic opening. In a breech birth the backside is not a problem, but the head may get stuck because it lacked the time to mold to the mother's pelvis (Batshaw & Perret, 1992).

Cord Prolapse

Prolapse of the umbilical cord has been a major cause of fetal death in the past, but current obstetrical practices have decreased its likelihood. It occurs in less than 1 in 200 labors. It is most frequently associated with breech and other malpresentations (Steer & Danielian, 1994). When the cord is wrapped around the fetus' neck during the process of delivery, fetal deaths occur because not enough oxygen reaches the fetal brain. Even when there is knowledge of a prolapsed

| Figure 3.4 | **Malpresentations and Breech Positions** |

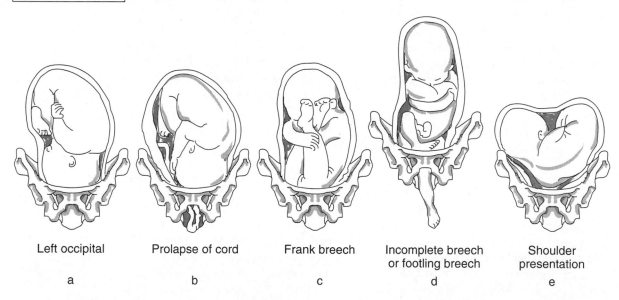

| Left occipital | Prolapse of cord | Frank breech | Incomplete breech or footling breech | Shoulder presentation |
| a | b | c | d | e |

Most infants move into position for birth with their head low in the abdomen and close to the mother's cervix. Typically, the chin is tucked and the head slightly rotated. Other presentations make birthing more difficult. Sometimes the forehead is the presenting part, called a "soldier" presentation (a); when the umbilical cord appears first it is called a prolapse of the cord (b); other times the buttocks are presenting, called a frank breech (c); one or two feet first, called a footling breech (d); or even the shoulder (e). The latter is called a transverse lie, where the fetus is actually lying horizontally in the uterus.

cord, the mode of delivery is controversial. In some cases a cesarean section will be done; in other cases positioning of the mother will be used to relieve pressure on the cord or the cord itself may be moved (Steer & Danielian, 1994).

Fetal Distress

Fetal distress is a widely used but poorly defined term. Although the term is only used for the fetus *in utero*, its implications are for a poor birth outcome. Most commonly, fetal distress is used to refer to fetal **hypoxia,** or lack of oxygen. The fetal heart rate should be monitored every 30 minutes during the first stage of labor, ideally, every 15 minutes. It should be checked just after a contraction. If the baseline is above 150 beats per minute or below 110 beats per minute, follow-up is needed (Steer & Danielian, 1994).

Fetal monitoring keeps track of the fetal heart beat, intermittently or continuously. This can be done by a health-care professional listening to the heart rate through a fetoscope (a modified stethoscope). When monitoring it on a continuous basis, an electronic fetal monitor is typically used. Some obstetricians use this routinely, others feel it is unwarranted in uncomplicated, low-risk women. Electronic fetal monitoring can be done externally or internally. An external electronic fetal monitor is physically noninvasive. It is a beltlike contraption that is placed around the abdomen and plugged into a monitor. There is a continual visual display of the fetal heart rate as well as an audible one. Some mothers find this comforting. For others it may be distressing, because of irregularities based on the function of the machine, movement of the fetus, or changes when contractions take place.

Internal electronic fetal monitors can be used after the membranes have ruptured and the cervix is at least 2 to 3 centimeters dilated, and the fetal presenting part can be reached. An electrode is attached to the fetus and then to a leg plate on the mother. The internal electronic fetal monitoring is more accurate but also more invasive. Many obstetricians question whether it should be used as a routine practice or whether it is only justified in high-risk deliveries. The use of electronic fetal monitoring has failed to show better neonatal outcomes, but has been related to an increase in cesarean sections when it has not been used with fetal blood sampling.

One problem is that fetal distress is rare and difficult to detect accurately. A reading that looks abnormal may occur frequently. Hence, for every infant with real fetal distress, three infants show false signs of fetal distress. Additionally, obstetricians do not agree on the interpretation of what constitutes fetal distress. Overall, there has been no clear improvement in birth outcomes for monitored and unmonitored births (VanTuinen & Wolfe, 1992).

Meconium Aspiration Syndrome

The presence of meconium in the amniotic fluid can cause fetal distress. **Meconium** is the waste product of the fetus and is passed through the anal sphincters. It is not clear why in some cases meconium is excreted into the amniotic fluid. In adults involuntary defecation is related to emotional stress. Some hypothesize that the process of labor emotionally stresses the fetus and hence causes the problem of meconium. This appears to be an untestable hypothesis. Others view it as a maturational issue as the passage of meconium into the amniotic fluid is rare before 34 weeks, is about 30 percent at term (40 weeks), but increases to 50 percent at 42 weeks (Steer & Danielian, 1994). Intestinal hormones have also been implicated.

The presence of meconium itself is not the issue, but rather the aspiration of the meconium into the fetal lungs. This results in mild to severe respiratory distress, which occurs in about one-third of the cases. Aspiration of meconium occurs because of fetal breathing movements. Gasping in the fetus is brought on by hypoxia (lack of oxygen). Fetal deep breathing becomes more frequent with advancing gestation. Suctioning the infant directly after the delivery of the head, before the first breath, was initially thought to control this problem, but apparently it is not successful in cases where the aspiration has happened *in utero*. Meconium aspiration syndrome has a wide range of outcomes, from those that require little or no therapy to infants needing long-term administration of oxygen and mechanical ventilation (Steer & Danielian, 1994).

Drugs Used to Ease the Pain of Delivery

Pain serves to provide a warning. It is not clear what the value of pain in childbirth is, but it may be nature's way of telling a woman to prepare for impending birth so that birthing does not happen unexpectedly. Some feel that once this warning has been acknowledged, there is no need for further maternal pain or distress. The major function of pain relief in normal labor is to make the birthing experience a positive one for the mother (Morgan, 1994).

During hospital deliveries mothers are often given drugs to reduce pain and decrease anxiety. Different drugs are given at different stages of labor as the nature and cause of pain changes. Pain builds. In the early stages of labor pain is visceral and is caused by the dilation of the cervix. Tranquilizers are frequently given, not to ease pain, but to reduce the woman's reaction to it. Sedatives are also given which make the woman drowsy and reduce her reaction to pain. Pain occurs in normal labor, but severe pain in early labor may be a precursor of a difficult labor and delivery (Morgan, 1994). Analgesics are given to reduce pain. Pain in the second stage of labor is different. It is caused by vaginal and perineal tissue trauma.

Increasingly, women are using psychoprophylactic techniques of pain control. This is a method of minimizing, but not eliminating pain. First and foremost the techniques emphasize having mothers prepared for the birthing process and having the mother actively involved in her own pain reduction techniques. Success is dependent on the mother's willingness to attempt it, her determination to succeed, and a normal labor and delivery (Morgan, 1994).

Like psychoprophylactic techniques, the purpose of general analgesics during labor is not to eliminate pain, but to reduce it. When mothers have not been educated about the pain of normal labor and do not have strong emotional support during labor, they may have a difficult time coping. Methods of pain reduction that do not impact the fetus are being explored. For example, transcutaneous electrical stimulation (TENS) is a method of controlling pain early in labor. The TENS unit excites the sensory receptors in the skin and decreases the perception of pain. It has no effect on the fetus and provides partial pain relief for some women. This is often used with entonox (nitrous oxide in 50 percent oxygen) a rapid acting analgesic that can be intermittently self-administered for pain (Morgan, 1994).

Any drugs given to a pregnant woman during labor cross the placental barrier and affect the fetus. They can cross the blood–brain barrier and hence directly affect the brain of the fetus. Since the amount of the drug is based solely on the woman's size or body weight, the concentration reaching the fetus is far greater. The liver and kidneys of the fetus are immature; so it takes a much longer time for the fetus to excrete the drugs than the mother. Despite concerns, the exact impact of drugs during delivery is not well documented. All drugs that affect the mother's central nervous system will produce central nervous depression in the fetus. The neonate whose mother received analgesics will probably have reduced Apgar scores, respiratory depression, decreased alertness, abnormal reflexes, and decreased social responsiveness and self-quieting for at least 24 hours (Morgan, 1994).

When the goal is to eliminate pain, a pudendal block is typically used. A **pudendal block** is a regional anesthetic that prevents sensations from the area of the vulva or lower birth canal from reaching the brain (unlike a general anesthetic which affects the whole body). Pudendal blocks are typically given by spinal injection. The most commonly used one is the lumbar epidural block. The woman feels no pain nor has any voluntary control of the area below the injection. This block is used for pain relief in labor and for cesarean sections. It requires an experienced anesthetist for the remainder of labor and delivery. Although it does not slow down the first stage of labor, it does make the second stage longer. Contractions often slow down, and the urge to push is lost. This results in doubling the number of instrument deliveries (Morgan, 1994). It is now possible to administer the epidural block on a continuous basis where one can stop the administration and allow the woman to push and then administer more of the drug. Epidural blocks can cause abnormalities in the fetal heart rate. As with other drugs administered during delivery, studies of long-term effects on the infant are inconclusive. In general, no long-term adverse effects have been found (Morgan, 1994).

In addition to the particular drugs used, the overall level of medication is of concern. In general, the research suggests that low levels of medication are less likely to result in problems in the neonatal period than high levels. It is not clear if drug-free newborns are necessarily better off, especially if the mother becomes anxious and this level of anxiety reduces the blood flow to the uterus.

Overall, the amount of the medication may be the most important variable. Then, perhaps, low levels of medication are an asset. Although there are short-term consequences to some of the drugs, there are few long-term documented problems. Most physicians believe that the effects of these drugs are transitory.

Others are not as sure. We need more research in this field, coupled with an exploration of ways of making childbirth without drugs a more pleasant, satisfying experience for expectant mothers, fathers, and newborns.

Childbirth Practices

The first part of this chapter focused on the more mechanical and medical aspects of childbirth. It also brought up points of controversy. Concern about childbirth practices and their implications for families have made changes in the system. The old tradition was that the father would take the mother to the hospital and, as labor became more active, he would leave her. The father then paced the floor, while the mother went to the labor room, which she might share with other women for several hours. When she was deemed ready, she was taken to the delivery room, probably given a general anesthetic, and woken up in the recovery room to be told that she had just given birth to a 7-pound daughter. She could typically see her husband then and, at some later point, her daughter. She could plan on spending almost two weeks in the hospital. In general, childbirth was considered a medical issue and those procedures were devised to make childbirth as safe as possible for both mother and child. Many people were dissatisfied with these procedures.

Although few expectant parents wanted to revert to the practices of earlier times, with consequent risk of death to both mother and child, they were seeking a more satisfying experience in childbirth. Concerns focused on several issues. The most controversial was the focus on pregnancy as an illness and childbirth as a medical/surgical problem. With pregnancy thought of as an illness, women were told to refrain from many things, from driving an automobile to exercising. They were often angry with, but also dependent on the doctor. If the woman chose to ignore the advice and something went wrong, then she was blamed. There was little effort to find out which restrictions were legitimate and which were not. During the delivery process itself, women were depersonalized and treated as if they were having an appendectomy. Related to the concept of a medical illness was the length of time women stayed in the hospital, often up to two weeks, again reinforcing the idea that the women were ill and needed medical attention to recuperate.

The exclusion of significant others was another controversial issue. Although many cultures traditionally exclude fathers from the birthing process, often there are relatives and neighbors who remain with the mother and support and coach her. Another issue was the separation of the mother and newborn. Those concerned with maternal bonding to the infant were especially vocal in their objections to this practice. Traditionally, the infant was only brought to the mother for feeding, and then whisked away, and this feeding was based on the hospital schedule, not that of either the mother or newborn.

Today birthing patterns have changed and are continuing to change. In the 1990s, in a noncomplicated delivery, women frequently go home in less than 48 hours. In some hospitals birthing is considered in the outpatient category, and the mother and infant stay less than 24 hours. This is a concern because conditions such as jaundice peak at the third or fourth day. The yellow tinge of the skin is an indication of excess bilirubin levels. If the new mother does not know this, it may go untreated and result in kernicterus (encephalopathy). This leads to neural deafness and brain damage often resulting in cerebral palsy (Weiner, 1994). If treated, this is entirely preventable. When infants stayed in the hospital longer, this was routinely monitored and treated.

Length of stay is complicated by issues such as insurance, or lack of it. Hospitals are expensive, so those without insurance coverage want to remain in the hospital for as short a time as possible. Even those with insurance have policies that pay for only 24- to 48-hour hospitalization following an uncomplicated vaginal delivery.

Some hospitals have birthing rooms as well as rooming-in situations where a mother has access to her infant. Fathers or significant others are often present and encouraged to be present during labor and birth, even cesarean births. Many couples decide to train the father to be the expectant mother's coach during labor. He helps her relax, leads her in the special breathing techniques, and is a companion, support, and distraction for her during the birthing process, especially during the time no staff attendants are present. Although popular literature supports father–infant bonding during the birthing process, the professional literature does not support presence at birthing as the method through which fathers bond with their infants (Palkovitz, 1992).

Some of the changes in birthing practices have been brought about by rising medical costs, others by different beliefs about childbirth. It is difficult to know the long-term effect of these changing patterns on infants and their families.

Changing Patterns in Childbirth

The technocratic model of childbirth sees it as a hospital ritual with the health of the fetus insured through drugs, tests, and techniques; time is an important variable; and the doctor is responsible for delivering the infant. A wholistic model of birth sees pregnancy and birth as an inherently normal process that needs nurture and support from significant others. Action is based on knowledge and intuition and the health of the infant is insured through the physical and emotional health of a mother attuned to her baby. A mother births a baby with the help of a skillful guide (Davis-Floyd, 1992).

The wholistic approach supported by Grantly Dick-Read (1959) in his book *Childbirth without fear: The principles and practice of natural childbirth* was one of the first steps toward moving away from a purely medical model of childbirth. For most women it went too far.

However, dissatisfaction with the technocratic model and unwillingness by many to fully buy into the wholistic model opened the door in the 1960s for other models of "natural" childbirth where the core of the model was not the hospital or obstetrician but the role of a "prepared" mother as an awake, active participant in the process whose feelings in labor and active efforts resulted in the birth of an infant (Davis-Floyd, 1992).

The concept of preparing a mother and a significant other to take an active part in childbirth has changed the system. By the mid 1980s, almost all hospitals in the United States allowed fathers in the labor and delivery rooms and were also recommending some type of childbirth classes for the expectant mother.

The Lamaze Method

Lamaze childbirth techniques or variations of this method are now used by many mothers and their significant others. The **Lamaze method,** developed by the French physician Ferdinand Lamaze (1956) and popularized in the United States by Marjorie Karmel (1965) in her book *Thank you, Dr. Lamaze,* is geared more to U.S. hospitals and their way of birth than the method proposed by Dick-Read. The challenge Lamaze offered was over the use of analgesia and having a significant other present during the birthing process (Davis-Floyd, 1992). Classes are frequently taken at the beginning of the third trimester. The basis of the approach is threefold, knowledge about what is going to happen, experiences in relaxation and breathing exercises, and teaching another adult to help in the process. The goal is to help the woman during the birthing process so she can be alert and awake and enjoy the baby, and at the same time not have the infant be the recipient of unnecessary drugs.

While the Lamaze approach ideally avoids the need for drugs, the approach supports their use if needed by the mother or in response to a physician's request. If a cesarean section is necessary, women are encouraged to accept that decision and not regard themselves as having failed in their approach. There has not been much research on this method, and what has been done frequently focused on the use of anesthesia and other medications, rather than evaluated the effect on the family as a unit. Some fathers did not want to participate in childbirth and reported feeling very stressed by the process; others felt that this method finally provided them with a necessary role.

The Leboyer Method

Frederick Leboyer (1975), another French obstetrician, focused on the environment into which the infant is delivered; his method is frequently known as "birth without violence." Leboyer argued that infants were sensitive to noise, bright lights, rough handling, and bad vibes (Congdon, 1994). The goal is to minimize infant trauma by having people speak in low voices, replace glaring lights with dim ones, and warming the room so there is no need to worry about the baby being too chilly as he is placed on the mother's naked skin directly after birth. The newborn is handled gently and slowly and the cord is cut only after it stops pulsating.

Many women who use the **Leboyer delivery** have also participated in a Lamaze-type of preparation for childbirth. As with Lamaze preparation, there are few well-controlled studies; instead, the few known studies support the claims of the advocates.

Delivery Positions

There is a growing body of evidence that lying on the back may not be the best position for either labor or delivery (Caldeyro-Barcia, 1975; Liddell & Fisher, 1985; Lupe & Gross, 1986). Labor is shorter for first-time mothers who stand and walk (Caldeyro-Barcia, 1978; Diaz, Schwarcz, & Caldeyro-Barcia, 1980) and they tend to require less pain medication (Flynn, Kelly, Hollins, & Lynch, 1978). Gravity increases the efficiency of contractions when a woman is vertical. In most cultures, lying down on one's back is not the traditional position for labor and delivery. Even side-lying is more efficient than back-lying (Roberts, Mendez-Bauer, & Woodell, 1983). There are many forms of vertical delivery, and when this option is available, women often have the opportunity to pick their preference from sitting in a birthing chair, being propped against pillows or another person, squatting on the floor, or squatting in a clean wading pool or tub. Interestingly, although research evidence supports vertical positions as being good for both the mother and infant, it has had little medical support in the United States (Davis-Floyd, 1992).

Other Birthing Trends

Both low- and high-risk pregnant women have explored a variety of alternative types of birthing for a variety of different reasons. Birthing centers, a compromise between hospital and home delivery, provide an alternative for some low-risk pregnant women. These are centers that may or may not be associated with hospitals, which provide a safe "homelike" atmosphere for women who want such an environment.

Home deliveries are becoming more prevalent in the United States for two very different groups of people: One group is typically well educated, with strong opinions about the birth experience, whereas the other is at high risk—particularly women who use drugs. In some states women in the latter group know they will be arrested after the birth (for illegal drug use). So they make the decision to have the infant at home. Thus, women choosing home deliveries are making two very different social statements. The former supporting childbirth as a natural, family-centered experience who will probably have the help of a midwife; the latter, themselves in a high-risk category, may give birth, without experienced guidance, to an infant who is at risk and may need special care. The prognosis for the former is very good, the prognosis for the latter very poor.

There is also a growing use of nurse-midwives in the birthing process. Certified nurse-midwives have an R.N. degree plus additional special training in obstetrics. However, they do no surgery. Some hospitals allow midwives to use their facilities; others do not. Midwives are more likely found in birthing centers and more likely to be present at home deliveries. With the shortage of physicians working in clinics and urban areas, many see nurse-midwives as the only alternative to providing the necessary prenatal care and support to the growing numbers of at-risk pregnant women.

Summary

This chapter covered labor and the birthing process. It focused on the different stages of labor and the factors influencing labor at each stage. It discussed both operative vaginal delivery and cesarean section deliveries and mentioned current concerns about the increasing number of cesarean sections. Birth was viewed from the perspective of the fetus and the transitions that were necessary to move from the liquid environment of the womb to an environment with air, light, and varying temperatures.

Complications related to labor and delivery were explored, including concerns about both the mother and the fetus and the strategies that are used to counteract these birth complications. The use of drugs to influence the speed of delivery and to offset the pain were also covered, as well as the assessment of the newborn at delivery. Changing patterns and trends in childbirth practices and the reasons for these changes were discussed.

Application Activities

1. Talk with a mother who has recently given birth. Ask her how she viewed the process initially, how these views changed the closer she got to delivery, and what actually happened during her delivery. Introduce another perspective and ask how she decided against that view.

2. Talk with your mother about your birth and what the experience was like for her and your father. Find out if she thinks things are "better or worse" now. Ask her what role she would expect to play if or when you or your significant other has an infant.

3. Discuss with your female and male friends their expectations about childbirth and how they formed these views.

Chapter 4

The Newborn

The birth of an infant marks the start of a new period in the lives of a couple. They have just moved up a generation and become parents. In Western civilization we symbolize the significance of this event by giving the newborn the age of zero. Birth is really a transition from the prenatal environment to a new postnatal environment. Newborns come into the world as marvelously complex individuals with a variety skills, many of which were functional during the prenatal period. The adjustments of the first month are so different for both parents and the newborn that this chapter focuses exclusively on those first 28 days.

Transition to Parenthood

The month following the birth of an infant is unique. It has a name: the **postpartum period.** It is often a period of emotional upheaval and adjustment. Parents feel profound joy while struggling with lack of sleep. Mothers are most subject to the "postpartum blues," but fathers, too, may feel depression, mood shifts, irritability, and fatigue as they come down off the birth high and reality settles in. Americans have a very romanticized view of babies and parenthood. We picture a smiling, gurgling baby who is undemanding and on a schedule that is compatible with our own. The reality is that a tiny new "addition" can require drastic changes. This is a surprise to most parents, even those who thought they were prepared.

The transition to parenthood is often difficult, for a variety of reasons. It is influenced not only by the birth of the baby but also by the relationship the couple had before the birth and even before the pregnancy. For many couples the decision to have a baby was well planned, for others it just happened. Parenthood is irrevocable: There may be ex-spouses but there are no ex-children. Although the process of labor may seem long and difficult, what comes later may be even be more demanding. One day there is no baby and the next day there is one. One day you can spontaneously run a half-hour errand, the next day you will need to negotiate having an adult at home to do the same thing. There is no time to ease into parenthood. Some view the transition to parenthood as a crisis.

Some of the radical changes in lifestyle that parenthood brings include less sleep, sometimes chronic fatigue, less time together as a couple, and perhaps less social life. Infants are expensive and can bring about changes in one's financial situation. They require special equipment such as car seats, cribs, highchairs, and so on. They outgrow clothes in a matter of months, but can get them dirty in a matter of moments. Both parents may suffer from insecurity and intimidation when faced with the demands of their new baby and concerns about living up to unrealistic standards of being a "good parent."

Although most couples are able to reorganize their relationship over the first few months, many factors influence how easy or difficult this reorganization is. Variables include the marital and family organization at the time of birth, preparation for parenthood, the length of time the couple has been married prior to the birth, and whether or not the child was planned (McCubbin & Dahl, 1985). The baby himself is a variable! To the extent that he is quiet, healthy, and sleeps and eats well, the adjustment is easier. A difficult delivery, or the birth of a premature or at-risk infant causes greater anxiety at this normally stressful time.

Whether having a baby is considered a crisis or a normal developmental event, having a baby definitely requires many profound changes. Couples or individuals who are unprepared or unable to make these changes experience a great deal of stress both in dealing with the baby and each other. Many couples feel that having a baby will pull them more closely together. This is unlikely to happen. Only 19 percent of 250 couples that participated in the Penn State Child and Family Development Project had more feelings of love toward their spouse, increased communication, or decreased feelings of ambivalence and conflict. Thirty percent remained unchanged, but did not gain a new sense of closeness. And 50 percent of the couples felt less love and communication, and more ambivalence and conflict (Belsky & Kelly, 1994). The Project identified six abilities that were important to making the transition to parenthood a positive one for couples:

- "Surrender individual goals and needs and work together as a team.
- Resolve differences about division of labor and work in a mutually satisfactory manner.
- Handle stresses in a way that does not overstress a partner or a marriage.
- Realize that however good a marriage becomes post-baby, it will not be good in the same way it was pre-baby.
- Maintain the ability to communicate in a way that continues to nurture the marriage." (Belsky & Kelly, 1994, 16)

Because the transition to parenthood is so tumultuous and fraught with many difficulties, it is surprising then that 90 percent of fertile couples do have children, and that this event is anticipated with such positive expectations. Some feel that the birth of a second or later child is less stressful than the birth of the first, but each birth brings its own unique stresses. With later-born children, parents must cope with siblings' reactions to the new baby, plus having extra work to do and trying to make sure they give adequate attention to the other children.

One frequent, but erroneous, assumption is that the transition to parenthood is the same for the mother and the father, or that it is done as a couple. Some aspects of the transition are gender specific. Although men and women become parents at the same time, they do not become parents in the same way (Belsky & Kelly, 1994).

Mother's Transition to Parenthood

For mothers the transition to parenthood may begin with "love at first sight" as she gazes into the eyes of her newborn. Some women find this love so consuming that they can't think about anything except the infant. Part of the transition for the new mother is worrying about the physical changes in her appearance. Mothers frequently become worried that they are unattractive; housekeeping demands seem daunting, and the dirty diapers endless. About 50 to 70 percent of mothers experience "postpartum blues." This is often a transient period of weepiness, mood instability, anxiety, and irritability that may last a week or two after delivery (Still, 1994b). Postpartum depression is experienced by 10 to 15 percent of mothers and is initially difficult to distinguish from postpartum blues. It lasts longer and involves ambivalent feelings toward the infant and an incapacity to love her family (Still, 1994b). These feelings complicate the transition to parenthood and, when severe enough, may require intervention.

Caring for very young infants takes tremendous amounts of time and energy. If employment outside the home is added to this, there is additional stress. One of the top priorities in a mother's transition to parenthood is an equitable division of labor. New mothers want their husbands to be a supportive, understanding partner, not a helper. She wants him to be willing to be neglected emotionally and physically as she adjusts to the role of motherhood and regains her emotional balance (Belsky & Kelly, 1994). One of the major findings regarding the transition to parenting is that the household division of labor and marital relations become more traditional. That is, women end up doing the cooking, cleaning, and child care (often in addition to working). During that time fathers "help" mothers, but the major responsibility for parenting and housework lies with the mother (Collins & Coltrane, 1995).

Women are often anxious about the potential competition between marital and maternal roles. Those who work have added pressure from that role and more than one-half (53 percent) of these women will return to work before their infant is a year old (U.S. Bureau of the Census, 1990). In the 1960s, the average father devoted 11 hours per week to being with his infant and caring for the home; in the 1990s this has increased to 15 or 16 hours per week. A working mother exceeds this contribution to child care by 300 percent (Belsky & Kelly, 1994).

Many mothers believe that there should be more shared emotional responsibility for the new infant. Emotional responsibility goes beyond a willingness to pick up a child or change a diaper. This challenges the assumptions that mothers are the only ones who can schedule pediatrician visits, oversee child-care arrangements, and so on. The longer women have been married, the better their health, and the easier their pregnancy, the easier is their adjustment.

Breast or Bottle Feeding

One decision a mother should make before the infant arrives is whether or not she is going to breast-feed her newborn. The production of milk by the breast is called **lactation.** Most physicians encourage mothers to breast-feed infants, or to at least try it, as one can later decide not to breast-feed, but it is difficult, or even impossible, to begin breast feeding if the decision is made too late. Until the 1940s, breast feeding was common in almost all societies. With improvements in packaging, a variety of formulas, and arrangements between physicians and infant-milk manufacturers, breast feeding has decreased.

After an upswing in breast feeding in the United States in the 1970s there has been a decrease beginning in the early 1980s. Ironically, this decrease occurred at the same time that researchers were finding increasing long-term health benefits for breast feeding. The primary health benefits of breast milk for infants are immunologic protection from gastrointestinal infection and disease as well as protection from certain chronic diseases later in life. Infants are not allergic to breast milk (although they can be allergic to the foods the mother ingests), and since milk production responds to the infant's consumption, it is rare to over- or underfeed a breast-fed infant (Morris, 1995). In 1989, 52 percent of hospital-born infants received some breast milk, but by 6 months only 18 percent were still receiving any breast milk. Proponents of breast feeding point to the well-documented nutritional and emotional advantages:

- Colostrum, the premilk fluid, passes on the mother's antibodies which protect the infant against disease.
- Breast milk is the ideal food for infants. It contains sugar (lactose), easily digestible protein (whey and casein), and fat (digestible fatty acids) and numerous minerals, vitamins, and enzymes. Formulas can approximate the nutrients but not the enzymes and antibodies.
- Breast feeding is positively correlated with lower rates of gastroenteritis, ear and upper respiratory infections, wheezing, diarrhea, vomiting, and eczema in infants.
- Breast feeding is a safety net against ill-prepared, watered-down, or too hot formula. It is also free (although the mother may eat more).
- Hormones produced during breast feeding enhance mothering and the mother–infant relationship and delay the return of fertility.
- Lactation also provides health benefits for the mother. It helps the uterus tighten up and return more quickly to its normal size; it uses up about 500 calories a day; and it helps the mother get back into shape physically. It reduces risk of breast, ovarian, uterine, and cervical cancer. It also appears to reduce urinary tract infections. (Adapted from Morris, 1995; Shelov, 1993).

Concerns related to breast feeding arise if the mother is extremely ill and may not have the energy, or if there are medications or disease (such as AIDS) that would pass into the breast milk and be dangerous to the infant. Relative to the transition to parenthood, the concern is that the mother is the only one who can nurse the infant. This may increase the new father's sense of isolation if other ways are not found to involve him. Another concern mothers may have is whether or not the infant is getting enough to eat. During the first month the best way to tell if a breast-fed infant's diet is adequate is through his elimination patterns. He should urinate about six to eight times a day and have several small bowel movements daily (usually after feeding). Because infants often lose up to 10 percent of their birth weight during the first week of life, weighing the infant is not a good indication. Once this weight is regained, infants should gain about two-thirds of an ounce a day during the first three month; this drops to about half an ounce a day after six months (Shelov, 1993).

The primary reasons for stopping breast feeding are nipple trauma, breast engorgement, mastitis, and insufficient milk (Still, 1994b). These problems have been extensively studied and can be remedied or prevented, except for an inadequate milk supply. There are some ways of accommodating that as well, from increasing liquid intake to a nursing trainer that provides formula though a small plastic tube while the infant is nursing at the breast (Shelov, 1993). When a mother chooses not to breast-feed, or stops breast feeding early, active steps must be taken to suppress lactation.

There are many reasons for the decline in breast feeding. More women with younger children are working, although some find through flexible scheduling, the use of a breast pump, or using a combination of breast and bottle feeding, they can continue breast feeding. The length of hospital maternity stays has decreased to a day or two or less. Short stays mean that there are few opportunities for mothers to learn how to breast-feed their infants. They assume full-time child care while they are physically recovering from the birthing process.

Infants who are bottle-fed by mothers or caregivers that love, hold, cuddle, and make eye contact with them while enjoying a feeling of togetherness have a positive experience as well. The issue is not so much breast or bottle feeding but the quality of the relationship.

Father's Transition to Parenthood

The transition to parenthood for fathers seems to be more even. They experience fewer lows, but also fewer highs. Rather than falling in love instantaneously, it may take fathers weeks or even months to fall in love with their child. It happens more gradually. Fathers are often concerned about the decline in their wife's sexual responsiveness (McCubbin & Dahl, 1985). The father may also feel left out and imagine that he is competing with the baby for his wife's attention. His priority may focus on concerns about work and money. Although realizing that the work load has changed, and perhaps even feeling guilty about his lack of participation, and although willing to modify his priorities, he still wants affection for himself, an active social life, and freedom to pursue his interests and see his friends (Belsky & Kelly, 1994).

From a father's perspective, he probably feels that he contributes far more to caring for his child than his father did for him. He feels that he should be appreciated for his help, rather than chastised for not contributing more, or criticized for any inadequate skills. One of the relatively consistent research findings has been that although many fathers need to learn how to nurture and care for young infants, early participation in infant care by fathers is more likely to lead to later sharing of child care (Coltrane, 1990). Fathers who are older and see the role of "father" as an important one in comparison to other roles have an easier adjustment.

The transition to parenthood is dramatic, but different for the mother and the father. The challenge is to move from a couple relationship into a family. The transition for the fetus from the womb to the family is also a dramatic one.

Transition from the Womb

From the perspective of the newborn, the universe has also changed radically. His senses are bombarded with new stimulation. He has been pushed from a world where he was curled inside a sac that gently supported his body. Now his body is stretched for the first time and he is poked and prodded. The noise is far higher pitched than what he heard before, but the biggest difference is light. The newborn can see, and there are things to look at that move.

The newborn's first contact with the full force of light comes at his emergence from the birth canal. Although his visual system is immature, he can see, but even low levels of light make him squint (Maurer & Maurer, 1988). The womb kept the fetus at an almost constant 99 degree temperature. At birth he emerges soaking wet into a room that is cooler than he is used to. The newborn has disproportionately more surface area from which to lose heat and less fat to prevent heat loss, so his body temperature cools quickly unless he is kept warm.

Newborns

Newborns are technically referred to as **neonates** for the first 28 days of their life. Newborns rarely look like their parents' dream baby. Instead the newborn is wet with amniotic fluid, his skin is wrinkled, and he may still be covered with the white cheesy substance called *vernix*. He may or may not have hair. His face may be asymmetrical from his trip through the birth canal, and his head may be cone-shaped from having been squeezed. His legs are bent or flexed and froglike. His skin may be a bit blue, his breathing rapid and even a little irregular, and his hands and feet will be cold (Shelov, 1993).

But when he open his eyes—suddenly, he becomes beautiful! If he is alert, he will be curious and gaze with long intensity. Mothers usually have two conflicting responses—how could anything this "enormous" have possibly fit inside her body, let alone get out, and how could anything this "tiny" be so perfect, especially those little hands, fingers, and fingernails.

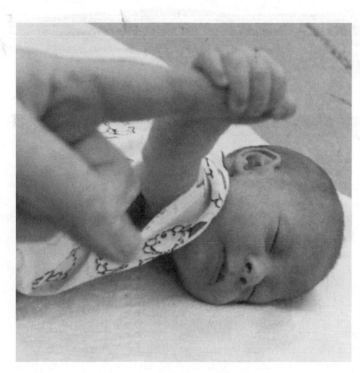

Although tiny, newborns are complete down to fingernails and eyelashes.

Physical and Motor Development

Although a newborn has all his body parts, he is not just a miniature version of an adult. The newborn is about 20 inches long and weighs about 7.5 pounds, with males being slightly longer and heavier than females. The body proportions of the newborn are different from the adult. His head constitutes about 25 percent of his body length, whereas in adulthood this is about 10 percent. The circumference of his head exceeds his chest and his lower jaw is quite small, giving him a receding chin. His limbs are disproportionately short, and typically flexed, and the fists are closed. There is no semblance of a waist; rather, he has a small chest and a protruding abdomen.

The newborn's body has a higher proportion of water than does an adult's and he will lose a few ounces of this water before he begins to gain weight. The newborn will grow about 1.5 inches and gain about 2 pounds during the first month. His motor development is dominated by reflexive behaviors.

Reflexes

The neonate has an amazing repertoire of responses called **reflexes.** These are controlled by the brain stem and the spinal cord. Some of these reflexes will disappear as the cortex of the brain matures and overrides them; others form the basis for coordinated, voluntary movement; and still others, such as the knee jerk, remain throughout life.

The first observable reflexes are called **primitive reflexes.** Some of the most primitive reflexes develop during the fetal period, such as rooting and sucking, the palmar grasp, and the Moro reflex. These are present at, or soon after, birth. Reflexes are predictable responses to specific stimuli. For example, an infant sucks whenever a nipple, finger, or pacifier is placed in his mouth. It is unrelated to hunger or the nutritive value of what is being sucked.

The newborn is in a reflexive action stage; he sucks, grasps, cries, roots, and swallows. These reflexes become modified over the first month. The sucking reflex becomes more efficient, that is, the infant learns how much sucking is required for liquid to get into his mouth and he coordinates sucking, swallowing, and breathing more efficiently.

Reflexes are useful in the diagnostic assessment of the newborn. They are primarily assessed to test the integrity of the central nervous system. If a reflex is absent, develops much later than it should, or persists long after it should disappear, there is the possibility of a dysfunctional central nervous system. Table 4.1 provides a summary of the reflexes, information on how to elicit each one, and the significance attached to the reflex.

There are a variety of theories about reflexes and their value and what happens to them. They may have survival, protective, or adaptive value. Some feel that all reflexes are innate and that at some point they had survival value in the evolution of the species. Others feel that these behaviors are controlled by the lower brain (brain stem and spinal cord) and that as the cortex develops it inhibits the reflexes or modifies them and they come under voluntary control. Still others contend that perhaps they are not reflexes at all but rather behaviors learned by the fetus in the womb (Bremner, 1994). We really don't know.

Some explanation of reflexes are less controversial than others. Sucking and rooting, both have obvious survival value. It seems likely that palmar and plantar grasps had a purpose earlier in evolution, perhaps for the young to hold on to their mother. The Moro or "tree climbing" reflex might have value if the response to being dropped is to hold on. However, the asymmetrical tonic neck reflex seems to have little survival value. Although we ponder how reflexes come about and then adapt or disappear, they are useful initial diagnostic tools, and as we learn more about fetal development we may increase our understanding of reflexes.

Although newborns are in a reflexive stage for the first month, they come into this world with the essential equipment they need to makes sense out of their environment. Newborns are not the helpless creatures we once thought.

Sensorimotor Organization

In the past we viewed the neonate as poorly developed and unable to control or adjust to his environment. William James stated "The baby, assailed by eyes, ears, nose, skin and entrails at once, feels it all one great blooming buzzing confusion" (1890, 488). Because the neonate was regarded as primarily a physiological organism, research concentrated on physiological aspects of development such as growth (Hepper, 1992). Neonates are no longer regarded as incompetent just because they do not match adult standards of sensory perception. One of the changes in studying young infants has been the acknowledgment of the interrelationship between sensory and motor development. During the 1960s and 1970s research focused on eye movements, head turning, and nonnutritive sucking. In the 1990s the emphasis is more on sensorimotor organization. These sensorimotor behaviors were reframed as actions which were organized, goal-directed, and intentional (Pick, 1989). Additionally, these sensorimotor actions needed to be viewed in organismic and environmental context.

A **sense** is a system by which information outside the nervous system is translated into neural activity and thus gives the neonate information about the outside world. Before looking at sensorimotor behavior, a brief overview of the sensory capacity of a normal infant at birth helps us set the stage. Newborns, although dependent, are amazingly competent beings who are not at the mercy of their environment but have a diverse repertoire of behavior that enables them to adjust and adapt to their environment (Hepper, 1992).

Vision

Infant vision is different from adult vision, but it serves the infant well and your knowledge of it will help you understand what to show very young infants. The newborn can see at birth. However, since this is his first experience with light, he is hypersensitive to bright lights. Neonates do not have normal adult visual acuity (20/20). Normal visual acuity at birth is about 20/600 (Batshaw & Perret, 1992). Although inhibiting for an adult, for infants this low visual acuity may have a protective quality and prevent overstimulation.

Newborns see best in dim lighting with high-contrasting colors. They are most attentive to black-and-white bull's eyes, stripes, and checks. Pastels are really washed out, and infants do not notice them. Infants focus best on objects that are close to them. Newborns do not yet have binocular vision or the range of peripheral vision that adults have. Rather, it is almost as if they are looking through two separate tunnels that do not come together. The newborn can focus on the human face and have a field of vision of about 90 degrees. To get an approximation of what a newborn sees, take a piece of wax paper and hold it about 8 inches from your eyes and look around. You will notice that everything looks blurred.

The eye is connected to the visual cortex of the occipital lobe of the brain by the optic nerve. During the neonatal period the visual cortex is very immature. This immaturity influences his gaze and ability to follow objects. The infant watches whatever part of an object catches his eye, but he does not visually explore the object. If the frame of a picture is of higher contrast than the picture itself, the neonate will focus on the frame and not see the picture. Thus, the neonate will focus on your chin or hairline, but will probably not see your whole face until he is 2 to 3 months old (Haith, Bergman, & Moore, 1977). He sees slow-moving objects as photographs spaced at intervals rather than as a film or videotape that is continuous. Neonates also lack the coordination to follow rapidly moving objects.

Researchers have wondered whether or not a newborn can see colors. The conclusion seems to be that he can see some colors at birth but he does not see col-

Table 4.1 Reflexes

Reflex	To elicit	Significance
Rooting	Stroke the corner of the infant's mouth. The infant will turn toward that side. This is easier to elicit when the infant is hungry.	May be depressed in newborn because of drugs given in the birthing process. Absence indicates neurological problems. Disappears at about 4 months.
Sucking	Place finger in infant's mouth and infant will suck. Easier to elicit when hungry.	May be depressed in newborn because of drugs given in the birthing process. Absence indicates neurological problems. Changes into voluntary behavior.
Palmar Grasp	Using your finger, put pressure on the palm of the infant's hand. The hand will close, grasping your finger. Premature infants have stronger and more persistent grasps.	Stronger in infants with cerebral palsy, absent where there is a lesion in the spinal cord. Disappears by about 2 to 3 months.
Babkin	Put pressure on the palms of both hands. The infant's eyes will close and mouth open.	Weak response, or return after it disappears, may indicate central nervous system dysfunction. Diminishes after the first month; is completely gone by 3 to 4 months.
Plantar	Place your finger or a pencil on the sole of the foot just below the toes and press. The toes will curl.	Strong in infants with cerebral palsy. Diminishes gradually but is gone by a year.
Withdrawal	Use a toothpick to prick the sole of the foot. The foot will withdraw.	Absence on one side indicates sciatic nerve damage; may be weak or absent in breech deliveries if legs were extended. Continues throughout life.
Babinski	Draw your finger up the sole of the foot from heel to toe. The toes fan out, the large toe flexes.	Absence indicates dysfunction of the lower spinal cord.
Asymmetrical Tonic Neck Reflex (ATNR)	With infant on back, turn head to one side; the arm and leg will extend, the other side will flex (fencer "on guard" position). Difficult to elicit in term neonates, easier at 2 to 3 months.	Concern is if this happens on one side but not the other. Persistence beyond about 7 months may indicate motor immaturity or cerebral palsy.
Symmetrical Tonic Neck Reflex	First flex head, then extend it. Both legs flex and the arms extend. Disappears as infant learns to crawl.	Helps infants get onto hands and knees. Persistence of reflex prevents extension of legs when head is raised.

Moro	While infant is on back, remove head support and allow head to drop about an inch. This is followed by complex movements where the arms are extended with the fingers curled, then flexed with the hands in fists (almost as if hugging a tree). It can be elicited by banging the table next to the infant's head, causing the head to move.	Absence indicates disfunction of the central nervous system. Persistence beyond 4 months (6 months in preterm) indicates brain damage and mental retardation.
Startle	Make a sudden loud noise. The infant will flex his elbows, hands in fists. Infants may elicit this reflex themselves as they startle ir response to their own cries, creating a vicious cycle.	May not be present at birth but will be after several weeks. Merges with the adult startle reflex.
Placing	Hold infant so the front of his leg just above his foot touches the edge of a table. He will lift his leg and place the foot on the table.	Disappears at about 1 year.
Stepping	Hold infant upright on a solid surface and tilt from side to side; infant will support weight and take alternating steps.	Usually disappears about 2 months, but if used frequently can continue until voluntary walking.
Standing	Place soles of feet on solid surface. Gradually allow infant to bear weight while maintaining his balance. Infant's hips and knees extend and he supports his weight.	Disappears in most infants around 3 months but may persist until voluntary standing.

SOURCE: Adapted from Barclay, 1985; Brazelton, 1983.

ors as an adult does. However, his ability in this area develops quickly, and by about 3 to 4 months his color vision is similar to an adult's vision (Maurer & Maurer, 1988). For an infant then, the world "would look like a badly misfocused snapshot that has been fading in the sun for so many years that you can barely identify the subject" (Maurer & Maurer, 1988, 127). The newborn, however, is not at all disturbed by this, as it is the only vision he has ever known. It is not until about 2 to 3 months that infants can distinguish mother from father visually. Since perception changes with distance, in his mind the mother that is across the room is different from the mother that holds him.

Hearing

The auditory system of the infant is among the most well-developed bodily functions at birth (England, 1990). By 20 weeks, the hearing apparatus of a fetus is functional, although it is not completely mature (Batshaw & Perret, 1992). Although infants cannot see in the womb, they can hear. Using real-time ultrasound has increased our understanding of the fetus in action and the skills that he brings with him at birth. Fetal auditory responsiveness has been repeatedly documented. Although it was initially thought that the fetus did not hear until 24 weeks, more recent work has shown that hearing may start even earlier. Hepper, White, and Shahidullah (1991) found that the fetus can respond to auditory stimulation at 16 weeks, perhaps even 12. This is before the hearing apparatus is functional. They hypothesize that perhaps very early in fetal life there are specific receptor cells that are responding to a stimulation by an undifferentiated neural system. In other words, the very young fetus responds to sensation but it is not sorted out into the specific sensory modality. Obviously, if the fetus can hear and has been hearing for quite some time there is little doubt that the newborn hears.

Hearing basically occurs when sound waves, or vibrations, travel through air or amniotic fluid and hit the ear drum, causing it to vibrate. This causes the small bones in the middle ear to vibrate; the vibrations then move to the inner ear where tiny hair cells carry the wave to the organ of Corti where they become electrochemical impulses that are sent through the auditory nerve to the brain.

The newborn has some disadvantages in this system. First, his outer ear (the visible part) is disproportionately small; secondly, his ear canal is plugged with a creamy white substance called vernix, which disappears in about a week; and, finally, the middle ear has extra fluid from the womb that it takes the body a while to absorb. He is functionally hard-of-hearing; what he hears is thinner and duller than what adults hear, but he can hear.

The auditory cortex, like the visual cortex, is fairly immature. The newborn's brain does not have the ability to sort out the reverberations of sound waves so that what he hears is not exactly the same as what we hear, much like what we see is not what the infant sees (Maurer & Maurer, 1988). He hears not only an initial sound like the slamming of a book on a table, but continuing vibrations as well. As adults, our brain ignores these further vibrations and "hears" a single sound. The newborn hears sound, after sound, after sound, after sound.

Because what is heard is so different for newborns, some of the initial testing that was done using pure tones led to conclusions that newborns could not hear at birth (Maurer & Maurer, 1988). However, given the right stimulus, such as rattles, they do respond and turn toward the rattle. Maurer and Maurer (1988) consider this not as locating a sound, but rather almost a reflexive orienting to the sound. That is, in response to a prolonged noise the newborn will hesitate, then turn very slowly toward the source of the sound. He is not looking for the sound source, as he does this in the dark with his eyes closed. Maurer and Maurer have labeled this the "Benny" reflex, (for the characteristic timing of entertainer Jack Benny). It usually disappears by 2 or 3 months.

Newborns locate sounds based on the high frequencies. As women's voices are higher pitched than men's, the newborn may seem more responsive to his mother than his father. Although he can hear both parents, he cannot accurately locate his father by his voice (Maurer & Maurer, 1988). Strangely, given all the newborn's disadvantages in the area of hearing, he has the ability to distinguish speech patterns and even has a preference about whom he listens to. He can distinguish between "pa" and "ba," quickly learns to recognize his own voice when played to him, and prefers his mother's voice to other female voices. One question you might ask is "How do we know this?"

DeCasper and his colleagues have been curious about what the fetus hears in the womb and whether or not it influences his preference for sounds as a neonate. For one thing, it is obvious that the fetus hears his mother's voice. DeCasper and Fifer (1980) used the neonate's pattern of sucking to determine their voice preferences. First they determined the neonate's baseline. (Sucking in infants occurs in bursts: The pattern is something like *suck, suck, suck,* pause, *suck, suck, suck,* pause, and so on.) Based on this pattern, the researchers calculated the average time of the pause for each infant. Then the neonates were divided into two groups. In the first group, if the infant had a shorter than usual pause, he heard his mother's voice, and if the pause was longer than usual, he heard an unfamiliar female voice. In the other group, the procedure was the same, but the voices were reversed (mother's voice was after a longer pause). The neonates did alter the length of their pause to hear their mother's voice. Neonates did not show a preference for their father's voice (DeCasper & Prescott, 1984).

DeCasper and Spence were also interested in finding out whether or not the fetus processes what he hears. They had 16 pregnant women read Dr. Seuss's *The Cat in the Hat* out loud twice a day during the last 6 weeks of their pregnancy. When the infants were born, the researchers studied their hearing preferences using nonnutritive sucking behavior. An apparatus was arranged so that when the infants sucked they heard one of two recordings: their mother reading *The Cat in the Hat* or reading *The King, the Mice and the Cheese* (which has a different tonal pattern and pace). They preferred *The Cat in the Hat,* that is, they sucked more to continue hearing this book (DeCasper & Spence, 1986). A related question was whether neonates would prefer their mother's voice as they now heard it, or would they prefer it filtered to sound like it did when they were *in utero?* Neonates preferred the sound of the mother's voice as they had heard it *in utero* (Fifer & Moon, 1989).

In order to eventually speak, the newborn needs to hear speech, and the speech that best suits his needs is "baby talk." In all cultures when adults talk to very young infants their speech patterns change. They speak more slowly, more clearly, in a higher pitch, and have more variability in their pitch and intensity, an almost singsong tempo. Their sentences are short and simple. This is what infants need. The pitch and rhythm gets their attention, the slow speed helps them sort out the sounds from the echoes, and the pauses help the infant hear the components of speech (Maurer & Maurer, 1988). Amazingly adults do this automatically with very young children. Perhaps we are programmed to respond to infants in this way!

Touch

The sense of touch is the first sense to develop in the early fetal period. With increasing size, the fetus comes into contact with the uterine wall, the fetus touches himself, especially his face, and the umbilical cord is constantly touching the fetus (Hepper, 1992). Newborns are not as sensitive to touch as adults; that is, they may not respond to a very light touch that an adult would feel. However, many early reflexes are stimulated through tactile sensations: rooting, Moro, sucking, and stepping reflexes. Through the combined integration of motor responses and reduction of immediate reflexive responses to tactile stimulation, the young infant's involuntary response to touch will decrease and be replaced by voluntary responses.

For a long time there was a question about whether or not neonates felt pain. As the perception of pain is typically viewed as a subjective phenomenon, and newborns could not relate their feelings, the assumption was that they could not feel pain. For this reason, circumcisions were done to male newborns without anesthesia. We are far clearer today that newborns do in fact have at least painlike responses (Anand & Hickey, 1987) and that circumcision should be done, when it is necessary for religious or medical reasons, with anesthesia (Balfour-Lynn & Valman, 1993).

Tactile stimulation plays an important role in the emotional development of neonates. They crave tactile stimulation and like to be held. Touching is also an important element in the development of visual attentiveness and attachment behaviors.

Smell

The percentage of the human brain devoted to smell is much smaller than in most other mammals, leading one to believe that it is a less crucial sense for humans. In addition, researchers have found the senses of hearing and vision more intriguing than smell. Consequently, relatively little is known about the infant's olfactory skills. Neonates appear to have a remarkably well-developed sense of smell. They can discriminate between pleasant and unpleasant odors. They also show a preference for fragrant odors and displeasure for noxious ones. Newborns can distinguish their mother's smell (from the smell of other mothers) by the end of the first week (Porter, 1991). They like the smell of their mother. By 6 days they can also distinguish between the smell of their mother's milk and another mother's milk (MacFarlane, 1975). Some researchers (Blass, 1990; Engen, 1986) hypothesize that smell may be more important to the very young infant than previously thought. It may be that the infant's ability to learn and associate smells with familiar individuals and places is an important mediator of social behavior. This may be initially how neonates "know" familiar people, as their vision is not yet adequate to distinguish faces.

Taste

Taste was the subject of early investigations of newborns, but little research is currently being done in the area. The newborn has an adequate number of taste buds. Neonates can discriminate between sweet, acidic, salty, and bitter tastes. Infants much prefer sweet tastes and will spit out sour tastes. They like salty fluids also. They can discriminate between intensities of these tastes also. Apparently the preference for sweet tastes is innate. Some research has shown that sugars, especially sucrose, may reduce the reaction to pain (Blass, 1990). A variety of measures have been used to determine preferences in taste. Some observe facial expressions, others sucking rates, and still others, heart rate. The latter two seem to be more reliable indicators (Lipsitt & Behl, 1990).

Cognition

Before the 1960s, there was little interest or research on the psychological capacities of the neonate. One of the challenges of studying cognition in the neonate is the rapid changes that are occurring in the brain itself, and the rate of physical and motor development. Some of the interest in neonate cognition goes back to sorting out the nature–nurture issue. Researchers study the neonate to better understand the structure of the mind. The neonate comes with an unexposed mind. If environment were the sole factor in determining the structure of this mind, then the environment would be the focus of early research. Likewise, if the unexposed mind was already structured to organize sensory and perceptual input into representations, then the only thing the research would discover would be cognitive universals (Mehler, 1985). That is, the mind would be essentially the same in everyone, with the impact of the environment in organizing the mind negligible.

Research on neonate cognition still focuses on the interaction of nature and nurture, but particularly on *initial acquisition devices.* Infants appear to come preprogrammed to learn language, logic, mathematics, and other cognitive information, and scientists study neonates to learn about the properties of the initial state of these acquisition devices (Mehler, 1985). The question becomes "What is the initial state of the infant?" and "How is this initial state modified?" One confounding problem in learning about initial states is that they may not all be operative at birth. Some may be dependent on biological maturation, others may be triggered by the environment (Carey, 1984).

Some researchers interested in the neonate have focused their attention on whether or not infants can "learn." **Learning** is typically defined as any relatively permanent change in an organism that results from past experience. Because learning is central to the way humans function in the world, it has been the subject of much investigation. The conclusion seems clear that neonates, even premature ones, can and do learn (Lipsitt, 1986), and they can learn even before birth (Hepper & Shahidullah, 1992).

Habituation

The neonate is able to habituate. Habituation is one of the simplest yet most essential learning processes. Habituation is the decrease in response that occurs to repeated stimulation. For example, if the young infant cried when the telephone first rang, and after repeated rings did not cry, one would say that the infant had habituated. Habituation is a central nervous system function that involves a primitive type of learning and memory. Habituation is essential for efficient function, for it is this ability that allows humans to ignore familiar stimuli and pay attention to new ones. In doing research, one of the challenges of interpretation is to determine if the decrement in response is a result of adaptation, habituation, or motor fatigue. Appropriate methodology, and the use of novel stimuli to elicit the response again, can distinguish among these responses (Hepper & Shahidullah, 1992). Habituation allows the newborn to "tune out" some stimuli and not react to them. One of the stimuli neonates rarely tune out is the human voice when someone is talking to them.

Language

Language begins with the newborn's first cry. Neonates have different cries that parents learn to distinguish. In addition to crying, newborns can make gasping sounds and vegetative sounds (murmurs and gurgles), which often accompany feeding. Newborns are responsive to the human voice, regardless of the language of the speaker. They prefer vocal music over instrumental. They also move to the rhythm of adult speech: If the speech is fast, the infant's motion increases and likewise, if the speech slows, the infant's motion also slows (Barclay, 1985). The sounds that the newborn makes are relatively easy to identify and quantify. There is a challenge, however, in understanding the infant's reception of speech and how she learns to make sense out of the spoken word.

Perceiving speech is a complex process. First the neonate must be able to structure acoustical space and locate sound sources in it; speech must be distinguished from background noise; and sounds must be kept apart from each other when they originate from different sources but occur at the same time. Neonates apparently can locate a single sound source, but they do it slowly (Mehler, 1985).

Social and Emotional Development

Some people believe that there is a critical period for mothers to bond to their infants and that this period is during the first hours or days after birth. Proponents of having fathers present at birth feel that fathers, too, bond during this period. Belief in bonding is one of the reasons people feel that mothers and their infants should not be separated in hospitals. The research does not consistently support this position but rather a variation on it. Both timing and duration of contact seem to be more important than whether or not the father was actually present during the birthing process. Palkovitz (1982) found that the longer after delivery the father held the infant, the longer he held the infant in that first encounter. And, the longer he held the infant at the initial encounter, the more likely he was to be engaged in caregiving at 5 months. This would support the proposition that the duration of contact, rather than the contact being at the birth process itself, was the more important variable.

The newborn has the rudiments of feelings. He feels pleasure with sweet tastes and odors and discomfort from intense lights and sounds, as well as bitter tastes and smells. He does not like being cold or exposed to vigorous stimulation (Maurer & Maurer, 1988). It is often clearer what an infant does not like than what he does like. Mostly he sleeps, and when a newborn does react, it is often negatively. This, too, changes quickly.

The neonate does not really have an emotional attachment to anyone, as he cannot distinguish between himself and others. He prefers "familiar." To adults it may seem that he prefers his mother because she is typically the one who is most familiar with the infant and his routine; however, it is the familiarity the infant is responding to, not the mother.

Much research has focused on the impact of parents on their newborn infant. Increasingly, we are beginning to look at the impact of the infant on the parent. One of the areas which influence this impact is the "state" the infant is in and his temperament.

State

The newborn's self-organization is probably best reflected in his capacity for state regulation. Infant states vary from types of alertness to levels of sleep. Interest in state was generated by Prechtl and Beintema's (1964) interest in obtaining optimal responses from newborn infants. These responses can only be obtained when an infant is in a quiet alert state.

When we as adults think broadly about what we do we can distinguish at a gross level that we sleep and we are awake. In general, newborns sleep about 17 to 18 hours a day. They are awake and quiet for 2 to 3 hours, active for 1 to 2, and cry or fuss the remainder of the time. It is the pattern of how these states occur that influences the family. On the one hand, the infant who sleeps for long periods at night, cries little, and is in a quiet alert state when awake is considered easy. On the other hand, the infant who sleeps only for short periods, cries a lot, and is rarely quietly alert is challenging for families. Although this information is useful, it is the infant's capacity for regulating these states that intrigues researchers, as well as matching the state of the infant with appropriate adult behavior. The state an infant is in determines to a large extent how available he is for contact with the environment. Many researchers are interested in classifying infant states. However, not all agree on the number and definition of these states.

Most researchers describe several sleeping states, distinguished by the amount of movement. All seem to agree that there is a state between sleep and wakefulness. The awake states vary more and relate to the amount of activity, focus, and crying. Table 4.2 highlights some of the major aspects of state.

The neonate's ability to respond to the environment is influenced by the state she is in. Neonates differ in the amount of time they spend in each state. The

Newborns are only momentarily in a quiet alert state and easily drift into drowsiness.

degree to which a newborn can be in an alert state and respond to adults is important for learning and establishing relationships. It is up to the adult to read the neonate's state, determine whether or not there is a pattern, and respond accordingly. One of the most difficult tasks adults face is trying to help newborns change states. Different infants respond to different soothing techniques. The most frequently used tactics to lower the state of arousal (typically that means to stop an infant from crying) are picking the newborn up, some type of auditory stimulation such as soothing words, restraining her limbs (swaddling), and changing the infant's position. Giving her a pacifier also affects her state. As you might expect, the state of the neonate is influenced by the amount of light and noise as well.

Table 4.2	Aspects of State
Deep or Regular Sleep	Eyes are closed and breathing is regular; very unresponsive to external stimuli; full rest and little movement
Disturbed Sleep	Irregular sleep in which the eyelids may flutter; infant stirs, may grimace, chew, and respiration may periodically be irregular; there may be sobs or sighs
Drowsiness	Appears when the infant is waking up or going to sleep; the eyes open and close but are unfocused; the infant is not alert; little movement
Alert Inactivity	Eyes are open and bright, the face relaxed; little motor activity; focused alert state is uncommon in newborns
Alert Activity	Eyes open, bright; bursts of motor activity; many free movements
Inflexibly Focused	Awake but not available for external stimuli; wild crying, thrashing, a lot of free activity; eyes may be squeezed tight; concentrated sucking
Indeterminate	This may reflect times where states are changing or the inability to classify a particular state

SOURCE: Adapted from Brazelton (1979), Brown (1964), Korner (1972), Prechtl (1965), & Wolff (1966).

The newborn's state influences researchers who want to learn more about neonates. For example, if you wanted to find out how well newborns saw something, obviously you would not attempt such experiments with a sleeping baby. But what could you conclude about a drowsy one or a crying one? The ideal is the quiet alert state, which is difficult to schedule. The infant's state influences not only the family and researchers, but potentially even such things as medical care. It is difficult for physicians to examine sleeping or crying infants and to focus on the questions mothers might have, and obviously impossible for parents to anticipate an infant's schedule and plan appointments around it.

Crying

Crying, as an aspect of state control, is of particular concern to parents. An infant's cry is a signal to parents that she is in distress. This distress is disturbing to parents, particularly when they do all of the obvious things to provide comfort—such as picking up and holding the infant, rocking her, changing a wet diaper, and soothing her—and still she cries. Some newborns, especially premature ones, have unusual cries, particularly high-pitched and piercing. These may indicate central nervous system disorders (Lester, Zacharaial Boukydis, Garcia-Coll, Hole, & Peucker, 1992).

All normal infants cry and most new parents are surprised at how long and how frequently newborns do so. During the first 6 weeks most newborns cry about 2 hours each day, or about 15 minutes for each hour that they are awake. Crying peaks at about 6 weeks, with infants crying between 2 to 3 hours daily (St. James-Roberts & Halil, 1991; Shelov, 1993) and then the overall amount of time spent crying gradually decreases although the number of crying episodes stays constant. By the end of the first year, infants cry slightly less then an hour a day (St. James-Roberts & Halil, 1991). Infants tend to cry most between 6 p.m. and midnight.

Some infants cry more than others. **Colic** is a condition in newborns indicated by a high-pitched cry accompanied by grimacing, clenched fists, knees that are either pulled up or rigid and extended, the passing of gas, and inconsolable crying. Colicky infants cry for more than 3 hours a day, 3 days a week, for 3 weeks during the first 3 months of life (Steinberg & Meyer, 1995). We don't really know what causes colic. Suggestions run from an immature gastrointestinal tract to food allergies to anxious mothers. About 20 percent of infants develop colic, usually between the second and fourth week (Shelov, 1993). The inability to stop an infant from crying is the most common reason given for abuse of infants. The most common abuse is to shake the infant. Shaking the infant hard can cause blindness, brain damage, and even death (Shelov, 1993).

Neonates at Risk

The neonatal period has the highest infant mortality rate, with three times more deaths than the remaining year of infancy. The highest number occurs the first day, followed by the first week (Rossetti, 1986). Birth weight and gestational age are the most widely used factors in determining neonatal risk. Neonates weighing less than 2,500 grams (or about 5 pounds and 8 ounces) are considered *low birth weight* (LBW). Those weighing below 1,500 grams (about 3 pounds and 5 ounces) are *very low birth weight* (VLBW).

The average length of a pregnancy is 40 weeks. An infant born between 37 and 42 weeks is considered born *at term*. Infants born before 37 weeks gestational age and after 20 weeks are considered *preterm*. Approximately 7 percent of live births in the United States are preterm (Svigos, Robinson, & Vigneswaran, 1994).

The relationship between gestational age and size is an important one. Infants who are born *small for gestational age* (SGA) are particularly at risk. These are infants whose birth weight is below the 10th percentile for their gestational age. Infants below the 5th percentile are particularly at risk. The smallness of the infant indicates fetal growth retardation unless the infant is simply genetically small (Steer & Danielian, 1994). An infant who is born at 40 weeks gestation weighing 4 pounds would be considered small for gestational age as he ought to weigh about 7.5 pounds. If this infant had been born at 34 weeks gestational age, he would just be considered low birth weight and preterm as his weight is appropriate for his gestational age. On occasion infants are born weighing about 7 pounds yet are technically preterm because they were born before 37 weeks. In cases like these it is likely the gestational age was miscalculated or the parents are large.

Preterm and low-birth-weight babies account for about 50 percent of neonatal deaths. Very-low-birth-weight babies have almost 200 times greater risk of neonatal death than full-birth-weight babies, and the risk of postneonatal death is 20 times greater (Semmler, 1989a). In addition to increased infant mortality, they are more likely to show increased morbidity, that is, developmental disabilities and chronic health problems (Semmler, 1989a).

Why some infants are born before term is unknown. Known factors were discussed in earlier chapters. Being born too soon means that a neonate has to make the adjustment from a uterine to an extrauterine life with a less developed body and body systems. Typically, infants weighing 1,500 grams or less stay in the hospital two to three months.

Preterm and Low-Birth-Weight Infants

Preterm infants look different than term infants. They typically have fine hair, or lanugo, over their body (which disappears by 38 weeks); their skin has a reddish tinge because the blood vessels are closer to the surface; the skin is more translucent; and they may lack breast buds, skin creases, and cartilage in their ear lobe because these do not appear until about 34 weeks gestation (Batshaw & Perret, 1992). Muscle tone develops gradually in the fetus and those born before 28 weeks may appear very floppy and "double-jointed." Some premature infants may not have primitive reflexes at birth (Batshaw & Perret, 1992). Physicians use characteristics such as these to assess the maturity of an infant especially when an accurate gestational age is not known.

Being born too soon means that not all systems are ready. Premature infants face risks that other infants do not face at birth. Although distinct, the problems of neonates born prematurely and those with low birth weight are similar and often additive. The problems typically relate to temperature control, nutrition, (both coordinating sucking and swallowing, and the ability of the digestive system to absorb nutrients), respiration (immature lungs), and excess bilirubin (a by-product of breaking down red blood cells). Common problems are briefly described in the following section.

Respiratory Distress Syndrome

Although a premature infant may appear to have normal breathing patterns at birth, approximately 20 percent of all premature infants develop respiratory distress syndrome (RDS), formerly known as hyaline membrane disease. RDS is the leading cause of death for premature infants (Batshaw & Perret, 1992). The younger the infant, the more likely RDS will develop. The respiratory system in premature infants does not work as easily or predictably as it should. The lungs do not expand properly because of the lack of an essential chemical called pulmonary **surfactant.** In a mild case, infants are given supplemental oxygen to help them until their system can produce enough surfactant. Surfactant is not produced by the fetus until 35 weeks.

Chemical research has produced synthetic surfactants that can be directly dripped into the infant's lungs. Another approach, if the birth process can be delayed 24 to 36 hours, is to give medication to the mother to stimulate the fetal production of surfactant (Batshaw & Perret, 1992). These procedures have tremendously improved survival rates in premature infants as well as their long-term development. Most neonates who have respiratory distress syndrome are off oxygen or ventilators in two to three weeks. Some infants, however, develop a chronic lung disease (bronchopulmonary dysplasia) that requires the use of oxygen therapy and artificial ventilation for an extended period (Batshaw & Perret, 1992). With the development of the surfactant therapy, it seems likely that this will be a much less frequent complication than in the past.

Other Circulatory Problems

For some premature infants certain necessary changes in the circulatory system may not take place. One of the most important is the closure of the ductus arteriosus, which the fetal circulatory system used to bypass the lungs. In about 30 percent of premature infants this closure does not take place. The closure is stimulated by the oxygen level in the blood, and, particularly if the premature infant has respiratory distress syndrome, this opening may not close. There is medication which stimulates the closing. If medication does not work, surgery must be performed to close the opening (Batshaw & Perret, 1992).

The premature infant is also troubled by an immature central nervous system which controls respiration and circulation. Getting oxygen into the lungs is a challenge. Some infants cease breathing entirely for 20 to 30 seconds at a time **(apnea).** This is further complicated by a fall in the heart rate called **bradycardia.** Apnea and bradycardia are a problem for about 10 percent of preterm infants, and the smaller the infant, the more likely there is to be a problem (Batshaw & Perret, 1992).

Persistent apnea may indicate some damage to the brain. These infants are also at much greater risk for sudden infant death syndrome (SIDS). Infants who have persistent episodes of apnea and bradycardia are sent home from the hospital attached to cardiorespiratory monitors or apnea monitors that sound alarms if the infant stops breathing. Parents are trained to give cardiopulmonary resuscitation (CPR).

Retinopathy of Prematurity

Premature infants may be at risk for an eye problem, retinopathy of prematurity, (ROP), that can lead to the detachment of the retina and blindness. Initially, this problem was thought to be caused by too high concentrations of oxygen used to treat respiratory distress syndrome and was called retrolental fibroplasia. However, changing the levels of oxygen, although decreasing the prevalence, has not eliminated the disease. Premature infants who have been treated for respiratory distress syndrome should have their eyes examined by an ophthalmologist frequently during the first months of life.

Intracranial Hemorrhage

Premature neonates have a very fragile system of blood vessels that supplies blood to the two sides (ventricles) of the brain. Most premature infants have some degree of intraventricular hemorrhage within a few hours after birth. During the first few days, the major concern is whether the hemorrhaging is life threatening. When hemorrhaging is limited, there seem to be no adverse outcomes.

The more severe hemorrhages result in a greater incidence of brain damage, seizure disorders, cerebral palsy, retinopathy of prematurity, and developmental delays, particularly in language and cognition (Semmler, 1989b). As a rule, the lower the birth weight and the earlier the gestational age the greater the probability of hemorrhaging. Approximately one-third to one-half of neonates weighing 1,500 grams or less have intracranial hemorrhage, which is the primary cause of death in these neonates (Semmler, 1989b). These very-low-birth-weight neonates account for approximately half of neonatal deaths.

A major concern after discharge from the hospital is the implication the hemorrhaging will have on the infant's long-term development. Infants who have had severe hemorrhages are at very high risk for developmental delay, and should receive frequent developmental assessments (Semmler, 1989b). They may profit from early intervention and therapy.

The ability to classify hemorrhages is relatively new, somewhat arbitrary, and constantly changing as new technology provides more accurate information. Ultrasound is the most widely used method for diagnosing and classifying intracranial hemorrhage.

Biochemical Abnormalities

In addition to the problems that are primarily related to prematurity, preterm neonates are more susceptible than full-term neonates to problems such as hypothermia, hypoglycemia, and jaundice. Losing body heat, or **hypothermia,** occurs because the premature neonate does not have as much subcutaneous fat and his higher ratio of body surface to body weight causes him to lose heat faster. This is why premature neonates are placed in warmed incubators. Premature infants have smaller reserves of glucose, which puts them at risk for **hypoglycemia** whose symptoms include lethargy, vomiting, and seizures. Providing early feedings, monitoring glucose levels, and administering glucose intravenously are solutions to the problem. Because the liver of the preterm infant is less developed, bilirubin begins to build up in his system giving him a yellow, jaundiced appearance. Treatment typically involves phototherapy. The newborn's eyes are shielded and he is put under a light source. When the bilirubin concentration is no longer at a dangerous level, the neonate is removed from the lights. In about 25 percent of the cases the therapy must be repeated if the bilirubin concentrations rise (Donn, 1992).

Nutrition

Many low-birth-weight babies cannot feed from a nipple. The sucking reflex is often poorly developed and so is the swallowing mechanism. The preemie has a small stomach and an immature digestive system so he gets fewer calories and nutrients. These infants are sometimes given a special formula through a nasogastric feeding tube. The high-caloric formula is less likely to precipitate **necrotizing enterocolitis,** a gastrointestinal disorder that is life threatening, and that affects 2 to 5 percent of very-low-birth-weight infants (Batshaw & Perret, 1992). Over time they will be able to feed orally. However, feeding may be a lengthy process and occur every two to three hours day and night.

Intensive-Care Nurseries

Different hospitals have different levels of care that they can provide for newborns. Level I facilities can handle routine newborn care. They are the typical well-baby nurseries that can be viewed from the hall and are associated with any hospital that delivers babies. Level II facilities can manage the problems of high-risk mothers and neonates that do not require artificial ventilators for more than 48 hours. They do not perform major surgical procedures. Level III facilities can provide services to all mothers and infants regardless of risk. They have the expertise and equipment to care for the seriously ill neonate. If a neonate that requires more extensive care is born at a Level I facility, he typically is transported by ambulance or helicopter to a Level III facility.

Women at risk for low-birth-weight infants are advised to have their deliveries in hospitals that have Level III care, even if this requires moving a mother while in labor. The outcomes are better than waiting for the infant to be born and then transferring him. As about half of the infants needing this level of care are born by cesarean section, the transport itself becomes a risk factor, especially if it is a long distance. Level III facilities are called intensive-care nurseries (ICN) or neonatal intensive-care units (NICU). Some premature infants and virtually all very-low-birth-weight neonates will need a Level III nursery (Semmler, 1989a).

Neonatal intensive-care units are designed for high-volume, short-term acute care. They focus on medical concerns rather than social concerns. They are used in specially designated hospitals with highly trained staff and they have very advanced technological equipment. They are staffed not with pediatricians and pediatric nurses but with **neonatologists,** medical specialists who concentrate only on the first month of life, and neonatal nurses, also specially trained to work with very small sick newborns.

A typical NICU might have 20 beds, serve 300 infants each year, and have four attending physicians and 200 nurses (Gilkerson, Gorski, & Panitz, 1990). Because these units are so specialized, they draw from a wide geographic area; small states may have only one such facility.

The intensive-care nursery is a threatening place for most parents and not at all what their idea of parenting is all about. The equipment itself is daunting, as is the noise level with monitors beeping and personnel moving quickly to handle emergencies. The infants in the intensive-care nursery are often very small and are hooked up to equipment to help them perform a variety of life functions from breathing to eating. They are also connected to equipment to monitor their life functions.

Instead of being alone in a dimly lit room getting to hold, cuddle, and love their baby, these parents must learn to look through a maze of equipment in order to see their baby who needs the same love, cuddling, and holding.

Bringing an Infant Home

As threatening as the intensive-care nursery is, the thought of bringing their premature infant home can be even more frightening to parents. Most premature infants come home around their due date. This, however, is not the same as bringing a full-term infant home. Premature infants are not well organized internally. They do not give clear signals about when they are hungry, sleepy, or overstimulated. They may go from soundly sleeping to loudly screaming in a matter of seconds. It takes full-term infants several weeks to begin to establish predictable patterns of eating and sleeping. It takes preterm infants even longer.

Because the infant is not well organized, the adult needs to be. The easiest way to do this is for parents to keep a chart of what the baby does 24 hours a day. This may seem unreasonable given the total situation, but the long-term payoffs are high. The infant's various states and when they occur, that is, when and how long the baby sleeps, when he cries and fusses, when he was alert, when his diaper was changed, and how much he ate or how long he nursed should be noted. After two or three days a pattern may emerge.

Preterm infants will usually sleep 18 hours a day or more. However, if they have been in an ICN, there probably has been no attempt to mold their sleep preferences into a pattern of day and night. The ICN is very different from a home and the adjustment for both parents and infant is a major one. It may be necessary to experiment with the environment to help infants adjust. Some infants like the new peace and quiet, for others the adjustment is too great. Some infants may need to have the lights on when they go to sleep and the radio playing softly. Both parents and infants will need the support of a visiting developmental nurse to work through this adjustment process.

Long-Term Implications of Prematurity

Socioeconomic factors have a significant impact on the predicted outcome for at-risk infants. The stress of coping with premature infants is exacerbated by limited parental resources (money, transportation, education, and so on). Problems of developmental delays and neurological problems are greater for very-low-birth-weight infants whose mothers are 17 years or less, have less than a high school education, and are not married, than for babies born to middle-class families (Heyne, 1989). Premature and low-birth-weight babies have a three times greater risk of being abused by parents or caregivers during infancy and early childhood (Schmitt & Krugman, 1992). This is true even when social class is held constant.

Developmental delays are also a possibility. Overall, there appears to be a correlation between birth weight and developmental delay: the lower the birth weight, the greater the probability of a developmental delay. Delays appear more likely in the perceptual-motor areas than in verbal areas (Bird, 1989). The birth weight itself does not seem to be the major factor, but rather the complications such as hemorrhaging and other medical risk conditions.

Sudden Infant Death Syndrome

Sudden infant death syndrome (SIDS) is one of the most perplexing and frightening causes of death in infants. SIDS is the leading cause of nonaccidental death for infants between 1 and 12 months of age. It affects approximately 7,000 infants in the United States annually (McKenna, 1990). It is the sudden and unexpected death of a healthy infant without an apparent medical reason. It is most likely to occur at night while the infant is asleep on her stomach. Premature infants account for 20 percent of all SIDS (Gyco & Beckerman, 1990). Siblings of infants who die of SIDS are also at risk.

Research suggests that SIDS infants may not have been as healthy before death as previously thought. Within 2 weeks of death, many had colds, with diarrhea and vomiting and seemed listless and irritable shortly before death (Hoffman, Jacobson, Padgett, Brumitt, & Billings, 1988). These infants tend to be bottle fed rather than breast fed. At greatest risk are infants from 1 to 5 months born to poor single adolescent mothers who smoked during pregnancy (Hoffman, et al., 1988).

For many years it was recommended that infants sleep on their stomach to avoid aspiration in case of spitting up. The American Academy of Pediatrics is now recommending that infants be placed on their sides or backs as this position is viewed as safer. The relationship between sleeping on the stomach and SIDS is not clear. It may be that the infant gets less oxygen or eliminates less carbon dioxide because she is rebreathing air from a small pocket of bedding. By the time infants can roll over independently, they will typically choose what sleeping position is most comfortable for them, but by then (4 to 7 months) the highest incidence time for SIDS is over.

At-Risk Infants

It is difficult to tell which infants are most likely to need early intervention. It seems that medical risk factors are the best predictor during the first year, while environmental risk factors are more useful predictors at older ages (Bird, 1989). In general, developmental testing overpredicts those who will have problems. However, it is important to note that a disproportionate number of low-birthweight babies who have normal IQs are diagnosed as having reading problems or learning disabilities when they reach school age.

Infants born preterm demonstrate more abnormal variation in their physical development than those born at term. Typically, they are delayed in several areas in early infancy. Studies suggest that premature infants demonstrate motor delays up through the first year of life. The relationship is less clear at later stages of motor development. Hanson (1984) suggests carefully watching and assessing at-risk infants over time and working closely with their families. Risk factors are cumulative and interactive. One must evaluate not only the infant, but also socioeconomic and familial factors that determine developmental outcomes. Without looking at both biological and environmental factors, it is not possible to determine whether intervention will be helpful or inappropriate.

Neonatal Assessment

The most widely used neonatal assessment tool is the **Neonatal Behavioral Assessment Scale** (NBAS) developed by T. Berry Brazelton in 1973, revised in 1984, and again in 1993. It can be used with infants from the first day of life through the first month. It is designed to provide an assessment of the neonate's neurological responses and behavioral repertoire. It evaluates the infant's potential for self-organization and ability to control state as a response to the environment (Tirosh & Scher, 1993). It requires a trained examiner and is only done on infants who are in the at-risk category. The examination takes 20 to 30 minutes and the examiner typically does the testing while the parents are present to help them understand how skillful neonates really are.

Unlike most previous measures, the NBAS was conceptualized as an interactive assessment. The role of the examiner was to draw out the organizational skills of the neonate. The emphasis is on establishing the newborn's capacities and limits, especially as they affect interaction with a caregiver. The assessment acknowledges the importance of state in the infant and looks at state changes and the predominant state of the infant during the assessment process. The infant's best scores are used, rather than his average performance. Because of the requirements of the testing, the examiner, in addition to being knowledgeable of infants, must also receive specific training on how to administer this particular test.

The NBAS requires the observation of six states of arousal: deep and light sleep; three levels of alertness (drowsy, alert, and active states); and, finally, crying. Ideally, the infant starts the assessment asleep and his response decrement, or habituation, to various stimuli is noted (light, bell, rattle). As the infant rouses, tactile responses are determined. Some reflexes are tested, and, as the neonate moves through light sleep to a drowsy state, additional reflex testing is completed. By this time, a state of sustained alertness is reached, and the neonate's ability to orient to a rattle, ball, face, and voice are determined. When the infant is placed on his back, his face is covered with a cloth to see his reaction. The tonic neck reflex and Moro reflex are elicited. This is often disturbing, and the examiner then observes the neonate's ability to self-quiet and helps him attain a lower level of arousal if he cannot do this himself. The examiner continually monitors and observes a variety of changes in the neonate's behavior (Worobey & Brazelton, 1990).

There are detailed scoring instructions that use the responses of the neonate and the observations of the examiner to determine optimal, normal, or inadequate performance for each dimension: interactive processes, motoric processes, state control, and response to stress. Repeated assessments are necessary to construct a meaningful profile (Worobey & Brazelton, 1990).

The NBAS was developed to assess full-term neonates. The assessment of preterm infant's behavior (APIB) is a refinement and extension of the NBAS for premature and high-risk neonates. It includes many of the same items with a different presentation and varying demands. The five subsystems are physiological, motor, state, interactive and attentional, and self-regulation (Widerstrom, Mowder, & Sandall, 1991). With a well-trained examiner, the APIB can identify some intervention targets for these very vulnerable infants.

Summary

The transition to parenthood is an abrupt one for both the parents and the newborn. Newborns are far more capable at birth than we once thought. They can gather information from all of their senses, but those senses are not as acute as an adult's. Although they cannot do complex problem solving, they are capable of simple learning, and do have preferences. Their language, although not well differentiated, is effective, and they are tuned in to human language. Neonates have different states and are unique in the amount of time they remain in each. They do get bored or habituate to stimuli that are repeated.

Some infants are born before term or with low birth weight. These neonates are different from term neonates in a variety of ways and have more complications than those infants born at term. They need specialized care that is given in an intensive-care nursery where medical specialists are trained to meet the specialized needs of these infants. The most obvious aspects of early growth and development appear in physical and motor development.

Application Activities

1. Talk with couples who have children about their transition to parenthood. Ask them about the best and worst aspects they remember. Ask each partner to characterize their own transition and that of their spouse. Think about the differences, if any, and how these relate to the literature covered.

2. Talk with your parents about their transition to parenthood and ask about their experiences. Discuss with them some of the current challenges that couples face and find out how they feel about these.

3. Think about your own expectations for the postpartum period. What do you know now that you didn't before reading this chapter? What could you do to make the transition easier for you, your spouse, and your newborn?

Chapter 5

Patterns of Physical and Motor Development

All children are unique, yet they share many commonalities in their patterns of growth and development. Growth refers to the physical changes that occur in children over time. Growth can be measured in inches or centimeters, and pounds or kilograms. Development, however, is more concerned with the acquisition of skills, such as walking and talking. Understanding the underlying principles of growth and development allows us to make predictions about whether future growth and development will fall within the normal patterns, and also allows us to plan in a developmentally appropriate way for infants and toddlers. Children come into the world "prewired" to grow and develop in a certain predictable pattern. Most children follow this pattern, some follow at a slower or faster rate, and a few do not follow the pattern at all.

Physical Growth

Prenatal development is by far the most rapid growth period, but we cannot see it. From a visual perspective, the most rapid period of growth comes during the first year of life.

Height

The average full-term infant is 19 to 21 inches long, with boys being slightly longer than girls. Length at birth has little relation to adult height and is actually challenging to measure accurately. Up to age 2, children are measured while lying on their back. Birth height increases by 50 percent during the first year, with the infant gaining about 10 inches (attaining a height of about 30 to 33 inches).

(By age 2, toddlers have reached approximately 50 percent of their adult height.) The pattern of decelerating growth continues, with an average gain in height of 5 inches between 12 and 24 months, and about 3 inches between 24 and 36 months (to about 38 inches).

Weight

At birth infants weigh about 7.5 pounds. Again, boys are slightly heavier than girls. Eighty percent of term infants weigh between 5 pounds 12 ounces and 8 pounds 6 ounces (Shelov, 1993). Infants typically double their birth weight in five months (to about 15 pounds) and triple it in a year (to about 22 pounds). The rate of change in the first year is startling if compared to similar changes for an adult. What would you be like if comparable changes happened to you? If today you were 5 feet 6 inches tall and weighed 120 pounds, in a year you would be 8 feet and 3 inches. And you would weigh 360 pounds!

It is no wonder that infants need several sets of clothing during their first year and spend time adjusting to their body and learning how it acts and reacts. Growth gradually decelerates, as toddlers gain about 6 pounds between 12 and 24 months and 3 to 4 pounds between 24 and 36 months (National Center for Health Statistics, 1976). The timing of growth is largely genetic. The ultimate height and body type of an individual are largely determined by the genes she inherited from her parents. Some variation is not genetic, because genes interact with factors such as general health and nutrition patterns. Children who do not get enough calories or adequate nutrition may not reach their genetic growth potential.

Overall, children who are born to large parents are longer and heavier at birth than those born to smaller parents. Growth patterns are predictable and deviations from them are significant. Growth is often plotted on a chart that compares an infant's actual growth with predicted patterns. Figure 5.1 shows predictions made by the National Center for Health Statistics that are frequently used to plot heights and weights of children from birth to 36 months. Although the patterns are the same, gender differences are clear, as is the decelerating rate of growth.

The expectation is that a child who is born weighing in at the 75th percentile will continue that pattern, and there is cause for concern if his weight should drop to the 10th percentile. There is far less concern about an infant who is born at the 10th percentile and continues on that growth pattern, especially if her parents are relatively small individuals.

Premature infants are measured against percentiles designed specifically for this purpose, as their rate of growth is an important measure of risk factors. Long-term expectations are that their growth will plot normally, but during the first year at least they need different charts. When using norms for development with premature infants, we often use an adjusted age, that is, the age of the child calculated from conception. (A 5-month-old infant who was 2 months premature would be compared to 3 months' expectations.) This adjusted age is used to modify expectations for premature infants.

Figure 5.1 | Height and Weight for Infants from Birth to 36 months

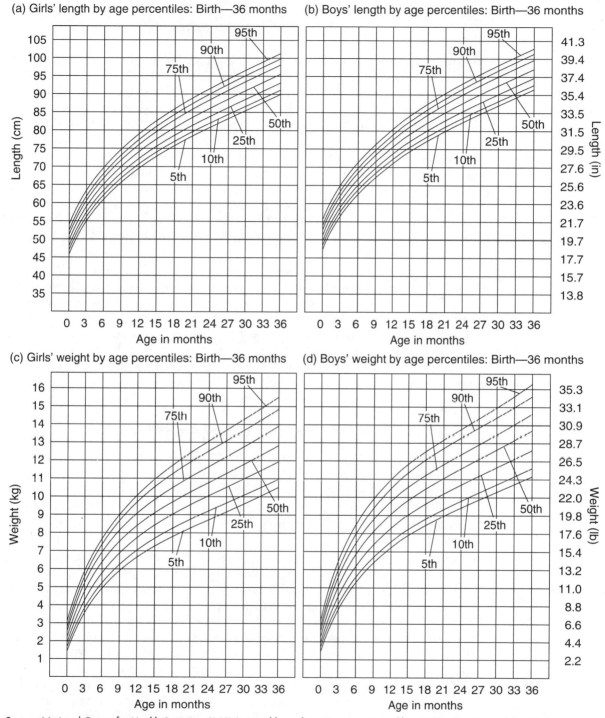

(a) Girls' length by age percentiles: Birth—36 months

(b) Boys' length by age percentiles: Birth—36 months

(c) Girls' weight by age percentiles: Birth—36 months

(d) Boys' weight by age percentiles: Birth—36 months

Source: National Center for Health Statistics. (1976). *Monthly vital statistics report: Health examination survey data. 25, 3* (supplement), 1–22.

Head Circumference

Another growth measure that is systematically taken by physicians is head circumference. As with height and weight, charts have been developed that determine what an average head circumference is for a newborn (about 14 inches) and how much head circumference should change over time (about 17 inches at 6 months and 19 inches by a year) (National Center for Health Statistics, 1976). These measures have diagnostic significance. If the head circumference itself is abnormally small, there is concern about mental retardation. If it is more than two standard deviations below the average size, a diagnosis of microcephaly is made. Infants with microcephaly have brains that are too small, malformed, or elements of the brain itself are missing. When the head grows too quickly there is concern about hydrocephalus.

The brain contains a watery liquid called **cerebrospinal fluid** that helps to nourish and cushion the brain. If the flow of this fluid is obstructed, it begins to create intracranial pressure. Because the bones of the infant's head are not fused (or joined), the head expands at a faster rate than it should, causing a condition called hydrocephalus (literally, water on the brain). Physicians are checking for hydrocephalus when they measure the infant's head circumference. This condition can be treated through medication or by surgically implanting a shunt (or drain) to decrease the pressure. If diagnosed early, many children will not have their lives restricted other than avoiding contact sports. For other infants, hydrocephalus may be related to other conditions that cause mental retardation.

The Brain and Nervous System

The nervous system consists of the brain, the spinal cord, and the nerves. The development of the nervous system impacts the actions of the muscles, glands, and organs of the body, as well as motor and cognitive activities.

In early fetal life the brain consists of only one layer, whereas the adult brain is arranged in six layers. The brain's weight at birth is about 25 percent of its adult weight (about 12 ounces). It grows to 50 percent of its adult weight by 6 months, and 75 percent by 2 years (Rosenblith, 1992). As the brain expands in size, the number and complexity of the nerve-cell layers expand as well. Between 6 months and 2 years, the cerebral cortex of the brain becomes increasingly complex. This complexity develops because of increases in the number of connections between neurons (not an increase in the number of neurons) and *myelinization*, the "insulation" of the nerve fibers with a fatty sheath of myelin that speeds up and improves the efficiency of transmissions (Morrell & Norton, 1980).

The brain is made up of nerve cells called **neurons** which have a spider like appearance with **dendrites** reaching out from the cell body. The **axon,** a snakelike fiber, also reaches out from the cell body. The axon carries impulses away from the nerve-cell body while dendrites receive impulse and carry them toward the cell body (Batshaw & Perret, 1992).

As shown in Figure 5.2, the axon of one cell body does not actually touch a dendrite of another cell body, rather, there are spaces between dendrites which

Figure 5.2 | Nerve Cell or Neuron

This simplified, idealized picture of a nerve cell shows how dendrites carry impulses to the axon.

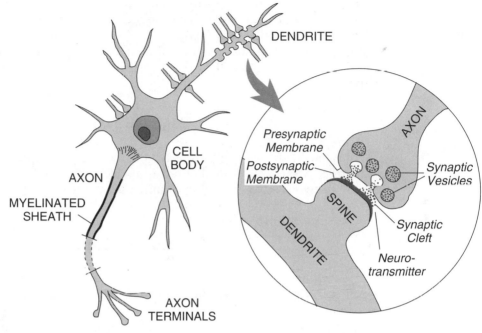

are called **synapses.** The electrical nerve impulse cannot cross the synapse. It stops at the end of the axon where it is converted to a chemical (neurotransmitter) to cross this gap, and then the dendrite converts it back to electrical energy until it reaches another synapse where this process continues until it reaches its destination (Batshaw & Perret, 1992). This seems like a long, complicated, laborious process, and with all these steps it becomes clear why speed is important. For infants who have immature dendrites, the process is very slow. It takes a long time for the perceived sensation to reach the brain, get processed, and then return with a message. This is why infants seem to react in slow motion.

In addition to layers, there are two distinct regions in the brain: the gray matter and the white matter. The gray matter consists of the nerve-cell bodies, which are grayish in color. The white matter is the axons, which are covered in a protective coating called a myelin sheath. One of the major changes during the first year of life is the development of the **myelin sheath.** At birth most axons have little or no myelin. The sheath aids in speeding up nerve impulses.

Although we cannot see the increasing complexity of the development of the nervous system, we can observe some of its effects. As the cerebral cortex develops, it influences motor and sensory development. Voluntary actions begin to replace reflexes, and the senses—particularly vision—become more useful to the infant. The brain does not develop in isolation. In addition to the development that is determined genetically, the brain needs stimulation. More specifically, it requires two types of stimulation: sensory input and self-directed activity (Bornstein & Lamb, 1992).

The brain, in its early development, appears to allow for some flexibility in development. That is, if some cells are damaged then others can substitute for them by offering alternative pathways. Much of the work in early intervention with infants with disabilities, and particularly occupational therapy, is based on this flexibility (Ayers, 1979). This is not true of damage that happens in adulthood.

Dental Growth

Teeth typically begin to break through the infant's gums somewhere around 4 or 5 months. Usually the two bottom front teeth appear first, followed about a month or two later by the four front upper teeth. These are followed by two more lower teeth. By about 30 months, children have their full set of 20 primary teeth.

Asynchronous Growth

The previous discussion may have made it appear that growth is a smooth process. In reality, growth is uneven; different parts of the body grow and change at very different rates. This process is referred to as **asynchronous growth** or the proportional phenomenon. The most obvious example of asynchronous growth is in body proportions. The head of the 2-month-old fetus comprises one-half (50 percent) of his total body length, by birth it has decreased to one-fourth (25 percent), and in adulthood it is about one-eighth (10 to 12 percent). The head doubles in length between birth and adulthood. The limbs, at birth, are disproportionately short. To reach adult stature, the arms quadruple in length and the legs quintuple. Trunk length triples. These differences are shown in Figure 2.3 in Chapter 2. Internal differences are more difficult to see, but overall, the proportion of the body that is water decreases and the amount that is made up by muscles increases.

Motor Development

There are few areas that give parents, infant specialists, and infants themselves more joy than the achievement of motor milestones. Motor development pervades all areas of development during infancy. Sensory stimulation provides the impetus for much motor development. Motor skills enhance social behavior and both benefit from and support cognitive development. It is important to know when different motor behaviors occur. Such knowledge increases the infant's safety, and helps in providing an interesting environment for growth and development.

The infant moves from having little control over his body at birth to sitting, standing, walking, and even awkward running, in a little over a year. He goes from randomly flaying his arms to accurately reaching for something he wants, and from having his fist closed to being able to pick up a pea. The development of these behaviors happens in predictable patterns.

The way in which motor development unfolds has long fascinated researchers and parents. The debate over nature versus nurture was intense regarding the development of motor skills. We know that infants acquire skills slightly earlier than was established in the 1920s and 1930s, but the patterns of development researchers found then are still valid today.

Studying Motor Development

The methods we use to study infants and toddlers today and some of the technology employed are different from earlier studies. Researchers choose different methods depending on what they are studying, their own theoretical background, and even the level of financial support and time they have to complete the study.

Naturalistic and Laboratory Studies

One can study infants in their natural setting or in a laboratory setting. A natural setting can be a house or apartment, a child-care setting, a neighborhood park, or even the local mall. Naturalistic settings are those where children frequently spend time. Laboratory settings are new and unfamiliar to an infant. If a researcher wanted to observe how adults and children typically interact, a naturalistic setting would be preferable. On the other hand, if a researcher is interested in finding out how adults and children interact when there are no toys available to play with, a laboratory setting would be preferable.

Naturalistic settings have the advantage of being familiar to infants and toddlers. However, if a researcher were observing 50 different infants for one hour each in their homes, the home settings themselves might be so different that generalization would be impossible. That is, there might be several siblings in one home, whereas other infants have no siblings but a grandmother is present. In some homes the observation might be interrupted by a telephone call, in others a visit by a neighbor. Some homes may have many toys and books, others may have very few; in some homes children may be in playpens, whereas in others they are free to roam. All of these variables may confound the observation and hence the conclusions. However, if a researcher wanted to know what happened in the home, naturalistic observation would be the only way to find out.

Laboratory-based studies are easier to control. The setting can be kept uniform for all the infants. Additionally, the setting can be described in detail so that other researchers can replicate the study to verify the information. Researchers may first observe infants in naturalistic settings to determine what they want to study, and then set up the laboratory to observe particular behavior that interests them. They then can bring infants into the laboratory where the controlled setting allows quantification of their findings.

Experimental and Observational Studies

Observational studies look at what occurs, when it occurs, and under what circumstances it occurs. Experimental studies are concerned with cause-and-effect relationships and systematically alter conditions to find out the results. A researcher interested in how two siblings play together might simply observe these children playing together. If she were not only interested in how they played together but wanted to know how they would interact if there was some stress involved, she might have the children put two puzzles together (one easy and one difficult) in a particular time frame. This would be an experimental study.

Experimental studies are useful in studying unique conditions and are more easily replicated. Observational studies ensure that the behavior being studied is spontaneously produced and focus on environmental factors. The ability to videotape studies has improved the reliability of observational research. Often observational studies are done in naturalistic settings and experimental studies are done in laboratory settings.

Studying Change over Time

Three approaches for gaining information about infants and toddlers have evolved: the longitudinal, cross-sectional, and cross sequential. The *longitudinal* method looks at one child or a group of children over time, the *cross-sectional* approach studies different children at each age, and a *cross sequential* study is actually a combination of the two approaches, studying groups of children for shorter periods of time. Table 5.1 illustrates the differences between these methods.

Cross-sectional studies are faster to complete because you do not have to wait for the infants to grow to collect the information, and it is easier to locate families who are willing to have their infant studied once rather than make a commitment for several months or years of periodic study. However, it is more difficult to identify patterns or precursors of behaviors when different infants are used.

Longitudinal studies require contact with a family for a long time and their willingness to continue to have their infant and toddler studied. Families may lose interest or may move in the middle of data collection, causing information to be lost. Also, if you discover a particular behavior at 6 months that is intriguing, you cannot go back and gather information on that behavior at earlier ages. Likewise, it is extremely difficult to change if you discover that you do not like the measures or techniques you are using.

The cross-sequential approach is a compromise, as it starts with groups of children of different ages (for example, 1 and 8 months) but also studies these children again. Because the same children are studied over a period of time, patterns may emerge. Yet the research can be completed in less time because children of different ages are in the original sample. Sometimes significant events (such as a depression or war) might influence the particular cohort being studied. A **cohort** is a group, based on time of birth and generation rather than age per se. Individuals born after World War II, the "baby boomer" cohort, have had very different life experiences than those of the cohort of infants born during the Depression of

Table 5.1		Longitudinal, Cross-Sectional, and Cross-Sequential Samples				
Age	Date	Longitudinal	Date	Cross-sectional	Date	Cross-sequential
Birth	1/96	Raelynn, Jennifer, Mark, Juan	1/96	Jamela, Suling, Inti, Roxanna, Isidro	1/96	Raelynn, Jennifer, Mark, Juan
4 months	4/96	Raelynn, Jennifer, Mark, Juan	1/96	Kristina, Hank, Myrtle, Giovanni, Don	4/96	Raelynn, Jennifer, Mark, Juan
8 months	8/96	Raelynn, Jennifer, Mark, Juan	1/96	Nancy, Jack, Aura, Humberto, Bethel	1/96	Jamela, Suling, Inti, Roxanna, Isidro, Raelynn, Jennifer, Mark, Juan
12 months	12/96	Raelynn, Jennifer, Mark, Juan	1/96	David, Peggy, Alex, Bung, Min	4/96	Jamela, Suling, Inti, Roxanna, Isidro

Using the longitudinal method requires a year for data collection. The cross-sectional method may require only a month, and the cross-sequential method may take 4 to 8 months, depending on how long children are studied.

the 1930s. Likewise, the cohort of infants who attend child day-care centers from an early age may be different from those who stay at home. Researchers use the cross-sequential approach to solve some of these problems.

Patterns of Behavior

There are individual behavioral differences in all children. For this reason, when we look at norms for behavior, such as walking, we give a range of ages when we expect this behavior to occur. In assessing how a child is progressing, a pattern is typically more useful than looking at isolated behaviors. Rather than only looking at "walking independently" and deciding whether or not a child's behavior is on target, we might look at the progression of walking. For example, we would expect the following pattern of walking:

> Walks holding on to furniture; walks with both hands held; walks with one hand held; walks alone two to three steps; walks without support for 6 feet.

If an infant were in the slower range in "walking holding on to furniture" and "with his hands held," we would expect that he would continue this "slower" pattern and not expect him to "walk without support" until about 15 months, the upper end of the normal range of independent walking. An infant on the fast track in this pattern walks without support by 12 months or earlier (Furuno et al., 1991).

Descriptive studies served important practical purposes in the past and are still valued today. We use the information about developmental patterns and ages at which typical behavior develops to decide what types of materials to use with infants of various ages, as well as to determine whether infants are showing delayed or atypical patterns of development.

Research by Wayne Dennis (1935, 1938, 1941), who restricted infants' ability to practice reaching, sitting, and standing, and who also investigated with his wife (Dennis & Dennis, 1940) the Hopi practice of placing their infants on cradle boards, found that, given the opportunity to practice skills they are maturationally able to perform, the infants acquire these skills quickly. This gave rise to the question of whether or not intensive training could produce skills before they could be maturationally expected. Researchers such as Gesell and Thompson (1929) and McGraw (1935) looked at such skills as learning to climb stairs, cut, or ride a bicycle. These co-twin control studies trained one twin in a skill before it was maturationally expected and not the other. Hilgard (1932) used preschool children as his subjects. Overall, they concluded that motor development depended on the maturation of the brain and the development of muscles in the body. Yet, these conditions were not sufficient, the study showed. There had to be some opportunity to practice the behavior, but intensive practice before maturation was not effective. Patterns of development discussed later on are largely based on the findings of these early researchers. Their results were confirmed and reconfirmed and as a result there has been minimal research interest in the topic for several decades. Cross-cultural studies of infant development show some differences in timing of motor events that are based on child-rearing customs and practices. For example, infants in Baganda sit early, a skill that mothers encourage in order to free them from carrying the infant while they garden; however, these infants rarely crawl or creep early, as they spend little time on the ground (Kilbride & Kilbride, 1975).

Principles of Motor Development

Children follow similar patterns in all areas of development. What makes children different are the varying ages at which specific skills are acquired. The first year of life sees rapid growth in acquisition of motor skills. During the next several years, the young child devotes much time and energy to "fine-tuning" these motor skills to the point where intricate motor processes are possible. Much of what we consider to be motor development occurs as a result of maturation and practice.

Having good motor abilities is important for very young children. The infant learns from sensations acquired through movement. The acquisition of new sensations occurs through active involvement with the environment, rather than through passive interactions. The infant is constantly receiving information from the environment from many sensory modes including hearing, sight, and touch. Early motor development then is not only motoric but rather a more coordinated development effort integrating the senses and motor skills (Bloch & Bertenthal, 1990).

Several principles underlie the development of motor skills in infants. The principles apply to all infants and toddlers, regardless of culture or race. Knowledge of these aids in understanding the normal developmental process and is essential for developmentally appropriate programming. They are applied to the acquisition of motor skills. They are:

- Motor development is continuous. It begins *in utero,* with birth being only a marker in the process. Maturation of the motor system goes from gross-motor activities to fine-motor activities. It involves the breaking down of gross movements into finer, coordinated, and voluntary motor responses. Complex motor skills build on simpler motor skills.

- There is a general pattern that all children follow in the development of motor abilities. The rate of development, however, differs among children. Some children may acquire skills more quickly and some more slowly than others. But the sequence of skill acquisition is similar. The acquisition of higher motor skills is based on the infant's first having acquired previous lower-level motor skills. Sitting is a basic skill acquired by most infants. However, every young child must first acquire the ability to control his head before sitting can occur.

- Motor development, like physical development, proceeds from the head down to the feet (cephalo-caudal), and from the midline or spine outward to the extremities (proximo-distal). Infants gain head control first, then arm coordination, and finally control of their legs. Coordination of motor skills first develops close to the center of the body, with control of the neck and the shoulders. Then body parts further away from the midline, such as the arms, and eventually, the fingers develop coordinated movements.

- Control of body movements occurs first in the horizontal position and then moves to vertical orientation. Children first learn head control while lying on their stomach (*prone*). This skill is gradually integrated while sitting and then later standing.

- Motor sequences are overlapping. Mastery of a skill is not necessary before others can begin, although skill ability does need to reach a functional level. Children begin to experiment with new motor skills as they are fine-tuning others.

- Generalized mass activity is replaced by specific individual movements. An infant's early motor acts are characterized by total body movements. Much of this is involuntary motion. The development of motor abilities involves the disaggregation of gross movements into finer, coordinated, voluntary, specific motor responses.

- Development is related to the maturation of the central nervous system.

Although practice is necessary for skills to emerge, no amount of practice will cause a child to display a skill before the necessary maturation occurs (Adapted from Barclay, 1985; Connor, Williamson, & Siepp, 1978; and Fetters, 1984).

Patterns of Motor Development

Motor development focuses on patterns of behavior rather than the attainment of a single skill or part of a skill. Patterns of development can be normal, delayed, or atypical.

Defining the "normal" developmental pattern poses some difficulties. Children vary in the ages and rates at which they demonstrate abilities in certain skill areas. A specific skill one infant may accomplish at one age, another infant may not accomplish until one, two, or even three months later. However, the later acquisition of skills does not necessarily mean that the second child is delayed. He may, in fact, be developing normally. The normal variation window depends on the particular skill. Walking has a very large variation in initial age acquisition, whereas lack of ability to uncurl one's fingers, or eye-following patterns that were not established within two months of expectation, would be of concern.

The skill of walking is a good example of the variation of ages at which children acquire an ability. We know that, on the average, most children begin walking around 13 months, and that almost all children can walk by 15 months. However, some children walk at 9 months of age, whereas others do not begin until they are 15 months. This difference in age of acquisition indicates only that some children learn to walk early and some later. Those who do not walk at 18 months are of concern.

Keeping this in mind, we can begin to get a picture of what constitutes the normal range of development. In a formal sense, we define normal growth and development as that which falls within the range of variation defined as normal for any given population. We add the phrase "given population" because there are many factors that contribute to variation in developmental norms. These factors include such things as individual learning styles, cultural norms, and environmental variables. For a large majority of the young population these differences constitute minor variations in expected-age skill acquisition.

The general sequence of motor development can be viewed as the infant moves from prone, to supine, to sitting, and to standing.

Prone.   Infants develop head control when, in a prone position, they lift their head to see what is happening around them. This is the beginning of the infant's struggle against gravity. At this point, the hands are still in fists and the forearms are tight against the body. As the infant's muscles strengthen and equilibrium responses improve, it is not just the head that is moved off the surface but the trunk as well. Gradually the forearms are used to bear weight. Two further variations occur: The infant can lift the head, arms, and legs off the surface at the same time, and he can use one forearm for balancing while he uses the other to reach for an object. Because of lack of control, infants sometimes flip onto their back. This is not true rolling, and once infants gain more control, this rarely happens.

Infants now begin to pivot when prone. *Pivoting* is moving the upper body in a circular pattern with the arms while the lower body stays at one spot. Infants then begin to use their arms and sometimes their legs to make forward progress or crawl. Infants crawl with their stomach on the floor. As control over the lower trunk and legs improves, the infant pushes up so that his weight is supported on his hands and knees. First he will hold this position, then begin to rock back and forth, and finally begin to make progress. This is creeping. The infant may go backward before he goes forward. The weight bearing and reciprocal movements required for creeping are important for later movements (Fetters, 1984).

Infants learning to creep first, support their weight with their arms, then push up so that the weight is supported on their hands and knees. Then they begin to rock back and forth, and finally begin to develop the reciprocal movements required for creeping.

Many people use the terms *crawling* and *creeping* interchangeably. Technically, they are being inaccurate. Think of snakes *crawling* as a way of reminding yourself that when infants' stomachs are on the ground they are crawling.

Supine.   The infant is fully supported in the supine (lying on back) position, so the arms and legs can be freely moved. Waving and kicking are the movement patterns most frequently seen in a supine position. The infant does a lot of visual following in this position, as objects and people move in and out of her range of vision. She may gaze at her hand before she gains the coordination to bring her hand to her mouth. Infants begin to roll from supine to prone at about 6 months. Infants who spend much of their time on their back, or in positions where their head is supported, may not develop head control as quickly as infants who spend more time in a prone position (Fetters, 1984).

Sitting.   Newborns look like the letter *C* when placed in a sitting position. Their body is in flexion. As body control improves, infants placed in a sitting position are able to raise their head. As head righting, equilibrium responses, and protective responses mature, the infant is able to sit independently (Fetters, 1984).

Initially, infants sit like a tripod, with their weight supported on their outstretched hands as well as their body. As trunk control increases, hands are used primarily for balance, and then the hands become available for exploration.

Although young infants can maintain a sitting position when placed there, it is not until much later that they can push themselves into a sitting position. Once they can maintain a position on their hands and knees, infants can move from creeping to sitting. Then an infant creeps to a desired object, moves to sitting, and picks up the object and plays with it. Infants typically get into a sitting position from a prone or side-lying position, using their hands to push, rather than from a supine position. Their abdominal muscles are not strong enough for them to sit up from a supine position.

Standing.   Although newborns can support their weight on their feet, this reflexive weight bearing does not remain. It is not until infants have attained a sitting position that they attempt standing. This upright control usually begins with the infant kneeling. He may get there by pushing back from a creeping position or change from a sitting position. From this kneeling position, the infant uses furniture to pull to a standing position, using the strength of his arms. Over time, this technique is replaced by one where the infant, from a kneeling position, shifts his weight to one knee, thereby freeing the opposite leg. He extends it, and, again shifts his weight. Initially a struggle, this movement becomes fluid with practice.

Walking.   Walking starts with a few toddling steps and then an inevitable fall. The toddler spreads his feet wide in an effort to establish a firm base, and holds his arms up and out about shoulder height to protect himself against the fall that will surely come. With time, the base narrows, the arms lower, and the traditional heel-toe pattern of walking develops.

Types of Motor Development

Early motor development involves three interrelated aspects: gaining control of the gross, or large, muscles of the body; then developing the fine, or small, muscles; and finally integrating the developing motor skills with information from the senses.

Gross-Motor Development

Large- or **gross-motor development** refers to the development and coordination of the large muscles of the body, including neck, trunk, arms, and legs. These muscles are necessary for all antigravity positions such as sitting, standing, and walking. They also are necessary to stabilize the body as finer movements are performed.

The following skill areas are generally considered in gross-motor development.

- Integrating reflexes
- Increasing head and trunk control
- Advancing sitting skills

- Progressing in standing
- Developing mobility
- Climbing stairs
- Learning on a balance beam
- Enjoying active play
- Jumping (Furuno et al., 1991).

An infant's motor development is dependent on the complex coordination of muscle strength and muscle tone. As with all developmental skills, opportunities to practice the skills enhance their likelihood for development. A weakness in the muscles or the inability to practice skills can significantly affect a young child's motor abilities.

The young infant spends time in both the prone and supine position for the first several months of life. The most important early motor skill developing is head control. First the infant lifts his chin up; this occurs around 4 weeks. By 3 months, the infant can begin to lift both the head and shoulders, with legs extended. By the 4th month, he can support himself on flexed elbows, chest off the surface. At the same time, the infant develops head control while in an upright position. Repeated practice while being held and placed in a seated position helps build muscle strength.

The second significant stage of development is sitting. Once the infant has gained adequate head control in an upright posture, he is able to support the uppermost part of his body. Between the 3rd and 5th month, the infant struggles to keep the head in midline, and needs adult support to stay in the sitting position. Between the 5th and 6th months, the infant is developing back strength. Around the 6th month, the infant can sit on the floor with arms forward for support, and by the 7th month he can sit unsupported. The child eventually gains strength and equilibrium so that by the 9th month he can begin to securely manipulate items, rotate and pivot, and complete coordinated tasks while in the sitting position.

A further major stage in the child's motor development occurs when she is able to place herself in an upright position. The infant is able to bear her weight around the 6th month, with support. Infants begin bouncing, when held, by the 7th month. Around the 8th month, the child can begin to pull herself up to a standing position, using a secure piece of furniture. Once the child feels secure and has gained some sense of balance when upright and standing, she begins to take cautious steps. By the 11th month, the child is cruising around furniture, holding on for support. She can also walk with one or both hands held, depending on balance. Finally, at around the 13th month, the child begins to take steps unsupported. Walking ability slowly develops as the child practices and experiments.

The toddler has the wide stance of the beginning walker. As the toddler progresses, he obtains a smoother gait, and walking becomes automatic. After walking, the additional skills to develop are considered coordinated actions to the skills already in place. Toddlers add running, jumping, and climbing to their large-motor repertoire. They begin to walk up and down stairs with help around the 18th month. By 2 years they can go up and down independently, two feet per step. They can kick a ball, and begin a form of running with occasional falling.

As young toddlers become more secure in their basic walking skills, they begin to experiment.

By the time a toddler approaches his third birthday, he can broad jump at least 2 feet, run on his toes, avoid obstacles in his path, walk down stairs using alternating feet, and climb jungle gyms and ladders. He can peddle a tricycle and catch a large ball. All of these later skills are evidence of muscle strength, good balance, and coordination. Figure 5.3 depicts these progressive patterns of development and their implications for fine-motor development.

Fine-Motor Development

The second area of motor development is small- or **fine-motor development.** This involves the coordination of small muscles. The development of fine-motor skills is dependent on several interrelated skills existent within the child. Vision

Figure 5.3 | Motor Development in Infancy

Motor development proceeds in a predictable sequence, and there is a normal range in the timing of the marker events.

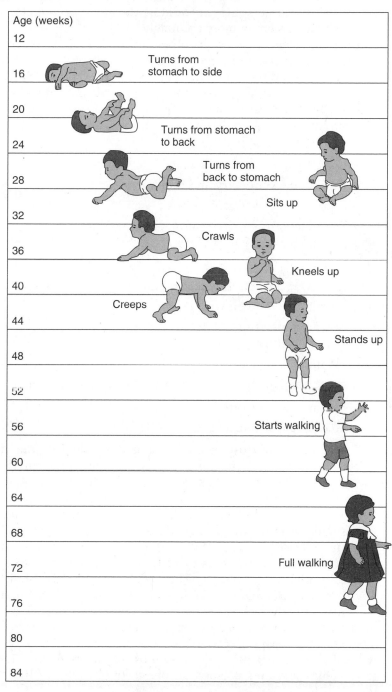

Age (weeks)

12	
16	Turns from stomach to side
20	
24	Turns from stomach to back
28	Turns from back to stomach
	Sits up
32	
36	Crawls
	Kneels up
40	
	Creeps
44	
48	Stands up
52	
56	Starts walking
60	
64	
68	
72	Full walking
76	
80	
84	

plays an important role in early fine-motor development. Though vision is not a prerequisite for fine-motor development, visual abilities function as a motivator for reaching and grasping. In addition, the ability to see objects allows children to direct their reaching more accurately.

Fine-motor development involves the child's ability to use the small muscles of the arms, hands, and fingers. The major accomplishment during this time is the precise use of the hands for reaching, grasping, and manipulation of objects (Fetters, 1984). Reaching goes from gross movements of the arm to directed, precise touching of objects. Grasping proceeds from swiping at and missing objects to accurately picking up tiny pellets and small items. The following skills are considered fine-motor skills:

- Looking and visual following
- Developing symmetry and midline orientation
- Using arms, wrists, and hands
- Learning to reach, grasp, and release
- Developing hand grasp
- Developing pincer grasp
- Removing and putting objects, and then smaller objects, into containers
- Learning to hold crayon/pencil
- Learning prewriting skills
- Building with cubes
- Playing with pegs
- Stringing beads
- Cutting with scissors
- Folding paper (Furuno et al., 1991)

The infant's early use of the hands is dominated by the grasp reflex, where everything placed in his hand causes the hand to securely close around the object. This reflex is visible until around the 4th month. Around this time, the hand remains open and the infant begins to attempt to voluntarily reach toward objects. However, it is not until the 10th month that the infant can voluntarily release objects in his hand. A child must be able to successfully and voluntarily pick up and release an object if finer eye-hand coordination skills are to develop.

Once the grasp reflex is integrated, the child can begin to concentrate on purposefully picking up objects. The development of the ability to grasp objects occurs in a specific sequence observable in most children. Children are not skilled at grasping early in life. The first stage in grasping is identified as a "raking" motion in which the infant uses the whole hand in a fisted motion, raking up objects. This grasping pattern is also described as ulnar-palmar prehension, whereby objects are held in the palm by all fingers flexing. If you placed a sock over your hand and grasped an object, this would be the characteristic palm grasp.

The next stage in grasp development is characterized by the use of the ulnar (little finger) side of the palm and the ulnar three fingers (middle, ring, and small fingers). Objects still appear to be raked-in, but there begins to be some distinction between finger usage. The next stage sees a shift in the use of the hand from the ulnar side to the radial side (thumb). The infant begins to use the thumb and first two fingers to grasp objects. This appears at about 6 months and is like grasping with a mitten on. This skill then progresses to the use of the index finger and thumb, identified as the inferior pincer grasp, by 7 or 8 months. Finally, the infant uses the tips of the fingers and thumb to pick up fine objects. This is called the superior, or neat, pincer grasp. The superior pincer grasp can be expected to emerge around 10 months. Figure 5.4 shows this progression. It is also about 9 or 10 months that the infant is finally able to voluntarily release objects in the hand.

Given the progress in grasping skills, infants around 7 to 8 months old can hold onto and feed themselves crackers, bang objects on the table, and transfer objects from hand to hand. But it is not until about 10 or 11 months that infants become interested in placing objects into containers and taking them out. Preference for a particular hand appears at about 1 year, and by 2 years most toddlers have a decided preference. About 90 percent will be right handed. Further development refines and perfects the process.

A second skill important to fine-motor development is the ability to direct the arm to reach for specific objects. Reaching is dependent also on the child's head and trunk control and adequate balance. Early reaching is seen when the child is

| **Figure 5.4** | **Progression of Grasping** |

Grasping gradually progresses from the palmer grasp of the 4-month-old to the neat pincer grasp of the 12-month-old.

Palm grasp	Mitten grasp	Raking with middle finger to grasp object in palm
4 months	6 months	7 months
Beginning thumb-forefinger grasp	Dropping an object voluntarily (release grasp)	Advanced thumb-forefinger grasp
8 months	9 months	1 year

supine. The child attempts to swipe at mobiles and objects directly over the head. *Swipes* are characterized as reaches in an arc pattern (Fetters, 1984). More directed reaching appears as the child gains better head and shoulder control. Initially, skill development occurs close to the midline of the body and slowly moves to the outer extremities. Around the 4th month, the child is able to bring the hands together in play. The infant also begins to reach for objects placed directly in front of him. When held in a supported sitting position, the infant can begin to reach for and touch objects on the table by the fifth month. Inability to reach for objects will greatly interfere with the child's ability to grasp and pick up objects.

A related concept is described as *pronation to supination*. Initially, all activities involving the infant's hand involve use of that hand with the palm down (pronation). As the child gains strength in the wrist, the hand rotates so that the child is able to accept objects with his palm up (supination).

Sensorimotor Integration

The third area, **sensorimotor integration,** involves the coordination of motor responses with sensory input. Motor skills are often used in conjunction with vision and hearing. In sensorimotor integration both sensory and motor components are integrated in the brain to facilitate smooth movement and the ability to learn new skills. Sensorimotor integration is necessary to pick up tiny objects, to draw pictures, to cut with scissors, and to perform many self-help activities such as buttoning and snapping.

The following are considered sensorimotor skills: auditory processing, body awareness, coordinating body sides, motor control, motor planning, ocular control, perception of movement, perception of touch, and visual-spatial perception (Bissell, Fisher, Owens, & Polcyn, 1988).

Auditory processing involves the ability to understand what is heard. It is not hearing per se, but rather the ability to sort, remember, and sequence auditory information. A young infant may cry at a loud noise but stop crying when he hears his mother's voice. He is processing auditory input. Processing auditory information begins before birth and continues throughout life. Over time the infant's responses become more selective and he learns to block out irrelevant sounds in his environment.

Body awareness requires the interpretation of sensations that come from the muscles and joints of the body. This is how you know what position your body is in without visually scanning yourself. Body awareness helps a young child know how much pressure he is exerting on an object. A young child with poor body awareness may break toys because he does not know how much pressure he is using when putting things together or pulling them apart (Bissell et al., 1988). When the toddler is using tools, he may press a crayon too hard or too softly because of lack of feedback about how his arm, hands, and fingers are moving.

Coordinating body sides is necessary for the development of a dominant hand and also for the hands to work independently of each other on a given task; for example, for one hand to hold the jack-in-the-box and the other to turn the handle. The ability of the infant to cross the midline of the body with his hands is an indication that this coordination is developing. Infants also show the coordination of body sides when they transfer objects from hand to hand or bang two blocks together.

Motor control involves muscle and joint stability, especially the muscles in the neck, trunk, and upper extremities (Bissell et al., 1988). Good control in the hands and fingers is necessary before young children can be expected to use "tools" such as crayons, markers, or pencils.

Motor planning is the cognitive conceptualization of how a skill is performed that occurs before movement. An infant learns to motor-plan as he is exposed to variations of familiar activities such as shaking three or four different types of rattles or when he plays imitative games like pat-a-cake and peek-a-boo. Young children need motor-planning skills to figure out how to climb, build a block tower, or cut with scissors. Motor planning is particularly important in learning new skills.

Ocular control is the ability of the eyes to smoothly track objects. Controlled eye movements are necessary to find and track moving objects, to scan a room, to sustain eye contact with a person, and to shift focus from one object to another. It underlies all activities requiring eye-hand coordination.

The **perception of movement** requires the processing of vestibular information originating in the inner ear. Vestibular information tells the child where he is in space. Children who do not process enough information about their own movements may have trouble maintaining balance and need to spend conscious energy just to sit in a chair. Those who process too much movement information may become fearful or overstimulated. Vestibular information helps to regulate attention as well as posture and balance.

The **perception of touch** involves both a protective and discriminative aspect. The protective tactile system is what makes us withdraw our hand quickly from a hot surface. Young children can either overreact or underreact to touch. Children who are hyposensitive may not feel pain from bumps and bruises, and also may not be able to manipulate materials well. Children who are hypersensitive may avoid tactile input by not participating in tactile experiences such as sand and water play. These children are sometimes labeled "tactilly defensive."

Visual–spatial perception is more than seeing. It involves assessing the relative distance between one's body and a particular object as well as between objects. The toddler with deficits in visual-spatial perception may bump into objects, and have trouble matching his gait to go down or up a step.

In addition to gross- and fine-motor development and sensorimotor integration, there is a set of reflexes that protects the body as it uses these new-found skills.

Automatic Reaction Reflexes

There is a group of reflexes that are not present at birth but instead emerge as the child's motor skills mature. These are called **automatic reactions.** They are an important group of reflexes that protect the body from harm. These responses are automatically elicited in response to the child's specific position in space and movement needs. Though these responses are generally reflexive in nature, the child does have some control over their use. One of the first reflexes to appear in this category is the defensive blink that appears at about 2 months. The infant now quickly closes his eyes as an object approaches that might enter the eye.

One of the most commonly observed automatic responses is called the parachute reflex. When an infant is held in ventral suspension (parallel to a surface face down) above a surface and quickly lowered almost to the surface, a 3-month-old infant will do nothing, whereas a 6-month-old infant will extend both arms, as if to break her fall, in response to the perception of losing balance. This response will appear even if the infant is blindfolded, so it is not in response to a visual stimulus. This is a basic safety reflex. The reflexive behavior is observed from about the 6th month through adulthood. It appears about the time infants begin to sit independently. A related reflex, called propping reflex, appears about the same time. If the reflex is present when an infant is sitting and gently pushed, she will use her arm to prevent herself from falling to the side. It is not until about 9 months that the infant demonstrates the protective extension of both arms to stop falling backwards (Furuno et al., 1991).

Another automatic response is a righting reaction appropriately called tilt. This response is elicited when the child's body is placed out of line with gravity, or tilted. The head is moved so it is held upright. This reflex begins to emerge around the 6th month and persists. This helps the child to sit and stand. Absence of this reflex suggest a central nervous system disorder (Barclay, 1985).

The predictability of patterns of motor development in infants enables us to use delayed or atypical patterns of development to identify young children at risk. Many parents bring the lack of developmental milestones to the attention of physicians and early care and education professionals. Sometimes these concerns warrant further assessment; many times they are normal variations in growth and development.

At-Risk Physical and Motor Development

It is often difficult to accurately assess whether a young child's development is an uneven or asynchronous growth pattern or, in fact, a developmental delay. Norms related to motor development are frequently used to determine whether an infant or toddler is developing at an appropriate rate. There is concern about mislabeling children who are developing in their own unique way. On the other hand, if the infant really does have delayed development, early intervention might actually solve the problem or at least improve it. Infants and toddlers are particularly difficult to classify because they grow and change so quickly and yet have such a small repertoire of behaviors. We were far more confident of our ability to sort, classify, and label young children in the 1970s and sometimes we were wrong. We were wrong in two different ways: We labeled children who were not disabled as disabled or we labeled children as having one disability (for example, mental retardation) when in fact they had another (cerebral palsy). Acknowledging these assessment problems, we now try to use broader classifications with young children, such as "developmentally delayed" or "at-risk." The **at-risk** term in particular is ambiguous. At-risk for what? Hrncir and Eisenhart (1991) propose three cautions to keep in mind before a child is labeled as at risk: "Risk is not static, standardized test scores are not effective predictors of risk, and children are not isolated entities, but develop within an ecological context" (Hrncir & Eisenhart, 1991, 24).

In the case of less clearly identifiable motor dysfunction, a framework must be used to examine and look for the signs of motor problems. Fetters (1984) groups atypical developmental patterns into three categories that include normal variation, atypical variation, and pathology.

There is some normal variation in the age of acquisition of motor skills. Some children may add or complete motor sequences in a slightly different way. Some children develop skills early in one area and use that to compensate for another area. For example, an infant who talks early may request objects, and consequently may not walk at 18 months since objects are brought to him. This may be an acceptable variation in the acquisition of motor skills. The developmental pattern is somewhat atypical, but not dysfunctional. However, one would suggest to the family that they stop bringing the infant what he requests, and see if in a matter of weeks he does, in fact, walk. If he does, this would be seen as a normal variation.

The second category, atypical variation, includes children whose motor development is observably atypical yet no pathology is identified. Many of these children are motor delayed, or demonstrate a weakness in muscle strength. There may be no clear reason why they are having motor problems. Fetters (1984) indicates that the apparent motor dysfunction may be a transient problem for many of these children and will disappear without any intervention. The problem may also be a sign of more involved motor difficulties that will appear later.

This second category is the most difficult category and the one in which early childhood specialists play the largest role. The following signs may be associated with atypical variation and cause concern for further examination:

- The presence of abnormal reflex patterns beyond the times they should have been integrated
- The absence of expected reflexes such as the automatic reactions (eye blink, protective arm positions)
- Poor coordination, lack of balance or equilibrium, or unexplained weaknesses
- Unusual muscle tone that may include either extremely tight or exceptionally loose muscles
- Signs of motor regression in which the child's motor skills appear to be deteriorating
- Children with prenatal and perinatal histories that put them at risk for later delays

In the third category, pathology, Fetters (1984) identifies motor problems associated with known disabilities, such as cerebral palsy or spina bifida. Children with pathological motor problems are frequently identified early. However, symptoms associated with disabilities vary among individuals.

Developmental Risk

Before deciding that a child is "at-risk" developmentally it is important that the term be clarified. It is also important that parents be informed of the criteria used to determine risk and how their child's situation will be different based on this label. Additionally, as children change and grow and develop, so do their environments change. Therefore, risk needs to be reevaluated (Hrncir & Eisenhart, 1991). Caution should be used before labeling a child as developmentally at risk, and when this labeling is done it should consider not only the child, but the family as well.

The term *at-risk* does not mean that a child will inevitably be delayed or affected but rather that the probabilities are higher than normal. Children can be placed in this category because of biological conditions, the family in which they live, or the physical environment in which they are raised. Children with established biological problems (for example, Down syndrome) who may be functioning within the normal range at an early age are considered "at risk" for later developmental delays because experience has shown that their rate of development will be slower.

Families have the potential for increasing or decreasing the risk for the child. Families that abuse or neglect children put them in a risk category medically, psychologically, and educationally. Infants born prematurely and those with disabilities are particularly vulnerable to abuse and neglect. On the other hand, families who love and respond to their infants, spend time playing with them in developmentally appropriate ways, and keep the infants safe and healthy, decrease risks for their children.

Environments can also cause infants and toddlers to be at risk. Some environments are more conducive than others for developing motor delays or patterns of behavior that make learning difficult. Substandard housing, crowded conditions compounded by poor nutrition, and lack of medical treatment increase the risk for very young children of having developmental problems. Environments where infants and toddlers can safely and freely explore inside and outside, where a wide selection of toys and materials are available for the child to play with, and where adults support and facilitate play and learning, reduce risk.

Children born prematurely are at greater risk for demonstrating abnormal variation in their physical development. Typically, children born prematurely are delayed in several areas of development in early infancy. Studies suggest that premature infants demonstrate motor delays up through the first year of life. Early intervention programs can have a significant positive impact on development for premature infants (Infant Health and Development Program, 1990). The impact varies with the infant, and those premature infants who weighed less than 1,500 grams benefited least from early intervention. When premature infants reach school age, they may still need supportive therapies such as speech and occupational therapy, and perhaps reading tutors to maintain gains achieved through early intervention (Ross, Lipper, & Auld, 1990). Fetters (1984) suggests that clinicians carefully watch and assess the prematurely born child over time and work closely with the family. In some cases intervention may be helpful, but for others it may be unnecessary.

Summary

Physical and motor development over the first three years of life is phenomenal. There is no time in later life when the child will again grow at this rate. Growth, however, is not even, and some parts of the body grow at different rates than others. Although there are variations in *rates* of development the *pattern* of development is relatively predictable.

Automatic reactions come in as they are needed by the infant as protection against being hurt from using newly evolving motor skills. The chapter described the sequences of both gross- and fine-motor development, and discussed the integration of these skills with the senses. Normal and abnormal patterns of motor development were described. Biological conditions, families, and environments can put infants and toddlers at risk for a developmental delay or can improve a child's chances of dealing with problems.

Knowing and understanding patterns of growth and development help adults assess whether or not infants and toddlers are following normal patterns and allows them to plan environments that stimulate and match these emerging skills. Increasingly, motor skills are paired with sensory information and provide feedback for the infant and toddler.

Application Activities

1. Sit in a place where you feel comfortable: a playground, a child-care setting, a religious facility, or the eating area of a mall. Watch the infants and toddlers and see if you can determine how old a particular child is based on your observations of the child's size and motor development. Then, ask the parent how old the child actually is. Continue watching to see how to refine your skills in this area.

2. Play with a young toddler (12 to 18 months) and try variations on creeping (different surfaces, over a pillow, and so on and walking (furniture, holding one hand, two hands, pushing something, and so on). Play a fine-motor game of exchanging 1-inch cubes, putting them in a container, and then try having him mark paper with crayons. Note the energy involved and the quality of the movements. If possible, do the same activities with a child a year older and make a comparison of both the quality and quantity of their movements.

3. Go to a toy store and evaluate the available toys for their usefulness in promoting small- or gross-motor development in young children. Note the cost, and the age range given on the box, if any. Decide which, if any, of the materials you think are worth the price and give your rationale for your decisions.

Chapter 6

Sensory and Perceptual Development

Infants receive information about their world from motor and sensory feedback, but how do they go about making sense out of all this information? Objects come in and out of their field of vision. They hear the sound of their mother's voice, smell her perfume, and feel their own wetness before their diaper is changed. How do they develop patterns to make their world more predictable? How do they decide what to pay attention to, that is, what is relevant and what isn't?

Vision provides the infant with information about what is interesting. Seeing objects and events motivates the infant to reach and locomote. Hearing provides the infant with information about his environment and the model to develop speech and language. Touch allows the infant to cuddle and mold his body to that of his caregiver and also to learn how different objects feel—a cuddly blanket, cold water, mushy food, hard plastic, and so on. Taste is part of mouthing. Thus the infant receives sensory information about objects by placing them in his mouth. The infant is sensitive to smells and develops associations with the sense of smell, particularly about his mother and other familiar caregivers.

Researchers have approached infant perception from very different perspectives. Two of the oldest theories present two very different points of view of how infants gain knowledge.

The **Associationist Theory,** first formulated by Aristotle, contends that infants are born with a blank slate and that their only mental ability is to receive information from their senses and to form associations from these perceptions. These associations are formed in one of three ways: similarity, contrast (opposites), and things that are experienced together (at the same time and place). Associationists believe that everything an infant knows has to be learned. Infants would first have to learn that objects exist in a three-dimensional world before grasping an object.

Nativism is the belief that infants are born with certain structures of knowledge. This theory assumes that knowledge is not based on experience but that the infant comes "prewired" in certain ways. Nativists believe that infants come knowing about objects and their existence. Additional support for this theory is derived from animals' innate responses to predators.

Although interesting, these theories are too general to guide research in sensory and perceptual development and go back to the nature–nurture issue that has haunted the field. Infant researchers are trying to move beyond this argument and leave it to the neurobiologist to solve.

One question that does intrigue researchers is whether infants' senses develop independently and coordinate with maturation or whether stimulation is more generalized and the sensory modalities are only differentiated later. Although infants have five senses, research has concentrated on only two of them: vision and hearing. Hence we know much more about these two senses than the other three. Researchers are concerned about not only the infant's ability to respond to sensory input, but also how he perceives it.

Sensation and Perception

The sensory aspect of development is related to the responsiveness of the sense organs to stimulation, that is, **sensation.** Perception is far more than sensation. **Perception** is a cognitive process in which information from the senses is organized and interpreted by the brain. To some degree perception is dependent on motivation and memory. All of the infant's senses are functional at birth. However, all need to mature in order to function in the same way that adult senses do. We are interested in how this maturation occurs and what role the environment plays.

Researchers want to know if perception is present at birth. Is the infant born with this ability, or does it develop from interactions with the environment, or as a result of maturation? They are interested in the information that infants receive from their senses and how they learn to utilize this information. Do infants get more information from one sensory modality than another? Researchers are also concerned about infants whose senses are impaired, the impact of the impairment on their development, and what can be done to compensate.

Studying Sensory and Perceptual Development

How can you tell what an infant hears, and, beyond that, how can you tell if he has preferences in what he hears? Questions such as these have tickled the imagination of researchers for many years.

Young infants are not ideal subjects. They have a very short attention span and no social conscience. In the middle of experiments, they cry, fuss, and even fall asleep. They also may get hungry or wet. Their state at the time of testing can greatly impact the results. Infants have a very small repertoire of behavior; they can't write, talk, or even point. Since most research on infant perception is done in the laboratory, infant researchers are dependent on parents bringing infants into the laboratory. The inability of infants to verbalize makes research challenging and accounts for many of the inconsistencies in the research. What we know about infant perception is indirect and based on the assumption that infants behave similarly to the way adults would in the same circumstances.

The following techniques are typically used in studying perception.

Orienting

Orienting is the process of attending to or noticing a stimulus. The orienting response is demonstrated by infants looking at a stimulus, listening to it, or a change in breathing or heart rate. Orienting behavior is a prerequisite for studying perception. Even if an infant looks at a picture or turns in the direction of a sound, it is not clear whether or not there is any internal processing going on. One can only know that the infant is aware of the stimulus.

Preference

Researchers are interested in finding out what infants prefer, whether in looking or sucking. The underlying assumption is that infants look longer or suck harder on what they "prefer." Especially with looking, researchers are careful to present two stimuli side by side and to change the visual object's position between left and right to ensure that they are not finding out the infant's position preference rather than his visual stimuli preference. Sophisticated researchers use photographic techniques which determine when infants are actually looking at a stimulus by measuring its reflection on the infant's eye. It is difficult to know what to conclude from infants who show no preference. Do they not perceive differences or do they just not have a preference?

In testing taste discrimination, instead of two stimuli being offered simultaneously, they are alternated whereby the amount consumed is measured to determine the infant's preference. In a case of fluid test preference for half of the infants, one fluid is presented first and for the others the comparison liquid. Otherwise, you might again be looking at the temporal equivalent of visual position preferences, because infants might always like the first fluid regardless of what it was. Or the infant might simply become satiated with the first fluid.

Conditioning

Conditioning provides more information about infants and how they learn. One reason why we are interested in finding out whether infants can learn is to determine the impact of early events. Psychoanalytic theory assumes that early events have enduring psychological effects. However, unless very young children can be shown to learn, it seems doubtful that early events could have a significant psychological impact. This issue spurred early research.

Conditioning is the learning of new associations. Infants can be conditioned, but the younger they are, the longer conditioning takes to accomplish.

Researchers study two types of conditioning with infants: operant and classical. **Operant conditioning** involves forming an association between a behavior that the infant already has in his repertoire and increasing the probability that this behavior will occur frequently by rewarding that behavior. If the behavior is positively reinforced, it is likely to recur; if it is neutral or negative, the behavior is less likely to happen. When the behavior occurs frequently, it can be used in operant conditioning. The use of conditioned responses provides more information about how infants perceive their world, but they are time consuming to establish in very young infants.

Operant conditioning with very young infants involves behaviors such as head turning or sucking. When the infant displays the desired behavior, he is rewarded or reinforced for his behavior. Because of the reward, the infant is more likely to repeat the behavior. In operant conditioning the object is to see if the infant can learn to perform a particular behavior in response to a particular stimulus, and how long it takes to establish that learning. Operant conditioning looks at behavior in the context of the environment, that is, the consequences of behavior. Skinner (1969) proposed the following operant conditioning relationship:

$$S \longrightarrow R \longrightarrow S$$
(discriminative stimulus)   (operant response)   (contingent stimulus)

In this relationship, the contingent stimulus determines what happens to the response, that is, whether or not it is reinforced. If positively reinforced, it is likely to continue. If punished, or if the reinforcement is removed, the response will weaken. Researchers have used this paradigm to learn about infant preferences. If, for example, researchers wanted to know if infants could distinguish between a tone that was 50 decibels loud and one that was 60 decibels loud, they would first need to establish an association between a behavior, that is, head turning to the right (discriminative stimulus), and the initial sound (50 decibels). The first problem is to get the infant to turn his head to the right frequently. To accomplish this, researchers might place an interesting picture (the reinforcement) on his right side and a dull gray picture on his left side to encourage the infant to turn to the right. When he does turn to the right, the tone is played (operant response). When the pairing of the tone with the turning is established, the picture is only used some of the time (intermittent reinforcement). Later, the reinforcer may be gradually faded. Eventually the infant turns to the right in response to the tone alone. Once this conditioning has been established, researchers can then use this to study infant perception. In this case, they may want to know if infants can distinguish between a tone that is 50 decibels and one that is 60 decibels.

Infants, like adults, form a generalized concept of a tone. This is, if the infant perceives 50 decibels and 60 decibels as the same, he will turn his head to both; if he does not, he will only turn his head to the initial tone (50 decibels) that was conditioned. The closer the variation is to the original stimulus (50 decibels versus 51 decibels), the more similar the response; and as the infant perceives the stimuli as being less similar, the response is less. These changes are the *generalization gradient*. At some point the contingent stimulus is so different from the original (discriminant stimulus) that no response is given (the infant does not turn his head to the right). This behavior helps researchers know what infants perceive as the same, similar, and different; that is, how well they discriminate between different stimuli.

Very young infants can be conditioned, but the process is slow. By about 4 months, however, it takes only a matter of minutes. By 4 months, infants' repertoire of behavior is also much larger. Beginning at that age, vocalizations and social responses can be used to study perception. Researchers are interested in using operant conditioning as part of an intervention program. They want to teach colicky babies not to cry by reinforcing the quiet alert state and to teach infants with Down syndrome to increase their vocalizations by reinforcing them.

In **classical conditioning** the learning is an association between two previously unrelated events in which the response to the original event (unconditioned stimulus) also is produced to the new event (conditioned stimulus). Pavlov was intrigued with the fact that dogs salivated not only at food but at the sight of the trainer who brought the food (Driscoll, 1994); that is, some neutral stimuli (the trainer) elicited the reflexive response (salivation). Classical conditioning is less frequently used with infants because it requires a longer time frame to establish. However, it is still a useful research technique and practical tool. The question posed would be a different one: If the infant stopped crying when he was fed, would he also stop crying at the sight of the breast or bottle or even the person having or bringing those? The classical conditioning paradigm looks like this.

Unconditioned Stimulus ⟶ Unconditioned Response
(food) or (milk)   (salivation) or (cessation of crying)

After conditioning, the conditioned stimulus is able to evoke the same response as the unconditioned stimulus.

Unconditioned Stimulus ⟶ Unconditioned Response
(food) or (milk)   (salivation) or (cessation of crying)
        ↑
Conditioned Stimulus ⟶ Conditioned Response
(bell) or (sight of mother)   (salivation) or (cessation of crying)

Conditioning is one of the tools through which researchers have learned about infants' senses. Infant learning has a sensory base. To better understand perception, it is necessary to look at the senses and understand how they work and how they are coordinated.

Vision

Though young infants do not have good visual acuity, they can see. To support infants' visual exploration, adults need to know how infants see, what infants are most likely to look at, how they visually explore objects, and how they process this information. From the infant's perspective, he needs something to look at, to keep it in his range of vision, and to focus on it.

The Eye

The visual system is very complex. The following is a brief description and overview of its components and how it works. The eye sits in a socket of the skull. When light enters the eye, it passes through the **cornea** (a transparent membrane), the **aqueous humor** (a watery fluid), the lens, and the **vitreous humor** (a jellylike substance that fills the eyeball). The amount of light that enters is controlled by the **iris,** a set of muscles which expands or contracts the **pupil,** the hole through which the light enters, regulating the amount of light. The image focuses on the **retina,** a layer of nerves that transmits impulses through the optic nerve to the brain. The most sensitive part of the retina is the **fovea;** the only insensitive part is the **blind spot,** where the nerve fibers come together. The eye does not actually "see." It receives light, turns light into electrical impulses, and sends them to the occipital lobe of the brain. It is the brain that actually perceives visual images. See Figure 6.1.

Visual Acuity

Measures of visual ability are based on **acuity** (how well a person sees) and their field of vision. In general, we compare what an infant can see to what a normally sighted adult sees. Normal adult vision is 20/20. At birth visual acuity is about 20/600, meaning that the infant sees at 20 feet what the adult sees at 600 feet. Everything beyond about 12 inches is a blur for the newborn. One reason for this is that the point of sharpest vision, the fovea centralis of the retina, matures slowly (Mehler & Dupoux, 1994). Visual acuity improves to about 20/100 at 6 months, 20/30 by 3 years, and 20/20 by 5 years (Boothe, Dobson, & Teller, 1985).

Figure 6.1	**The Eye**

The visual system is complex and involves the components of the eye itself, the optic nerve, and the occipital lobe of the brain.

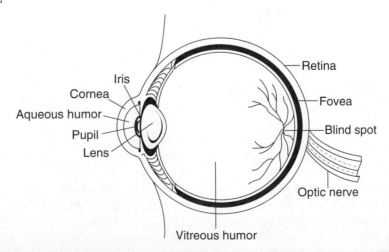

There are many different definitions of blindness. The legal and medical definition is visual acuity of 20/200 or less in the better eye or a visual field of less than 20 degrees with the best possible correction (Batshaw & Perret, 1992). The normal visual field is about 105 degrees. Obviously, by these definitions newborns are legally blind although they do have usable vision.

Actually, blindness is relatively rare in young children, with about 1 in 3,000 children identified as blind. About half of these children were born blind; another 40 percent lose their sight during the first year. Of children born blind, about one-fourth have no usable vision; another fourth can distinguish some light; and the remaining half have enough vision that they can read enlarged type (Nelson, Calhoun, & Harley, 1991). Although the causes of blindness are varied, for children who are born without sight the most common cause is interuterine infection such as rubella and malformation of the visual system. Although infants can have blindness as their only disability, in about half of these children there are other developmental disabilities as well.

If you wanted to determine an infant's visual acuity, how would you go about it? Held and his collaborators (Gwiazda, Brill, Mohindra, & Held, 1980; Hayes, White, & Held, 1965) used two discs with equal illumination, one grey and the other with black lines (horizontal, vertical, or slanted). Infants prefer looking at the disc with stripes to the grey one. When the lines or stripes are wide enough the discs look different; however, as the stripes get narrower and narrower, the discs look identical. The process of narrowing the stripes until the discs look the same is how visual acuity is measured. When infants can see no difference, they show no preference. This is their threshold of visual acuity. By repeating this procedure with infants during the first year, we learned that their visual acuity gradually improves; that is, they can see increasingly finer distinctions in the lines.

Scanning Patterns

What do you see when you look at a picture or someone's face? Obviously, a face is typically composed of eyes, nose, and mouth. You have the ability to scan and integrate the entire face. Neonates may not be as skillful as you are. They tend to get stuck (fixate) at relatively predictable spots such as the chin or hairline of a face, the corner of a triangle or square, or the external contours of an object. Although his scanning is not well developed, the neonate can regulate his looking behavior and avoid looking at visual stimuli as well as fixating on an object. Neonates tend to scan horizontally because this requires fewer eye muscles (Haith, 1980). Not surprisingly, neonates prefer looking at a vertical pattern of black and white stripes. These colors have the highest contrast and the stripes are interesting for horizontal scanning.

Around 2 months, the scanning pattern changes and the infant scans more of the total picture. The infant now scans all the corners and sides of a triangle and square and is drawn to explore the internal contours of the face, primarily the eyes and mouth. At 2 months, his ability to make complex visual discriminations improves dramatically; also, he begins to remember these patterns (Salapatek, 1975). Researchers believe it is at this point that infants begin to look for meaning

Figure 6.2	**Scanning Patterns at 1 Month and 2 Months of Age**

At 1 month, infants scan the high-contrast periphery of a face, whereas by 2 months they begin to scan the interior contours as well.

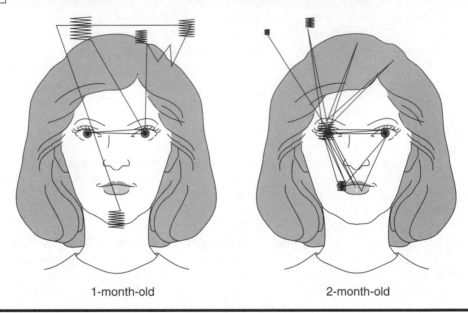

1-month-old   2-month-old

in visual stimuli. These changes are thought to be related to the maturation of the cortex of the brain (See Figure 6.2).

Beyond the age of 2 months, infants are increasingly interested in looking at more complex patterns. They become bored with stripes and find a checkerboard, a bulls-eye, or a picture of a person or object more interesting. Too much complexity, such as a very small checkerboard, or lack of contrast, will not sustain scanning.

Visual Tracking

In addition to scanning stationary objects, infants need to be able to track moving objects. It takes neonates longer than older infants to find and focus on a moving object and even then the movement of the object must be slow. Within these limits, neonates can track. However, the process is jerky. By 2 months, the infant's tracking is smooth and continuous with some anticipation of where a movement is going. By about 6 months, the infant can easily accommodate various speeds. Eye control starts on the horizontal plane (looking from side to side). Therefore an infant can follow a horizontal arc by about 3 months. Eventually, by 4 or 5 months he can follow movement using just his eyes and not turning his head as part of the process. By 5 or 6 months, the infant is visually attracted to more distant objects (Furuno et al., 1987).

Facial Perception

There is much debate in the field about infants' desire to look at faces or "face-like" patterns at a very young age. This goes back to the recurrent nature–nurture question. Some researchers feel that neonates are prewired to focus on faces in preference to other objects. Others feel that this interest in faces is a function of general maturation and is not innate. As the infant increases in age, there is far more agreement about his actual behavior. Research suggests that by about 2 months infants can discriminate between a typical facial pattern and one in which the features (eyes, nose, mouth, and eyebrows) have been rearranged. By 3 months they can distinguish a picture of their mother and father from that of a stranger. The general consensus seems to be that facial perception is part of perceptual development.

Perceptual Invariants or Constancies

Facial perception has also been used to determine what infants perceive of as unchanging or invariant in an object. Researchers are intrigued to find out when infants begin to abstract these invariants. Before 2 months it is unlikely that infants have this ability. Beginning by about 3 months, however, infants begin this process with very familiar objects, like their mother's face, and continue with this process until about 7 months when they can recognize the invariant aspects of a stranger's face.

Size is another aspect of perceptual constancies. When a person in the distance appears to be very small, although this is reflected in retinal size, we do not expect the person to be very tiny. We have an expectation that there is some constancy in the size of individuals. Apparently, infants too have this visual size constancy by 6 to 8 months and perhaps at birth (Mehler & Dupoux, 1994).

Depth Perception

Researchers have long been interested in whether or not infants perceive depth at birth. Current indications are that depth perception has a variety of aspects and is not a single entity that appears at a particular time. Some aspects of depth perception begin to appear about 4 months of age. It is unclear whether depth perception develops as a function of experience, or is governed by a biological timetable, or is a combination.

Despite the fact that we have two eyes, through a process called **fusion** we see one image. This is called **binocular vision.** Fusion occurs when two images are aligned on the retinas in corresponding positions (Held, 1985). A variety of methods are used to determine when binocular vision occurs, including eye patterns that follow motion equally to both left and right, and responses to illumination where one eye is initially covered; when the eye is uncovered, the pupil of the first eye adjusts slightly to accommodate the second eye. In infants under 4 months and individuals with strabismus this adjustment does not occur (Birch & Held, 1983). Precisely localized reaching is another indication of honed binocular vision, spatial sensitivity, and depth perception.

Four months is also a transition point in the development of depth perception. **Stereopsis** involves the comparison of small differences between the images in the two eyes which results in depth perception. Stereopsis, called **stereoacuity,** appears in about 20 percent of full-term infants by 2 months and 80 percent before 5 months. Once it appears, stereoacuity develops in a matter of weeks to adult levels (Held, 1985). Binocular vision, which develops about 4 months of age, is a source of depth perception for adults. Because the eyes are separated, we see a slightly different vision in each eye. The differences in these two "visions" gives clues to depth. The development of binocular vision would seem to be a prerequisite for depth perception.

Some of the research on depth perception focuses on **looming.** A looming object is one that keeps coming closer and looks as if there will be a collision. The clue is the perceived increasing size of the object as it gets closer. Infants under 2 months of age generally stare at looming objects but do not blink. About 2 months of age, some infants began to blink; and by 4 months, virtually all infants blink and move their heads backward as objects approach. This argues that the 3-month-old infant has depth perception based on kinetic information (Yonas & Ganrud, 1985). Motion-carried information is a fundamental aspect of the visual system early in life.

Some aspects of depth perception are based on environmental cues or pictorial cues. These can be observed in both two- and three-dimensional objects. In a picture, if one person is much smaller than another the assumption is that the smaller person is "in the distance." This is not related to movement as in "looming," or to binocular vision, since even if you looked at the picture with one eye closed you would reach the same conclusion. The ability to relate size and distance develops between 5 and 7 months. It is not exactly clear how it develops, but it seems that visual experience plays a part.

One of the most interesting ways that researchers have studied depth perception is with the use of an apparatus called the visual cliff. Basically, the visual cliff is a glass table divided in half. On one side it appears that the surface is directly under the glass and on the other side the surface appears to be several feet below the glass table. The floor under the cliff is typically patterned, so the depth is easy to perceive. A board is placed in the middle of the table on top of the glass. Then the infant is placed on the board. Crawling infants, about 6 to 9 months, avoid the "deep side." Even if their mother is placed by the "deep" side and calls the infant, the infant will not cross the "deep" side of the table to get to her. Infants do cross the "shallow" side to get to their mother. These results lead researchers to conclude that infants have depth perception.

The visual cliff has also been used to measure related visual information. Infants at about 2 months could tell that the two sides of the visual cliff were "different." When researchers used heart rate measures (accelerated heart rate indicated fear), infants up to 5 months of age showed no acceleration of their heart rate when on the "deep" side, whereas infants of 9 months did.

Visual Impairments

Infants who have a total loss of sight caused by structural damage to the eyes are usually diagnosed at birth or soon thereafter. Notable lack of visual responsiveness to the environment is identified by parents and medical personnel. Decreased visual abilities affect a child's capacity to receive vital information. A young child depends heavily on vision for many later skill developments. All other developmental areas are affected by a child's lack of visual skills.

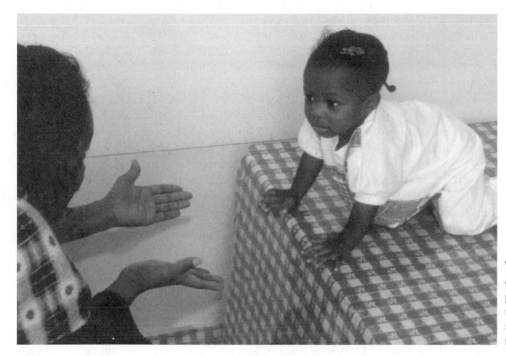

When an infant develops depth perception, she will not cross the "deep" side to get to her mother.

There are four major categories of visual problems. These include injury to or deficiency in the physical mechanisms of the eye, problems with visual acuity, impairments to the muscular structure of the eye, and problems in visual perceptions or the message pathway between the eye and brain. Each category of visual problems can be further broken down into specific areas. For most infants and toddlers, problems involving the physical mechanisms, acuity, and muscular structure can be corrected with medical techniques, glasses, or surgery. Problems involving the nerve pathways are difficult to remedy with medical intervention. Although there are a number of problems, only three will be discussed as they affect many infants and toddlers and must be dealt with at an early age to prevent negative long-term consequences.

Retinopathy of prematurity (ROP; previously called retrolental fibroplasia) occurs primarily in premature infants. The normal blood vessel development in the retina is disrupted. Therefore they stop growing, leaving scars that contract. If there are enough of these affected vessels, they detach the retina from the eye, causing blindness. It affects about 7 percent of very-low-birth-weight infants (less than 3.5 pounds).

Strabismus occurs in about 3 to 4 percent of all infants, but in as many as 15 percent of prematurely born infants (Nelson, Calhoun, & Harley, 1991). There are six muscles that control the eye. One is on each of the four sides of the eye; the other two muscles help rotate the eye. The muscles controlling the eyes must work in coordination to result in clear vision. When the muscles are weak and lack coordination, the child develops strabismus. At some point during development of binocularity, the eye appears to be subject to imbalance. Strabismus is usually identified when a child is about 18 months to 3 years old. The most common type of strabismus is esotropia where both eyes turn in toward the nose (cross-eyed). **Exotropia** is when both eyes turn out. Some infants and toddlers only have these problems intermittently, usually when they are tired. This is not a concern.

Amblyopia occurs when the vision in one eye is blurred or lacks retinal images. Just as an unused muscle atrophies, unused neural pathways deteriorate. About 2 percent of young children have amblyopia. It can be caused by a number of conditions that interfere with vision: cataracts, unequal refraction errors, and strabismus. In the latter two cases, the brain receives two different pictures, as each eye is seeing differently. In order to avoid double vision, the brain "turns off" the weaker eye, which leads to amblyopia. If treated early, the prognosis is good. To strengthen the weaker eye, the stronger eye is typically covered with a patch during the child's waking hours, thus forcing the child to focus with the weaker eye. This is done as early in a child's life as possible. This can also be corrected with surgery.

Development of Infants and Toddlers with Visual Impairments

Infants and toddlers who are visually impaired often show delayed development. These infants typically have low muscle tone, since children are stimulated to use their muscles by sight. Gross-motor skills are consequently delayed. Therefore infants and toddlers with visual impairments tend to sit later and may not crawl. They will typically walk with a wide stance for added support, and may not walk until age 2 or later. Speech also develops later, with less body and facial expression and little nonverbal communication.

The emphasis in working with these infants is the development of ear-hand coordination rather than eye-hand coordination. Toys that make a variety of sounds are used. Adults must talk more and help these infants interpret their world. Although it is tempting to keep these infants in play pens where they will be safe, that is not the best way for them to learn about their world any more than it is for a child who can see. A conscious effort must be made to motivate these children to reach and grasp and explore objects. They may need help using both hands to explore. From an early age they need to be active in their world.

Hearing

The auditory system of the infant is among the best developed bodily functions at birth. As the infant matures, she can localize sounds, initially by turning her head to search for the sound and then by looking directly at the sound source. Infants are capable of discerning subtle variations in both intensity and frequency of sound (Mehler & Dupoux, 1994).

The Ear

The ear is the organ of the body that we think of when we think of hearing. The ear has three parts: The outer ear, or auricle, is the only part that is visible. It is connected to the middle ear by the ear canal. The oval window separates the middle ear from the inner ear. See Figure 6.3.

Sound waves, or vibrations, enter through the auricle and travel through the inch-long ear canal until they reach the ear drum (**tympanic membrane**), causing it to vibrate back and forth. The ear drum is attached to one of the three small bones in the middle ear (the *ossicle*). These three bones transmit vibrations to the oval window, the beginning of the inner ear. In addition to transmitting sound, the combination of the tympanic membrane and ossicle amplifies the sound by about 30 decibels (Batshaw & Perret, 1992). When there is fluid in the middle ear, this amplification does not take place. The **eustachian tube** connects the middle ear to the back of the throat and serves to equalize air pressure in the middle ear. If the eustachian tube is not operating correctly, there can be a painful build-up of fluid which puts the middle ear at risk for infection and hearing loss.

The inner ear converts the mechanical sound waves to electrical energy. Only about the size of a pea, it contains the vestibular apparatus (which controls balance) and the **cochlea.** As vibrations cause the oval window (a thin membrane) to move, pressure is changed in the inner ear. The cochlea contains two types of fluid, the perilymph and the endolymph. Pressure changes cause the tiny hair cells in the endolymph to move. They move differently depending on the frequency and intensity of the sound. These hair cells convert the mechanical energy to electrochemical impulses and send these impulses through the nerve

---

Figure 6.3 | **The Ear**

The auditory system includes the outer, middle, and inner ear, as well as the auditory nerve and the auditory cortex in the temporal lobe of the brain.

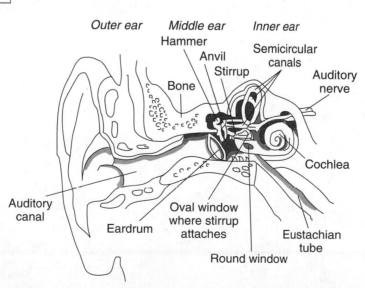

fibers to the **auditory nerve,** which is connected to the cochlea, and then to the auditory cortex in the temporal lobe of the brain (Batshaw & Perret, 1992). The brain does not really hear per se, but rather combines sound with other sensory information to allow perception and interpretation.

The loudness, or intensity, of sound is measured in **decibels** (dB), while pitch or sound pressure levels are measured in cycles per second, or **hertz** (Hz). The closer the sound waves are to each other, the higher the pitch. Humans can hear frequencies between about 20 to 20,000 cycles per second, or hertz. A hertz equals one cycle per second. We are particularly interested in the speech frequencies, which range from 250 to 6,000 hertz. **Intensity** is defined by the height of the sound wave with the higher waves being the loudest sounds. On that scale, 0

Many infants like the sound of a bell, especially when they are the ones ringing it.

decibels is the faintest sound a person with normal hearing can detect. Although speech varies, normal conversation ranges from 40 to 60 decibels.

To support auditory development, adults need to know something about how infants hear, what infants like to listen to, what role audition plays in their development, and how infants perceive and localize sounds and process auditory information.

Auditory Perception

We know that infants hear and that the auditory nerve is well myelinated at birth. The myelination of higher parts of the brain such as the auditory cortex will continue for several years. Researchers are interested not just in how well infants can hear, but whether or not they can detect differences in intensity and frequency, and whether or not they have preferences relative to the intensities or frequencies of auditory stimuli.

Intensity

Studying an infant's auditory perception, like studying his visual perception, is challenging. Infants respond differently to sounds depending on the complexity of the sound itself, how suddenly it begins, and the pitch of the sound. Once the newborn's ears are cleared of fluid, they can hear sounds of about 40 decibels. Since conversation typically is this loud or louder, the infant can hear the human voice.

Frequency

Infants apparently have preferences regarding the frequency of noises they respond to. They appear to like low-frequency sounds (200 to 500 Hz) which, interestingly, are the same frequencies as the human voice. Researchers have found that they prefer a human voice to silence and that they prefer their mother's voice to all other voices. They find very high (over 4,000 Hz) and very low (70 Hz) sounds distressing, and can be soothed by complex low-frequency noise. Complexity is related to how many frequencies a given sound has. A pure tone has for practical purposes a single frequency. Obviously, infants can distinguish between low and high frequencies.

Localization

Researchers now agree that newborns turn in the direction of some sounds, which is a primitive form of localization. What researchers finally realized was that infants did in fact locate a sound when they were given 12 seconds to respond, kept in a position where they could turn their head, and the tone itself was produced by a rattle. The duration of the tone (1 to 20 seconds) did not seem to matter (Mehler & Dupoux, 1994). This ability to orient to sound appears to drop out around 2 months and to be replaced by voluntary localization about 4 months. The reason that it was so difficult to confirm these results experimentally was that researchers did not give infants enough time to respond and, erroneously, concluded that they did not respond.

By the time toddlers are about 18 months old, they are able to locate a sound source quite precisely. The interest in localization is spurred by curiosity about whether newborns know that sounds are typically made by objects and whether an infant turning his head to the source of a sound indicates an expectation of visually seeing a sound-producing object. Although there is evidence that infants have this knowledge by 3 or 4 months, it is not clear whether or not younger infants do.

Hearing Impairments

Infants with hearing impairments make noises and babble like other infants up until about 6 months of age. They do not, however, respond to auditory stimuli out of their range of hearing. Auditory impairments severely impact the development of speech and language skills. Both speech and language depend heavily on hearing in the early years of development. Language is acquired through listening, imitation, practice, and correction.

There are two major types of hearing impairment: **conductive** hearing losses that result from damage to the external or middle ear, and **sensorineural** losses that result from damage to the cochlea or auditory nerve. If there are both conductive and sensorineural losses, they are referred to as a *mixed* loss.

Conductive Hearing Impairments

A conductive loss is one in which a problem in the outer or middle ear prevents sound from getting to the inner ear. This can be caused by something lodged in the ear canal, excessive ear wax, or fluid in the middle ear. Many young children who experience frequent ear infections have periodic conductive losses. Conductive losses reduce the child's ability to hear speech sounds through air-conduction. Sounds transmitted through bone conduction are heard normally. Most conductive losses can be corrected through antibiotics or surgery.

Most children (76 to 95 percent) have at least one ear infection during their early childhood years. In fact, ear aches are the second most commonly diagnosed disorder in young children during an office visit. It is estimated that over half of all antibiotics given to children are for ear infections, or otitis media (Hallahan & Kauffman, 1991). There are usually few long-term implications from these occasional ear infections (Bluestone & Klein, 1988). Children who have repeated bouts of otitis media are at risk for permanent hearing loss, poor acquisition of language skills, and learning disabilities (Denk-Glass, Laber, & Brewer, 1982; Ralabate, 1987).

Middle ear disease, or chronic otitis media, is the build-up of thick fluid in the middle ear that does not drain through the eustachian tubes. It is difficult to accurately measure the prevalence of middle ear disease. However, some estimates are that as many as 50 percent of young children have this condition (Denk-Glass, Laber, & Brewer, 1982). This thick fluid is a prime target for bacterial growth and causes a hearing loss of about 60 decibels or less. Antibiotics can cure the infection, but the fluid may linger on for days or even weeks, causing a hearing loss.

Middle ear disease is often undetected until the infant or toddler shows signs of physical illness. Irritability, lethargy, and inattentiveness are the most typical symptoms. Once the infection sets in, the infant may pull at his ear or the fluid may be seen draining from the ear. Because of the intermittent nature of the problem, it can be missed even among children who have their hearing checked.

Middle ear disease can be treated medically by antibiotics. If the problem persists, a surgical procedure called a myringotomy is used: First the ear drum is cut; then tubes are inserted to allow the fluid to drain. If untreated, persistent temporary losses could become permanent (Mollick & Etra, 1981).

Sensorineural Impairments

A sensorineural impairment involves damage to either the inner ear, the nerve to the brain stem, or both. In cases of sensorineural impairments, sound vibration is properly transmitted through the outer and middle ear, but something happens to the sound within the cochlea or auditory nerve pathway. A new surgical procedure for this condition, *cochlear implants,* allows some children over the age of 2 who are profoundly deaf to hear sound they previously could not perceive. It may enable children who cannot benefit from amplification to hear environmental sounds such as the telephone and car horns and makes speech reading easier for them. The results at this time are quite variable. A learning process is required, since the child needs to differentiate and identify sounds she hears for the first time (Hallahan & Kauffman, 1991).

Hereditary deafness can be inherited as an autosomal recessive disorder. Infections in infancy and early childhood can also lead to sensorineural hearing impairments. Bacterial meningitis carries the greatest risk, but common viral diseases like chicken pox, measles, and mumps can also cause hearing loss. Sensorineural impairment is also part of many different syndromes such as rubella.

Amplification is prescribed for children with moderate losses. Typically, a hearing aid is prescribed to make sounds louder. A device is fitted as soon as the loss has been established. Even with amplification, however, sounds are unclear and distorted to the child.

Development of Infants and Toddlers with Auditory Impairments

It is extremely difficult to identify an infant with a hearing impairment. Infants and young children cannot tell us they cannot hear, and for the first six months there is little developmental difference between them and other children. Unless there is a family history of deafness, or children were born prematurely, they are rarely tested. Generally, it is only when children miss speech and language milestones that a hearing impairment is suspected.

In general, the less severe the loss, the later it will be diagnosed. Only profound losses are detected in the first months of life. The initial stage of testing is usually observational. Parents are watching to see if the infant responds to sound, particularly, whether a sleeping infant blinks or moves at a sound, typically a horn or bell. Responses of infants under 6 months of age are also measured by using auditory brain-stem responses. Electrodes are pasted on the sleeping infant's forehead and behind his ears. Via earphones tones are presented and recorded and the responses are analyzed for abnormality. This procedure evaluates the integrity of the hearing pathway from the inner ear to the brain (Warren, 1989).

In testing for auditory impairments, children from about 6 months to 2 years are usually conditioned to respond to a visual reinforcer paired with a sound (Batshaw & Perret, 1992). Toddlers and older children are usually tested with earphones and taught to do a simple task every time they hear a sound, such as putting blocks in a container in response to a sound. With the earphones, differences between hearing in the right and left ear can be ascertained.

Impedance audiometry is used to assess the functioning of the middle ear. This is used in conjunction with other audiometric testing to detect the occurrence of otitis media in children over 7 months. A microphone attached to a probe is sealed in the ear canal and air is pumped in or removed. A written record of this procedure is a **tympanogram.** The shape of the tympanogram is useful in diagnosing when infants and toddlers are retaining fluid in their ears (Batshaw & Perret, 1992).

Conductive losses in infants and toddlers prevent them from hearing sounds effectively. A majority of conductive losses are not severe enough to totally block sound transmission. Instead, sound is muffled in transit. An infant with fluid build-up hears sounds as if he were underwater. An infant with excessive wax hears sounds similar to a person having ear plugs. In each case, sound is heard, but acuity is poor. Infants and toddlers experiencing frequent conductive losses are susceptible to impairments in the area of speech and language. Conversations are muffled and good language modeling cannot occur as the children cannot hear much of what is spoken. Children with conductive losses frequently omit initial and final sounds of words. Children with mild to moderate losses are usually delayed in the development of speech and language and may need specialized help with articulation.

Children experiencing a severe to profound sensorineural hearing loss may have little understandable speech. They are likely to babble like other children up until about 6 months. Then, while a hearing child's babbling becomes more complex, the child with a sensorineural loss babbles less. In addition to delays in expressive language, infants and toddlers with severe and profound losses will also have problems with receptive language. They may need both oral and manual methods of communication.

Touch

Infants are born with sensitive tactile abilities. There are a variety of sensory nerve endings just below the surface of the skin whose purpose is to convert mechanical energy to electrical signals that go to the brain. Some reflexes, like the rooting and stepping reflexes, are elicited by touch. Through the combined integration of motor responses and reduction of immediate responses to tactile stimulation, the young child's primitive reactions to touch decrease to mostly voluntary responses. Infants respond to tactile qualities and explore objects differently depending on whether the objects are soft or hard, rigid or flexible.

Another question that has intrigued researchers is whether or not infants recognize an object visually that they have explored orally based on its texture (smooth or not smooth; hard or soft). By 1 month they apparently do (Gibson & Walker, 1984). There is, however, some question about whether oral exploration is actually part of **haptic perception** (touch) as infants explore very differently with their hands than with their mouth (Streri & Molina, 1994). This is further complicated because of the use of the hand in transporting objects as well as touching them. It appears that infants 2 months of age have difficulty gaining tactile information because of their unimodal grasp. That is, they can only grasp an object but not explore it because of their lack of coordination. There does not seem to be a transfer of information from vision to touch at this age. This seems to be true until about 5 months. Observational data from reaching patterns of 4-month-old infants support this. When infants this age reach for an object and miss, rather than adjusting their reach they tend to start the reach over from the beginning (Streri & Molina, 1994). Between 4 and 5 months, infants explore objects using both hands (Streri, Molina, & Rameix, 1993). By 6 months of age, infants can visually recognize felt objects (Rose, Gottfried, & Bridger, 1981).

The relationship between haptic perception and motor skills illustrates the ways in which development interacts. As the infant gains control of his body, his hands are freed to explore objects. This exploration provides infants with additional information about objects that cannot be obtained by vision or hearing.

Atypical Tactile Responses

Young children with atypical tactile responses reflect a very diverse group. Some infants display extreme forms of tactile defensiveness. For these children, it is unpleasant or even painful to be touched or receive any form of tactile stimulation. Eating can be a difficult task, as the defensiveness produces the bite reflex, the gag reflex, or can result in infants who refuse to eat.

Infants with physical impairments, such as cerebral palsy, react with primitive reflexes when they are touched. These reactions interfere with normal motor movements. Atypical tactile development is also part of some emotional-behavioral disorders. Autistic children, for example, tend to find tactile stimulation very unpleasant and in fact will try to avoid situations that may result in touching. Some infants exhibit low sensitivity to touch. They do not feel pain. These children frequently have severe emotional problems or profound disabilities.

Taste

The young infant is born with an adequate number of taste buds. Therefore, it is assumed that young infants have a fairly well-developed taste sensation at birth. A variety of measures have been used to determine preferences in taste. Some researchers observe facial expressions, other sucking rates, and still others heart rate. The latter two seem to be the most reliable indicators. Infants can discriminate between sweet, acidic, salt, and bitter tastes; most of them prefer sweet tastes. Newborns do not show a preference between water and a saline (salt) solution; around 4 to 6 months a preference begins to appear.

There is little information available regarding any disorders in the area of taste problems and infants. There are groups of infants who refuse to eat and others who decline any intake of fluids. Although there has been no determination to date indicating any relationship between nutritional intake and taste sensation problems, little research has been completed examining the taste sensory input. Though not much is known about the taste sensation, taste may be an important area of early child development. Young infants spend a great deal of time mouthing objects they encounter in their environment and the taste sensation may affect this activity.

Smell

Little is known about the infant's olfactory abilities, since most of the research has been done on neonates, which has been reported earlier in Chapter 4. Once it was determined that the sense of smell is well developed at birth and that young infants are capable of discriminating between pleasant and unpleasant odors, most researchers lost interest. Infants appear to show preference for fragrant odors and a displeasure for noxious odors.

Since little is known about the infant's olfactory abilities, even less is known about any problems associated with this sensory ability. There is some indication that learning is an important variable in reaction to different smells and that females may be more sensitive to odors than males.

Intersensory Perception

Although we have some understanding of the sensory abilities of infants, there are still many questions about what they do with the sensory information they receive. There are two opposing theories about how the senses become coordinated: integration theories and differentiation theories.

- **Integration theories** posit that the senses are independent at birth and that with maturation intersensory coordination gradually emerges. They see each sense modality as a separate "tunnel" of information that emerges at about the fourth month into an area where the transfer of information between the senses is possible.
- **Differentiation theories** consider the senses unified early in development responding to stimulation and that gradually the senses become differentiated. In this theory information is viewed as coming into the child and being acted upon without reference to specifically modalities. Thus, intersensory perception is possible at birth. They feel that it is not until about four months

that the senses become differentiated and the infant is aware that he is gaining information by "looking" at it or "hearing" it (Bahrick & Pickens, 1994).

Piaget's (1952, 1954) theory of infant sensory development is one of the best-known integration theories. He feels that at birth infants have modality-specific inputs and that it is not until about 4 months of age that something "to look at" also becomes something "to touch" and something "to hear." Piagetian theory suggests that it is the infant's active engagement with his environment through his increasing motor control that is the foundation for sensory integration and coordination.

Gibson (1969), a proponent of the differentiation theory, feels that infants have an innate perceptive capacity. According to this theory, infants do not have to integrate inputs from various senses; rather they are perceived simultaneously. Only later does the infant distinguish among his senses to determine how he obtained the information. Gibson feels that even very young infants can respond to both qualitative and quantitative aspects of stimulation.

A variation on differentiation theory is the Intensity Hypothesis (Lewkowicz, 1994) which suggests that infants respond to the quantitative aspects of stimulation—the overall amount of stimulation. Properties such as loudness, brightness, size, and so on, are undifferentiated and lumped together as intensity. Qualitative aspects of stimulation such as rhythm, texture, and shape are not differentiated until about 4 to 6 months (Lewkowicz, 1991).

Researchers are curious about how infants perceive and integrate their world, but figuring out what infants do to make sense of their world is still a challenge.

Categorization

Knowing the skills infants have still does not truly answer the question of how they make sense out of their world. It appears that they organize information by categories. Adults use categories to make sense of sensory information. This is true even when the information is continuous, such as wavelengths; we categorize it into discontinuous units called colors and we see boundaries between these colors.

Researchers mention different types of categories. Perceptual categories allow us to differentiate among objects, whereas linguistic categories relate to specific aspects of categories. Perceptual categories related to color would include red, yellow, green, and blue. Linguistic categories might be teal, aquamarine, turquoise, and so on. There are also natural and technical categories. Natural categories are learned by children without specific teaching and they occur in the vocabulary of all languages. Technical categories occur later and are dependent on the family and culture in which one is raised (Mehler & Dupoux, 1994). Thus the perception of color (natural category) is the same for all humans, whereas the labels given to the perceived colors are different (technical category).

If color, then, is a perceptual category, the question is do infants differentiate among colors in the same way that adults do? To find out, infants under 4 months were presented a color adults call blue (480 nm wavelength) until they habituated.

Infants were then presented with two stimuli equidistant from the original wavelength, another shade of blue (450 nm wavelength), and what adults call green (510 nm wavelength). The infants had a much greater reaction to the green than the new blue, indicating that they found a qualitative change in the green but not the blue (Mehler & Dupoux, 1994). Using the same model, the researchers investigated other color relationships and concluded that although infant categories were broader than adults, they divided wavelengths into four principal categories, as did adults. Color was then viewed as a natural category. Interestingly, children can rarely name colors before about age 4. This may be because the cortex is not mature until about this age. Infants also seem to have natural categories relating to orientation (vertical and slanted lines), form, and part-whole relationships (Mehler & Dupoux, 1994).

As with colors, infants divide up their auditory world. They differentiate rhythmically much the same way as adults do (Mehler & Dupoux, 1994).

Researchers sometimes have different views about how infants perceive their world. Piaget contends that young infants have no concept of object permanence. Bower, on the other hand, feels that infants have a concept of object that is independent of their own actions. He found that infants expect objects with a regular trajectory to reappear at a particular exit point, that at 2 months infants reach for a toy they have seen even when the lights go out, and about 5 months they are surprised when an object disappears and reappears a different color (Bower & Patterson, 1972; Bower & Wishart, 1972).

Summary

Researchers are interested in the infant's sensory abilities at birth and how these change. They are interested in understanding what the infant's world is like and how he makes sense out of it. Infants, however, are challenging to work with because of their behavioral states and their small repertoire of behaviors. Researchers have to make assumptions about the infant's preferences through indirect means. Habituation and conditioning are used to learn about the infant's perceptions.

Overall, in the area of sensation and perception we know the most about visual perception, and secondarily about auditory perception. We have very little knowledge about touch, taste, or smell. Infants can see at birth, but their vision, compared to adults, is blurred and they have problems changing focal length. With increasing age, their acuity improves and they become aware of depth and its implications for their safety. Visual impairments in infants and toddlers are often difficult to identify unless the visual loss is profound.

Infants can also hear at birth, but again, not with the same level of acuity as adults. They are sensitive to different intensities and frequencies of sound and they make attempts to localize sound soon after birth. Their ability at localization improves as they get older. Children with hearing impairments are difficult to identify until they begin to miss some of the language milestones. Although we know less about the senses of touch, taste, and smell, they are certainly operational in very young infants and affect their development.

Application Activities

1. Design an experiment where you will determine the color preference of an infant. First write it down and then do it. Decide the colors you will use, how you will present them, how many trials you need, and how confident you feel with the results.

2. Explain to a parent what her infant's sensory capacities are and what type of stimulation the infant might like.

3. Use a conditioning paradigm to teach an infant something. Write down your design, how long conditioning took, and what you learned.

4. Explain to a parent why a 1-month-old infant would find large newspaper headlines more interesting than the pastel prints that are typically used on crib sheets, bumpers, and baby blankets.

Chapter 7

Cognitive and Intellectual Development

We know that infants come into the world seeing, hearing, feeling, tasting, and smelling. What we do not know is how they construct meaning out of their world. Do they come "knowing," or must they interact with their environment to learn about it? Is this learning linear, incremental (where a "bit" at a time is added), or does knowledge sometimes spurt ahead and become qualitatively different from previous knowledge?

A great many changes in cognitive processing occur during the first three years of life. The child progresses from the involuntary motor responses of early infancy to symbolic and abstract forethought. He takes a giant leap for such a small period of time.

Cognitive Development

The study of cognitive development has intrigued researchers for many years. The act of knowing is called **cognition.** Cognition is the process of knowing in the broadest sense. It involves gathering information, categorizing this data, interpreting it, comparing it to previous data, and organizing it. Organization is critical for cognition; information and symbols must be organized so they can be retrieved in the future. Cognition involves a variety of other functions, including perception, memory, and learning. Cognition also involves nonmental processes such as personality, emotions, and social conscience. Cognitive researchers have focused on universals, rather than individual differences. The literature that does focus on individual differences falls in the area that is referred to as intelligence (Meadows, 1993).

Intelligence is the capacity of an individual to adapt to the environment. When one thinks of the characteristics of an "intelligent" young child, one thinks typically of a child who talks early, has a good vocabulary for his age, attempts to solve problems in interesting ways, is curious about the world around him, and adapts. Less intelligent children do these things less well. Intelligence is different from cognition in that it depends on judgment about what is necessary to adapt. Intelligence is therefore somewhat relative, depending on the demands of varying cultures and the eras in which one lives. Researchers are interested in both the general aspects of intelligence as well as the specific ones. The latter part of this chapter focuses on intelligence.

Perception is the aspect of cognition that involves organization and interpretation of sensory data. For perception to be effective, you need memory. **Memory** is the mental process whereby information is stored either for a short or long time so that it can be retrieved. Without memory, learning cannot occur. There are three aspects to memory. *Recognition* is the simplest form of memory and the aspect that is most used by very young infants. It involves recognizing a person or object that has been previously known. **Associative memory** involves connecting information about two events. For conditioning to be effective, there must be some associative memory in young infants. Memory also involves *recall*, bringing back an experience without any cues. Recall is more complex than recognition because it requires the child to think symbolically. Symbolic thinking apparently begins to occur about the time that an infant begins to use words, at about 1 year.

As you might guess, there are many different theories about how children learn about their world. Increasingly, these theories are becoming more complex. Theories, like knowledge, are not static. Theoretical modifications occur because of new information about growth and development and new insights by the theorists. Theories are far more comprehensive, sophisticated, and relevant to the real world with real people than they have been in the past. Some theories overlap and find general points of agreement, others do not. Some theories seem to have a central focus, such as cognitive development, yet also have implications for other areas, such as language or social development. Before looking at specific theories, there are some issues that all theories about early development must address.

Developmental Theories

Theories about development and issues related to these theories are changing. There was a time when theories were designed solely to help people think about issues in the field and were viewed as basic research. In the 1990s, with increased interest in intervention and concern about the health and welfare of children, particularly as it is reflected in social policy, there is a renewed interest in applied research and theories that help focus this research. Changing demographics have brought the question of the role of culture in development to the fore and have questioned the assumption of universals in cognitive and language development.

There is much debate about whether development is continuous or discontinuous. If discontinuous, is it divided into stages? If so, how many? And how does one make a transition between stages?

Stages in Development

Questions about the theoretical usefulness and validity of the concept of stages and transitions in cognitive development challenge many researchers. Piaget's theory uses a stage-based model. He implies that when one behavior in the next stage is exhibited, then the child moves into that stage. Others (Feldman & Snyder, 1994; Flavell, 1971), although acknowledging different internal organizations in individuals at different points in time, see stages as more gradual with transitions between them and they also contemplate the reality that young children may be in different stages in different aspects of development. That is, at any moment in time a child exhibits behavior from several stages of development depending on the domain. Although Bijou (1992) uses stages in his behavior analysis, his stage distinctions are totally arbitrary and are only used as ways of dividing time rather than being related to development.

Feldman and Snyder (1994) agree that developmental domains can be best understood and characterized in stages. However, they admit that there are limitations "because the behavior of any given child (and the system that generates and governs this behavior) is never as consistent, orderly or stage-appropriate as the hypothetical ideal would predict" (1994, 19). Feldman and Snyder (1994) summarize the underlying assumption of stage-based theories in four categories:

Universal Achievement. An assumption of stage-based theories is that all children from all cultures will pass through these stages. Aspects of culture or of individual uniqueness are of little interest.

Universal Acquisition. The achievement of universals is possible because no special environment or teaching is necessary for the acquisition of these behaviors. The suggestion is that children are born intrinsically motivated to construct their view of the world and that the environmental conditions are available in all cultures for this to happen. The child will move through all stages without specific interventions.

Invariant Sequence. There is a specific sequence that development must follow and all individuals must follow that sequence. Stages cannot be skipped, nor does one move backward in the process. The time one spends in each stage may, however, vary.

Hierarchical Integration. There are rules that govern movement from one stage to another and how information from each stage is reorganized and transformed as the basis for the next stage in the hierarchy.

Feldman and Snyder (1994) believe that if the focus of development broadens to include behaviors that are not universal, then the first two assumptions are called into question or need to be modified to only pertain to that portion of development which is universal and to allow the exploration of other domains using the remaining principles of a stage-based model (sequence and hierarchical organization).

Universal to Unique

The decision to focus on universals has impacted not only the cognitive domain but language as well, and has taken the focus away from individuals and their families and the impact of culture to focus only on the "common" aspects of development. With the focus on universals, questions arise as to whether we have missed some important aspects of unique development (Feldman & Snyder, 1994).

The focus on the universal aspects of cognition, which is characteristic of most cognitive theories about infants and toddlers, has not taken into account how infants and toddlers acquire other knowledge such as that about their culture and ethnic identity.

Culture refers to the behavior patterns, values, beliefs and products of a particular group of people that are passed from generation to generation. Cultural groups can be very large or small. A group's culture influences the identity, learning, and social behavior of its members (Lonner & Malpass, 1994). Ethnicity is based on cultural heritage, national characteristics, race, religion, and language. Ethnic identity is a sense of group membership based on an individual interpretation of these variables. Cultural domains, for example, include the three R's— "Reading, 'Riting, and 'Rithmetic"—as well as the understanding of political and economic systems. Although one cannot expect that all individuals in a given culture need to achieve the level of mastey of each of these areas, there is the expectation that despite cultural differences, all group members will have some level of knowledge in each of these areas (Feldman & Snyder, 1994).

The comparison of one culture with other cultures is called **cross-cultural studies.** The goal of these studies is to provide information about the universals in child development, that is, the degree to which behavior patterns, values, beliefs, and products of a particular cultural group are similar and to what degree they are unique or culturally specific.

There is also knowledge that is discipline based. The discipline that you are currently studying is an aspect of child development. Many individuals have no course work and little academic knowledge about infants and toddlers, regardless of their cultural background. Others may have advanced degrees with infancy as a speciality. We know little about this specialized kind of knowledge and how it is acquired. Even within disciplines at an idiosyncratic level, it is not at all clear why some physicians become surgeons and others neurologists. Child prodigies are the most striking examples of idiosyncratic cognitive development. They move through the stages of development in the predicted pattern, yet at an extraordinarily rapid rate (Feldman & Snyder, 1994). Cognitive theories in general are not concerned with, nor do they explain, unique cognitive achievements. Their focus has been on the universal, not the unique aspects of cognitive development.

A pioneer in studying cognitive development was Jean Piaget. His work dominated the field for many years. Piaget's theory provides a great deal of information about development during infancy and toddlerhood. Many later theorists compare their principles and findings to his. Piaget's ideas are discussed below, including the modifications that more current research suggests. This is followed by a brief discussion of other theories of cognitive development.

Piaget's Theory of Cognitive Development

Jean Piaget called himself a **genetic epistemologist** because he studied the basis of knowing, or cognition. His conclusion was that cognitive development (the growth of the child's thinking skills and abilities) encompassed a complex variety of factors and variables that can affect development. Although later scholars challenged parts of his theory, there is no doubt that he changed our view of infants.

Piaget introduced the idea that there were two kinds of knowledge: logicomathematical knowledge and physical knowledge. Knowledge is based on the focus of the child. If he is focusing on the organization of his actions, their order, and what happens when he acts on objects, he is learning about logicomathematical knowledge. If, on the other hand, he is concentrating on the properties of the object itself, he is learning about physical knowledge (Sinclair et al., 1989).

Piaget made very careful observations of the behavior of his own three children and other Swiss children. From these observations he developed a theory about how infants learn. His writing recast the infant in the role of an active participant and problem-solver in his world. Current researchers see young children as even more competent than Piaget theorized (Gelman, 1979; Lewkowicz, 1994; Mehler & Dupoux, 1994). He focused on aspects of infant learning that others had not even considered. He reached two conclusions that greatly influenced his work and hence the entire field. The first was that children's mistakes were more interesting than their correct answers. The second was that children had to be understood from their point of view, not from that of an adult, and that it was possible to find out what that point of view was (Gratch & Schatz, 1987).

Piaget's theory is a biological model that rests on two basic hypotheses: that cognitive mechanisms are extensions of organic biological regulations; and that these mechanisms become specialized and differentiated through interactions with the external world (Piaget, 1970). Piaget focused on the universals in behavior and developed a stage-based theory.

Piaget's goal was to use his observations to understand how infants define concepts that are precise, logical, and consistent. This goal not only influenced what he observed, but how he then organized his observations and made sense out of them. Present views of cognitive development are broader than this one aspect of cognition and are more context bound; that is, researchers today are more reluctant to make broad generalizations from limited specific information. They believe that there are consistencies but that these are loose and general and that specific behaviors need to be viewed in context.

Piaget emphasizes that cognitive development, like motor development, occurs in a recognizable and predictable progression, and that later development is based on the information the child received during earlier stages of development and interactions (Flavell, 1963; Piaget, 1963, 1970). He believes that the child's intellectual development begins at birth and that intellectual growth is a function of consistent interactions with the environment. The majority of early behaviors of infants are sensorimotor. His theory is detailed below with some later modifications and criticisms noted.

Components of Piaget's Theory

Piaget (1970) divides cognitive development into stages of intellectual growth composed of learning processes. This is how he describes the key components in the learning paradigm:

Assimilation. Young children come to know about their world through experience and active participation. Their minds funnel all this information into the brain for processing (**assimilation**). All knowledge is connected with an action, whereas assimilation provides the basis of meaning. It is different from a stimulus response (S–R) association in that it is S–(AS)–R. AS stands for the assimilation of the stimulus into a scheme (Beilin, 1992). For example, an infant grasps all rattles the same way regardless of their size or shape. This grasping information is treated as "old" knowledge. That is, the child will use the same grasping motion for a cube that he did for a rattle. If the result is too divergent from his "old" knowledge, he will ignore it. He can make minor changes and adjustments but not major ones. Likewise, requiring the infant to stretch to reach the rattle provides slightly different information, setting the stage for accommodation.

Accommodation. Accommodation occurs when new information necessitates restructuring of what was already learned. If the infant cannot efficiently grasp the block using the previous pattern, then the infant will have to adjust. This is accommodation. Accommodation is an inner reality. One might think of assimilation as a process of generalization, and accommodation more as a process of discrimination.

Adaptation. Assimilation and accommodation are separate yet complementary processes that result in new levels of adaptation. Adaptation involves change and is an ongoing process. With adaptation the infant might have two versions of grasping a rattle based on his experience; that is, he might develop different grasps depending on the shape and size of what he is grasping.

Considering his assimilation, accommodation and adaptation ideas led Piaget to conclude that the key to cognitive development is an environment in which there are a variety of similar, but not the same, experiences. This limited variety allows the child to assimilate past experiences. He will then accommodate a new experience (if it is not too divergent from his past experience), and he will develop a new level of adaptation which will expand his repertoire of knowledge. The next key to cognitive development is the organization of knowledge in a meaningful way.

Organization. Organization is the individual's interpretation of reality. It is concerned with systems of relationships among elements. Experience and knowledge are categorized, sorted into meaningful bits, and relationships between those "bits" are established. These are complex, ordered relationships. Organization involves a stabilizing process, as these "bits" or variations become tied to one another.

Equilibration. Central to Piaget's theory is the understanding that assimilation, accommodation, adaptation, and organization exist together in a balanced state called **equilibrium.** Equilibrium is dynamic; it requires almost constant recalibration and adjustment. The process of building and maintaining equilibrium is call **equilibration.** The interaction of assimilation and accommodation that requires more complex organization also produces a new state of equilibrium. As the infant interacts with her environment, reality must be constantly reinterpreted; new adaptations are therefore required. This is how Piaget sees the infant as successfully adapting to a more complex environment.

The following example shows how these processes work. A toddler learns that green things outside are called plants. Later, the child learns that not all green things outside are plants, but can be other things such as cans, cars, and so on. He also learns that there are different types of plants, some you can eat, some that hurt, and some that look pretty. Later, the child learns that small, green things called plants are also called plants when found inside the house. And finally, the child learns that different kinds of plants also have individual names (cactus, fern), that distinguish one plant from another. In each case, the child adapts previously learned information into a new ever-expanding category of information.

Schemes.   Children develop patterns of behavior, or **schemes,** that function as organizing responses to environmental interactions. Schemes are built by the process of assimilation and accommodation. A scheme develops as an organized behavior pattern that is repeated frequently. Infants have a sucking scheme. The young infant may first suck on a breast or bottle, then a pacifier or finger. As the infant adapts to these different objects, the sucking scheme is expanded and modified. The infant abstracts the commonalities in the sucking into a mental representation of sucking that is a scheme. Infant schemes are based on sensorimotor actions. As the infant is provided with widening opportunities to interact with different materials and to practice skills already learned, he slowly progresses to higher levels of learning or cognitive activity.

A scheme, then, is a mental representation, or intellectual structure, referring to a particular behavioral action sequence. Schemes are organizations of elements or ideas that are coherent, adaptive, and purposeful. Networks of schemes are developed that guide what the infant perceives and does about the world. With increasing age, schemes become increasingly based on mental activity as the individual develops knowledge from concept formation, reasoning, and language or symbols.

Active Learning.   Learning is a result of interaction with the environment. Infants acquire new information by actively experimenting with materials and objects. Active learning is essential for the child to practice and refine previously learned skills and to acquire new schemes. Children need appropriate materials to experiment with. These learning tools need to be matched to their level of sensorimotor development. Piaget feels children need a wide range of experiences in order to learn. What the infant learns about the world derives from physical experience. Thus all children acquire this knowledge through active participation. Children also learn and develop socially. However, social experience is learned from people and to some extent can be taught. Social learning is not the same for all children as it is culture based.

Piaget believes that for children to learn they must actively engage in their environment.

Stage-Based Development

All children progress through *stages* of cognitive development in the same order, but not necessarily at the same rates or ages. Cognitive development is hierarchically based; that is, what is acquired at a later stage is dependent on what was learned in earlier phases of development. Each sequence, or stage, in development is a prerequisite to the next. Qualitative changes in the child's intellectual abilities occur as the child progresses through these developmental stages.

Piaget divided the child's cognitive development into four periods. Each period is identified and characterized by the occurrence of specific cognitive processes. The four periods are the sensorimotor period, the preoperational period, concrete operations, and formal operations. Piaget did not emphasize age levels, but rather emphasized the qualitative differences in cognitive abilities that occur in each period. The sensorimotor period and the beginning of the preoperational period are the two periods experienced by infants and toddlers.

Sensorimotor Period

Piaget called the first stage of development the **sensorimotor period.** This period is characterized by infants exploring their world with their senses and motor activity. This usually takes place from birth until about 2 years. He identified six individual substages in the sensorimotor period of development. The first three stages concentrate on the infant's own body and the latter three describe schemes that relate to practical intelligence as it relates to space and objects (Beilin, 1992). The end of the sensorimotor stage is marked by the emergence of symbolic functioning—that is, the ability of the infant to mentally represent events and objects and to solve problems through mental activity. The first two years of life create the need as well as the capacity for representation. Infants need to link present experiences to past ones; then they need to represent objects, people, movements, and so on; and, finally, they need the means to solve problems (Sinclair et al., 1989). People in the environment serve to verify judgments of what infants and toddlers are learning.

Newer research has proposed changes to Piaget's six stages of sensorimotor development and identified four stages that are based on both behavioral changes observable in the infant as well as changes that occur in the brain itself. Noted are significant changes in brain waves, sleep cycles, and perceptual abilities that coincide with behavior changes noted at transition points at 3, 8, 12, and 18 months (Bornstein & Lamb, 1992; Fischer, 1987; and Fischer & Silvern, 1985). This provides a remarkable congruence with Piaget's stages if one ignores the reflexive stage and focuses on the transition markers.

A discussion follows about the characteristics of the sensorimotor stages, the modifications, the individual skills acquired in each stage, and the transition marker.

Stage 1: Reflexes (0 to 1 Month)

According to Piaget, the first month of life is primarily a reflexive stage. The neonate knows very little; however, he has reflexes that he practices and repeats. Reflexes such as sucking, crying, and grasping undergo some assimilation and accommodation as the infant practices these skills.

Some later research does not view the infant as being quite so dominated by reflexes as Piaget characterized him. The neonate's visual scanning, response to sound, taste preferences, and memory for smell, suggest he may be somewhat more capable and complex than Piaget thought (Lewkowicz, 1994; Mehler & Dupoux, 1994).

Stage 2: Primary Circular Reactions (1 to 4 Months)

Gradually the infant's reflexes begin to come under control as sensorimotor cognitive structures replace reflexes. **Circular reactions** are sequences of behavior, such as sticking the tongue out or thumb sucking, that are repeated several times in succession. These reactions are primary circular reactions because they do not require external objects. They involve the infant's body. Primary circular reactions are the repetition of actions that initially happened by chance. Therefore the focus of the infant is on the action sequence, not on the object. The goal seems to be the repetition of the behavior sequence, not exploration of the object. Over the four months of this stage, these primary circular reactions increase in number and seem to become easier, requiring less concerted effort.

Accidental interactions with the environment, combined with reflexive actions, frequently lead the baby to continue the actions. Through this repeated practice a new skill is learned. For example, the infant who accidentally comes into contact with a toy and sets it in motion through an arm movement may continue to make such arm movements. Through repetitive swiping actions, the arm movements become more accurate. Eye-hand coordination also improves.

Infants at this stage are curious; they begin to imitate behavior and vocalizations of others when others imitate them. If the infant performs a certain behavior such as uttering a sound, and an adult then imitates the sound the infant made, the infant will then repeat the sound. Some researchers feel that the infant cannot distinguish between herself and others at this time so that it really is not imitation at all but merely continuing a circular reaction. Others feel that this is true imitation (Rosenblith, 1992). Piaget suggests that the infant is assimilating the model behavior, as the infant's imitation is not an exact one, and is using it as a learning device.

The third aspect of this second stage is typified by the gains in coordination and integration that the infant makes. Infants now know that objects can be explored in a variety of modalities. The infant turns her head to look at an object that made interesting sounds. When the infant hears her mother, she also expects to see her. She now reaches for interesting objects to explore, although some of the exploration is still with the mouth.

Stage 3: Secondary Circular Reactions (4 to 8 Months)

Infants become more goal directed and repeat motor activities that are interesting over and over during this stage. Secondary circular reactions begin as infants purposefully explore objects to see what happens, rather than for motor action itself. An infant shakes a toy and it rattles, the infant makes it rattle again and again. The term *secondary* implies that the reaction is elicited from something in the environment other than the infant herself. When a new toy is offered, the infant tries out all her available schemes: The toy is sucked, banged, grasped, dropped, shaken and so on. If the child becomes intrigued with one of these schemes, it is repeated. (Dropping always seems to be the most intriguing!) Infants may show abbreviated schemes; that is, if a child sees a rattle which he usually shakes in a certain way, he may use his hand to make part of the shaking motion used when playing with the rattle (Barclay, 1985).

Infants begin to imitate simple actions; but only those actions they can see or hear themselves complete. An example of this is hand-waving or babbling. According to Piaget, facial expressions cannot be imitated because the infant cannot see his own face.

The first signs of object permanence occur during Stage 3. **Object permanence** is a memory skill whereby infants remember that objects still exist even when they cannot see them. This is important for the acquisition of later, higher-level skills. During this stage, the infant shows signs of partial object permanence. For example, if a toy is partially hidden, with a portion showing from under the cover, the infant will search and may find the object. But if the toy is completely hidden, the infant loses interest in the object, and will not search for it.

Newer theories that focus on the transition at 3 months see primary circular reactions as the major marker of this stage and view them as the earliest awareness of cause and effect. They also see these reactions as the foundation for many later skills. They see the infant coming into this transition still heavily under the influence of reflexes and leaving with accidentally discovered knowledge (Steinberg & Meyer, 1995).

Stage 4: Coordination of Secondary Circular Reactions (8 to 12 Months)

Now the infant puts together two secondary circular reactions: The infant may combine pulling and dropping. The infant now shows true "means-end" behavior. He moves a toy out of the way (means) to get to a favorite doll (end). Means-end behavior indicates the ability to understand how one goes about getting what one wants—knowing the means, or procedures, for solving the problem of achieving a particular goal. The child who jostles an adult's leg to continue the horsey ride, or pulls the adult's hands together to continue a pat-a-cake game, or holds up his arms to get picked up, understands this concept. The infant's imitation skills improve. She can now begin to imitate new sounds. Later in this stage single words appear. The child can begin to imitate unseen gestures such as facial gestures, or patting the top of the head.

The infant's ability to remember that toys and other items still exist when out of sight improves. The infant will search for objects he sees being hidden. He begins to show distress when he searches for something and it is not there. Yet, if the object is not where he initially searched for it, he will stop looking. His problem-solving skills have not fully developed yet.

The transition that takes place around 8 months is characterized by a change from the accidental discovery of the previous time to intentional behavior. The focus is on objects as opposed to the self. Objects are used in secondary circular reactions and as the focus of object permanence. Objects are seen as significant in that they are a mark in the infants' knowledge of the differentiation of self and object, and that objects can be acted on in intentional ways. Researchers struggle to understand the dimensions of object permanence and try to understand why infants this age show only partial object permanence. Piaget believed that infants stop searching because they think that the object no longer exists. Others offer different explanations: perhaps the infant gets "stuck" on one aspect, such as the location where the object disappeared (Flavell, 1985); perhaps it is a memory problem (Harris, 1983); or even that the infant has no other behaviors in his repertoire to call upon.

Stage 5: Tertiary Circular Reactions (12 to 18 Months)

The circular (repetitious) quality of the past continues, but the tertiary stage involves first experimentation and then variation. Entirely new ways of doing things are learned through *active* experimentation. This is variation on repetition. Alice Honig characterized this as the "What will happen if . . ." stage. It is a wonderful stage of experimentation. Toddlers manipulate and explore materials to solve problems. Toddlers repeat actions and modify their behavior to see what happens in this tertiary circular reaction stage. Problem-solving abilities develop, but involve trial and error rather than using forethought. Causal thinking is developing. Object permanence development continues. Toddlers will search in new places for hidden objects. They must still watch the object being hidden to look for it.

The toddler builds entirely new schemes during this stage. Mobility opens up new arenas for learning. As memory improves, children can learn from watching an event. With the advent of language, the toddler can and does ask questions.

The transition at 12 months is marked by a move from just intentional behavior to more systematic exploration and a more mature understanding of object permanence. Young toddlers use their entire repertoire of behavior to explore their environment. Frequently, the box is more intriguing than the new toy.

Stage 6: Beginning of Thought (18 to 24 Months)

This is a transitional stage between the sensorimotor and preoperational period. It is the stage of symbolic representation. Toddlers can now solve problems in their mind, without going through the actual external problem-solving process. They can mentally represent objects and actions and invent new means to get objects without using trial and error. They can imitate models that are not present; wave "bye bye" even if no one is waving back. She can imitate gestures she cannot see herself make, such as facial gestures like scrunching up her face. She can search without needing to see the objects hidden. Pretend play begins!

The transition at 18 months marks the shift in cognitive development from the sensorimotor orientation of infancy to the symbolic thinking that characterizes early childhood. Symbolic thinking allows the toddler to mentally represent, manipulate, and combine information, objects, and events. Growing memory skills allow the toddler to call upon his past experiences to solve present problems. The challenges of object permanence are conquered as toddlers know that objects exist whether they are hidden or removed.

Sensorimotor Period Themes

Piaget theorized that children's cognitive development could be analyzed by studying certain consistent themes that appear with developmental variation throughout the sensorimotor period. These themes include circular reactions, means-end behavior, object permanence, spatial relationships, causality, imitation, and schemes for relating to objects.

Circular reactions provided Piaget with a means of understanding how cognitive development is influenced by behavior, that is, how the infant makes sense out of new experiences, reorganizes them, and ultimately brings them under control (Gratch & Schatz, 1987). One way of viewing circular reactions is practice in skill development. From self-directed activity the infant increasingly uses circular reactions to explore and act upon the environment.

Means-end behavior involves the child's ability to understand and work through the problem-solving process. The process includes the ability to understand how to get what one wants. The means-end behavior slowly develops from a basic reflexive behavior to becoming a complex problem-solving process. The infant initially uses trial-and-error actions to solve problems such as how to get a square shape into the shape box. The infant is then finally able to mentally figure out a solution to a problem without having to actually complete the task.

Object permanence is the child's ability to know that objects and people exist even though the child is unable to see or hear them. Object permanence develops slowly. It develops from the child's being able to remember the existence of objects seen partially hidden and progressing to the ability to remember the existence of objects not in sight. The child then has a mental image of the object or person in his memory.

This sequence is one of the most challenged aspects of Piaget's theory. Scholars argue over different variables which may affect this process. Some feel that it may be the infant's perception, rather than cognition, that influences the results, or that whether the objects are stationary or moving influences the results (Bower, 1975). Others have focused on the relationship between what is hidden and what hides it (Dunst, Brooks, & Doxsey, 1982), and again others on events that are possible versus impossible (Spelke et al., 1992).

Other researchers have reached different explanations about why young infants fail search tasks (Baillargeon, 1994). These explanations relate to the infants' inability to manipulate objects. They also relate to refinements in the nature-nurture issue. Some researchers (Spelke, 1991) have proposed that infants are born with substantive beliefs or core principles about the physical world that guide their reasoning relative to the effects of principles such as force, penetrability, and continuity (conservation). Others believe that infants are equipped with more general learning mechanisms that allow them to make generalizations about the physical world. Baillargeon (1994), a proponent of the latter model, believes that young infants first form an all-or-none concept about a phenomenon and then slowly identify the details that relate to this phenomenon. To test this model, based on the knowledge that infants look at novel events longer than familiar events, infants are shown a possible and an impossible event. Because infants as young as 3 months look longer at the "impossible event," Baillargeon (1994) concluded that infants possess many of the same fundamental beliefs about objects as adults do. This research also challenges Piaget's ideas about infants' knowledge of the physical world and how it is acquired.

Another aspect of object permanence that has provoked a good deal of research is the particular search error that infants make when looking for objects that are out of sight or hidden. Some feel that the problem is one of memory; that is, the infant at this stage can remember that the object exists, but he cannot remember where, especially if there is a delay between the hiding and the search (Gratch et al., 1974). Other researchers see the problem in relationship to how infants code (or don't code) positions in space. It does appear that infants make fewer errors if the positions used are well separated in space and different covers are used to hide the objects (Bremner, 1994).

Overall, research confirms that initial indications of object permanence occur about 4 months and major improvements occur at approximately 8 and 12 months. It also seems clear that situational variables related to the objects them-selves—what they are covered with and where they are placed—and the response required of the infant influence infants' reactions.

Spatial relationships relate to the child's ability to recognize an object's posi-tion in space (where it is located) and to have a sense of where he is in relation to the object. Initially, the infant has no idea or notion of spatial relationships, but quickly begins to track objects and turn to sounds. He begins to be able to reach for objects, later quite accurately. As he gets older, tasks such as block-building, walking, and running develop and he gains a sense of where objects are in rela-tion to himself and the environment.

Causality is the child's recognition and understanding of the causes of events, and that specific behaviors can produce changes. Very young infants show no awareness that their behavior can cause anything. Later, the infant begins to understand that a given action can cause an event to occur; that is, shaking the rattle causes the noise.

Imitation is the ability of a child to "copy" either the gestural or verbal actions of another person. In the beginning, the infant is a gross imitator. He is not capa-ble of modeling very well, though he will try imitating actions. The very young infant can only imitate actions already in her motor schemes and which she can see herself produce. This level of early imitation is present until about 8 months. At that time the infant begins to imitate motor actions she cannot see herself make as well as new sounds. By 18 months, the toddler is capable of deferred imitation, that is, imitating an action seen in the past. The child may imitate a behavior on Wednesday that he saw on Monday but did not imitate at that time.

Piaget believes that imitative ability is part of cognitive development. He sees imitation as a way of learning new behaviors or knowledge. Once imitation has developed, he sees the process as primarily one of accommodation. When the infant imitates behaviors that are not part of his repertoire, first accommodation takes place, then adaptation.

In general, the research supports Piaget's position that children's ability to imi-tate is dependent on their cognitive skills and that imitation increases in fre-quency and becomes more detailed and exact over time. There is some contro-versy over whether newborns and very young infants can imitate unfamiliar acts. Very young infants cry more in response to the cries of other young infants than they do to cries of older infants, synthetic cries, cries of chimpanzees, or silence (Martin & Clark, 1982). Is this imitation? It is not clear. Some say yes, others no. A number of studies have investigated whether infants can imitate actions they cannot see before Stage 4. Most have used tongue protrusion or mouth opening, as the infant can perform those behaviors and yet not see them. Most researchers found that infants in Stage 2 could imitate tongue protrusions (Jacobson, 1979).

It may now occur to you to ask "So what? Who cares?" Why should we be so concerned about imitation or object permanence? Fundamentally, the issue is whether or not infants must construct their own reality, as Piaget believes, or

Although infants at 6 months can make funny faces, Piaget does not believe they can imitate these faces until about 8 months.

whether they are born with some innate knowledge. Additionally, developmental information about imitation and modeling has direct relevance to working with infants. Knowing that infants imitate behaviors that are at, or just above, their cognitive level facilitates developmentally appropriate planning.

Preoperational Period

Piaget sees a major change in cognitive functioning beginning about age 2. The toddler is no longer tied to a sensorimotor representation of the world. The child can now think using mental representations, or use symbols to represent the environment. In the process, words take on the form of signifiers of objects and events.

Piaget designated the second major developmental period the **preoperational period** (about 2 to 7 years). The most obvious transition to this period is the rapid acquisition of language (Beilin, 1992) which supports mental representation. Thoughts are egocentric, with symbolic imagery highly individualized. This egocentrism differs from the sensorimotor period. However, the child can not yet take a perspective other than his own, and assumes that everyone likes what she likes. Understanding of the concepts of past, present, and future begins to take shape. However, children have trouble seeing how steps of a project fit together to make a whole. They see each step of a process as separate. The child's play skills expand into more creative activities.

Although children in this preoperational period have advanced far above the sensorimotor-based learning of the previous period, their thought processes are still immature. Some of the significant changes that occur during this period are detailed below. Toddlers from 24 to 36 months are just emerging into this 5-year-long period. Consequently, many of the characteristics of the period will not be obvious in those toddlers.

Preoperational Period Themes

Like the sensorimotor period, the preoperational period also has themes that appear with developmental variation throughout the period. These themes include egocentrism, centration, irreversibility, transductive reasoning, and concept formation. Each of these themes are discussed here.

Egocentrism.   The child is not able to view things from another's perspective. Children's language reflects this egocentrism. Children seem to believe that others know what they are thinking and they leave out important pieces of information. On the other hand, they can't put themselves in another's place to figure out the strategies that someone else might use in a game or in problem solving.

Centration.   This concept typifies the ability to concentrate on only one attribute of an object at a time. To solve problems successfully, children must be able to attend to many attributes of an object at the same time. The preoperational child's centration in thinking does not allow her to think of multiple attributes simultaneously. If presented with a liquid in a tall narrow glass that is then poured into a short fat glass she will assume that the volume has changed even if she watched the pouring. She cannot see that the volume in one glass is both lower and wider. She will center on one attribute or the other. As a further example, suppose that a child is given 10 wooden blocks, 6 of which are yellow and 4 are red. She will probably be able to name the color of the blocks, and which color is most represented. However, having centered on the color, she could probably not answer whether there were more yellow blocks or wooden blocks. She cannot focus on the attributes of both color and type of material (wood).

Because young children focus on appearances, they may be frightened by people wearing Halloween costumes or who dress up as holiday or cartoon characters, even if they watch them put on the costume. They do not realize that someone can simultaneously be two things and they overwhelmingly center on visual appearance.

Irreversibility. The preoperational child is not aware that logical operations are reversible. She is not aware that the ball of clay made into a pancake can be "reversed" into the original ball of clay. The knowledge that shape does not affect mass, volume, and other qualities is called **conservation.** Conservation requires that a child focus on the transformation from state to state in relation to mass, length, number, volume, and area. Of these, number appears first but that is long after the child is 3 years old.

Transductive Reasoning. Logical reasoning requires the child to use both inductive (from specific to general) and deductive (from general to specific) reasoning. Transductive reasoning requires the child to recognize the stable commonalities of attributes despite perceptual changes.

Concept Formation. With the emergence of logical thought, the child's problem-solving and decision-making abilities change dramatically. She can put events and objects in some useful order. She begins to understand the concepts of class (animals) and subclass (dogs) and the relationship between these.

Conclusions About Piaget's Theory

Researchers today do not see Piaget's stages as being as "tidy" as he described, nor do they see the demarcations between stages as being so clear cut. There seem to be more shades of grey and variations on themes than Piaget acknowledged. The stages are a useful way of organizing information. They serve as "ideal types," but their qualitative significance is not as well documented as is the progression of development that they portray. Piaget was a pioneer whose work laid the foundation for later research. Today there are many studies with many variations to compare and contrast to his work. Researchers have taught young children to make distinctions that Piaget would have believed they were too young to make. Overall, however, it appears that Piaget's theory has generated a tremendous amount of interest and research in very young children.

Other Theories of Cognitive Development

There are a variety of other theories of cognitive development. Some theories focus solely on cognitive development, others are more general theories. Brief descriptions of other relevant theories follow.

Vygotsky's Theory

Lev Vygotsky was a Russian developmental psychologist who died prematurely in 1934. His successors have continued to develop his ideas, yet are not necessarily in agreement about how he would have continued (Meadows, 1993). His writings have only recently been translated into English.

Vygotsky's emphasis is different from Piaget's. Vygotsky's focuses on the social world and social interactions and language as the foundation for cognition (Berk, 1994). Social experiences are seen as shaping the child's way of thinking and interpreting the world. Language plays a critical role because that is how individuals communicate with each other and it is an indispensable tool for thought (Vygotsky, 1934 [trans. 1987]). Vygotsky sees adults dialoguing with children as the way in which higher forms of mental activity are constructed and transmitted (Berk, 1994).

Vygotsky distinguished three stages in cognitive development characterized by: preintellectual speech, preverbal thought, and the use of external symbolic means. He sees children under age 2 in a *primitive* stage of preintellectual speech where they use vocal activity as a means of attaining social contact and emotional expression. They can perform systematic and goal-directed activities which do not require verbal operations. *Practical intelligence* begins around 2 years of age as the child's language reflects syntactical and logical forms. The third stage sees the child beginning to use external symbolic means (such as language) to help with internal problem solving. Language can now be used to reflect and develop thought. Initially, language is used to express emotions and maintain social contact, then to communicate, to make reference, to represent ideas, and then to regulate one's own actions (Meadows, 1993). Children who talk to themselves are viewed as regulating and planning mental activities. What Piaget would consider "egocentric speech" Vygotsky would call "overt self-regulation." With age these verbalizations are replaced with inner speech which serves the same function but is no longer observable.

Vygotsky views language as a multifunctional medium. Language can focus on the relationship between signs (learned conventions such as words) and reality, and as a symbol system can analyze the relationship between signs (Deleau, 1993). Language serves a planning function and allows children to solve problems through speech and then carry out the activity. Through the interweaving of thought and language children move from a fragmentary use of a representational system to mastery of a representational system and sophisticated cognitive skills (Vygotsky, 1934 [trans. 1987]).

According to Vygotsky's theory, cognitive development occurs because of social interaction with more competent partners. This adult guidance, called **scaffolding,** facilitates learning. More mature partners who create a dialog with young children support the children's cognitive and language learning by expanding and extending their knowledge base (Meadows, 1993). The support provided by adults is most effective if the child can use the same strategies to solve similar problems himself (Berk, 1985). For example, if a toddler is trying to force a triangle into a form board, it is more useful to suggest he turn the triangle or try it in another place than it is to tell him that it is a triangle and does not go there.

Another important concept that Vygotsky has contributed to the field is his idea of a **zone of proximal development** (ZPD). This refers to the range of tasks that a child cannot yet accomplish alone but can accomplish with the help of adults or more competent peers (Vygotsky, 1987). Learning cycles then consist of zones of proximal development in different experiential domains. To find the ZPD, the adult must assess the child's abilities, plan activities which are slightly in advance of the child's development, and then provide the necessary scaffolding for the child to perform the task. As the child's competence increases, the adult takes less responsibility for the task and allows the child more, while at the same time introducing increasingly difficult tasks that require scaffolding.

Maturation Theory

The **maturation theory** was widely accepted in the United States until about the 1960s. Arnold Gesell and his colleagues were the major proponents of the theory. They believed that children are primarily influenced by their genetic inheritance and that environmental influences are secondary. Children are seen as moving from one stage to another based on their biological "readiness." Based on this theory, norms were developed about predictable stages of cognitive development. Gesell focused his theory on two critical characteristics: behaviors that are universal and occur as a function of age (Gesell, 1928). The theory fostered little interest in intervention.

Behavior Analysis

According to the **behavioral analysis** view of learning espoused by B. F. Skinner, learning occurs because children systematically interact with a structured environment and are rewarded or positively reinforced for their successful accomplishment of tasks. (Bijou, 1992; Morrison, 1988). This perspective suggests that adults need to plan the "right" environment for young children and should respond to children's desired or appropriate behaviors with immediate rewards. Responses that are rewarded will continue; those that are not will be extinguished.

Behavior analysis principles are used to analyze development during infancy. Bijou and Baer (1965) concluded that although infants are unique, the stage of infancy is universal. They also found that the changes that took place were similar for all children in a given culture. Based on that, they felt that personality structure began developing about age 2 and continued to age 5. Having singled out personality, they focused their analysis on exploratory behavior, curiosity, play, cognitive abilities, problem solving, intelligence, competence, and the roots of moral behavior (Bijou, 1992).

Bijou and Baer revised their theory in 1978 to focus more on the impact of the individual and his social, emotional, and affective interactions, with the concept of stimulus and response being viewed within the context of a person's interactional history. When an infant is creeping, a chair leg (stimulus) is an obstacle to go around (response). Later this chair leg (stimulus) might be something to pull up on (response), and still later the chair leg (stimulus) might be maneuvered when the chair is pulled into the table (response). Increasingly, they included factors relating to the setting in which behavior takes place as having an interactive impact on the stimulus-response sequence.

The principles of behavior analysis are used extensively in the study of infant perception, one aspect of cognition. Behavior analysis highlights the factors that each problem has a unique history and hence needs a unique solution tailored to the specific problem behavior. The goal is to assist individuals working with young children to use empirically based learning procedures to modify or change targeted behaviors. Applied behavior analysis is used extensively in working with young children with severe and profound disabilities.

Social Learning Theory

Social cognitivists also emphasize the impact that the environment (both physical and human) has on an individual's cognitive development (Bandura, 1992). Like behaviorists they see the person strongly shaped by individual experience. Genetic factors and neural maturation are considered important, but social cognitive theorists view humans as having vast potential, with behavioral outcomes being heavily influenced by the person's specific interactions with the environment.

Social-cognitive theory examines the interaction of external environment with behavior, cognitive, biological, and other internal events that can affect perceptions and actions. Each of these factors is seen as both acting on and reacting to each other component. Looking more closely at these interactions gives more insight into the cognitive development of infants and toddlers.

The social-cognitive approach focuses on people in the learning process. Bandura (1992) suggests that learning occurs through modeling, observation, vicarious reinforcement, and self-regulated behavior. Social-learning theorists differ from behavioral theorists in that the former believe in a motivational aspect to learning and that children will learn more if they are interested in what they are learning. In the behavioral perspective, the child's interest is not important. Behaviorists believe rewards for achievement determine learning, not the child's interest in the material.

What people think, believe, and feel influences how they act. Parental expectations about their new infant influence how they treat him. If they believe that toddlers need support in becoming autonomous individuals, they will behave in a way that provides time and activities to support independent behavior. People are both producers of and products of their environment (Bandura, 1992).

Information-Processing Models

The information-processing approach to cognitive development sees cognition as a matter of remembering information and organizing it to solve problems. Researchers focus on how information is selected, represented, stored, and retrieved. They view the human brain much as they might the central processing unit of a computer. They sometimes use computers to test their hypotheses (Meadows, 1993). They are intrigued with memory, both storage and control processes.

They are interested in the particular strategies that children use in relation to the demands of the task (Simon, 1981), in particular how young children encode and transform information in solving problems. Young children seem to have small and nonflexible repertoires of strategies for problem solving which they use somewhat randomly. Young children often remember familiar events as part of a sequence or script. They often have a "getting up" and a "going to bed" script. Very young children who don't have the language skills to explain these scripts can demonstrate them by using a doll. Two-year-olds can fill in missing words from favorite picture books and even correct tired adults who say crocodile instead of alligator. With increasing age, children begin to use deliberate strategic approaches to problems and increased flexibility in applying strategies. Knowledge bases too, increase with age (Meadows, 1993). Many of the cognitive tasks used by information-processing models have a Piagetian base (Case, 1985).

Theories of cognitive development seek to describe children's cognitive capabilities and limitations on a developmental continuum and explain how more advanced understanding grows out of less adequate comprehension. This chapter to this point has discussed how infants develop cognitively and has focused on the universals rather than on individual differences. Intelligence highlights the differences in cognitive development.

Intellectual Development

Most researchers make a distinction between cognition and intelligence. Cognition has to do with knowing, whereas intelligence is the use of knowledge. Cognition is the abstract concept; intelligence is what we measure. Confusion about the meaning of *intelligence* and cognition is compounded because different people use the word intelligence in different ways. Psychologists view intelligence as the biological foundation for cognitive functioning that is responsible for individual differences in intellectual competence. The public view of intelligence relates to how individuals conduct their affairs and solve problems in their life and achieve success in academic, cultural, and career pursuits. The third meaning of intelligence is what the tests measure, and what we usually refer to as IQ (Eysneck, 1986).

Tests can be designed to measure the first or second definitions of intelligence. The tests are very different. Cattell (1971) tried to distinguish between these two aspects of intelligence when he looked at "fluid" and "crystallized" intelligence. He saw crystallized intelligence as an individual's accumulated knowledge base from schooling and other learning experiences. Crystallized intelligence increases from infancy through adolescence, and depending on the intellectual challenges of an occupation, potentially through adulthood. Crystallized intelligence is measured through knowledge-based tests and vocabulary tests. Fluid intelligence is independent of education and cultural influences. It increases to adolescence but then remains constant. It is measured through such things as novel tasks, inductive reasoning, and the classification of squiggle shapes (Meadows, 1993).

Theories of Intellectual Development

The child development field has many different theoretical models of intellectual development. A common model relates to the contribution of heredity to intelligence. Some believe that intelligence is primarily inherited or genetic; others believe that the main contributors to intelligence are environmental; and again others emphasize an interaction between heredity and the environment. That is, genetics determines the upper and lower limits but the environment influences where in those limits an individual falls. Although the argument about the sources of intelligence is well known, it is important to realize that opinions held about the role of genetics and environmental influences on intelligence have a profound effect on the field of child development.

If intellectual development is a genetic unfolding process, then infants who are born full term and healthy should grow up to be healthy adults. If they do not, then it is our inability to detect a subtle genetic problem at birth. Likewise, if an infant is born with a genetic disability such as mental retardation, then there is little point in early intervention because the environment cannot overcome the genetically determined outcome. The genetic approach looks at heredity as setting a trajectory for intellectual development that is relatively uninfluenced by the environment.

The environmental view argues that the infant grows and changes in response to environmental factors. This view predicts that an infant who grows up in a functional family where he is loved and cared for and given good nutrition and a stimulating environment would have a very different life outcome from the same infant who grows up in a dysfunctional family which neglects the infant and presents an unstimulating environment.

Neither of these views places much emphasis on the infant as an individual. There is a debate about whether the infant is an active or passive player in his own intellectual development. Sameroff (1993), using Riegel's model, characterizes the passive infant–passive environment combination as the basis for learning theories that look at such factors as the frequency of stimuli that determine what an individual will "learn." The passive infant–active environment model is the foundation for the behavior modification approach. In this approach the environment is actively manipulated to obtain specific responses from the individual. The active infant–passive environment is most compatible with Piaget's view. The infant constructs knowledge based on experience. The active infant–active environment model is a transactional view in which there is interaction between the infant and the environment which influences both the infant and the environment. The infant is seen as changing over time. The process is continuous and dynamic. However, even though this is a dynamic process, major differences are found between young children who grow up in high-risk environments and those who do not. Sameroff (1993) concluded that environmental conditions limit or expand the opportunity for development and that infants need to be viewed in the context of their environment.

Measuring Infant Intelligence

How do we measure infant intelligence, and for what purpose? Infants are assessed to obtain information about whether or not an infant is developing normally and also to make predictions about how well infants will do intellectually later in life. However, before looking directly at infant assessment measures, it is important to look at general issues related to infant assessment.

History

One issue in measuring intelligence is defining it. Some researchers, for example Galton, believed that intelligence was a fixed inherited capacity. Later researchers like Spearman focused on general cognitive or intellectual ability and wanted to measure this "g" factor without contamination from different experience, knowledge, or education (Meadows, 1993). Other definitions of intelligence were related more closely to educational needs.

Much like Piaget influenced the way we view an infant's cognitive development, Alfred Binet influenced the way we assess intelligence. Binet was an experimental psychologist who worked in Paris with a colleague, Theodore Simon, to develop a test to identify children in the schools who were mentally retarded and could not profit from regular education. (Interestingly, Piaget also worked with Simon when he was in Paris. Binet had died by that time.) Binet believed that children who had normal intelligence and those who were mentally retarded shared the same trait of intelligence. He viewed intelligence as being measurable, and that scores measured a point on a continuum (Meadows, 1993). This assumption challenged the concept of fixed intelligence and presented the possibility that someone who was developing slowly at one point in time might be able to catch up. Likewise, someone who was very advanced might slow down.

Rather than defining intelligence in terms of sensory and motor abilities as his predecessors had, Binet defined intelligence relative to higher-order mental functions such as memory, comprehension, attention, judgment, and imagination (Teti & Gibbs, 1990). His definition has had a profound effect on the conceptualization of intelligence and on intelligence testing.

The test Binet and Simon developed was administered so that the least difficult items were given first, followed by increasingly more difficult items. The test gave an overall score called an intelligence quotient (IQ) and had standardized administration procedures. It also resulted in a mental age. If a child who was 36 months old took the test and answered correctly all of the items that the average child his age did, he would have a mental age (MA) that was the same as his chronological age (CA), in our example 36 months. The IQ was then based on the mathematical formula: $IQ = MA \div CA \times 100$. In this case, since the MA and CA are identical, the IQ is 100. If the MA were higher than the CA, then the child would have an IQ above 100; if the reverse were true, the IQ would be lower than 100.

Although the test was revised several times, the most well-known revision in English was done by Terman at Stanford University. He standardized the scale in the United States and used the intelligence quotient (IQ) as the index of test performance (Teti & Gibbs, 1990). In the United States, the test was (and is) known as the Stanford-Binet. Many intelligence tests have been standardized and patterned after this test. The Stanford-Binet was considered useful for children as young as age 3, up through adulthood. In the 1920s, researchers began looking for a test that could be used for younger children. Arnold Gessell at Yale, Mary

Shirley in Minnesota, and Nancy Bayley in California, all made important contributions to the development of such an infant assessment measure (Teti & Gibbs, 1990). Gesell and Bayley both developed tests that are still used today. The Cattell was developed as a downward extension of the Stanford-Binet.

Issues in Measuring Infant Intelligence

There are two major dimensions that relate to the accuracy of infant intelligence measurement; the first has to do with issues relating to the test itself, the second is the challenge of the infant herself. One reason for testing an infant is to determine whether or not there might be long-term problems that could respond to intervention. In this case, the concern is the test's ability to detect problems that have long-term negative outcomes. Infant intelligence tests do a good job identifying infants and toddlers with severe and profound developmental delays. They are not, however, very effective in identifying young children with mild to moderate delays.

One critical testing issue concerns the relationship between scores obtained on infant intelligence tests and intelligence tests given at a later age. This is a major problem. What we consider "intelligence" in infancy is not the same as "intelligence" in elementary school children or adults; that is, patterns of cognitive activities that constitute intelligence change at different ages (Meadows, 1993). Newer lines of thinking focus on infant alertness as shown in habituation tasks and attention as a predictor of intelligence test scores in early childhood (Bornstein & Sigman, 1986), and tests that use visual recognition memory (McColl & Carriger, 1993). These types of tasks tap basic cognitive abilities that underlie intelligence at any age. Because of the need to use longitudinal data to confirm this hypothesis, it will be a while before we know the results of this approach.

The Infant

The infant himself poses concerns about accurate testing. The mother is almost always present so that she is part of the testing process. Regardless of whether her role is active or passive, she may affect outcomes. Scheduling is also an issue. An infant may only have 1 to 2 hours of alert time in a day, which is obviously the ideal time for testing. At the very least, regular nap and feeding times should be avoided when testing. Flexibility is also a key ingredient. Because there is so little time, the examiner must be calm, gentle, and very efficient (Kamphaus, Dresden, & Kaufman, 1993).

Psychometric issues relate to the quality of measurement of intelligence or any other characteristics that are being measured. The question is how does one differentiate between "good" measures and "bad" ones? There are some basic characteristics about tests that determine the quality of the test regardless of what it is measuring.

Reliability and Validity

Reliability focuses on the consistency of a measure. One way of determining if a measure is reliable is to give it again and compare the results. If the measure is reliable, the results should be the same or very close to the same. The infant who obtains a developmental quotient of 100 on Tuesday should get the same score or one very close to it on Wednesday.

Validity is established when a test is measuring what it claims to measure, in other words, that it gives the information we want. In reality, tests do not have validity; rather, it is the use of the test that determines whether or not it is valid. Since there always are degrees of validity, the question really becomes whether or not there is enough validity for a particular use (Smith, 1990). There are many aspects to validity. With infants we are most concerned with predictive validity. Predictive validity tries to project the same or related characteristics in the future. We desire to know how infants will perform in the years to come and whether the problems we are seeking to solve will impact their future.

Reliability is related to validity. If you cannot consistently get the same results each time you measure something, it cannot be valid. Conversely, just because you can consistently measure something does not mean that it is valid.

Objectivity and Bias

Objectivity is important in looking at measures and who is using them. To the extent that the requirements of a specific measure are not adhered to and that subjective evaluations are used, a test is less valid and reliable. A related issue is **bias.** There is concern about individual bias in a testing situation and cultural bias in the test itself. If clean, attractive, cooperative, and highly verbal young children consistently score higher than children who are dirty, poorly dressed, shy, or disruptive, bias might be operating. Cultural bias can occur if all children taking a particular test have not had equal exposure to the material.

Norm-Referenced and Criterion-Referenced Measures

In norm-referenced measures, scores by an individual child are compared with scores by other children of the same age. Norm-referenced measures may be standardized or nonstandardized. When they are standardized, there are specific instructions relative to the administration and scoring of the measure. In standardized instruments, the "norm" for developmental quotients (DQ) is 100. Infants scoring more than 100 are considered developing faster than the "norm"; those with DQs less than 100 are developing slower than the "norm." The norm was established by testing and retesting thousands of infants. Norm-referenced tests are used to identify infants and toddlers with developmental delays. A concern with norm-referenced tests is that they may not accurately show the abilities of children with disabilities (Noonan & McCormick, 1993).

A criterion-referenced test relies on an absolute standard and provides information about the child's performance relative to a specific skill or activity. For programming purposes, criterion-referenced measures are usually more useful. It is more helpful to know whether to expect an infant can sit independently for five minutes or stack three cubes than it is to know that he has a developmental quotient of 110.

Types of Measures Used with Infants and Toddlers

The major reason that infants and toddlers are assessed is to identify those who are developmentally at risk. The three types of measures used in these assessments are: screening measures, norm-referenced measures, and criterion-referenced measures.

Screening measures such as the *Denver II* (Frankenburg & Dodds, 1990) are used to decide which children receive further testing and which ones do not. This is a crucial decision. There are two types of errors that can occur during the screening process: false positives and false negatives. Screening results that indicate children need additional testing, when in reality they do not, are considered false positives. Such results create overidentification, concern and stress in families and children, and a workload problem for professionals. False negatives occur when children who are at risk pass through the screening and are not identified for follow-up. This results in under-identification and hence lack of early intervention for infants and toddlers who could profit from early intervention. False negative results cause parents and professionals to assume that infants and toddlers are developing normally when in reality they are not. It also denies them access to early intervention programs from which they might benefit.

Standardized norm-referenced measures like *The Battelle Developmental Inventory* (BDI; Newborg et al., 1984) and *The Bayley Scales of Infant Development* (Bayley, 1993) often form the core of a diagnostic assessment. These measures are used to get an overall picture of the infant or toddler and to determine whether further, more specialized assessment is necessary. Given the lack of high-quality screening measures for young children, norm-referenced measures may also serve a screening purpose. These measures are standardized and require a trained examiner.

Criterion-referenced measures like the *Brigance Diagnostic Inventory of Early Development* (Brigance, 1991), the *Learning Accomplishment Profile—Diagnostic Edition* (LeMay, Griffin, & Sanford, 1978), and *The Hawaii Early Learning Profile* (Furuno et al., 1988), are often used after screening and diagnosis has been completed. These measures are useful in program planning and in measuring small increments of development. There are also assessments designed for particular populations that are difficult to test, such as infants and toddlers with motor or sensory impairments who may not be able to respond to standardized test items. Other assessment instruments look at particular areas of development or interaction patterns.

Delayed Cognitive Development

Delayed cognitive development is intellectual growth that does not follow the expected rate of cognitive development. Children with cognitive delays follow the same sequence of cognitive-skill acquisition as other children, but the rate of acquisition is slower. Also, these children will rarely reach the higher level of abstract thinking skills.

It is often difficult to identify infants and toddlers with delayed cognitive development, especially when these delays are mild. Other variables, such as speech and language delays, or lack of environmental stimulation, may adversely affect the test scores. Because of these identification problems, infants and toddlers who show delays in cognitive development are called developmentally delayed. This is a more tentative diagnosis than mental retardation and it does not carry the same impact. Since it focuses on the child's developmental rate, it leaves the possibility for alternative diagnoses, for example, learning disabilities.

Infants and toddlers with developmental delays have a slower rate of learning, poor memory skills, problems in abstract thinking, poor generalization skills, and lack of learning strategies (schemes). They may have a short attention span and sometimes be highly distractable. Language skills are also delayed as is the acquisition of basic daily-living or adaptive skills (for example, feeding, toilet training, and dressing). Children with more severe delays may lack social interaction skills, motivation, and a striving for independence.

Infants and toddlers exhibiting extremely delayed development or when there is a known cause or etiology may be diagnosed as mentally retarded. The American Association on Mental Deficiency has developed the most widely accepted definition of mental retardation:

> *Mental retardation* refers to substantial limitations in present functioning. It is characterized by significantly subaverage intellectual functioning, existing concurrently with related limitations in two or more of the following applicable adaptive skill areas: communication, self-care, home living, social skills, community use, self-direction, health and safety, functional academics, leisure, and work. Mental retardation manifests before age 18. (American Association on Mental Deficiency, 1992, 5)

Because of concerns about labeling per se and criticism of the assessment process, the Association explains the assumptions behind their definition and how it is to be applied.

1. Valid assessment considers cultural and linguistic diversity as well as differences in communication and behavior factors;

2. The existence of limitations in adaptive skills occurs within the context of community environments typical of the individual's age peers and is indexed to the person's individualized needs for supports;

3. Specific adaptive limitations often coexist with strengths in other adaptive skills or other personal capabilities; and

4. With appropriate supports over a sustained period, the life functioning of the person with mental retardation will generally improve. (American Association on Mental Deficiency, 1992, 5)

Changes in the definition and its application have moved the emphasis from just the IQ score to including concurrently existing limitations in adaptive skills. Although an IQ of 70 to 75 or below is considered subaverage, there is a consensus that additional measures should be used to verify these results and the results should be reviewed by a multidisciplinary team.

Sources of Cognitive Delays

The type and severity of a child's cognitive delay vary greatly, based on what is interfering with the development of cognition. Children with cognitive delays are not all the same. Each child's development is influenced by a multitude of factors, including the individuality of each child and the environment in which he lives. However, children with cognitive delays can be grouped according to the cause or factors associated with the delay:

- Brain or neurological problems. These include damage to the brain, malformation of the brain, absence of certain parts of the brain, as well as other neurological problems difficult to identify specifically.
- Medical syndromes. Some medical diagnoses have established risk for having cognitive delays. These include Down syndrome, certain genetic abnormalities, and metabolic disorders such as phenylketurnia (PKU).
- Unknown causes. These children usually demonstrate mild to moderate developmental delays and have no known etiology. Many of these children come from extremely impoverished environments, with a lack of adequate early stimulation. (Peterson, 1987)

It is not only the cause of the delay that affects the level of cognitive impairment, but the extent to which the child is able to interact with his surrounding environment and the type and quality of that environment (Connor, Williamson, & Siepp, 1978). For example, a child with a physical impairment who could not take part in early motor-learning activities, like shaking a rattle and mouthing, lacks vital early learning experiences to build on. Consequently the development of later, higher-level skills may be affected.

Cognitive Development and Program Planning

Your beliefs about how young children learn will influence how you interact with them and the expectations you have for them. Some people believe that learning is primarily a matter of maturation. According to the maturational perspective, based on the work of Arnold Gesell, children's development is biologically based and determined. Adults who support this philosophy would focus on providing a developmentally appropriate environment and expect that children would develop according to their innate abilities. Rather than rushing to develop skills, adults following this view would look for "readiness" signs from children that indicate that they are physically and behaviorally ready to perform more advanced tasks. If these signs are not apparent, the only antidote, according to the maturational perspective, is to wait until the child is ready.

Adults whose philosophy agrees with Piaget's cognitive-developmental perspective need to be aware of both children's innate abilities and stages of cognitive development and the quality of the environment available to the children. Teachers need to provide a stimulating environment in which children can learn by doing activities that interest them and match their level of adaptation.

When teachers plan developmentally appropriate environments, they can match children's individual needs by providing scaffolding for one child while encouraging others to explore independently.

Vygotsky's ideas contrast with Piaget's and would provide a different model for the basis of early care and education. Children would be in multi-age groupings; the teacher-child ratio would be approximately one to one; and teachers would have to have extensive training in detailed diagnosis of skills, what skills fall in the ZPD, and how to scaffold for and sensitively teach the required skills (Meadows, 1993). Teachers would engage in more dialogues with children and mixed age peer groups would be encouraged. Opportunities for play within a sociocultural context would be supported and encouraged (Berk, 1994).

Although the philosophies themselves are different, most caregivers develop an eclectic philosophy that incorporates aspects of several of the different theories. For example, if a caregiver uses Piaget as a guideline, she puts a favorite toy inside a hula hoop and encourages the child to pull the hoop. If the infant does not pull the hoop, she models the behavior and exclaims when the child gets the toy (social-learning theory). She again encourages the child to try; when he is successful, she rewards the behavior with a big hug (behavioral theory).

Summary

Infants come into the world seeing, hearing, feeling, tasting, and smelling, but it is not clear whether they come as a "blank slate" or they come "knowing," prewired to learn certain things. The child progresses from the involuntary motor responses of early infancy to the use of symbols and abstract thought in three years. There is disagreement about how and why these changes occur.

The work of Piaget focused on infant cognition and emphasized that cognitive development occurs in a recognizable, predictable progression with later development dependent on earlier stages of development. He believed that cognitive development begins at birth and is a function of sensorimotor interactions with the environment. Vygotsky's theory places greater importance on the role of language in cognitive development and social interaction.

Researchers make a distinction between cognition and intelligence. Some believe that intelligence is primarily genetic; others feel environmental factors are primarily determinant; and again others see that there is a strong interaction between heredity and the environment. More complex views take the infant's role more into account. Recognition of the importance of early experience and the role of the environment have led to the development of measures to assess infant intelligence. The hope is that early assessment can lead to timely and productive intervention. Some of the issues related to infant assessment include the infant herself, definition of intelligence, and the reliability and validity of the measures.

Three types of assessments are typically used with infants: screening measures, which help determine which children need further testing; norm-referenced measures, which compare the child's development to others of the same age; and criterion-referenced measures, which are useful in program planning and in measuring small increments of development. Assessments are used primarily to identify infants and toddlers with delayed development.

Delayed cognitive development does not follow the expected rate of cognitive development. Infants and toddlers with delayed cognitive development are called developmentally delayed. It is difficult to accurately identify very young children who are mildly delayed since each infant and toddler's development is influenced by a multitude of factors, including the individuality of each child and the environment in which he lives.

Although cognitive development has been the focus of this chapter, the use of symbols and the overlap with other areas of development, particularly language, influences cognitive development in a variety of ways.

Application Activities

1. Play with an infant who is about 8 months old and use Piaget's ideas about object permanence. Hide objects that interest the infant. Repeat this with both younger and older children. What conclusions did you reach about object permanence, age, and the usefulness of Piaget's theory?

2. Talk with a parent of a toddler. Ask the parent how intelligent they feel their child is and what behaviors they use to come to that conclusion.

3. Develop an item that might be part of an infant intelligence test. Write an operational definition for the item and procedures for carrying out the item. Ask a friend to give your item to an infant. Note whether the friend performed the task the way you had envisioned it. Repeat the item with revisions if necessary and then score the item. Did you and your friend agree on the results? If not, can you account for differences?

Chapter 8

Early Communication and Language Development

The first cry, the first word, the first sentence! The infant's ability to move from no language to an understanding of the complex rules of grammar in three short years has fascinated researchers. Some researchers think infants come prewired to learn language; others that it is simply a matter of maturation; others again feel children learn by imitating people in their environment; and still others hold that language is learned through basic social and emotional drives.

Language and Communication

Language refers to a system of intentional communication that is understandable to others. It traditionally consists of sounds, signs, and symbols. The infant can understand language long before he can use the formal language of his culture. Language involves a system that includes a set of acceptable rules whereby messages and ideas are transmitted between individuals. It refers specifically to the child's ability to comprehend and understand what is transmitted and the child's ability to express those messages and ideas in some acceptable and logical format.

Language can be divided into two general categories: receptive and expressive. **Receptive language** implies the ability to understand the meaning of the message. **Expressive language** is the ability to adequately and acceptably communicate messages in a way that others can understand them. There is agreement that comprehension, or receptive language, precedes the production of words and sentences, that is, expressive language. Because the relationship between understanding and production of language is somewhat asymmetrical, some feel that the bases for comprehension and production may by be different. There are three major components to expressive language: (a) **phonology,** the speech sound system; (b) **semantics,** (meaning associated with words and speech; and (c) **syntax,** the grammatical rule system for generating sentences (Tager-Flusberg, 1994).

Although there are language areas throughout the brain, there are two main areas that are involved in language: Broca's area and Wernicke's area. Broca's area for most people is located in the left hemisphere of the cerebral cortex near a motor cortex that controls the muscles of the tongue, throat, and face that are involved in speaking (Wilson, 1990). Damage to this area results in a disruption of the ability to speak (expressive aphasia). Individuals with this type of aphasia speak slowly and laboriously. However, their understanding of language is unimpaired. Wernicke's area is also located in the left hemisphere but it is close to the auditory cortex. It seems to be essential in understanding the relationship between words and their meanings. Damage to this area makes it difficult to comprehend ideas and to think of words to express thoughts although the speech itself is fluent.

Communication is a broader term that includes both speech and language and the many variables that make up the communication process. Communication involves giving and receiving information, signals, and messages. It involves not only the process of speaking, but includes such aspects as understanding simple to complex gestures, imitation of new sounds, awareness of subtle communication cues, and comprehending what has been said, to name just a few of the factors involved.

Communication is not limited to vocal expression. It involves a larger concept, including communicating ideas, wants, and needs through some mode: physical gestures, facial expressions, grunts, crying, words, and complex phrases. Individuals can communicate with other individuals who speak a different language, with individuals who are hearing impaired and have no speech, and with animals.

Theories of Language Development

Billions of children learn to talk. They learn the language spoken by their parents. The question is how do they do it? Interest in identifying universals in language acquisition goes back to the familiar nature–nurture issue. Do infants learn language by imitating adults or do they learn because they have an innate biological propensity to develop language?

Researchers have approached the issue of language and its acquisition from a variety of theoretical and research perspectives. Some have studied the acquisition of a second language; others have looked at it from an evolutionary perspective; and still others have looked at children born without some of the senses considered necessary for language acquisition. Many of the theories of cognitive development include language development.

Maturation Theory

Early studies of communications (1950s and before) used a normative, or maturational approach, supported by Gesell (1928). Researchers looked for patterns, or norms, by categorizing the sounds that infants made, counting the number of words children acquired, and looking at the length of sentences that children could utter in relation to their age. Later research, beginning in the 1960s, is more complex and concentrates more on the acquisition of language, the function of early communication, and the infant's ability to understand language.

Behaviorist Theory

Theorists supporting the behavioral model contend that infants learn language through the processes of imitation and reinforcement. These two processes together explain why children who are reared in homes where English is spoken learn to speak English, whereas those in Spanish-speaking homes learn to speak Spanish. Children utter some sounds and sound combinations through imitation and some are random. As adults reward, correct, ignore, or punish the young child's emerging language, they influence the quality and quantity of language as well as the child's attitude toward communication (Osgood, 1968).

The role of reinforcement is a generalized one. As infants coo and babble, adults reinforce sounds that are close to words. A sound sequence such as "mamama" is reinforced and becomes the word "mama." Sounds that are not reinforced fade into extinction. As children utter sounds that are closer to adults' words, they "shape" these sounds into words by reinforcing sounds that successively approximate words until they are true words. As utterances increase in length, imitation takes a more important role in the process.

It is not as obvious from this theoretical approach why young children use words in ways that adults do not. For example, toddlers say "Me go," "Mommy car," and "Sit chair" which they probably have not heard even in the simplified language that adults often use with young children. Most scholars feel that this behavioral approach is too simplistic to explain language development (Chomsky, 1959).

Nativist Theory

As with cognition, a major goal of some researchers was to identify the "universals" that characterize language acquisition for all languages and all children (Thal & Bates, 1990). Identification of invariant universals across languages would support the theory that there was some kind of innate, unitary "language acquisition device," or LAD (Chomsky, 1968). Chomsky hypothesized that individuals have a predisposition to learn language and that this LAD has sets of language system rules (grammar) for all languages. Not finding universals would bring this "innateness" into question. Support for this position uses the fact that infants babble sounds and noises used in languages they have never heard. According to Kuhl, between birth and four months infants are capable of distinguishing each of the 150 sounds made in all human speech (Grunwald, 1993). Two-year-olds can utter complex yet understandable sentences they have never heard.

To the extent that the "normal" patterns for language acquisition are variable, it makes it more difficult to identify and predict atypical patterns. It also brings into question the "norms" that we have in language development and requires that we consider a broader range of age norms and styles of acquisition than was previously accepted (Baron, 1992).

Thal and Bates (1990) argue against the position that innateness and universals necessarily go together. They feel that variation is endemic in nature and that lack of variation in language development would bring "innateness" into question. They hypothesize that individual differences in the rate at which subcomponents of language ability develop support the position that language processing involves a number of different component processes, which can apparently develop at different times. Differences in rates or individual variations in language acquisition do not mean that language is not innate.

Psycholinguistic theory holds that there is an inborn tendency for children to learn what Chomsky (1990) refers to as the "deep structure of grammar," which is universal for both children and languages. This deep structure consists of the rules for transforming ideas into sentences. The surface structure differs with the language itself as well as the person speaking it. The surface structure focuses on vocabulary and grammar.

Research to date has found variation in patterns both within and among infants and languages. Some of this variation seems to be related to the structural differences among natural languages. However, within the same language group there are also different patterns of language acquisition. For example, Thal and her colleagues found great variation in the period when infants began to talk. However, comprehension appeared to be equal between early and late talkers (Thal, Tobias, & Morrison, 1991).

Interrelationships among Language, Cognitive, Social, and Emotional Development

Researchers tend to study language separately from cognitive, social, and emotional development because of procedural, philosophical, and practical problems (Bloom, 1993). Nevertheless, it appears that they are related. Language is no longer seen as an isolated domain that develops independently of cognitive development. Many of the biological markers discussed in cognitive development are reflected in language development. Language represents our thoughts, yet also shapes and directs our thinking (Honig 1982). Social interaction is viewed as an important factor in language development. Emotional development is a motivator for language development, just as emotional expression is one of the first uses of language.

Researchers primarily interested in cognition focus on language as a way of finding out about a child's knowledge or how young children attach the forms of language to what they know about the objects, events, and relationships in their world (mapping). They are also interested in the developmental changes in thought processes that make the acquisition of knowledge possible, primarily symbolic capacity for representational thought (Bloom, 1993).

Vygotsky's theory of development relies heavily on language acquisition as the impetus for development of more complex cognitive and social interaction.

He found that when children encountered obstacles and cognitive difficulties in tasks, their incidence of egocentric speech almost doubled (Vygotsky, 1962).

Language is a transactional process. Individual differences in language development appear to be related to cognitive development. Language, then, may be best viewed as a "window on the mind" (Thal & Bates, 1990, 379). Language is a reflection of cognitive development as well as a communication device. Language is a tool. It allows the child to express her private world, to influence other people, and to get things done (Bloom, 1993).

Characteristics of Human Language

Fromkin and Rodman (1974) have pointed out four characteristics of human language that are not part of the communication systems of other animals: creativity (or generativity), arbitrariness, displacement, and discreteness.

Creativity, or **generativity,** determines the arrangements and rearrangements of parts of language (sounds, words, and sentences) to create new meanings. "Pat" has a very different meaning from "tap," and "Paige called her mother" has a very different meaning from "Her mother called Paige." **Arbitrariness** in language relates to which words stand for which objects or events. Although onomatopoeia, the formation of a word by imitating the natural sound of an event or object (such as tinkle or buzz), adds interest to speaking and writing, it does not alter the arbitrary nature of words.

The concept of *displacement* in the language of humans allows us to refer to things occurring in different time frames and other places. Language can be used to refer to events that have happened in the past, might happen in the future, and might be here or elsewhere. Language parts can be separated into *discrete units* such as sounds, words, or sentences. We often use these units to analyze language development. **Phonemes** are the smallest units of sound that distinguish one utterance from another. They are usually letter sounds. For example, the meanings of *h*at and *c*at are distinguished by the phonemes /h/ and /c/. Morphemes are the smallest units of a language that contain meaning. They are usually words or meaningful word parts. **Morphemes** are words as well as the prefixes and suffixes attached to words ("block" is one morpheme, but "blocks" is two). The **mean length of utterance** (MLU) measures the number of morphemes, or units of meaning. It is a useful and frequently used measure of language acquisition.

Prerequisites for Communication

Infants can communicate from birth, but their ability to use language grows gradually. Its initial foundation is in play. The first games that infants play with adults help them to focus on sounds, gestures, facial expressions, imitation, and turn taking. It is enhanced by adults who respond to infants' communication long before it is goal directed.

Three elements must be present before children use words or gestures to refer to objects: intentionality, reference, and convention (Bates, O'Connell, & Shore, 1987).

Intentionality in infants is signaling behavior that suggests that the infant knows something about the communicative process. It appears at about 9 months of age. Intentionality is difficult to capture because there is a fair amount of interpretation on the part of the adult. For example, a 7-month-old infant who wants a cookie looks directly at the cookie. A 9-month-old infant gazes alternately between the cookie (the desired object) and an adult, as though she expects the adult to help her attain the object. We interpret this latter behavior as intentionality. Appeals may be made directly to an adult for help rather than the object itself if it is unattainable. If an infant is not successful in attaining her goal, she may repeat the action or modify it in some way until it is attained or there is an indication that the adult will comply.

Referential communication refers to the relationship between objects or events and words. Initially, the young child playing with a toy may show it to an adult. Over time, and often with the support of adult comments and labeling, the infant then gives the toy to the adult. This showing and giving behavior is seen as the infant's working through the principles of referential communication. This sequence is followed by pointing (at about 9 or 10 months) at objects; naming them follows several months later.

Convention is an aspect of arbitrariness (Fromkin & Rodman, 1974) that refers to shared, ritualized, arbitrary behavior that conveys meaning. There is no intuitive link between the word *red* and the color red. But when you talk about a red object, there is a "conventional" understanding of the color of the object. At about 10 months, the infant begins to imitate new sounds and gestures. Imitation becomes a method of learning new conventional behavior. At this time some traditional behaviors also become ritualized such as "bye bye," "peek-a-boo," "soooo-big," and others. Children will frequently perform these behaviors on request, initially with physical support but eventually with just verbal requests. The joint processes of imitation and routinization are necessary for the acquisition of cultural conventions (Bates, O'Connell, & Shore, 1987).

Many changes occur in the infant's language development at about 9 or 10 months. Many researchers feel these changes are tied to concomitant changes in cognitive development. Cognitively, children are mastering means-end behavior and object permanence. Simultaneously, their memory skills are improving. These changes set the stage for understanding the symbolic function of naming.

The infant faces some enormous tasks in deciphering language. First she must determine what the meaningful units in an utterance (morphemes) are, then the meaning of units when they are used in combination (grammar). For example, she must relate the word *ball* to the object ball, and then *get ball* to the action of retrieving the ball.

Biological Prerequisites for Speech and Language

We don't expect newborns to walk. Visual inspection of the infant's legs leads us to the conclusion that he is not physically able to walk. Biologically, the newborn is no more ready to talk than walk, but the parts of the body that must mature for talking are less visible. A newborn's vocal apparatus is not just smaller than an adult's, it is also different in that the relative placement of the components does not allow the sounds necessary for speech.

The newborn's tongue is short and broad. It is contained within the oral cavity, whereas the back third of an adult's tongue is in the throat. The newborn's **hard palate** (front part of the roof of the mouth) is also broad and wide, unlike the arched palate of adults. The most critical differences are in the **larynx** (voice box), which is located just below the bottom of the oral cavity, and the **pharynx.** The pharynx goes from the mouth and nasal passages to the larynx and esophagus. This positioning allows the infant to breathe and swallow at the same time (which adults cannot do). Although the arrangement is useful for nursing infants, it makes it impossible to articulate some sounds used in speech (Baron, 1992). With growth, the child's vocal tract gradually looks more like an adults, until finally the child is capable of accurately pronouncing all the sounds in the English language.

The configuration of the nonhuman primate's vocal tract is very similar to an infant's, which is one reason why researchers could not teach chimpanzees to talk. The incomplete maturation of the vocal tract influences children's ability to articulate sounds until about age 6 when maturation is complete. Infants born prematurely will show delays in some areas of speech due to delayed maturation of the vocal apparatus.

An additional area where maturation affects language is the central nervous system itself. Verbal abilities are primarily centered in the left hemisphere of the brain. The key issue here is the lateralization of the brain. With maturation the brain becomes more differentiated and the hemispheres more specialized. Lateralization apparently begins at birth and takes about 10 to 12 years to complete. The greatest changes in lateralization take place early in life and probably influence language development. However, exactly how this happens is not known (Baron, 1992). Children who have injuries to the left hemisphere of their brain before this process is complete recover some of their ability to speak, whereas adults having the same injury do not. Because of brain development, linguistic theorists feel that the period from about 18 months until puberty is a sensitive period for language learning.

Early Communication

There is no doubt that the infant's first verbal communication is the cry and that this is the most frequent form of vocalization for about the first six months of life. Early crying vocalizations seem to be related to the infant's physiological state, in other words, comfort or discomfort. With increasing time, these vocalizations begin to be more like communication. Although there are many ways of studying the development of communication, a chronological approach seems to make the most sense. Looking at major milestones creates some logical divisions: early vocalizations, first words, first phrases, and development of grammar (Bates, O'Connell, & Shore, 1987). Despite variations in the timing of language acquisition, there are major language milestones that predictably occur. However, different researchers find different stages and ways of dividing these stages (Brown, 1973; McLean, 1990).

Early Vocalizations (0 to 10 Months)

There is much preparation for speech before the first word is uttered. The young infant attempts to communicate discomfort, displeasure, and contentment. Early communicative acts are primarily reflexive in nature or used to express basic bodily needs or states, such as hunger or pain. No specific words are used to express needs or wants.

During the first few weeks infants primarily cry and make "vegetative noises." At about 2 to 3 months, cooing and laughing are added to the infant's repertoire. Contentment produces coos and vowel sounds. Discontentment produces crying.

Are babies' cries different depending on whether they are hungry, wet, or unhappy? The jury is out. Maybe some infants do have different cries, but it is also possible that adults read meaning into cries that is not really there. For example, if an infant cries about the time he is expected to be fed and stops crying when he sees the bottle, we are likely to conclude it was a hungry cry. This conclusion might be more in response to context than to the crying itself. When researchers have studied crying they have not found differences in crying based on pain or hunger. In one experiment, they played tapes of infants crying and asked adults to predict why the infant was crying. Adults could not predictably differentiate among the cries. However, as part of their controls they had kept the length and intensity of the crying constant. It may be that the length of crying and a pattern of growing intensity are relevant signals for parents that were not part of the experimental conditions (Baron, 1992).

From birth until about 2 to 3 months, the infant's communication consists of reflexive reactions to internal and external stimuli. The caregiver responds to these signals or cues by increasing or decreasing stimulation, and talking to the infant in "motherese." **Motherese** is a universal language adaptation where sentences are short, speech is slow, high pitched, and exaggerated. The infant in turn reacts to the tone of voice and facial expression by producing more consistent signals, and calibrating his states or moods (McLean, 1990).

At about 2 to 3 months, infants become more purposeful in their actions and signaling. Infant cooing and laughing, which begins at about 2 months, is very pleasurable to adults. Researchers disagree about whether early cooing, once thought of as the prelinguistic phase, is in fact related to the development of language, the linguistic phase. The /ku/ (coo) and /gu/ (goo) sounds are physiologically very easy-to-produce sounds from the back of the throat. Even those who feel cooing is related to early communication have not delineated the role it plays in the development of language. This vocal play may be a transitional stage before babbling begins (Tager-Flusberg, 1994).

At about 2 months, both the cries and other verbalizations start to take on the structure of human speech and by about 3 months there are patterned vocalizations that are vowel-like, such as /ah/, /ee/, and so on (Stark, 1986). By about 4 months babbling comes in. These babbling sounds are produced when the infant is happy. They continue to be internal-state responses and do not need stimulation to be present, since even infants with profound hearing losses babble. About this time infants also get the idea of turn-taking in communications: The adult speaks and then pauses; the infant vocalizes and waits; and then the adult speaks again. These become "conversations" between adults and infants. As the infant's vocalization sounds more like communication, sensitive adults respond to this cue and begin the turn-taking process.

Infants appear to interpret the intonation contours of adult speech accurately by about 4 months as well. Infants are now upset by angry voices and soothed by friendly ones. Around the 5th month infant utterances seem to take on the intonation and speech patterns of their native language (Bates, O'Connell, & Shore 1987). And infants now yell, squeal, and have more of a variety in their repertoire of vocalizations.

At about 6 months infant babbling makes a significant change to canonical, or reduplicated, babbling. **Canonical babbling** is the systematic pairing of a consonant and vowel ("ma" or "dah") and then the repetition of that sound ("ma-mama"). Different than spontaneous babbling, the infants seem to find pleasure in recreating sounds they have heard themselves make like the repetition of the circular reactions noted in cognitive development. The initial consonant sounds used are those most easily produced including /m/, /d/, /b/, and /g/. These sounds are easily produced by simple oral-motor manipulation. Eventually, the child develops the ability to voluntarily produce sound-blend combinations—/ma/, /ba/, /ge/, /ga/, /da/, and so on.

Parents typically notice this change in babbling and may think that the infant's babbling is associated with words. This is unlikely; however, it is still an enjoyable thought. Infants will repeat over and over the sounds they find pleasing. Infants who cannot hear do not develop canonical babbling. Babbling has no meaning, but it does provide verbal exercise and exploration. It is verbal play at

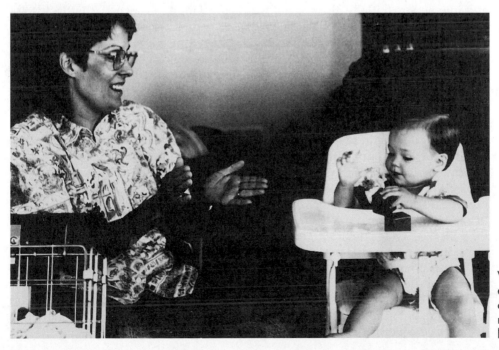

When infants' attempts at communication are reinforced, they are likely to increase.

its finest. It is also a way of making social contact and expands the earlier turn-taking into longer conversations.

The infant's sounds progressively become more refined. He begins to repeat sounds heard in the environment. He copies sounds and begins to experiment more with rhythm and inflection. About 8 months, babbling goes through another phase called **variegated babbling,** where the infant varies the consonant vowel pattern (dah-de, ba-be).

As with motor development, infants have much variation in their babbling. Infants vary in the amount they babble, the variety of sounds they babble, and the amount of time they babble. Some cease babbling when they begin to speak (about 12 months), others babble until they are 2 years old. It appears that the sounds of late babbling do become the sounds of early speech (Baron, 1992).

First Words (10 to 16 Months)

The infant now begins to make purposeful gestures and sounds to obtain wants, to comment on some event or object, and to answer simple questions. He also imitates adult speech.

However, deciding when a "first" word occurs is almost as difficult as deciding when the "first" step takes place. First words are usually double syllables and consist of easily made sounds using the consonants /m/, /b/, /d/, and vowel sounds. The words typically include mama, dada, bye-bye, and so on. Many of the earlier "words" spoken by the infant were not words at all, only blends of sounds. However, they were approximations of real words like "mama" or "ba-ba" that resulted in attention given to the child, with accompanying stimulation and interaction. Initially, there is not word association, but eventually the idea of a relationship between word and object develops. In most instances, the child learns the meaning of the word before he begins to use it while communicating.

Comprehension of words (receptive language) begins before the production of words (expressive language). Comprehension and production are quite different processes. Comprehension requires that speech-sound sequences be related to objects or events, whereas production requires retrieving from memory and articulating a sound sequence that relates to these object or events. Around 10 months, infants begin to respond predictably to some words. The first of these are traditionally the infant's name and "no."

Why "no"? Why not "yes"? One reason is that children are likely to be told "no" far more frequently than "yes." One role of adults is to protect the new investigator from harm. This may require many no's which one hopes are followed by suggestions of what can be safely done. Additionally, the /n/ is far easier than the /y/ for the infant to say.

As infants show understanding of language, many adults begin to point out and name objects as infants interact with them, "Look, that's your ball" or "Here comes Daddy." If the infant responds with "Dah" or "DaDa" a word is born. It is reinforced by excitement and requests to say it again. "That's right, you said Daddy. I'm going to give you a big hug!" When it becomes a word for an infant, and what the word really means to him, is unknown.

The child continues to use single words but also engages in vocal activity where the sounds resemble connected speech but are not real words. This is called *jargon*. The child uses adult rhythm and inflection in the expression. A real word or two may be discernible within the context of the jargon, but it is largely a connection of vocal sounds, with meaning only to the child.

As infants acquire words, it is interesting to speculate how and why some words become part of the young child's vocabulary and others do not. Bloom (1993) gives three principles that govern what words are learned. The first principle is that of *relevance*—children learn words pertaining to objects or actions that have meaning to them. First words are often nouns and are the names of objects that children act upon such as *ball* and *shoe* (Genishi, 1988). Initially, children seem to move from action, to concept, to words. Some young children place the most relevance on objects (nouns), whereas others learn words that help them initiate or maintain social interactions such as greetings (Nelson, 1973). What children are learning, however, is not just words, but the mental representation of what the words are about.

The second principle, *discrepancy*, has to do with the difference between the world as it is and the world as the child wants it to be. To the extent that the child wants something, it creates the demand for language. The third principle, *elaboration*, reflects the increasing complexity of the child's world. With his increasing knowledge he needs increasingly complex words and structures to express these ideas (Bloom, 1993).

Some sounds are difficult for toddlers. The placement of the lips in /b/ and /p/ is clear. It is far less clear how far apart the lips should be to produce the /y/ sound. Some sounds are universally difficult because of the needed position and coordination of the mouth, tongue, lips, and breath. Other sounds are difficult because of their position in words or the length of the word itself.

Emerging speakers use a variety of strategies in coping with words that are difficult for them to say. Sometimes they just lop off syllables. "Banana" may become "nana." Other times they replace difficult sounds with easier ones; "wawa" for "water." Toddlers are not bound by the convention of labels we use. They will sometimes make up names for items if they don't know the name or it is difficult. They may use sound as a clue. A vacuum cleaner may be a throaty "vooom" in imitation of the noise of the vacuum cleaner.

Toddlers learn words for what they know personally: the people in their lives, their possessions, and events they participate in. They seem to learn words about events that change and motion verbs that are associated with change such as "go" and "stop." These may be some of the earliest words that are linked together as in "car go." Certain adjectives such as "more" are also useful to toddlers (Baron, 1992). As children learn new words, they often make two words into one, such as "moo-cow."

As interesting as the words that toddlers use are, the context in which they are used and the multifunction of the words are even more intriguing. Initially toddlers are restrictive in their use of words. Toddlers sometimes refuse to generalize. This is called **underextension.** The label "book" refers to one and only one book. Other books must have another label. Later, children's overextension or overgeneralize is sometimes the most revealing aspect of their cognitive classification system. An interesting example is a poster of a toddler petting a collie dog saying "nice kitty, nice kitty." For her, everything that was furry and had four legs was "kitty." For most adults this is a humorous example of overextension. Parents find it less humorous when all men are called "Daddy" and all women "Mommy." Yet these are similar situations of overextension.

Sometimes toddlers are confronted with dilemmas over labeling. One toddler had a favorite blanket that she called, appropriately, "favorite." As she became attached to another blanket, the adults in her world joked about an appropriate label for the *other* blanket suggesting "Favorite II." She ended the appropriate label discussion by simply calling the *other* blanket "*other*." Another toddler, after being told what a whopper of a doll she had, named the doll "whopper."

We are curious about how many words toddlers know. Our interest in this focuses on counting the number of words. Yet, achieving an accurate word count is extremely difficult. Does the toddler stroking the collie know "kitty?" Does the toddler who labeled her blankets "favorite" and "other" know those words? What do you do about "wawa" and "vooom"? If you wonder why there is so much variation in the reported range of words that we think children know at young ages, it is because researchers make different decisions about what to count. In addition, some words children know are transient. The toddler vacationing at the beach learns the word "crab"; two months later the child may no longer remember the word.

Single words that are used to express complex thoughts are called *holophrases*. Their interpretation leaves a lot to the adult's imagination. The word "favorite" may mean "This is my favorite," "I want favorite," or any of a variety of other meanings. The words themselves may be augmented by gestures as context may help in interpretation. Toddlers frequently become very frustrated when adults do not interpret their phrases accurately.

Stringing Words Together (14 Months to 28 Months)

Around the 14th to 18th month, the child begins to experiment with new sound blends, using sounds heard in the environment, combining them, and producing new words. As children transition into two-word utterances, the word order is not fixed. A child may say "little doll" or "doll little" and the words themselves may not be related. Toddlers put two single words together, without the intention of word combination, "cookie— —mommy." Gradually this is followed by two-word utterances that do relate, "Fall down." Utterances that leave out many words are often referred to as **telegraphic speech.** Early two-word phrases tend to request: "Mommy come?" "Daddy ball," "Want juice." With the few words that toddlers can put together they can convey an amazing amount of information. Typically the adult has little difficulty understanding the meaning of the utterances. Toddlers have a small group of functional words that are used frequently. These pivotal words frequently include "no," "more," "mine," "go," "all gone" (Machado, 1990).

Like other developmental areas, growth in language is asynchronous. Language development has intermittent spurts and these spurts vary with individual children. Toddlers around 15 months frequently experience such a developmental burst. Some have this burst as young as 10 months, others as late as 20 months (Cawlfield, 1992). During this language burst, the toddlers show a decreased interest in toys and playing independently and an increased interest in the primary caregiver. They are interested in books and labeling objects in pictures. They attempt to say words and concentrate on watching the adult's mouth. This period usually lasts about four months. The culmination seems to be the emergence of symbolic thinking, along with increased interest in toys and a longer attention span (Cawlfield, 1992).

The toddler's vocabulary is increasing. New words are learned quickly, though the correct pronunciation is not necessarily acquired during the initial stages. The toddler begins to enter into simple conversations and initiate communication with another peer or adult. Communication expands to two-, three-, and four-word utterances. These may contain nouns and verbs, and even adjectives. However, the toddler's speech may not be fully intelligible. Practice helps the development of the child's expressive skills. He needs adult support for this burst of language and continued support as he uses this language with peers and in his play.

Grammar (24 Months to 36 Months)

Throughout the second year, vocabulary increases dramatically, fluency progresses, and grammar and syntactic skills improve. The toddler uses many new consonants. However, the most interesting aspect of language now is how children learn the structure of language. We know a lot about how children learn grammar from the mistakes that children make using irregular verbs and plurals.

Children begin to use the past tense around 2 years. They sort out some of the rules, such as adding "ed." You are likely to hear the child say "I goed home," "I blowed hard," and "I weared it today." This is a delightful stage as it is clear by these mistakes that young children have generalized the rules of the language. Initially, they may use some irregular verbs correctly out of imitation. They have similar problems with irregular plurals that they do with irregular tenses: "Look at the mans." Word placement is a challenge, particularly with negations. "Why you aren't coming?" Some of the creativity is delightful as children grope to express themselves and become master "wordsmiths."

As toddlers grow in their ability to use language, the interaction of cognition and language is apparent. The 2-year-old who approaches the stove and says to himself "Don't touch" is using language to guide his behavior. This "private" speech emerges shortly after social speech and provides the 2-year-old with both practice and pleasure. By the end of the preschool years, although private speech still exists, he doesn't need to say the words aloud (Machado, 1990).

Adult Speaking Adaptations for Infants and Toddlers

Most adults modify their speech when talking with infants and toddlers. Although they do it in idiosyncratic ways, there tend to be predictable principles that they follow in these modifications. Baron (1992) has categorized the following modifications.

Sound.   Adults pitch their voice higher, speak both louder and slower (commonly called "motherese"), and enunciate more clearly when talking with infants. They also use a greater range of frequencies and more animation. When they talk to toddlers, they may use an unusual pattern of emphasis (Yes, that is **Sam's** truck.). They may use unusual pronunciation of words (Sooo big) or they may echo a toddler's incorrect pronunciation. Thus adults might echo a toddler's assertion that her sister played the "fa-lute." When mispronunciations are humorous, the attention they get is reinforcing.

Meaning.   When talking with toddlers, adults frequently use diminutives such as kitty, doggie, bunny, and so on, and substitute words such as *choo choo* for *train*. They may use nonstandard combinations such as "choo choo train" and "moo cow" or use the words that the toddler has made up: "I have to get the vooom and clean this up." They frequently generalize in trying to make concepts easier for children to understand.

Grammar.   Adults typically both shorten and simplify their utterances. They also frequently use nouns and pronouns in unusual ways. Instead of saying "I'll do it," they may say "Mommy do it." They may use plural pronouns instead of singular ones: "Let's eat up all our dinner." They may even purposefully misuse grammar, such as telling a combative child, "no hit!"

Conversations.   Adult conversations with young children generally relate to the immediate present and the child's immediate surroundings. Many conversations involve adults pointing out and naming items for toddlers. They also ask toddlers many simple questions. They may provide both the question and the answer "Are you hungry? (and when the toddler makes a positive signal) Why yes, I can see that you are." Adults also repeat, expand, and extend toddler's utterances. A toddler's request for "More" might be responded to with "Do you want more milk?"

Many of these practices are useful for young children. Problems occur when adults continue with these speech patterns when they are no longer necessary or useful. For the young toddler all "fish-like" creatures might be referred to as "fishes." However, between 2 and 3 years children are ready to learn about minnows, whales, and dolphins.

Sources of Variation in Language Development

Not all children learn the same "language." Learning language is complicated by a number of variables such as the intelligence and personality of the child himself and the situation of the family in which he lives. Family factors include whether the child is a first, later, or only child; how responsive the family is to his verbalizations; and the family's beliefs about how children are reared.

Families in which language is supported and books are introduced at an early age are likely to have children who become eager readers.

Families

As children are different, so are families. They have different expectations for their children and different ideas about their role in language development. Some families think children basically learn to talk on their own, and they are responsive to the child but do little initiating. Other families make more conscious efforts to stimulate language by pointing out and naming objects and reading to young children.

Adults provide most of the modeling and examples for young language learners. Parents who respond to a toddler's communicative attempts support and encourage these attempts. When adults do not respond to a toddler's sounds and gestures, they send a message that communication behaviors are not important. It is important that the toddler's communicative efforts be responded to so they continue to communicate with the world around them. Lack of reinforcement extinguishes behavior. Adult interaction is necessary for the development of the child's language abilities.

Parents are rarely the cause of delayed language, but they, as well as teachers, can often help children develop good language. Some types of adult speech, such as asking divergent questions and showing approval of children's attempts at communication, are conducive to language development. Convergent questions that can be answered with a "yes" or "no" are less likely to stimulate representational abilities and constructive thinking (Honig, 1982), whereas making disparaging remarks about children's language has negative effects on children's language development. Focusing on their deficits and not allowing children time to respond reduces children's self-esteem as well as their language output (Dumtschin, 1988). Modeling grammatically correct speech, asking open-ended questions, recasting, and expanding their statements, all encourage language development.

Position in the Family

Infant language development varies with the infant's position in the family, the educational level of the mother, amount of reading and television watching, and other variables. As children begin to use identifiable words, they appear to take one of two approaches in learning additional words: a referential approach, or an expressive approach (Baron, 1992). First children, especially those from middle-class homes, usually have a referential approach. These children often use words early (9 to 10 months) and generally the words refer to objects or people in their immediate surroundings. Other children begin talking a little later (12 to 14 months) and have more diverse utterances of an expressive style, such as a version of "please" or "thank you." They tend to add to their vocabulary more slowly.

The child's style may reflect the parent's style. If the mother names objects for the infant, the infant will probably learn the names of objects. The presence of other children mediates the language that mothers use with infants. Older children are more likely to answer questions posed and "take over" experiences than younger children. With other children in the home, the mother may focus on having children play together in harmony and, in an effort to request similar things of both older and younger children, may make more socialization requests. It is not clear how children who spend time in child care are influenced.

Gender

In general, adults talk to boys differently than they talk to girls. There is some evidence that mothers talk to girls more than to boys and that they are more likely to use words that relate to feelings and emotions with toddler girls than with their male counterparts. Mothers of girls asked more questions, repeated their child's utterances, and used longer sentences than did mothers of boys. Mothers of boys used more imperatives (Gleason, 1987). These differences show great cultural variation.

Bilingual/Bicultural

The number of children with a non-English language background in the United States, 4 years and younger, is steadily rising and was estimated to be about 2.6 million in 1990 (Soto, 1991). There are a variety of misconceptions about how young children learn a second language. One misconception is that young children learn language more easily than adults. This idea is based on the assumption that infants are prewired to learn language. Adults learn second languages faster than young children do. Actually, adolescents are the fastest learners of a second language (Krashen, Long, & Scarcella, 1979). Young children who are naturally exposed to a second language are likely to be more proficient than adults. However, initially the process slows them down in acquiring language. Young children who hear two languages typically mix the languages and are not aware of the distinctions between the languages until about ages 3 or 4 (Garcia, 1983).

There are basically two approaches to learning a second language. The **additive approach** focuses on enrichment by the addition of a second language, but primarily communication is carried out in the native language. The **subtractive approach** teaches the second language as a replacement for, or at the expense of, the native language. This approach is the pervasive one in the United States today (Soto, 1991). Infants and toddlers need to be accepted and supported in their language-learning time. Children learning two languages need time to acquire, explore, and experience a second language. They need to practice both languages. A second language should be viewed as an addition to their native language. Young children need to have both their native language and their culture valued.

Personality

A child's personality influences how language is learned. Socially outgoing infants tend to vocalize more than quieter infants. Risk-taking toddlers are more willing to attempt new words regardless of their ability to say them, whereas more cautious toddlers may wait until they are more confident in saying a word. Some toddlers patiently listen as adults expand and use utterances that they have mispronounced. Others are quickly off to another topic or area.

Language Assessment

There are a variety of approaches to language assessment. A traditional approach is to determine whether or not a child's language development is "normal" and, if it is not, to identify the areas in which it is deficient. Another approach is to use language as a vehicle for finding out what children know and how they use this knowledge in everyday contexts (Lund & Duchan, 1993).

One must first determine the purpose of a language assessment. If the language assessment is done to determine if a child has a language delay, then a standardized norm-based assessment or a developmental scale designed for this purpose is probably the wisest approach. There are several language measures available that have been standardized on "normal" children so that we do know what the mean length of response (MLR) is for a child of a given age; what consonants should be mastered; and whether or not children should use pronouns, prepositions, plurals, past tense, and so on. Examples of measures that fall in this category are the *Preschool Language Scale* (Zimmerman, Steiner, & Evatt, 1979); the *Sequenced Inventory of Communication Development* (Hedrick, Prather, & Tobin, 1984); as well as the traditional developmental screening measures with subtests in the language area, such as the *Denver II* (Frankenburg & Dodds, 1990), and the *Battelle Developmental Inventory* (Newborg et al., 1984).

Once data has been obtained, it is up to a professional to determine how much of a delay there is, and whether it is of concern. For example, is a child who is "below average" a concern? What about the child who is in the 25th percentile? The 10th percentile? Or the child who has a six-month delay? Test results have to be interpreted to be useful in making decisions and they should be used with other measures to get a broader picture of the whole child and the context in which he grows and develops.

If a problematic language delay is determined, the next step is to find out what is causing the problem. Often a case history is taken from the parent or parents to gain some insight into what the probable causes might be. The delay may be related to a psychological or physical problem (such as a hearing impairment, mental retardation, or autism). There may also be information about a "forceps delivery," "teenage mother," "low-birth-weight infant" and so on. Although this information may be helpful, knowing the cause of a language delay may not be useful in remediation unless that cause can be changed in some way.

It is then necessary to determine more specifically what the areas of deficit are. At a global level one might look at receptive versus expressive communications. The context in which the language is used is also important. One cannot necessarily assume that a child who shows an inability to make a plural on a test does not use plurals in spontaneous language or vice versa (Lund & Duchan, 1993). Also it is important to figure out the discrepancies between what the child intends to communicate and what is actually communicated. Since children's language varies in different contexts, it may be necessary to gather more information about the child's language performance in a variety of contexts before reaching conclusions.

The next step is to determine what the patterns or regularities in a child's language behavior are. Again, this not only examines the language per se, but also the different contexts in which language is used. One may have to look at activities or events, the level of the child's familiarity with the events or individuals, the purpose of interactions, the child's role in the activity, and so on (Lund & Duchan, 1993). This knowledge may influence the child's language production.

Using the gathered information, a professional can better assess a child's communication skills and, if necessary, design a program that will enhance the child's language development. Assessment with infants and toddlers is an ongoing process. Therapy is typically done in the social context where the language will be used.

Communication and Language Delays

The child's ability to communicate is a critical factor in development and functioning. Communication is the key process through which individuals transmit and receive information, needs, wants, knowledge, and emotions. Disorders in the area of communication, consequently, may affect cognitive, social, and emotional areas of development.

Risks for Early Communication Delays

Many variables can affect a child's speech and language development. First, the child must have an intact sensory system for picking up relevant information in the environment. Second, the child must have the capabilities for processing the information, understanding what was seen and heard, and remembering the important facts. Third, the environment must be such that adequate stimulation is provided for the child to learn. Fourth, the environment must be reinforcing to the child to stimulate further communication (Peterson, 1987).

At a more specific level, hearing impairments are the leading cause of speech delays in young children (Billeaud, 1993). Infants born with chromosomal anomalies are at risk for communication disorders as are those exposed to drugs and alcohol. One criteria for the diagnosis of autism is a severe speech/language impairment beginning before 3 years of age. It is estimated that between 4.5 percent and 10.1 percent of premature, low-birth-weight infants survive with a major disability (McCormick, 1989). Infants who have self-regulatory problems beyond the 6th month are also at risk for communication disorders. Some children in their first 36 months have diseases, traumas, and injuries that adversely affect their communication abilities (Billeaud, 1993).

It is estimated that about 3 to 7 percent of children will develop or be diagnosed as having a learning disability, which frequently involves a communication disorder. Those children who are later identified as having dyslexia may exhibit language characteristics as early as 30 months that are indicative of these problems.

It is often difficult to diagnose an infant with a communication disorder at an early age unless it is related to a high-visibility disorder such as severe cognitive disabilities or neuromotor abnormalities. Communication disorders are high-incidence, low-visibility disorders and are often not identified in infants and toddlers. Looking at the records of school-age children in special education programs with high incidence problems including communication disorders, only one child in six was identified before age 3 and only one in four before age 5 (Palfrey et al., 1987). To the extent that young children with communication disorders are not identified, the opportunity for early intervention is gone. Although many young children who are slow to talk do catch up, only about half of them reach normal skill levels without intervention (Thal, Tobias, & Morrison, 1991). Children who exhibit only atypical language are unlikely to be accurately diagnosed as infants and toddlers, and will probably not be identified until school entry (Billeaud, 1993).

Speech and language delays are not synonymous. They involve two distinct areas of disorders. Within each category there is a further classification of disabilities that assists the clinician and interventionist in knowing the general characteristics of the disorder as well as some possible intervention options. Some of these specific disorders do not affect very young children, and they will not be discussed here.

Speech Disorders

Speech disorders are an interference in the production of specific sounds or sound blends that result in speech sounds that are inappropriate, irregular, or missing. Unless there is a physiological basis for a speech disorder, such as a cleft palate or cerebral palsy, it is very unlikely that infants and toddlers will be classified as having a speech disorder. They do not yet have the ability to produce all of the speech sounds. The lack of sounds when expected is used more as an indication of other impairments (such as a hearing loss) than as an indication of a speech disorder per se.

Fluency concerns the toddler's ability to develop a regular flow or rhythm of speech. The development of fluent speech is dependent on motor coordination and timing, linguistic and cognitive knowledge, and emotional maturity. "Fluent speakers are those who speak easily (without much muscular or mental effort) and continuously (without interruption), at a rapid rate" (Gottwald, Goldbach, & Isack, 1985, 9). The most common fluency disorder is *stuttering*. Stuttering involves abnormal repetitions, hesitations, and prolongations of sounds and syllables. Associated with stuttering are characteristic body motions such as grimaces, eye blinks, and gross body movements.

Occasional dysfluency is common in older toddlers and is often situationally specific. It increases when toddlers talk with someone who speaks rapidly, when language use is more formal, when they answer questions, use more complex sentences, or use less familiar words (Gottwald, et al., 1985). The most common normal dysfluency is the repetition of whole words or phrases. "Me-Me want." These occur most frequently at the beginning of sentences. Boys show more repetitions than girls, but both sexes show fewer repetitions with increasing age.

Some toddlers become stutterers. There are signals that adults can detect before toddlers reach this stage. One indicator is the frequency of dysfluencies. More than two sound or syllable repetitions or more than one sound prolongation per 100 words spoken is a danger sign. Additional signs include part-word repetitions ("Da-daddy"), especially if these repetitions are repeated more than twice or have an irregular rhythm ("D-da-da daddy"), and a sound held for more than one second ("Da——ddy") (Gottwald, et al., 1985).

Children who are tense and fearful are also at risk for developing stuttering. Ignoring stuttering is only appropriate with early dysfluencies. Maintaining eye contact and listening to the content of the message is helpful. The cause of stuttering continues to be debated between an organic versus learned behavior origin. Language therapy can help children overcome stuttering as well as teach techniques to diminish the intensity of the stuttering. Toddlers stutter less when adults speak slowly and clearly and do not press for "on the spot" answers.

Language Delays

Language delays are the failure to acquire language skills at the normal rate and within expected age ranges. Children with language delays acquire language along the same developmental patterns as normal children, but the acquisition of skills occurs over a longer period of time. Language delay can include a general delay in all dimensions of language or it can relate to skills in specific areas such as semantics or syntax. Causes for delay in the acquisition of language can include physical or structural problems such as a hearing impairment, physiological or neurological problems such as cerebral palsy, mental retardation, or emotional problems (Dumtschin, 1988). Some language delays have no specific cause, but may be environmental.

The two most common organic causes of language disorders are mental retardation and hearing impairment. Mental retardation characteristically results in delayed language development. The more severe the retardation, the less language that is acquired. Delayed language is not, however, indicative of mental retardation. Mental retardation includes the learning characteristics of poor memory, short attention span, poor classification skills, and poor abstract thinking skills, all of which contribute to delayed language development.

Brain damage is an organic cause of language disorders. Brain damage can interfere with children's ability to receive, understand, remember, and recognize communicated information. These types of disorders are referred to as **receptive language disorders.** Under these conditions, a child can hear adequately and has no expressive disorder, but the messages, once heard and transmitted to the brain, somehow encounter interference and the message is not understood.

Hearing impairments usually lead to some delay in language acquisition. A toddler with a profound hearing impairment cannot understand speech, even with a hearing aid. A child who is hard of hearing can understand speech (with difficulty) using only the ears, either with or without a hearing aid. The child's ability to receive and express verbal communication varies according to the type and severity of hearing loss (Neisworth & Bagnato, 1987).

Physical disabilities can also affect both speech and language development. Motor impairments can prevent children from becoming involved with their environment; that is, the child who is unable to actively manipulate materials and receive sensory inputs, will lack experiences that help to build semantic language skills. Children with these impairments may be delayed in language acquisition and will require assistance in helping them acquire the knowledge or experiences to compensate. Physical disabilities can also affect the oral-motor structures and musculature of the body. These infants and toddlers are capable of developing language but may be unable to verbally express themselves in ways that others can understand. Alternative methods must be developed for these toddlers to express and communicate their thoughts and wishes.

Impact on Development

Social and emotional development can be significantly impacted by language delays or disorders. Difficulty in communicating interferes with social interaction. Interactions usually require a give-and-take situation. The inability to engage in social interactions can lead to isolation and the development of poor interpersonal skills. Social isolation or weak interaction skills may lead to a lack of social interactions, which are models for later social interaction skills and help to build strong self-concepts.

Inappropriate environmental responses can make children unmotivated to communicate. Early communication development is intricately related to adequate and appropriate amounts of social interaction. During the cooing and babbling stages, adult responses to a child's vocalizations stimulate further vocalizations. The failure of the environment to interact with the child can result in a child uninterested in communicating. If attempts at communication continuously receive no response, the activity loses its appeal and fades away. Poor language models can also contribute to language delays. Language is learned through imitation and experience. The lack of appropriate language for modeling will result in children deficient in language skills.

Infants and toddlers who have spent significant amounts of their lives in hospitals may demonstrate delays in language acquisition. Prolonged or frequent hospital stays prevent them from taking part in many of the normal, active learning experiences that help to build a good language repertoire. Medical interaction often lacks some of the reinforcing and motivating factors present in home environments. The combination of these medical-related factors may contribute to delayed language development.

Emotional disturbances can also lead to language delays. Young children exhibiting moderate and severe emotional difficulties typically have problems in language expression. Emotional disorders may result in children lacking the expressive language skills to make their thoughts known; others may lack the inner language with which to think about the information received; and again others may develop their own language form which is unintelligible to the outside world. Young children with autism and severe psychotic disorders typically demonstrate severe language disorders, though they may not experience speech difficulties.

Language is essential in the learning of cognitive skills. If the environment is causing the language delay, then it will most likely have the secondary effect of limiting cognitive development due to lack of adequate early stimulation. Understanding language helps children build a foundation on which later learning is based. The inability to understand and process what is communicated will interfere with learning. Brain damage that results in language disorders may affect cognitive processing as well.

The inability to communicate ideas and thoughts can be very frustrating to young children. This is especially true for children with intact language systems but defective speech output. If children know what they want to say but are unable to express their message, extreme frustration and stress can result. This can lead the children to develop behavioral problems or withdraw from interactions. In both situations, the children need to have alternative means available by which to communicate their messages.

Summary

As is true with the development of other skills, language development is hierarchical. Infants must first be able to produce simple sounds, such as cooing and babbling, before they will be able to coordinate the tongue and mouth to produce more complex sounds such as words and sentences. Language acquisition is a major accomplishment achieved during the first three years of life.

Adequate communication and language play an important role in children's learning and subsequent cognitive and social development. Likewise, motor development, cognitive ability, and the environment influence early communication and language development. Failure to develop appropriate language skills, therefore, can have profound effects on the development of important learning and social skills.

Application Activities

1. Observe a toddler and write down the words that the toddler uses. Count the number of different words used. Determine his mean length of utterance and how the words were used. Compare this information to the normative information given in the text.

2. Play with a toddler and choose a word that you would like to teach her. Develop a plan for doing this, and then follow through and do it. Analyze your success or lack of success.

3. Choose a book and read it to an infant or toddler. Think about the language characteristics of the book and modify your style based on the child's responses to the book.

4. Talk to an infant or toddler. Tape your conversation. Describe your speech patterns. Did you modify them? If so, in what way? Did you take turns? How did you know when to lead and when to follow?

Chapter 9

Social Development

Social development is an important process that begins at birth. Human newborns are surrounded by a vast social network. One of their major life tasks is to adapt to this environment of people. Infants seem to come with the ability to tune into their social environment. They appear to be particularly aware of their mothers and from an early age recognize their mother's smell, voice, and face.

Social development focuses on relationships: their establishment, maintenance, and role in human life. The development of appropriate social responsiveness and emotional well-being in infancy lays the foundation for later social interactions with both adults and peers.

Social development has been broadly categorized into several areas which include attachment, parental relationships, (primarily mother–child relationships, although there is now father data too), other adult–child relationships, and sibling and peer relationships. Some of these relationships develop simultaneously, one depending on the other for further development, whereas others develop independently of each other.

As distinguished from social development, emotional development defines the growth of the infant and toddler's own self-concept and individual well-being. Social and emotional development are intrinsically tied together, as are other areas of development such as language and cognition. Although there is some overlap as well as disagreement about social versus emotional development, the field's current emphasis on infant mental health and current concerns about the lack of prosocial behavior in young children warrants treating social and emotional development as separate chapters.

In attempting to make sense out of social development in infancy, we are frequently looking for a theory to guide our thinking, much as Piaget provided a way to think about cognitive development. Regretfully, there has been far less focus on social development, as no single theory has had the impact on the field that Piaget had on our understanding of cognitive development. Early work in the area of infant social development was influenced by the behaviorist John B. Watson and the psychoanalyst Sigmund Freud.

Early Theories of Social Development

Both behavioral and psychoanalytic theory view infancy as a critical time for the child to be socialized by adults to fit into adult society. Their views of the infant himself and the socialization process differ with behaviorists viewing the infant as a passive being shaped by the external world and psychoanalytic theory seeing the infant as an active player in his development with instinctual drives that must be molded by society. However, neither theory was concerned with individual variation nor the interactional aspect of development, that is, the impact of the infant on the adult (Feinman & Lewis, 1991).

Behaviorism

From the behaviorist perspective, the child is socially a blank slate. The role of adults is to expose the child to the right values so that the infant grows into being a productive, self-sufficient member of society. Behaviorism focuses on power differences in the infant–adult relationship. The infant's dependency on the adult increases the probability that the infant would seek rewards and try to avoid punishment. Child rearing is seen as an almost businesslike arrangement. Parents are even cautioned not to become too involved with their young children. "Never hug and kiss them, never let them sit on your lap" (Watson, 1928, 81). Child rearing is viewed as a job: There is a correct standard of behavior that children are expected to adhere to. And it is the parents' job to see that they do.

Parents are seen as responsible for their children's behavior. Nurture clearly won the nature–nurture debate as seen in the following statement by Watson:

> Give me a dozen healthy infants, well-formed, and my own specific world to bring them up in and I'll guarantee to take any one at random and train him to become any type of specialist I might select—doctor, lawyer, artist, merchant chief and, yes, even beggar-man and thief, regardless of his talents, penchants, tendencies, abilities, vocations, and race of his ancestors (Watson, 1924, 82).

Current behaviorists do not have such an extreme position. However, it was the view of behaviorism put forth by Watson that influenced early research on socialization.

Psychoanalytic Theory

Sigmund Freud was the initial architect of psychoanalytic theory. Freud was a medical doctor who specialized in neurology. He practiced in Vienna, Austria. Freud was born in 1856 and died in 1939. His stage-based model placed great importance on the early stages of development. Rather than the passive infant of Watson's conception waiting to be molded, Freud (1940) saw the infant as active and filled with instinctual drives that placed him at odds with society. Withdrawal of parental love is the motivator of Freud's model. Freud believed that all individuals go through five stages in their psychosexual development. He hypothesized that at each stage of development there was one part of the body (erogenous zone) that gave more pleasure than other parts. According to Freud's theory, there was inherent conflict between these sources of pleasure and the demands of society. Personality development was based on how these conflicts were resolved.

Oral Stage.   This first stage of development lasts from birth until about 18 months. The infant's pleasure centers around his mouth as evidenced by his sucking, mouthing, and biting. He uses these oral actions to reduce tension. If weaned too early or too late, he might become fixated at this stage of development. Freudians would expect then that he might begin to suck his thumb or fingers as a way of relieving tension. Early researchers did find that infants who had been nursed less (whether breast or bottle) did suck their fingers more (Goldman-Eisler, 1951; Roberts, 1944). (Behaviorists would have expected children who had been weaned later to show more thumbsucking because it was a learned and positively reinforced behavior.) Freud felt that either too much or too little sucking interfered with attachment.

Anal Stage.   The second stage, beginning at about 18 months and lasting until about age 3, focuses on the eliminative functions. In Freud's view, during this time span exercising the anal muscles reduces tension. Conflict at this stage revolves around toilet training, with training that is too early or too strict causing later personality problems. (Behaviorists would expect problems related to toilet training to cause bowel or bladder dysfunction, for example, constipation.) There was some evidence to show that harsh toilet training was related to negativism and aggression (Sears et al., 1953). The development of the characteristic anal character (punctual, precise, parsimonious) was the long-term expected outcome.

Phallic Stage.   The third stage begins about age 3 and lasts until about age 6. The child's pleasure during this stage focuses on the genitals. The young child typically finds that self-manipulation is enjoyable. This stage has great importance for Freud's theory, whereas feminists found it highly objectionable (Horney, 1937; 1945). The conflict at this stage for the boy is that he falls in love with his mother and has an intense desire to replace his father in her affections. This incestuous wish is often called the Oedipus complex. (In Greek mythology Oedipus unknowingly kills his father and marries his mother.) This results in castration anxiety because of fear of punishment by the father. As a response, this conflict is resolved by identification with the same-sex parent. The girl at this stage develops penis envy and holds her mother responsible for her lack of a penis. She becomes attached to her father (Electra complex) with the resolution at about age 5 or 6 through identification with her mother. Lack of resolution results in fixation which is characterized by aggressiveness and narcissism (the individual himself is the object of his erotic pleasure).

According to Freud's theory, young boys need to identify with their fathers to successfully resolve their psychosexual development.

Latency Stage.   This is a stage of repressed sexuality in which children's energy focuses on social and intellectual skills. It lasts from about age 6 to puberty.

Genital Stage.   This is a time of sexual reawakening, but now the source is from someone outside the family. Unresolved conflicts with parents reemerge.

In addition to stages, Freud (1940) believed that personality has three basic structures which also have a developmental base. The most primitive structure of the personality is the **id.** The id consists of instincts and contains an individual's psychic energy. The id is unconscious and pleasure seeking. Freud felt that infants are controlled by their id. As children grow, they have to deal with the demands of reality. They begin to develop their **ego.** The ego is partially conscious and partially unconscious. The ego is the structure which develops from experience and therefore is the child's rational mind. The ego solves problems, evaluates risks, and makes rational decisions based on information. Neither the id nor the ego have a sense of morality. The **superego,** or conscience, is the last structure of the personality to develop.

The development of the superego is gradual and is accomplished by 5 or 6 years of age, although it may be modified later. The young child is subjected to frustration, some of which arises from parental demands. This frustration generates hostility in the child. Yet because of anticipated punishment, especially loss of love and abandonment, the child represses the hostility. To maintain this repression as well as to gain parental affection, the child adopts parental rules and prohibitions. He tries to emulate his parents' behavior to the point of punishing himself when he violates (or is tempted to violate) a prohibition. This self-punishment is experienced as guilt. Guilt feels like fear of abandonment. So the young child tries to avoid this feeling by acting in accordance with parental demands and by developing defense mechanisms to control impulses that may get him into trouble (Hoffman, 1970).

While Freud focused on problems related to fixation, Bowlby (1952) focused on the function of attachment for the development of the ego and superego. Bowlby felt that the infant is dependent on his mother to aid him in this capacity. She is his psychic organizer. If the mother–child relationship is continuing and satisfactory, the child takes over this controlling and planning function. As long as the mother and child have a positive relationship, things proceed smoothly. When this positive relationship is lacking, Bowlby felt that the child is at risk for impaired ego development (Bowlby, 1952). Bowlby placed great importance on the first two years of life.

Like Bowlby, Erik Erikson appreciated the contribution of psychoanalytic theory, but he reframed the stages into psychosocial stages that changed throughout the life span. His theory is discussed in detail in the next chapter.

Early Research in Social Development

Early research in social development was based primarily on psychoanalytical and behaviorist theories. These theories greatly influenced the topics that researchers chose to explore. Attachment and dependency received a tremendous amount of research, as did child-rearing techniques, sex-typing, socialization, and aggression.

Early research on attachment focused solely on mother–infant relationships. Research about attachment was based on the model of a middle-class "nuclear" family of European descent where the mother stayed at home and the father worked (Crockenberg, Lyons-Ruth, & Dickstein, 1993). Viewing this narrow range of family representation, it is easy to see why there was so much emphasis on the importance of the mother's role and so little interest in the father.

The classic work of Sears, Maccoby, and Levin, *Patterns of child rearing* (1957) focused on issues related to how and when parents wean, toilet-train, and discipline their children. They also looked at how parents deal with sexual expression and aggression. Much of the concentration was on whether parents used power assertion which included physical punishment, deprivation of objects or privileges, or the threat of these (behaviorism), or whether they used nonpower-assertive techniques such as love withdrawal (psychoanalytic).

Baumrind (1967) in another classic study with 134 preschool children and their parents, using observations of children, parent–child interactions, and parental interviews, described three general categories of parental control:

- Authoritarian parenting—Restrictive parenting style that includes many rules and expectations of strict obedience and relies on punishment or love withdrawal to gain compliance.
- Authoritative parenting—More flexible style in which children are allowed a degree of freedom within set limits and which relies on power or reasoning to gain compliance.

- Permissive parenting—A laissez-faire style of parenting which includes few limits and a great deal of child freedom and few attempts to control behavior or gain compliance.

Data from her observations indicated that parenting style was related to patterns of children's behavior (Baumrind, 1967): Those parents who were authoritarian were more likely to have children who were classified as conflicted-irritable (fearful, moody, passively hostile, and so on). Parents who were authoritative generally had children who were energetic-friendly (self-reliant, cheerful, cooperative, and so on). And those parents who were permissive were likely to have children who were impulsive-aggressive (rebellious, low self-control, domineering, and so on).

Concerns with Early Theories and Research

Research centered on the idea of parental control predominated in the 1950s and continued into the 1960s. However, by the late 1960s and early 1970s it became clear that this view of socialization was not embraced by all infancy scholars. Opposition to the theories centered on three themes: infant competence, individual differences in infancy, and mutuality of influence (Feinman & Lewis, 1991).

Behaviorists viewed the infant as incompetent and undirected, whereas psychoanalytic theorists saw the infant as incompetent and misdirected. With new research on infants' sensory competencies and their ability to learn, even while still in the womb, earlier views of incompetence could no longer be considered valid. Researchers began to focus on the competent infant.

Individual differences and variations in infants finally caught the attention of researchers, as opposed to the continuing search for universals. Some of the early work of Thomas, Chess, and Birch (1968) that focused on differences in temperament of infants helped in the move away from universals.

Finally, researchers were beginning to look at the role of the father and to include information on a range of family constellations. This led to a growing recognition that the mother–child relationship exists in the context of family relationships that affect the way the mother cares for the infant and hence impacts the infant's development. As the focus has moved from the centrality of the mother per se and now looks at infant development in a broader context, there has been expanded interest and research in the father's role in infant development. Further research has also emphasized the impact of grandparents and siblings. In essence, the move has been toward viewing the effect on the infant of all his caregivers. Additionally, researchers began to consider the impact the infant himself had on those caregivers.

The realization that infants were competent, active, and unique complicated and fragmented the research in social development. Researchers recognized the problems with previous conceptualizations, but there was no replacement. Researchers in infancy then began to move closer to a developmental-psychology framework, whereas those interested in social aspects of early childhood moved closer to social psychology (Feinman & Lewis, 1991). Early childhood research began looking at the effects of television, superheros, and war play on children's socialization. Infancy researchers are still struggling to rework the behaviorist–psychoanalytic model of socialization or build an alternative model (Feinman & Lewis, 1991).

Rather than developing a general theory of social development, researchers now tend to focus on a specific aspect of social development, such as relationships or attachment, and concentrate their work in that one area.

Relationships

There are a variety of ways to look at relationships. One can focus on the individuals involved, such as adults, peers, and infants and toddlers. There is little doubt that gender and age influence relationships beginning at birth. One can also look at relationships based on the degree of intimacy or connectedness between individuals, such as infants and fathers. One might look at the intimacy of relationships as ranging from love relationships to friendship, acquaintances, and strangers (Lewis, 1987). Obviously all these categories of relationships can be subdivided. When we add that relationships must be viewed as complex, transactional, and embedded in a social context, we seem to have muddied the waters even more.

Development of Relationships

To understand different types of relationships, it is necessary to look at how relationships develop. There may be some innate genetic basis for the formation of social relationships or they may grow out of early adult–child social interactions. Focusing on social interaction, the question becomes how these initial adult–child interactions transform into a relationship. Lewis (1987) sees the emergence of self-concept as the mediating variable that supports this transition.

The first step in the development of relationships for infants requires *self-differentiation*. Initially, the infant considers himself as part of his mother; until he can view himself as a separate entity, he cannot develop relationships. A second necessity is for the infant to develop the concept of self-permanence. This concept is similar to object permanence, wherein the infant knows that objects exist even when he cannot see them. The concept of *self-permanence* is established around 8 to 9 months. With the establishment of self-differentiation and self-permanence, the infant conceives of himself as an independent person regardless of the settings, the people he is with, or the interactions that are taking place. This process results in the establishment of the "self–other" schema. This schema is necessary for the development of other aspects of "self" and provides the basis for more complex social cognitive processes.

What aspects of "self" must infants develop? If I asked you to describe yourself what would you tell me? You might start by telling me you are a 20-year-old female with red hair, brown eyes, and so on. This idea of "self" as defined by a combination of characteristics is called the **categorical self** (Lewis, 1987). This is the way we think about ourselves and includes such aspects as gender, age, physical features, competence, and so on. As toddlers grow in self-awareness, this can lead to self-consciousness. Young toddlers are interested in aspects of themselves and may point out features like their nose in a mirror. However, they might become embarrassed looking at themselves in a mirror, whereas as infants they loved to admire themselves. They may also show intense concern about losing their mother, another indication of their concept of self and their awareness that their mother is separate from them.

One part of the development of "self" is *gender identity.* By age 2 most children can tell you whether they are boys or girls and use the terms boys and girls to talk about their peers. However, they are still visually grounded and can be confused by appearance. A girl with a boy's name who looks boy-like would be a "boy." Although they are aware of their gender, they have not yet attained *gender constancy,* the belief that they will remain the same gender for life (Huston, 1983). However, by age 3 they are beginning to know the *sex* or *gender stereotypes* (social expectations for male and female behavior) and behave following those patterns: Boys like rough-and-tumble play and use trucks and blocks; girls like housekeeping and play more quietly with dolls (Huston, 1983). Two-year-old boys may play in the doll corner, but by 3 and beyond this is less likely. Overall, boys tend to be more stereotypic in their play than girls. Some believe that this stereotypic concept of gender roles may be necessary and serve as the foundation for later nonstereotyped behavior (Lobel & Menashin, 1993).

The development of the categorical self or a *self-schema* allows toddlers to relate to others, particularly their peers, in different ways. Toddlers learn that they are beings with wants and needs and desires as well as likes and dislikes. As they attribute these feelings to themselves, they begin the process of learning that there are also other "selves" who have wants and needs and feelings. Other children are not inanimate objects. In cognitive theory this process is called **decentration.** The toddler must overcome his egocentric idea that he is the only person in the world and begin to attribute the same feelings, wants, and needs that he has to others. This knowledge is necessary for the development of two prosocial skills: empathy and sharing, the foundations for building relationships (Lewis, 1987). Having either empathy or sharing requires that toddlers develop not only self-awareness but awareness of others.

Piaget argued that these schemes developed in the late preschool years, whereas others see them beginning as early as 2 years of age (Lewis, 1987). The child's use of the word "no," and his interest in establishing his autonomy and actively doing things himself, are seen as indicators of both self-awareness and awareness of the intent of others.

Attachment

Attachment is the development of the human bond between infant and adults. Attachment has been studied in more detail than any other early childhood relationship. Some see the development of attachment as the most important early social event to occur in the child's life. Attachment is not present at birth but develops over time and progresses through stages. Much of the research in this area has focused on the mother–infant bond.

Theories of Attachment

Psychoanalytic theory was the basis for much of the early work in attachment. Freud believed that the mother–child relationship was unique and that the mother was the child's first and strongest love object. Additionally, this relationship was the prototype for later love relations. He believed that the basis of this relationship was sucking. Because of the importance of sucking, weaning was a threat to the mother–infant relationship: If weaning were either too severe or too lenient, the infant's later interpersonal relationships were at risk.

Erikson extended, revised, and reframed Freud's ideas. He felt that interactions other than sucking influenced the development of relationships, and he generalized it to a "trust–mistrust" continuum. He felt that good mother–infant relations promoted basic trust, whereas poor mother–infant relations led toward mistrust. His trust and mistrust concepts related not only to individuals but extended to generalized trust in institutions.

Both Freud and Erikson placed great importance on the mother–child relationship not just because of the relationship itself, but as a prototype for relationships through life. Those who had insecure attachments were forever doomed (without specific intervention) to inadequate relationships, especially in their own marriage and parenting. Although the concept is central for them, neither Freud nor Erikson actually used the specific term *attachment* for this mother–child relationship.

Ethological theory, which looks at behavior in evolutionary terms, views attachment as a biological survival mechanism for animals and humans. Species with long periods of immaturity need some way of keeping their young safe until they are old enough to care for themselves. Infant attachment to mothers is seen as providing this necessary protection. As infants became more mobile, the attachment figure becomes a secure base from which infants can explore their environment (Bowlby, 1989). Similarly, being wary of strangers and protesting separation increased chances of survival.

Current thinking about attachment is influenced by the work of ethological theorists, primarily the work of John Bowlby and Mary Ainsworth. Ethological theorists suggest that to ensure the survival of the species, infants are equipped with behaviors that increase their probability of survival: the ability to cry, cling, call, smile, lift their arms to be picked up, creep, and follow after a departing adult. These behaviors are the basis for the attachment of adults to infants.

This may not sound startling today, but consider that when Bowlby first presented his conceptualization of the attachment process (*The nature of the child's tie to his mother,* 1958) the assumption was that the basis of attachment was feeding. Bowlby's paradigm was very different. He defined attachment behavior as follows: "Attachment behavior is any form of behavior that results in a person attaining or maintaining proximity to some other clearly identified individual who is conceived as better able to cope with the world" (Bowlby, 1989, 238). The biological function attributed to attachment is protection, and this behavior can be seen throughout life, particularly in emergencies.

Bowlby (1989) envisioned two interrelated processes: attachment and exploration. When a child of any age feels securely attached, he can freely explore his environment. For young children these explorations are limited in time and space. The concept of a secure base is the fundamental foundation underlying this exploration. When a close, caring, intimate relationship is formed, infants can balance feelings of security with their need to explore. Deep security in being cared for allows free exploration and focused play. When this security is lacking, the infant's quality of play suffers (Honig, 1993). As children get older, they increase their time and distance of separation. So children can productively be away from their attachment figure for increasingly longer times.

For the attachment process to operate efficiently, the infant must have information about himself and also the attachment figure. He needs to know how likely the other is to respond as environments and conditions change. By the end of the first year, the infant has a considerable amount of knowledge about his world and organizes this knowledge to form a "working model" that includes models of self and mother in interaction with each other (Bowlby, 1989). The infant uses these models to plan his behavior. The more accurate and adequate the model, the better adapted the behavior.

Stages of Attachment

Like cognitive development, attachment is considered to have several stages. The first three stages occur during infancy and toddlerhood (Ainsworth, 1967). These three stages are widely accepted and appear to be invariant. Bowlby (1969) suggested a fourth stage that appears at the end of toddlerhood.

The first stage of attachment is called **indiscriminate attachment,** or *undiscriminating social responsiveness,* and is present from birth to approximately 4 to 6 months. The infant enjoys being handled, being approached by people, and being drawn into social interactions. There is no special responsiveness to the primary caregiver; young infants enjoy being held by anyone. The infant produces orienting behaviors (tracking, listening, postural adjustment) and signaling behaviors (smiling, crying, and vocalizations).

Once the infant develops the ability to identify familiar adults (3 to 4 months), the process of **discriminate attachment,** or *discriminating social responsiveness,* can begin. During this second stage children show a marked change in social behavior. They respond differently to one (or a few) familiar individuals than they do to strangers. The infant may visually follow an attachment figure, fuss when she leaves, and smile more at that person than others. Although the initial attachment figure is usually the mother, there is no biological reason for this. Attachment develops through contact and familiarity.

Although these two stages are well documented (Ainsworth, 1969), they have not intrigued researchers the way the third stage has. The third stage builds on earlier attachment behaviors, but is characterized by the infant's initiative in seeking proximity and contact with the attachment figure, and is referred to as **active initiation.** The timing of this phase is dependent on specific motor and cognitive developments. First, to seek proximity, the infant has to have some locomotion skills. At a cognitive level he needs the concept of object/people permanence. Both of these skills begin to develop around 8 or 9 months. Because this stage is so intriguing, it is discussed in further detail below.

A final stage is identified as **goal directed,** or *goal-corrected partnership,* and usually appears in the third year. It is characterized by the child's understanding of factors that influence the adult's behavior. This knowledge allows the child to interact with adults in a more sophisticated way (Ainsworth, 1973; Lyons-Ruth & Zeanah, 1993). Children play as more equal partners in games where the adult might be the "baby" and the child might leave to go off to work telling the "baby" she will be back to get her soon.

Active Initiation Stage

Because of the importance placed on secure attachment, researchers have been interested in not only describing attachment and its evolution, but measuring it. In an attempt to quantify attachment at the active initiation stage Ainsworth (1963) developed the *Strange Situation.* It works something like this: A mother and child (between 12 and 24 months) enter an unfamiliar room that has two chairs and a few appropriate toys for the child to play with. The mother stays with the infant for 3 minutes and then leaves. A stranger enters and stays for 3 minutes. Then the mother returns and the mother and infant are reunited (Honig, 1993). This procedure allows observation of the child's behavior before, during, and after separation. Observations focus on behaviors related to proximity seeking and maintaining contact as well as more negative behaviors of protest. Theoretically, a securely attached child would protest strongly at separation as well as score high on proximity-seeking at reunion. However, once having connected with the secure base, the child would then be ready to leave the security of his mother and go back to exploring the toys.

Some have questioned whether a child's protest when his mother left or when he was approached by a stranger are adequate measures of attachment. Part of the concern is that these negative behaviors are used as an indicator of positive attachment. Others even question whether protests are a measure of attachment at all. Many feel that stranger anxiety may not be a valid measure of attachment because young children have had very different experiences with strangers. Young children in child care have seen many different caregivers, as well as the parents of the other children. Ainsworth (1973) herself raised some of these questions. It may be that fear of strangers is more related to fear of the unknown than attachment per se.

Leaving aside problems of evaluating the role of the stranger, there were some additional problems. One was that from a theoretical perspective attachment should be a stable trait. That is, the behaviors of a "securely attached" child at 12 months should remain at 2 years. Likewise, the attachment should hold in a variety of settings. This did not happen. Ainsworth (1973) argued that the problem was not the concept of attachment but rather the measurement of it. Further, that attachment was more wisely thought of as a pattern of behavior rather than a particular behavior.

Ainsworth described three patterns of attachment: securely attached infants, ambivalently attached infants, and avoidant infants. A fourth pattern, disorganized/disoriented attachment, has also been established (Main & Solomon, 1990). All infants are attached to their caregivers. The differences are in the security of the attachment and the particular pattern an insecure attachment may take.

Secure attachment. Infants showing secure attachment show some protest at being left alone, or with a stranger in an unfamiliar place. This may be the obvious distress of crying or fussing, the disruption of play behavior, or unwillingness to be comforted by a strange adult. When the mother returns, the child calms quickly, seeks proximity, and returns to play and exploration. Parents of securely attached infants appear to be sensitive and responsive to the infant's signals. They seem to feel secure in their own attachment patterns.

Avoidant Attachment. An infant who displays avoidant behavior does not protest when the mother leaves the infant in an unfamiliar setting, nor does she immediately acknowledge the mother's return. Rather, she becomes busy exploring the surroundings and makes overtures to the unfamiliar adult. At first glance, these look like mature behaviors. However, most feel that this is a strategy for dealing with the stress of separation rather than lack of stress per se. It is viewed as an organized defensive strategy. Parents of these infants tended to minimize or dismiss the importance of attachment and to avoid confronting negative affect (Lyons-Ruth & Zeanah, 1993).

Ambivalent Attachment. Infants displaying this type of attachment are distressed at separation from the mother and contact her when she returns, but the contact is one of anger. They don't seem to be comforted by the mother's return and they don't seem to be able to resume play. This behavior has been interpreted as the infant's exaggerated response to a less responsive caregiver. Parents of ambivalent infants showed similar ambivalent feelings about their own parents, saw them as being overinvolved, and felt unable to please their parents. They appeared preoccupied with attachment relationships (Lyons-Ruth & Zeanah, 1993). Both avoidant and ambivalent attachment patterns are seen as organized, consistent strategies of response to stress.

Disorganized/Disoriented Attachment. Infants with disorganized/disoriented attachment lack a consistent pattern in response to stress. Their response may be idiosyncratic, but typically includes alternations of approach and avoidance of the mother. They lack an organized way of seeking comfort and security when stressed. Parents of these infants appeared stressed and seemed to be dealing with unresolved loss or trauma. Some of the mothers were depressed, abusive, alcoholic, or having serious psychosocial problems (Lyons-Ruth & Zeanah, 1993).

Patterns of attachment in children appear to be far more stable over time than specific behaviors. However, they were less stable for infants from economically vulnerable families or in families where mothers entered into employment during the attachment process. It appears that the mother–child relationship has to be renegotiated at this time. Research continues in the area of attachment in an effort to understand and classify attachment behavior. At this point there is both support for the importance of the concept of attachment in understanding long-term relationships and challenges to it, and how it is measured.

Attachment and Early Care and Education

Some researchers feel that the early use of non-maternal care for very young infants may disrupt the attachment relationship. They see infants in child care as having internal models of attachment that are characterized by insecurity and avoidance. Although the data are not completely consistent, there appears to be an overall pattern that infants who are in non-maternal care for more than 20 hours a week are more likely to be insecurely attached. The data is less clear on the type of this attachment but it shows an increased incidence of avoidant attachment (Barton & Williams, 1993).

Although there are few studies of father–infant attachment, the findings did show some consistency, but only with boys. Male infants who were enrolled in child care more than 35 hours a week were more likely to be classified as insecurely attached to their fathers (Belsky & Rovine, 1988; Chase-Lansdale & Owen, 1987). In looking more carefully at child characteristics, it may be that males and difficult infants are more vulnerable to insecure attachment when in child-care settings (Belsky, 1988; Belsky & Rovine, 1988).

What does this mean? Some argue that repeated separations cause the infant to regard the mother as inaccessible. However, that does not explain the data related to the fathers because in the sample fathers went to work on a daily basis. Nor does it account for the fact that a majority of infants (65 percent) in non-mother care are securely attached to their mother (Barton & Williams, 1993). In hopes of finding some explanation for these data, researchers are beginning to look at family variables.

In general, the literature reveals few differences in parent–child interactions between employed and nonemployed mothers. Differences that were found had discrepant findings with little evidence favoring one set of mothers over the other (Barton & Williams, 1993). Researchers have not looked systematically at maternal psychological variables. It may be that working mothers feel stressed, tired, and may be less available to their children when they are home with them. If infants are insecurely attached, it may not be related to child care per se, but to the fact that mothers are not available to their infants when they are with them. Hence, what is important may be the quality of time spent with infants not the quantity of it (Clarke-Stewart, 1989).

It appears that infants who are insecurely attached to both parents are at greater risk of social-emotional problems than those infants who are securely attached to one parent and insecurely attached to the other. Infants who are securely attached only to their mother seem more competent than those securely attached to only their father (Belsky, Farduque, & Hrncir, 1984). It is also suggested that infants who are insecurely attached to their mothers, but are securely attached to a substitute caregiver, are more socially competent than infants who are insecurely attached to both mother and caregiver. These patterns were more likely to happen when children were in high-quality care that was characterized by smaller child-to-adult ratios and responsive care (Howes et al., 1988). Although there is some suggestion that high-quality settings might ameliorate long-term consequences of insecure infant–mother attachments, infants who were insecurely attached to their mothers were more likely to be placed in poor-quality care arrangements (Howes et al., 1988).

It appears that substitute care is associated with a greater rate of insecure attachment of infants. The reasons for this pattern are less clear than are the implications that these data have for the infants' long-term adjustment. Some have argued that non-maternal care is associated with later social maladjustment, particularly increased incidence of aggression and noncompliant behavior (Belsky, 1988). At this point the data are too limited and inconsistent and there are a

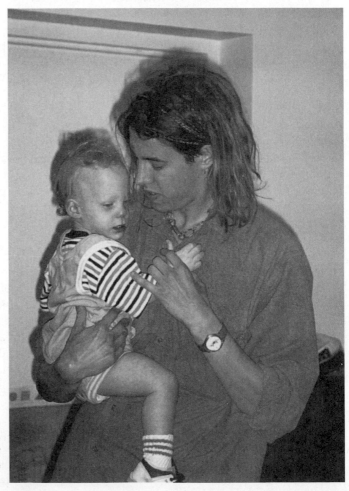

We know much less about children's attachment to their fathers or male caregivers.

variety of methodological problems which limit the generalizability of the findings (Barton & Williams, 1993).

One might ask, "Are we asking the right questions?" What we need to know is what infant/toddler outcomes are associated with what patterns of maternal and non-maternal care, under what conditions, and what are the variables related to these outcomes (Barton & Williams, 1993). Quality appears to be the overriding variable, not whether or not infants are in child care.

Child's Perspective of Attachment

From the child's perspective, the goal of attachment is to keep the attachment figure close. He attempts to use the skills he has that are likely to bring or maintain contact. Attachment is typically studied through the separation process, that is, leaving the child for a specified period of time and evaluating his reaction. Children typically experience many separations, from being left at home with one parent while another goes to work, to being left with a babysitter, or to staying with an adult relative. Separation also occurs when children enter early care and education settings.

All young children react to separation. Some children cry, others want their mothers to stay; some withdraw and some act out; some hesitate to enter a care setting and, when left, keep returning to the door; some look stressed and some bring attachment or transitional objects (Gottschall, 1989). We use separation reactions in the laboratory to evaluate attachment. In naturally occurring situations the goal is to use what we know about attachment to support the child.

Young children want a sense of predictability and control over their world. Explaining to young children what is going to happen before the parent leaves gives them this information but may produce a predictable separation reaction. Children whose parents try to "sneak out" to avoid this reaction are likely to have increased separation anxiety (Powell, 1989). Even young children who initially seem to separate easily may have problems at varying points, for example, with the birth of a sibling or if parents go away for a weekend.

Toddlers can use symbolic play with adult guidance to play out the separation paradigm. This involves games of having objects disappear or hide and then reappear. These games, with sensitive verbal support, help children cope with fear of abandonment. The major issues involved are whether or not the parent will return and who will care for the child in the interim. Children need repeated reassurance on both of those issues.

Symbolic play also offers children the opportunity to play out their feelings about being left. Many young children think they are placed in early care and education settings because they were "bad." Parents may inadvertently support this idea by telling children they are going to child care because they got "so big" (Gottschall, 1989). Young children may play out this theme (sending things away because they get too big) as a way of coping with separation anxiety. Explaining to children that they are in care so their parents can work is rarely useful and does not address the child's concerns or misconceptions.

Many children use transitional objects as a way of coping with separation. As young children become attached to people, other objects that are part of the child's daily life also become invested with meaning. Eventually, the child develops an emotional tie for the object (Jalongo, 1987). This transitional or attachment object gives them visual, tactile, and olfactory memories of comfort. Children often want additional security at naptime or bedtime which is why blankets or "blankies" are the traditional attachment object. Attachment objects are most important to toddlers and the need peaks between 2 and 3 years as they provide portable comfort as children encounter new situations (Jalongo, 1987). Teachers need to be empathetic and supportive of children's need for an attachment object. It is not something to be shared. When it is placed in a locker or cubbie, children often check on it periodically just as a younger securely attached child checks on the presence of a valued adult.

Attachment objects help children make transitions easier. They serve as a home base for young children venturing out into the world. Disparaging remarks by adults about the object typically only increase the child's need for it and fear of losing it. As children's confidence and competence grow, the need lessens. As children become more familiar with a new setting, some are willing to replace the attachment object with a visual reminder of their family. Children can be encouraged to bring photographs to school as reminders of home rather than the attachment object (Jalongo, 1987).

The question then becomes when does the reliance on an attachment object become atypical? The principles are the same that we use for other areas of development: duration, intensity, and emotional distress.

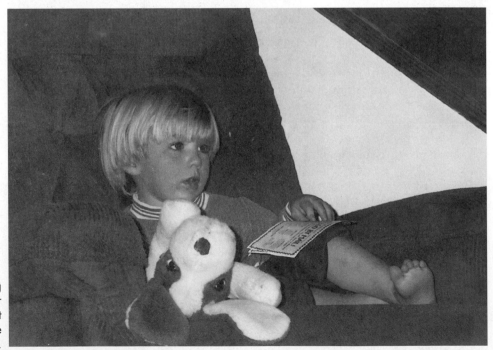

When young children are sick or upset, attachment objects become more important.

Sensitive Period

One aspect of attachment is timing. If the purpose of attachment is survival and learning social interactions, the question arises as to whether there is an optimal time frame for attachment to occur. Researchers distinguish between sensitive and critical periods. **Critical periods** are fixed periods of time, early in life, biologically determined, of short duration, with long-lasting implications. This is a "now or never situation." Critical periods for imprinting in animals are well documented. Imprinting in greylag geese can be used as an example (Lorenz, 1965). A young chick (12 to 14 hours after hatching) will follow a moving object presented at this time far more than one presented earlier or later. As most chicks see their mother at this time, they are imprinted with their mother's image and follow their mother. If, however, they were to see another moving animal, such as a human, they would follow that animal as if it were their mother. This is true even if the mother is available after this time (Lorenz, 1965).

An application of this critical-period concept to humans resulted in modification to the idea of **sensitive periods** that are longer lasting and provide an optimal time frame for development. Attachment does not fall into the critical-period category because attachment requires some learning, the time frame (first 18 months of life) is too long, and it appears that some early problems in attachment can be ameliorated. Many, however, view infancy as a sensitive period for the development of secure attachment (Bowlby, 1952). If infants do not become securely attached, or in Erikson's (1989) framework develop trust, their psychosocial future development is at risk.

One reason that there is such concern about the development of attachment is that secure mother-infant attachment has been linked to positive outcomes in later years. Infants who have secure attachments seem to find it easier to welcome younger siblings (Volling & Belsky, 1992). These securely attached children apparently grow into socially skilled, secure preschoolers. Whereas insecurely attached infants seem to have more behavior problems as preschoolers (van der Boom, 1990), a secure attachment does not prevent behavior problems in preschool children any more than insecurity causes them. The concern is when insecurely attached infants live and grow in families with few social or emotional resources.

Atypical Social Development

Some infants fail to develop secure attachment patterns with adults. They do not respond as expected to social stimuli. They may be irritable, not easily comforted, dislike affection, and may be withdrawn. These infants may have difficulties in their signaling systems that interrupt the early attachment process. They may cry continuously, have a piercing scream, arch their bodies to physical touch, and show no response to soothing interactions from adults. They may have poor eye contact and lack interest in social interaction. They are frequently described as "difficult" infants. The presence of one or more of these behaviors can cause parents or caregivers to think that the infant does not like them. They may also find it unpleasant to be around the infant due to these behaviors. The result may be the failure of the adult and the child to develop secure attachment.

The identification and detection of atypical social development is difficult with young children. Diagnosis includes a subjective judgment of what is appropriate or inappropriate (Peterson, 1987). Cultural and child-rearing differences must be included in the evaluation.

The first signs of atypical social development are identified as infants and toddlers try to master basic developmental skills or social responses. There is concern when an infant cannot be comforted, when a toddler does not talk and continues to show extreme anxiety around strangers, or when a young child does not demonstrate any responsiveness to adults. These responses are warning flags for social development. What differentiates atypical social development from normal development is when the behaviors are exhibited more frequently, persistently, and at ages when they are no longer appropriate, typically past the stages at which these behaviors are expected.

Attachment Disorders

Failure to develop appropriate attachment patterns will likely lead to children who are withdrawn or shun social interaction. They may exhibit cranky and whiny behaviors. Social responsiveness may be limited. These children fail to develop appropriate interaction patterns with adults and peers. They do not respond as expected to social stimuli. The combination of these behaviors typically results in further isolation as both adults and peers tend to ignore or dislike these children and refrain from interaction.

Attachment problems can also be related to problems in the behavior patterns of the caregiver. The caregiver plays a crucial role in the development of attachment. Mothers who are depressed or under great strain may find it difficult to respond to their infant's cues, or they may respond in inappropriate ways. Approximately 50 to 70 percent of women experience postpartum blues. This is usually limited to 10 to 14 days after delivery (Still, 1994b). In cases where this develops into depression or psychosis, there is typically a preexisting history of mental illness. Separation between the child and caregiver during early infancy can also affect the attachment process. Children needing frequent hospitalizations when young are at great risk for attachment difficulties, which may manifest themselves in social withdrawal and lack of social interactions with the environment.

Adapting to a new infant requires complex and competent functioning. Some families do not adapt well to infants. Families who do not have accurate expectations about infant behavior and development find it difficult to adapt. Caregivers with the ability to predict and "preview" upcoming developmental changes were more supportive of infants' developing skills than caregivers who lacked such an ability (Trad, 1994). Caregivers who are under stress, regardless of the source of stress, find adaptation difficult. Families with fewer resources, whether they are financial, social, or educational, find it more difficult to adapt.

Adapting is an interactive process. Infants themselves can increase the amount of adaptation required. Infants who are premature, low birth weight, and biologically "at risk" because of a disability or complications of pregnancy, labor, and delivery, often give less clear cues and are less responsive to caregivers. Obviously, the most vulnerable situation is when both infants and their caregivers are at risk.

Mothers who are psychologically unavailable or hostile are likely to have infants who are not securely attached. In cases of physical abuse the children are anxiously attached; with psychological unavailability the children are avoidantly attached (Honig, 1986). Anxiously attached toddlers are typically more aggressive and frustrated and show more negative affect. In addition to the psychological consequences of such maternal behavior, research showed that the toddlers' developmental or intelligence quotient declined precipitously. A group of infants whose mothers were psychologically unavailable when tested at 9 months had an average developmental quotient of 118; by 24 months this had declined to 87. Those infants who were also experiencing physical abuse had a mean mental development score of 121 at 9 months; this declined to 83 at 24 months (Honig, 1986). Obviously, the effects of such treatment on infants are pervasive and devastating for young children.

Patterns of Atypical Social Development

Children's social behavior needs to be interpreted in light of their developmental level and the specifics of the situation. Some behaviors are present and appropriate only during certain stages of development. As the children progress through developmental stages and new information is acquired, their behavior should be modified so that old behaviors disappear and new alternative behaviors take their place. Stranger anxiety appears around 8 months of age, but is later replaced with more developmentally appropriate social skills as children develop security and trust.

Peterson (1987) lists seven general factors which should be evaluated to help distinguish between normal social behavioral patterns and atypical behavior development. These include:

- The situations in which the behaviors are exhibited
- The developmental ages at which the behavior appears and continues to be manifested
- The intensity of the behavior, excess or deficiency
- The duration or persistence of the behavior
- The extent to which others can alter the behavior
- How much the behavior interferes with progress in other developmental areas and
- How much the behavior interferes with the lives of others (Peterson, 1987, 226).

Differences in parental styles of child-raising and interactions can significantly affect a child's social and emotional development. They can affect both children's social skills and their personality development. Parental factors that affect development include the degree of permissiveness; the manner and atmosphere under which children are allowed to express behaviors such as anger, frustration, and pleasure; parental expectations for performance; amount of parental control; degree of emotional responsiveness of parents to children; and types of discipline implemented (Peterson, 1987).

Victimization and Its Developmental Implications

In an effort to move beyond the literature that focused solely on child abuse and neglect and to find a developmental framework for viewing social situations in which children are at risk, Finkelhor (1995) proposed the concept of "victimization." He saw the need to develop a means for understanding social traumas within a developmental framework.

The initial thrust was to develop a typology of child victimization. Using national statistics, victimization was grouped into three broad categories: pandemic, acute, and extraordinary. **Pandemic victimizations** occur to a majority of children in the course of growing up, yet they receive very little public or professional attention. This includes such things as assault by siblings or peers and physical punishment by parents. Children are far more likely to be hit by someone than to be abducted, and in fact, children worry more about this because of its alarming frequency and the influence that it has on their everyday lives (Finkelhor & Dziuba-Leatherman, 1994). The probability of peer violence increases for children in child care settings. However, we rarely think of it in this light. **Acute victimizations,** which affect far fewer children, would include physical abuse, neglect, and family abductions. Finally, **extraordinary victimizations,** which affect even fewer children yet receive a great deal of attention, include homicide, child abuse, and nonfamily abduction (Finkelhor & Dziuba-Leatherman, 1994).

Children are disproportionally victims of violence. The National Family Violence Survey (Straus, Gelles, & Steinmetz, 1980) found that children were the victims of severe violence (beating up, kicking, hitting with a fist or object) twice as frequently as an adult partner. With the frequency of siblings and peers assaulting younger children, it appears clear that this is an area that needs more attention (Finkelhor & Dziuba-Leatherman, 1994).

As children grow and develop, they both acquire and lose characteristics that put them at risk for victimization. Because young children are dependent on the adults in their world to fulfill their basic needs, they are vulnerable in ways that older children are not. The most clearly dependency-related form of victimization is neglect (Finkelhor, 1995), for which parents are the most responsible (Sedlak, 1991). Even when others are aware of neglect, it is the parents' responsibility to care for their children. Young children are also victims of child abuse, homicide, and abductions by parents in custody cases.

Assessing the results of victimization for young children is different than when dealing with adults. When adults are victimized, they typically display post-traumatic stress symptoms which are relatively short term and primarily affect the behavior associated with the experience. Young children, too, show such behaviors as fearfulness, nightmares, avoidance of violence on television, fear of adults who resemble the offender, and fear of returning to the place where the victimization occurred (Finkelhor, 1995). Almost all traumatic situations result in some increased sense of fearfulness. In addition to traditional post-traumatic stress symptoms, victimization of very young children can interfere with normal developmental processes (Shirk, 1988).

Although specific developmental problems vary, the effects of victimization can result in impaired attachment (Cicchetti & Lynch, 1993); problems relating to others; poor peer relationships (Wolfe & Mosk, 1983), often in the form of aggression toward peers with lack of remorse (Friedrich, Beilke, & Urquiza, 1988; George & Main, 1979); and problems coping with stress and anxiety (Briere, 1992).

This view of victimization uses the disruption of developmental tasks of childhood as a basis for understanding vulnerability (MacDonald, 1985). Development of attachment to a primary caregiver is a major social task of infancy. Victimization interferes with this task when abuse is perpetrated by the caregiver. The result is insecure attachment and the expectation is that the effects of this insecure attachment will be carried into later phases of development and other relationships (Cicchetti & Lynch, 1993). There may also be physiological alterations in endocrine functioning and neurological processes that permanently affect a range of cognitive and behavioral development (Putnam & Trickett, 1993).

As children become a little older and are capable of mental representation, they develop the ability to dissociate. They do this by fantasizing, developing imaginary playmates, and denying things they clearly have done (Putnam, 1991). Children victimized as twos or preschool children use dissociation as a defense mechanism and develop chronic patterns of dissociation which may include memory loss, a tendency for trancelike behavior, and auditory or visual hallucinations.

The child's level of cognitive development impacts victimization. Cognitive appraisal (what a child believes about what happened) may mediate the victimization experience (Rutter, 1988). This process is believed to work differently in young children than adults. Young children do not have the cognitive maturity to objectively assess all situations. Therefore parents can reframe the experience and model behaviors to buffer some of its negative impact (Kendall-Tackett, Williams, & Finkelhor, 1993). When parents are part of the victimization process, the results are not mediated.

In the extreme, children can be diagnosed as having a reactive attachment disorder. This is associated with grossly pathological care that disregards the young child's physical and social/emotional needs. Children show one of two responses: They become inhibited and fail to respond socially or they are disinhibited and indiscriminately form attachments (American Psychiatric Association, 1994).

Failure to Thrive

Failure to thrive is the modern day equivalent of marasmus, or wasting away, of an infant without a biological reason. Some infants have parents who are psychologically unavailable to them. These infants may develop a pattern of refusing to eat or drink and refusing social interaction. Their weight can suddenly drop dramatically and necessitate medical intervention including intravenous feeding.

If the malnutrition has persisted beyond 6 months of age, the effects are irreversible and normal brain growth may not be achieved (Marzek, 1993).

The main cause of failure to thrive is that the infants do not get enough food. In most cases (70 percent) there is no organic reason for their not being able to eat. Of these cases 50 percent are cases of neglect; the infants are simply not fed enough. An additional 20 percent are accidental, based primarily on errors in formula preparation. As children become older, around 2 years, failure to thrive is less of a problem because children can obtain food for themselves by asking for it or finding it in the home (Marzek, 1993).

Adult–Child Interactions

Social development is an interactive process that involves the infant and adult attending to and responding to each other.

Social Referencing

Social referencing is a process whereby one person utilizes another's interpretation of a situation as a knowledge base (Feinman, 1992). It is a form of active communication that occurs when an infant or toddler encounters a situation of uncertainty and looks to a trusted adult for an emotional signal to resolve the situation (Emde & Buchsbaum, 1987). For very young children this facilitates or reduces stress in everyday life. For example, an infant may be startled or frightened by a jack-in-the-box, but a sensitive adult will make an exaggerated face showing surprise and say "Did you see that clown?" This then provides the infant with information on how to respond to this new experience.

During the first six months the infant presents emotional information. The caregiver uses this information to meet the infant's needs. By the latter part of the first year, the infant uses emotional expressions from adults to resolve uncertainty. Facial expressions of familiar social partners provide information to infants. By the end of the first year, infants use the facial expression of adults as a form of social referencing. When encountering an unfamiliar situation, infants will turn toward an adult to determine whether or not to approach. If the adult looks wary, the infant is less likely to approach. Infants vary in their use of social referencing; securely attached infants are more likely to use this behavior. Infants look most often at adults who are themselves more emotionally expressive (Camras & Sachs, 1991).

Infants' Cues

Obviously infants cannot control their world; they cannot get their own food or change their own diapers. Infants send cues to their caregivers to modify their environment. However, they do not have a vast repertoire of behavior with which to work. They depend on such cues as sleepiness, fussiness, alertness, hunger, changes in body activity level, distress, and several others. Some infants send cues that are clear and easy to read. Other infants send ambiguous or confusing cues that make it more difficult for the caregiver to respond appropriately. The infant whose eyelids get heavy, yawns, cuddles up, and then falls asleep is easier to read than the infant who opens his eyes, appears to be awake, yet when picked up fusses, and returns to sleep. Premature infants and those with disabilities often are less alert and responsive in their early months and their cues are more difficult to interpret (Hussey, 1987).

Responding to Infants' Cues

Caregivers must be able to read the infant's cues to respond to the infant's needs. Some adults are more sensitive to infant cues than others. However, this is a learned skill. Therefore, even those who do not seem to be innately sensitive can improve their ability to read infant cues by being given specific information about these behavior cues. Some cues that infants use signal distress—such as crying. The caregiver must recognize the distress signal, and decide on an appropriate action to alleviate the distress; that is, determine whether the baby needs to be changed, fed, or held and comforted.

The faster, more accurately, and more sensitively caregivers respond to and alleviate distress, the more quickly the infant will be comforted (Honig, 1993). Caregivers who are under stress may not be as sensitive to infants. Infants respond to "depressed" caregivers and may mirror that depression (Honig, 1986). Some caregivers believe that responding to infants quickly will spoil them and make them more demanding. This is not correct; in fact, the opposite is true. When infants are responded to quickly, the infant even begins to anticipate help and may stop crying at the sight of the caregiver, knowing that his needs will be met.

Alleviating distress is important for the infant's well being; however it is only a small part of the challenge of working with very young children. The ability to play with the infant and to respond to and initiate social interaction and support cognitive growth requires far more caregiver adaptation than mere disaster relief.

Joint Socialization

When adults respond accurately to the infant's cues, an interaction takes place. The infant then "reads" the adult's response so that he can modify his behavior. That is, the infant cries to signal the caregiver; the caregiver responds by picking the infant up, cuddling him, and then changing his diaper; the infant in return responds by a cessation of crying and perhaps making eye contact. If the infant does not respond to the caregiver, then adaptation is not possible. No infant responds every time; likewise, no caregiver always accurately interprets infant signals. However, to the extent that interactions are consistently inappropriate, because of either the infant or the caregiver, the relationship becomes a concern.

The progressive development of the interaction patterns between the infant and adult is the result of several factors. These include the child's temperament, the child's communication cues or signals, the adult's interaction style, and the adult's personality, skill, and emotional investment in the child's upbringing. The development of social behaviors within children is a result of a combination and interaction of these factors. A fussy infant with a calm and caring parent can develop into a relatively stable preschooler. A fussy infant with an intrusive, abrupt, and unaffectionate parent may develop into an older child with emotional difficulties and social behavior problems.

Another framework for understanding this interaction is Vygotsky's (1962;1978) zone of proximal development. In Vygotsky's model the infant or toddler uses the adult as a guide to learn about her world. The adult role is to help the young child find connections between what they already know and what is necessary to deal with a new situation. With very young children this scaffolding might include modeling, verbal labels to help classify objects and events, nonverbal emotional cues to help assess the situation, and so on. Young children are very astute observers and use social referencing as an effective means of learning information.

Initially, young children require a great deal of redundancy in scaffolding to understand a concept (Rogoff, 1991). If an adult were playing ball with a young toddler, the adult might show the toddler the ball, slowly roll the ball, encourage the toddler to roll the ball, while at the same time saying "Do you want to play with the ball?" "Can you roll the ball?" "This ball is red. The ball is round and red." The continued use of the word *ball* when one would normally substitute a pronoun, and the verbal and nonverbal support are the redundancy in the scaffolding. As the child becomes knowledgeable about the properties of balls, the redundancy in the scaffolding is faded. Success depends on the skill of the adult in matching the child's changing world.

Fatherhood

Fatherhood is a hot topic of the 1990s. Professional and popular literature portrays a "new breed" of fathers who have high involvement, increased commitment, and spend greater amounts of time and energy in child-centered activities (Palkovitz, in press). The new style of fatherhood has been labeled "involved fatherhood," "highly participant" fatherhood, "androgynous fatherhood," or simply "new fatherhood" (Griswold, 1993; Lamb, 1986; Palkovitz, in press). At the same time the public is also being inundated with stories about the uninvolved "deadbeat" father who ignores his parenting obligation, resulting in a "good dad–bad dad" dichotomy (Furstenberg, 1988). Griswold (1993) feels that the "new father" is largely a middle-class phenomenon and represents a male survival strategy to accommodate their wives' careers and to compensate for their own decline in bread-winning capabilities. Additionally, this "good dad–bad dad" image is confounded by race and social-class variables. Scholars have focused their research on poor African American fathers and reinforced the stereotype of the macho-man who is financially irresponsible and uninvolved in his children's lives rather than looking at the middle-class African American father (McAdoo, 1986).

Talk of more equality in gender roles within the family has not necessarily meant increased involvement of fathers with young infants (Lewis, 1987). Despite much rhetoric there seems to be no general evidence that parents participate equally in the care of very young infants. When interviewed prior to the birth of the infant, couples told the researcher that they expected the mother to do approximately twice as much caregiving as the father. However, three weeks after the birth the mother was doing four times as much caregiving as the father (Palkovitz, 1992). Although maternity leave may account for some of this difference, it seems unlikely that the caregiving will become equally distributed.

Lamb, Pleck, and Levine (1987) found four factors crucial to understanding variations in degree of father involvement: motivation, skill, support of the mother, and cultural and institutional support. Motivation, that is, the extent to which the father wants to be involved with his children, impacts involvement. Motivation, however, is not enough. Men also need skills and sensitivity, along with the self-confidence to use these skills to interact with their young children. Level of paternal involvement is also related to support, particularly from the mother. There is some question about how much mothers actually want fathers to be involved. This may be related to the fathers' perceived lack of skill; it may be the

Fathers play with children differently than mothers.

one area where mothers feel they have authority and don't want to give it up; or it may be related to attitudes and values. Middle-class cultural values are clearly changing in this area. The fourth factor is related to institutional practice; the father's need to work. One might expect that fathers whose wives worked would be more involved; however, paternal involvement levels show very little relationship to the mother's employment status or work schedule (Marsiglio, 1991).

Studies of fathers and infants show that fathers play and interact with infants differently than do mothers. Mothers tend to spend more time in routine caregiving behaviors (like diapering and feeding), whereas fathers tend to play more often in physical ways. Fathers are more likely to bounce and tickle younger infants and engage in more rough and tumble play as infants turn into toddlers. However, men are in no way inherently deficient in their ability to parent. A father's qualities as a parent are far more important than gender (Griswold, 1993; Starrels, 1994). Some studies have found that toddlers prefer their fathers as playmates (Lamb, 1977).

Fathers typically become more involved as their children become older and less of their time is spent in routine care and there is more time to play and explore. The different interactions of mothers and fathers are important and work together to enhance a child's development. Although father attachment has been studied far less than the infant's attachment to the mother, it seems clear that children are attached to their fathers and that fathers can be involved, sensitive caregivers (Lamb & Oppenheim, 1989).

In addition to the direct effects of fathers on their children, there are also indirect effects as parents can learn from and support each other. Mothers observe and imitate fathers' positive interactions with infants and vice versa. Mothers often feel more supported when their husband is actively involved in parenting and, in turn, interact more positively with the child themselves.

Siblings

Siblings play an important role in the socialization of children. Young children are attached to their siblings, particularly younger siblings to older ones (Lewis, 1987). Sibling relationships are the longest-lasting family relationship. Siblings play a variety of roles depending on gender, age, spacing of siblings, and family and cultural expectations. Siblings share the same parents and the same environment. Therefore the infant's early experiences of sharing and turn-taking often occur with siblings. Infants and toddlers learn many skills through watching and imitating older siblings. Siblings often serve as playmates.

Given the positive potential of sibling relationships, it is interesting that much of the research on siblings has focused on the more negative aspects of those relationships. One area that has received attention is the impact of later siblings on the first. It seems clear that with the birth of a second child the parents' attention, time, and energy must be divided between the two children. Nevertheless, it appears that first-born children still receive more attention and affection than later-born children (Lewis, 1987). Information on cognitive competence is somewhat variable. Some studies have shown an initial drop in children's IQ scores with the birth of a sibling and that this decrease vanishes a year after the birth (Feiring & Lewis, 1982). However, it has also been found that children who have younger siblings, regardless of their birth order, are smarter than those without. (A third born with a younger sibling is smarter than a third born without a younger sibling.) Some hypothesize that the opportunity of teaching the younger sibling is a positive cognitive experience (Lewis, 1987).

Much research on siblings focused on such family structure variables as gender and birth order to explain either similarities or differences in sibling socialization. In general, the contribution to our understanding was not great. More recent research has begun to view siblings as experiencing a microenvironment within the family. In trying to elucidate differences in the socialization of siblings, researchers have identified four different classes of sibling experience: (1) differential parenting; (2) differential experiences with other siblings; (3) differential experience in peer groups; and (4) differential exposure to life events (Bussell & Reiss, 1993).

Research seems to support the observation that parents react differently to each child in the family and that children feel they are treated differently from their siblings. Very young children closely monitor the mother's interactions with siblings and react to those interactions. Young children who experienced greater maternal control or less maternal affection than their siblings were more likely to be anxious or depressed (Dunn & McGuire, 1994).

Parenting changes over time. In their longitudinal study Dunn and McGuire (1994) noted that although parenting with a single child was not consistent over time, the parenting of a child when he was 2 was similar to the parenting of his sibling when he was 2. Therefore, it may be that parenting is more consistent based on age of the child than previously thought. And although we see parents behaving differently with each of their children, it may be that we need to think of parenting varying appropriately with the age of the child rather than overall consistency. This may also be why children perceive their parents as treating them differently from their siblings.

As children increase in age or go to early care and education centers, they encounter children their own age who are unrelated to them. These interactions are often different from interactions with siblings as the children are now frequently the same age.

Child-to-Child Interactions

Little child-to-child interaction occurs early in infancy. Infants do not have the necessary social or motor skills to interact with each other, although by 6 months they do observe each other with interest and may gesture and vocalize at others. It is not until toddlers can safely venture away from adults that the potential for more involved social interactions begins.

A majority of early social interactions center around play and play activities. The quality and type or level of interaction that occurs between children in play activities develops sequentially, increasing with age and maturation. Researchers have been intrigued with this process. Mildred Parten (1932) constructed a developmental categorization of play in 1932 that is still used today.

Classification of Play

Parten classified play based on the child's level of social participation and the level of organization of the play itself. She saw a social developmental progression in play, but noted that even older children could be in different levels of social participation at different times.

For about the first two years, children participate in unoccupied, onlooker, or solitary play. Infants need adult involvement in play as they are unable motorically to play independently. The length and quality of independent play increases as their motor and cognitive skills develop. Early play is centered on sensory exploration of materials and the environment. See Table 9.1.

Around 18 months, many children begin to view other children with interest, but interaction is typically minimal. At this stage, children see other children as objects rather than persons. Toddlers may pull, pinch, hit, or bite others. This behavior may last up through 30 months or later for some children. Around the 24-month age level, toddlers often become involved in parallel play activities, in addition to maintaining their interest in more solitary play activities. At this time, children are not yet ready for cooperative play situations. They are still involved in independent play activities, but these activities now occur in close proximity to other children. Children closely watch each other's play activities and imitation of play actions is common.

Table 9.1	**Parten's Classification of Play**
Level	**Definition**
Unoccupied Behavior	The child is not playing in the usual sense, but watches activities of momentary interest or plays with his body.
Onlooker Behavior	The child watches others play. He may talk to, question, or offer suggestions to the children who are playing.
Solitary Play	The child plays alone with toys that are different from those used by other children; there is no verbal communication with other children.
Parallel Play	The child plays independently, but among other children with similar toys and materials.
Associative Play	The child plays with other children, all are engaged in similar activities, however, there is no organization or roles assigned.
Cooperative Play	The child plays in a group that is organized for a purpose, to obtain a goal or to dramatize adult life; formal games are included in this classification; there is a definite division of labor and a sense of belonging to the group.

SOURCE: Parten (1932).

Howes and Matheson (1992) note some variations between Parten's level of parallel and associative play. In **parallel-aware** play, children not only use similar materials but they become more social and make eye contact with each other. As contact increases, children may smile at and talk to each other and perhaps exchange toys, turning it into **simple-social** play. Children will want to use the same object and attempt the same play activity. Two children can both be in the block area, using the same-size blocks and building roads, yet the entire play activity occurs independently for each child. With increasing age, 2-year-olds play with other children in small groups but they don't reach the cooperative level of play.

Smilansky and Shefatya (1990) conceptualized play differently from Parten. They, too, focused on the child's development, but they were more interested in cognitive aspects of play. They used Piaget's ideas about cognitive development as the basis for their stages. This conceptualization of the development of play meshes well with Parten's levels of social interaction. In the Smilansky and Shefatya framework, children can engage in functional, constructive, or dramatic play alone, near others or with others (Rubin & Howe, 1985). See Table 9.2.

As children's play develops, their social interactions move away from caregiver to peer relationships. The child is developing both motor skills and his cognitive ability to decenter, that is, focus on more than one aspect of an object, which allows for the manipulation of toys and objects in a social context. Increasingly, children learn to participate in reciprocal relationships with peers. The development of symbolic play goes through a predictable sequence.

The ability to "pretend," or pretense, emerges at about 1 year (Fenson & Ramsey, 1980). Pre-pretense is more in the mind of the adult than the child. As the 1-year-old lies down, the adult says "Oh, you're sleeping, I better be quiet" and then tiptoes away. In Vygotsky's zone of proximal development this represents a nudge into symbolic play (Gowen, 1995). Initially, actions are directed toward the child himself (self-pretend) as he "pretends" to comb his hair or drink from a cup. Over the period of several months, this ability at pretense extends to beyond the self (other pretend). Now a toddler might pretend to

Table 9.2	Stages of Play
Level	**Definition**
Functional Play	Repetitive movements that appear playful and usually involve objects (shaking a rattle, dump and fill, and so on)
Constructive Play	Using objects or materials to make or create something (putting together a puzzle, using playdough, painting, and so on)
Dramatic Play	Pretend play which may or may not have props and frequently involves assuming a role (eating/drinking pretense, family role play, using dolls, and so on)
Games with Rules	Activities that require compliance with particular requirements and may involve competition (simple board games, ball games, hide and seek, and so on)

SOURCE: Smilansky and Shefatya (1990).

comb a doll's hair or even have the doll hold the comb and pretend to comb her own hair.

An important aspect in the development of symbolic play is the ability of the child to participate in substitutional behavior; that is, a child can pretend that one object is another, such as a block for a car (object substitution). The ability for single substitutions (block for car) appears at about 24 months. The ability for double substitutions (a block for a car and a string for a gas hose) emerges later (Gowen, 1995; Trawick-Smith, 1991).

Around age 2, children incorporate imaginary objects and beings into their play; however, they need the support of real objects. They can imagine the tea, but they need the teapot and cup to pour it into. Toddlers become capable of a different form of object substitution (active agent). They "animate" the object. Instead of just feeding the doll, they become the doll and say "yucky" in response to being fed. Puppets, dolls, and stuffed animals support the emergence of this level of symbolic play (Gowen, 1995).

As children's symbolic play develops, it becomes more integrated. The transition to integration is where the child repeats an action with different recipients (sequence no-story) (Gowen, 1995). She feeds different dolls or the doll and herself. This develops into related behaviors (sequence story) when she pretends to put the food in a dish and then eat, or pour the tea and then drink it. These sequences begin to appear at about 15 months but increase in frequency and complexity (Gowen, 1995). Asking questions about the child's drama is one way of increasing the complexity. As children gain sophistication, planning plays a more important role. Planning is an important aspect in play by age 4. Children decide what they are going to do and how they will go about doing it before they actually do it.

The ability to participate in symbolic play has cognitive underpinnings. Work with young children with mental retardation found that children who had mental ages less than 20 months did not participate in symbolic play (Hill & McCune-Nicholich, 1981). Even then, these children typically showed more functional qualities (pretend play was based on their everyday experiences) and less creativity in their play than did other children.

Smilansky and Shefatya (1990) make a distinction between dramatic play and sociodramatic play. In dramatic play the child takes on a role and imitates a person with the aid of real or imagined objects. For toddlers, these roles are typically self-related; often they pretend to be their mother or father. Sociodramatic play involves a theme of some type and at least one other child to participate (Smilansky, 1968; Smilansky & Shefatya, 1990). As children progress from age 2 to age 3, they go from self-based to shared make-believe play, and they begin to participate in shared play themes. Their play becomes increasingly more complex over the preschool years.

Promoting Prosocial Behavior

Social development was seen as the core of the early childhood curriculum until the 1960s when the emphasis shifted to cognitive development. The goal of early childhood programs was to promote prosocial behavior and positive child-to-child social interactions. Prosocial behaviors include helping, giving, sharing, and showing sympathy, kindness, affection, and concern for others (Wittmer & Honig, 1994). For many programs prosocial behaviors are no longer core goals.

Concerns about prosocial behavior have arisen for a variety of reasons. Some researchers have found that full-time child care beginning in infancy may be associated with increased aggression and noncompliance (Honig, 1993). There are concerns about war play and superheros (Carlsson-Paige & Levin, 1987) and how this play is moving down to include younger children, and overall concerns about the amount of violence young children are experiencing (Osofsky, 1993/1994).

Since the Federal Communications Commission deregulated children's television in 1984, there has become an increasing concern about the amount of violence on television. Young children watch an average of 4 hours of television a day. In low-income homes this figure rises to 6 hours (Miedzian, 1991). Programs designed for children are less likely than others to show any long-term negative consequences (5% do), and they often portray violence in a humorous context (67%) (National Association for the Education of Young Children, 1996). Many are concerned about the values that children are developing through television. When the television is not chosen for developmentally appropriate programs, there is concern that instead of infants establishing a sense of trust and safety, they learn that the world is dangerous, enemies are all around, and that weapons are needed to keep one safe (Levin & Carlsson-Paige, 1994). Instead of helping children develop a sense of autonomy and connectedness to each other, television portrays autonomy as being related to fighting and the use of weapons. Conversely, helplessness and altruism are related to connectedness. Other concerns revolve around empowerment and efficacy, gender identity, appreciation of diversity, and morality and social responsibility (Levin & Carlsson-Paige, 1994). Television in and of itself is not bad. Rather, television programs need to be viewed for their appropriateness in a developmental framework, and the amount of time children spend watching television needs to be regulated. Young children need time to actively engage in their world.

Toddlers struggle with the ideas behind sharing, turn-taking, and ownership. Teachers who promote prosocial behavior specifically identify these behaviors "I like the way you and Connie are taking turns using the markers." Comments should be specific; however, they should not be used to the point that the purpose of prosocial behavior becomes external reward rather than an internal standard. Programs that emphasize cooperation rather than competition promote prosocial behavior (Honig & Wittmer, 1996).

To promote prosocial behavior, adults often help children take the perspective of another child, especially in situations where one child hurts another. "She's crying because you hit him. What can you do to help her feel better?" This both points out the consequences of the behavior as well as helping children understand what might make a distressed child feel better. Children need to accurately identify the emotional state of another child before they can act in a prosocial way toward them (Wittmer & Honig, 1994). Most toddlers respond prosocially to peers in distress (Howes & Farber, 1987). Toddlers, however, who have been abused are impassive or react with anger (George & Main, 1979). Vulnerable children need support in specifically developing prosocial behavior. Choosing children's literature with prosocial themes may be a place to start (Honig & Wittmer, 1996).

Prosocial behavior does not just happen—it must be learned. Modeling prosocial behavior sets the tone for young children. Empowering toddlers by giving them choices enhances their prosocial behavior. Likewise, making them conscious of other children and their feelings promotes prosocial behavior as well.

Summary

Social development begins at birth. It focuses on relationships: their establishment, maintenance, and role in human life. Social development lays the foundation for later social interactions with both adults and peers. Behaviorism and psychoanalytic theory provided the theoretical basis for early work in social development. Early research focused on such areas as child-rearing techniques, sex-typing, and socialization. As the knowledge base about infancy increased, scholars began to question the efficacy of these theories.

Current research focuses on relationships and the development of these relationships. The area of attachment is an essential element in social development. Infants come with behaviors that support attachment, but they need sensitive adult support for secure attachment to develop. Not all infants develop these secure attachment behaviors to their primary caregivers. Some infants do not display attachment because of the infants themselves, others because of the inadequacies of caregivers. Some infants display avoidant attachment, others ambivalent attachment, and still others disorganized/disoriented attachment. Infants are not only attached to their mothers or primary caregivers but also to their fathers and siblings. Research is increasingly focusing on the role of fathers, siblings, and culture in early socialization, and the joint socialization of the infant and caregiver.

Not all infants display typical social development. Atypical social development is difficult to diagnose because of the natural variability of infant behavior. Problems relating to attachment as well as child victimization are concerns. Infants and toddlers not only experience short-term problems but the potential for long-term development risk.

As infants become toddlers, their social interactions reach beyond their family to peers. This interaction is based on play behavior. As toddlers learn to use symbolic play, they increasingly interact with peers. Play becomes a basis for social development. This interaction increases in complexity with age. More complex interactions demand new levels of self-awareness from young children.

Application Activities

1. Explain how you would support secure attachment with your 6-month-old child when you place her in an early care and education setting and return to work.

2. Using Vygotsky's concept of the zone of proximal development, determine the type of scaffolding you would do for a toddler in a pretend play situation.

3. Think about your expectations for fathers relative to their motivation, skill, and support in caring for infants. Decide what you believe, then talk with a male about his expectations. Compare the expectations and reasons for them.

4. Talk with the mother of a young child about the amount and type of television her child watches. Note any concerns she expresses. Are these related to the developmental appropriateness of programming?

Chapter 10

Emotional Development

Emotional development is one of the least studied areas of early child development, especially compared to areas like language and cognitive development, but even in comparison to social development. Many texts link social and emotional development together in their coverage and refer to social-emotional development. There is little doubt that social and emotional development are related, and that emotional development needs to be viewed in a social context. However, combining social and emotional development obscures the specific ties that emotional development has to cognition, language, and other developmental areas (Hyson, 1994).

Rather than a belief that it is less important than other developmental areas, the lack of information about emotional development reflects the complexity of studying such a complicated elusive area. Recently, however, there has been increased professional interest and acknowledgment of the importance of this area. The focus is on the development of emotionally healthy children. Increased interest derives from looking at emotions as a motivator of development, concern about the impact of early care and education settings on infant and toddler development, the impact of poverty on emotional development, the amount of stress many young families face, and the cumulative impact these conditions have on infant and toddler development.

Theories Relating to Emotional Development

Few theories focus directly on emotional development. Consequently, the underlying basis for our knowledge and beliefs about emotional development originates in more general theories. Much early thinking about emotions was not developmentally oriented, but related more to the evaluation and significance of the expression of emotions, causes of emotions, or sequences of physiological events related to emotions (Izard & Malatesta, 1987).

The various theories about emotional development are not necessarily incompatible, but they do focus on different aspects of emotional development. In any case, it is apparent that emotions are easier to describe and feel than to define. How many are there? Which emotions are the basic ones? When do children first feel emotions? Lack of agreement about these issues has led different researchers to conceptualize emotions differently. Some have focused on the expressive characteristics of emotions, particularly facial expressions. Their research has looked at infants' facial expressions to determine when emotions are expressed. Some have looked at the cognitive aspects of emotions and focused on empathy, others at the physiological aspects of emotions and heart rates, and others at the subjective experiences of emotions.

Psychoanalytic Theory of Psychosocial Development

Eric Erikson's work provides a foundation for understanding emotional development as it relates to psychoanalytic theory. He expands and reframes Freud's psychoanalytic theory. Erikson proposed a stage-dependent theory in which each stage depends on the previous stage and contains the seed for succeeding stages. The stages are developmental and viewed as a series of psychosocial crises, with the successful resolution of these crises having positive social-emotional outcomes. Table 10.1 describes these stages.

Erikson frames the conflict inherent in the psychoanalytic model as related to psychosocial crises rather than stemming from the erogenous zones that Freud proposed. Erikson felt that the crises were more responsive to the social context in which individuals grow and develop. Individuals struggle with the conflicting pulls of each crisis, with the resolution of each crisis resulting in basic strength of character or "ego" quality (Erikson, 1989). If the struggle is not successful, then the individual psychologically withdraws and future psychosocial development is at risk. Thus, if infants do not develop trust in infancy, it will be difficult for them to establish autonomy in early childhood. Infants learn trust when they cry and an adult responds quickly. However, if they cry and no one comes, over time they do not develop trust.

Erikson sees the infant's ego, or concept of self, develop through the internal struggle to establish basic *trust* versus *mistrust*. To develop, this trustfulness must be nourished by responsive and sensitive care. To some extent this is viewed in the psychoanalytic context of sucking and weaning, with concern that if infants are weaned too early or too late it interferes with their overall development. The development of trust is related to the development of hope. "Hope is, so to speak, pure future; and where mistrust prevails early, anticipation, as we know, wanes both cognitive and emotionally" (Erikson, 1989, 61). When trust is not developed, the infant withdraws and loses hope. Erikson's explanation for infant deaths in foundling homes would be that the infants did not develop trust, and hence

Table 10.1	Psychosocial Crises	
Age	**Psychosocial Crisis**	**Successful Resolution**
Infancy	Trust vs. Mistrust	HOPE
Early Childhood	Autonomy vs. Shame, Doubt	WILL
Play Age	Initiative vs. Guilt	PURPOSE
School Age	Industry vs. Inferiority	COMPETENCE
Adolescence	Identity vs. Identity Confusion	FIDELITY
Young Adulthood	Intimacy vs. Isolation	LOVE
Adulthood	Generativity vs. Stagnation	CARE
Old Age	Integrity vs. Despair, Disgust	WISDOM

SOURCE: Adapted from Erikson (1989, 49).

hope, that they psychologically withdrew from this environment and, even with good medical care, died from lack of hope.

During early childhood the focus moves to the toddler's growing independence and his need to establish his own autonomy to exercise choice. This stage is characterized by the toddler's struggle between *autonomy* versus *shame* and *doubt*. The toddler bounces back and forth trying to balance free choice and self-restraint. The toddler develops his will as he struggles between doing what he wants to do when he wants to do it (impulsiveness), and regulating his behavior and emotions in a socially acceptable way (compulsion). The toddler is moving from "oral sensory dependence to some anal-muscular self-will and to a certain trust in self-control" (Erikson, 1989, 60).

Although psychoanalytic/psychosocial theory does not have the support it once did, it has had a tremendous influence on the field of early childhood. There is a great emphasis on self-help skills during early childhood and on giving toddlers the satisfaction of completing tasks and viewing themselves as competent. There is also grave concern about caregivers who shame toddlers into compliance and the effect that this type of discipline has for toddler development.

During the play age, or preschool years, the third psychosocial crises is played out as the child works through relationships with parent figures in an atmosphere of play. The child comes to grips with the opposing pulls of *initiative* versus *guilt*. Positive resolution of this conflict results in purpose. Young children who do not work through this conflict between initiative and guilt are extremely inhibited. Lack of a positive outcome at this stage is seen as the foundation for many of the psychoneurotic disturbances, such as hysteria, which are rooted in this stage (Erikson, 1989).

Differential Emotions Theory

Differential emotions theory has been conceptualized primarily in the work of Caroll Izard and his colleagues. The central premise of this theory is that emotions, which are characterized by neurochemical, expressive, and experiential components, are the fundamental motivators of human behavior. There are basic emotions that have unique adaptive functions. Interest allows the infant to learn about his world; disgust keeps him from eating things he should not have; and distress brings someone to care for him. Like the ethological theory that was the basis for the attachment research, the theory of differential emotions emphasizes the survival value of emotions, and delves into them in detail.

Differentialists feel strongly that emotions are the critical building blocks and prime movers in organizing and motivating developmental processes and all significant human behavior (Izard & Malatesta, 1987). They denote seven principles that serve as the foundation of this theory.

Principle 1.   Facial expressions connected to basic emotions have regular forms, emerge at predictable times, and have adaptive functions.

Facial expressions are the result of particular facial muscle movements and consequent changes in facial appearance that signal emotion. Physical emotional expression is an integral component of emotions. This is the neuromuscular component of emotions. It is innate but modifiable. Three facial expressions are present at birth: interest, disgust, and distress (Izard & Malatesta, 1987). Enjoyment, signified by a social smile, emerges at about 1 month. When the smile appears, it encourages social interaction. The emotions of surprise, sadness, fear, and anger emerge as a result of biological maturation by about 7 months. These too have signaling value for the infant.

Young infants not only use their face to express emotion, but often their whole body conveys how they feel. The joyous infant may not only smile and have bright eyes, but she may laugh and move her arms and legs in anticipation (Hyson, 1994). The shy toddler may avert his gaze downward and suck his thumb. A fearful toddler may "freeze." With increasing age, some of these body signs may even become standardized adult forms of expression, such as "high five" and "thumbs up" gestures. Sound and voice quality also convey emotional messages.

An assumption that underlies this conceptualization is that there is a natural concordance between expression and feeling; that is, that the infant's facial expression is an accurate representation of his internal feelings, that they are congruent. When an infant is feeling distressed, his facial expression will show this distress. Likewise, when he is feeling joyous, his face will show that as well.

Principle 2.   The emotions system can function independently. Therefore the interaction and interdependence between the emotions system and the cognitive system increase and become more complex with development.

Expressive behavior changes in both function and form because of maturational changes in the nervous system and interactions with the social world. Over time infants learn to regulate their expression of emotions. They also use, and learn to respond to, expressive behavioral cues of others.

Principle 3. Infants change from having instinct-like expression to more restricted and controlled expressions because of maturation and interaction with the environment.

Newborns express their inner states and do not seem to have the ability to do much else. Self-regulation is initially the ability to feel calm and relaxed and not be overwhelmed by the environment. Emotions change in predictable ways with increasing age. An event that might have elicited the basic emotion of distress in a 2-month-old might elicit a more specific response of anger or fear in a 12-month-old. Predictable changes include: frequency, range, discreetness, and integrity of expression (Izard & Malatesta, 1987, 513). As infants get older, negative affect decreases; that is, the amount of time spent in disgust and distress states decreases and there is proportionally more positive affect, especially interest and smiling.

The ability to regulate emotional expression develops gradually and unevenly (Hyson, 1994). Through interest and self-regulatory capacities working together, the infant gradually gains control over his emotions. His "interest" prompts him to visually explore his environment so as to provide stimulation. However, if his environment becomes too stimulating he can use his skills in self-regulation to avert his gaze, to visually find a caregiver's face, to listen to a soothing voice, or to respond to gentle stroking and rocking to help regulate his state.

Young infants learn what they can do to comfort themselves. Before the end of the first year, many have individualized these strategies. By about 1 year infants can exercise conscious, voluntary control over their emotions and even deliberately intensify or reduce their emotional expression (Hyson, 1994). Children also learn to respond to cultural norms for the expression of emotion.

Infants display discrete emotions, but with increasing time, as children gain more control over emotional expression, they show more blends. Blended expressions may signal mixed emotions, or a conscious attempt to mask a particular feeling. There are even suggestions that children as young as 2 years can use a social smile as a mask for other feelings. However, they frequently cannot control their facial expression to conceal all of the negative affect as they smile (Izard & Malatesta, 1987).

Principle 4. Infants are born with an innate expression–feeling concordance, but with development there is increased flexibility in expression–feeling relations.

Differential emotions theory hypothesizes that there is an initial link between the infant's expression and feelings at birth; that is, what an infant feels internally and how he expresses that feeling are congruent. One task of the infant is to learn to uncouple this link and self-regulate the expression of emotions. The ability to do this is a result of cognitive development and social interaction. Toddlers spend a tremendous amount of time learning to manage the expression of emotions in everyday life. As their behavior repertoire increases, they conceal feelings in order to not hurt others, as well as for personal gain, or to avoid punishment. They learn to express sadness when another gets hurt, even when they don't like the child who is injured, and they learn to constrain their anger when their turn is over or they must wait for their turn (Izard & Malatesta, 1987).

Principle 5.   The socialization of emotional expressions contributes to the regulation of emotional feelings.

The facial expressions of the infant influence the caregiver and likewise the expressions of the caregiver influence the infant. These expressions help share feelings through matching and empathy, and serve to motivate social interactions. As infants learn to exercise some control over emotions, they begin to bump up against the social conventions of their family and culture. Many of the rules that govern how emotions are expressed are culture specific. Young children learn to express, transform, inhibit, or mask emotions based on their socialization. This learning teaches them to conform to the customs of the larger culture relative to the regulation of emotions. Some of this socialization is gender specific.

Principle 6.   Emotion-feelings are the same over the life span but the causes and sequences of these feeling change with development.

Although emotional development changes with increasing age, the emotion-feelings do not. Pain is probably the best example of this. Whether it is the cry of the infant getting a DPT shot or the stoic acceptance of a terminally ill patient, pain is still the feeling. The causes and expressions of the feeling, however, differ. The cue-producing characteristics of pain, disgust, and fear help to keep one safe throughout the life span. Some feel that empathy should also be emphasized as a basic emotion that meets the evolutionary criteria as the basis for acts of altruism. This certainly has value to the species. Thus helping behavior, although manifested differently, appears at all ages (Izard & Malatesta, 1987). Because feelings themselves are stable, with repetition infants learn to identify feelings such as joy or sadness. Feelings may be the first element of "self."

Izard and Malatesta (1987) distinguish between emotion-feelings and the external expression of emotions. The facial expressions of emotions are often brief. Therefore one cannot assume that when the external expression of an emotion is over that the feeling itself is gone. The duration of an emotion is far more complex and it includes cognition as well as biochemical processes of the body, in this case particular hormones and neurotransmitters.

With increasing age, children's available responses to emotions increase. An infant experiencing fear will try to escape or avoid the situation. An older toddler might use language to deal with fear. A child shouting "You don't scare me!" at a taunting peer is an indication of his coping with fear in a more complex way.

Principle 7.   The concordance of facial expressions and expression-feelings help the child develop emotion-cognitive relations and affective-cognitive structure.

Differential emotions theory sees emotions as the primary motivator for the acquisition of language and cognitive development. Likewise, growth in understanding and language enhances the complexity and flexibility of emotional development.

This principle suggests that the first affective-cognitive structure is the association between positive affect and the image of the caregiver's face. It is through experiences that allow the association of a facial expression with a feeling state that infants develop mental structures related to emotions. It is these expression-feelings sequences, literally viewed as cause-and-effect sequences, that help infants identify feeling states. With growing awareness, the children can recognize these states, own them, regulate them, and, ultimately, use the state to elicit change in their environment.

Emotional Stages and Milestones

Greenspan and Greenspan (1985) identify six stages, or major milestones, in emotional development. Their conceptualization might be viewed as a stage-based theory, with overlapping stages or milestones. While the infant is working on mastery of a particular stage, he is also simultaneously exploring another stage of emotional development. The Greenspans do not focus on distinctions between stages of emotional development for classification purposes, as was done, for example, in Piaget's theory of cognitive development; rather, they see a continuous flow wherein the end of one stage is blending into the next.

After approximately nine months in the darkness of the womb, infants emerge into a world full of sensory stimulation. There are three components to the *first stage* or emotional milestone for the infant: He must feel tranquil in the midst of this stimulation, organize his sensations, and reach out actively into the world. This reaching out leads into the *second stage*. The infant must be interested in the sights and sounds of his new world and find them pleasurable. The *third stage* brings the infant further into the human world, as events are not only intriguing, but enticing, pleasurable, and exciting. At this stage infants between about 3 and 10 months want to interact with their world. They want to take turns with their parents and respond. They want to be part of actions and reactions. Their emotions are evident as pleasure produces a smile, while anger and protest are seen in their refusal to give up, a tight grasp, or tears (Greenspan & Greenspan, 1985).

By about 10 to 12 months the *fourth stage* begins to emerge. Infants connect small units of feeling and social behavior and learn that these bits develop into more complicated patterns of behavior. By about the middle of this stage, toddlers are capable of more complex behaviors. Now the toddler can go beyond simply being able to express pleasure or displeasure. If a toddler wants a particular toy that is out of reach, rather than just being able to cry to express his displeasure at not having what he wants, he can organize and focus his feelings on what he wants (the toy), develop a plan of action based on his intentions (take his mother's hand and lead her to the desired toy and point to it), and have a sense of satisfaction at getting his needs met through his own planning and actions (playing with the toy). He realizes the symbolic meaning of objects. He also realizes that objects have functions as do people. If you place a telephone in his hand, he will talk into it. He more clearly comprehends the distinctions between animate and inanimate objects and that these serve different functions. All this occurs before the age of 2 (Greenspan & Greenspan, 1985).

The *fifth stage* incorporates the advances the toddler has made in cognitive development to reconceptualize his world. This stage is characterized by the tod-

Now toddlers can separate make-believe from reality and enjoy imaginative play.

dler's ability to move from understanding how objects function to being able to imagine the objects in his mind. He can create in his mind's eye a picture of his mother or father or pet. He can play imaginatively and even dream. However, he has difficulty distinguishing dreams from reality (Greenspan & Greenspan, 1985).

During the *sixth stage* of emotional development children are able to separate make-believe from reality, since they can play with ideas, plan, and even anticipate what will happen. They are expanding their world of ideas to include emotions. They have moved beyond the more generalized emotions of pleasure to curiosity, the ability to set their own limits, and to express empathy and love. Three-year-olds want emotional dialogues that are increasingly complex (Greenspan & Greenspan, 1985).

Another developmental milestone is the association of verbal symbols to feeling states, that is, emotion-cognition relations. Toddlers begin to label emotions during the second year and by 18 months most toddlers have considerable skill in this area. By age 3 children can demonstrate rather sophisticated knowledge of not only emotions but the causes and sequences of emotions.

The Greenspans believe that children, like adults, may reach different levels of functioning in different emotional areas because of emotional constrictions or limitations. That is, a young child may show warm trusting feelings, but be unable to lead or assert himself. They may show overall adequate functioning, but have setbacks in a particular area. There are also children who do not reach adequate levels of functions. They do not know how to relate to others and so they often play alone. Or they may vent their frustration through aggression and temper tantrums, their only way of expression, since they are not able to talk or even scream about their problems. Successive failures to attain emotional milestones are associated with the likelihood of difficulties at subsequent emotional stages (Greenspan & Greenspan, 1985). Helping children attain emotional growth and development from the earliest stages is the best way of ensuring the likelihood of positive emotional development.

Defining Emotional Development

Izard and his colleagues and the Greenspans have probably helped focus the field on a definition of emotions more than any other professionals.

> "An emotion is experienced as a feeling that motivates, organizes, and guides perception, thought, and action" (Izard, 1991, 14).
> "... emotions—characterized by neurochemical, expressive, and experiential components—are the fundamental motivator of human behavior and each of the basic emotions has unique adaptive functions including a significant role in the organization of the developmental processes" (Izard & Malatesta, 1987, 494).
> "... we view emotions as complex, subjective experiences that have many components, including physical, expressive, cognitive, and organizing, as well as highly personalized, subjective meanings" (Greenspan & Greenspan, 1985, 7).

What seems clear in these statements is that emotions play a role in the organization of, and motivation for, development. This takes the study of emotions far beyond just facial expressions and accelerated heart rates.

Based on this complex view of emotions, it seems important to take advantage of the similarities in the various theories and to make them easier to apply in early childhood. The following themes flow through all of the theories.

Developmental Domains Are Interrelated

In attempting to understand development, scholars have tended to separate it into component developmental and skill areas. Although this separation makes the developmental process easier to conceptualize, it sometimes neglects the interrelatedness of developmental areas. The long-term consequence of this disaggregation approach is that assessment, treatment, and intervention have focused on particular developmental areas as if they could be treated in isolation.

For example, an infant with cerebral palsy would probably be referred to a physical therapist to help him achieve motor milestones that he was slow in reaching. It is unlikely that he would be referred to a mental health professional to support the motivational and internal mental organizations needed to perform motor tasks.

Recently, scholars interested in emotions have focused more on functional interrelationships among the different domains and are recognizing that one domain may affect functioning in other domains. They are not referring to the more obvious overlap between social and emotional development, but rather the role emotions play in the cognitive, language, and motor domains. This multi-domain approach increases the complexity of viewing children's development, which is further complicated by the need to look at the infant or toddler as part of a family system that embraces certain cultural values, and who lives in a specific geographic area, and at a particular point in sociohistorical time.

Although it is useful for our understanding to study cognitive, language, motor, social, and emotional development separately, when we look at the whole child we cannot separate these domains because they interact and influence each other.

Emotional Development Has a Biological Basis and Is Adaptive

There seems to be a consensus that infants are born with qualities which may be called drives, motives, or inborn tendencies, or even "prewiring," which have certain adaptive survival skills. At a general level these include skills for self-regulation, activity, becoming interested in the world, participating in human interactions, and seeking positive affect (Poisson & DeGangi, 1992). Another way of stating this is that nature equips infants with loud cries and the ability to cling to a caregiver, to give dazzling smiles, to lift their arms to be picked up, and other behaviors that are designed to elicit caring and close relationships from significant adults (Honig, 1993).

Emotions Develop in a Social Context

Infant and toddler emotions develop in the context of relationships. It is through imitating, initiating, and responding to adults that young children learn about their emotions and the full range of emotional functioning. Infants seem to have a built-in tendency to become attached to their caregivers. They are capable of establishing relationships with several caregivers. Sibling bonds, too, are characterized by strong emotions. With increasing age, children develop friendship patterns and have ties to a peer group.

The contagion of crying that occurs when one infant sets others off is probably not empathy. However, over time children do respond to the distress of others, the precursor of empathy. Some scholars feel that the capacity for empathy, the tendency to vicariously experience emotional states another feels, has evolved in humans and is the basis for biologically based altruism (Hoffman, 1981). The process of social referencing begins at about 8 or 9 months and continues through the preschool years. This occurs, for example, when toddlers deliberately look at an adult to predict what will happen if they were to take another child's toy (Hyson, 1994). Toddlers seem fascinated by the emotions of others and put on displays to elicit emotions, sometimes laughter and sometimes anger.

Patterns of Emotional Development

Emotional development changes with increasing age. As with motor development, infants develop an increasing array of emotional resources as they grow older. Emotions can be viewed as having various components (Lewis, 1992). *Emotional states* are the feelings related to different emotions. *Emotional expressions* include facial expressions, physical posture, movement, as well as other nonverbal ways to convey emotions and verbal expression of emotions. *Emotional experience* has to do with how a person interprets and evaluates their emotions. Emotional experience is the most cognitive aspect of emotions because it requires the individual to bring these experiences to a conscious level and reflect on them (Lewis, 1992).

It is difficult to know when young children begin to understand emotions. Some studies report infants as young as 6 weeks can distinguish between facial expressions (for example, happy versus angry), but there is little indication as to what this ability actually means to the infant. Identifying developmental patterns involves two related issues. The first issue concerns identifying the links between children's early understanding of emotions and language. The second relates to how children's understanding of emotions is linked to interactions with others (Kuebli, 1994). The developmental timetable for the emergence of emotional states is fairly well agreed upon.

- Birth to about 7 months—displays emotions (interest, distress, and disgust at birth; enjoyment emerges at about 1 month) and responds to emotions in others (Izard & Malatesta, 1987).
- Seven to 18 months—surprise, sadness, fear, and anger emerge about 7 months. Shame, shyness, guilt, and contempt emerge between 12 and 18 months (Izard & Malatesta, 1987). Infants use emotional cues of others (social referencing) to guide their responses to situations. They label or comprehend few emotion terms (Kuebli, 1994).
- Eighteen to 24 months—embarrassment and pride emerge. The first emotion words are beginning to appear (happy, sad). At this point toddlers begin to use emotion words spontaneously in conversations with others (Kuebli, 1994). They can reliably associate facial expressions with simple emotional labels. Happiness appears to be the easiest emotion for them to label (Hyson, 1994).
- Two to 3 years—children's emotions vocabulary increases rapidly. They can correctly label simple emotions in themselves and others. They can talk about emotions they have experienced in the past, what they are currently feeling, and how they might feel in the future. They can identify emotions associated with certain situations and talk about the causes and consequences of emotions (Kuebli, 1994). By 3 years children can imagine how

they might feel in various hypothetical situations. They use emotion language in pretend play.

We are less knowledgeable about the emergence of emotional experience. Emotional experience probably develops gradually with the child's self-differentiation and becomes integrated into his self-concept. Adults often take an active role in the socialization of young children's emotions. Adult behavior can reinforce the child's expression of emotions. Telling Nadine "I like your smile" rewards that behavior. On the other hand, saying "It can't hurt that much" sends the message that displaying emotions is not okay (Ford, 1993). Adults can also directly teach children about social conventions for expressing emotions. The obvious, but ill-advised, "boys don't cry" is a prime example of direct teaching. Emotional expression is also taught indirectly through "contagion" (when one child laughs others "catch" it), through social referencing and through observation and modeling (Kuebli, 1994). Sometimes emotional beliefs are influenced by expectancy or foreshadowing as when adults tell children they are going to "love" a new experience whether it is a new book or a new teacher.

Forms of emotional expression are embedded in cultures and subcultures. Different cultures support or condone the expression of certain emotions and when, how, and with whom these emotions can be expressed. For example, Japanese culture has more emphasis on shame than does United States culture (Lewis, 1992). Families, too, differ in their acceptance of emotions and language they will allow to express emotions. Within families there are gender differences in how parents talk to young children about emotions. Both fathers and mothers have been noted to talk about a greater number and variety of emotions with daughters than with sons (Kuebli & Fivush, 1992).

Talking about emotions with young children provides them with a foundation to learn about feelings. Hyson (1994) identified seven major trends that characterized children's emotional growth:

- Wider, more complex emotional relationships
- More varied, complex, and flexible ways of expressing emotions
- Better coordination and control of emotions and emotion-related skills
- More ability to reflect on their own feelings and those of others
- Representation of emotions through language, play, and fantasy
- Linking individual emotions to culturally valued skills and standards
- An integrated, positive, autonomous, but emotionally connected, sense of self (Hyson, 1994, 59–60).

Temperament

Although the basic processes by which children learn about and develop emotions are similar, there are vast individual differences in the display of emotions and emotional states in young children. Temperament is one aspect of emotional development that has received much attention. Infants are born with a unique temperament. Temperament is a pattern of responsiveness and moods and is

All toddlers get upset on some occasions. It is the pattern of these reactions that reflect personality and temperament.

present at birth. Some infants smile all the time—no matter what happens—and some infants are difficult to soothe once they are disturbed or frustrated. Some toddlers are shy around strangers, while some feel comfortable and secure wherever they are. An infant's temperament impacts on how he reacts to the people in his world and how those people respond to him.

Personality develops over time. It is shaped by experience. At birth infants have only temperament; personality develops as infants live and grow in their world. Temperament affects how an infant relates to his world. Temperament includes the infant's general mood (happy, fussy, and so on); activity level (adventurous, cautious); adaptability (flexible, routinized); intensity of reactions (appropriate or not); persistence; distractibility; reactions to new situations; and regularity of sleeping and eating cycles. Just as adults respond to situations in fairly predictable ways, so too do infants. It is her predictable pattern of response and preferences that makes up an infant's temperament.

Thomas, Chess, and Birch (1968), in their New York longitudinal study, collected data from parent interviews and child observations and identified nine dimensions and three styles or types of temperament that they felt had stability over time. Children who were categorized as "easy" or "difficult" at age 3 were still in that category in young adulthood (Chess & Thomas, 1990). These particular characteristics are useful to observe. Soderman (1985) described these characteristics and observations in children.

- *Activity level:* This refers to the percentage of time an infant or toddler is active or not active. The child who is always on the go and can't sit still is at one end; the child who just sits is at the other extreme. Children need a balance both in themselves and their programming of both active and less active times.
- *Rhythmicity:* Children have an internal biological clock that can be either regular or unpredictable. For those children who are regular, it is important to look at the match between adult expectations and the child's typical pattern. To the extent these mismatch, this child can be more difficult than the unpredictable child.
- *Approach/withdrawal:* Children have a typical response to new experiences. The extremes are to approach without caution (no fear) or to avoid at all costs through crying or clinging to adults. Most children approach new experiences with some degree of caution. For children who have had many or recent encounters that were painful, the response of clinging or crying is understandable.
- *Adaptability:* Some children find it easy to adapt to change, others find it very difficult. Young children who are change resistant may find new routines, a different caregiver, a new sibling, or even a new child entering the class extremely stressful. Especially at celebrations, holidays, and transitions these children need extra time and support.
- *Intensity of reaction:* Many situations evoke reactions in young children. Some are happy; others are sad or angry. It is the intensity and length of the response in relation to the event that needs to be evaluated. The child who violently cries for 20 minutes when another child takes a toy and the child who shows little or no reaction when all the toys are taken are examples of extremes.
- *Responsiveness threshold:* This is the amount of stimulation necessary to obtain a response. For one child, to be lightly touched will result in a cry of pain; another child may have to be told to take his hand out of the water which is scalding him. Children who have low response thresholds can become overstimulated by too much noise, touch, light, and so on. They need support in regulating their environment.
- *Mood:* Children have a range of moods that are a balance of happy and less positive moods. Some children seem to be in a predictable mood most of the time; others vary considerably. Infants and toddlers who have predictable negative moods that include frequent crying and fussing may make adults feel guilty. Rather than receiving the extra attention, love, and support they need, these children may be avoided.
- *Attention span and resistance:* The amount of time a child remains interested in an activity increases with age. Some children are consistently able to complete tasks, while others flit from activity to activity in a scattered way. Resistance is the ability to return to an activity if interrupted and to settle back in. This ability also varies from child to child.

■ *Distractibility:* This relates to how the child reacts to extraneous stimuli. Can the child block out distracting sights and sounds or does he easily lose concentration? Some young children become so involved in projects that they do not allow themselves enough time to get to the bathroom; others cannot become absorbed in any activity and their attention continually wanders.

Most young children, and adults for that matter, have some "difficult" traits, or have days when the traits are displayed. It is only when the infant or toddler's predictable patterns of response are extreme that there is a need for concern.

Temperament Types

■ *Easy children* are those who rate moderate in intensity, adaptibility, approachableness and rhythmicity, and have predominately positive moods. They are usually calm and predictable and tend to eat and sleep on a schedule, although they can adapt the schedule to some extent. They typically approach new experiences positively and show little negative emotion. Often they are easy going and tend to be highly sociable. Chess and Thomas (1977) classified about 40 percent of their sample as easy children.
■ *Difficult children* are at the other end of the temperament scale. Difficult infants show a lot of negative emotion—they cry a lot, are fearful of new experiences, and are easily distracted. They are unpredictable and have irregular schedules and mood shifts. Although they set their own eating and sleeping pattern, they do not follow a predictable schedule. They shift states quickly and may go from sleeping to screaming in seconds. These children are slow to adapt, non-rhythmical, have intense reactions, and often have negative moods. They are also movers. They crawl, walk, or run, rarely staying in the same place for long. Even before their movement is purposeful they are moving. They are also less sociable than other children. Chess and Thomas (1977) found about 10 percent of their sample to be difficult children.
■ *Slow-to-warm-up children* have the characteristics of difficult children but do not show the intensity or persistence of the difficult. Initially their response to new events is negative, but, given time, they do in fact "warm up." Although it takes them longer to adapt than easy children, they do not show the intensity in reactions of difficult children. The remaining 35 percent of the sample did not fall into one of these categories and were considered of "average" temperament. Fifteen percent of Chess and Thomas's (1977) sample fell into this category.

Infant temperament is sometimes a challenge to adults. Some parents find this information comforting in that by accepting that children come with different temperaments, they are not the cause of their children's temperament. Temperament does, however, affect the infant's development because it impacts how the infant approaches his environment as well as how the environment affects the infant (Brazelton, 1992). Difficult and easy children evoke different responses from adults. However, they don't get the same response from all adults. The key is the interaction pattern between the child and the adult, or the "goodness of fit"

(Thomas & Chess, 1980). *Goodness of fit* looks at the mesh between the expectations and interactions of the adult and the child's behavior in relation to the expectations. A mother who is up and on the go and is not disturbed by crying and temper tantrums might be delighted by a *difficult* child and find an *easy* child a bore. A parent who has a cautious approach to new ideas and patience may find a *slow-to-warm-up child* enchanting, whereas with either a difficult or easy child she may feel overwhelmed or unnecessary.

It is not possible to evaluate child outcome on temperament alone. Chess (1983) stresses that the interaction between the adult's expectations and the child's responses is a key factor in assessing the quality of the adult-child relationship. Concern focuses around children with difficult temperaments who need extra adult understanding but who may actually receive less positive responses from adults who do not know how to work with difficult children. These "difficult" infants may be at risk for a variety of developmental problems, such as attachment disorders and problems relating to learning (attention deficit hyperactivity disorder), behavior, and socialization (Goldstein, 1992).

Crying and Temper Tantrums

All children at one time or another cry or throw temper tamtrums without being physically hurt. The tantrums are usually strong expressions of anger characterized by crying, screaming, and perhaps hitting, kicking, or destroying of materials. Older toddlers may also hit others or use language to express frustration. Prior to developing adequate language abilities to express anger or frustration, children use tantrums as their way to vent "pent-up" tension.

Although a pattern of excessive crying is considered a symptom of stress (Honig, 1986), crying is increasingly being viewed in a more positive light. Some view crying as the natural repair kit all individuals are born with and consider it an important and beneficial physiological coping mechanism. Crying not only reduces tension but also removes toxins from the body (Solter, 1992). Emotional crying is a response to "the straw that broke the camel's back." Tension has been building, and at some point something triggers the tears. It is often difficult to figure out specifically what caused the crying. The event which was the direct antecedent of crying may seem trivial, yet the emotional build-up may have been coming on for a long time.

Although crying is viewed as positive and healthy, just as shouting for joy is, there are times and places when children need to learn to control their emotional expression. This becomes increasingly true as children get older. Adults sometimes have problems accepting children's crying. They see their role as keeping young children happy and when they cry they may feel that they are not doing their job well. They may try to make crying children "happy up" by telling them not to cry or conversely threatening to give them something to cry about. In reality, "crying is not the hurt, but the process of becoming unhurt" (Solter, 1992, 66). Crying is the solution, not the problem.

Some children like to be held while they cry, others do not. Sometimes crying turns into raging and tantruming. If others are likely to be hurt, the behaviors need to be stopped. The goal is to stop violence while encouraging the expression of feelings. Firm but patient contact with a tantruming child can often move the behavior into crying. Children with delayed language skills often continue tantruming behaviors after others have stopped. Physical outbursts of emotions are one of the few ways available for young children to express anger or frustration.

Tantrums can also be attention-seeking behaviors, especially for children raised in environments severely lacking in social stimulation. Reinforcing appropriate behaviors, while providing consequences for negative behaviors, has been the accepted method for dealing with tantrums. As toddlers develop better language skills, they are able to use speech rather than tantrums as a viable way to express frustration and anger.

Biting, Pinching, and Hitting

Most children go through a stage during which they bite, pinch, or hit others, whether they be children or adults. The expected age at which this behavior occurs is between 1 and 2 years. During this time children are still very egocentric. They notice other children, but see them as objects, not people. There is frequent tension over possession of objects. As a child is learning control over his emotions, and saying "no," tantruming and biting can be used to get what he wants. Since language skills are still developing, children do not yet have a good repertoire of words to always express anger or frustration in acceptable ways. It is during this time period that biting and pinching occurs.

Toddlers need verbal direction as to how to redirect their anger in socially appropriate ways, giving them the verbal phrases to use. It is when children persist in biting, pinching, and hitting well past the expected ages, or when the behaviors are excessive (such as biting that breaks the skin), that the behavior becomes of concern to adults.

Shyness

Occasional shyness is expected, as all children require moments for being alone. *Shyness* is characterized by an ambivalent approach/avoidance quality (Hyson & Van Triest, 1987). Shyness is different from wariness and social disengagement; those behaviors do not share the ambivalent characteristics of shyness.

Shyness in infants is often seen in response to new adults, and, as greater cognitive advances bring greater social sensitivity, in toddlers. Cultural differences may account for some shyness (Honig, 1987). Shyness in young children is often characterized by thumb sucking or alternately smiling and hiding (Izard & Hyson, 1986). Avoidance of gaze, an unwillingness to respond to friendly social overtures, and even blushing are also associated with shyness (Honig, 1987).

Some aspects of shyness are learned by children, some appear to be culturally based, and others are genetic. When shyness is a temporary solution to a novel or overwhelming social situation, it may well be adaptive. When shyness is extreme, it may be related to a poor self-image or a lack of social skills. Shy children may not be noticed and may not have the opportunities or skills to interact with other children or to gain an adult's attention. Elective mutism in school may be an extreme form of shyness, especially if the child displays very different behavior in the family setting (Honig, 1987).

A shy child needs to be given time to warm up in new situations. He may need to be taught social skills for joining peer groups. He may need support in feeling good about himself and the talents he has to offer other children. He needs the subtle support of caring adults who encourage him but don't take over and act for him.

Shy children may need to learn skills to gain access to groups and maintain group membership. Children who grow up in authoritarian families are more likely to be shy. Caregiving styles that support democratic decision making and respect may help young children (Baumrind, 1971). Shyness can be reduced by helping children feel more attractive, supporting them in small groups after having taught them social entry skills, and even by teaching them muscle relaxation games (Honig, 1987).

Withdrawal

Children differ in how introverted or extroverted they are. Children who are introverted need more time to be alone whereas children who are extroverted like lots of social interaction. It is important to respect the rights of children to be introverts (Morris, 1994).

Concern arises when there is a pattern of excessive withdrawal, characterized by the inability to develop relationships with parents or peers, inactivity, excessive social isolation, and lack of affect. If these characteristics occur individually or in combination, there is a cause for concern. Consistent lack of interaction will cause a child to miss experiences that lead to improved social competency, better self-esteem, and increased overall development. Children may need to be taught social-skill techniques and be reinforced for all social initiatives.

Atypical Emotional Development

Professionals concerned about atypical emotional development are primarily in the field of infant mental health. The focus of infant mental health has been prevention and an attempt to identify long-term risk factors (Edme, Bingham, & Harmon, 1993). This is a fast growing field and one that is different from adult mental health. From its inception the field has been multidisciplinary as no one profession has all the knowledge or skills needed to work with these infants.

One of the challenges to the profession is the task of classifying problems in this area. Problems must be classified with a developmental orientation because young children change so quickly that what would be normal at one time may be atypical at another. Classification must also be done with an understanding of the dynamic exchange between the young child and his environment. This requires a systemic and multigenerational point of view.

Classification of infants with atypical emotional development is a challenge. However, its purpose is to communicate knowledge among professionals and to help people. Several different organizations have developed classification systems including the American Psychiatric Association, the World Health Organization, and the National Center for Clinical Infant Programs (NCCIP). The NCCIP classification identifies five major diagnostic categories: Disorders of Social Development and Communication; Psychic Trauma Disorders; Regulatory Disorders; Disorders of Affect; and Adjustment Reaction Disorders (National Center for Clinical Infant Programs, 1991).

Disorders of Social Development and Communication

Disorders in this area include atypical pervasive developmental disorders. Pervasive developmental disorders are characterized by severe deficits in many areas of development (American Psychiatric Association, 1994). Early childhood schizophrenia, Rett's Disease, and autism would be examples of a pervasive developmental disorder. Autism has received more attention and empirical study than other emotional/social disorders of infancy. For this reason it will be dealt with in greater detail.

Autism

Infantile autism is considered a form of childhood psychosis. Autism affects 4 to 5 out of 10,000 individuals (American Psychiatric Association, 1994). Males outnumber females 4 to 1 (Batshaw, Perret, & Reber, 1992). At birth the autistic infant appears similar to other children and often shows normal developmental patterns. Some warning signs such as stiffness when being held, or lacking or infrequent eye contact are subtle and often recognized only in hindsight (Segal & Segal, 1992). Between 18 and 36 months the signs of autism manifest themselves prominently and this is when a diagnosis is likely. About 70 percent of individuals with autism are also mentally retarded (American Psychiatric Association, 1994).

Autistic infants begin to withdraw and are unresponsive and unaffectionate. They often engage in excessive repetition of body movements, including head banging and rocking. There may be some functional speech, though children with autism typically use repetitive, jargony speech patterns or rely on gestures or motoric actions. There is an absence of peer interaction. These children may exhibit stereotyped behavior such as spinning objects, hand whirling, rocking, echolalic speech, or excessive orderliness.

The exact etiology of autism is unknown, although researchers seem to be in agreement that autism is caused by an abnormality in the brain or brain damage (Batshaw, Perret, & Reber, 1992). Previously, researchers felt that autism was caused by cold, uncaring mothers. Current research does not support this finding, but some families still feel a stigma.

Early intervention has been shown to be very effective in dealing with early autism. Intensive behavior modification, individual attention, and structured learning environments are essential components for a successful early intervention program for children with autism. Lovaas (1982) reported that 50 percent of the children in his study who were provided with an intensive one-on-one behavior modification program prior to age 3½ made a complete recovery, and were able to enter regular elementary school and attain normal IQ scores. From the parents' perspective many readjustments in lifestyle are necessary, as the young child with autism displays unpredictable behaviors, many of which are potentially life threatening. There is little doubt that these families have increased stress levels.

Psychic Trauma Disorders

Disorders in this category are classified as to whether the disorder is related to a single event (acute, single event) or whether it is a connected series of traumatic events and those events are repeated (chronic, repeated). A child who broke his arm in an automobile accident and had to be taken to the emergency room would be expected to have short-term disturbances such as nightmares and probably would be fearful of riding in cars for a time. A child who is repeatedly abused or neglected is at risk for more pervasive interference with developmental tasks (Finkelhor, 1995).

Regulatory Disorders

There are a variety of ways in which infants need to regulate their behavior to adjust to the world around them. Infants with trouble doing this are often referred to as "fussy." Sometimes these behaviors are beyond "fussy" and infants need help in regulating themselves. Regulatory disorders are characterized by disturbances in sensory, sensorimotor, or organizational processing (Edme, Bingham, & Harmon, 1993). Infants in this category would have trouble regulating their states, gaining control over sensory input, having efficient motor functioning, and perhaps some problems in social relatedness (Edme, Bingham, & Harmon, 1993). Six specific types of regulatory disorders are identified: hypersensitivity type, underreactive type, active-aggressive type, mixed type, regulatory-based sleep disorder, and regulatory-based eating disorder (National Center for Clinical Infant Programs, 1991). These subcategories help focus on the specific area of the disruption. This classification system allows one to identify disorders in the area of sleeping and eating/feeding as infant disorders rather than as symptoms of other disorders that are more typical of older individuals.

Treatment is very individualistic. However, infants are typically helped to regulate their states by such things as swaddling and rhythmic music and self-comforting techniques. Speech and language therapists work with children with feeding disorders finding textures, consistencies, and techniques that increase the likelihood of food consumption.

Disorders of Affect

This category reflects both generalized negative states as well as disorders that are related to specific environmental circumstances. Disorders in this category include anxiety disorder; mood disorders, including prolonged bereavement, depression, and labile (unstable) mood disorder; mixed disorder of emotional expressiveness; and deprivation syndrome. Some of the disorders are concerned with relationships and growth disturbances. Although the emphasis is typically on infant–parent relationships, it is possible that a child who is distressed in a child-care setting would show a disorder in this category. Adults are helped to read infant cues more accurately and to increase the order and predictability in the young child's environment and the availability of a primary caregiver.

Adjustment Reaction Disorders

Concerns in this area focus on the length of time it takes infants to adjust to change. The expectation is that if the adjustment takes more than four months, then infants may be having more problems that should be expected. An infant or toddler who cannot adjust to child care after four months would be a concern in this area. Specialists in infant mental health may have to be consulted to work with infants and their caregivers to provide support and guidance to work with these problems.

Summary

Emotional development is one of the least studied areas of child development. Lack of information about emotional development reflects the complexity of studying emotions, rather than a belief that it is less important than other developmental areas. Although few theories focus directly on emotional development, many general theories about behavior form the underlying basis for our knowledge and beliefs about emotional development. For example, Erikson proposed a stage-based developmental theory within which psychosocial crises and the resolution of these crises are seen as affecting social/emotional outcomes in children.

Differential-emotions theorists believe that emotions serve as a foundation for organizing and motivating developmental processes including cognitive, language, and motor functions, and all significant human behavior. The Greenspans discuss emotional development in terms of a stage-based theory with overlapping stages or milestones.

These theories are not necessarily incompatible, but focus on different aspects of emotional development. However, it is apparent that emotions are easier to describe than define. There is interest in looking at the functional interrelationships among the different domains, and recognizing that one area of development may affect functioning in other areas.

One aspect of emotional development that has received much attention is temperament. Temperament affects how an infant relates to his world. Based on their characteristic patterns of behavior, children can be classified into three basic temperament categories or types: easy, difficult, and slow-to-warm-up.

Some patterns of emotional behaviors cause concern whereas others are viewed as atypical. When behaviors persist beyond expected ages or the behaviors become excessive in nature, they may be signals for concern about an emotional disorder. Those who are concerned about atypical emotional development are primarily in the field of infant mental health. The National Center for Clinical Infant Programs identified five major diagnostic categories of atypical development. Infant mental health specialists find these categories helpful when treating infants and toddlers with atypical emotional development.

Application Activities

1. Have a conversation with a young toddler that focuses on emotions. Draw a simple happy and sad face and see if the toddler can identify the emotions. Then see if she has developed a causal relationship between events and emotions. Ask how she would feel at her birthday party, and so on, and then how she might feel if she fell and hurt herself.

2. Using the information given in the text, talk with a parent who has more than one child. Try to determine the temperament types of her children and how the parents act and react to them differently because of this.

3. Observe a toddler from another culture. Can you pick out obvious differences in emotional expression and preferences from those of your own culture?

Chapter 11

Infants and Toddlers and Their Families

The birth of an infant is a momentous occasion that affects all family members. At birth the infant begins an individual course of growth and development. However, he is born into a family. His first relationships and first experiences of the world are with family members. However, he joins an existing family unit whose development is already in progress. As the family incorporates the infant into its system, certain changes and adjustments are necessary in the ongoing process of family development. The life cycle of the family is different from the life cycle of its individual members. To understand infants and toddlers in the context of their families, it is necessary to view the family unit as it changes over time.

Defining the Family

Defining families has become complicated by changing views of changing families in a changing society. Perhaps, like emotions, families are easier to describe than define. For data gathering purposes the Census Bureau defines families as "a group of two or more persons related by birth, marriage, or adoption and residing together in a household" (U.S. Bureau of the Census, 1991, 5).

The census is concerned about legal and biological relationships; scholars are more concerned about commitment. Zilbach notes "A family is a small natural group in which members are related by birth, marriage, or other form which creates a home or functional household unit" (Zilbach, 1986, 6).

Others emphasize different aspects of family. "Families comprise those that have a shared history and a shared future. They encompass the entire emotional system of at least three, and frequently now four generations, held together by blood, legal, and/or historical ties" (McGoldrick, Heiman, & Carter, 1993, 406).

For infants and toddlers the idea of a functional household unit seems to be more relevant than concerns over blood lines and legal ties.

Family Characteristics

Families are diverse. There are many different family types, and even within a type families differ in the number of parents, children, step-children, the sex of these children, and their position in the family. To understand the impact a particular infant will have on a particular family, one first needs to understand the characteristics of the family itself. This requires a variety of information about both the family and the infant. Information about the size of the family and its configuration, as well as knowledge of the family's cultural and ideological background is helpful. The personal styles of its members also influence a family and how it operates. All individuals have personality and temperament characteristics which can be strengths or challenges for families with very young children.

A family's economic resources, education, and occupation combine to form the family's socioeconomic status (SES). Families with a higher SES frequently can afford formal support systems, such as help with cleaning and child care. This does not necessarily mean that these families cope better than families with lower SES, but they do have more resources available to manage stress. The cultural background, in combination with ethnic and religious differences, determines foods eaten, rituals and celebrations, and values and perspectives. Increasingly the United States is becoming multiethnic and multiracial. Infant specialists need to be aware of and value cultural differences, be cognizant of family values, and use culturally sensitive communication.

There is little doubt that metropolitan areas have a wider range of child-care services than rural areas. Families with an infant or toddler living in a rural area might have only a single choice in a child-care setting and it might or might not be a good one. A long drive might be necessary to obtain needed specialized or complex medical care. Problems in getting needed care also exist in large urban areas with primarily poor populations.

Infants and toddlers make great demands on adult time. The health status of all family members is an important variable in coping. To the extent that adult family members have repeated or chronic physical or mental illnesses, or use drugs or alcohol excessively, their abilities to cope in general and to care for an infant or toddler are reduced.

Adding an infant to a family increases stress. Individuals within families have different ways of reducing stress and coping with situations. Some members are more skillful than others, but all family members need to learn methods of coping with stress. If both parents work outside the home and care for young children, their stress increases and the amount of personal time they have decreases. Some parents rely on formal support systems such as counseling to cope with this stress; others use informal support networks such as family and friends; and still others simply ignore the stress in hopes that it will go away or cure itself. It rarely does.

Different infants make different demands on families, and every infant's demands will vary over time. Some infants, such as preterm infants, may require high levels of medical intervention at various times. Others may only see a physician for well-baby check ups. Some infants cry and are difficult to console, whereas others rarely cry. Some spend their time awake and alert, whereas others spend most of their time sleeping. Some toddlers are very active and into everything, while others are less active. It is important to understand how the family perceives the infant. Whereas some families view having a baby as a major crisis, other families see the infant as requiring relatively minor adjustments to family life.

Family Functions

Families have fundamental needs that must be met for their existence to be maintained. To survive, all families must perform certain functions. These functions serve to meet the needs of family members and also have the long-range goal of helping family members become self-sufficient and independent. These functions are the same for all families, although families may fulfill these functions at different levels (Turnbull & Turnbull, 1990; Zilbach, 1989). Infants and toddlers have a special impact on these functions as explained below.

Economic. Families must generate income and pay bills. The addition of an infant to a family increases expenses and may decrease income. Increased expenses can come from the cost of new equipment, clothing, food, diapers, and child-care expenses. Income may be lost if a parent takes maternity leave, if a parent stops working, or if a parent must take time off to care for a sick child.

Maintenance. All families must perform tasks of daily life, such as cooking, cleaning, laundry, and so on. Infants and toddlers, because of their dependence, require more care than older children, and increase the number of daily tasks that must be performed. Families must also decide how to divide up these tasks.

Social. Most families find their social life and outside leisure activities affected by having a new infant. Yet, families need to be part of the larger social system. They need an informal support network of friends and neighbors to provide opportunities for infants and toddlers to develop and practice social skills. Parents also need a social life apart from their children. Overall, families with better social support networks find the adaptation to parenthood easier than those who lack such support systems.

Affection and Self-Image. Families meet the needs of their members for physical intimacy as well as support and love. Infants and toddlers need to develop trust, be securely attached to their parents, and be loved and cared for. A positive self-image is important for all members of the family. Parents themselves may develop a negative self-image if they feel their parenting skills are not effective. All family members need to see themselves as having competence and worth. Parents of infants and toddlers need to support their accomplishments. This may be difficult when parents have worked all day, have daily house-related work, and may be stressed for other reasons.

Educational/Vocational. With infants and toddlers, concerns about education include deciding what constitutes quality child care and the type of care setting

Families need to spend time with their children as well as forming an adult social support network.

in which to place a child to receive such care. As infants become toddlers, the question arises as to whether or not the ideal setting for the infant is also the best setting for the toddler.

Recreation. Families need recuperation time, rest, and relaxation. This is frequently the family activity that is most often eliminated under stress. Sometimes families don't meet recreational needs because of finances, other times because including an infant or toddler makes the activity more difficult. It is important that families find recreational activities they can enjoy as a family, as well as to meet individual recreational needs.

A household unit is created as families fulfill the basic family functions. In varying degrees all family members participate in fulfilling these functions. Caring for children and other dependent members, and meeting individual growth needs, are concerns of all family members through the family life cycle (Zilbach, 1989).

Just as theories are useful for guiding our understanding of cognitive and emotional development, so too can they guide our understanding of infants and toddlers in the context of their families.

Family Theories

There are many different family theories. However, only three that are most relevant to understanding infants and toddlers within the context of their families are presented here.

Family Systems Theory

The family systems framework is a theoretical umbrella that makes assumptions about how families function. Family systems theory focuses on the family as a unit as opposed to the individual infant or toddler himself. The idea that families function as a system is based on the work of Ludwig von Bertalanffy (1934). Bertalanffy, a biologist, viewed organisms as having mutually dependent parts and processes as well as mutual interactions. Social scientists reframed this and conceptualized that all living systems, including families, are internally interdependent (Gladding, 1995). Family members constantly interact and mutually affect each other. It follows then, that when there is a change or movement in one member of the family, or when the family circumstances change, all aspects of family functioning are affected. In the family systems framework the focus is more on the relationships between family members than on the family members themselves.

Family systems theory posits that families operate under the same rules that govern all systems. (A *system* is a set of objects that interrelate with one another to form a whole.) In family systems theory families are viewed as powerful forces that can work for the good or detriment of individual family members (Gladding, 1995). Systems can be either open or closed. In a closed system there is no interaction with outside forces. Living organisms, including infants and toddlers, are parts of open systems. They must interact with their environment to live. Families are viewed as continuously changing and reconstituting themselves. They are open and self-regulating systems. Families also interact with the larger social system. Families have times of stability and times of change and a major family task is to maintain some balance between these two. This stability, or **homeostasis**, is maintained by feedback loops. Negative feedback loops support stability while allowing for minor modifications of the family system. When the need for change is greater, such as when an infant is born, positive feedback loops support change.

Like most systems, families are divided into *subsystems*, which are in fact systems within systems. *Boundaries* define who is part of the system and who is not.

Boundaries vary on a continuum from very rigid to very diffuse. At the one extreme, very "rigid" boundaries are so inflexible that people cannot join or leave the system. Even communication cannot move between subsystems. In this type of family the entrance of an infant might be a crisis. At the other "diffuse" extreme it is difficult to figure out where one system ends and another begins and who belongs to what system. In this type of family system it might be difficult to organize the care of an infant. Optimally, there are clear boundaries where rules of relationships are spelled out, there is good communication between the subsystems, and the subsystems can function without interference from each other.

There is a hierarchial structure of subsystems as they interact with each other. The husband and wife, or couple, constitute the **marital subsystem**. This is the executive subsystem that should be in charge of the family. The ability of the **marital subsystem** to establish a clear boundary allows them to grow and develop as a couple. These same people also constitute the **parental subsystem.** The parental subsystem allows the parents to effectively run the family. When the bond across generations (for example, the mother–child bond) becomes stronger than the marital bond, the marriage is at risk.

Olson, Portner, and Levee (1985) have developed the circumplex model of family functioning focusing on *how* people interact. There are three important elements: cohesion, adaptability, and communication. The Family Adaptability and Cohesion Evaluation Scale (FACES III) measures these elements and is now in its third revision.

Cohesion.   Cohesion, as defined by Olson, Portner, and Levee (1985), is based on the emotional bonding family members have with one another, how they handle distance and closeness, and the degree of autonomy a person has in the family system. The dimension of cohesion focuses on how much independence family members have, how decisions are made within the family, the amount of time families spend together, whether family members share interests or hobbies, and so on.

Families that are extremely high on cohesion are *enmeshed*; that is, the bonds are so close that there is little individual autonomy and family goals and needs are put before individual goals and needs. These families are characterized by overinvolvement and overprotection. At the other extreme of cohesion, families are described as *disengaged*. These families have high autonomy and individuality but experience very little closeness as a family and are not high on family solidarity. These families may be underinvolved; so an infant or toddler might be neglected. Most families fall somewhere between enmeshment and disengagement, with healthy families with young children being closer to enmeshment and moving more toward disengagement as the stage of adolescence approaches.

Adaptability.   Adaptability refers to the ability of the family system to change or modify its power structure, role relationships, and rules in response to different situations (Olson et al., 1983). All families differ in their ability to cope with change and instability—and all families experience these periods.

Families with little control or structure are *chaotic*. These families have few rules but even these change frequently and are rarely enforced. It may not be clear who is part of the family and who is not and there may be no one in charge of the family. Family members come and go apparently at will with little notice or planning. These families are unpredictable and sometimes stressful; they offer little opportunity to develop relationships and common meaning. Family members cannot count on each other nor do they plan together for the future of family members. These families frequently have trouble complying with complicated care routines for infants and toddlers.

Rigid families are the other extreme. They have a high degree of control and structure. They tend to repress change and growth. Roles are rigidly, and often traditionally, defined. The power hierarchy is clear and there is little room for negotiation. Rules are handed down and enforced. However, rules that are appropriate for infants may not change to meet needs as infants move into toddlerhood. Well-functioning families function between chaotic and rigid.

Communication. Communication is seen as the facilitating dimension in the circumplex model and it both characterizes families as well as helps them change degrees of adaptability and cohesion. Communication allows well-functioning families to move from being close and cuddly with infants and toddlers to gradually opening up to allow more space for older children.

Family Life Cycle

In theories relating to the family life cycle, families are conceptualized as a unit of interacting individuals that move through time with predictable stages, tasks, and transitions. Some changes are predictable (*normative*), such as when family members are born, grow up, and leave the home. Sometimes changes cannot be predicted (*non-normative*), such as an infant being born with a disability, or an untimely death. The family life cycle is one method for understanding the family unit as it moves through time.

Researchers studying the family initially tried to identify a "universal" progression for families, that is, regular stages through which all families passed (Duvall, 1977). Life course variations are so great that some have questioned the validity of a universal family life-cycle concept. Others have reframed it (Carter & McGoldrick, 1993; Combrinck-Graham, 1985). In the United States the structure, stages, and form of the family have changed radically since the 1950s. Also, the length, sequence, and composition of transitions tend to vary with social class as well as sociohistorical time (Gladding, 1995). Some reasons for changes are related to later marriages, decreasing birth rates, increasing divorce and remarriage, and longer life expectancy.

Family structure has also changed, challenging the "normal" family life cycle even more. People are living together without marrying (about 3 percent), and women are having children without marrying (about 26 percent). More women are choosing never to marry (about 12 percent), and even more never to have children (15 to 25 percent). Approximately half of all marriages in the United States will end in divorce and an additional 20 percent will have two divorces. About 6 percent or more of the population is homosexual (Carnegie Task Force on Meeting the Needs of Young Children, 1994; Carter & McGoldrick, 1989; McGoldrick, Heiman, & Carter, 1993). Untimely deaths, family members with a chronic illness or a disability, or abusers of drugs or alcohol reduce the number of "normal" families even more. Cultural variations, migration, and poverty reduces the number still further.

Among all the changes that have occurred, the changing role of women has probably had the most dramatic effect on the shift in family life-cycle patterns (Carter & McGoldrick, 1989; Piotrkowski & Hughes, 1993). The role of women as both wife and mother has been central to the concept of the family life cycle. The phases of the family life cycle were the markers in women's lives as they focused on childbearing and child rearing. Child rearing was expected to occupy a woman's active life span. Reality has changed. Therefore we must view infants and toddlers in the families in which they will actually be raised.

Given the great changes that have occurred, what is the value of studying stages based on a model of an intact middle-class family? Regardless of variations, the model focuses on the negotiation of underlying processes of family expansion, contraction, and the realignment of the relationship systems to support the entry, exit, and development of family members in a functional way (Carter & McGoldrick, 1989). Another value of the family life cycle is that it shows the different tasks family units must accomplish at different points in time; how difficult it is to meet the needs of all the family members; and how patterns can change based on the developmental needs of the family and as family members interact with a changing society.

Some theorists think of the family life cycle as a kind of dance. There are times when families are very close (centripetal) and other times when families open up to give their members more freedom or personal space (centrifugal) (Combrinck-Graham, 1985). Childbirth is one of the centripetal, or coming-together, times. Even adult children who had not previously been close with their parents frequently find ways of resolving issues as the first child/grandchild is awaited.

The family life cycle approach is stage based and looks at families over time. At each stage there are developmental tasks that families need to accomplish; if these tasks are not resolved during a particular stage, later stages will be more difficult. A developmental task arises within a family when a family member has needs that converge with societal expectations (Duvall, 1977). For example, a universal developmental task is that infants need to be cared for by adults. When developmental tasks are not met, stress is produced in the family. An infant who cannot be comforted or a toddler not walking by 18 months can create stress in families.

Stages are typically long, whereas the transition between stages is relatively short. The transitions, however, are often stressful as family members are required to change and adapt in response to new situations. The stages, changes required by transitions, and challenges to the family life cycle are discussed below, as well as the concerns when developmental tasks are not met.

Launching the Single Young Adult

It may seem strange to begin the family life-cycle discussion with young adulthood. However, this stage has the potential for beginning a new family life cycle. As the single adult leaves home, he or she must accept emotional and financial responsibility for him or herself. The primary developmental task for this stage is for young adults to develop a sense of self in relation to the family in which they were raised. They need to consider the powerful influence their family has on their perception of reality of who they are and if, who, when, how, and where they will marry. Families also influence their expectations for the remaining stages of the family life cycle including marital roles, choices about childbearing, and child rearing (McGoldrick, Heiman, & Carter, 1993). Additionally, young adults need to develop intimate peer relationships and establish themselves in relation to work or a career and financial independence.

This young adult stage is the cornerstone for later development of both self and family. Successful completion of this stage requires that the young adult separate from his family of origin without cutting them off or continually fleeing to them for emotional support. It is a time to formulate personal life goals, to establish a sense of self before joining with another, and to find new and different ways to relate to the family of orgin. When this developmental process does not come to successful completion, young adults remain emotionally or financially dependent on their family or they cut them off (Carter & McGoldrick, 1989).

The Joining of Families through Marriage: Coupling

The beginning of a family unit can be viewed as the establishment of a common household by two people who may or may not be married, but have the expectation of becoming an interdependent couple. Coupling, whether a first or later marriage, or without marriage, involves renegotiating personal issues that previously were decided individually. Although we usually think of coupling as the joining of two individuals, in reality it is the joining of two family systems with the creation of a third family system. While coupling situations differ widely, current male–female relations are more difficult than in the past because of the changing role of women, the joining of couples from different cultural backgrounds, and physical distance between family members (Carter & McGoldrick, 1989).

Trying to achieve a successful couplehood is challenging, especially when couples are moving toward equality of the sexes. The transition to couplehood requires a commitment to this new family system. Many of the challenges at this stage are related to separating from the family of *origin* and establishing boundaries that allow the couple the space to grow as a twosome while at the same time maintaining connections to the extended family systems (McGoldrick, Heiman, & Carter, 1993). Major issues, such as deciding whether to have children or not, and minor issues, such as putting the cap on the toothpaste, are negotiated. The successful completion of this stage requires the couple to develop a mutually satisfying relationship and see themselves as a unit separate from, but related to, their families of origin.

There is a fairly uniform set of tasks that all couples must negotiate. Their decisions will vary, depending on their views of the proper role for the members of the couple and the family. These roles can be performed by one individual or they can be shared on some basis (50–50, 20–80, and so on). The important issue is that these roles are negotiated during this period and that each partner agrees on the resolution. These roles are typically renegotiated at each stage of the life cycle and the framework for their negotiation needs to be established.

- The provider role—who earns the money to support the family, and whether this role will change with the advent of an infant.
- The maintenance role—who does, or is responsible for, the cooking, cleaning and in general looks after the house. Note that the decision in some cases may be to not assign these tasks to family members but to hire someone to perform these tasks.
- The child-care role—who will be responsible for the infant and his material needs as well as where he will be in care if not at home.
- The child-socialization role—who will be responsible for teaching the child socially acceptable behavior.
- The recreational role—who has responsibility for recreation. Is this done together or individually and is the time equal?
- The sexual role—who is responsive or assertive as a sexual partner. Does the advent of a child change this responsibility?
- The therapeutic role—who is the listener, the sounding board, who offers support and encouragement.
(Adapted from McCubbin & Dahl, 1985).

To the extent that couples reward and complement each other in these roles, the better the relationship is likely to be. Successful and amicable negotiation of these roles provides a positive base for the next stage in the family life cycle, should the couple have a child. To the extent that these issues have not been successfully negotiated, they will reappear as stressors in the next stage.

Becoming Parents: Families with Young Children

This stage of the family life cycle is characterized by adding a dependent member to the family. Becoming parents requires that people add the role of parent to the role of partner. They move up a generation and perform the task of caregiving for the infant and young child (Combrinck-Graham, 1985). Parents may struggle with each other relative to taking responsibility for the infant. They may have made decisions in the previous stage about how they were planning to handle child care and household responsibilities and discovered that planning and reality were different. Parents struggle with issues related to taking responsibility for young children, setting appropriate limits, and developing patience to allow children to express themselves.

Transition to Parenthood.   All family life-cycle transitions, such as marriage or retirement, bring some accompanying stress—the transition to parenthood is no exception (Belsky & Rovine, 1984; Entwisle & Doering, 1981). Becoming parents causes adults to clarify and reconsider their values and the decisions they made in young adulthood. The reality of the infant may be different from the expectation. A mother who initially planned to take a six-week leave from work and then place the infant in child care may decide that she does not want to do that. But, if financially she must go back to work, her situation becomes stressful. Conversely, a mother who quit her job to be with the infant full time may decide that infants are not as much fun as she thought, and so she again seeks a job. As with all joint decisions, the partner may not have changed his thinking or may have changed in different directions. Many changes in a short period of time, especially if the changes are conflicting, are stressful in families.

The extent to which the newborn is divergent from the family's hopes and expectations can be particularly stressful. Children both affect and are affected by the systems in which they develop. The characteristics of the infant and the interaction of these characteristics with parenting styles ("goodness of fit") are particularly important factors.

The central struggle of this stage in the family life cycle is different than it was in the 1950s. Many contemporary couples try to manage child-care responsibilities and household chores while both parents work full time. The problem of finding and affording high-quality child care and negotiating issues of gender-related roles related to child care and the maintenance of the household are at the core of this phase (Piotrkowski & Hughes, 1993).

Some theorists see having school-age children as a continuation of having young children. Others consider this a separate stage marked by the entrance of a dependent family member into the larger extra-familial world (Zilbach, 1989). Today most children enter school with some experience in early care and education settings. However, the transition to school may still be a major event.

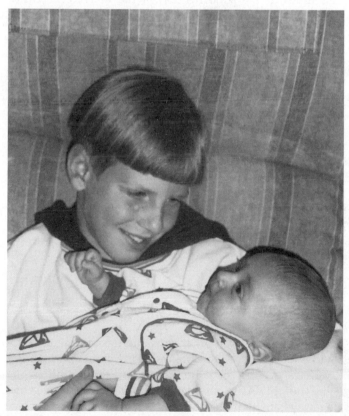

Some families have both school-age children and very young ones.

The Family with Adolescents

As children move into adolescence, families must evaluate and establish qualitatively different boundaries than they used when children were younger. Adolescents need freedom with guidance (McGoldrick & Carter, 1982). Adolescents want to be like their peers; thus parental authority is often challenged. Adolescents need flexible boundaries that allow them to be dependent and nurtured when they cannot handle things alone, yet also allow them to experiment with increasing degrees of independence. The complexities of adolescent sexuality are also added at this time.

Families at Midlife: Launching Young Adults and Moving On

This is the longest phase in the family life cycle. With low birth rates and longer life spans, parents now launch children almost 20 years before retirement. The process of launching young adults is a very gradual one that actually begins in infancy. The launching process began when parents took an infant to a child care setting or preschool (Zilbach, 1989). This midlife stage is characterized by the most family member exits and entrances. Parents have to be ready to both move up a generation and become grandparents as well as develop a different type of relationship with their own parents who may become dependent on them and require caregiving responsibilities. If the solidification of the marriage has not taken place, they may try to hold on to the last child, or the couple may move toward divorce.

The Family in Later Life

Adjusting to retirement is the major task of the later life stage in the life cycle. This may put strain on a marriage. Financial insecurity and dependence are also issues that elderly people face. It is also a time when couples must cope with the loss of friends, relatives, spouse, and perhaps a child. Grandparenthood, however, can offer opportunities for relationships with young children without the demands of parenthood.

Viewing the family from this family life cycle perspective has highlighted some of the tasks that families must perform at various stages in the development of the family and how these tasks change over time. Bronfenbrenner (1992) incorporates elements of family systems theory and the family life cycle into his ecological theory.

Ecological Systems Theory

Ecology is the study of relationships between organisms and environments. Ecological systems theory provides a framework for looking at the child and his family in a societal context. Ecological studies focus on infants and their families, the neighborhoods they live in, the child-care settings they attend, their parents' work places, the social/legal system that influences their lives and the sociohistorical conditions under which they live. Bronfenbrenner defines it in the following way

> The ecology of human development is the scientific study of the progressive, mutual accommodation, *throughout the life course*, between an active, growing human being, and the changing properties of the immediate settings in which the developing person lives, as this process is affected by the relations between these settings, and by the larger contexts in which these settings are embedded (Bronfenbrenner, 1992, 188).

The ecological systems model examines the ever-changing process of interactions between the infant (or toddler) and the environment. These interactions affect both the infant and the environment through mutual feedback (Howe & Briggs, 1989). The ecological systems model views the world as being made up of increasingly broader social systems. Bronfenbrenner (1986, 1993) terms these the *microsystem, mesosystem, exosystem, macrosystem,* and *chronosystem.* Others (Howe & Briggs, 1989) see these as starting with the individual and moving into other more complex environmental layers. The views are essentially similar, the terminology different.

Microsystems are the smallest units of the ecological system. They are the immediate settings in which individuals develop. For infants this is typically the biological family, although it could be a foster home or a neonatal intensive-care nursery, neighborhood, and child-care setting. Bronfenbrenner defines a microsystem as

> . . . a pattern of activities, roles, and interpersonal relations experienced by the developing person in a given face-to-face setting with particular physical and material features, *and containing other persons with distinctive characteristics of temperament, personality and systems of belief* (1992, 227).

This definition is expanded from his previous writings (changes in italics; Bronfenbrenner, 1979) to include the characteristics of the other individuals in the environment. It allows one to focus on the quality of the setting. Quality is dependent on "its ability to sustain and enhance development, and to provide a context that is emotionally validating and developmentally challenging" (Garbarino, 1990, 81). In general, this microsystem level is concerned with personal care, whereby caregiving roles are primarily shared by family members. An infant or toddler is potentially part of many microsystems: the family; an early education and care setting; a religious setting; the neighborhood play area; and so on. The microsystem is continually changing. So it is not useful to look at single events, but rather at the pattern of events over time.

Mesosystems are the relationships between microsystems in which the individual acts and reacts. The mesosystem is a system of microsystems and the linkages and processes between them (Bronfenbrenner, 1992). This system focuses on the home/child-care relationship, home/school relationship and so on rather than on the entities themselves. For infants and toddlers this system is relatively small.

Exosystems are systems that influence the microsystem but in which the individual plays no direct part. In this context, we are referring to settings that influence the development of infants and toddlers, but where they play no direct part.

The exosystem looks at "the linkage and processes taking place between two or more settings, at least one of which does not ordinarily contain the developing person, but in which events occur that influence processes within the immediate setting that does contain that person (e.g., for a child, the relation between the home and the parent's work place)" (Bronfenbrenner, 1992, 227).

The exosystem directly affects children by the policies that are set as well as indirectly affecting children through their parents. The parents' workplace usually has policies regarding parenting leaves, sick-child care, family transfers, and so on. Likewise, the parents' salaries and, importantly, the level of their medical and dental benefits, have a tremendous impact. These policies can support families or they can make having young children very difficult.

The exosystem also includes the extended family, neighbors, and friends of the family. A strong support network of friends and relatives can ameliorate some of the stressful effects of living with an infant or toddler. Conversely, not having a support network can increase the perceived stress. Typically, support networks are evaluated by the number of linkages within the system; that is, how many friends or relatives are available to support the young family and whether or not the people in the support network know each other. It adds depth to the system when people know each other. Regardless of the quantity or depth of the support system, systems vary in how helpful they are.

Macrosystems are the broad ideological and cultural patterns within which mesosystems and exosystems operate. Decisions at the macrosystem, or belief system, level affect a vast number of people. It is at this level that laws are made. For example, if there were going to be universal standards for child care or welfare reform in the United States, they would be made at the macrosystem level. Cultural beliefs are part of the macrosystem.

> The *macrosystem* consists of the overarching pattern or micro-, meso-, and exosystems characteristics of a given culture, sub-culture, or other broader social context, *with particular reference to the developmentally-instigative belief system, resources, hazards, life styles, opportunity structures, life course options, and patterns of social interchange that are embedded in each of these systems.* The macrosystem may be thought of as a societal blueprint for a particular culture, subculture, or other broader social context (Bronfenbrenner, 1992, 228).

Macrosystems encompass all other systems, and these patterns of beliefs are passed on from one generation to the next through socialization by families, schools, religious institutions, and the government. From this perspective, social class, religious groups, and in some instances neighborhoods and communities, could constitute a macrosystem. Macrosystems overlap with culture, yet provide a different framework (Bronfenbrenner, 1992).

The **chronosystem** looks at the life course relative to sociohistorical time. It focuses on the environmental events and transitions that occur for a particular cohort. Major events such as depression, war, and so on affect individuals; likewise, the increasing probability that mothers of young children will work outside the home and the divorce rate also impacts the lives of children. Bronfenbrenner (1992) feels that research on infants and toddlers needs to be done in the context of the ecological systems in which it occurs.

At the microsystem level the developing child is seen as an active agent whose developing processes influence and are influenced by the personal attributes of significant others. A critical element for understanding development is the degree of stability, consistency, and predictability of the systems over time. There is concern when systems at any level are highly disorganized or extremely rigid (Bronfenbrenner, 1992).

Variations in Family Types

There are currently many variations in family types that contain infants and toddlers. Some of these occur because of divorce and remarriage, some because of single-parenting situations. These variations have implications for infants and toddlers and how they grow and develop.

Divorce

The largest variation from the traditional family life cycle comes through divorce. At its current rate in the 1990s, about half of all marriages in the United States end in divorce. The divorce rate peaked about 1980, has declined slightly since then, and stabilized (Collins & Coltrane, 1995). Divorce is becoming more a norm than an exception to the norm. Of these divorces, approximately 60 percent involve children (Hetherington, Law, & O'Connor, 1993). In divorcing families the children are likely to be very young. Moreover, approximately 10 percent of the births take place after the divorce and before remarriage (Rindfuss & Bumpass, 1977). High rates of divorce have been attributed to a variety of causes such as the greater participation of women in the labor force with its concomitant economic independence, improved contraception, the welfare system, the increasing proportion of marriages involving premarital births, the changing ideology of the women's movement, and the liberalization of divorce laws (Hetherington, Law, & O'Connor, 1993).

Divorce almost always involves marital conflict and an accumulation of grievances and unhappiness. Regardless of the specific conflict event, which is usually a minor issue such as who is going to change the baby, most conflicts in marriage are related to certain basic issues: children, sex, money, use of leisure time, relatives, and infidelity (McCubbin & Dahl, 1985). Many couples in the United States fight more frequently over children than any other subject. Differences in attitudes toward child rearing go to the very core of relationships because parents frequently find it difficult to compromise.

Families with young children are in what is often called the "pressure cooker" stage of the family life cycle. The most common time for divorce happens during this stage, about six years after marriage, with rates peaking in the second and third years (U.S. Bureau of the Census, 1992). Many of these divorces are initiated by women (Carter & McGoldrick, 1989). These are also the years when families are most likely to have infants and toddlers. Estimates are that between 40 and 60 percent of infants born in the 1990s will spend some time in a mother-only household (Furstenberg & Cherlin, 1991).

The decision to get divorced is a complicated one with many interrelated factors. Economic conditions are crucial. Marriages are most likely to stay together during periods of economic depression and least likely to during periods of sustained economic growth (Collins & Coltrane, 1995). The role that children play is not clear. However, one can make some assumptions based on the reasons typically given by men and women for divorcing. Men typically give sexual incompatibility and in-law problems as reasons, whereas women are more likely to complain of physical as well as verbal abuse, financial problems, drinking, neglect of home and children, and lack of love (Kitson & Sussman, 1982).

As researchers try to explain why there are so many divorces, they also are looking at why marriages fail. Neither marital satisfaction nor frequency of disagreements is a good predictor of divorce. However, styles of conflict resolution are associated with divorce. The most common pattern of marital relations leading to divorce is one where one spouse, usually the wife, is conflict-confronting; that is, she wants to deal with areas of concern and disagreements and express her feelings about these. When she is married to a spouse who is conflict-avoidant, that is, he responds with defensiveness, avoidance, and withdrawal, but if prodded responds with resentment and anger, the pattern is one that is likely to lead to divorce (Hetherington, 1989). A second pattern associated with divorce is one where couples have little overt conflict but have different expectations and views of family life, marriage, and children, and have few shared interests or friends (Hetherington & Tryon, 1989).

These patterns are likely to operate within a family for a long time before the divorce. This means that children have been exposed to unresolved disagreement, anger, and a model of ineffective problem solving. Troubled marital relations frequently make parents unavailable to their children for parenting. Therefore children from such marriages have high rates of behavioral problems before the divorce. This is a vicious circle in that the stress of dealing with a difficult, noncompliant, and antisocial child adds stress to a fragile marriage and may precipitate a divorce (Hetherington, Law, & O'Connor, 1993). Whatever the cause, it seems clear that families in the process of divorcing have disrupted family relationships, that both parents and children display disordered behavior, and that these behaviors will affect them as they move into the changes and challenges of establishing separate one-parent households.

Divorce is a loss of a way of life for young children. The predictable patterns of everyday life are replaced by different expectations and life experiences and a profound degree of uncertainty about what is happening. Household rules and routines change, and a single parent typically experiences task overload as he or she takes on the tasks that previously were shared by two. Although divorce is a major disruption in children's lives, viewed in the context of these lives over time it is not as traumatic as early researchers first thought. The experience of conflict in the home seems to be the more important variable. Children in families where two parents persistently quarrel were found to have higher levels of distress than children from disrupted marriages (Demo & Acock, 1991; Furstenberg & Cherlin, 1991).

Of the post-divorce strains the economic ones appear to be the most vexing. In the first year following divorce, the average family income of women decreases by almost 40 percent. One cause of this is the partial, intermittent, or nonpayment of child support by 70 percent of fathers (Hetherington, Law, & O'Connor, 1993). The average amount of child support received was under $3,000 (Ahlburg & DeVita, 1992). Lack of child support is a major reason why six times as many female-headed households live below the poverty line as compared to male-headed households (U.S. Bureau of the Census, 1992). This income remains low for many years after the divorce (Hoffman & Duncan, 1988). However, five years after divorce, regardless of who initiated the divorce, most women feel more satisfied with their family situation than they did during the last year of their marriage (Wallerstein & Blakeslee, 1989).

Parents who divorce typically have two young children. The first years after divorce are associated with diminished parenting by custodial mothers. These mothers are frequently preoccupied, irritable, nonsupportive, and use erratically punitive discipline. Most children show some problems in the first two years following divorce. These problems are primarily in the social and psychological area. Young children demonstrate increased noncompliant, angry, and demanding behaviors (Hetherington, Cox, & Cox, 1982). Sibling relationships are problematic, with conflict, aggression, rivalry, and disengagement (Hetherington, 1989).

In most situations mothers are awarded custody of children. Only 10 to 13 percent of fathers are awarded sole custody of their children at the time of divorce, and in these instances it is usually because the mother is considered incompetent, she does not want custody, or there are male adolescent children (Emery, 1988; Hanson, 1988). Very young children, regardless of sex, are almost always in the custody of their mothers.

There seems to be some consistency in the pre- and post-divorce quality of parenting for mothers but little for fathers (Hetherington, Cox, & Cox, 1982). Noncustodial mothers usually remain in contact with their children, whereas noncustodial fathers become increasingly less available to their children. Furstenberg and Cherlin (1991) identified three factors that impacted the child's adjustment to divorce: (a) the effectiveness of the custodial parent in parenting the child; (b) the level of conflict between the mother and father; and (c) the relationship of the child with the noncustodial parent. When the custodial parent is effective, levels of conflict are low and the relationship between the child and the noncustodial parent is maintained. The outcome is more positive for children.

Parental conflict does not end with divorce, and is indeed often accelerated after a divorce. Conflicts often revolve around issues related to visitation rights and child-support payments. Children are caught in the middle of these conflicts. Older children seem to be able to adapt and negotiate, whereas young children don't have these skills.

For many young children divorce is the first in a series of changes from a two-parent family to a one-parent family and frequently (with the remarriage rate for women at 65 percent), again to a two-parent family (Carter & McGoldrick, 1989). About half of divorced adults remarry within three to five years of divorce. If both parents remarry, children will have four parental figures. Divorce, single parenthood, and remarriage has many implications for young children.

Single-Parent Families

Single-parent families are those with one parent and dependent children. One of four children in the United States lives in a single-parent family. The number of single-parent families has more than doubled since 1970. Likewise, the reasons individuals become single parents have changed. In 1970 approximately one-fourth of single parents were widows or widowers. The majority of single parents in the 1990s are single parents because of separation (19 percent) and divorce (42 percent), or because they have never been married (29 percent; Karmerman & Kahn, 1988). The fastest-growing group of single-parent families is headed by women who have never been married (Mulroy, 1988). More than 90 percent of all single-parent families are headed by women.

Single-parent families are as diverse as two-parent families. Despite the increased number of single-parent families, there is still a tendency to look at these families as deviant, unstable, or dysfunctional. Society has had difficulty accepting single-parent families as viable family units with variability in style, structure, and values (Lindbland-Goldberg, 1989).

Never Married Adolescent Single-Parent Families

The number of unmarried teenage mothers is consistently rising. This group accounted for 9 percent of all births in 1991 (Annie E. Casey Foundation, 1994). Estimates are that 80 percent of teenage pregnancies are unplanned (Alan Guttmacher Institute, 1993). Adolescent pregnancy is a complex and serious problem. Adolescent pregnancy occurs more frequently in the United States than in any other developed country (twice as high as England and seven times as high as the Netherlands). Over 1 million adolescent girls become pregnant annually, and about half of these pregnancies go to term. Virtually all of these mothers keep their infants (Carnegie Task Force on Meeting the Needs of Young Children, 1994).

Single parenthood is complicated by being an adolescent. During adolescence women experience multiple biological, social, cognitive, and psychological transitions and challenges. If an event such as an unwanted or unintended birth occurs during adolescence, school-aged adolescents are likely to be developmentally unprepared to adjust socially and psychologically to parenthood (Ketterlinus, Lamb, & Nitz, 1991). The concern is not just for the unexpected pregnancy, but also for its implications for the child. Women who have unintended pregnancies are less likely to provide good prenatal care, less likely to reduce or quit the use of drugs, alcohol, and smoking, and, after the child is born, less likely to follow up on immunizations (Public Health Service Expert Panel, 1989). Additionally, the risks of child abuse and neglect, low birth weight, and infant mortality are greater (Zuravin, 1987).

Those who were raised in single-parent households, and who themselves were born to teenage mothers, are also more likely to experience early childbearing. Adolescent parenthood, especially among low-income African Americans, has serious negative implications for long-term marital stability and ultimately for the economic well-being of a young mother and her children (Hayes, 1987).

Women who begin having children as adolescents tend to have, on average, one more child per family than do women who begin their families later in life (Moore & Burt, 1982). Infants born to adolescents are more likely to be premature, have low birth weights, have low Apgar scores, and die within the first month and first year of life. Low birth weight is a major cause of infant mortality and also contributes to serious long-term consequences, such as mental retardation, cerebral palsy, and other disabilities and medical conditions.

Risks do not end with the birth of a full-term viable infant. Adolescent mothers tend to be less verbal and less supportive of the infant's social/emotional development (Pope et al., 1993). Negative long-term child developmental outcomes have been found in the areas of intellectual development, social/emotional development, and school achievement (Harel & Anastasiow, 1985). If an adolescent enters into motherhood in poverty, it is unlikely that she will ever break free from the poverty. Even if teenage mothers do not start off in poverty, the outlook for their future is uncertain: Fifteen years after giving birth, teenage mothers were more often the head of single-parent households, and their children were more likely to be living in poverty (Mercer, 1990).

Families are
increasingly diverse.

Among all the responsibilities parenting brings, the new mother is called upon to fulfill the functions of socialization and education for her child. This can be a very difficult task for an adolescent who is still working out her own socialization. A teenage mother may not even understand that this duty exists. The mother's reactions to her child may focus more on discipline for individual acts and less on developing social skills as a whole. Many young mothers have difficulty understanding the reasons underlying the aggressive behavior of their children, and consequently have difficulty setting limits for the child's behavior. The teenage mother needs family support and guidance. "The complexity of assuming adult roles without cognitive, emotional, and social maturity can be catastrophic for both the young mother and her infant when there is not an extensive supportive environment" (Mercer, 1990, 72).

Although the move away from the marital dyad is increasing for all families in the United States, it is most apparent for African American teenage mothers. Among white teenage mothers, 52 percent were married at the time of delivery, whereas only 10 percent of teenage African American mothers were married (Hardy & Zabin, 1991). Grandmothers or other family members often take on parenting responsibilities. This provides a collective responsibility for the child, but often adds stress to the household (Annie E. Casey Foundation, 1994).

Remarried Family Systems

Remarried family systems are complex and highly variable, and no longer an unusual alternative form of the family in the United States. In 1987, 33 percent of the population was in some step situation and 20 percent of children under 19 were stepchildren or had half-siblings (Visher & Visher, 1993). Researchers predict that by the year 2000 there will be more step families than any other type of family in the United States (Glick & Lin, 1986). The remarried family system includes more than one household unit. All family members are affected emotionally, financially, and legally by the actions of the other household. The coparenting team is complex as it includes both biological parents and their respective spouses or committed live-in partners. Extended families include multiple grandparents and step-grandparents, and siblings consist of biological siblings, half-, and stepsiblings from both households (Whiteside, 1989).

There are a variety of types of step families. When the man is the stepparent, these are called stepfather families; when it is the mother, they are stepmother families. Complex stepfamilies are those where both adults have children from previous marriages living in the households, and these comprise about 7 percent of stepfamilies (Visher & Visher, 1993). Approximately half of stepfamilies have a mutual child. The timing of the birth of this child impacts the outcome for the child and family. If the child is conceived before the stepfamily has been successfully integrated, the birth is likely to cause increased stress and difficulty. If the child is born after the couple has formed a solid relationship, the birth of the child makes a positive contribution to the integration of the family (Bernstein, 1989).

Remarried families are different from first married families in a variety of ways. Stepfamilies form after a process of loss and change. Members of stepfamilies come together at different phases of their individual, marital, and family life cycles. Children, as well as adults, have experienced different traditions and ways of doing things, so all members of the household have ideas about how families "should" work. Parent–child relationships have preceded the couple relationship, rather than followed it. Children have a parent elsewhere, if not in reality then in memory. As about half of the children in stepfamilies have contact with their other parent, there are shifts in household membership when the children move between households. There is little or no legal relationship between stepparents and stepchildren.

During the early stages of remarriage the structure of the family remains divided, primarily along biological lines. The challenge for successful family reorganization requires adult family members to deal adequately with relationships with former spouses. Children for their part must give up the hope for parental reunion. There are many property rights and turf issues that need to be resolved. As a consequence, families have to work out issues relating to power and conflicting loyalties. This reorganization stage lasts approximately two years (Visher & Visher, 1993).

The middle stage of remarriage (three to five years) is characterized by significant structural reorganization. This is the time when the boundaries around the marital couple are strengthened. The parental biological ties must be loosened and the role of the stepparent clarified. If these issues are not resolved, the family will remain in a stalemate, divided along biological ties, or move toward divorce (Whiteside, 1989). Couples in stepfamilies may form strong couple bonds but good stepparent–stepchild relationships do not necessarily follow. Apparently these two types of relationships are separate from each other. Divorce rates are higher for second marriages than first marriages and even couples who are happy together may divorce because of stepparent–stepchild problems. The later stages of successful remarriages are characterized by established patterns of relationships that allow for intimacy and authenticity. The family structure is well integrated.

Regardless of the type of family or microsystem in which infants and toddlers live, some face more challenges than others. One of the most pervasive macrosystem situations facing infants and toddlers and their families today is poverty.

Poverty

In 1990, families with children under 3 years of age were the single largest group of families living in poverty in the United States. "Across all ethnic groups and family structures, more children under age 3 live in poverty than do older children, adults, or the elderly" (Carnegie Task Force on Meeting the Needs of Young Children, 1994, 17). Between 1987 and 1992 the number of children 6 years and under living in poverty grew from 5 to 6 million, putting the poverty rate at 26 percent. In 1995, the poverty line was $10,030 for a family of two, $12,590 for a family of three, and $15,150 for a family of four (Children's Defense Fund, 1995c). Poverty figures available for 1993 showed the highest rate of child poverty in 30 years, 15.7 million children (Children's Defense Fund, 1994b).

Poverty is complex and multifaceted. It undermines families and the well-being of young children. Poverty affects parents who are overwhelmed by the work and cost of caring for very young children; it impacts health issues such as inadequate nutrition, overcrowded housing, and lack of health care; and it adds to the stress that trying to cope with these problems produces.

The human cost of poverty to young children is devastating. Low-income children are:

- Two times more likely than other children to die from birth defects;
- Three times more likely to die for all causes combined;
- Four times more likely to die from fires;
- Five times more likely to die from infectious diseases and parasites; and
- Six times more likely to die from other diseases
  (Children's Defense Fund, 1995a, 19)

Of families with young children living in poverty, 38 percent did not receive any public cash assistance, approximately 20 percent had their own earnings and some cash assistance, and 32 percent had only public cash assistance. The remaining 10 percent had income from a variety of other sources (National Center for Children in Poverty, 1995). In 1992, even full-time employment was not a guarantee against poverty. If an adult worked 35 hours a week at a minimum-wage job ($4.25 in 1992) he would earn $7,438. This amounts to 66 percent of the poverty line for a family of three and 52 percent for a family of four (National Center for Children in Poverty, 1995). Although it would be possible for both parents to work in a two-parent household, the second salary, if minimum wage, would almost be negated by the cost of child care for one child and would be financially disadvantageous if there were more than one child.

Poverty is highest in urban areas, 35 percent, as compared to 19 percent in suburban areas. Statistically, children of color, living in inner cities, and having single mothers are overrepresented. Twenty-nine percent of children under 6 are Hispanic or African American; yet they represent 55 percent of all poor children. Children born to unmarried mothers are more likely to be poor (National Center for Children in Poverty, 1995). The Hispanic population with very young children is the poorest segment of the population; 73 percent of single mothers and 30.8 percent of married couples live below the poverty line. African Americans with very young children fare little better, with 69.7 percent of single mothers and 21.4 percent of married couples living below the poverty line (Einbinder, 1992, in Carnegie Task Force on Meeting the Needs of Young Children, 1994).

Poverty increases the probability that risk factors will be present simultaneously in the child himself, the parent, the parent's informal support system, and the neighborhood. The disadvantages of poverty permeate all of life from health care and nutrition, to quality of housing and neighborhoods, to educational opportunities. The cycle of poverty is associated with poor maternal nutrition, low birth weight in babies, and increased substance abuse by pregnant women. These are all potential causes of developmental problems and additional potential stressors in an already stressed system (Children's Defense Fund, 1995a). Women with low incomes have the highest rate of depression of any group in the

United States (Halpern, 1990). Mothers who are depressed are less responsive and nurturing, less aware of their children's moods, and more restrictive. Children raised in extreme poverty are at risk for developmental problems. The causes are complicated, but include poor cognitive/language stimulation, poor nutrition, exposure to safety hazards, and poor health care. Adverse financial circumstances affect the entire family and include increased risk of marital dissolution, family disorganization, physical abuse, and neglect (Conger, Elder, & Lorenz, 1992).

Overall, 61.5 percent of single mothers with children under 3 live in poverty as compared to only 12.8 percent of married couples. The number of children receiving food stamps increased by 50 percent from 1989 to 1993, reaching 13 million children (Children's Defense Fund, 1995b). Poverty is rarely eliminated by public assistance: The combination of Aid for Dependent Children (AFDC) and Food Stamps only raised the income levels of families to 65 percent of the poverty line in 1993 (Annie E. Casey Foundation, 1994).

Homelessness

In the latter part of the 1980s, families with young children became the fastest growing segment of the homeless population. Reports indicate that about one-third of the homeless population are families, with the percentage being even larger in cities such as New York and Philadelphia (VanRy, 1993). Homeless families are diverse, but young single-parent, female-headed households represent the largest portion of the homeless population nationwide (Kryden-Coe, Salamon, & Molnar, 1991). Accurate statistics of how many children are homeless are difficult to obtain because of the nature of the population and differences in definitions of homelessness. Estimates are that on any given night 100,000 children are homeless, with the majority of the children under 5 years of age (Carnegie Task Force on Meeting the Needs of Young Children, 1994).

Many of these homeless families have experienced high rates of violence and report that family violence was the primary cause of the homelessness. Often the mother took the children and left the abusive situation without time, emotional strength, or financial resources to find another secure place to live. Concern about additional violence may make having a permanent address an impossibility (Kryden-Coe, Salamon, & Molnar, 1991). Statistically, homeless mothers had children before the age of 20, their children were under 10 years of age, and they had experienced unstable housing before they became homeless. They moved an average of 2.6 times in the 12 months before they became homeless (Winkleby & Boyce, 1994).

Living on the streets or in shelters has many effects on homeless infants and toddlers and their families. In general, there are physical health problems related to homelessness; colds, tiredness, and generally not feeling well, are the most frequent and common health problems of the homeless, as well as feelings of depression (VanRy, 1993). Homeless infants and toddlers may be hungry and have poor nutrition and increased health problems. When they are homeless, their parents may not have places to put their children. Therefore there is little opportunity for the children to play and explore their environment.

For an infant or toddler the trauma of becoming homeless may be devastating.

> . . . the disruption of existing social networks, family routines, and emotional ground-
> ing in one's own home; the anxiety of an uncertain future and the fear and violence
> often associated with shelter living. For a child who is homeless, the play yard can
> mean a motel hallway; the bedroom, a back seat of the car (Klein, Bittel, & Molar,
> 1993, 23).

Conditions related to homelessness frequently lead to developmental delays for
infants and toddlers; these are most apparent in motor, cognitive, and language
development.

In the United States an increasing number of early care and education settings
are including homeless children. Their programs must be modified to help children feel safe and to help them develop age-appropriate skills and concepts. This
is difficult, because although many of the children are in programs when their
family is in a shelter, rules about how long a family can stay in a shelter vary, and
programming is based on unstable funding sources and whether or not space is
available. Some shelters have on-site child care settings; others use settings
within the community. Regardless, child care is seen as an essential element in
helping young children whose families are homeless (Klein, Bittel, & Molnar,
1993). Many young homeless children are fearful. They frequently display emotional and behavior problems such as a short attention span, withdrawal, aggression, speech delays, sleep disorganization, difficulty in organizing behavior,
regressive behaviors, awkward motor behavior, and immature social skills (Klein,
Bittel, & Molnar, 1993; VanRy, 1993).

Parental roles may change as families move, and parents may not be emotionally available to their children when they are trying to cope with problems
related to food, shelter, and finances. Poverty and homelessness are inextricably
tied to the family and community. In many instances these problems are compounded by violence.

Violent Environments

No one likes to think about violence and young children. When violence does
occur, we want to believe that it is the exception and that it is reported to make
headlines and sell newspapers. When we read these articles, we also want to
believe that infants and toddlers don't understand what is happening and therefore won't remember the experiences. Research findings negate such optimistic
views.

Researchers categorize violence in terms of three aspects: (a) community violence; (b) domestic violence; and (c) physical and sexual abuse (Osofsky,
1993/1994). As stress to families increases, the probability for violence increases.
Very young children are exposed to this violence and frequently are the victims
of it. Infants and toddlers do experience violence and try to understand it.
Because they don't have the language to express their feelings, it is the professional's role to comprehend what the meaning of this violence is for young chil-

dren (Osofsky, 1993/1994). In addition to being the victims of violence, children are exposed to violence on television, in their homes, and in the community.

Community Violence

The United States is one of the most violent nations in the world. This violence has reached down to our youngest and most vulnerable citizens. Almost 4 million children are growing up in "severely distressed neighborhoods." These neighborhoods are characterized by poverty, female-headed families, high levels of school dropouts and unemployment, and a reliance on welfare (Annie E. Casey Foundation, 1994). In these neighborhoods fear of crime and violence undermines security and increases isolation. Many young children have witnessed a stabbing or shooting either in their home or in the neighborhood (Osofsky, 1993/1994).

Parents worry about their inability to protect their children from violence and to keep them safe even when they are home or in their own neighborhood. Low-income and minority parents report the most worries (Osofsky & Jackson, 1993/1994). Protecting their children is a basic family function. When they cannot do this, parents feel helpless and threatened. Although very young infants may not be aware of violence in the community, they are aware of their caregivers' fears and anxiety, and will be influenced by the adults' coping strategies (Osofsky, 1993/1994). Parents who raise children in violent environments may be depressed, sad, and anxious. Adults who are depressed tend to talk to infants and toddlers less, and to be less responsive to their needs. They have difficulty controlling their emotions and their young children experience more scoldings and shouts than hugs and kisses (Osofsky & Jackson, 1993/1994). Infants and toddlers reflect this same depression and smile less and begin to withdraw into themselves. Adults may cope with violent environments in a variety of ways. They might put young children to sleep in bath tubs to avoid random bullets, and they rarely take children outside or allow them to play on the playground. They may become overprotective of their children as a way of keeping them safe.

Young children who are exposed to violence think about their world differently. Repeated exposure to violence is likely to have an even more significant effect and it is likely to be more pervasive as infants' and toddlers' understanding of events changes with increasing age. It will be difficult for such children to learn to trust others or to think about their environment as dependable and predictable.

Unlike older children, infants and toddlers have a very small repertoire of behaviors with which to show their distress. The symptoms children display are related to the child's age, gender, and circumstances. Some very young children who have been maltreated or exposed to violence withdraw and may become depressed, others may become aggressive (Cicchetti & Lynch, 1993). Among young children who see parents fight, boys are more likely to become aggressive and girls to withdraw (Cummings et al., 1993). Other symptoms may include disrupted patterns of eating, sleeping, and fearfulness (Drell, Siegel, & Gaensbauer, 1993).

Domestic Violence

Domestic violence is viewed as a systematic pattern of gender-related abuse. Definitional problems and underreporting make it difficult to ascertain the actual extent of abuse. The National Coalition Against Domestic Violence estimated that 3 to 4 million women are beaten by their male partners every year (Alsdurf & Alsdurf, 1989). However, domestic violence cases only get reported when victims seek assistance. It is estimated that for every call made to the police about domestic violence there are ten instances when the abuse goes unreported (Davis, 1988).

Domestic violence impacts young children in three ways: It makes their primary caregiver less available to them; they may witness the abuse; and they may be injured by the abuse. Domestic violence is the leading cause of injury to women of childbearing age (15 to 44) (Ingrassia & Beck, 1994). It is estimated that 20 percent of adult women (15 million) have experienced physical abuse at least once from a male partner (Stark & Flitcraft, 1991). Twenty-one percent of all pregnant women are battered and 30 percent of all battered women are abused while pregnant (National Coalition Against Domestic Violence, 1994). At least 3.3 million children witness parental abuse each year, including fatal assaults with guns or knives as well as hitting or slapping (Jaffe, Wilson, & Wolfe, 1988).

Domestic violence is a pattern of behavior rather than an isolated event. An abusive event typically starts out with conflicts and arguments. Next there is a tension-building stage. Hostility increases. At some point the abuser's rage can no longer be controlled and he lashes out in physical aggression. After the aggression the abuser is often kind and affectionate to try to make up for or minimize the seriousness of the abusive event (Alsdurf & Alsdurf, 1989). Abuse is not limited to physical force but can include the threat of force, coercion, intimidation, withholding financial resources, and isolation from friends and families (Fishbane, 1993). The effects of violence can make women emotionally paralyzed, submissive, and victims of learned helplessness, all of which have not only negative effects for the women themselves, but for the young children they care for (Gondolf & Fisher, 1988). When there is violence in the home, there is also more likely to be maltreatment of children. Children in families with a history of violence or abuse and neglect in the home are at risk medically, psychologically, and educationally.

Child Abuse and Neglect

Child abuse is an umbrella term used to encompass many forms of child mistreatment. Honig (1986) identifies four kinds of abuse that occur to young children:

> Severe *physical abuse* leaves bodily scars and results in death for several thousand children annually; some children suffer from *psychological unavailability* of the mothering one; some are *neglected* and hungry; and some are emotionally scarred by bitter hostility, shaming, chronic verbal abuse, and criticism (Honig, 1986, 49).

Young children can also be the victims of sexual abuse. Child sexual abuse is any activity between a child and an adult (or much older child) which sexually excites or satisfies the adult's needs or desires. Some categories of children are more likely to be abused than others. Infants born prematurely and those with disabilities are particularly vulnerable to abuse and neglect. In Florida, for example, low-birth-weight babies represent 7.7 percent of all births, but 20 percent of abused children (Task Force for Prevention of Developmental Handicaps—1991 update).

Although many would like to believe that abuse of young children occurs infrequently, the reality is strikingly different. Physical abuse is the leading cause of death among children less than 1 year of age in this country. Homicide accounts for 10 percent of all deaths of children between 1 and 4 years (Mrazek, 1993; citing Waller, Barker and Szocka, 1989). One-third of all victims of physical abuse are under 1 year of age (U.S. Department of Health and Human Services, 1992). Almost 90 percent of children who died as a result of abuse or neglect were under the age of 5 and, in 1993, 46 percent were under 1 year of age (Children's Defense Fund, 1995a). One-third of all sexual abuse cases involve children under 6 years of age (Schmitt & Krugman, 1992). In 1993, there were an estimated 2,989,000 reports of child abuse and neglect to the child protective service agencies in the United States. About 45 out of every 1,000 children were reported as victims of maltreatment (National Committee to Prevent Child Abuse, 1993). However, it is estimated that unreported cases could be two to three times that number (Bowdry, 1990).

For infants, physical abuse often takes the form of being shaken by adults. They are most frequently shaken because they are irritable and will not stop crying. Parental inability to be successful with their infants causes some to strike out at the infant. Physical abuse also includes excessive corporal punishment, misguided attempts at teaching children, and battering children. Some parents use physical punishment rather than reasoning with children in the belief that it takes physical measures to make children into good people. These measures include whipping, face smacking, hitting with boards, belts, and cords. Injuries that result from such punishment are typically bruises, welts, and cuts. Parents who discipline children in this way frequently report having received similar punishment in their own childhood. They may agree that the punishment is excessive, but remain convinced that the child may grow up to be a delinquent if he does not learn right from wrong in this way from the very beginning. Some people feel that this is acceptable behavior, not child abuse.

Some parents harm their child as they attempt to teach her certain behaviors. They might burn the child's finger tips as a way of teaching her that stoves are hot and she should not touch them. These parents will readily admit what they have done, but they do not see it as abuse and may be offended that you consider it as such.

Of the almost 3 million reported cases of child abuse and neglect in 1993, 1 million were confirmed. Neglect is the most commonly reported form of child abuse, constituting 49.9 percent of reported and confirmed cases (Children's Defense Fund, 1995a). Parents simply may not have the money to buy enough food and clothing for their children. Or, their priorities for spending money may not include necessities for the child. Sometimes infants and toddlers remain home alone while their parents are at work because the parents cannot afford child care. In many cases neglect is the result of a larger dysfunctional pattern that includes adult drug abuse. In these cases all the "family" income is used to buy drugs. Unfortunately, problems associated with drug-related abuse and neglect are frequently compounded by the child's prenatal exposure to drugs and alcohol. This condition, plus a neglectful or abusive environment, increases the child's risk for multiple social problems.

Emotional abuse is the most subtle and often unrecognized form of abuse. However, it can be extremely damaging to a child's self-esteem. Sometimes this abuse is based on parents' perceptions that if they fail to degrade the toddler he will get a "big head." The toddler is perceived and portrayed negatively by the parents and the toddler may perceive himself in the same light and describe himself as "bad."

Both boys and girls can be victims of child sexual abuse. Although the child is never at fault, children often do not report what has happened. The perpetrator frequently tries to keep the secret by convincing the child that it is her fault and that no one would believe her anyway. Sexual abuse is further complicated because the most frequent perpetrators are natural parents, stepparents, adoptive and foster parents (Faller, 1989). Abuse by nonfamily members is the least frequent type to occur.

Infants and Toddlers in Foster Care

Sometimes child rearing becomes so complicated by other stressful conditions, such as physical or mental illness, domestic violence and abuse connected with alcoholism or drug addiction, and other exceptional circumstances that the social service system decides that a child's safety is threatened (Lee & Nisivoccia, 1989). Abandonment and removal of infants and toddlers from their biological family is occurring more frequently in society. Families may have no financial means to support children and therefore give them up. "As poverty has grown so has child maltreatment . . . . Maltreatment and poverty are clearly connected" (Lee & Nisivoccia, 1989, 5). The increase in the number of children in out-of-home placements is also related to increases in substance abuse and AIDS. Infants born into dysfunctional family systems are at high risk of abuse and neglect. Their removal is often an emergency response for their safety. On the last day of the fiscal year in 1993 in the United States, there were 442,218 children in foster care (Children's Defense Fund, 1995b). "Nationally, 75% of the foster children are returned home, but one study points out that 32% of them return to care" (Lee & Nisivoccia, 1989, 3).

The attachment process is often affected when infants and toddlers are removed from their home. As attachment is based to some extent on day-to-day interactions and having needs met for physical care, nourishment, and affection, families who cannot fulfill these functions place young children at risk (Solnit & Nordhaus, 1992). These infants and toddlers are in double jeopardy. They live with caregivers who are unavailable to them, and are hence at risk for the long-term implications detailed above, yet removing them from their homes may have negative consequences relative to attachment. "As a practical guide, for most children between the ages of two and five, a separation for more than two months is upsetting to the degree that it may lead to psychological harm" (Solnit & Nordhaus, 1992, 16).

More than half of all children placed in adoptive or foster homes have siblings (Solnit & Nordhaus, 1992). Young children may be very attached to their siblings. Although siblings cannot take the place of a caring adult, they offer the potential for support and consistency for the young infant and toddler. There is concern when these siblings cannot be placed in the same setting. The struggle for attachment is the basis of permanency planning (Kagan & Schlosberg, 1989).

Summary

Infants and toddlers are now usually studied within the context of their families. The individual is viewed as an open system who acts and reacts with the environment. For families to survive, they must carry out certain functions. And infants and toddlers have a definite impact on how these functions are fulfilled.

Professionals frequently divide the life cycle of the family into stages of family life that have specific developmental tasks for the family to perform. The various stages have differing impacts on infants and toddlers. The "traditional" stages in the family life cycle may be altered by events such as divorce and remarriage, and being a single parent.

All families are different. To understand a family, one must know about the particular characteristics of the family and its members, including the infant or toddler. Important variables include family structure and cultural background, the socioeconomic status of the family, geographical location, the personal characteristics of members of the family, health of family members, and their coping style. Different families have different patterns of interacting and communicating; these are important variables.

Having put the infant in the context of the family, it is next necessary to put the family in the context of society. Using an ecological framework, the infant and family are viewed in ever widening circles. One considers first the family itself and then the immediate social environments where the infant is raised, the relationships among these environments, the rules that govern them and, finally, the cultural and ideological systems that influence the larger decisions of society viewed in the context of sociohistorical time.

Families are changing and the changes pose challenges for professionals working with the nation's youngest children. Research increasingly stresses the importance of the early years for a child's development, and that infants and toddlers need to be viewed in an ecological framework that is family centered and that takes into account the environment in which the child lives. At the same time that we are becoming aware of the critical importance of the early years for a child's later development, we also find that an increasing number of our youngest children are being raised in conditions of poverty and are facing risks that no other group of children in our history has had to face: the prevalence of teenage mothers, single-parent families, and lack of quality child care. Professionals must be aware of and meet these challenges for infants and toddlers and to the society in which we all live.

Application Activities

1. Drive around the town in which you live. Are there neighborhoods in which you feel uncomfortable? Describe these neighborhoods. Think about how you would raise an infant or toddler in these neighborhoods as compared to neighborhoods in which you feel comfortable.

2. Take one issue such as child care and look at it using an ecological framework. If you were going to tackle such an issue, discuss how your strategies would be different at the micro-, meso-, exo-, and macrosystems levels.

3. Talk to a friend or acquaintance whose parents are divorced. Talk with her about the timing of the divorce, custody arrangements, low and high points. Find out how this experience has influenced his or her expectations about coupling and families.

Chapter 12

Collaborating with Families of Infants and Toddlers

"**W**e are family-centered," "we support family empowerment," "we believe in family support," "we look at parents as partners in the educational process." What does all this mean? It is certainly part of the new rhetoric. However, is it new and different or just a rehash of the same old system which publicly acknowledges parents as the primary caregivers, teachers, and socializers of their children? But then professionals, after having made that acknowledgment, tend to tell families how they think parents should raise their infants and toddlers. Really working collaboratively with families can offer advantages to teachers, parents, and young children.

Renewed interest in working with families stems from two different aspects of our changing society. The first is the dramatic increase of mothers of very young children in the workforce and the resultant increase of infants and toddlers in child care. The second is our growing recognition of the importance of the first three years of life, the role that family plays in those years, and society's concern about a family's ability to play that role optimally. The first concern has led to interest in parent/staff collaboration, the second to interest in parent education and strategies to support families with young children (Powell, 1990).

There are also new realities in the 1990s that are refocusing how we think about infants and toddlers. In the 1940s, because of a national emergency, young children were temporarily and valiantly cared for outside their homes. The expectation was that when the emergency was solved the situation would return to the status quo. It has not. Child rearing is now viewed as a shared experience with both parents and other adults raising young children. Changes in family demographics are also presenting challenges to the system. These new realities relate to the structure of families, their life styles and their cultural and ethnic characteristics (Powell, 1990).

Ecological Systems Theory

Bronfenbrenner's ecological family systems models provide a framework for understanding, organizing, and making sense out of the information relating to families and early care and education settings. Both families and settings are part of the young child's microsystem. At the mesosystem level, the focus is on the relationships between microsystems: families and early care and education settings, as well as other settings in which young children participate such as religious training, neighborhood play areas, and so on. Although the principles that Bronfenbrenner (1979) proposes apply to all relationships within the mesosystem, the focus of this discussion will be solely on the relationship between the family and the early care and education settings.

Bronfenbrenner was interested in formulating general principles or hypotheses in which the relationships between microsystems would be optimized. He proposed the following:

- frequent interaction and face-to-face communication between the family and staff
- communication designed to motivate and support the capacities of those who deal directly with children, not to degrade or undermine them
- consensus on goals for children and roles for adults
- both the family and the setting are supportive of each other, regardless of the family member or child's competence, experience, race or cultural background
- when a child enters a new microsystem he is accompanied by a familiar adult (Bronfenbrenner, 1979).

Using the Bronfenbrenner model, it seems clear that one goal of family/staff collaboration is to increase the continuity between the home and early care and education microsystems. Obviously, some discontinuities exist between the home and early care and education settings, but is that good or bad?

Continuity and Discontinuity

Although researchers in the field are concerned about the effects of continuity and discontinuity on young children, the terms have not been well defined nor have the conditions under which they are beneficial or harmful been well enumerated (Peters & Kontos, 1987). In an attempt to rectify this problem, Powell (1990) has operationalized the terms to allow a closer scrutiny of them. He proposes that *continuity* be used to refer to the linkages and congruence between families and early care and education settings. Linkages focus on the structural aspects of the relationship that look at the level, type, and frequency of communication between the settings as well as the amount of time that individuals from one setting spend in the other setting. *Congruence* refers to the substance of the relationship relative to the degree of similarity between the family and settings in such areas as child-rearing practices, values, goals, expectations, language, and adult-child relationships. For example, a family might have close linkages with their child's setting because an adult spends time there and communication is frequent. However, there might be little congruence if the family members are not native English speakers, have a different ethnic heritage and cultural values that focus on survival skills. Children whose families are neither middle class nor Anglo are likely to experience discontinuity between home and school regardless of the ethnicity and social class of their preschool teacher (Powell, 1990,1).

Continuity and child care interact in a variety of ways. Parental values interact with child-care decisions because given a choice, parents choose settings that reduce levels of discontinuity. When looking at variables that relate to satisfaction, Whitehead (1989) found that shared values between the mother and caregiver increase maternal satisfaction in child care. Parents who value educational enrichment tend to choose settings where this is encouraged (Clarke-Stewart, 1987). This can, however, be viewed both positively and negatively. Parents who have less stressful lives tend to choose higher-quality centers than parents with more stressful lives (Howes & Olenick, 1986). There is also congruence at the other end of that spectrum. Parents with few resources tend to choose child-care settings that are less adequate (Goelman & Pence, 1987).

We know less than we would like to about the impact of continuity and discontinuity on very young children. Discontinuity provides both opportunity and risk. Peters and Kontos (1987) suggest four variables that relate to the impact of discontinuity on young children. One variable relates to the magnitude of the discontinuity, with greater discontinuity posing a greater threat. A second variable is the duration of the discontinuity. A third relates to the timing of the event. To the extent that the discrepancy happens at a vulnerable or sensitive time, the impact is greater. Many people believe that infancy is such a period. A related concern is whether these changes are viewed as "on time" and "off time." Again, many question whether young infants should be in full-time child care (Belsky, 1988). The fourth variable relates to the preparation that the child has had for understanding the situation and the communication that has occurred about the transition.

Parent education is one method that has been systemically used to increase continuity. Initially, the goal was to change family values to be closer to those of early care and education professionals. Current efforts in this are more collaborative, with families examining their values and settings in how they interact with and care for very young children.

Parent Education

Parent education is a form of collaboration. Parent education offers exciting possibilities for working with parents to potentially enhance the development of their children as well as giving them the support of others who are sharing a similar experience. The goal of most parent education groups is to develop parenting and decision-making skills. Parents are adult learners and may reflect a wide variety of experiences, attitudes, and values. All levels of expertise need to be supported in a risk-free environment (Berger, 1995). Evaluations of intensive family-oriented education programs have shown short-term positive effects in increased child competence and positive maternal behaviors as well as longer effects on increased levels of education, smaller family size, and an increased probability of the family being self-supported (Powell, 1989).

Parent education groups vary significantly in their structure and purpose. They vary on a continuum from parent groups in which a parent is the leader and there is little structure to groups where a professional teacher runs the group. The meetings themselves can range from unstructured meetings with no specific goals or curriculum to a discussion led by a professional teacher who controls the curriculum and the level of participation (Berger, 1995). In and of themselves these different structures are neither inherently good nor bad, but the match between the parents and the structure may influence participation as well as what is learned.

One challenge for parent education is the different value systems that parents bring to the child-rearing situation. The academic field of child development has some clear guidelines regarding the types of parenting that are most likely to produce children who do well in school. This field supports reasoning over corporal punishment, authoritative rather than authoritarian parents; responding to infants as quickly as possible in a gentle responsive way rather than letting them cry it out, and so on. These views are not accepted by all parents. Thus it is often difficult to work with parents who have different values and do not want to be told how to raise their children (Theilheimer, 1994). Yet parent education programs are adapting. The stereotype of the child development professional lecturing a group of mothers on how to raise their children is no longer an accurate portrayal of many of the programs (Powell, 1990). High-quality parent education programs are now characterized by

- Equal relations between parents and staff with the intent of the program to empower parents in their child-rearing roles. Professionals do not take the role of expert and tell parents the *best* way to rear their children.
- Time devoted to open-ended, parent-dominated discussions.
- A balanced focus on the needs of the parents and the needs of the children. Programs include information to support the parents in strengthening their social support networks and community ties.
- Being responsive to the needs and characteristics of the population served. Good programs are different and they are designed to match the parents they serve. They are responsive to cultural characteristics and values of the populations they serve and to the income level and risks that families face (adapted from Powell, 1990).

Working with Families in a Cultural Context

Individuals do not develop their language, rituals, rules, and beliefs in a vacuum. They are part of the cultural heritage handed down to them through their family. Culture is a way of life, a blueprint for living. It is both learned and internalized by being part of a particular culture (Berger, 1991). Infants and toddlers come to early care and education settings with a cultural background as do their parents. Infants and toddlers and their families must be understood within the context of their cultural and ethnic background.

The analogy of the United States as a "melting pot" has been replaced by that of a "salad bowl." The growth of diverse cultural groups has increased to the point that the term *minority* is no longer useful. Hanson, Lynch, and Wayman (1990) present some interesting information about the changing demographics of the United States population. There is especially dramatic change among families with infants and toddlers. The overall percentage of children in the United States population is decreasing, but the proportion of children from non–Euro-American populations is increasing.

> In the years between 1985 and 2030, the total number of ethnolinguistically diverse children will have increased by 53%, and the proportion of children in those groups compared to all children will have risen from 28% to 41% (Hanson et al., 1990, 115).

By the year 2010, one of every four children in the United States will be from racial minorities (Chan, 1990). This is accounted for by increased immigration, by higher birth rates, and by earlier ages of child bearing in these populations. It is also likely that this population will have a greater proportion of children "at risk," as these figures interact with environmental risk factors, particularly poverty and its concomitant lack of early medical support (Rounds, Weil, & Bishop, 1994).

Keeping in mind the growth of cultural diversity, it is important to know each family's view of child rearing, and their expectations, both personally and culturally, for children of various ages. For example, to set up programming that promotes independent functioning and self-help with a family that values dependency is almost certain to fail. Also, you need to know families' basic views about having children in the first place, and their feelings about discipline and child rearing.

In developing cultural sensitivity, knowledge about different cultural groups is necessary. However, this limited knowledge may not be sufficient because all individuals and families are different and embrace different aspects of culture. Knowledge of culture has to be both generalized and individualized. "Families from racial and ethnic minority groups are faced with the task of raising their children to live in their own culture as well as to function effectively as a minority member in a majority culture" (Rounds, Weil, & Bishop, 1994, 8).

When the person gathering the information and those giving it are not proficient in the same language, the communication process can be very difficult. Even when information is translated, there can be confusion, especially if there is conflict between verbal and nonverbal messages. To be culturally sensitive, competent teachers must learn four tasks:

> First, they must clarify their own values and assumptions. Second, they must gather and analyze ethnographic information regarding the cultural community within which each family resides. Third, they must determine the degree to which the family operates transculturally; and finally, they must examine each family's orientation to specific child-rearing issues (Hanson, Lynch, & Wayman, 1990, 126).

Cross, Bazron, Dennis, and Isaacs (1989) identify five elements that contribute to cultural competence.

Acknowledging and valuing diversity.   This involves the recognition that there are cultural differences and that these differences play a role in what families believe about infants and toddlers and how they should be reared.

Conducting a cultural self assessment.   Before one can become aware of other cultures, one needs to take a close look at one's own culture and how this has shaped values and beliefs about infants and toddlers. This is the lens through which you will view infants and toddlers and their families, and you need to be aware of the biases you hold. Other than Native Americans, we are all here through past immigration. This is an important part of the culture of all of us, and it influences how we value and care for infants and toddlers and how we respond to their families. Becoming aware of one's own culture and its values increases the probability of becoming a culturally sensitive individual who can validate the differences among people and appreciate their commonality.

Recognizing and understanding the dynamics of difference.   Cultural differences contribute to both obvious and subtle differences in individuals. Obvious differences include such things as the language spoken, amount of eye contact, and body language used, whereas more subtle aspects of culture may influence the amount of self-disclosure someone is comfortable with.

Honoring diversity.   Child-rearing practices are designed to socialize infants and toddlers into their own culture. Daily caregiving routines for infants and toddlers reflect a culture's fundamental, deeply felt values and beliefs (Nugent, 1994). Since infants absorb their culture as part of the caregiving process, the early care and education of children is important to many parents. Child-rearing practices may provide the key to understanding socialization practices in different cultural contexts. However, if early care and education settings reflect only the values of the dominant culture, parents may be concerned about the practices used. Likewise, infants and toddlers may be deprived of a part of their own culture, or they may experience inexplicable discontinuity between care at home and that in a child-care setting.

Acquiring cultural knowledge.   Learning about different cultures is an ongoing process. There are many books written that describe different ethnic groups with some focusing on practices that relate to early childhood (Lynch & Hanson, 1992). This is the foundation from which more individualized knowledge must build. Additional family information is necessary about variations within the cultural group:

- Reason for immigration. What was the family seeking or leaving behind? Were they fleeing from political persecution, poverty, or war, or were they brought against their will as slaves?
- Length of time since immigration. How many generations has the family been in the United States?
- Place of residence. Does the family live in an ethnic neighborhood?

- Order of migration. Did the family come as a unit or did one member come first and others join later?
- Socioeconomic status. What is the socioeconomic status of the family and their attitudes toward education and upward mobility?
- Religiosity. What are the family's religious ties to the ethnic group and are there strong political ties?
- Language. What languages are spoken by family members and what are their levels of comfort and fluency in different languages?
- Intermarriage. To what extent do family members have connections to other ethnic groups and how frequently have intermarriages occurred?
- Attitudes. What are the family members' attitudes toward the ethnic group and its values? (Adapted from McGoldrick, 1993)

Adapting to diversity.   The final element in cultural sensitivity is using the information and insights acquired to adapt early care and education practices to meet the needs of infants, toddlers, and families. This may challenge you to expand your definition of "family" and their participation to include grandparents and various significant others in conferences. It will be useful to focus on the strength that a particular cultural background brings to infants and toddlers and work with the strengths and priorities that families have set. At another level, adapting to diversity may cause you to look at the bulletin boards, books, and even dolls in the dramatic play area in a new light and to wonder about how comfortable families from various cultures feel in the early care and education setting.

We don't have research results to resolve issues related to continuity and discontinuity. However, it seems imperative that family/staff relationships and communication be positive and supportive to help infants and toddlers cope with the discontinuities in their lives.

Parent-Staff Collaboration

There is general consensus among early care and education professionals that parent-teacher collaboration is important. Parents of infants and toddlers may have experience with parent-teacher relationships if there are older siblings. If there are no older siblings, the opportunity to set the stage for parent involvement arises during the first encounters with parents of infants and toddlers. Parents and teachers agree that collaboration and partnership is the goal and this is particularly important for very young children (Berger, 1995).

To support collaboration, early care and education personnel need training in working with parents as well as infants and toddlers. With a focus on viewing infants and toddlers in a family-centered way, it becomes important that personnel be sensitive to the needs of families as a unit (Seefeldt, 1985). It is useful to start out with the assumption that most infants and toddlers are in early care and education so that their parents can work. This may limit the level of involvement that parents have as well as their personal preferences. One way of looking at parent involvement is to view the different ways or levels at which parents can be involved. The *first level* of involvement is the obligation that parents have to bring their young children to school safe and healthy and to work out routines for continuity in care. The *second level* involves the basic communication necessary to convey and receive relevant information from child-care providers. The *third level* requires participation in the care setting, from attending parent meetings to volunteering. An expectation that the parents can be regular volunteers is probably unrealistic and may cause stress if viewed as an essential part of parent involvement. The *fourth level* of collaboration involves extending the learning to the home and making conscious decisions to support children's learning at home. The *fifth level* has to do with governance or educational decision making in the setting, such as sitting on a parent advisory council that participates in the hiring process, determines hours the setting is open, costs and so on, of a particular setting (Epstein, 1987). This *fifth level* is more relevant to center-based situations.

The ambiance of the setting itself influences levels of collaboration. Parents are more likely to become involved if they know they are welcome in the early care and education setting. Having an open-door policy as well as formal times when parents can get to know and talk to staff increases the likelihood that parents will be involved (Berger, 1995). Also, having regular speakers on topics suggested by parents may make parents feel the setting is responsive to their needs. Having a parent advisory council for the setting also increases parent involvement and even parental satisfaction.

Parents with young children, especially single parents, have many demands placed on them. If parent activities occur in the evening, the reality is that parents may be tired after working all day and that someone will need to stay home and care for the child or a babysitter will need to be hired if child care is not provided. If activities are held on the weekend, parents may feel that their only free days are being consumed. Expectations for parent involvement need to be couched in terms of the realities of dual-earner families and single parents. Levels of collaboration that do not require attendance at the center itself need to be acknowledged.

Parent-Staff Roles

The respective roles and expectations of parents and teachers or caregivers are much clearer with older preschool-age children than with infants and toddlers. With older children parents are expected to provide love and affection while teachers and caregivers provide support and stimulation. With infants and toddlers, the role distinctions are much less clear. Infants and toddlers need love, caring, and affection from all caregivers. Conflicts between parents and staff may be based on this role confusion and the expectations that the traditional roles that teachers/caregivers play with older children are the same as with infants and toddlers. Although caregivers do not usurp a parent's role, for optimal child development there needs to be a strong, loving relationship between infants and toddlers and their nonparental caregivers.

Parents and caregivers both approach the caregiving situation with expectations about their roles. Information must be communicated about these roles. As

Families have expectations about how their children should be raised and the roles that caregivers play.

a parent places an infant or toddler in an early care and education setting, she may feel that caregivers are evaluating her as a parent (Furman, 1995). This may influence what information she chooses to share. This may be a particularly stressful time for a parent as she is trying to help her infant or toddler adjust to a care situation at the same time that she herself may be experiencing pressure in returning to the "regular" work routine while adjusting to the added responsibility that a child entails. Parents will need support during this transition.

Parents want to know about the child from the caregiver's perspective, and caregivers need to know about the infant and toddler from a parent's perspective in order to collaborate effectively. Good communication skills are essential for this exchange, whether they are used in a parent-teacher conference, on home visits, talking with parents about concerns, or providing information. Developing clear and open lines of communication and being clear about the roles that are expected of parents and caregivers benefits everyone. During the infant and toddler years, the distinctions between caregiving and parenting roles is sometimes overlapping, and may cause additional stress if not acknowledged.

Parents may worry that their child will love the caregiver more than them (Gestwicki, 1992). Parents play all roles related to the care and education of their child. For parents, having children is a marathon. They are in it for the long haul, and may have to pace themselves and balance concerns related to other children in the family, marital relationships, work, and other issues. Parents are expected to love their children unconditionally and to favor their child and to look out for him or her. Parents may find the level of caregiver emotional involvement a concern.

Early childhood professionals interact with infants and toddlers only in the classroom or child-care setting. They may see the child from the perspective of a sprinter. Their involvement is shorter; thus what is not accomplished immediately may be gone forever. They may feel strongly about the infants and toddlers they care for, which can be problematic if their views differ from those of the parents. Caregivers are expected to love and care for young children but also remain somewhat removed and objective. They are expected to show no favoritism for a particular child. Teachers sometimes feel that parents believe there is only one important child in the classroom: obviously theirs (Gestwicki, 1992).

The differences in roles, as well as the ambiguity of the roles for early childhood professionals, may be a source of tension. In one study it appeared that parents and teachers in child-care settings agreed on what constituted good parenting. However, teachers viewed parents as having far poorer parenting skills than parents felt they had (Kontos, 1984). Additionally, teachers in child-care settings feel that they work very hard but that this is not appreciated by parents (Galinsky, 1988). Such feelings can cause tension in the parent and teacher/caregiver relationship.

Parental Stressors

Parents and teachers typically see each other on a regular basis at their worst times: in the morning when parents are trying to get to work on time, and at the end of the work day when they are tired from a day's work and are going home to the "second shift." Some aspects of jobs are likely to increase parental stress. The more hours parents work, the more likely they are to feel conflict between their job and family responsibilities. Parents who had little control over scheduling their work hours experienced more stress, as did parents with very demanding, hectic jobs. When supervisors are not supportive of work/family needs, there is likely to be lower job satisfaction and a higher degree of stress (Galinsky, 1988).

Parents of young children may feel insecure about their parenting skills as they try to decide how to respond to the demands of their rapidly changing infant and toddler. They may also feel very possessive of their infant and are not sure they want to entrust anyone else with his care. They may not want their infant to form a strong attachment to the caregiver, as this makes them feel more insecure. They may even feel jealous of the caregiver who spends so much time with their child. Placing an infant or toddler in an early care and education setting may be very stressful for parents.

Teacher/Caregiver Stressors

Teachers and caregivers in early care and education settings also experience stress from working long hours, and they may feel more stressed when parents are detained or unavoidably late at the end of the day. Taking care of young children is physically demanding and hard work. It requires knowledge, intelligence, flexibility, creativity and caring (Ryan, 1990). While trying to be helpful to parents and responsive to their children, some caregivers begin to feel burned out as they find themselves trying to be "all things to all people" (Galinsky, 1988, 6). As with parents, staff working relationships are important to the health and well-being of teachers/caregivers. The same ambiguity about roles that affects parents also affects teachers and child-care providers.

Some early childhood professionals feel that parents who leave children in care so they can work may think that caring for young children is not important—if it were important, then mothers would all stay home with their children. Likewise, some caregivers feel that parents who leave their young children in care are abandoning them. These judgments can get in the way of caregiving. If your personal philosophy includes feelings such as these about parents then you might want to care only for older children or find an aspect of the profession that does not include working directly with parents and young children.

A care provider's feelings that her work is not appreciated is further complicated by society's evaluation of the job status of those who care for infants and toddlers. This low job status with high levels of responsibility and low pay may cause stress. As caregivers evaluate the differences in financial status between themselves and the parents whose children they care for, they may feel resentful that parents are willing to spend money on a new car or expensive home but not willing to pay more for child care (Galinsky, 1988).

Early care and education professionals often receive little training in how to work with parents. This means that when everything is going well, there are few perceived communication problems. However, when there is a conflict with the parents, the caregivers have few skills to resolve these conflicts. Adults typically rely on methods that result in verbal aggression and defending, withdrawal without resolution, or blaming. Particularly if a teacher has had a difficult day, she does not want to take it out on the child but may well blame the child's parents or any available parent (Galinsky, 1988).

Although teachers and caregivers may not do it openly, many of them make judgments about the parents of the children they care for. Generally, parents held in low esteem were those who limited their conversations with staff to talk about their children and were more likely to be authoritarian in their control of their children. They were also more likely to be single minority parents with low incomes. These parents, who are likely to be the most stressed, have the fewest resources, and although most in need of social support, they are unlikely to receive social support from the early care and education system (Kontos & Wells, 1986).

As parents and teacher/caregivers begin to communicate, they each come with a past history that needs to be acknowledged. Each has concerns and a perspective about the cause of those concerns and some potential solutions. The communication skills of the teacher/caregiver can exacerbate or allay these underlying tensions. Communication is the key to successful collaboration (Shea & Bauer, 1991).

Communicating with Parents

Communication is the process we use to get and give information. It refers to nonverbal as well as verbal processes and includes the social context in which the communication occurs. It is an indicator of interpersonal functioning. To get and give information, clear communication, both verbal and nonverbal, is essential.

Communication includes speaking, listening, reflection of feelings, and interpretation of the meaning of the message (Berger, 1995). Communication is a complicated process because it takes into account not only the words spoken, but nonverbal information such as the tone of voice and the body language that accompanies the words. Relying only on the content of the spoken word is not effective. Researchers believe that, when interpreting communication, only 7 percent of the meaning of a conversation is conveyed by the verbal message (spoken word); 38 percent of the information is gleaned from the way the words are spoken (the vocal and tonal quality of the message accounts for); and 55 percent of the meaning is gathered from the visual message, the body language (Miller et al., 1988).

Knowledge of the communication process leads to the conclusion that important information should be conveyed face to face with parents and that telephone conversations should be limited to nonemotional factual information. In addition to the general aspects of the communication process, there is also an individual factor in that people filter messages through their values and past experiences so that different people may interpret the same information differently.

Berger (1991) identifies characteristics of teachers who are good communicators:

- They give their attention to the person speaking, using eye contact and body language.
- They listen to parents to gather both the feelings and meaning behind statements. They clarify, reframe or restate parental concerns, and distinguish between factual information and feelings.
- They do not criticize, moralize, blame, or judge others. They discuss the infant or toddler's good qualities before bringing up concerns.
- They match their style of giving information and the amount of information they share with the parents' ability to handle the information. They don't "dump" all the information on the parents at one time if they feel the parents will not be able to handle the information.
- They emphasize that concerns are no one's fault. They work together to solve problems and plan for the future.
- They focus on one issue at a time and have enough specific information to document both concerns and progress, but keep the focus on strengths.
- They become allies with parents, viewing them as partners and working to empower them to help their children.
- They focus on the topic at hand, encourage parents to talk and share information, and only talk 50 percent of the time (adapted from Berger, 1991, 156–157, 175–176).

Words are abstractions which stand for ideas. They make communication possible but also confound it. Clarity is especially difficult when people from different cultural backgrounds communicate. Context is important in determining the meaning of words. The word *orange*, for example, can be a fruit or a color. The context of usage allows us to distinguish between the two meanings. However, as ideas get more abstract, clarity is more difficult. A parent might consider herself to have been a "little" late for picking up her daughter. The caregiver may have considered her "very" late.

Communication Techniques to Avoid

There are some ways of communicating that are likely to be counterproductive with parents, or with anyone for that matter.

Avoid Giving Advice.   It is often tempting to give parents advice on how to solve problems that they are having with their infant or toddler; it is rarely wise. It is appropriate to offer constructive suggestions, but even these should be rare. Before giving suggestions, it is necessary to gather enough information about the situation to make the suggestions relevant. You need to find out about the problem, when it occurs, how frequently it occurs, what parents have already tried to do to solve the problem, and whether or not these solutions were effective. Try to get as much specific information as possible before you offer any suggestions. Then offer your perception of the problem to see whether or not it is the same as the parents'. Support the parents in their efforts to solve the problem by commenting positively on what solutions they have tried (if this is appropriate). If you do find the need to offer suggestions, do it in a casual, tentative, nonjudgmental way. Offer more than one suggestion.

Avoid the Word *Understand*.   Sometimes caregivers respond to a parent's problem by saying "I understand exactly what you mean." Such a response is not particularly helpful. The response is likely to trigger thoughts in a parent such as "How can she understand? She isn't me. She doesn't walk in my shoes. She isn't the one getting up in the middle of the night" and so on. People who respond by "understanding" usually convey the impression to others that they really don't understand at all. An empathetic response is far more appropriate— "It must be difficult to get up in the night when you know you have to go to work the next day."

Avoid Judging and Blaming.   Although we consciously try not to judge parents, sometimes our language gives us away. When parents feel they are being judged or blamed, they frequently become defensive. Starting out a conversation with "As you know . . ." is almost always offensive. Using words such as *ought* or *should* also implies judgment. "You should always leave extra diapers in Chunga's locker" is different than saying "Chunga is out of diapers; could you bring some tomorrow please?" The former statement is likely to evoke a defensive reaction from a parent such as "If you were more careful with the diapers you wouldn't go through them so quickly. I know how many I use at home and I left plenty here." This can end up being a no-win situation. It is easier to avoid it.

Avoid Mind Reading.   Mind reading is assuming what another person wants to know or should know without asking. When a parent says "Tell me what I need to know," they are assuming that you can read their mind. If you respond to that statement, you will tell them what you find interesting or what you would want to know if you were the parent. For example, you may tell a parent the particular activities that her son enjoys when what she really wants to know is whether he cries when he is put down for his nap. If he does not, you are unlikely to mention it. It is unlikely that you will figure out what the parent wants to know and she will ultimately be dissatisfied with the exchange. It is more useful to help parents clarify what it is they want to know than to assume you can read someone's mind. Do this by asking the parent for more specific information "I want to tell you about what concerns you. Can you ask me questions about certain parts of the day?" If the mother persists in wanting to know about what you think is important, then you may have to offer her choices—"Would you like to know about his activities, his sleeping, eating, how he gets along with the other children? Help me decide where to start." This will usually get a parent to at least state a preference (adapted from Deiner, 1993).

Much of the communication that takes place between parents and caregivers is on a daily basis. In addition to these daily exchanges, it is important to have regularly scheduled conferences that look at the infant's or toddler's overall development, and to think about the information gathered as part of a whole picture rather than on a daily basis.

Parent-Staff Conferences

Traditionally, there are at least three occasions for parent-staff conferences. The first occurs near the beginning of the year. The second conference occurs about the middle of the year, with the final one near the end of the year. If there is an expectation that the infant or toddler will change placements in a setting or move to a different setting, another conference may be used to plan for the transition. These are usually routine conferences, and the basic technique is frequently known as the "sandwich":

- Talk about the infant or toddler's positive qualities and how he has adjusted and the developmental strides he is making.
- State your concerns about the child, if there are any, and give concrete examples.
- Conclude on a positive note.

Conferences don't just happen. They require much gathering and organizing of information and reflection about the meaning of the information gathered.

Preparing for the Conference

Gather and organize the notes you have about the child. Provide examples of the planning that you can share with parents. Give careful thought to the infant or toddler as an individual, his likes or dislikes, personality traits, temperament, and the special qualities that you enjoy. Have some of his favorite toys available so parents can see them. (This also gives them information about developmentally appropriate toys they might use at home.) Think about how to make parents physically and psychologically comfortable. Many adults are not comfortable on toddler-sized chairs!

Conferencing with Parents

If the conference is held at the early care and education setting, the parents might view this as "teacher territory" and they may need help feeling relaxed and comfortable. Avoid jargon, accentuate the positive, and talk in terms that are specific enough so that parents can correctly carry out suggestions if they choose (Bjorklund & Burger, 1987).

Being an active listener is an important skill for teachers and caregivers. Parents may not ask the questions they really want to know the answers to, and it may be up to the teacher/caregiver to reframe their questions. A parent might ask "Do you think Pat is happy here?" To simply say "Yes" probably does not answer the question that the parent really wanted to know about. It may take some exploration on your part to find out what the parent is concerned about such as "Can you tell me more specifically what you want to know?" The parent may say "I worry because he always cries when I leave him and I wonder if he cries all day?" Then you can appropriately respond "Pat continues to cry for about five minutes after you leave. A teacher holds him and she walks around the classroom with him as she tries to figure out what may interest him. She typically finds something and he gets involved playing. He is involved until nap time and he frequently withdraws and gets a little weepy. Someone rubs his back until he settles down. The other difficult time for him is when the other children's parents come to pick them up. He becomes anxious for you. I can see why you might think he was unhappy all the time when you only see his most difficult times. Do you have suggestions for ways of comforting him that work well for you that we might try?" Suppose, on the other hand, you had said, "Pat really enjoys using playdough. That keeps him happy for a long time." Although a truthful answer, the parent might come away from the conference feeling that you did not answer her question (even though she never really asked it). Mind reading lets you think you know what others want to ask without their asking.

Parents genuinely want to know about what their infant or toddler does during the day. With older children, examples of work they do at school plus their verbal comments help parents understand how they spend their time. With infants and toddlers, this parental understanding is more difficult as the children do not convey the necessary information and they have few "products" as examples of their activities. It is often helpful to take pictures of the infant or toddler throughout the day to show parents how time is spent, or videotape a child at various points throughout the day as a way of sharing information with families.

Problem-Solving Conferences

On occasion you will request a conference with the parents, or they with you, to discuss a particular concern. These conferences are different from the routine ones in that they are problem related and usually have one definite topic. A problem-solving conference should be scheduled when you notice a consistent change in an infant or toddler's behavior or when his behavior deviates far enough from the norms of development and social/emotional behavior that it consistently comes to your attention. A deviation is more than just having a bad day. A different, although overlapping, set of techniques is used for this type of conference.

Scheduling the Conference

Arranging a problem-solving conference is a delicate matter. You don't want to alarm parents, but they do need to know the purpose of the conference. It is important to keep the time frame between scheduling the conference and holding the conference as short as possible. Parents are likely to be anxious when you request such a conference either at arrival or pick-up time. Plan what you will say ahead of time. State your concerns generally. "I have been observing Kate for several weeks and tried to adapt the program to better meet her needs but she still seems to cry when you leave and spends a great deal of time sitting in her locker. Could we set a time to meet and talk about this?" Parents may push for additional information. Give them general information, but don't have the conference. Explain that you have things to show them to help them to better understand what is happening and that then you can jointly work on solving the problem. Schedule the conference as soon as possible.

Preparing for a Problem-Solving Conference

As with all conferences, being well prepared is very important. In these problem-solving conferences, however, a lot of the preparation has to do with preparing yourself. After you have made your observations and gathered together all the information you have, go through the following steps:

Define the Problem.   The most important aspect of this part of the preparation is to separate facts from assumptions or generalizations. It is important to be specific and precise. To say that Brian doesn't get along with the other children is not precise enough. However, knowing that Brian bit Sally while they were both using playdough and that he hit Juan, knocking him off the tricycle, helps define the problem more clearly.

Express the Concern.   At this point it is useful to express concerns of how the behavior makes caregivers feel. "I am worried that one of the children will get hurt and also worried that Brian has some problems we aren't addressing."

Generate Hypotheses.   It is useful to both describe the problem and express your concerns before you begin generating hypotheses about the cause of the problem.

It is also important to gather information from the parents about how they feel about the situation. Parents may share your concerns or have very different ones. Parents may respond that they don't view this as a problem "He is all boy just like his Dad." Another parent might be appalled that his son is being aggressive with others and agree to "straighten him out at home." It is futile to try to solve problems without knowing how the parents perceive the problem. Although the "facts" might be agreed upon, the interpretation of these facts may be different. Ask parents their hypotheses about the child's behavior. In general, behavior does not have either a single cause or a single solution. It is wiser to think through the problem fully the first time than to have a second conference over the same issue, having made no progress toward a solution. Problem solving generally involves generating hypotheses about the cause of the problem and potential solutions.

Generate Suggestions.   Once you have at least four hypotheses about the cause of the problem, it is necessary to generate suggestions for solving the problem. It is important that all participants generate suggestions and that all suggestions are considered. Examine each suggestion, critique them, and then prioritize them. This may be a time when negotiation is necessary as the long- and short-term advantages of solutions are weighed (Brandt, 1995).

Develop a Plan of Action.   After defining the problem and looking at potential causes and solutions, the time has come to implement the suggestions. A plan of action must be developed and then implemented. Trouble-shooting approaches must also be developed and potential problems anticipated. (If the solutions were easy and obvious, you would not have needed a conference). The question you must now work through in your plan is why the easy, obvious solutions have not worked and what will now be different. Verbally work through potential solutions and their consequences and decide on an initial plan of action.

Try out the Plan.   Agree to try out the plan for a specified period of time and see how it is working. Don't modify the plan or evaluate the results until it has been tried several times. Know that change is difficult; if it were an easy problem, your help wouldn't be needed.

Modify the Plan.   Most plans need some modification to work effectively. It is important to think of problem solving as a process and not an event. Consider generating additional hypotheses about the cause of the problem and consider other solutions to see if they look any better in light of experience. Being prepared to try out a plan and then to modify it based on new information is very different from expecting a plan to work the first time and to continue working. The modification may be done on an informal basis.

Evaluate the Plan.   Schedule a time to evaluate the plan and to determine if it is working. If it is not working, modify the plan or generate a new one. Even if the plan seems to be working effectively don't expect that the issue will stay solved forever. Circumstances and people change.

It is useful and empowering to share the process of problem solving with parents. All people face problems and having a plan is often useful. Framing problem solving as a process that changes makes it less likely for people to decide that they failed to solve the problem.

Problem-Solving Conferences on Developmental Concerns

This is a particular type of problem-solving conference that is challenging to both caregivers and parents. No one wants to be the one to suggest that a child might have a developmental problem; however, at some point the early care and education provider may have to do so. The role of the early care and education provider in this instance is to provide parents with the information they need to make a decision about whether follow-up is necessary and if so, how to do it. This type of problem-solving conference requires substantial preparation, observation, and factual information.

With a strong developmental background and good observational skills, providers may become concerned when they observe a particular infant or toddler. When you first suspect a developmental problem in an infant or toddler, you may have only a vague feeling of uneasiness. You may feel that something about this child's behavior is outside your category of "normal." Trust yourself. Watch the child more closely, write down what you observe in order to determine what is bothering you. These notes are for you. They need not look beautiful and they might include the questions your observations generate as well as the observations themselves. Your notes may look similar to these:

Shawn seems to have trouble separating from his mother (More often than the other toddlers? Has this always been true? Was it true in his previous setting?). He cannot (will not?) stay at one activity for over a minute or two. He doesn't seem to be involved with the activities of other toddlers (bored? over his head?).

Does Shawn have an emotional problem? Maybe he does, and maybe he doesn't. Your role is that of gathering information, not providing a diagnosis. It is the parents' decision as to what to do with the information you gather. You can contribute valuable information that may start a diagnostic process.

Your first goal is to gather the information that you need to make a decision about your "hunch"; that is, either to talk with the parents, or to dismiss the hunch. While gathering information, consider whether the problem is related to the child, or to the program. Are there modifications that could be made in the program that would make a difference in the child's behavior? Also, it might be useful to have another set of eyes look at the child. The director or administrator of the program or another teacher might have suggestions as well as additional insights and observations about the child (Abbott & Gold, 1991).

Gathering and Organizing Information

If after further observation of the situation you still believe there is a problem, the next step is to gather enough information about the child to talk with the parents.

Effective teachers
can videotape
children in the
classroom as well as
taking time to
answer another
child's question.

Prepare yourself by keeping the following questions in mind: "What do I need to know?" After that, "How will I use this information?" Then, "What is the most effective way to gather and convey this information?" Be creative and thorough in gathering your information.

Videotape.   If the infant or toddler's behavior is of concern to you and you want to point it out to the parents, videotape it so you can show them specifically what concerns you. With older children work samples are often used, but with younger children a videotape may be more effective in making your point, as there are few "products" with young children.

Work Samples.   As infants move into toddlerhood, there may be some samples of their work you can use. Collect these and perhaps those of a child of a similar age if there are differences that you want parents to see.

Anecdotal Records.   Have available the records that you have kept on the child to share with the parents and document your concerns.

Program Modifications.   Be prepared to talk with parents about the ways you have modified your programming for the child and the results of these modifications.

Informal Consultation.   Plan to share with parents your initial concern and how you worked through the process and the people with whom you shared your concerns and the feedback they gave you in the process.

Agencies, Parents, and Other Professionals.   If parents share your concerns they are likely to want to follow up on your suggestions. If they do this they will probably ask you for suggestions about referral sources. Think about the types of services that parents may need and have the name of a contact person as well as a phone number for them. They may want to know about Child Find or other agencies that serve children up to 3 years of age. They may also want to know about private resources. They may even want to know if there are parents or parent groups that might provide some insights for them (adapted from Abbott & Gold, 1991).

Your role is one of expressing concern and helping parents develop a plan of action that will either confirm or disconfirm your concern for a particular child. This process of confirmation will require referral services. Public Law 99-457 provides free evaluation for children 3 to 5 (Part B); some states also provide these services free to children up to age 3 (Part H). The Child Find specialist is a contact person who knows the regulations for the state, the services provided, and the cost. Parents may make different choices about assessment processes, but Child Find is a good initial source of information.

Know going into the meeting that this may be the first of a series of meetings if parents do not have the same concerns as you do. The parents may need time to consider what you say and to look at their infant and toddler in a new light. It is important to give them time as well as information. Although you may have prepared all of the information for the conference, you may not use it all at the first conference. Conferencing is part of a process and the follow-up is as important as the conference itself (Bjorklund & Burger, 1987).

Conferencing with Parents about Developmental Concerns

Welcome parents, state your general concerns, then get input from the parents about their perception of the child's behavior both at home and at school. If they share your concerns and are appreciative that someone else has noticed, the conference will probably move quickly. If they don't share your concern you need to find out the basis for their perceptions. These are frequently based on experience with other siblings (Jack didn't talk until he was 3 and he was always a loner), or lack of information about developmental norms or experience with other children. Sometimes learning about developmental norms can influence their understanding of the situation and help them differentiate between age-appropriate behavior and that which is not (Morgan, 1989). They may attribute the behavior to particular circumstances (Dottie's grandmother was in the hospital and now is in a nursing home). How you proceed is dependent on the parents' perception of the situation. They may provide you with information that causes you to rethink the situation.

The goal of the conference should be to develop a plan of action. This plan may be additional observation or it may be that parents follow up on referrals. It should be clear who is responsible for doing what, and when you will conference again. It may be that parents want to observe the child in the setting and watch more carefully at home and that your role is to help guide their observations. You, too, will observe and plan to meet again in two weeks to evaluate what you each have learned.

Assessment, if parents make that decision, is a process that takes time. Keep open lines of communication with the parents and support them in their efforts. This may be a stressful time and they may be reluctant to talk with others until they know the outcome of the assessment process. Parents may disagree about whether or not to follow through on the assessment and this may add to family stress. Remind yourself to avoid giving advice, mind reading, judging and blaming, or telling them you understand what they are going through. At times like this it is very tempting. Support the process and the concerns that parents have.

Some interactions with parents are very factual, or parents and staff agree on the situation and how it should be handled. Sometimes parents make decisions or request staff to do things for their children that they are not sure are in the best interests of the child. For example, parents might request that an infant not be given a morning nap so that he will sleep better at home. The staff may face an ethical dilemma if members believe that the infant needs a morning nap, all the other infants this age do take a nap, and they find the infant very fussy and difficult to cope with when she has not had a nap. If the center has a policy about napping it can be evoked. If not, staff must make a decision about what they will do.

Ethical Behavior in Early Care and Education

Ethics comes from the Greek word *ethikos,* meaning moral or ethical. Codes of ethics are statements about the right way to conduct oneself in a profession. Some might ask why ethics are important for individuals who work with and study very young children. Katz (1991) focuses on four aspects of the profession that give rise to ethical problems.

Multiplicity of clients.   Who is served by child care and early education? The off-the-top-of-the-head response is typically "the child, of course." However, if that were solely true there would be fewer concerns about the cost of child care. In reality, the parent may be the first client group served, and then the child. At another level, there are organizational concerns and the interest of the community at large. Sometimes these can be in conflict. Parents may want accommodations that the administration is unwilling to support, staff may feel that what parents' request is not in the best interest of the child, and so on.

Power and status.   The staff of early care and education settings, as well as all adults who interact with infants and toddlers, have tremendous power over them. An infant's self-protective repertoire is very limited. He is dependent upon the adults in his life for his care and safety. Power can also be an issue between parents and staff. Because individuals who care for young children do not have high status, parents may make demands on them that they would not make with other professionals, such as their pediatricians.

Ambiguity of data base.   Although the field of early childhood education has a set of beliefs about what constitutes "best practice" in the field, there is little proof about the efficacy of some procedures. For example, if someone were to ask you the effects of child care on infants and toddlers, what would you tell them? When answers are not clear cut, a code of ethics is necessary to deal with the temptations of those in the field.

Role ambiguity.   Are teachers of infants and toddlers more mother-like or more teacher-like? To the extent that they responsible for the whole child, not just his academic life, it may be unclear where boundaries should be drawn. What happens when parents and caregivers disagree over issues related to child rearing, discipline, toilet-training, socialization, and so on? From the child's perspective, if they do disagree what are the effects of this discontinuity on his development?

These are truly dilemmas, and increased diversity in the population increases the concerns of all. Staff must decide how they will handle the parent who does not want her son to play with dolls, as well as the parent who wants her daughter disciplined for her "bad" behavior by being slapped. This parent agrees that you can't do this at school, but requests that you keep her informed so that she can punish her when she gets home. Do you tell her when the child has misbehaved?

The National Association for the Education of Young Children has developed a Code of Ethical Conduct and Statement of Commitment that was adopted in 1989 (Feeney & Kipnis, 1991). This code includes sections on ethical responsibilities to children, to families, to colleagues, and to the community and society. Although a code of ethics does not provide answers to specific questions, it provides a framework that can be used to structure these answers.

Summary

Parent involvement is viewed as a positive aspect of early care and education, but changing demographics make it challenging for parents to be involved. Programs and philosophies of parent education are changing and are more responsive to the characteristics of the population served. Collaborating and communicating with parents are essential parts of working with infants and toddlers. Parents need information about their children and you need to know about the infants and toddlers from their perspective. The roles and expectations of parents and caregivers are not always clearly defined. The differences in expectations about these roles as well as the ambiguity of the roles may be a source of tension between teachers/caregivers and parents. Additionally, parents and teachers typically see each other on a regular basis at their worst times: in the morning rush and at the end of the work day. Caregivers often receive little training in how to work with parents. When everything is going well there are few problems. However, when there is a problem, teachers or caregivers have few skills to resolve it. Developing good communication skills is important. Caregivers who are good communicators listen to parents and attend to them, focus on issues, and become allies with them. Communication can be improved by avoiding some common mistakes. Caregivers and parents schedule routine conferences as well as conferences devoted to solving particular problems and developmental concerns. The latter conferences require more preparation and more detailed follow-up.

Infants and toddlers in early care and education settings come from a variety of ethnic and cultural backgrounds. Increasingly the importance of culture for infants and toddlers and their families is being recognized, and there is increased need for caregivers to be aware of their own cultural values, to be sensitive to those of others, and to adapt their communication and programming to accommodate diversity.

Application Activities

1. Observe a parent–teacher/caregiver conference. Discuss with the teacher before the conference her goals and strategies. After the conference talk with her again about how she felt about the conference.

2. Talk with a parent about parent-teacher/caregiver conferences. Ask her to tell you about her most memorable conference (positive or negative) and what made that particular conference stand out in her mind.

3. Role-play with a friend the telephone call to set up a problem-solving conference. Evaluate your performance.

Part II

From Theory to Practice

Planning Programs and Activities for Infants, Toddlers, and Twos

Part II of the book links together the developmental-theory base contained in the first part of the book with prototype activities which apply the material on program planning for young children. The first chapter in Part II looks at early care and education settings: different types of settings, issues related to quality and cost, and the impact of child care on young children. The next six chapters are specifically devoted to planning programs for young children. The division of these chapters reflects the major developmental milestones of the first three years. The chapters are in pairs. One chapter presents the necessary information for program planning and the following chapter provides a selection of developmentally appropriate activities. Enough prototype activities are provided to help you determine individual appropriateness as well. The first pair of chapters focuses on the early months of development when the infant has few skills in independent purposeful movement (birth through 8 months); the second pair is designed for infants and toddlers who can crawl and walk (8 to 18 months); and the third pair is for toddlers and 2-year-olds (18 months to 36 months).

Some information, such as guidelines for planning activities and using activities in a developmental framework, involves principles that apply regardless of the age of the child. Those principles are given here and not repeated in each chapter.

Using Developmental Guidelines in Planning Activities

Developmental guidelines are used differently for programming purposes than for assessment. When you plan activities, it is important to know what skills are likely to emerge soon, what skills the infant is practicing, and what skills have been mastered. Developmental norms are used to determine when skills are most likely to emerge. For programming, the goal is to encourage the development of emerging skills. These are the skills that are in Vygotsky's zone of proximal development. They are skills a young child cannot do alone but can accomplish with adult scaffolding. Some infants and toddlers grow by the norms and their skills appear at the predicted times. Others, however, have unique patterns where some skills or behaviors may appear earlier and others later than predicted. The format of these activities is designed to accommodate developmental differences.

Emerging Skills

If a skill is likely to emerge in a given time frame, then it is important to provide activities that support and encourage this skill. For example, if you know that at about 1 month an infant's arms become active when he sees a toy. When he is lying on his back he can bring his hands to the midline. Knowing this, you might hold a toy above the infant and talk to him to encourage him to reach for the toy. By 2 or 3 months, he may grasp the toy. The goal is for the adult to provide the necessary scaffolding to allow the infant to do the activity.

Practicing Skills

Once skills emerge, they need to be practiced. When an infant can grasp one toy, then he needs to practice using differently shaped toys. Toys need to be presented in different locations so that he has to reach up, down left and right. Adults need to vary materials so infants have a broad base of experience to work from. You will note that many activities are entitled "Variations on . . .". These activities are designed to be repeated with variation many times. They appear for the first age group for which they are developmentally appropriate, but are used over a wide age span. Here the goal is for the adult to provide enough variation to broaden the skill base.

Mastering Skills

Infants do not have to have completely mastered one skill to learn others so that some skills may be in all stages. (For a 1-year-old walking might be emerging, creeping may be at the practicing stage, and sitting might have been mastered.) Infants who have mastered a skill profit from using that skill activity in a variety of interesting ways or sequenced with other skills they are learning. When skills are mastered, infants need similar but more challenging experiences. They also need opportunities to move on to related, but more complex, skills. Thus infants who are mastering creeping may also be practicing standing and walking (walking with both hands held). At the mastery level, the infant is "grooving" the skill so it becomes automatic. In this instance the goal is to provide enough opportunities for practice that the task is mastered.

Using Activities in a Developmental Framework

The activities that are given in the chapters are designed as models or prototypes for the types of activities that are appropriate for infants and toddlers in a given age range. Activities are arranged by developmental/planning areas; within areas, those activities that have a similar purpose (such as to improve sensorimotor integration) are grouped together. The accompanying activity index contains a list of all the activities, their developmental/planning area, designated age range, and page number.

All activities are formatted in the following way:

Developmental/Planning Area designates which area the activity focuses on. For infants the focus is developmental, for example, cognitive or language. For toddlers more traditional planning areas are used, such as Creative Arts or Discovery. Particularly for young infants the developmental areas overlap, however, only one designation is used per activity.

Activity Name is the descriptive name given for each activity.

Purpose is a statement about what the activity does. This relates to, but is more specific than, the developmental area, and includes information about overlapping areas. For example, the activity "Bounce and Sing" is in Creative Arts, and the purpose of the activity is "To encourage creative movement, rhythm, and imitation."

Materials provides a list of the materials/objects necessary to perform the activity.

To Make provides information on how to make the materials/objects.

Procedure tells the adult how to carry out the activity. In general, the activities are designed for a level where infants are *practicing* skills.

Easier is a section which gives ideas for making the original activity easier for the infant. This is usually accomplished by varying either the materials used or the procedure. This section is useful when skills are *emerging*. This section also includes ideas to accommodate infants and toddlers with disabilities.

Harder is a section that gives ideas for making the original activity more difficult. This is also accomplished by varying either the materials used or the procedure. This section is useful when infants have *mastered* skills and need to expand them and for older infants and toddlers who enjoy particular materials or who want to join the play of younger children.

Comments are additional remarks that may be advice on what parts of an activity to emphasize, hints on making clean-up easier, or ideas for further expanding the activity.

Notes contain safety cautions.

Activity Index

Developmental/Planning Area	Activity	Age Range in Months	Page Number
Sensorimotor	Variations on Tummy Time	0–8	400
Sensorimotor	Variations on Sitting	0–8	401
Sensorimotor	Variations on Rattles	0–8	402
Sensorimotor	Variations on Rolling	8–18	438
Sensorimotor	Variations on Push and Pull	8–18	439
Sensorimotor	Variations on Walking	8–18	439
Sensorimotor	Variations on Creeping and Crawling	8–18	440
Sensorimotor	Dump and Fill	8–18	441
Sensorimotor	Obstacle Course	18–36	494
Sensorimotor	Variations on Balancing	18–36	494
Sensorimotor	Variations on Throwing	18–36	495
Sensorimotor	Variations on Balls	18–36	496
Cognitive	Infant Massage	0–8	402
Cognitive	Scrunchies	0–8	403
Cognitive	Mousie	0–8	403
Cognitive	Hidden Toy	0–8	404
Cognitive	Red Ring	0–8	404
Language	Black-and-White Books	0–8	405
Language	Talking Walk	0–8	406
Language Arts	Nursery Rhymes	8–18	445
Language Arts	Puppets	8–18	446
Language Arts	I Can Do It	18–36	497
Language Arts	Hats	18–36	497
Language Arts	Flannel Board Stories	18–36	498
Language Arts	Tape It	18–36	498
Social/Emotional	Anticipation	0–8	406
Social/Emotional	Touching Songs	0–8	407

Developmental/Planning Area	Activity	Age Range in Months	Page Number
Social/Emotional	Mirror	0–8	407
Social Awareness	My Book About Me	8–18	448
Social Awareness	My Baby	8–18	449
Social Awareness	Cups and Spoons	8–18	449
Social Awareness	Gelatin	8–18	450
Social Awareness	Hand Lotion	8–18	450
Social Awareness	Dressing Book	8–18	451
Social Awareness	Big Picture	18–36	505
Social Awareness	Celebrations	18–36	506
Social Awareness	Tools	18–36	506
Social Awareness	Dress Up	18–36	507
Adaptive/Self Help	Find the Fist	0–8	408
Adaptive/Self Help	Teether	0–8	408
Adaptive/Self Help	Textured Mat	0–8	409
Discovery	Cardboard Blocks	8–18	441
Discovery	Variations on Peek-a-Boo	8–18	444
Discovery	Hide It	8–18	445
Discovery	Banana Grahams	18–36	499
Discovery	Goop	18–36	500
Discovery	Variations on Playdough	18–36	500
Discovery	Outdoor Treasure Box	18–36	502
Discovery	Boxes, Boxes, Boxes	18–36	503
Creative Arts	Doing It Song	8–18	446
Creative Arts	Pudding Finger Paint	8–18	447
Creative Arts	Scribbling	8–18	448
Creative Arts	Shaving Cream Fingerpaint	18–36	504
Creative Arts	Torn Paper Pictures	18–36	504
Creative Arts	Mood Dancing	18–36	505

Chapter 13

Early Care and Education for Infants, Toddlers, and Twos

Increasingly, research has shown that an infant's early experiences are critical for healthy growth and development. The time directly after birth is one of adjustment, infant to parents and parents to infant. It is a time to learn signals and learn the interpretation of these signals and to develop attachments. Most physicians recommend that women need at least six to eight weeks away from work to recover after pregnancy and childbirth. Child development experts recommend four to six months as the length of time critical for fostering healthy infant attachment and development. Most mothers would like to remain home about six months. (Carnegie Task Force on Meeting the Needs of Young Children, 1994). Why then, given the feelings of mothers and recommendations of professionals, are children as young as 6 weeks of age in early care and education settings? Although some children have always been cared for by others, the magnitude of the number of young children in care has increased as women need to rejoin the workforce. Economic needs require women to go back to work far earlier than they did in the past.

History of Early Care and Education

Early childhood programs have a long history in the United States, dating from the mid-1800s. There were several overlapping movements: "the kindergarten movement, the nursery school movement, the day-care movement, and more recently, the early intervention or compensatory education movement" (Spodek, Saracho, & Peters, 1988, 3).

Organized group care of children did not begin in the United States until the mid-19th century. It was initially a philanthropic endeavor by upper-class women to care for children of the working poor and recent immigrants. Such group care later became part of the social welfare movement, when social workers trained paraprofessionals to care for young children (Klein, 1992).

The federal government became involved in child care during the depression of the 1930s. Child care was one aspect of the Works Progress Administration (WPA) program. Its purpose was three-fold: It provided work for unemployed teachers, care for children whose mothers were working because their husbands were out of work, and it used up surplus food the government was buying from farmers. The federal government's interest in child care continued through the end of World War II. Then, although some child-care centers remained, the majority of them closed in the late 1940s (Barclay, 1985). During the 1950s in the middle class, the expectation was that infants and toddlers would be cared for by their mothers at home and, as preschoolers, would attend a half-day nursery school before enrolling in kindergarten. As more women began reentering the workforce in the 1960s, child care again became, and continues to be, an important issue.

Issues relating to child care have changed. In the 1960s we asked whether or not children should be in day care. In the 1980s we asked what constituted quality child care and what the effects of early care and education were on young children and their families. In the 1990s we are asking how to provide high-quality child care for infants and toddlers and focusing on work/family issues. Child care is viewed in the context of other relationships (Pawl, 1992). The quality of these relationships impacts the quality of care children receive.

Issues in Early Care and Education

The early history of child care has had a direct impact on the issues in the field. Some important issues remain unresolved; both relative to the impact of care settings on the infant or toddler, and issues related to the settings themselves. It is difficult to differentiate these issues cleanly because the quality of a setting influences the impact on the infant or toddler. The distinction between child care and early education is one such issue. The historical connection of child care to the welfare system caused much stigmatization. Child care was viewed as part of a service system that provided custodial care for children of families who need help. Child care allowed mothers to work and hence kept them off "welfare" while at the same time preserving the family unit (Klein, 1992).

Over time, the nursery/kindergarten movement began to overlap with the child-care movement. An important distinction between the two is that the nursery/kindergarten movement was based in education, not social welfare. This grounding significantly influenced child care in two ways: Educators were interested in impacting the curriculum for children so that it moved beyond custodial care; and, at the same time, such education was recognized as a service to the general public, not as a welfare issue (Klein, 1992).

Some professionals in the field see child care and early education as different, but overlapping, services for young children. Others, such as Spodek and Saracho, see no distinction. "Indeed, children's development is considered at risk if they are denied an educational program while they are attending a child care center" (1992, 189). Lack of agreement about the relationship between child care and early education has led to confusion and disagreements about quality, particularly in relation to personnel preparation, staff training, and teacher-child ratios.

Some confusion also relates to the "target population." Who are services provided for? From an early-education perspective it was clear that services were designed for young *children*, typically between the ages of 3 and 5. Child care, on the other hand, was seen as a service designed to meet the needs of *parents* of young children. Sometimes the needs of parents and children are pitted against each other when funds are limited: High-quality care is better for children but more costly for parents. To keep costs for parents down, quality for children is often sacrificed.

Having infants and toddlers in care presents additional challenges. Do infants and toddlers need teachers or "mother substitutes"? Infants and toddlers are just forming their identity and learning about themselves. Adults play a role in this definition of self. Infants develop a sense of self, not based on educational activities, but based on caring, sensitive relationships (Lally & Phelps, 1994). To support infants in this process, caregivers need a sound grounding in the developmental aspects of infancy as well as having knowledge and experiences with infants and toddlers in group situations. Does this now make them highly trained caregivers or teachers? As a society we value "mothering" and more recently "fathering" and in a more generic sense good "parenting". We offer classes to teach parenting skills and acknowledge the stresses involved in parenting. Regretfully, we label caregivers as "unskilled."

In April of 1993 a voluntary partnership of national organizations joined to share information and see if they could develop a set of guiding principles for a unified and comprehensive system for early education and child care that they all could endorse. After working for more than a year, they developed a document that was endorsed by 14 national organizations (as of November, 1994). These organizations include such diverse groups as the National Association for Family Child Care, the Children's Defense Fund, Child Care Law Center, Quality 2000, and Early Childhood Policy Research (NAEYC, 1995c).

The Guiding Principles for a Child Care/Early Education System supports quality community-based care and an infrastructure necessary to support it, including a range of quality services, a well-compensated staff, and affordable prices for families. The principles affirm that child care and early education are a shared responsibility among the public and private sectors and families and providers. The underlying principles include the following:

- Families should be able to chose from a variety of diverse early care and education options and have the primary voice in planning and delivery of services for their children.
- All options should be high quality with culturally competent, well trained, stable staff who work with children in safe, healthy, age and developmentally appropriate environments.
- Government regulation should serve as a consumer protection mechanism.
- Communities should offer a continuum of services beginning with parenting education and continuing through supports for adolescents. Communities need to meet and serve families needs differently over time. Systems should be responsive to the unique needs of their community.
- The early care and education system should be integrated with other family support programs and should include children with disabilities and children from all income levels. It must provide resources and referrals, community planning, ongoing assessment, and evaluation.
- Leadership and staffing of the early care and education system should reflect the diversity of families in the community and nation. The staff should have adequate salaries that reward training, fringe benefits, effective mentoring, and career development opportunities. Leadership development should be promoted at all levels.
- Early care and education systems must be financed from multiple sources to provide high quality and what families can afford to pay. (Adapted from NAEYC, 1995c)

The 105th Congress (1996) has put child care in the limelight of a national debate over the role and responsibility of government to its youngest citizens. One of the concerns is the availability of quality child care.

Availability of Child Care

The stereotypical picture of the breadwinner-father and stay-at-home mother of the 1950s typifies less than 7 percent of families in the United States in the 1990s (Silverstein, 1991). In 1965, only 17 percent of mothers of 1-year-olds worked. In 1991, 53 percent of such mothers were in the work force. Estimates are that by the year 2000 nearly 7 in 10 mothers of young children will be employed outside the home (Children's Defense Fund, 1990). Single parents and families belonging to the lower socioeconomic classes have always needed child care (Klein, 1992). The combination of the women's movement of the 1960s and 1970s and an increasing cost of living provided the impetus for mothers of all social classes to join the work force.

With an increasing population of infants and toddlers and an increasing number of mothers in the workforce, there is an increased need for child care. Between 1976 and 1990, the number of child-care centers tripled and the number of children in center-based care quadrupled (Willer, 1991). It is estimated that in 1990 there were approximately 80,000 child-care centers, about 118,000 regulated family child-care homes, and from 555,000 to 1.1 million unregulated family child-care homes. About 3.3 million children are estimated to be in unregulated family child-care homes (Research and Policy Committee of the Committee for Economic Development, 1993).

One question then is, "Is there a gap between the demand for and the supply of child care?" Hofferth (1992) says "no." The rationale given for this answer is that (a) we do not have a large number of preschool children caring for themselves and (b) the cost of child care has only shown a slight rise since 1975 (Hofferth, 1992). Others disagree. Galinsky and her colleagues (1994) found that 65 percent of parents believed they had no other alternatives when selecting child care and 28 percent reported that they would have used other care if it was available.

Quality in Child Care

Although the supply of child-care settings seems to be adequate, there is concern about the quality of the settings and whether or not families have a choice of child-care settings.

Quality is a relative concept, not an objective reality. Quality is also a dynamic concept that changes over time. Different stakeholders define quality differently; quality has become an international buzz word (Moss, 1994). The quality of child care directly affects the welfare of children in care.

There are few objective measures of quality of care. The *Early Childhood Environment Rating Scale* (1980), the *Family Day Care Rating Scale* (1984), and the *Infant/Toddler Environmental Rating Scale* (1989), developed by Harms and Clifford, are the most widely used measures. Although these scales are formatted in the same way and serve the same general purposes, the content of the scales is different. The scales require that an outside observer rate items on a scale of 1 to 7, with 1 being inadequate and 7 being excellent.

The *Early Childhood Environment Rating Scale (ECERS)* organizes 37 items under seven subscales: personal-care routines; furnishings and display for children; language-reasoning experiences; fine- and gross-motor activities; creative activities; social development; and adult needs (Harms & Clifford, 1980). The *Family Day Care Rating Scale (FDCRS)* organizes 32 items under six major headings: space and furnishings for care and learning; basic care; language and reasoning; learning activities; social development; and adult needs (Harms & Clifford, 1984). The *Infant/Toddler Environmental Rating Scale* (Harms & Clifford, 1989) focuses solely on this age group.

These instruments are designed to be used in a single visit, which is good for research purposes. However, the "snapshot" is influenced by when the visit takes place and the particular staff that are observed (Brophy & Statham, 1994). It is also difficult to judge the dynamic nature of the environment and how responsive it is to children's changing needs and desires.

The National Child Care Staffing Study (Whitebook, Phillips, & Howes, 1990), using multiple assessments, studied 227 centers that served infants and preschool children in five major metropolitan areas. Some centers refused to participate, and one might conclude that these centers were of less high quality than those who did agree to participate. The results were not encouraging. The authors stated that "the quality of services provided by most centers was rated as barely adequate" (Whitebook, Phillips, & Howes, 1990, 4).

The Cost, Quality, and Outcomes Study Team (1995) evaluated 400 child-care centers, and surveyed parents of 826 children. For infants and toddlers the outcome was devastating. Forty percent of infant classrooms were rated as poor quality, 52 percent as mediocre quality, and only 8 percent as developmentally appropriate.

An overarching issue relative to quality is whether the amount and quality of individual attention provided is enough to meet the needs of infants and toddlers. Another major issue concerns the amount of and the appropriateness of the planning and following through on plans by providers.

Defining Quality Child Care for Infants and Toddlers

What determines quality in child care for infants and toddlers? Parents and early childhood professionals agree that they want children in child-care settings to be healthy, safe, have warm relationships, and to learn. They disagree about whether or not these conditions exist in a given setting and have very different perspectives on achieving these outcomes.

Early Childhood Professional Considerations in Quality Care

Most developmentalists agree on a common set of elements when considering the characteristics of high-quality child care.

Table 13.1	NAEYC Accreditation Criteria for Staff–Child Ratios and Group Size

	Size of Group				
	6	8	10	12	14
Age of child					
B to 12 months	1:3	1:4			
12 to 24 months	1:3	1:4	1:5	1:4	
24 to 30 months		1:4	1:5	1:6	
30 to 36 months				1:6	1:7

SOURCE: Adapted from Willer (1990, 64).

Environments for toddlers should include such things as fish tanks that are at a height where children can not only enjoy feeding the fish but easily view them as well.

The Environment. Environments can support or impede relationships among caregivers, infants and toddlers, and their parents. All children need an environment that is safe, healthy, and comfortable. Environments need to include supports (place and flexibility of schedule) to encourage parents to visit, and to meet the needs of mothers who want to continue breast-feeding their infant. Pleasant surroundings help set a positive mood for young children and caregivers alike (Lally & Phelps, 1994).

Group Size and Adult–Child Ratios. Children need to receive care in small groups. Recommended group size is dependent on the age of the child being cared for (the younger the child, the smaller the group). Table 13.1 summarizes the recommended relationship between the age of the child and the size of the group. Infants and toddlers with disabilities can be included when group size is kept at these levels. In situations where there are mixed age groupings, for example, family day-care homes, there should never be more than two children under age 2 (Lally & Phelps, 1994).

As groups get larger, adults not only have to respond to the caregiving demands of more infants and toddlers but they also have to deal with the other adults in the room. This need for organization leads to more restrictive management techniques and less social interaction and language stimulation (Howes,

1992). Infants and toddlers need an intimate environment where they can share and discover their world with the support of caring adults. For young children there are too many distractions in large groups, including increased noise level, stimulation, general confusion, and not enough intimacy.

Educated Caregivers.   Adults who care for infants and toddlers need training in early care and education in general, and specifically in relationship to expectations about growth and development during the first three years. The skills of the caregiver are paramount. Because infants and toddlers are so dependent on the adult in the environment, that adult must be well trained. Infants change so quickly that what is appropriate for a 4-month-old is not appropriate for a 9-month-old. The caregiver needs to know how infants and toddlers change and grow from birth to 3 years, not only their physical and motor development but also their social and emotional development (Provence, 1992).

Designated Primary Caregiver.   In addition to limitations on group size, there should be an adult who is designated as having primary caregiving responsibility for each particular infant, someone with whom the infant can develop an intimate relationship and who learns the infant's cues and patterns. When toddlers are able, they will choose their own primary caregiver. This request should be honored when possible. This does not mean that one person is exclusively in charge of a particular child, but rather that there is a team, and each caregiver is primarily assigned to particular children. This gives parents a person to contact when they have a question about the infant or toddler and it means that fewer things will fall between the cracks (Lally & Phelps, 1994; Carnegie Task Force on Meeting the Needs of Young Children, 1994).

Continuity in Care.   As infants and toddlers develop intimate relationships with caregivers, it is important that this relationship continue. Infants are learning to develop trust. Security is a prime issue for young infants. The most serious threat to that security is the loss of a primary caregiver (Reinsberg, 1995). From an infant's perspective, staff turnovers or reassignments are viewed as a loss. The national annual turnover rate among child-care providers is 40 percent (Carnegie Task Force on Meeting the Needs of Young Children, 1994). Although some of this cannot be prevented, the child-care setting needs to be designed to allow infant-caregiver relationships to be maintained over time. Changes, when they happen, should be planned and gradual. A child-care setting that moves children or caregivers every few months is not acting in the best interest of the child (Lally & Phelps, 1994).

Parent Involvement.   Good early care and education programs encourage parent involvement and input. Although recognizing that parents also have other commitments, they actively seek their advice about their own child and about the setting in general. They find creative ways for busy families to be an active part of the system. Ideally, these programs are linked to a comprehensive "wellness" program of which child care is only part of the support system available for families with young children. Unfortunately, this ideal is rarely realized. In the United States, child care is a fragmented system, if it is a system at all, with little regulation or support for either the child-care setting or the families (Carnegie Task Force on Meeting the Needs of Young Children, 1994).

Culturally Sensitive Care.   The number of infants and toddlers from nonwhite, non-Anglo families is increasing in the United States. In 1970 approximately 12 percent of the population under 18 was nonwhite. Estimates are that by the year 2000 approximately 38 percent of children under 18 will be nonwhite, non-Anglo (Research and Policy Committee of the Committee for Economic Development, 1987). These numbers are expected to grow. Caregiving values are rooted in a person's childhood, their child-care training, and the culture in which they were raised. One goal is continuity between the family and the home, particularly as it relates to culture. Ideally, there are caregivers who speak the same language and come from the same culture as the children in the setting. It is extremely difficult to care for young children when caregivers cannot communicate important information to their parents. For the infant cultural sensitivity is even more basic as he is developing a sense of self.

There is no national set of standards that can be used to evaluate child-care settings in the United States. State governments have been charged with setting such standards, but the standards vary widely. For example, 23 states do not set any standards for group size; one state requires one adult for every three infants; and another state allows one adult to care for 12 infants (Carnegie Task Force on Meeting the Needs of Young Children, 1994).

Although there is diversity in group size and staff ratios, there is consistency in training requirements. Virtually all states allow infants and toddlers to be cared for by providers who have not completed high school, have no training specific to infant and toddler development, and have received less than 6 hours of annual in-service training. Few states have standards for the amount, content, or quality of training for individuals working in early care and education. "Many early care and education practitioners in America are not required to have any early childhood training to work with young children" (Morgan et al., 1994, 80). State governments do not consider training important, quite contrary to professionals and parents.

Parent Considerations in Quality Child Care

Although parents and early childhood professionals share an interest in high-quality child care, their perspectives are very different. Parents focus on their own children. They want caregivers to see their infant or toddler as special and to hold and cherish that child as if it were their own. They want their child to get sensitive, individualized care. They want "good parenting" from a provider who delights in their child. Overall, they are interested in the caregiver as a person. Most parents believe that government regulations and standards are not related to quality. They see the government's role in setting health and safety standards but little else (Carnegie Task Force on Meeting the Needs of Young Children, 1994).

There is a great deal of consensus among parents regarding some aspects of high-quality child care. They agree on the following:

- Attention to children's safety
- Provider's communication with parents about their children
- Cleanliness
- Attention children receive
- Provider's warmth towards children (Kontos et al., 1995, 127)

Parents also differ from each other in what they want in child care. Some parents want a homelike setting with a "mom-like" caregiver. This situation can be viewed as an extension of the family; that is, it is identical to a home except that the provider cares for children other than her own. Other parents want a program of activities for their infant and toddler which is provided by a caregiver who has had training in early childhood education. This situation can be thought of as a mini preschool and the caregivers are often former teachers who have decided to stay home with their own young children. The third model is a combination of the two: a "mom-like" caregiver who provides an educational program, or a more extended family with planned activities (Jones & Meisels, 1987; Whitehead, 1989).

Children's Perspective on Quality

In the United States we rarely think about children's views of quality, especially very young children. Such views, have, however, been considered in Denmark. Denmark has a long-standing organized system of publicly funded early childhood services that include both centers and family day-care homes. The Ministry of Social Affairs laid down a set of principles that all settings must observe:

1. Children's development, well-being, and independence must be encouraged.
2. Children must be listened to.
3. Parents must have influence.
4. Centers must be regarded as a resource in connection with preventive work, i.e., the staff must, in cooperation with other professionals, ensure the special support that is needed for some families with children.
5. Centers must be regarded as one of each neighborhood's facilities for children, i.e., the staff must cooperate with other facilities in the neighbourhood, both public and private. (Langsted, 1994, 30)

Following up on point number two, Denmark began an extensive program on 'Children as Citizens' as a way of listening to and including children. Children's comments on their child-care settings pointed out the need for some structural changes in centers. Children noted that they were not all hungry at the same time, that sometimes they did not want to go out to play at the designated time or they wanted to stay outside and play longer, and they felt it was unfair that children could only have water between meals while adults stood around with a cup of tea or coffee if they wanted it. Accommodations were made. Juice was always available, the playground was staffed with one adult throughout the day, and the common lunch time for all was dropped (Langsted, 1994).

Discovering the needs and desires of children under 3 was more challenging. Many programs for very young children had been preoccupied with rules and prohibitions. Where these rules were challenged, it was difficult for both caregivers and parents. Young children were given the right to say "no". If a child did not want to eat he didn't have to, and he could leave the table and do something that interested him. What he could not do was "yo-yo" back and forth. Rules that dealt with safety remained; most other rules were abandoned. One consequence was that there were fewer conflicts between adults and young children. There were, however, more conflicts among the children. This was viewed in a positive light—children had the right to try to solve their own conflicts. Parents were concerned that because their children were now allowed to jump on the furniture at the center they would want to do so at home. Meetings between staff and parents and observations over time helped parents realize that children are able to make more decisions for themselves than adults typically allow them to make. They were able to distinguish between home and center rules (Langsted, 1994).

The goal of this section is not to advocate the use of the Danish model, but rather to mention it as an alternative, and to broaden your thinking about quality and the relative aspects of it, and to encourage you to include children's values in your thinking about quality.

Joining Parent and Early Childhood Professional Concerns for Quality Child Care

Parents and professionals both want infants and toddlers who are happy, healthy, and learning in child-care settings. Most parents find the quality of their children's child care "very good," whereas trained observers viewing the same setting evaluate the quality as mediocre to poor. There are several explanations for this discrepancy. One obvious one is different operational definitions of quality. Another explanation is that parents use different information to evaluate child-care settings. Still another explanation is that parents, too, have concerns about the quality of care settings but that they are reluctant to voice these concerns to themselves or others. From a parent's perspective, it would be very difficult to rate a child-care setting as "poor" and then leave their child there. It is difficult to know what part each of these aspects plays in the different views of parents and early childhood professionals relative to high-quality child care.

"Research suggests that parents pay relatively little attention to the indicators of quality that professionals suggest they use to screen child care options, such as licensing and caregiver training" (Larner & Phillips, 1994, 51). Howes (1992) discusses the concept of quality child care, and also considers the different orientations of parents and professionals. She looks at quality as having two aspects: structural quality and process quality. "Structural quality generally refers to variables that can be regulated, including adult–child ratio, group size, and education and training of adult caregivers" (Howes, 1992, 33). On the other hand, "Process quality refers to the providers of developmentally appropriate activities and to warm, nurturing, and sensitive caregiving within the child care arrangement" (Howes, 1992, 33). Process quality is certainly more difficult to quantify than structural quality, but it is an equally important component of quality. Fortunately, the qualities overlap.

Warm, nurturing teachers model behavior for toddlers and enthusiastically support their accomplishments.

Teacher/Caregiver Characteristics

Parents and professionals agree that the most important element in any early care and education situation is probably the teacher. The relevant structural characteristics of this individual include the amount and type of formal education she has had, whether the education was related to infants and toddlers, her experience in child care, and the length of time she has served in the early care and education system. To be most effective, teachers of infants and toddlers need both formal education as well as specialized training in infants and toddlers.

It is very difficult to quantify the process quality of caregiving. It is hard to operationalize qualities like warmth, caring, and responsiveness. However, when these are agreed to be high, there seems to be greater attachment and social play, and language scores are higher. The experience of the caregiver does not seem to be a good predictor of child outcomes. However, the long-term stability of the caregiver-infant relationship seems to be an important variable that relates to child outcome. Infants and toddlers do better if caregivers are consistent. The children spend more directed time and have better language skills when the attachment aspect of child care is not at issue (Howes, 1992).

The quality issue does not appear to be what standards should be set, or whether parents or professionals should decide on the standards. Rather, the problem focuses on the cost of implementing those standards so as to provide quality child care that is affordable.

Cost of Quality Child Care

Parents who have the most resources seem likely to secure the best child care. The question is: Do parents with the most resources actually get the best child care? Is good child care basically dependent on the ability to pay? Family factors heavily affect child-care outcomes for infants and toddlers. Good experiences in child care are related to: parental knowledge of child development, which influences their choice of settings; family income, which allows them to choose among settings based on variables such as quality programs; stress levels, which are usually lower when parents have more resources; and child-rearing values and practices, which usually coincide more with what developmentalists consider to be best practice in early care and education (Howes, 1992). Even for parents with many resources, success in obtaining high-quality child care depends partly on luck; that is, finding the setting of choice in an acceptable location, and one that has an opening for the age level of the child who needs care. In general, families with the fewest resources have the most problematic child outcomes.

Research has shown a relationship between high-quality child care and cost. In 1993, high-quality care for infants and toddlers cost $185 to $200 per week in many communities. Thus, families might pay as much as $8,000 to $10,000 annually for quality child care (Carnegie Task Force on Meeting the Needs of Young Children, 1994). NAEYC estimates the figures at slightly less: $6,364 to $8,345 (Willer, 1990). Even these costs are out of reach for many families, particularly those who have more than one child in care.

What do families actually pay? In 1990, the average yearly price for preschool children with employed mothers was $3,150 (Galinsky & Friedman, 1993, 89). Families pay an average of $2,565 for *family day care* or $3,173 for *center-based care* for each child. Care for children under 1 year is more expensive in most settings (Carnegie Task Force on Meeting the Needs of Young Children, 1994).

Families who cannot afford high-quality child care spend a disproportionate amount of money on poor to mediocre care for their children. Families who make less than $15,000 annually spend 23 percent of their income on child care, whereas those who make $50,000 and over spend 6 percent of their income on child care (Carnegie Task Force on Meeting the Needs of Young Children, 1994). Children from low-income families are in lower quality child care as are children from minority families (Galinsky, et al., 1994).

To move from a system of "barely adequate care" to one of "high quality care" basically doubles to triples the cost of child care. The money goes into increasing the salaries of caregivers and lowering the teacher-child ratio. As of 1992, salaries for teachers and providers in child-care settings averaged about $10,000 annually. This low figure is compounded by the fact that real earnings have declined since the mid-1970s by almost a quarter (Bellum et al. 1992). The result of low pay is a decline in the consistency and quality of care and high teacher turnover. Understandably, individuals with college degrees and experience in caring for infants and toddlers are not attracted to employment in most child-care settings.

There is concern in the field regarding the qualifications of some professionals who work with very young children. Many of these individuals have little preparation, low status, and receive low pay. In 1977, the Department of Labor's *Dictionary of Occupational Titles* classified day-care workers and nursery school attendants on a par with kennel keepers (Hostetler & Klugman, 1982). Given the importance of these individuals in the lives of young children, it may be time to add momentum to the "movement" in the field related to the preparation of individuals who work with the nation's youngest children.

In 1992 the National Association for the Education of Young Children reaffirmed its commitment to addressing the problem of inadequate compensation. "This statement affirmed that inadequate compensation, low status, and poor working conditions in many early childhood programs are rooted in three interconnected needs: *quality for children, equitable compensation for staff, and affordability for families*" (NAEYC, 1992, 43).

Professional Preparation

The concept of professionalism can be used to distinguish between individuals who are engaged in an occupation and those who do similar tasks in a nonvocational way. Both mothers and other adults care for infants on a regular basis. However, practitioners who work in early care and education are considered professionals, whereas a mother is not. This concept, as defined, is unrelated to either skill or training.

Professional preparation for those who work with infants and toddlers is considered part of early childhood education. Early childhood is usually defined as birth through 8 years. Many different types of programs in early care and education include infants and toddlers, which include a variety of professionals within each type of program. This variety confounds the problem of a professional identity. Are we talking about child-care providers, infant and toddler teachers, preschool teachers, early interventionists, or early care and education practitioners? Bettye Caldwell coined the term *educare* but it was not adopted (Daniel, 1995). The president of the National Association for the Education of Young Children, Jerlean Daniel, proposed the term *developmentalist*. She feels that this term serves three functions: It presents an accurate view of our way of working with children and providing services for children and their families; it allows for a variety of program delivery modes; and it provides a rationale for involvement in child and family public policy issues (Daniel, 1995). The developmentalist perspective allows one to simultaneously look at the child himself, his experiences and maturational level, and the interaction of these within the larger societal context. It is too early to tell if others will adopt her recommendation.

Several professional organizations have issued a joint position paper on personnel standards for individuals working in early childhood and early childhood special education. This shared vision was developed over three years and recommends: (a) a common core of knowledge and skills needed by all early childhood educators; and (b) a specific set of knowledge and skills that expands upon and exceeds the common core in relationship to children with significant learning needs (Smith, 1995, 2). The common core was adopted by the National Association for the Education of Young Children (NAEYC) and the Division for Early Childhood (DEC) of the Council for Exceptional Children in 1994. It is entitled *Guidelines for Preparation of Early Childhood Professionals* and is distributed by NAEYC. *Guidelines for Licensure in Early Childhood Special Education* was adopted by these two groups in 1994 and by The Association of Teacher Educators in 1995. This publication is available through DEC. The three groups agree that there should be "a free-standing credentialing process . . . for persons who work with young children separate from the credentialing of general educators or of special educators (NAEYC, 1995, 1). They feel that children birth to 3 are so different from older children that specialized knowledge is needed, not simply a downward extension of other knowledge. The Division for Early Childhood is also concerned about quality, and through a task force developed *DEC Recommended Practices: Indicators of Quality in Programs for Infants and Young Children with Special Needs and Their Families* (DEC Task Force on Recommended Practices, 1993).

The content revisions to the *Guidelines* reflect many changes in the field during the 1980s and 1990s. Previous guidelines focused on "teacher education," whereas the new guidelines look at "professional preparation." This change highlights the variety of roles, in addition to teaching in a classroom, that many early childhood educators play. It reflects the emphasis on preparing professionals to work in inclusive environments, to work in partnership with families, particularly vulnerable families, to work collaboratively with other adults as mentors or supervisors, or in a consultation model with specialists such as psychologists and therapists. The new guidelines call for more emphasis on "cultural and linguistic diversity, individualization of curriculum and instructional practices, and knowledge of the central concepts and tools of inquiry in various curriculum content areas" (Bredekamp, 1995). These changes reflect the association's support for including children with disabilities in early care and education settings, the use of technology with young children, and concerns about young children's increased exposure to violence. The changes also reflect a more family-centered orientation, the need for more reflective thinking in the field, and support for child and family advocacy. These guidelines provide a framework for building an early childhood professional development system that includes early childhood professionals at the associate, baccalaureate, and advanced degree levels (Bredekamp, 1995).

Because of the diversity of settings and roles within these settings, individuals can enter the field of early care and education with a variety of educational backgrounds that reflect many different levels of knowledge and experience. Some settings have no requirements, others focus on the individual's age and moral standing, whereas again others are concerned about specialized skills and knowledge and how these were obtained.

In an effort to acknowledge many ways of learning and credentialing in the field of early childhood, the Child Development Associate Credential (CDA) program was developed by representatives from the American Association of Elementary/Kindergarten/Nursery Educators, the Association for Childhood Education International, and the National Association for the Education of Young Children. Their task was to develop the assessment and credentialing system for the CDA credential. This credential was developed as part of a career ladder for individuals in early care and education who do not have standard academic credentials. As defined, a Child Development Associate is a professional who

> assumes primary responsibility for meeting the specific needs of a group of children in a child development setting by nurturing the child's physical, social, emotional, and intellectual needs; sets up and maintains the child care environment; and establishes a liaison relationship between parents and the child development center (CDA Pilot Projects, 1978, 1).

This program focuses on the credentialing of individuals in the field who have primarily an experiential background. The program has delineated six competencies and divided these into 13 functional areas that can be used to guide personnel preparation and also be used to evaluate those currently practicing in the field. The CDA competencies include the following abilities:

1. To establish and maintain a safe, healthy learning environment
2. To advance physical and intellectual competence
3. To support social and emotional development and provide positive guidance
4. To establish positive and productive relationships with parents
5. To ensure a well-run, purposeful program responsive to participant needs
6. To maintain a commitment to professionalism (Phillips, 1990.)

The first award of the credential was given in 1975 and more than 30,000 had been given by 1990 (Phillips, 1990).

Early Care and Education Career Continuum

Early care and education professional development could ideally be viewed as a continuum with different levels of preparation and responsibility at each level and a prescribed amount of training that would allow professional mobility. However, at this point "No coordinated system exists across delivery systems to develop well-trained practitioners to work with young children in homes, centers, Head Start programs and schools" (Morgan et al., 1994, 80).

In an effort to define levels of early childhood professional development, NAEYC has designated six stages on the continuum of professional development which provide both academic levels and statements of equivalent achievement. *Level I* includes individuals who work under the supervision or with the support of higher level professionals. These individuals usually work directly with children or serve as paraprofessionals in a classroom. With additional training, such as a one-year early care and education certificate program or completion of the Child Development Associate Credential, they may move to *Level II*. Individuals at *Level III* would have an associate degree that conforms with NAEYC guidelines or have demonstrated proficiencies that are equivalent to this level.

Individuals who are curriculum specialists and in administrative positions who hold baccalaureate-level degrees and, as part of their course of study, have had supervised teaching experience with infants and toddlers or older children are at *Level IV.* They may participate in the direct care of young children or serve in an administrative position relative to directing a program or working in the area of program planning. Professionals who hold masters *(Level V)* or doctoral degrees *(Level VI)* are less likely to serve young children directly but may serve in administrative positions or do research (NAEYC, 1994).

The early childhood education professional continuum can also be viewed from a different perspective beginning with the child and moving out. You can start with the child and look at how directly services are related to caring for a particular child. Some professionals serve children directly on a daily basis. Other professionals, such as social workers and family therapists, provide their services to the family rather than just to the child. Still other professionals pro- vide leadership in the field such as presidents and chairpersons of professional groups and organizations like the National Association for the Education of Young Children, the Association for Early Childhood International, and the National Center for Clinical Infant Programs. Others work in leadership posi- tions at the state and national level influencing policy decisions that affect chil- dren and their families. Some professionals such as professors, authors, and researchers focus on providing information about infants and toddlers. Other professionals provide goods and services to the field. These individuals might write children's books, help design developmentally appropriate toys or clothing for various ages of children, and so on. The variety of positions available in the early care and education field confound the issues of professionalism, but also offer varied employment opportunities at many different levels.

Consequences of Child Care on Children's Development

Being in child care has an effect on children's development. However, it is diffi- cult to determine exactly what that effect is for an individual child. Researchers interpret the data differently and have come to different conclusions about the impact of child care on infants and toddlers. In addition, we typically compare mothers who stay at home with their children to mothers who are employed and have their children in a child-care setting. The differences we see are usually solely attributed to child care. However, the impact of maternal employment is rarely dealt with—but this is a confounding variable. Another concern is that the centers studied are biased toward high-quality centers, particularly those spon- sored by universities.

Studies of the impact of child care on infants' and toddlers' development show some trends but the studies are less conclusive than those with preschool chil- dren. In general, preschool children in child-care centers do at least as well or bet- ter on tests of intellectual development compared to children who remain in their homes. The only exception is children from shockingly poor centers (Clarke- Stewart, 1992a). We are less sure about the impact of child care for infants.

Social class interacts with the impact of child care on infants and toddlers. A longitudinal study of 867 children in care during their first three years found that the effects of child care varied with the income level of the family. For infants from lower-income-level families, early care was associated with higher reading scores. Infants who were in center-based care also scored higher in mathematics. For middle- and upper-income children, the results are more variable. Children who began child care before 1 year, for example, were doing less well (Caughy, DiPietro, & Strobino, 1994). It appears that child care has the ability to compensate for the home environment of low-income children. However, entering care during infancy was not associated with gains for middle- and higher-income children; and in some cases the results were lower.

The implications of child care for social and emotional development are even less clear cut and more prone to different interpretations. Some studies have shown that preschool children in child care are more socially competent. They are more outgoing, assertive, self-sufficient, helpful, cooperative, and verbally expressive. Other data finds these children less polite, louder, more boisterous and rebellious, more likely to use profane language, and more aggressive (Clarke-Stewart, 1992a).

A confounding variable is the quality of the care children receive. For preschool children, research has shown a relationship between the development of social and intellectual skills with caregiving behavior. When caregivers are stimulating, educational, and respectful rather than being custodial in care, controlling, and demeaning, there were more likely to be positive outcomes (Clarke-Stewart, 1992a). Stability of staff also made a positive contribution to quality outcomes as did having better educated and trained teachers (Whitebook et al, 1990). An additional plus was having some type of curriculum; the nature of the curriculum itself was not as important as having a structure with some organized and supervised activities (Clarke-Stewart & Fein, 1983). Group size and adult-child ratios impact quality. With fewer adults and more children than recommended, children spend more time watching others, fighting, and imitating other children (Clarke-Stewart, 1987).

The research that focuses solely on infants is less conclusive. There has been debate about whether or not child care is good for infants or whether it places them at risk for emotional insecurity and social maladjustment (Clarke-Stewart, 1992a). The standard way of evaluating attachment between infants and their mothers is the Ainsworth Strange Situation (described in detail in Chapter 10). Data analyzed from 16 studies including approximately 1,200 children did find that more children who were in full-time day care were insecurely attached to their mothers (36 percent) than children who were not in child care (29 percent; Clarke-Stewart, 1989, 1992). The question is "Is this difference significant?" Clarke-Stewart is likely to say a cautious "no," Belsky (1992) a vehement "yes."

Belsky (1992) questions not only the differences but also the way in which data were collected. He found no negative effects associated with fathers caring for their children. However, he sees risks of insecure attachment for children "experiencing early and extensive nonparental care" (Belsky, 1992, 86). He accounts for some of his differences in interpretation to the age of the infant when the data was collected. "When families were enrolled before they knew how day care and family relationships were developing, rates of insecurity were found to be significantly higher among children exposed to more than 20 hours per week of non-parental care in their first year" (Belsky, 1992, 86).

Belsky sees the age of entrance into care as a critical variable in the impact of child care. The importance of being under 1 year of age when enrolled and being in nonparental care for more than 20 hours a week were seen as indicators of insecure attachment. His interpretation of the relative amount of insecure attachment moves from approximately 25 percent for young children in less than 20 hours of nonparental care to about 40 percent for infants with more than 20 hours of care to more than 60 percent for maltreated infants (Belsky, 1992). Belsky concludes that the "detrimental consequences of poor-quality day care are most pronounced when such care is initiated in the first year of life (Belsky, 1992, 90). Poor infant day care is associated with attachment insecurity, aggression, and non-compliance.

Bowman (1992) reframes the debate to focus on children's learning rather than their development. She also tries to move the debate from focusing solely on attachment to the mother to a broader context of children's psychological development. This may provide a more useful context for understanding and interpreting the available data rather than focusing solely on attachment as measured by the Ainsworth Strange Situation.

Overall, the evidence suggests that "Children are most likely to have positive and pleasant experiences when the child care is regulated, when it is not-for-profit, and when it is of high quality" (Howes, 1992, 43). Centers that have higher quality care include publicly sponsored centers, worksite centers, and centers with public funding tied to licensing standards—all have access to extra financial resources that they use to improve quality. High-quality centers hire educated staff and pay good wages that attract and retain good teachers, ensure that there are enough adults to pay close and caring attention to infants and toddlers, and train and retain competent directors.

The consequences of child care on development are not clear. However, child care is, and will continue to be a part of the way many children grow up. Professionals in early childhood continue to press for increasing the quality for child care to improve child outcomes and the need for federal regulation and a coordinated system for the delivery of services.

The Federal Government's Role in Early Care and Education

Although policy decisions about providing care for young children are provocative and bring forth deep-seated sentiments about the roles of government and family, many laws that are passed both directly and indirectly affect child-care programs. Many federal programs impact child care. They include Dependent Care Tax Credit (DCTC), Dependent Care Assistance Programs, Child Care and Development Block Grants, Social Services Block Grants, Aid for Dependent Children Child Care, Transitional Child Care, At-Risk Child Care, Child Care Food Program, and Head Start. Many of these programs provide subsidies in

It is difficult to assess the impact of early care and education without knowing the age at which children entered care, the number of hours they are in care, and the quality of the program.

some specific formula to help defray the cost of child care for particular groups. The Department of Labor cites 31 programs in 11 federal agencies that deal with child care in some way (Research and Policy Committee of the Committee for Economic Development, 1993). In an effort to deal with child care in a more responsive, coordinated, systematic way, in January, 1995, the federal government created the Child Care Bureau within the Administration for Children, Youth and Families which is in the Department of Health and Human Services.

The federal government also sets regulations that impact who is included or excluded from child care. Legislation such as Public Law 101-336 Americans with Disabilities Act of 1990 (ADA) supports the inclusion of children with disabilities in all child-care settings. Additional support for inclusion is provided by Public Law 102-119 Individuals with Disabilities Education Act, Amendments of 1991(IDEA). The intention of this legislation is that infants and toddlers with disabilities will be cared for in early care and education settings in their own neighborhoods, just like their siblings. Placing infants and toddlers with disabilities in regular early care and education settings is not a new idea (U.S. Department of Health, Education, and Welfare, 1972). During the 1990s, inclusion received a great deal of attention as more children were being identified as having disabilities. Simultaneously, increases in the number of non-Euro Americans focused concerns on racism, and with a changing philosophical environment, there was a legislative base calling for early intervention services for infants and toddlers at risk.

Including Infants and Toddlers with Developmental Delays

Not surprisingly, more early childhood programs of various types are enrolling young children with developmental delays and with diagnosed disabilities than they did in the past (Wolery et al., 1993). The benefits most frequently cited for including young children with disabilities in child care were the role that exposure played in helping all children learn to accept differences, and the fact that including children with disabilities provided them with more normalized experiences and opportunities for socialization (Wolery et al., 1993). That is, a young child with disabilities could learn, practice, and generalize skills in a normative environment designed to support his total development (Bruder, Deiner, & Sachs, 1992).

Although inclusion of children with disabilities is mandated by the Americans with Disabilities Act, there is resistance. The five most common barriers that were identified were in the areas of personnel preparation (untrained staff and lack of consultation); inadequate staff-child ratios; objections of parents, teachers, and administrators; lack of funds, space, equipment, and transportation; and architectural or structural restrictions (Wolery et al., 1993). Family day care probably serves more children with disabilities than any other care arrangement (Fewell, 1986). Issues that affect family child care in particular relate to liability insurance and the reaction of the care provider's family to having a child with a disability in their home (Deiner, 1992).

There are many successful models for including children with disabilities in child-care settings. The Bank Street Family Center uses a mixed age group of children 6 months to 3 years with groups of no more than 10 with one or two children with disabilities included (Balaban, 1992). Some programs such as Delaware FIRST and DelCare use a consultation model and invest heavily in both preservice and inservice training for family and center care providers, whereas the Day Care Training Project in Connecticut developed a model curriculum for including children with special needs in child care (Bruder, Deiner, & Sachs, 1992). In many ways the care issues for these children are the same issues that arise relating to quality of care for all infants and toddlers.

Types of Child Care

Child care comes in many varieties and sizes, but at least five distinct types of child care can be identified: 1) parental care; 2) child care by relatives (either in the relative's home or the child's home); 3) family day care; 4) child care centers; and 5) other types of care including babysitters, housekeepers, and nannies. The care of infants is more variable than for older children. Families determine the type of care they feel best fits their needs. This may ultimately be determined by what is available. Some professionals feel that family child care is preferable for infants and toddlers and, as children reach preschool age, that center-based care provides more variety.

Table 13.2 provides a comparison of the results of the National Child Care Survey 1990 (Hofferth et al., 1991) and the statistics based on the National Center for Educational Statistics (1992) and the U.S. Bureau of the Census (1990, 1992). The distribution of care is only shown for children under 3. Despite the disparities in the data, it appears clear that many infants and toddlers are cared for by indi-

Table 13.2	Distribution of Care for the 11.1 Million Children under 3 in the United States		
		NCCS	NCES
Parent		52.5%	25%
Non-parent		47.5%	75%
	Child-care center	12.0%	16%
	Family day care	11.2%	26%
	Relatives	16.5%	27%
	in their home	9.5%	
	in child's home	7.0%	
	In-home provider	3.6%	7%
	Other	4.2%	

SOURCE: The National Child Care Survey (NCCS) 1990, (Hofferth et al., 1991); National Center for Education Statistics (NCES), (1993).

viduals other than their parents and at least some of this care takes place in institutional settings. As infants and toddlers become preschoolers, the probability of this care being in a child-care center increases to 33 percent (Clarke-Stewart et al., 1995).

Parental Care

Approximately one-quarter to one-half of children under 3 in the United States are cared for by their parents in their own homes. We actually know less about this care and the quality of the care than we do about other types of care. At one level, we assume that biological parenthood automatically assures sensitive and thoughtful care; at another level we are well aware that this is not true (Pawl, 1992). The assumption seems to be that separation and attachment are a nonissue when parents themselves care for their children. Sometimes parents care for their children at home and work as well by juggling their work schedules so someone is always home; or sometimes the child is taken to work; or a parent does some work at home.

Relative Care

Many infants and toddlers are cared for by relatives, either in their homes or in the child's home. These arrangements are not subject to regulations of any kind. As with parents, we assume that the care given by relatives is automatically better than that given by unrelated people. (Again, we know this is not true in all cases.) Mothers who would not place their children in an organized care setting will leave an infant or toddler with an older parent or relative who may not have the energy to keep up with the child. Surprisingly, young children are not more securely attached to relatives than to nonrelative providers (Galinsky et al., 1994). Quality is dependent on the circumstances and the individual giving the care. In some of these situations grandmothers or aunts care for infants while the mother returns to school or work. In other situations it is more of an informal family child-care situation that happens to be run by a relative who, typically, also has young children. This arrangement is common for infants, children of mothers who work part time, and for poor children (Clarke-Stewart, Gruber, & Fitzgerald, 1994).

Looking at this group more closely, it appears that 60 percent of the relatives were taking care of the children to help out the mothers, not because they wanted to. Additionally, two-thirds of the children with relatives were living in poverty with its concomitant stresses (Galinsky et al., 1994). Intentionality was an important variable; that is, did the relative actually decide to care for children or was it still viewed as "helping out?" "Intentional providers offer higher quality, warmer, and more attentive care that helps children achieve their fullest potential" (Galinsky et al., 1994, 60).

Family Day Care

In family day care a single provider cares for a small group of children (typically one to six) in her home. Family day-care providers have a small business, caring for the children of others and often their own as well, in their homes. These sites are usually located near the cared-for child's home, and are easy to get to. Parents may feel that they have more control over what happens in this type of setting than they might have in a center-based program. They may also develop a close personal relationship with the provider. In this type of setting the provider may take a motherlike role. Many are willing to be flexible about arrangements. In some states family day-care homes are licensed, in others they are registered. In some instances there are no state regulations or many providers do not follow through on licensing or registration. This is the most common type of care for 1- and 2-year-olds whose mothers work full time (Clarke-Stewart, Gruber, & Fitzgerald, 1994).

Family day-care providers have diverse experiential and educational backgrounds. They are primarily adult women, most of whom are or have been married and who have had children of their own. Most care for their own children while they care for the children of others, or did at one time. Many have participated in some type of in-service training, but the training varies greatly in content and duration, from the minimum requirements for a license to college degrees in early childhood education. Much like the director of a child-care center, the family child-care provider must administer and manage her own program. At the same time she is often the sole teacher. "Family child care providers are among the loneliest and least appreciated of all professionals working with children" (Trawick-Smith & Lambert, 1995).

For children who are cared for outside the home, family day care is the most likely setting, as it constitutes at least 30 percent of child-care arrangements. If unlicensed and unregulated homes are included, the figure is much higher (National Center for Educational Statistics, 1992). The National Center for Educational Statistics (1992) found that almost twice as many parents used family day

Family day-care providers have the opportunity to work with children in more informal settings and the atmosphere is more homelike.

care for infants and toddlers as used center-based care. The National Child Care Survey (Hofferth et al., 1991), found them to be about equal sources of care. One reason for the discrepant figures is attributed to the regulation or licensing of family child care. In many instances family child-care homes are not licensed. Kontos (1992) estimates that between 85 and 89 percent are not licensed. Galinsky and her colleagues found 81 percent of family day-care homes "illegally nonregulated" (Galinsky et al., 1994). This confounds the reporting system and may mean that there truly are many more infants and toddlers in family child care than the surveys found and we have even less control over quality than we thought.

Family child care is a more informal service arrangement between the parents and individual providers than is center-based care. Family child care may be viewed as part of the social support system for infants and toddlers. As family day-care providers are the proprietors of their business, parents can easily deal with the person making decisions relative to the care of their child. They do not have to go through a bureaucracy of teachers and program administrators to obtain information or to seek change. Family day care provides more continuity of care for the infant and toddler and family than center-based programs. Parents have fewer worries that a primary caregiver will be shifted from one room to another or that, as caregivers change shifts, important information about their child will be lost. There are fewer children in the setting, the children may receive more individual attention, and there are fewer concerns about infection.

Family day-care homes may be able to provide more flexibility in scheduling. Some families may need only part-time care, others may need full-time child care to allow parents to work, which sometimes includes nights and weekends. Irregular work hours of some parents makes conforming to the requirements of a center difficult. Family day-care providers make individual decisions about whether or not to accommodate their schedules to these types of demands. Some family day-care homes also offer the potential for expanding the informal support network of the family by the addition of other parents and the family day-care provider herself (Deiner & Whitehead, 1988). Family day care creates relationships which can develop into friendship patterns.

Most family day-care providers care for children in a multi-age group with ages spanning 5 years or more. If they provide infant and after-school care, the age range is even wider. This means that providers must be able to care for children at a variety of different developmental levels at the same time, as well as to help children with different maturational levels interact with each other. Family child-care providers often care for their own children within their home. At times the parenting and caregiving roles collide. They have to resolve with their own children such issues as autonomy and separation, which materials and equipment are to be shared, and what does not have to be shared, and differentiating between child-care time and family time (Trawick-Smith & Lambert, 1995).

One concern about family child care is the lack of a back-up system. A sick family day-care provider would need to have another adult take her place. Many providers do not have these back-up systems in place and just close down their care. A related problem occurs if the family day-care provider's children become ill, especially if it is with a communicable disease such as chicken pox. If the setting is temporarily closed, parents are placed in the position of finding alternate care for their child on short notice.

An additional concern is whether or not the family child-care home will continue to provide service. The annual turnover among family child-care providers is estimated to be as high as 60 percent (NAEYC, 1985). Instability of child-care arrangements are difficult for infants and toddlers who are forming attachment relationships and stressful for parents who must renegotiate caregiving arrangements. Parents may also be concerned about the quality of care their child receives as there is usually no other adult in the setting and young children are not verbal enough to discuss their day.

There is no national system or consistent standards for the formal organization of family child-care homes. Most providers have not been regulated or connected to community child care, but this is gradually changing. In some communities an infrastructure to support family child care is developing. Such supports include family day-care associations, accreditation programs, the child-care food program, child-care resource and referral systems, education and training opportunities, and support organizations (Shuster, Finn-Stevenson, & Ward, 1992).

Child-Care Centers

Child-care centers are the most visible type of child-care settings. These can be public or private and either nonprofit or for profit. Some are individual centers, others part of chains. About half of the child-care centers in the United States are for profit (Clarke-Stewart et al., 1994). Approximately 40 percent of centers are administered by private community or charitable organizations, churches or parent cooperatives. About 9 percent of centers are part of day-care chains and 10 percent of centers receive government funding. Government-funded centers usually offer a wide range of services from meals to medical attention (Clarke-Stewart et al., 1994).

Child-care centers vary in size, from small centers with as few as 12 children, to centers that have several hundred children. Some centers have their own building, whereas others may share a setting. Frequently these latter are located in churches, housing projects, community agencies, industrial buildings, or colleges and universities. Settings vary in the ages of children served. Some group settings do not include infants, other settings may have children as old as 11 in after-school care.

Child-care centers must be licensed by the state and abide by their requirements. States vary widely in these requirements. Some states focus on health and safety regulations in their licensure requirements. There may be specific requirements relative to training of staff and administrators, and staff-child ratios based on the age of the child. Some states suggest curriculum guidelines. The level of quality of child-care centers is closely related to county and state requirements for licensing and their ability to monitor these requirements.

Other Care Arrangements

Families have a variety of other care arrangements. Some are informal, such as leaving children with a friend or neighbor; others are more organized, such as having a live-in nanny or someone come into the home on a regular basis. The least common type of care for infants and toddlers is to have an adult come into the child's home on a regular basis to care for the child or children. Although there are organizations that can and do provide such services, there is no regulation for this care and its quality is dependent on the person who is delivering the care. Some care of this type is probably exceptionally good, whereas other situations may be problematic. Like care given by parents and relatives, we know less about the quality of this care and the qualifications of the individuals who provide it.

In-home care is the most expensive type of care on a per-hour basis—the cost has almost doubled since 1975—whereas other child-care settings have remained relatively stable in cost (Hofferth et al., 1991). However, for parents with several young children at home this type of care may be particularly appealing as well as cost effective.

Child care is increasingly being viewed as part of the larger issues that relate to the interface of work and the family. Many corporations have become interested in child care as a way of increasing morale, stabilizing their work force, and reducing absenteeism.

Work/Family and Early Care and Education

In the past the expectation was that an individual's work and personal life were separate. Studies of absenteeism have shown that this expectation is an unrealistic one. Causes of absenteeism include such things as staying home to care for a sick child, finding child care, and the breakdown of child-care arrangements. Women are more likely to stay home than men. Economically, if they earn less money and must take the day off without pay, this makes sense (Research and Policy Committee of the Committee for Economic Development, 1993).

Work/family issues have become part of the total caregiving picture and these issues highlight the need for more reliable and responsive child care. Work/family conflicts cause stress in most families with single working parents or dual-career families. Stress resulting from child care-concerns was rated the number-one problem by employees of a Boston corporation (Friedman, 1986). In response to this concern many businesses and corporations are sponsoring child-care centers or providing child-care information and referral services as an employee benefit. Based on 16 studies of employer-supported child-care programs, both employers and center users feel that absenteeism and morale have been improved. Studies have shown that the greatest benefits were in the areas of personnel recruitment and reduced turnover (Galinsky & Friedman, 1993).

Large employers have taken the lead in improving their employees' access to affordable, quality child care. Initially, most focused on a strategy designed to meet the stated needs of their employees. They typically started out with a single strategy such as Resource and Referral (R&R) which helped them locate child care, making Dependent Care Tax Credits available so child care could be paid with pre-tax dollars, or even an on-site center. Some companies went beyond this stage and began to develop a more integrated approach to work/family benefits that might include adoption subsidies, creating and monitoring the quality of child-care settings, training providers, and so on. Some companies have moved beyond this and are implementing family-friendly workplaces. Leaders in this field are Corning Incorporated, IBM, and Johnson & Johnson. These companies provide a variety of innovative programs such as family specialists hotlines, alternative work schedules, (such as job sharing, work at home, compressed work weeks), and even seminars to sensitize management to work and family issues (Research and Policy Committee of the Committee for Economic Development, 1993).

Although many companies are responsive to their changing work force and work/family issues, others do not acknowledge the obvious overlap and interaction among the work system, the family system, and the early care and education system. Something as simple as the particular hours that parents work, or having to work overtime influences when they need child care. The interactions of work, family, and early care and education systems should be viewed as dynamic since a change in one greatly affects satisfaction with the others. For example, a change in work hours may not be accommodated by an existing child-care arrangement or the addition of a new baby, or a change in work location may make an existing child-care arrangement less satisfactory. Families might need to change what had previously been a satisfactory care arrangement in response to these situations (Whitehead, 1988). For infants and toddlers as well as families these changes may be stressful and disruptive.

Child care is also inextricably tied to welfare reform. Increasingly welfare reform is moving toward requiring all individuals, including mothers of young infants, to work or participate in work training. This will increase the need for both child care for very young children and for child-care subsidies (Cohen, 1996). The goal of welfare reform is economic independence for low-income families. For poor mothers to work they need care for their children. When the cost of this care consumes such a large part of their income, work becomes unfeasible. According to figures from the General Accounting Office, if child care were free (subsidized 100 percent), the number of working low-income mothers would rise from 29 to 74 out of every 100 poor mothers and 43 to 81 out of every 100 near-poor mothers (U.S. General Accounting Office, 1994). Partial subsidies have a more limited effect. The working poor and near poor are most in need of subsidized child care.

A combination of limited resources for funding child care and program mandates about who is eligible to receive such subsidies confounds the problem of subsidizing child care. For example, if a mother whose child care is paid for through At-Risk Child Care and Transitional Child Care loses her job, she also loses her child-care subsidy. In addition to the difficulty of searching for a job while caring for young children, when she finds another job she goes to the bottom of the list for subsidized child care and must pay the full child-care fee. However, if her funds get so low that she is eligible for welfare, she will get subsidized child care when she finds a job or participates in employment-related activities (NAEYC, 1995b).

Parental Leave

In an effort to deal with some of the problems related to work/family issues, the Family and Medical Leave Act (FMLA) was passed in 1993. This federal legislation requires employers of 50 or more people to provide eligible employees 12 weeks of unpaid leave to care for the newborn infant with their job guaranteed at the end of this period and with a continuation of existing health benefits.

The FMLA is a step toward promoting parental care for newborns but it only covers about half of the workforce. In addition, the unpaid nature of the leave does not solve the problem that most parents cannot afford to be without income for that length of time. Needing income, many parents return to work before the period of the leave is up (Carnegie Task Force on Meeting the Needs of Young Children, 1994).

Summary

There is little doubt that the questions we asked about child care 20 years ago are very different from the ones we ask today. Today there is increasing awareness of the developmental importance of the infant and toddler years. Consequently, there is increasing concern about the quality of care for infants and toddlers.

Widespread child care is a reality in the 1990s and families can choose from a variety of options as they consider care for their infant or toddler. They can choose to care for their child themselves, to place their child in an early care and education center, a family child-care home, have a relative take care of the child, or have someone come into the home to care for their infant or toddler. Family resources, both human and financial, will greatly affect their decision. Whatever their decision, they must make some decisions about what they consider quality among the available choices. Do they want another "mom" and home or a "mini preschool," or a combination. Family values and resources influence all these decisions.

Quality child care is an elusive term. Professionals and parents do not necessarily agree on what constitutes high-quality child care. Parents are more concerned with the situation of their own child and individual teacher, whereas professionals are more concerned with groups of children, regulations and licensing, and the programming that is planned for even the youngest children. Varying quality in child-care settings also has varying consequences for the children in care. There is agreement that quality child care for preschool children provides positive learning in the intellectual area. There is less agreement about the impact for infants and toddlers, particularly those who enter full-time care before their first birthday.

Increasingly, child care is being viewed in an ecological framework and as a work/family issue. Businesses and corporations are becoming more involved in child care in a variety of ways. The cost of high-quality child care is an issue. High-quality care is very expensive. Costs of care would double or triple if care were brought up to a level recommended by professional organizations. This is prohibitive for most lower- and middle-income parents.

Although there is no comprehensive national system of child care, the government has played a role in providing child-care subsidies in a variety of ways. It has also passed laws that support infants and toddlers with disabilities to be placed in neighborhood child-care settings as a move toward a more normalized view of development.

Application Activities

1. You are a parent of an infant and you must return to work when she is 6 months old. Decide on the type of care setting you will use and what you will look for when you visit possible sites. What will be the basis of your decision regarding her placement?

2. There is concern about some consequences of child care for infants. How will you cope with this at a personal level? What will you do to mitigate the negative effects, if any, of care?

3. You are campaigning for election to the U.S. House of Representatives from your district. Describe your child-care platform and how you will market it.

Planning for Young Infants: Birth to 8 Months

What kind of planning can you do for young infants? They just "are" until they begin to move and talk, or are they? Young infants have a surprising number of skills, likes, and dislikes, and can express both pleasure and disappointment. They like human faces, sounds, and smells. They see adults as objects of interest and a novelty in their environment. They may even favor them with a smile, a laugh, or babble at them. They like to look at them and then stop looking when they decide they have had enough. Although young infants have a limited repertoire of skills they do have them, and the objective of planning is to enjoy infants themselves and support the development of their skills.

Developing a Philosophy

What do *you* believe about infants? Should young infants be home with their mothers? Do you think that anyone at all can care for an infant, that it is "natural," and that it requires no training? Do you think that all young infants need is to be to safe, warm, and dry? Do you think all young infants are pretty much the same? Do you think that infants are really little adults who just have a lot to learn? Your answers to these questions will influence how you plan and form your philosophy for working with infants.

You already have a philosophy for working with very young children. It may not be well articulated, but it exists, and it influenced how you answered the questions above. It will also influence how you will interact with families, how you set up the environment, the type of preparations you make, the degree to which you individualize planning, and whether or not you base your planning on developmentally appropriate practices. There is no single correct philosophy, but it is important to be able to articulate your philosophy, to know how it developed, and to continually evaluate and modify it with your personal growth. It is also important to compare it with what early childhood teachers and researchers have found. This is true whether this is your first experience with infants and toddlers or whether you have taught for 30 years. It is true whether you are childless or have raised 12 children.

Developing a philosophy for working with infants, toddlers, and twos is a dynamic process. The philosophy is dependent upon a variety of variables. One variable is you as a person, your past experiences as a child, and the decisions you have made based on these experiences. Also, your personality, temperament, and way of being in the world impact your philosophy. Related to this are your attitudes toward young children in general and the role you believe that families and early care and education settings play in caring for and educating very young children. This combines with what your know about a variety of specific content areas: child development, particularly as it relates to infants, toddlers and twos; early childhood education; early childhood special education; and family studies. These variables interact to develop an initial philosophy.

This initial philosophy is shaped by personal experiences in working with infants, toddlers, and twos. This personal experience may be through working at an early care and education setting, babysitting for young children, or having children yourself. It is also affected by those who teach you about infants, toddlers and twos. Professionals choose which aspects of development to emphasize and what to skim over. Some professionals will emphasize the social and emotional aspects of early development, others cognitive development. This emphasis may influence your philosophy. If professionals voice opinions about aspects of the field such as breast-versus-bottle feeding, placing young infants in early care and education settings, and discipline, then these may impact your philosophy.

Your initial philosophy is modified and continually changing as it adapts to your personal growth and development and changing ideas about infants, toddlers, and twos. It is also affected by how you interact and plan programs for them, which is in turn modified by your increasing content and knowledge base. Your philosophy is continually evolving as you change, learn, and reflect on what you know and believe.

The question then becomes how does your personal philosophy determine what happens in the classroom? Another mediating variable is the realities of the early care and education setting. Your philosophy may initially impact the actual setting that you choose to work in. To the extent that a setting's philosophy lacks congruence with your philosophy, you may not seek employment there. Once working in a setting there may well be some differences between your philosophy and what happens in the classroom. For example, you might believe that young children should eat when they are hungry and sleep when they become tired, and the setting might have set times for eating and sleeping. How you will cope with these differences depends on your philosophy and how flexible it is, and even perhaps, how badly you need the job and the availability of other employment.

Developing a philosophy is an ongoing process but one that should happen at a conscious level so that it can be evaluated and re-evaluated. Many of the variables that relate to a personal philosophy are examined in Chapters 14, 16, and 18.

As your philosophy is such an important variable in how you teach, it is critical to examine it at a conscious level. You need to see where infants and toddlers fit into your philosophy, whether or not your philosophy includes infants and toddlers who are developmentally delayed, and how you feel about infants and toddlers who live in vulnerable families. Because infants change and grow quickly, it is useful to focus your philosophy on three distinct periods: the early months (birth to about 8 months); crawlers and walkers (8 until about 18 months); and toddlers and twos (18 to 36 months) (Lally et al., 1987). The chapters in the book reflect these divisions. Below are some criteria to help you clarify your philosophy.

What is the purpose of early care and education?   Is child care designed as a service for parents, or as a cozy place for infants to grow and develop, or both? If you care for very young children you need to decide what type of care these children need. Do they need only to be fed, changed, and kept safe? Most early childhood professionals believe that infants need much more. They need adults who play with them and enjoy caring for them. They need adults who respond to an infant's needs rather than expecting infants to respond to adult schedules.

How do you feel about parents who place infants in care?   Do you plan to work and have others care for your child? How do you feel about parents who place their infants in care? Most early childhood professionals recognize that adults have to make choices. They make the best choices they can at the time they make them. Our role is to honor those choices and to make care settings positive for all children.

Do individuals who care for very young children need specific training?   Some people believe that caring for infants is an innate ability. They believe that all adults, but especially women, automatically know how to do it. Early childhood professionals believe that teaching and caring for infants requires as much skill, if not more, than teaching calculus. Students studying calculus can ask teachers questions to clarify what they don't understand. Infants have much less ability to demonstrate a mismatch between the material and the learner. Although they can show distress by crying, inappropriate program planning rarely causes that level of distress. The infant is dependent on the astute observations of adults to provide sensitive care.

What is the role of the teacher/caregiver?   Many early childhood teachers feel that the roles of teachers and parents should differ. They feel that "preschool teachers should leave sensuous and intimate relations to parents" (Honig, 1989, 5). Most agree with this philosophy for preschool children, but what about infants? Early childhood professionals believe that infants need to be held, cuddled, and loved by caring adults. Working with infants is an intimate social relationship. It requires "tender, careful holding in arms; feedings that respect individual tempos; accurate interpretation of and prompt, comforting attention to distress signals; giving opportunities and freedom to explore toys on the floor; and giving babies control over social interactions" (Martin, 1981, in Honig, 1989, 5).

What is "curriculum" for very young children?   What kinds of goals do you have for working with infants and for yourself as you interact with infants? Infants need a learning environment that supports physical and motor growth and development and stimulates intellectual competence. They need support in developing positive social relationships with adults and others, as well as encouragement to develop emotionally. To be useful, these general goals need to be looked at in more detail and then translated into developmentally appropriate practices and individualized care.

How should adults interact with infants?   Should adults offer an infant two toys to see which he prefers, or should they choose one and give it to him? Early childhood professionals offer children choices. They watch where the infant looks and describe what is happening, rather than talking about what interests them. The adult takes turns with the infant, talking and then listening; she does not do all the talking.

Early childhood professionals are in general agreement about most issues related to a general philosophy. Individual variations in philosophy deal with the degree to which a particular practice is used. Exactly where an individual stands within the range of accepted practices is a matter of personal choice and one that frequently changes with time and experience.

Developmentally Appropriate Practice

The concept of developmentally appropriate practice underlies program planning for all of early childhood education. The concept has two major components: *age appropriateness* and *individual appropriateness*. Age appropriateness means that the learning environment, the teaching methods used, and the activities and materials chosen are based on what is generally expected for children of a particular age and stage of development. Individual appropriateness focuses on the child as a unique individual with his own personality, likes and dislikes, learning pattern, family and cultural background, and the adaptations that need to be made to accommodate the wide differences among individual children (Bredekamp, 1993). Adults use the concept of age appropriateness to decide what range of behaviors, activities, materials and methods to choose from, and individual appropriateness to make the specific choice. Developmentally appropriate practice enhances learning and encourages independence. The role of the adult is to match the particular activity to the developmental level of the infant while honoring the uniqueness of that particular infant.

Infants birth to 8 months are dependent on adults, not only to plan activities but also to bring the activity to the infant and often play on a one-to-one basis with the infant. Activities for infants this age are designed as lying or sitting activities. For infants with emerging mobility (8 to 18 months) the focus is on motion. They need both incentives to move and something to do when they get where they are going. Moving still requires concentration and effort, and children's skills develop at differing rates: the competent crawler may be late in walking or find it inefficient as a mode of transportation. Planning is still very individualized. Toddlers and twos (18 to 36 months) are reliably, independently mobile. They can actively choose what they want to do because they can seek out the activities that they want to participate in and leave when they are finished. The chapters in this textbook that focus on program planning and activities are divided into these three age ranges.

Fundamentals of Planning for Young Infants

Planning for nonmobile infants is very different from planning for toddlers or preschool children, yet many professionals don't realize the degree of expertise necessary. Planning for very young infants is very individualized and developmentally based. Activities are usually one-on-one, are planned for a particular infant, and executed when that infant is interested. Infants, especially when very young, have such a small repertoire of behavior that a single activity with slight variation is often repeated until the infant reaches another developmental level. For example, an activity such as "teethers" can be repeated many times, simply using different teethers and talking about their characteristics.

Planning for infants is more holistic than planning for older children. Their ability to attend to a task is dependent on their state and your ability to choose the appropriate time and activity to engage the infant. The ability to excel as a caregiver is dependent on accurate observations of the infant, knowledge of development, and the ability to bring these two sets of information together.

For purposes of planning, early infancy can be divided into three functional phases, based on large- and small-motor development. In general, the motor requirements of an activity determine which activities are appropriate for which infants.

- Infants from birth up until about 4 or 5 months of age do not have good antigravity skills. Therefore, activities are designed for an infant who is lying either prone (on stomach) or supine (on back) or in a supported sitting position. These activities are also appropriate for older infants who are at this developmental level.

- Beginning at about 4 months of age, infants need less support sitting (head control is greatly improved) and they are moving toward independent sitting. They show more independent exploration in their play. Their hands are now free to explore the environment.

- At about 8 months, most infants develop some form of emerging mobility. The infant begins to move independently by crawling, creeping, hitching, scooting, or perhaps walking.

The best materials are those which encourage active involvement of the infant. Active involvement differs; just looking is active involvement for a very young infant, but not for an older infant.

A major part of the day for very young infants is taken up in routine care and transitions. The challenge is thinking about these as potential learning experiences while at the same time making these experiences enjoyable and taking the opportunity to spend time with infants individually.

The Learning Environment

Learning environments for infants are indoors and outdoors and are at floor, stroller, lap, and shoulder levels. The learning environment changes during the day as infants play on the floor, are picked up and carried, are rocked in a rocking chair, are walked outside in a stroller, and bask on a blanket in the sun on the grass. Infants need a variety of learning environments. Their environment should contain both soft and hard elements. They need pillows and mirrors. Infants like bright, high-contrasting colors and interesting patterns to look at. They need cheerful, friendly pictures of infants, children, and adults hung at different levels. These pictures should depict a variety of ages and ethnic groups. Infants need space to be quiet by themselves and space to interact with other children. They need space to pivot, roll over, and crawl, as well as sturdy furniture to practice pulling to standing. The learning environment should include varied equipment and materials that are developmentally appropriate, and these materials should be organized in a useful way so that the materials are readily available, but are rotated so they are not all out at once.

A major consideration in setting up the environment for young infants is safety. A safe, secure environment is essential for optimal growth and development. Safety needs to be routinely reevaluated based on the age and developmental level of the infants. Safety has a prevention component. Safety equipment such as smoke alarms and fire extinguishers should be operable and adults should know how to use them. Fire drills should be practiced monthly so that all adults know the procedures. A current list of emergency services phone numbers—including poison control, fire company, and medical help, as well as numbers for contacting parents—should be easily accessible. First-aid supplies should also be accessible and adults should know how to do basic first aid as well as how to handle choking.

Beyond the obvious safety considerations, does the environment seem like a soft cozy place to play and relax? Do infants have their own cribs and bedding, and objects that are of special comfort to them? Are there child-sized furnishings and materials that are appropriate for infants, such as infant seats and textured pillows and mats? Are there pictures on the walls that infants can see and mirrors at a height where they can look at themselves? Are there rules or different physical areas to separate walking children from nonwalkers? Are diapering, feeding, sleeping, and play areas separated? Is the space generally calm with pleasant voices and soft music or are there loud noises and angry voices? How does the space feel to adults? Are there furnishings that encourage adults to hold and cuddle children? Do they want to get down on the floor and play with the infants or do they feel more comfortable standing? Can an adult see all of the infants easily so she can keep visual contact with one infant while playing with another? Can she respond immediately if an infant gets hurt or frightened?

Developmentally Appropriate Planning for Young Infants

This is it! The time when infants are not sleeping, eating, or participating in routine care. Optimally, this is a time when they are alert and interested in learning about the world around them. Young infants are not in this state for very long, so it is important to "catch" it. With increasing age, infants spend more time in this state and less time sleeping. As young infants are only just learning how to interact with others, your games with them may last only a moment or two. These interactive times alternate with times that infants play alone. Planned play time is not the only time you attend to the infant, but rather your other time is spent in a less planned way. Each infant needs some planned play times with an adult every day, as well as the times when you are caring for him and supporting him in other ways.

Particular planned play time activities should be written for each infant. Adults often find it helps them as much as the children to have a general theme around which they plan. Themes help adults decide which materials to use and help frame the language you use. Ideas for activities to use during play time for young infants are in the next chapter. They are grouped by developmental areas.

Planning for infants is so closely related to their growth and development that it is efficient to organize planning around these. The infant must interact with his world to learn and adjust his responses to accommodate different activities and materials. The interaction of development, experiences, and learning is the foundation for planning for young infants. The infant's development is the "given" for the adult to select experiences or activities within the infant's "zone of proximal development." When the match is accurate, learning takes place. This learning is then "grooved" to a level of mastery through variations of the experiences, and new and more complex experiences are introduced with adult scaffolding.

Developmental differences between a 4-month-old infant and an 8-month-old infant are so vast that activities for one are inappropriate for the other. As infants become predictably mobile and increase their repertoire of skills, less individualization is required.

Sensorimotor Development

Infants must learn to use both the large and small muscles in their body. They must gain control over the muscles that relate to stability in order to be able to sit and stand, the muscles which are used in creeping and walking, and the muscles related to manipulation of objects such as reaching, grasping, and releasing (Wilson, 1990). Additionally, infants must integrate the information they receive from their senses with their motor skills to understand that something to look at may also be something to touch. They need to integrate the use of muscles with information they receive from their senses to know how to move around objects without bumping into them and to know how far to reach to grasp a desired object.

Large-Motor Development

Some activities for young infants are designed to use the large muscles of the body such as those in the neck, trunk, arms and legs. These muscles are necessary for all antigravity postures such as sitting and standing. They also are necessary to stabilize the body as finer movements are performed. The pattern in which they develop serves as a guide for matching activities to children. Infants differ in the rate they acquire motor skills but the progression of development is the same:

- To support large-motor development, infants need a variety of materials that encourage both nonlocomotor and early locomotor movements. The strategies to encourage locomotor movements are similar to nonlocomotor except that the objects are placed at a greater distance so the infant has to actually move to get to the object.
- To encourage nonlocomotor movement (pushing, pulling, stretching, twisting, pivoting, and so on), place the infant prone and place a desired object slightly out of reach so that the infant has to stretch to get the object.
- Call to infants so they have to twist to visually make contact with you.
- When they are sitting, encourage infants to pick up items which they have to stretch and bend to reach.

Small-Motor Development

Small-motor development involves the child's ability to use the small muscles of the arms, hands, and fingers. Reaching begins with gross movements of the arm and progresses to directed, precise touching of objects with the fingers. Grasping proceeds from swiping at and missing objects to accurately picking up small items. The development of fine-motor skills is dependent on other related skills. Although vision is not a prerequisite for fine-motor development, the ability to see objects motivates infants and directs their reaching. Reaching is also dependent on the infant's head and trunk control, and adequate balance. Reaching is a prerequisite to grasping and picking up objects. An infant must be able to pick up and release objects for finer eye–hand coordination skills to develop.

Young children, particularly infants, learn about their world through exploring with their senses—looking, hearing, touching, tasting and smelling. Motor skills are often used in conjunction with sensory information. In sensorimotor integration both sensory and motor components of behavior are integrated in the brain to facilitate smooth movement and the ability to learn new skills. Infants need activities that encourage the development of both large- and small-motor skills and provide opportunities for integrating these skills with sensory input. They need a variety of materials that encourage all types of movements and reflect a developmental progression for skill building. Infants are very active. They want to practice emerging skills. Know and encourage the movements that infants are capable of. Be sure these movements are safe.

- Provide infants with interesting toys to reach for and grasp. With young infants these need to be large and soft. As they develop more precision, the toys can be harder and smaller.

With practice, infants' reaching and grasping becomes more precise.

- Encourage infants to both grasp and release objects. Asking infants to give you what they have grasped helps them learn to release.
- Give infants objects that are safe to drop and throw and encourage them to do so.

Cognitive Development

Cognition is very different in infants and toddlers than it is in older children. They begin with reflexive actions that develop into more organized and coordinated activities. These actions are then repeated intentionally and variation is added.

Infants, beginning about 4 months, become fascinated with what objects do. Infants now explore materials to see what they can do. Previously, the goal was simply motor action. Now, an infant who "discovers" he can make a toy rattle will repeat the shaking action again and again to hear the rattle. This is the beginning of means-end behavior. This is also science. The first signs of object permanence begin in the middle of the first year. So infants need many experiences with hidden objects and people. Sometimes the objects should be partially visible. Then, as the infant's skill improves, hide the object completely.

- As infants are developing object permanence, play games that involve looking for objects and hiding and seeking. Hide toys for the infant to find and play Peek-a-boo.

- When the infant drops objects from his highchair, see if he looks for them. Repetition is important; so the adult needs to retrieve the objects. This helps children learn what predictably happens.

- Talk to infants when you are out of their sight. Disappear and reappear in the same or different places.
- As infants learn about the effects of their actions, give them objects they can act on such as a ball that moves when they hit it. Encourage them to vary their actions (Push it harder), point out the effect actions have on the object (The harder you push it, the farther it goes).

Language/Communications Development

Learning to communicate is a major task for infants. Learning the underlying concepts of language and its usefulness begins during infancy. Infants need to learn that communication is a useful skill. This learning requires responsivity. Adults who respond to the infant's language initiations increase the likelihood of his continuing and increasing his language skills. Communication also requires listening skills and someone to listen. As the infant is learning to talk, he is also learning to use language as a way of internalizing and organizing information.

Infants begin the process of learning to talk at birth. In the first few weeks of life infants are learning to distinguish different sounds; that is, noise versus the human voice. By 1 month infants respond differently to speech than to other sounds and even begin to show awareness of the different speech sounds that people make. Young infants can hear speech sounds, but they are not yet able to make them because they lack the muscle coordination for speech. By the time the infant is 6 to 7 months old, he begins to practice sound formation by cooing and babbling. Talking to him and imitating the infant's babbling are good ways to foster language during this stage.

As infants begin to babble, they also initiate verbal contact with others. Infants need verbal stimulation at this time. You can support language development by responding to an infant's attempts at conversation (babbling). Introduce new words, but take turns with her. Infants are continually learning how to say new sounds and eventually new words.

- Initiate language with infants with the expectation that they will respond, whether or not they do.
- Talk to infants and offer praise and encouragement for their efforts.
- Model language by verbally labeling experiences and pictures for infants in addition to extending and expanding the infant's language.
- Encourage infants to coo, babble, make sounds, and say words by talking directly to them while you play. Describe in simple words what you are doing as well as what they are doing. Describe the materials you are using.
- Communicate with infants during caregiving routines, such as feeding, changing, and dressing as well. These are great times to talk to each child about how special she is.

Humming, singing, and talking are ways to help infants listen, make sounds, and begin to understand the give and take so important in communication skills. By providing stimulating materials for infants to listen to, touch, and play with, you give them many opportunities to listen and to make sounds. One of the most important methods of encouraging infants to make sounds is by interacting with them throughout the day.

Infants make sounds with objects, by hitting, banging, shaking, and even crumpling. They experience a wide range of sounds and noises, including voices of adults and other infants, doors opening and closing, kitchen noises, music, and outside noises. There are several ways to encourage infants to make sounds. One often-mentioned activity is playing "ping-pong"; that is, repeating a baby's sounds to her and making up sounds for the baby to copy. Watch and listen for her reaction!

Social and Emotional Development

Teaching young children how to interact socially with others begins almost at birth. The manner and style in which adults respond and interact with infants sets the stage for their later social skill development. Children take the cues and examples adults demonstrate for them and use them in their own interactions. Appropriate and positive social interactions will likely lead to the development of good social skills and a positive self-image. Infants may not yet be ready to learn social etiquette, but they are ready to learn the foundation skills that will lead to later social-skill development. The key to the development of these early foundation skills is social interaction.

Opportunities for social interaction skills occur during all of the activities that take place between adult and child. The process begins when an adult answers an infant's cry, talks to the infant during feeding, looks at the child during diapering, waits to interact during an infant's quiet times, and initiates interaction when appropriate. Though adults may not feel they are actively "teaching" children social skills, their respectful styles of interaction are powerful "incidental" learning experiences.

Adults who respond appropriately to an infant's communication attempts help the infant learn appropriate techniques to use later in response to communication from others. Adults who answer an infant's cry with calm understanding help him to acquire a sense of safety and security, knowing that someone is available to help when needed. Infants need to trust and feel secure with the adults who care for them. This is easier for some infants than others, both because of the infants themselves and the environments in which they live or are cared for. All infants are different. Each has a basic way of being in the world. We frequently refer to this as temperament. Temperament influences a variety of behaviors in the infant: activity level, mood, persistence and distractibility, and the ability to adjust to change. Caregivers should be sensitive to these differences in infant temperament.

Although infancy may seem to be stress free to an adult, to an infant it may seem very stressful. Being separated from the parent and adjusting to a new caregiver or caregivers may be stressful. Different surroundings, routines, and other children can cause stress. Even adjusting to her own emerging skills, especially locomotion, may place an infant in stressful situations. Infants need to be viewed as legitimately having stress. Therefore caregivers need to reduce that stress where possible as well as help infants learn to cope with stress.

- When the infant begins to stir from a nap, begin to talk in a soothing voice. Try to catch and maintain eye contact.
- When the infant cries, lift him to your shoulder, rub his back and help him to focus on an interesting object or your face.
- As the infant notices his hands and has fun making them move, play a gentle game of pat-a-cake or peek-a-boo, using the child's hands.
- During quiet time, place the infant on your lap in front of you. Smile and say "ah- boo" as you lean forward and gently bump your forehead to the infant's. Repeat this as long as the activity seems enjoyable to the infant.
- Carry on conversations with the infant whenever it is appropriate. Use different tones of voice: high, low, loud, soft, laughing, and soothing.
- The more you interact with the infant, and the more opportunity you give her to play turn-taking games, the more the infant will take part. If you play a babbling game with her, and wait appropriately, you will get more and more response as time goes on.
- The development of a secure relationship with an adult is critical to the development of the infant's health and competence.
- You do not spoil infants by responding to their cries! Crying is their way to express that something is not right. Not responding to cries can lead to children who do not initiate communication, because they think no one will listen! Respond to cries with a soothing voice, asking what is wrong. They won't be able to tell you, but it will make them feel better.
- Tell an infant before you are going to pick her up, put her down, change the diaper, or place her in an infant seat what you are about to do. This signals when a change is to occur.
- When the infant begins to experiment with his voice, he will repeat sounds over and over. You can repeat the sounds, too. While you are doing so, place his fingers on your lips. Let him feel the vibrations as each sound is made. This also helps to foster eye contact.
- Be alert to the subtle movements of infants to communicate thoughts or feelings. Each infant has a unique signaling system. So it is important to learn signals and their meaning.

Self-Help and Adaptive Development

For infants, self-concept begins with self awareness. Infants need to feel accepted for who they are. They need to feel that caring adults will set limits that will keep them safe. They need to be respected as individuals who have their own wants and needs. One need is support in developing skills that will allow them to function independently. Infants need your support in developing these skills, even though it is often easier to just do things for them.

- Help young infants find their hands and gently guide the hand to the mouth if this is something that will bring the infant comfort.
- Support infants in holding their own bottle, but you hold them.
- Give infants cups and spoons to explore and play with.
- Include finger foods in infant diets when they are old enough for some solid food.
- Encourage emerging mobility.
- Give infants choices and show delight and support when they chose.
- Praise infants as they learn to control their body and make it function in the way they want it to.

Planning for Transitions and Routine Care

There are two schedules that impact the day: the infant's and the adult's. Each infant has an individual schedule that responds to her physical and biological needs. This schedule changes over time (older infants sleep less than younger infants). Some infants have relatively regular internal schedules and settle into a routine easily, while others have difficulty and do not seem to have a pattern. With increasing age, almost all infants develop more predictable routines. Adults must develop a schedule which coordinates the caregiving for each infant (Wilson, 1990). The key to schedule planning is *flexibility* and organizing general time blocks that respond to infants' needs. Ideally, timing is flexible but sequences are predictable. This helps infants learn what will happen next. The younger the infant, the more imperative it is to respond to the infant's biological clock than to preset schedules.

Much of the time spent providing care to infants is made up of important and essential routines such as changing diapers, preparing meals, giving bottles, or helping infants settle down for a nap. These routines offer an opportunity for spending time individually with an infant and provide chances to communicate how much you like that infant by making eye contact, talking, singing, imitating the infant's sounds, or saying nursery rhymes. Routines give infants a sense of security and trust, as their most basic needs are being met in a consistent caring manner. Thinking about routines as part of the learning environment allows planning to be incorporated into the physical caring aspect of the routine situation.

Arrival Time

This is the time that infants make the transition from parent care to care from another adult. Adults need to be available to make this transition easier for infants. I sometimes think of this as the "hip to hip" transfer. This may be a difficult time for some infants, and it is likely that even infants who readily transfer will have some difficult days which will make this arrival part of the day particularly hard. Adults, too, may have trouble with this process. Mothers or fathers, concerned about leaving a child in care, often find this transition difficult. Their concern may make the transition even more difficult. They need a caring adult to reassure them that their infant will be well cared for while they are gone.

Arrival time is a time for parents to share information with caregivers about the infant's time at home and any concerns, joys, or unusual events that have taken place. For example, "Josh's grandparents visited last night and he didn't get to bed until very late and had trouble quieting down." Now, if Josh takes a longer than usual nap you will have an indication as to why that happened. Parents should be encouraged to put complex information in writing. When the parent actually leaves, infants need one-on-one time with an adult to settle in to the new situation. What the infant does next is dependent on his age and his particular schedule. If he has gotten up early, he may sleep; if he is not tired, he may play.

It helps if the caregiver and parent are each clear about who has what responsibilities, such as, who puts on or takes off the infant's outside clothing. Either the caregiver or the parent should regularly initiate the transition and leave taking. If both adults are undecided, the infant is likely to become restless and fussy, making it difficult for the adults to communicate.

Nap Time

Setting up a routine for sleeping is important. Soothing and calming infants helps them go to sleep. They have different preferences. Helping infants develop positive sleep patterns is crucial to the adults in their world. Problems in this area derive from what are termed *sleep associations*. There are events or patterns of events that become paired with sleep so that the infant associates these events or patterns with sleep and cannot go to sleep without them. A particular pacifier, being rocked or patted, or being walked, are some of the common associations. The result of these sleep associations is that if an infant awakens she does not have the skill to get back to sleep herself and so she needs adults to help (Family Resource Service, 1993).

Infants can *learn* to go to sleep. They can be put to bed awake, the adult saying something like "Have a good sleep" and move out of their range of vision. If infants cry, they should be checked on every 5 minutes. Unless there is some reason that they need to be picked up, it is not a good idea to do that. They need love, reassurance, and support, but they also need to learn to go to sleep. When infants are having problems in this area, the adults in an infant's life need to agree on a routine to help infants learn to go to sleep and to comfort themselves when they awaken at inappropriate times. Cribs are for sleeping. When they are not sleeping, place infants on the floor, in infant seats, or prop them up so they can play. Infants are typically fed when they awaken from sleep.

Eating

Very young infants eat every 2 to 4 hours. There is little doubt when they want to eat, as they fuss and cry to let you know. Most, however, have a pattern, and if you learn it you can feed them before they cry. Infants need to be held while they are fed. Eating should be a relaxed leisurely social time. When feeding the infant, gently massage her head, fingers, shoulders. Consider singing softly during feeding. This is a great time for working on eye contact, as infants will look at your face while you're talking or singing.

With increasing age, infants eat more at each feeding and the feedings become farther apart. Up until about 1 month, infants typically take 2 to 4 ounces of fluid six to ten times a day. Between 1 month and 3 months, the volume increases to 5 or 6 ounces and the feedings decrease to six to eight. By 6 months, the infant has four to six feedings of about 6 to 7 ounces each (Marotz, Cross, & Rush, 1993).

Propping a bottle, that is, placing an infant in a crib with the bottle propped so it is in his mouth, is not recommended as a feeding method for both social and medical reasons. Socially, infants need the close skin-to-skin contact with caring adults. Medically, infants who go to sleep with a bottle risk developing bottle-mouth syndrome which is characterized by a high rate of tooth decay. Although teeth are not visible, they are there and susceptible to decay. Propping a bottle can also lead to ear infections if the bacterial growth in the pooled liquid travels

Feeding a young infant can be a relaxed leisurely time. Yet, simultaneously, the adult can be aware of and available to older children in the environment.

from the infant's mouth to the eustachian tubes and into the ears. Allowing an infant to lie down with a bottle also increases the danger of choking (Marotz, Cross, & Rush, 1993).

Breast milk or formula contain all the nutrients needed by the infant for the first six months of life. At around 4 to 6 months, infants begin to produce enzymes that can digest complex carbohydrates and proteins other than those found in milk (Marotz et al., 1993). Pediatricians and parents typically decide when solid food should be added to the infant's diet and in what order.

Six months is a real demarcation in infant eating. This is when additional foods are usually introduced. Typically, iron-enriched cereals are introduced first (the infant's iron stores are exhausted by about 6 months), then fruits and vegetables, followed by meat or meat substitutes. Initially, individual foods are introduced rather than mixtures, so if food allergies develop they can be more easily identified. Finger food such as dry bread and crackers are also introduced around this time. In general, young children prefer sweet foods. The other variable is familiarity. At one point all foods are new to infants and they may reject these new foods. Rather than deciding that an infant does not like a particular food that is rejected, the key is to continue to offer a particular food. Looking and smelling is not enough. The infant actually has to eat the food before it enters the familiar category and is accepted (Birch, Johnson, & Fisher, 1995). This may have a biological, adaptive base. Putting food into the body is risky. What if you eat something poisonous and die? As you eat and stay healthy, you eat the same foods again. When you consider the vast variety of foods that infants eat throughout the world, there is some credibility for this position.

Teeth also begin to erupt about 6 months. This may be stressful for some infants and disrupt their eating pattern. They often want to use their teeth and may prefer foods that can be chewed such as toast or teething biscuits. The diarrhea that often accompanies teething is not caused by the teething process itself but by infectious organisms from items that the infant is mouthing and chewing (Marotz, Cross, & Rush, 1993).

Eating is a relaxed social experience, even for infants. Talk or sing to infants when they are eating. Name the foods they are eating, describe the tastes and textures. Encourage them and support their competence as they begin to feed themselves with finger foods. Allow infants to play with empty cups and spoons.

Diapering

An infant's diapers are changed many times each day. Some days caregivers feel that all they do is feed infants and change their diapers. This, however, is also one-on-one time when the infant is awake. Often, the stimulation of being partially naked will make an infant alert and interested. It is a wonderful time to talk to him, sing, or play. Talk about body parts, or what the infant was doing or will be doing next. The infant may look away occasionally, but continue the eye contact. She will come back to you.

When you are changing the infant, take the opportunity to develop body awareness by massaging her arms, legs, and feet with gentle pressure and light touches. Be sure to have pictures or a mirror at a height the infant can see while being diapered. **Keep one hand on the infant at all times. Never leave an infant alone on the changing table. Wash your hands immediately after diapering before doing anything else.**

Infants urinate as frequently as every 1 to 3 hours or as infrequently as four to six times a day. The darker the color, the more concentrated the urine. The stools of breast-fed infants are light mustard colored, whereas those of formula-fed infants are more tan or yellow and smellier. They are also firmer than those of breast-fed babies, about the consistency of peanut butter. The frequency of bowel movements varies widely from one infant to another with breast-fed infants having fewer, as there is very little solid waste to be eliminated. Infants frequently pass a stool after feeding as a result of a gastrocolic reflex which causes the digestive system to activate whenever the stomach is full (Shelov, 1993).

If formula-fed infants do not have at least one bowel movement a day, or have very hard stools, they may be constipated. As solid food (cereal) is added to an infant's diet, the first few stools may be very difficult for the infant to pass, an important reason to have good communication with parents. Infants can also get diarrhea, which is characterized by high liquid content in the stool and an increased frequency of bowel movements. This can be caused by a change in the infant's or mother's diet (if breast-fed), or it could be an indication of an intestinal infection. The major concern with diarrhea is that the infant could become dehydrated (Shelov, 1993). Noting bowel movements is also part of the record-keeping system. When stools are hard or very watery, parents should be informed.

Departure Time

Departure time is another major transition. Some infants are overjoyed to see their parents, others seem nonchalant about the transition, and others may find the transition a difficult one. They may need support and reminders of the routine. Toward the end of the day most caregivers reflect on the day and decide what information needs to be shared with an infant's parents. Important information should be written down. If there is more than one caregiver, all relevant information should be collected and communicated prior to departure. Know who has permission to pick up the child so there is no tension if someone besides the parent comes to get the infant. Have clear rules about when infants can be picked up and dropped off and be sure you and parents know what the emergency backup system is and how to use it.

Although much of an infant's time is spent in routines, the remaining time is for play and learning.

Methods and Materials for Working with Infants

Methods are the behaviors, strategies, and techniques that adults use to interact with infants and toddlers. *Materials* are the objects or things that infants and toddlers interact with. The methods adults use require a knowledge base that includes the ability to assess an infant's developmental level and state, a repertoire of behaviors, strategies, and techniques, and the ability to match these appropriately to a particular infant at a specific point in time. Then, the adult must evaluate whether the "match" was a good one by observing the infant's behavior. This is an ongoing process.

Since infants change and grow by actively interacting with their environment, materials are an extremely important part of planning. Nonmobile infants are dependent on adults to provide these materials. Infants learn through their senses by looking, listening, touching, smelling, and tasting. They need materials that can be held, dropped, thrown, mouthed, and shaken. They need materials of different textures, colors, weights, and sizes. Adults must choose appropriate materials to support infant learning. The following diagram (Figure 14.1) depicts this process of materials-methods interaction.

The materials you choose and the methods you use are components of the learning environment. Materials are specific to young infants; they are listed here along with guidelines for selection. Appropriate materials can enhance learning and encourage independence in infants and toddlers. When selecting materials, it is helpful to ask yourself the following questions:

- Is the toy safe and durable? Watch for sharp edges or small parts which infants could swallow or choke on. Consider whether the toy will stand up to banging, dropping, chewing, and so forth.

- Is the toy washable? Infants enjoy and learn from putting toys in their mouth. Washability is a must to prevent spread of germs.

Figure 14.1 | Materials–Methods/Adult–Infant Interaction

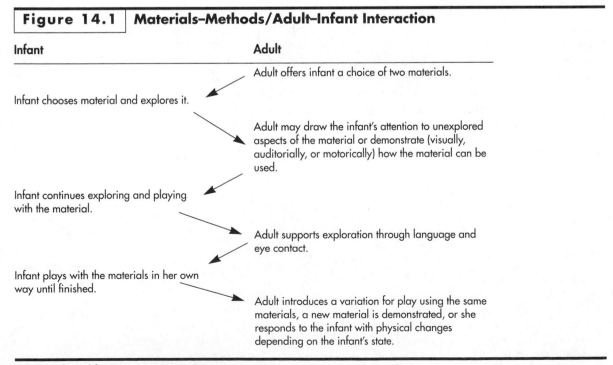

Infant

Adult

Adult offers infant a choice of two materials.

Infant chooses material and explores it.

Adult may draw the infant's attention to unexplored aspects of the material or demonstrate (visually, auditorially, or motorically) how the material can be used.

Infant continues exploring and playing with the material.

Adult supports exploration through language and eye contact.

Infant plays with the materials in her own way until finished.

Adult introduces a variation for play using the same materials, a new material is demonstrated, or she responds to the infant with physical changes depending on the infant's state.

SOURCE: Adapted from Deiner (1993, 116).

- Is the size, weight, and shape of the toy appropriate? Consider how easy or difficult it will be for an infant to hold and manipulate the toy. If the toy is heavy and hard to grasp, an infant is less likely to play with it. If it tips over easily or rolls away, the infant may become quickly frustrated. (Toys with suction cups on the base may avoid this difficulty.)
- Is the toy bright, colorful, and appealing?
- Does the toy stimulate more than one sense? For example, is the toy soft and textured *and* does it make noise as well?
- Is the toy appropriate to the infant's developmental level? In general, infants need experiences with toys they can successfully play with, but they also benefit from being challenged by toys and tasks slightly above their current level.

Some categories and examples of possible materials to consider when making selections are mentioned below. In looking at your overall variety of materials, try to include some from several categories rather than having more toys in just one or two areas.

- Materials that encourage awareness of self and others: toys with mirrors, dolls, and puppets.
- Materials with varied textures: textured rattles and blocks and fuzzy puppets.
- Materials that make noise: musical toys, rattles, squeaky toys.
- Materials that reflect ethnic diversity.
- Materials for cuddling: soft stuffed dolls, animals, toys and other huggables

Even the best materials are not a substitute for adult interaction. Although infants benefit from periods of independent play, their play with toys is almost always enhanced by an adult close by talking about what the infant is doing and offering encouragement and assistance as needed.

For infants birth through 8 months, a variety of materials such as the following is useful.

- Mobiles (evaluate them from underneath, as that is where the infant will be)
- Rattles
- Teethers (some of which are easy to grasp)
- Musical toys
- Unbreakable mirrors
- Soft-fabric toys of different textures that are sturdy and washable
- Fabric dolls or animals (huggables) with limbs that are easy to grasp
- Balls (soft, textured, clutch, and some that make noise when they roll)
- Toys with suction cup bases
- Toys that roll, or can be pushed or pulled
- Plastic measuring spoons
- Soft vinyl or cardboard books
- Water toys

Novelty is an important variable. Infants are attracted to new and different objects. Toys with different colors, designs, and actions add differences. Caregivers can provide novelty by adding to and changing crib mobiles and having a variety of similar toys so they can be rotated.

Organizing Materials for Infants

There are a variety of ways to organize materials for infants. The choice is dependent on personal preference and planning style.

1. Materials can be organized by general developmental levels. Materials might be categorized for infants birth to 4 months and 4 through 8 months. Materials themselves might be categorized; for example, all rattles might be placed together with the age noted (4 to 8 months).

2. Organize similar materials (all the suction-cup toys) in baskets, boxes, or other containers. This makes it easier to grab exactly what you want quickly.

3. Keep most toys out of sight, bringing out one or two activities at a time. Bringing out a few toys at a time keeps activities novel and maintains the infant's interest in them.

4. Another way of organizing materials is by themes. This may be a secondary level of organization and would determine which rattles are chosen to support the themes. If a theme were "My Body," then a rattle shaped like a foot might be included in the theme materials along with a mirror, a picture of an infant, and so on. All the materials that are used for a particular theme are kept together, being washed and returned when the theme changes.

There are a variety of ways to organize and plan for infants. Over time you will find the one that best fits your needs. A major decision is to decide whether to plan a week for each child or to plan a day and include each child in the plans for that day. This is a matter of emphasis and preference since your plans must be individualized regardless of which approach you use.

It is not necessary to plan for each developmental area every day but it is important to include all areas over the week. It is also important to note the infant's age as that is very relevant in your planning. For infants under 4 months, calculate the age in weeks; for infants between 4 and 8 months, knowing the age within two weeks is fine, or knowing that an infant is 6 and a half months old. Since infants change quickly, adults need to keep reminding themselves to keep their planning developmentally appropriate. Certainly learning will occur that is not part of this written plan, but it is important to plan specific learning episodes for each infant and have written comments about the learning experience.

Some adults, especially those who have only a few infants to care for, prefer to have all of a single infant's plans for a week on the same sheet of paper as in Chart 14.1. Chart 14.2 shows how you might arrange this type of planning for a number of infants on a daily basis. Again, age is noted for each infant. The number of infants cared for would determine how many entries you would need on the form. You would plan more activities for older infants than for younger ones.

Chart 14.1	Planning for a single infant for a week

Infant's Name _____ Age _____ Week of _____ Theme_____

Developmental Area	Materials	Method
Monday		
L		
C		
S		
E		
SM		

Tuesday		
L		
C		
S		
E		
SM		

Wednesday		
L		
C		
S		
E		
SM		

Thursday		
L		
C		
S		
E		
SM		

Friday		
L		
C		
S		
E		
SM		

Feedback/Comments:

Developmental Areas: communication/language (L), cognitive (C), social (S), emotional (E), sensorimotor (SM); circle area letter.

Chart 14.2	Daily plans for a small group of infants

Date _____   **Theme** _____

Infant's Name _____ Age _____

Developmental Area	Materials	Method
L		
C		
S		
E		
SM		

Feedback/Comments:

Infant's Name _____ Age _____

Developmental Area	Materials	Method
L		
C		
S		
E		
SM		

Feedback/Comments:

Infant's Name _____ Age _____

Developmental Area	Materials	Method
L		
C		
S		
E		
SM		

Feedback/Comments:

Developmental Areas: communication/language **(L)**, cognitive **(C)**, social **(S)**, emotional **(E)**, sensorimotor **(SM)**; circle area letter.

Including Infants with Disabilities

Most professionals in early childhood education and early childhood special education agree that the best setting for infants and toddlers with disabilities is one which also includes other children without disabilities. The Individuals with Disability Education Act (IDEA) of 1991 states that all infants and toddlers should have access to services that allow them to function in as "normal" an environment as possible; that is, they should be included in neighborhood schools (including child-care settings) along with other children. It is likely that most child-care providers will need to develop skills to include premature infants and infants and toddlers with disabilities. Because programming for very young children is so individualized, planning for these children is not very different than developmentally appropriate planning for any infant. What is different is the form that planning takes and the individuals involved in the planning itself.

Infants who are diagnosed with disabilities typically have moderate to severe disabilities or characteristics that are recognizable at birth such as Down syndrome or fetal alcohol syndrome. Other infants may be determined to be at risk because of low birth weight or because of their family situation. Some of the infants with disabilities will look different from the other infants; others will not.

Individualized Family Service Plans

Infants and toddlers (birth to 3) identified as having developmental delays or disabilities should have an Individualized Family Service Plan (IFSP). This is a plan that is developed by the child's parents together with a team that is working with the child. This team may have been instrumental in the selection of the early care and education setting for the child. The purpose of the IFSP is to identify, organize, and facilitate the attainment of a family's goals for themselves and their children with disabilities (Johnson, McGonigel, & Kaufmann, 1989). The components of this plan are laid out in Part H of the Individuals with Disabilities Education Act. States have different definitions about what constitutes a developmental delay, however. If the child meets the state's definition, he will probably have an IFSP. Although IFSPs vary, they all include the following information:

- A statement of the child's present developmental levels, including physical, cognitive, speech and language, psycho-social development, and self-help or adaptive skills

- A statement of family strengths and needs relative to enhancing the development of their infant or toddler

- A statement of major outcomes (goals) expected for the child and family, methods for achieving these, and a time line for measuring the degree to which desired outcomes are achieved and whether or not IFSP revisions are necessary

- A statement of specific early intervention services necessary to meet child and family needs, including information about the frequency, intensity and methods of service delivery
- Projected dates for starting and ending (if appropriate) services
- The name of the service coordinator who will be responsible for implementing and coordinating the plan
- A plan for supporting the child and family during the transition into programs for 3- to 5-year-olds.

Regardless of the specific requirements of the law, most good IFSPs also include the following information, which is extremely helpful in program planning:

- A statement of the child's strengths as well as needs
- An emphasis on functional abilities rather than a compilation of test scores
- A description of abilities within a developmental context
- Inclusion of all developmental domains (physical, cognitive, language and speech, psycho-social, and self-help), not just the ones where deficits are noted
- Information on behavioral and temperament characteristics
- A description of the functional limitations of the child that are relevant to intervention planning (Bailey, 1988).

In all cases where the infant has an IFSP there will be a designated service coordinator who will help gather the information needed to plan for the infant and to interact with the family. The caregiver, along with the family and other professionals, is a part of the team that works with this infant. Infants with disabilities may require more specific planning than other infants. They are likely to have particular developmental areas that need attention. Caregivers should be part of the team that decides on the plan for an infant with disabilities so that it is not only appropriate for the infant, but one that the caregiver knows how to carry out. Make sure to plan activities for the infant's developmental level rather than chronological age. Adapt activities to meet individual needs. Parents and therapists are likely to have specific suggestions for helping the caregiver with a particular child.

The idea behind the IFSP is that services should be family centered, not just infant centered. The most important idea behind the process and resulting product is that families decide what they want as outcomes on the IFSP. This means that families and other professionals working with the infant with a disability jointly plan for this infant. The parents and professionals provide guidance and support for those working with the infant. A statement about procedures and methods that will be used to produce the desired outcomes is a required part of the plan. See Figure 14.2 for sample IFSP.

Low-Birth-Weight and Premature Infants

Some infants who are born with very low birth weight are initially classified as having a developmental delay and need individualized programming planned by an early intervention team. Early intervention increases the probability that

Figure 14.2 Sample Individualized Family Service Plan (IFSP)

This Individualized Family Service Plan was developed when Lily was 14 months old. Because of her young age, the IFSP was reviewed by the team a month later and then at short but increasing intervals. The sample given here is for the review at 22 months.

Background Information

Child's Name: Lily

SSN: 222-66-6234

Date of Birth: 3/19/94

Age in Months: 14 months

Address: 201 Main St. Anytown, U.S.A.

Telephone: 717-322-0785

Family Members

Family Members	Relation to Child Being Served	Date
Cathy	mother	5/95
David	father	5/95
Sinsew	older sister	5/95

IFSP Team

Name	Title	Agency
Cathy	Parent	
David	Parent	
Evelyn	Service Coordinator	XYZ Infant Program
Kathy	Speech-Language Pathologist	XYZ Infant Program
Carolyn	Occupational Therapists	Children's Hospital
Wanda	Pediatrician	Medical College of Anytown
Michael	Assistive Technology Educator	State University
Elsie	Nurse	Department of Health

IFSP Team Review Dates

Review	Age of Child	Date	New Assessment? (Y/N)	New Outcomes? (Y/N)
30 days	1 yr. 3 months	6/95	Y	Y
90 days	1 yr. 5 months	8/95	N	Y
4 months	1 yr. 6 months	9/95	Y	Y
8 months	1 yr. 10 months	1/96	Y	Y
12 months				
18 months				
24 months				
30 months				

SOURCE: With permission of Michael Gamel-McCormick.

383

This page of the IFSP reflects Lily's strengths and functioning levels based on both observations and assessment. It also notes the assessment results from which these conclusions were drawn. The page also reflects the concerns and priorities of the family.

Child's Name: Lily   **DOB:** 3/19/94   **DOA:** 1/17/96

Child's Strengths and Functioning Levels:

Lily has much better stamina than she has ever had. She lets us know what she wants by pointing at things. She is able to make some sounds through her tracheostomy tube. She is able to finger feed herself and is eating more. She likes yogurt and applesauce and tender chicken. She recognizes all of her relatives and smiles when she sees her sister. She is getting interested in some toys but still does not play for more than 2 or 3 minutes. Lily is walking with her hands up high (still!) but is moving around quicker. She is able to hold small toys and a spoon. She is crawling up steps and will try to step up them.

Family's Concerns and Priorities:

We want Lily to begin to talk or at least make sounds. She seems to be getting frustrated with her trach and is sometimes pulling at it.

Our finances are in bad shape and both of us will need to work. We need to find care for Lily. Now that she is stable we're ready to do that.

We need some time together. The past year has been hard for us and we're not sure about our relationship because we've been spending so much time in the hospital with Lily.

Child's Assessment Functioning Results

Skill Domain	CA	Age Level/Range	Skill Domain	CA	Age Level/Range	Skill Domain	CA	Age Level/Range
Receptive	22 m	14 m (11-15)	Adaptive	22 m	19 m (15-22)	Personal-Social	22 m	17 m (16-18)
Expressive	22 m	12 m (10-13)	Gross Motor	22 m	17 m (15-21)			
Cognitive	22 m	16 m (14-19)	Fine Motor	22 m	18 m (16-20)			

This is a sample of an "action" page in an IFSP. The first column notes the date and the outcome number. The outcome number reflects the parents' priorities for that particular outcome. The outcome, or objective, is stated next, and the supports or resources necessary to achieve it are noted followed by the action plan designed to attain that particular outcome. The next columns reflect the parents' evaluation of the progress toward the attainment of that particular outcome and the date. The final column is for comments. Note that parents—not professionals—evaluate the progress in this IFSP form.

IFSP Outcomes

Child Name: _Lily_ **DOB:** _3/19/94_ **Service Coordinator:** _Evelyn_ **Page:** _1_

Outcome # and Date Identified	Outcome Statement	Supports and Resources	Action Plan	Family Evaluation		Comments
				Date	Rating	
1 1/96	Cathy and David will visit at least three family child care homes to find day time care for Lily.	Evelyn and Richmond Dept. of Social Services Neighbors and friends	Cathy and David will ask friends and neighbors about family child care providers. Evelyn will get a list of approved providers from Dept. of Social Services.	2/96 3/96 4/96	2 3 5	—got job for Cathy. Child care not good—need better
2 1/96	Cathy and David need time together away from the children.	Elsie Evelyn Relatives	David and Cathy will ask relatives if they want to be trained to take care of Lily. Elsie will provide training to relatives. David and Cathy will arrange to go out once a month without the children.	3/17/96	5	One family member (Aunt Thel) will get trained

Family Evaluation Ratings 1 = situation changed, no longer needed **2** = situation unchanged, still need outcome **3** = implementation begun, still need outcome **4** = outcome partially accomplished **5** = outcome accomplished but family needs more **6** = outcome mostly accomplished to satisfaction **7** = outcome completely accomplished to family's satisfaction

In addition to the service coordinator, the parents and older sister play an active part in carrying out the IFSP.

Child Name: _Lily_   **DOB:** _3/19/94_   **Service Coordinator:** _Evelyn_   **Page:** _2_

Outcome # and Date Identified	Outcome Statement	Supports and Resources	Action Plan	Family Evaluation Date	Family Evaluation Rating	Comments
3 1/96	Lily will use one word or approximations to ask for things in the house.	Kathy Evelyn Cathy and David Sinsew	Kathy will teach Cathy and David how to cover Lily's trach and encourage her to make sounds. Sinsew can play with Lily and get her toys when she makes noise.	2/96 4/96	3 3	Lily covering trach and making sounds.
4 1/96	Lily will play with toys for at least 10 minutes.	Cathy and David Sinsew Evelyn Kathy	David and Cathy will find toys and objects that Lily likes. Evelyn will watch Lily play with Cathy and give her ideas about how to lengthen Lily's play times. Sinsew can play with Lily with the toys she likes.	2/96 4/96	3 4	ID toys— Sinsew playing great w/Lily.

Family Evaluation Ratings 1 = situation changed, no longer needed   **2** = situation unchanged, still need outcome   **3** = implementation begun, still need outcome   **4** = outcome partially accomplished   **5** = outcome accomplished but family needs more   **6** = outcome mostly accompl. to satisfaction   **7** = outcome completely accomplished to family's satisfaction premature infants will catch up to their peers and no longer be classified as having a developmental delay. As with all infants, planning is based on developmentally appropriate practice. Initial judgments are made about age/stage appropriateness. For young infants gestational age may be most useful in planning. That is, an infant who is currently 5 months old who was born two months prematurely may be more appropriately planned for as a 3-month-old. Individual appropriateness supports the adaptation and modification of planning and programming to meet these infants' needs.

Infants born prematurely often have an especially limited repertoire of skills, so a variety of materials at the same developmental level is particularly important. Although many very-low-birth-weight infants catch up with their peers, at this young age there are predictable differences. The cues that these infants give are often subtle. With practice, these can be interpreted and responded to. The task of interpretation and response may not be easy.

- These infants may have trouble establishing a pattern of wake and sleep; their cry is often more high-pitched and frequent.

- A disorganized premature infant often cries 6 hours a day. (Full-term newborns often cry 2 to 3 hours a day for several months.) Colicky crying typically begins right after feeding and frequent burping is useful. Random patterns of crying are difficult to interpret. They may be just a discharge of excess energy, boredom, or overstimulation.

- Many premature infants have a low tolerance for stimulation. Therefore a setting with as much going on as in child care may tax their system. When they become fussy and irritable, try less, as opposed to more, stimulation.

Infants with Developmental Delays

We often classify young infants as having a developmental delay rather than trying to pinpoint a specific disability. It can be clear by comparing the infant's development to charts of normal development that the infant is not developing as quickly as most infants his age. It is often unclear whether this is just an individual growth pattern and the infant will "catch up" in his own time or whether the delay is of a more permanent nature. Until children are 3 years old and we are more sure about the nature of the delay, we often look at development in this more general way.

- Provide a visually stimulating environment, particularly mobiles, until the infant begins reaching and grasping.

- Use a great deal of variation and repetition of activities, especially those that intrigue the infant; it is likely to take these infants longer to "groove" an idea or skill.

- Encourage the efforts that the infant makes.

Infants with Physical Impairments

Most physical disabilities involve damage to the central nervous system. Although these cannot be cured through early intervention, alternative pathways may be developed through exercise, massage, appropriate positioning, and the use of prostheses (Krajicek, 1991).

- Provide toys that are interesting to look at and listen to.
- Bring objects to the infant and experiment to see if there is a way she can hold or control the object herself.
- Use soft or textured objects that are easier to grasp.
- Use toys with suction cups so the toys stay in one place if the infant has coordination problems.
- Positioning of the infant is very important. There are some positions infants should not be in and ways of carrying them that are not helpful. Talk with the physical therapist or parent about positioning.

Infants with Visual Impairments

In infancy the role of vision is to motivate and guide behavior. It also plays a major role in incidental learning and it extends the infant's world beyond his reach (Zambone, 1995). Because infants with visual impairments do not use eye contact to express and maintain interest, caregivers must use other senses to excite children into exploring their world. The classic work of Fraiberg (1965) showed the importance of early intervention, including touch, to prevent "blindisms" or secondary autistic-like behaviors in infants with visual impairments and the necessity of physical stimulation during critical periods of 2 to 3 months and again from 7 to 9 months for the development of attachment behaviors.

- Find out the infant's degree of vision and under what distance and lighting conditions she sees best.
- High-contrast colors such as black and white are often easiest to see and developmentally appropriate for this age.
- Use real three-dimensional objects to demonstrate with and teach concepts.
- Work through the infant's strengths by offering stimulation through other senses: sound, smell, taste, and touch.
- Keep in verbal contact with the infant as she will use your voice to know you are near if she cannot see you. Be sure to identify her by name when you talk to her.
- Provide as much verbal stimulation as you can, and use words as you normally would; that is, don't avoid words like "look" and "see" even though the infant may not be able to see.

Infants with Hearing Impairments

Early intervention can improve any residual hearing an infant has (Anastasiow & Harel, 1993). Infants with hearing impairments use hand movements as signs in much the same way that normal infants babble. These movements should be encouraged as one would encourage babbling (Petite & Marentelle, 1991).

- Support the infant's hand movements and learn the meaning of gestures that the infant and his parents typically use for communicating with each other.

- The sense of hearing and balance are related. Give infants many opportunities for large-motor activities that require and develop the sense of balance. Also, view balance as a safety consideration.
- Offer stimulation through other senses: sight, smell, taste, and touch.
- Use songs and fingerplays that have motions to go with the words.

A goal for all infants during the early months is to become more neurologically organized, which is often seen in the establishment of more predictable patterns of behavior. One way to determine these patterns is through interacting with and observing the infant and recording his behavior.

Adult-Infant Interactions

Adults interact with infants at different levels of involvement. The nature of adult-child interactions is one of the most important variables in determining quality in child-care settings (Klass, 1987). Whether adults are in their own home, a family day-care home, or a child-care center, they have different levels of involvement with children. Sometimes they are just in the vicinity of the infant; at other times they facilitate play; and still other times they actively participate with infants.

Levels of Involvement

The levels of involvement of adults with children is one measure of quality. These levels indicate the amount of adult involvement. Klass (1987) characterizes these levels of involvement in the following way:

Stabilizing Presence. Infants, when they are awake, always need an adult nearby to ensure their safety and to be available to them. An adult's presence has a stabilizing effect on an infant's behavior. An adult fixing lunch or reading to another infant should still be aware of what is happening to the children around her.

Facilitative Intervention. In this situation an adult moves in and out of an infant's play. It may be to pick up a dropped toy or to distract a mobile infant who seems intent on snatching a toy from another infant. This is not intrusive, but rather, the adult involvement extends, redirects, expands, or clarifies what the children are doing.

Shared Participation. This is when an adult and child actively participate together in an experience. These times may be initiated by infants and responded to by adults or they can be planned by adults who take advantage of a quiet alert time to interact with an infant. The younger the infant the more likely it is that the caregiver responds to the infant's invitation. Shared participation may be verbal turn taking or exploring a new toy. As infants get older, this may be looking at a book together, playing peek-a-boo, or searching for a hidden toy.

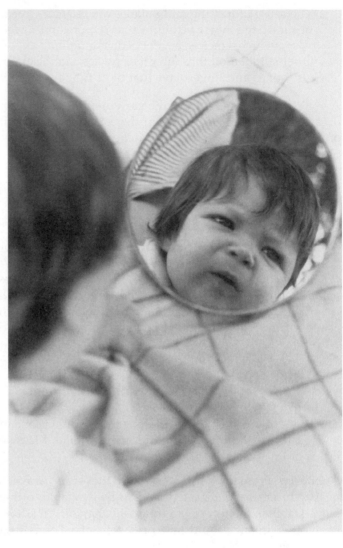

For young infants, adults must facilitate play by bringing toys and objects like mirrors to the infant and initiating an interaction.

Within the various levels of involvement, Klass (1987) delineates six distinct patterns of interaction: physical intimacy, spontaneous conversation, praise, assistance, structured turn taking, and understanding and following rules. These patterns, occurring throughout the day in various situations, are seen as central to quality adult-child interactions. The latter two are more characteristic of toddlers and twos and are discussed in Chapter 17.

Physical Intimacy. Infants need frequent opportunities for physical intimacy with adults throughout the day. Infants need loving, supportive, responsive adults who are in tune with their needs. They need adults who hold, carry, and cuddle them frequently and respectfully. With increasing concern about child sexual abuse, both parents and caregivers are concerned about cuddling children. Many feel that it is safer to keep "hands off." For young children this concern creates a major problem. Infants need physical contact with caring adults as much as they need food and clothing. It is not a matter of allowing physical intimacy but encouraging it (Hyson, Whitehead, & Prudhoe, 1988).

Spontaneous Conversation.   Infants need adults who look into their eyes when they talk to them, who use a soothing pleasant voice, and who call each infant by name. They need adults who use simple language, "motherese," to explain what the infant sees, hears, and what he is touching. Infants need adults who verbally prepare them for what is going to happen, describe what is happening, and then frame what will happen next.

Praise/Encouragement.   A positive, appreciative atmosphere is more helpful for an infant's growth than is a setting where negative, blaming comments are made frequently. Praise is one way of doing this. When praise is positive, general, and implying some judgment or evaluation of the infant's performance, it helps infants recognize their triumphs. Some examples of praise are "Great job, Alexis" or "Charday, you are getting so good you almost don't need any help." Adults use praise to make infants feel good about themselves, to encourage them to learn, and to promote appropriate behavior. Recent research, however, shows that indiscriminate praise does not always have these effects (Hitz & Driscoll, 1988). Praise can sometimes even have negative effects if not used appropriately. Inappropriate praise may influence young children to rely on others' opinions rather than judging for themselves, and to decide that they are only "good" when they are pleasing adults (they have become externally motivated rather than internally motivated), thus encouraging dependence on adults rather than independence (Hitz & Driscoll, 1988).

Encouragement may be a more appropriate word than praise. Encouragement refers specifically to responses to efforts or specific aspects of the infant's work or play. Encouragement does not place judgment. ("You really dumped a lot of sand.") Encouragement focuses on effort rather than on an evaluation of a finished product ("You worked hard getting that piece in" or "You look like you enjoyed that cookie)". Encouragement is designed not to compare one infant with another but rather to note individual accomplishment and improvement.

Assistance. As unpredictable as infants are, they need adults who predictably come when they cry and soothe them patiently. Infants need adults who are responsive to their individual needs and rhythms for sleeping, eating, and elimination. They need adults who support their curiosity while keeping them safe and who model the behavior they want infants to develop. They need adults who like themselves and who cherish infants.

Observing and Recording Infant Behavior

Planning is infant-centered. Thus, to learn about infants, you need to observe them and note your observations. Although it may seem that you are only noting eating, sleeping, and elimination patterns, it is important to establish a pattern of observation. You will have both formal and informal observations. Formal observations should be arranged on a regular rotating basis for all infants. Because infant behavior changes so quickly, it is important that these observations happen weekly for young infants and monthly for older infants. For young infants formal and informal observations may be similar in format with the major distinction that the formal observations occur on a regular basis and are part of the record-keeping system.

With young infants, one of the first uses of observation and record keeping is to determine the infant's biological rhythms. One way to determine the patterns of a young infant is to keep a round-the-clock chart of what the infant does at various times of the day and night. It is frequently easier to determine patterns when you have information for 24 hours than just the hours that the infant is in care. This is also a way of sharing information with parents and they with you. Although it is not necessary to keep a chart every day, it may be useful to do it for three consecutive days or until you can determine a pattern. Knowing patterns helps planning. If an infant is particularly fussy at a specific time of day, you may be able to arrange to be with him then or you may find out that he is fussy because there is a lot of stimulation going on at that particular time, and you can modify the environment. Infants' patterns change predictably around 1 month and 4 months, and unpredictably at any time.

If you make up a chart, you can include information that is useful to you and the parents. The easier the form is to fill out, the more likely it will be completed. Chart 14.3 is a sample of how you might collect this information. Although you lose information by using 15-minute intervals, you get enough information to establish the patterns you are looking for. Often parents don't fill in the chart at night, but in the morning will check what time they got up to feed their child and for how long.

Certain data is essential for all observations. It may be useful to duplicate observation sheets so that you will routinely record the information. Such data includes: infant's name, birth date, current date, and so on. The name has obvious significance; noting the birth date and then the date of the observation allows

Chart 14.3	Round-the-clock chart of infant behavior						
Name _____		**Birth date** _____		**Date** _____	**Recorder** _____		
Time	Sleeping	Eating (amount)	Diapering	Quiet Alert	Active Alert	Crying	Fussing
8:00							
8:15							
8:30							
8:45							
9:00							

you to precisely determine the infant's age. As children get older, knowing their age within a week or month is fine, but with a 3-month-old infant a month is a third of her life and more precision is necessary. Note who did the observation and the infant's state at the beginning of the observation. Infants have different patterns at different times of the day. Most infants are more alert in the morning, and if you are looking for optimal behaviors it is sensible to choose times when the infant is likely to be at her best.

Informal observations occur more frequently and mostly focus on events that are markers (Amelie rolled from her back to her stomach today for the first time), or that deviate from the usual pattern (Juan took an unusually long nap today). Note where the infant is during the observation, such as in an infant seat in the middle of the rug, who else is present (both children and adults), and what play-things the infant has available. Additional information can be added, notes written on the back, evaluative comments included, and so on. This chart is a working document and should be viewed as one.

Regardless of the level of formality, there are two important aspects to observation: detail and objectivity. To note that "Joshua had a hard day" is not useful. You need details to both understand what happened and to see what modifications might help Joshua. You should also be aware of your subjectivity in saying that whatever happened was "hard." It is more useful to note that "Joshua cried for 20 minutes after he was dropped off this morning. He also woke up from his afternoon nap crying."

Observations made during the course of the day are part of the ongoing teaching/caregiving process. You need to continuously monitor the match between infants and their environment and note where modifications are necessary. Additionally, your attention may be drawn to behaviors that are unusual for a particular infant, for example, an infant who slept longer or shorter than usual, fussed more or less, or even met some developmental milestone.

Interesting behaviors should be briefly noted and a method of discussing them with parents developed. Parents want to know what happened during their infant's day, and, as the infant cannot tell them, a system needs to be in place to convey this information on a regular basis. Likewise, you need to have a system of incorporating information from parents' observations that might influence your day. The methods you choose for recording the information gathered from your informal observations is dependent on both the setting and the purpose of the observations and the desires of the parents. Observations can be recorded for a variety of purposes. The goal of this type of observation is to share information with parents and to plan and individualize programming for infants.

Sharing Observations with Parents

Some caregivers find exchanging information verbally with parents at the beginning and end of the day works. This method is often most effective when there is just one caregiver and few parents, who stagger both their arrival and departure times. When there are changes in the caregivers over the course of the day, information frequently falls through the cracks. Even when the major method of communicating information is verbal, some system of written record keeping should be developed for each child as a permanent record-keeping system. Developmental milestones should be recorded as should general information about development that might be shared with parents at more formal parent-caregiver conferences.

Information for parents of an infant typically falls into one of two categories: temporary (daily) concerns and permanent records. Typical information that is exchanged on a daily basis includes eating (both time and amount), sleeping (beginning and end time noted), toileting (with bowel movements noted), and qualitative comments about the infant's day. Permanent record keeping focuses on entries related to developmental areas and reflects the infant's abilities and preferences. These observations are part of formal record keeping.

There should be two different systems of record keeping for this information. If there are multiple caregivers, they should use the same systems and have some general agreement about what falls into each category and how the information will be recorded. For daily concerns some caregivers use a message board where both they and parents can write each other brief notes that are erased at the end of the day. Some find that sending index cards home is useful; others send a notebook back and forth with each child; and still others develop sheets with categories already written on them and with categorized information filled in on a daily basis. Permanent records are usually filed in an office and include more generalized information, written observations, as well as photographs and videotapes.

Recording Observations for Individualizing Programming

Infants are dependent on the observations and insights of adults to choose toys that match their developmental level and their individual preferences. Noting what materials an infant likes is a necessary part of programming. It is also important to note the infant's ability level in playing with different materials in different developmental areas. Infants may be mastering some large-motor skills while at the same time other skills are just emerging. Planning needs to be responsive to such individual differences.

It is useful to compare your observations to a set of norms, such as those in the HELP Charts (Furuno et al., 1987). Comparison will help you focus on skills that are expected for a particular age. Charts such as these are used differently for programming than for assessment. For programming purposes it is useful to look at the age at which skills begin to emerge so that you can support the development of those skills with the materials you choose and the methods you use with a child. These are activities that require adult scaffolding.

A recording device such as Chart 14.4 could be used with 6-month-old infants. It contains only skills that are likely to emerge beginning at about 6 months. It frequently takes skills a month, or even two or three, to emerge. Similar charts from earlier months would overlap this one. This chart might be used at two-week intervals as a guide for deciding the types of activities to use with an infant this age. Develop a simple code such as plus /+/ for observing the behavior, minus /−/ for no observation, and /N/ for no opportunity.

Chart 14.4	Emerging skills at 6 months				
Name _____ Birth date _____		Date	Date	Date	Date
Follows trajectory of fast-moving objects					
Retains two of three objects offered					
Looks for family member or pet when named					
Slides object or toy on surface					
Finds hidden object behind 1, 2, and then 3 screens					
Plays peek-a-boo					
Smells different things					
Responds to facial expressions					
Plays 2 to 3 minutes with a single toy					
Says 'dada' or 'mama' nonspecifically					
Waves or responds to bye-bye					
Shouts for attention					
Body righting on body reaction					
Demonstrates balance reactions in supine					
Protective extension of arms to side and front					
Lifts head in supine position					
Holds weight on one hand in prone position					
Gets to sitting without assistance					
Bears large fraction of weight on legs and bounces					
Stands, holding on					
Pulls to standing at furniture					
Brings one knee forward beside trunk in prone					
Manipulates toy actively with wrist movements					
May show fear and insecurity with previously accepted situations					
Shows anxiety over separation from mother					
Distinguishes self as separate from mother					
Responds playfully to mirror					
Cooperates in games					
Struggles against supine position					
Bites food voluntarily					
Feeds self a cracker					
Drinks from cup held for him					

SOURCE: Adapted from HELP charts (Furuno et. al., 1987).

Given the information in this chart, you would probably not be surprised when an infant who had previously separated easily from his mother now began to cling; nor when a parent proudly tells you that her son calls her "mama" or that he is now pulling up on furniture. Knowing that an infant at this age may play 2 to 3 minutes with toys, you might encourage the infant who is distracted after 1 minute to play longer, whereas if an infant played for 4 or 5 minutes you might note what interested him for this length of time. You might make funny faces in the mirror with an infant, play peek-a-boo, and help him wave bye-bye to his parents. You might offer a prone infant a small toy so he has to support his weight with one hand while he reaches for the toy with the other and even dance with him as you provide the balance and sing music to bounce to. These are emerging developmentally appropriate behaviors. The adult's skill is to make them individually appropriate. The infant won't reach for a toy that does not intrigue him or play longer if he has no interest in the materials. He needs to be invited to participate and the play needs to be both fun and respectful of the infant's needs and desires. For some infants this is too much too soon. If you systematically use charts such as this and many of the skills are still being mastered, you may not want to move to the next chart until the infant is 6 1/2 or even 7 months old. There may be some developmental areas that are developing more quickly than others. Infants grow unevenly. The skill in teaching is the ability to individualize programming.

It is not enough to plan and program well; being an acute observer and keeping records of these observations is an important part of teaching and the basis for future planning.

Summary

Adults must determine their feelings about infants being in the care of adults other than their parents and determine their philosophy about working with infants. Planning for young infants is very different from planning for mobile infants or toddlers. Planning for infants is individualized and designed to meet the infants' changing interests and skills. It takes into account the intertwined developmental area and the infant's vulnerability. Infants are dependent on adults to choose developmentally appropriate materials and bring these materials to them when they are in an alert state. Adults need skills to include premature infants and infants with disabilities in their planning. They will need skills to be part of a team that plans for and supports these infants and their families. The adult must be aware of infant preferences and routines.

Routine care consumes a large part of the infant's day. Caregivers should make this quality time for social and emotional development as well as language stimulation. Adults should not only support learning, but should also model positive patterns of adult-infant interaction. Adults must develop both formal and informal observational and recording-keeping skills regarding infant behavior. Infants cannot tell their parents about their day, so caregivers must convey information about the infant's day, as well as other relevant information about what transpired in the infant's life while he was not home.

Planning provides the framework for working with young infants but it does not provide the activities. And although knowing about cognitive development is useful, it doesn't specifically tell you what the cognitive development level is for a specific 3-month-old. This knowledge is necessary to design both age appropriate and individually appropriate activities for young infants.

Application Activities

1. Using a chart similar to 14.3 for the care for a very young infant, make a chart for each 15-minute period and chart the infant's behavior.

2. Develop a written lesson plan for this infant, first based solely on age, and carry out the plan. Evaluate the lesson and describe how you individualized and modified your plan as you worked with the infant.

3. Talk with two mothers about a typical day in their lives. Choose one mother who works and has an infant in child care and another who stays at home with the infant. Have them "walk" you through their day starting with when and how they get up in the morning and the sequence of how they spend their time.

4. Visit a child-care setting during the departure or arrival transition and observe how parents and caregivers interact and share information. How would you feel about the interaction if you were a parent? A caregiver? What would you do to improve communication?

Chapter 15

Activities for Infants: Birth to 8 Months

There has been a dramatic increase in the number of very young infants who are in group care. Some infants enter the child-care system as early as 6 weeks of age but most enter between 4 and 6 months. These very young infants need adults who plan an environment that is interesting but not overly stimulating and who are experts at deciphering infants' cues and responding to them quickly, gently, and consistently.

Activities for Infants

Activities and materials for very young infants are chosen because they are interesting to look at or listen to. At about 2 to 3 months of age infants begin to reach for and grasp toys. For infants older than 3 months, materials and activities are designed to withstand active exploration, particularly mouthing, as well as constant washing. Although young infants don't have a lot of skills, they need to practice the ones they have. Therefore, having a variety of similar toys is useful and varying their use is a key for planning. Infants change and grow quickly. Be watchful that older children do not leave toys that are unsafe for infants where infants can reach them.

The activities that follow are prototypes designed for infants from birth to 8 months. Many of the activities are variations on caregiving routines and are included to show how to vary these routines and also the types of activities that are appropriate for young infants. It is important to think of these as activities and vary them, otherwise care can become solely custodial. If infants are in the younger range (1 month), use the section that makes activities easier; if they are in the older range (6 to 8 months) and the activity seems too easy, use the modifications designed to make it more difficult for them. The same principles apply to adapting activities to infants with developmental disabilities. The activities in this chapter are designed for infants who do not have efficient independent mobility. If an infant attains mobility more quickly than expected, move into the next set of activities. Likewise, if he is slow in gaining mobility, use these activities but increase the level of difficulty.

■ **Sensorimotor**

VARIATIONS ON TUMMY TIME

Purpose   To improve upper body strength and reaching and grasping

Materials   Rattles toys, including inflatable ones

Procedure   When the infant is prone, hold a toy that intrigues her above and to one side so that she needs to support her weight on one arm to grasp the toy with

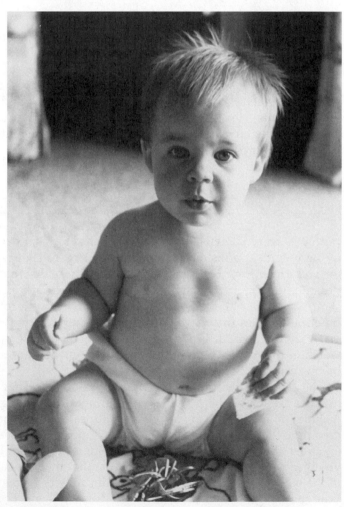

When an infant no longer needs her arms for sitting, give her something to play with or a cracker to eat.

the other. Offer toys on different sides so the infant practices bearing weight on each arm. Praise the infant for reaching the toy but don't make her work so hard she is frustrated.

Easier   Don't hold the toy as high and quit as soon as the infant tires.
Harder   Gradually increase the height of the toy to increase her reaching skills.

Comment   Infants sometimes need incentives for practicing skills. If there is nothing that requires them to push up on one hand and reach with the other, they may not do it. Use toys that vary in shape, size, and color but which can all be grasped.

■ **Sensorimotor**

VARIATIONS ON SITTING

Purpose   To improve upper body strength and balance

Materials   None

Procedure   Sit in front of the child and do the following "warm up" exercises. Encourage the infant to copy what you do. Talk about what you are doing as you do it.

Look over your right shoulder, then left; look at the ceiling, then the floor
Roll your shoulders
Put your arms out at shoulder height and flap them
Touch your toes
Pivot your shoulder left and then right
Look at the child and call his name
And so on. The infant will not be proficient following you, but it is good exercise.

Easier   If the infant begins to slump, sit behind her and place your hands around her hips and lower back for a minute or two. This will give added support. Help move her body gently as you talk about what you are doing. Sitting in a cardboard box may add variety and give slight support to some infants. It can also contain the toys they are playing with so they are easier for a nonmobile infant to find.
Harder   Add movements that are more subtle with hands, and facial expressions.

Comment   Gradually increase the amount of time and the number of opportunities infants have to sit independently. Trunk muscles need to be used to develop. Sometimes infants need encouragement to continue to develop these muscles. They need something to do while they sit. So be sure there are toys available to play with. If an infant is encouraged to use her hands to play with toys or copy your motions, she is less likely to need them to help with balance.

■ Sensorimotor

VARIATIONS ON RATTLES

Purpose   To encourage grasping and shaking

Materials   A rattle or toy that must be shaken or poked to make a noise

To Make   Take a plastic 35 mm film container. Put in a teaspoon of uncooked cereal, rice, or beans. Tape the cap on with colored tape and decorate the container with stickers. Make several rattles with different sounds. If using clear film containers, use food coloring to dye rice different colors, dry it and then put it in the clear film container and seal it.

   Tie a variety of plastic measuring spoons together with strong yarn or twine to make a different rattle.

Procedure   Shake the rattle and offer it to the infant. If the infant does not respond, demonstrate how to shake the rattle, verbally calling attention to what you are doing ("Look, I'm shaking the rattle. Hear the noise? Can you shake it?"). Again, give the infant the rattle.

Easier   Help the infant explore the toy or manipulate it for her, so she can see and hear how it works. Talk about what you are doing and the relationship between what you do and the sound. Use a Velcro bracelet to help the infant hold the rattle if necessary. A spoon-shaped or telephone-receiver-like rattle is easiest for young infants to hold.

Harder   Tie a sturdy string no longer than 9 inches onto the rattle and attach it to a high chair. When the toy falls off the tray, encourage the infant to pull the string to get the toy. Offer help if needed. You can also encourage the infant to imitate your behavior with the rattle. For example, make two sounds and see if the infant can make just two sounds. Make short, long, loud, and soft sounds and see if the infant can follow your lead. Verbalize what both you and the infant are doing.

Comment   Use a variety of rattles that make different sounds. Rattles with suction cups provide an interesting variation.

Note: Use the string only with direct adult supervision. The child should not be left alone with string. Keeping the length as short as possible (under 9 inches) is a safety precaution.

■ Cognitive

INFANT MASSAGE

Purpose To increase body awareness

Materials   Lotion, changing table, floor, couch, or bed

Procedure   Place infant on the changing table or floor. Undress infant (be sure it is warm enough). Place some lotion in one hand to warm it, then put the lotion on the infant's body. As you massage the infant's body with the lotion, talk to the infant about his body. "Adolpho, now I'm going up and down your arm. Let's check out that hand. You've got five fingers. I'm going to count them. One, two, three, four, oh, actually this one is a thumb." Continue to talk to the infant as you massage his body.

Easier   Just do one area of the infant's body, such as the arms or legs.

Harder   Talk in more detail about what you are doing.

Comment   Massaging the infant's body increases body awareness. It is also good for relaxation and for establishing closeness between infants and their caregivers.

■ **Cognitive**

SCRUNCHIES

Purpose   To increase body awareness

Materials   Brightly colored scrunchies (what women use to hold pony tails)

Procedure   Put scrunchies around each of the infant's wrists or ankles. Point these out to the infant by holding the infant's hand and saying "Look at you, this hand looks great!" Check to see if the infant's eyes focus on the hand (or on the scrunchies).

Easier   Use scrunchies made out of black-and-white striped or patterned materials. Securely attach a large bell to a scrunchy or circle of elastic that can go over the baby's feet.

Harder   Encourage the infant to bring his hands or feet to his mouth. Help him focus on the scrunchies for longer periods of time.

Comment   Infants need to become aware of and explore their own bodies before they can reach and grasp objects. Brightly colored or striped socks also call infants' attention to their feet.

Note: Adding a bell for sound provides an additional stimulus. It is a safety hazard if it is small enough to be swallowed. Use a large bell, attach it securely and check to be sure that it is attached on a regular basis.

■ **Cognitive**

MOUSIE

Purpose   To improve anticipation and attending

Materials   None

Procedure   Using two fingers of your hand, start at one of the infant's extremities and slowly walk your two fingers up the limb saying slowly "Mousie, Mousie,

Mousie" as you get closer to the trunk (belly button area), say quickly "Mousie, Mousie," and give the infant a gentle tickle.

Easier   Make the anticipatory time shorter by saying fewer "Mousies."
Harder   Make the anticipatory time longer by going back down the limb and up again before saying the quick "Mousie, Mousie."

Comment   Learning to anticipate what is going to predictably happen is an important cognitive skill. For variation use the infant's name instead of "Mousie."

■ **Cognitive**

HIDDEN TOY

Purpose   To develop object permanence

Materials   Small toy, cloth

Procedure   Get the infant intrigued with a toy. Then cover the toy completely with a cloth and encourage the infant to find it. If the infant does not find it, partly uncover the toy and again encourage the infant to look.

Easier   Only partly cover the toy with the cloth. Encourage the infant to find the toy. If he doesn't attempt to find it, point to the toy and again encourage him. If he still doesn't find it, take the cloth off dramatically saying "Here it is!" Play the game again.
Harder   Add an additional cloth. Again, start with a toy that intrigues the infant. Hide it quickly under one cloth, then move it to hide it under a second cloth (while the infant is watching), covering the toy completely. Initially, expect that the infant will hunt under the first cloth and then perhaps go to the second. Give verbal support for the search.

Comment   Activities such as this help infants develop the concept of object permanence. The concept has many aspects; so infants need increasingly challenging experiences to develop the concept fully.

■ **Cognitive**

RED RING

Purpose   To improve cause and effect reasoning as well as reaching and grasping

Materials   Ring with about a 6-inch diameter

Procedure   With the infant sitting, offer the ring to the infant to reach and grasp. Encourage the infant to explore the ring by mouthing or shaking it. Place the ring on the floor where the infant can just grasp it. Place a desired toy inside the ring and see if the infant will pull the ring to get the toy.

Easier   Move the ring closer and demonstrate how to pull the ring to get the toy. Then, place the ring and toy out of reach and verbally support the infant reaching for the toy.

Harder   Attach a 6- to 9-inch string to the ring. Place the ring with a toy in it out of reach but with the string reachable. Encourage the infant to pull the string to get the toy.

Comment   Infants need many opportunities to practice means-end behavior. Placing a toy out of reach on a towel or diaper provides a similar experience.

Note: When using a string, never leave the infant unattended and don't use a string longer than 9 inches.

■ **Language**

BLACK-AND-WHITE BOOKS

Purpose   To improve receptive language and visual coordination

Materials   Book of simple black-and-white designs or *White on Black, Black on White, What is that, Who are they?* by Tana Hoban

To make   Cut poster board into six pieces measuring about 5 1/2 inches by 6 inches. On page 1, using the marker, make a bullseye in the center and draw three thick concentric circles around the bullseye; page 2, using a ruler, divide the poster board square into 1-inch squares and color alternating ones black; page 3, using a ruler, divide the square into 1-inch stripes and color alternating ones black; page 4, using a ruler, divide the square into 1-inch diagonals and color alternating ones black; page 5, draw a smiley face with the wide side of the marker; page 6, draw a distorted face (mouth where eye should be) or caricature of a face. Place each poster-board page in a plastic bag, then staple plastic-bagged pages together to make a book. These can also be laminated instead of put in plastic bags.

Procedure   Sit in a comfortable place such as a rocking chair with the infant in your lap. Hold the book so the infant can see it (about 8 inches from his face) and watch to see if he focuses on the bullseye. If not, tap it lightly to draw his attention and say "Look, that's a bullseye." Then turn the pages and point out the salient characteristics of each picture.

Easier   Use only the first picture.

Harder   Talk more about each picture. Make another set of pictures where the designs are the same but the lines are a half inch wide.

Comment   The focus of this activity is on the experience of enjoying a pleasant, cozy reading experience with a young infant rather than the content of the "book." Make additional faces such as a distorted (nose where eyebrow should be and so on) or a stylized face on the poster board, or use black-and-white pictures of people faces. These can be laminated also and attached to the crib.

Note: If you use small zipper locking plastic bags, be sure they are securely closed and attached to the crib as plastic bags are an asphyxiation threat to infants.

■ **Language**

TALKING WALK

Purpose   To improve receptive language and environmental awareness

Materials   None

Procedure   Pick the infant up and hold her so she can see over your shoulder. Walk around the room and point out objects and events that are taking place and what other infants and toddlers are doing. "That's the telephone. Sometimes it rings and I talk to people on it. There is Roxanna, she is playing with Dot. This is one of my favorite pictures. Aura painted it. See the beautiful red she used."

Easier   Make the walk shorter and talk less. Use items that the infant is familiar with and start out with what she knows, like her own coat, then let her touch it. Use disparate items to continue, such as a book; allow her to touch this also. Only label one or two items and then stop.

Harder   Label more items for the infant and talk about their function. Encourage the infant to touch the items and to try to imitate what you say. Vary what you say to include a "What is that?" Wait a few seconds and then say something like "Those are Nathan's boots!" Use similar items such as sneakers, boots, slippers, and shoes to make it even more difficult and talk about the properties of foot gear and why they are different.

Comment   Infants need to learn about and feel comfortable in their environment. The view from your shoulder is very different from their view from the floor. So it is important they see this too and learn the language that goes with these new perceptions. Although infants will not understand all the words you use, they will hear the different tones of your voice and begin to make associations especially if you demonstrate what each object does.

■ **Social/Emotional**

ANTICIPATION

Purpose   To increase trust and attending

Materials   None

Procedure   Before beginning an event such as giving an infant a bottle, picking him up, or changing him, offer the infant verbal information and a visual cue about what will happen. Show the infant the bottle and say "Are you hungry? I have your bottle ready. Do you want it?" Then pause to give the infant time to respond. (Don't expect him to say "yes." You are giving him the time and respect to process information rather than just putting the bottle in his mouth.) Before picking up an infant, hold out your arms and say "I'm going to pick you up," then pause so the infant can anticipate what will happen. Then follow through on your action.

Easier	Keep the gestures and words you use consistent so the infant knows what to expect. Follow through with the action quickly; that is, if you show him the bottle and he responds, then feed him right away, don't wait several minutes.
Harder	Rather than initiating the cues, respond to the infant's cues. If he quiets when approaching his crib or infant seat, say "You know I'm going to pick you up." Then do it.

Comment   As infants learn that their world is predictable they are willing to wait longer for events to happen because they are developing trust.

■ **Social/Emotional**

TOUCHING SONGS

Purpose   To increase social interaction and improve trust

Materials   None

Procedure   Sing or chant songs or rhymes where you touch the infant, such as "This little piggy went to market," "I'm going to get your nose," and "Hickory Dickory Dock."

Easier	Sing or hum a song while you hold the infant and move him to the rhythm of the song such as "Rock-A-Bye Baby."
Harder	Help him do the motions to songs or rhymes like "Pat-A-Cake" or "Johnny Hammers with One Hammer" by holding him on your lap and gently moving his body.

Comment   Infants learn to feel secure through close sensitive contact. This should be a light, happy interaction.

■ **Social/Emotional**

MIRROR

Purpose   To increase social interaction

Materials   Unbreakable mirror (about 12 inches round or square)

Procedure   Hold the infant on your lap with mirror in front of her so she can see herself. Talk about what she sees in the mirror, "Look, there's Alison! I see you!"

Easier Place the infant in front of large mirror mounted where she can more easily see herself. Tap her image in the mirror. Say "Look, this is you. Don't you look gorgeous."

Harder Point to and name facial parts when she looks in the mirror. Ask the infant to point out these parts on his own face. Play imitation games in the mirror such as opening and closing the mouth, patting the head, tugging the ear, and making silly faces!

Comment Infants enjoy looking at themselves in the mirror. As many mirrors they encounter are too high for them to see, these accessible mirrors are a good way to show them what they look like. Mirror rattles, especially larger ones, are also very useful as the infant can manipulate them herself.

■ **Adaptive/Self Help**

FIND THE FIST

Purpose To improve self-comforting

Materials None

Procedure When the infant is fussy, gently guide his hand to his mouth to see if he needs some help finding it. Encourage him to suck on it. Talk in a calming voice and allow the infant to enjoy the sucking sounds he is making. Verbally support what is happening "Sometimes this makes you feel better."

Easier Help infants keep the hand available. Encourage the process.

Harder Give an infant verbal support for finding his hand and sucking before helping him.

Comment Infants suck for the sheer pleasure of it. Helping an infant find his hand does not set him up for years of thumb sucking. Infants suck as a way of "organizing" themselves. Many adults will want infants to suck on pacifiers rather than hands or fingers. There is no reason why infants cannot do both. It is important that infants can use their hands because these are always available whereas pacifiers may not be. A hand is under their control; use of a pacifier may be dependent on an adult.

■ **Adaptive/Self Help**

TEETHER

Purpose To improve self-comforting and eye-hand coordination

Materials Teether

Procedure Encourage the infant to reach, grasp, and mouth his teether. Say "This is a "foot" (if foot-shaped) teether. Do those toes taste good?" Touch infant's foot and toes and say "Here's your foot. I have your toes!"

Easier   Gently guide the infant's arm from the shoulder area to help him grasp the teether and bring it to his mouth if necessary. Talk to the infant and tell him about your actions as well as his. Confirm that it is sometimes comforting to suck on something even without hunger.

Harder   Encourage the infant to explore the teether in ways other than mouthing, such as banging, shaking, and throwing. Try to support the infant in simple imitation skills. For example, put a foot-shaped teether in a big sock. Take it out and encourage infant to try. Tap the teether on the surface or clap while holding the teether in one hand.

Comment   This activity uses a natural form of exploration (mouthing) to interest the infant and then expand on this activity. Have a variety of teethers so infants have experience with different shapes, colors, and textures.

■ **Adaptive/Self Help**

TEXTURED MAT

Purpose   To increase body awareness

Materials   Mats made of various materials (satin, cotton, fake fur, velvet, terry cloth). Textured mats are also commercially available.

To make   Sew together squares of various materials. Nine squares of 12 inches each make a good-size mat (36 inch square).

Procedure   Place infant prone on mat. If it is warm enough, have him in diapers. Take a corner of the mat and stroke his hand with it and talk with him about the texture of the material and how it feels. Use a different corner for another texture.

Easier   Place the infant on the mat clothed and let him explore independently with his hands.

Harder   Use more of the textures with the infant. Place him in different positions on the mat so it is easier to reach other textures.

Comment   Some infants might not like some of the textures, so go gently, using smooth, soft textures. You can also use unsewn fabric squares. Help the infants explore the fabrics and gently rub one piece of fabric on her arm and talk about how it feels.

Summary

Infants from birth to 8 months grow and change quickly. The nonmobile infant is dependent on the adults in her environment to choose developmentally appropriate activities and bring them to her. Initially, activities are primarily those that require the young infant to look or listen. As infants spend more time in alert states and gain more control, expand activities to include objects that can be grasped and mouthed as well.

As infants are able to sit, they have their hands free to explore materials and manipulate them. Since young infants don't have a large repertoire of skills, they need many variations in activities to practice skills without getting bored. As infants approach mobility, activities are used which encourage infants to pivot and to approach more interesting materials.

Application Activities

1. A friend has just had a baby and you want to buy a baby present. Describe what type of toy you would buy and what you would tell your friend about using the material with her infant.

2. Visit someone with an infant under 6 months and play with the infant. Pick a particular activity and try it out. Evaluate the activity. Try a more difficult activity from one of the other chapters and see how that works.

3. Following the format given in the text, write an activity for a 6-month-old infant and try it out. Evaluate your experience.

Planning Programs for Crawlers and Walkers: 8 to 18 Months

Planning for crawlers and early walkers is different from planning for either infants or 2-year-olds. This is a transitional time emphatically marked by developmental milestones: the first step and the first word! Children have a growing sense of self and an increased interest in their peers. They are interested in listening to adult language but may not be happy around unfamiliar adults. Sitting is old hat; crawling is being replaced by creeping and standing. Walking is emerging, to be followed by trotting and even walking backwards.

Receptive language far outstrips expressive language although the child may say several words. There are often long babbled sentences that "ought" to make sense but it is as if they are in a different language. Self-help skills are emerging as children want to dress and feed themselves, although they may be happier undressed and self-feeding is often very messy. Emotions are becoming more specific. There are smiles and hugs for affection, anxiety at separation, and anger at both people and objects that don't do what they are "supposed" to do.

Setting Up the Learning Environment for Crawlers and Walkers

Crawlers and walkers have a heightened awareness of the world around them and the ability to get to more of that world. But they lack experience. Much of the concentration for planning is the consolidation of emerging skills and building a foundation of trust in the world around them. With this new mobility, crawlers and walkers are moving from infancy to toddlerhood. Revisit your philosophy and determine what place crawlers and walkers hold and how they might challenge your philosophy or require that you expand it.

Adults are responsible for setting the stage for young children's play. In order to provide quality play experiences, adults must arrange: (1) time; (2) space; (3) materials; and (4) preparatory experiences (Johnson, Christie, & Yawkey, 1987). A schedule for young toddlers includes time for free play, indoors and outside, and for routine events such as eating and napping. Crawlers and walkers need space to play to practice emerging large motor skills. A good program should have areas for crawlers and walkers to create messy art work, a dramatic play corner for simple thematic play (primarily variations on housekeeping), a block corner for constructive play, a cozy book and language area for quiet reading, a fine-motor manipulative area, and a sensory area for exploring the properties of and playing with sand and water.

Crawlers and walkers also need materials with which they can play. A simple method for selecting toys is to provide materials for all the areas listed above. The actual materials will depend on the age and developmental level of the group. Crawlers and walkers vary greatly in skill level and need a variety of materials to choose and use. Adults must provide enough materials for each child; have duplicates of popular toys; and provide enough space for crawlers and walkers to use materials. Teachers should select toys that are: (1) safe, (2) durable, (3) cleanable, (4) appealing to crawlers and walkers, (5) realistic, (6) versatile, and (7) developmentally appropriate (Johnson, Christie, & Yawkey, 1987).

Some young children may need preparatory experiences to help them understand how to play certain roles. For example, a crawler or walker with experience accompanying his parents on grocery-shopping trips can usually act out the roles of shopper and clerk to some degree. But the one who has never been to the grocery store may have difficulties. He might carry out the roles mommy or daddy play when the groceries are brought home, that is, storing them or preparing food to eat, rather than the clerk-shopper roles. Field trips are good ways to expand the repertoire of real-life experiences on which the crawlers and walkers can draw (Johnson, Christie, & Yawkey, 1987).

How Crawlers and Walkers Learn

Young children learn through active exploration of materials and objects. They learn through the use of their senses of vision, touch, smell, taste, and hearing. They continuously absorb the sights and sounds of the world around them, whether events are planned or happen spontaneously. Building on what they have previously learned, they add new ideas, words, and thoughts. This building process results in learning. Learning happens during the active experiences children are involved with on a daily basis and when there are adults in the environment who provide the necessary scaffolding to support learning.

Every activity offers an opportunity for the crawler and walker to learn and how he can be more active in the selection of what he wants to do. The toys no longer have to be brought to him; he can go to the toys. Whatever the play activity, the purpose of the interaction with toys or materials is not just fun, but also to learn. Learning is not immediate. Instead, learning occurs at the point where crawlers and walkers are challenged between what they already know and something new: the "zone of proximal development."

Play is the work of childhood. The curriculum is play. Through play, children learn cognitive, social, emotional, language, motor, and adaptive skills. They perfect motor skills, they learn to cooperate and share ideas, and they learn practical aspects of math, science, reading, social studies, and communication skills. The secure play environment allows them to make mistakes and take risks without feeling pressure to be perfect. Additionally, play fosters a lifelong attitude whereby children learn to use play as a way to relax.

By 8 months infants have acquired the skills to engage in simple cooperative games with adults. These early social games consist of turn taking, offering a toy to an adult and then responding when it is given back, watching when it is another's turn, and so on. By 18 months the toddler can participate with peers in simple cooperative games like Ring-Around-the-Rosy (Hughes, Elicker, & Veen, 1995).

Activities can help them express their feelings in actions when they do not have the vocabulary to use words. It is important to think about play and the characteristics of play. Play is fun. Play is done for the process, not the outcome. However, there is more to play than mere fun. Play needs to be challenging, but not impossibly difficult, to hold interest. Play takes place in a relaxed environment.

From a Piagetian viewpoint, by playing with objects, exploring their different uses, and thinking about them, children come to understand objects and cause-and-effect relationships. The child's active involvement is an important aspect of play (Lawton, 1988). Understanding and knowledge develop when the child discovers "new" ways to accomplish something through manipulating the objects in her world. Johnson, Christie, and Yawkey (1987) suggest that play occurs when the child suspends reality-based uses for objects and creates unique uses for these objects based on his needs or desires. For example, the toddler who uses two blocks as a telephone is playing rather than exploring the properties of blocks.

Crawlers and walkers need more than nice toys and equipment to play with. They need to have warm, caring interactions with adults. Knowledgeable adults expand play by imitation, then modify and provide scaffolding for the play. They respond to the child's play, demonstrating that his behavior has consequences. If a young toddler is using playdough, the adult might expand the play by initially manipulating the dough and then making a pancake, snake, or little balls out of it. The child can decide whether or not to add these actions to his repertoire of playdough behaviors. A modification might involve adding a rolling pin or cookie cutters to help the toddler use the dough in a different way.

Crawlers and walkers are learning many things about their world. They may not understand at first that the water from the faucet sprays when they hold their hands too close. They require time to experiment as well as verbal scaffolding that helps them understand the relationship between where they hold their hands and what the water does. Likewise, if they are playing with the playdough, they will learn that the harder they roll the thinner the dough gets. They also need to learn that if they hit someone and hurt him he may cry or bite them. They learn more when adults elaborate on their play and are responsive to them.

Verbal interactions with adults encourage the child's language, problem solving, self-esteem, and social skills. Acknowledgment of a child's actions and choices helps focus his attention, and repeating his verbalizations increases the likelihood of his verbalizing again. Converse with children about what they are doing and ask them questions that relate to their play even though they are not able to answer them. Demonstrate different ways to play with an object. If children are hitting balloons with hands, casually demonstrate how to hit the balloon with an elbow, head, foot, or cardboard tube. This is the type of scaffolding Vygotsky feels is necessary for young children to learn in the zone of proximal development.

On busy days it is easy to forget how important individual time with a crawler or walker is. Spending time alone with a young child communicates to him that you like him and that he is important to you. This can be an important time for learning. Take advantage of special time you have with one child before the other children arrive, or when a child wakes early from nap. As in families, individual time is important for all children in early care and education. Young children just learning to move about on their own may want to spend their whole time crawling, cruising, or walking. An adult can follow them about and talk about what they are doing. The adult should spend some time working on developing skills. Try to achieve a balance, however, of planned activities and of following the child's choice or lead.

Adults are responsible for planning for children's play. This includes deciding on themes, generating goals and objectives for the group as well as individual crawlers and walkers, gathering appropriate materials, planning how time will be spent and the procedures that will be used. It also includes organizing materials so that only one or two special types of activities are available at a time. For instance, have several trucks and cars with play people to put in and take out of the vehicles. When this is no longer of interest, bring out a new activity, such as interlocking blocks. Toddlers need choices, so have other activities available if some crawlers and walkers are not interested in the main one, but don't have so many choices that they get overwhelmed.

Developmentally Appropriate Planning for Crawlers and Walkers

For crawlers and walkers there needs to be a combination of activities that are close by and those that are arranged on low shelves that crawlers and walkers can go to and choose. Be sure that activities are accessible, as crawlers will crawl to an area, then sit, make a choice, and then play. Be prepared that several minutes later (if that long) this process may be repeated. If the child initiates the activity, it will probably take place directly on the floor; if an adult chooses the activity, the child may be in a high chair or, as children get older, at a low table.

Language Arts

Language arts permeates the curriculum. For this age the opportunities for language input abound although a formal language arts program would be out of place for children this young. For crawlers and walkers, a major component of language arts involves learning the meaning of words. Often a child's first words depend on context for exact meaning. For example, when a young child says "ball," it is usually easy to understand from the situation whether he means, "Get me the ball," or "Catch the ball," or "Look what I found. A ball!" It's not until about 18 months that toddlers begin to string words together such as "Ball gone."

- When a young child talks to you, wait until their "sentence" is over before you respond. This helps foster the give-and-take rhythm of normal conversation. Don't interrupt, but instead wait for her to finish.
- Point to what you are talking about so children can learn the names of objects.
- Crawlers and walkers understand many more words than they can speak. Give them the vocabulary they need by labeling objects and actions for them. See yourself as a language model, and be sure to model good language usage.
- Give crawlers and walkers time to respond to your requests. Language is new to them.
- Select durable books. Many infant/toddler books are available with pages of heavy coated cardboard, cloth, or plastic. Expect to read these books in one-on-one situations, again, again, and again.
- Provide scribbling materials for crawlers and walkers such as large crayons and markers.

Discovery

Adults need to provide opportunities for learning about the world as well as the language labels that make these experiences meaningful to young children. This combination of experience and language is necessary to develop scientific and mathematical thinking. Although from an adult's perspective it may seem mundane, the experience of hearing songs and nursery rhymes that include numbers, and that designate quantity and size, are initial mathematical concepts. Science experiences for crawlers and walkers are based on what they do naturally. They look at things, touch them, taste them, smell them, and manipulate them. These skills are exactly what young scientists need to know in order to learn about the properties of the world around them. Discovery activities support a young toddler's natural learning processes. Provide opportunities for children to actively learn about their environment on a regular basis. Provide a variety of materials to facilitate self-discovery so children can construct their own knowledge. Crawlers and walkers learn competence when their behavior has a predictable outcome. They need practice discovering this in relation to both objects and people's behavior.

- To facilitate means-end learning, crawlers and walkers need a variety of sound toys: shakers, bells, rattles, clackers.
- Include materials that involve cause-and-effect relationships: wind-up toys, busy boxes, and jack-in-the-boxes.

■ Giving crawlers and walkers an opportunity to stack blocks can enhance their fine-motor development and concepts of spatial relationships. Initially, you can demonstrate stacking two blocks, then say, "Now it is Tammy's turn." This will also help develop skills in imitation. Remember that larger blocks will be easier to stack, but may be hard for small hands to manage.

Sensorimotor Activities

The development of sensorimotor skills is most rapid during infancy and early toddlerhood. The skills emerge and are refined with practice during these years. The pattern of motor development dictates that gross-motor development precedes fine-motor development. Crawlers and walkers who cannot pick up a large ball and lift it over their heads cannot be expected to print their names recognizably, regardless of the amount of time spent practicing printing. Crawlers' and walkers' motor skills need to be progressively challenged. As their sense of balance improves, they can progress from standing to walking, to walking on a line taped on the floor, to walking on a balance beam. They need many opportunities to integrate information that comes in from the senses with both large- and small-motor movement.

■ Take materials outside to play, such as riding toys, large balls, large trucks and cars, and large cardboard boxes.
■ Encourage crawlers and walkers to use the motor skills available to them, regardless of competence. They need the most practice in areas in which they are the least able. So emphasize process over product.
■ For different sensory input let the children play with the same items in different textures such as cornmeal, oatmeal, coffee, or rice.

Creative Arts

All children are unique. Each has his own special style of working, learning, and creating. Creativity is somewhat dependent on the developmental level of the child and his past experience with various media. What is creative for infants is not for crawlers and walkers, and what is creative for a young toddler who has never experienced a particular media is not creative for toddlers who have had much experience with it.

There isn't any hard-and-fast rule about when to introduce art activities into the planning process, however, children from about 1 year old can participate in simple art activities. First art experiences are characterized by exploration and experimentation. They focus on the use and texture of the materials. Crawlers and walkers are intrigued with what materials can do and what they can do with the materials. It is important to have a variety of media so they can discover the most important qualities of each.

Art for crawlers and walkers is a sensory experience. Scribbling develops from the first faint markings of an infant until about 2 years of age when toddlers begin random scribbling. These are jerky, erratic marks on paper. They may be

Young toddlers like to dress up in adult clothing and pretend.

just as interested in getting crayons out of the container or the tops off markers as they are in making marks. Because of their lack of concern about the product, the boundaries of paper are seen as arbitrary and rarely acknowledged. Crawlers and walkers need large sturdy crayons, chalk, and paint brushes. The paper, too, needs to be large enough to accommodate broad movements. Young children need to explore and use many different art media. They can paste collage materials and they can help tear them into pieces. They enjoy finger painting as well as using thick tempera paint, clay, or play dough. Crawlers and walkers are interested in exploring the media itself at first. Art activities provide them with the opportunity to develop and use their senses in a satisfying, constructive way.

Young children enjoy and learn from a variety of musical experiences. They learn new words, develop memory skills, and develop a sense of rhythm as they sing and listen to music. You can make up the words. They especially enjoy having their name included in the song. Songs can be as simple as "I'm going to get Sara's bottle, bottle, bottle. I'm going to get Sara's bottle, bottle, bottle. I'll be back in a minute." Even if you don't have a good voice, they will like your singing.

- Provide the crawlers and walkers with enough materials, space, and time to be creative.

- Let toddlers color with large markers or crayons and vary the color, size, and shape of paper used (but don't make it too small). Add accessories such as stamps. Use wet or dry chalk on paper and a chalkboard. Use sidewalk chalk and let the children see what happens when it gets wet.
- Sing simple songs throughout the day. You can make up the words.
- Use music to help transitions such as waiting to be picked up, eating lunch or going outside. Sing songs or play "following directions" games. Ask children to "touch their nose" or "clap their hands." Sing songs like "Put your finger in the air." Take advantage of these opportunities to add to children's learning and their self esteem.
- Pair music and movement to encourage young children to move in different ways and to explore body awareness.
- When introducing young toddlers to dramatic play, start with the house-keeping area. This is familiar and is the easiest to facilitate. Don't put all your props out the first day, but rather watch the play and gradually add materials in response to their interest.

Social Awareness

Crawlers and walkers first need to develop self-awareness, and then awareness of others and the roles those significant others play in their lives. This is the beginning of social awareness. First they learn about their family and care-givers. As they enter an early care and education setting, they expand their awareness of roles of adults. They may need to learn new ways to be with adults when they enter an early childhood program. They must learn the different expectations of staff and parents, and also the different expectations of the early childhood program versus home. They need to find ways of sharing adult attention. Likewise, they need to develop methods of interacting with peers. Throughout this process they are learning about themselves. These are difficult areas of growth.

Young toddlers will spend most of their social studies time reenacting the adult roles they are most familiar with, and situations that are meaningful to them. As awareness of the environment expands, these new roles will be incorporated into play. After a visit to a fire station, domestic play scenes may be interrupted by fire fighters who come to put out the fire.

Young children are often interested in learning to dress and undress themselves. The natural opportunities for dressing and undressing typically come during arrival and departure times, or other transition times when children are going outside or coming inside. These times are frequently stressful. Sometimes the thought of putting crawlers and walkers in snowsuits, boots, and mittens is enough to keep even the staunchest believer in outside play inside. The long-term solution is to have toddlers become more self-sufficient and independent in these tasks.

- Include materials that encourage awareness of self and others such as toys with mirrors, dolls, and puppets. Provide materials for cuddling such as stuffed dolls and toys as well as a cozy area to cuddle in.

- Bulletin boards or wall displays should include pictures of children from different ethnic groups, and of children with assisitive devices (eye glasses or wheelchairs) and visible disabilities.
- Work on the crawlers' and walkers' body awareness *and* motor planning skills as he figures out which leg goes where, how hats and mittens fit, and how to pull socks off.
- Undressing is easier than dressing, so begin with undressing. For undressing, have the child do just the last part of the task, such as pulling off her sock when it is around her toes. Gradually have the child do more of the task (pull off from middle of foot, get over heel and pull off) until she can completely remove the sock. Praise the child for her efforts. Starting with something the toddler can feel successful about encourages her to continue learning these skills and to try more difficult sequences.

Planning for Transitions and Routine Care

Much of the planning for transitions and routine care are continuations of patterns developed for younger infants. Adults are still responsible for communicating with each other about the time the crawler and walker spends at home or in child care. A much larger portion of the child's day is spent playing and proportionately less in routines, particularly sleeping. Sleep patterns are gradually changing. At 8 months most infants take a morning and afternoon nap; however by 18 months there may be only a longer afternoon nap, which begins earlier. However, sleep patterns and schedules are still very individual. Crawlers and walkers are usually starting to have teeth and bite, instead of just mouthing objects. With teeth and better arm and finger control they may drink from a cup independently or with some adult assistance and they can feed themselves using both their fingers and a spoon. Fingers are still more reliable. As physical growth slows, children may eat less than previously.

Including Crawlers and Walkers with Disabilities

Effectiveness of inclusion is still being evaluated, but evidence suggests that, if done well, inclusion can be a positive learning experience for all involved—the crawler and walker with a disability, his family, the child's peers, and the teachers (Bruder, Deiner, & Sachs, 1992). Peterson (1987) has found that, in order to successfully include children with disabilities, adults must be aware that social interactions do not occur spontaneously. Adults frequently must take the responsibility to facilitate positive social interactions between children with disabilities and those without. Some ways to encourage positive interactions include: (1) highlighting the achievements of all such children; (2) pairing for short time periods or tasks; (3) modeling appropriate play behavior for the child with a disability; and (4) encouraging empathy and prosocial behaviors in all the children. Beckman, Robinson, Jackson, and Rosenberg (1985) suggest that to meet the educational needs of young children with disabilities adults need to:

- Be responsive to cues from the crawler and walker that indicate understanding, interest, frustration, or fatigue.
- Provide appropriate verbal information that highlights the young child's attempts at behaviors and positive reinforcement for his successes.
- Maximize the crawler and walker's opportunities to manipulate and explore objects and materials. For some children with physical disabilities this may be difficult, but the adult is responsible for helping the toddler discover adaptive skills.
- Provide activities that are developmentally appropriate for the skills and goals for each individual child in the program.

Adapting Toys for Crawlers and Walkers with Disabilities

Most of the toys and materials you would use for any young child can be used with children who have disabilities; others may require minor modifications. If there are major modifications, parents or specialists will typically provide this equipment. In general, if there is no need to modify an activity, don't. When modifications are necessary, the toys and materials should be appropriate for the child's developmental level and chronological age, promote age-appropriate social and communication skills, and not interfere with regular routines or call undue attention to the child (McCormick & Feeney, 1995). Although specific alternative activities may be used, they should be interesting, varied, and available to other children in the class as well. Many simple adaptations suggested below will be useful for any crawler or walker who is challenged by an activity.

- Slightly deflated beach balls are easier than regular rubber balls for crawlers and walkers to grasp, throw, and catch.
- Toys can be hung above a child who is not moving independently but is interested in looking at or reaching for and grasping the toys. Toys can be hung from the upright handle of an infant seat, above a changing table, or (if you are really ambitious!), you can attach a pulley to the ceiling and hang toys from a rope. Use of the pulley allows you to easily adjust the height of the toys for various children. If toddlers are grasping toys and pulling them, be sure that this equipment is strong enough to be safe.
- Toys with several parts (such as simple puzzles) can be adapted by gluing magnetic strips onto the back of each piece. A cookie sheet can be provided on which children can move the pieces. Just moving the pieces and taking them on and off the cookie sheet provides some resistance at first.
- If the crawler or walker has difficulty grasping small handles, such as those on a jack-in-the-box, pop beads can be cut at their opening and pushed over the handle to make it easier to hold onto. Likewise, foam hair curlers can be placed over paint brushes or crayons to make them easier to hold.
- Experiment with different materials to see what works, and remember that young children change and grow quickly so that adaptations have to be monitored and evaluated on a continuing basis to be sure that they are developmentally and socially appropriate. (Adapted from Langley, 1985)

Crawlers and Walkers with Developmental Delays

With increasing age, differences among children become more apparent. Children with developmental delays may require some modifications in your planning and activities but these are minor and usually easy adaptations.

- Simplify your language and use short directions.
- Offer more difficult activities in small steps (if you are using pop beads have all except one together as opposed to having them all apart and expecting the child to put them all together).
- Demonstrate what you want the child to do. Then give the child a turn and encourage her attempts at imitating you. After watching her response, modify your demonstration and again take turns.
- Once a crawler or walker has developed a skill, work on variations of that skill; that is, if a child has learned to pound a red block to make a noise, vary the color and size of the block.
- Keep activities short, and expect crawlers and walkers with developmental delays to have shorter attention spans than others and to need more support and redirection as they move among activities. They may need more cues to interact with materials.

Crawlers and Walkers with Physical Impairments

Children need materials that support the development of large- and small-motor skills. When other children are beginning to crawl and walk, it is important that thought be given to other forms of mobility such as a creeper of some kind. Because motor tasks may be difficult for young children, it is important to provide scaffolding for these activities. You may need consultation to know the best way to provide that support.

- Correct positioning and holding of children with physical impairments are important. Specific information on materials and on positioning the child with a physical impairment should come from the child's parents or the physical or occupational therapists.
- Know and encourage crawlers and walkers to use the movements they are capable of.
- Be alert to the child's subtle movements that indicate communication of thoughts or feelings.
- Provide crawlers and walkers who have motor delays with opportunities to observe other children using motor skills that may emerge at a later time.
- Allow children the opportunity to touch materials as well as to look at them. This means you may have to carry an item to the child so that she can touch it, or actually place it in her hand and help her explore the material.

Crawlers and Walkers with Visual Impairments

With the advent of locomotion, young crawlers and walkers with visual impairments may need additional accommodations. Consult with a vision specialist, orientation and mobility specialist, or others involved in providing services to the child about room arrangement, activities, and so on. These specialists have information about long-term expectations for the child; that is, whether the child will read using large print or braille, and useful hints as well.

- Use materials that make sounds when manipulated. Balls with bells in them or pull-toys that make a noise when they move are useful. Be sure rattles make noise for these children to orient to and reach for.
- Encourage the development of auditory localization skills. Make a noise, and when the child turns to the sound encourage him and give him the noisemaker. Verbally praise him as well. "Friedrich, I can't fool you. You know where that noise is coming from don't you. Here is the ball."
- Use whatever sight the crawler or walker has available. If she can make distinctions only among toys with high contrast like black and white, be sure you have toys like this.
- Locomotion is different with children with visual impairments. They frequently walk later than other children and they often use hitching as a means of locomotion. (Children hitch when they scoot on their bottom. This protects their head.)
- Provide materials such as large manipulative toys that require two hands or activities that prohibit self-stimulation behavior, if this is a problem.

Crawlers and Walkers with Hearing Impairments

Consult with speech and language specialists, audiologists, the child's parents, and others involved for information on how to accommodate and adapt your programming.

- Use vision and visual cues as the primary input source for information. Show the child what you want her to do. Model behavior.
- Provide activities that encourage the child to use the hearing she has. Find out what the child is most likely to hear and incorporate these sounds in your curriculum.
- Be aware of extraneous noise in the classroom. Hearing aids amplify all noise, so the child may actually have a hard time concentrating on specific sounds if there is loud background noise.

Crawlers and Walkers with Social/Emotional Disorders

Consult with the psychologist, parents, and other therapists on the best ways to adapt programming and to include these young toddlers in your program.

- Realize that the child may be overly sensitive to noises and evaluate your environment in this respect. Noisy vacuum cleaners or other children playing noisily may disturb crawlers and walkers with social/emotional disorders.
- Respect the child's tactile defensiveness if this is an area of concern. However, be sure to find other ways of letting the toddler know you like him.

Verbal support such as saying "Brett, I'm glad to see you this morning" may be wiser than a hug.

Methods and Materials for Working with Crawlers and Walkers

Crawlers and walkers need toys to support their newfound mobility, their autonomy, and their emerging skills at imaginative play. They need toys to push, pull, and climb on and over. They need toys for solo play and some toys that are more social. There should be a variety of toys from several categories rather than just one or two types, including

- *Toys that encourage movement:* pull toys, push toys (including ones that don't tip easily for beginning walkers), balls, small vehicles
- *Toys with pieces that fit together:* shape sorters, simple puzzles (3 to 6 pieces with and without knobs), blocks, stacking rings
- *Toys that require pressure to put together or take apart:* large interlocking blocks that fit together, "pop" beads, rubber puzzles, pegboards and plastic-knobbed pegs, giant blocks or links that snap together
- *Toys with varied textures:* texture rattles, balls, and blocks, fuzzy puppets
- *Toys that make noise:* musical toys, squeaky toys
- *Toys that involve cause-and-effect relationships:* wind-up toys, "Busy Boxes," building blocks
- *Toys with hidden parts:* jack-in-the-boxes
- *Toys that encourage talking:* toy telephones, puppets, cardboard boxes
- *Toys that encourage pretending:* play dishes, picnic supplies, hats, dolls, pounding benches
- *Toys for cuddling:* stuffed dolls and huggables

Even the best toys are enhanced by adult interactions. Infants need time to play alone, but they also need your encouragement and assistance.

Health and Safety

The role of the adult in particular, and the environment in general, is transactional. The child influences it and is influenced by it. It is important that caregivers create a positive, inviting environment for the child, even if he does not seem to respond. Crawlers and walkers with their new mobility skills need to play in places where they are safe, feel secure, and can master the skills they will need throughout their lives. This environment must be designed with their biological needs in mind. They will use new mobility skills to perfect them. However, they may have few inhibitions or concepts of safety.

As infants increase in age, their newfound mobility presents new challenges for planning and programs. The mobile infant is learning to get what he wants himself, although initially, the energy and concentration that it takes to get there may make him forget the purpose of the venture before he reaches his goal. This mobility requires increased vigilance and "child proofing" of the environment. Issues of safety are more easily solved in settings that are designed solely for young children. Adults in family day-care homes must reach some compromise about this issue.

Indoor and outdoor areas raise different issues for child safety. Survey the learning environment visually. Look for obvious safety concerns such as sharp corners or exposed edges on tables or chairs. Look at the tables, chairs, and shelves and see how sturdy they are. Could an infant pulling up on them tip them over? If so, they need to be replaced. Now, get down on your hands and knees or even lie down. Are there things you have overlooked, such as an exposed electrical outlet without a safety plug, a cord that could be pulled, a piece of a broken toy that could be swallowed? Are crib rails locked in the "up" position when children are napping? Is an adult always with an infant when he is on a changing table or being bathed? Outdoor areas pose additional safety challenges, as they are frequently shared by older children. Areas should be fenced in and functionally organized. Grass is probably the best surface area. Concrete and asphalt get very hot in the summer and are dangerous for infants who are sitting and creeping, and they are not very resilient when children fall.

Proper nutrition is an important part of being healthy. Infants are born preferring sweet over bitter or sour tastes, yet too much sugar in the diet contributes to dental caries and also excess weight. As adults help establish children's eating habits, it is important to choose snacks wisely, foods that are low in fat and salt and high in complex carbohydrates. Snacks are a major dietary factor providing over 20 percent of children's caloric intake (Rogers & Morris, 1986). When you make snacks with the children as part of your programming, make sure they adhere to good nutritional standards. Find ways of celebrating special events that do not always include cupcakes and candy.

As children become more independently mobile, issues of health and safety take on new importance. Before taking toddlers on field trips you can begin to teach safety concepts by verbalizing what is happening. When on field trips, talk to them about safety practices while you pull them in a wagon or push them in a stroller. "The light is red, we have to stop until it turns green." "Look both ways before you cross the path."

Health, safety, and nutrition are closely related and affect one another. We track these in infants by gains in height and weight and the achievement of developmental norms. Health is more than the absence of disease. It is a dynamic state of physical, social and mental well-being. Preventive health care instills good health habits beginning in infancy. Inoculations are part of this prevention, as is hand washing. Planning the environment to avoid accidents and injuries is another aspect of prevention.

- Avoid pull-toys with springs and strings that crawlers and walkers may try to eat. For safety reasons pull-strings should be no longer than 9 inches. Reevaluate your environment for unsteady walkers.

- Special care must be taken with toys that have trailing loops and cords. Infants should be taught never to put these loops or cords around the body in such a way as to cause tripping or choking. Toys such as these should be stored where infants can't reach them and used only under adult supervision.
- Make sure riding toys have widespread wheels and a low center of gravity to prevent tipping over.
- Stuffed toys should have sturdy seams. Infants can choke on stuffing. Check labels to see that toys are non-allergenic, machine washable, and machine dryable.
- Balloons are treacherous for young children. They can be sucked into the windpipe and cause a child to choke to death.
- Metal or plastic toys should have smooth, rolled edges. Avoid toys with jagged edges where parts are imperfectly fitted together or toys that look as if they might break into sharp, jagged pieces.
- Spot-check toys occasionally for minor damage. Often a spot of glue, a tightened bolt, a few drops of oil, or even a bit of adhesive tape will prevent further damage that could lead to an accident.

Uncovered foam balls and blocks are not recommended for infants this age. Because infants put everything in their mouth, they are likely to ingest the foam and may choke on it.

Choking

As infants begin self-feeding and have the ability to purposefully put small things in their mouth the probability of choking increases. If an infant is choking, first check to see that he can still breathe. If so, wait for the object to come up. If not, turn the infant so his head is facing down and it is lower than his buttocks then slap him firmly between the shoulder blades. If nothing happens, try again. If the infant still can't breathe when upside down, try to remove the object with your finger. Chances are one of these steps will remove the object. If the infant can breathe but keeps choking, rush him to the hospital. All people who care for children should know the Heimlich maneuver for young children and CPR.

Discipline

Crawlers and walkers are mobile. Adults need to reevaluate their feelings about what young children should or shouldn't be allowed to do and how they will deal with infractions. Feelings about conflict and its resolution need to be incorporated into your philosophy as you expand it to include crawlers and walkers. There is inherent conflict between the young toddler's growing need for autonomy and the adult's need to maintain control and inculcate values and socially acceptable behavior. One might view this inherent conflict as a continuum between giving the child complete autonomy and breaking his will. This conflict appears first with crawlers and walkers. Adults make a conscious or unconscious choice about where they stand on this issue. Your philosophical position about dealing with conflict has both short- and long-term implications for the children you work with. The skills children learn in dealing with conflict set the groundwork for conflict resolution during their later school years.

Setting limits is part of an adult's commitment to a child, not just a reaction to an immediate behavior. The discipline should fit the child and the infraction, and should be accompanied by a conviction that setting limits is an important part of caring for young children. When caring accompanies discipline, it is positive; when there is no caring, it is just punishment. The goals of discipline, then, are two-fold: stopping inappropriate behavior as it occurs and developing long-term inner controls for behavior. Adults can facilitate the development of these inner controls by using positive discipline effectively.

How children act or respond affects the way adults interact with them (Brazelton, 1979; 1992). Children are different and some are easier than others. These differences in temperament are relatively permanent and impact adult-child interactions. One key to discipline is the "goodness of fit" between adult expectations and what the young toddler is emotionally and developmentally capable of doing. What is easy for one child may be close to impossible for another. The child himself is a variable.

Easy children (those who show moderation in intensity, are adaptable, approachable, have generally positive moods, and a sense of rhythmicity), may stop an inappropriate behavior with only a "teacher look." Slow-to-warm-up children (those who have low activity and intensity levels and take longer to adapt than easy children) may initially require physical cues, but as they become aware of the rules, they will become more self-controlled. Teachers need to realize this and pull back to give them more opportunities to establish self-control. Difficult children (those who have intense reactions, are slow to adapt, nonrhythmical, and often have negative moods) may require physical prompts to stop the same behavior and they may continue to need these prompts. Regretfully, children who have difficult temperaments need more adult understanding yet may actually receive fewer positive responses from adults who do not understand them nor know how to work with difficult children (Chess, 1983).

Sometimes toddlers, especially difficult ones, will make adults angry, particularly when they hurt another child. Sometimes it's appropriate to tell the toddler that their actions made you angry. However, it is imperative to *discipline,* not punish, the child's behavior. For example, say to Rochelle "I don't like it when you bite Todd. It hurts him and it makes me angry. You need to play by yourself away from the other children. I don't want you hurting other children." Come back in several minutes and coach her on the skills she should have used when she resorted to biting. It is important to follow up with a child and teach her what the acceptable behavior is.

Guidelines for Crawlers and Walkers

■ Keep the child's developmental level in mind. Expect behavior that is appropriate to his developmental level.

- Take into account the child's cultural and environmental background when deciding how to deal with particular behaviors. In some instances it may be necessary to preface rule statements with reference to a behavior. "When you are in school you must wash your hands before you may have a snack."
- Be firm, persistent, and consistent. Being firm lets children know you are serious and what they are doing is inappropriate. Be persistent—follow through with your consequences. Be consistent—every time the child rips pages, she should be disciplined. (If the adult is firm and persistent, a child usually will only try an inappropriate behavior a few times.) If the adult is wishy-washy, a child is likely to try the behavior more often because he has not learned the limits for his behavior.
- Set reasonable limits. Young toddlers are just learning to share. It is not realistic to expect them to share an especially desirable toy with a friend.
- Let children know that you care for them and are proud of who they are and what they can do. Reinforce them when they act appropriately, or make attempts to please. For example, "Kaitlin, I'm so proud of you. You put the blocks away all by yourself".
- Set up the room so the physical space encourages appropriate behavior. Avoid long paths that encourage running.
- Help children label their feelings verbally when they are upset, angry or hurt. You might say, "Shawntell, you're really angry because Jacy took your doll".
- Provide reasons for the limits you set. "Marco, you need to walk when you are inside, the floors are slippery."

Anticipatory Guidance

Following the adage that it is better to prevent spilled milk than to clean it up, consider a preventive approach to discipline. Prevention, or anticipatory guidance, is broad based. It ranges from developmentally appropriate planning to who sits beside whom in a small group. It includes reinforcing appropriate behavior and knowing the cues individual toddlers give before they "lose it."

Reinforcing Appropriate Behavior

One aspect of anticipatory guidance is looking for "the good stuff," that is, catching children doing something good. The magic is for adults to comment on the desired behaviors they see as much as they can. Children want attention and tend to repeat the behaviors for which someone gives them attention. So, if many comments are made on positive behaviors, children should be showing more of those behaviors.

Comment on the behavior you want to reinforce in a matter-of-fact way. "What a good idea! You got a puzzle for José, so that you and he could each have one." Think carefully before making a comment to see if you can turn a potentially negative comment into one that looks at the positive part of what the child is trying to do. When one child takes a toy from other child don't say "Don't grab that from him, Connie." Try instead to reframe the situation and say "Oh, I see you want to play with a puzzle. Let's see if we can find one for you." or "Were you trying to help Chris put that puzzle piece in? It looks like he wants to do it by himself. Let's find a puzzle for you." By interpreting part of a behavior as positive, the child can look at himself in a more positive light also. He may feel a relief that an adult saw what he really wanted and helped him get it.

Labeling the Behavior, Not the Child

It is better to label the *behavior* as "bad" rather than the child. For instance say, "I don't like it when you bite Jamie," rather than "only bad girls bite." The child will eventually learn that you don't like her behavior (biting), rather than thinking that you do not like her.

Young toddlers are just beginning to understand the feelings of others. You can help them with this process. One way is to give the child who was bitten a lot of caring attention rather than paying negative attention to the child who did the biting. You may also want to verbalize the hurt toddler's feelings to increase awareness in others of how it felt. For instance, "Oh, Jamie, that bite must have hurt. How can we make you feel better?" Hold and cuddle the hurt child and attend to her needs. Give less attention to the child who did the biting. Try to be understanding of both children's feelings, and try not to make a big deal of the child who did the misdeed. Rather, include that child in the conversation of figuring how to make the hurt toddler feel better.

Another way to help toddlers understand others' feelings is to notice and label different feelings, expressions, and behaviors during the day as you see them occur. For example, "Ryan, you look angry. Do you want *that* truck? You can play with *this* one now or wait until Anna's turn is over." "Oh, Brennan, how thoughtful of you to bring Paten's blanket to her. You know that makes her feel good and helps her go to sleep."

Adults need to actively look for and comment on the positive (good) things toddlers do every day. Crawlers and walkers like attention and want to please adults. If they are rewarded with positive comments and hugs, they will feel good about themselves. If, however, they only hear from adults when they do something they're not supposed to do, then expect that they will continue to behave negatively to get attention. Children will have conflicts occasionally. You cannot prevent all negative experiences. However, if you are positive most of the time and turn conflicts into learning experiences, more positive behavior is likely to follow.

Transitioning Between Settings

As infants and toddlers get older, they often move to new rooms or settings and new children join the original group. It is frequently difficult for the young children to leave familiar surroundings and people to face an unknown situation. It may also be stressful for an adult when a child she likes very much leaves and is replaced with an unknown child with whom she has to build a relationship. Changing just one child in a group can change the entire group's dynamics.

When children are moving from one group to another within the same setting, for example, from an infant to a toddler group, there are steps you can take to make the move easier. Similarly, these procedures can be taken when a child first joins the group.

Decisions as to when to move children out of a particular grouping are made for a variety of reasons. Some of these decisions are based on expediency (there is space); others have a more philosophical base. Crawlers and walkers are typically moved out of an infant setting between 12 and 18 months, perhaps before this if their large-motor skills are very good. If moved in the younger age range, it is typically to a "tweenie" group of toddlers about 12 to 24 months; if the move is later, the age range is often 18 to 36 months.

Infant and toddler programs are different. Infant programs are more individualized and personalized and there are fewer infants and more adults. In infant programs, typically an adult is assigned to an infant as a primary person. Crawlers and walkers typically choose their own primary adult based on their preferences. Toddler programs also have more complex social demands from peers and a different daily routine (Daniel, 1993).

Changes in settings cause stress for all the individuals involved: the toddler joining the group, the parent leaving the child in a new setting, and the adult receiving the new child. To make this transition easier for everyone, try to:

- Encourage parents to visit the new toddler setting before the transition and talk with staff about the transition process.
- Expect the transition process to take four to six weeks. Begin the transition gradually with a short visit (about half an hour) to the new room with a trusted adult. This time is gradually extended and the child is drawn into the new group. The adult may leave, but will return for the child. When all feel comfortable, the child will become a permanent member of this new group.
- Have children who know each other go through this group transition at the same time, if feasible.
- Borrow some toys the toddler is familiar with, particularly ones that are huggable and more "home-like", from the infant room.
- Support toddlers in dramatic play. Toddlers will often "play out" their concerns, or give you insight into what it is that they are concerned about.
- Read stories about children beginning school, or about the beginning of any new event.

Entering a new classroom is a difficult time for all, especially as it is accompanied by internal growth in the child himself. It is unwise to begin this process at a time when other major changes are likely to happen in the family (the birth of a new baby, family separations, vacations, and so on). The transition should be made either before or after these events (Daniel, 1993).

Although the suggestions given above won't entirely eliminate difficulties at transition times, they should reduce them. Anticipating possible problems and planning strategies to avoid them is useful. Some thoughtful planning which deals with your individual situation and the needs of the toddlers is likely to be helpful as well. Having toddlers understand exactly what you expect of them during transition times is a first step. Children need to feel secure and know that there are rules and that the adult is in control. Expect some testing behavior at transition time. A calm but firm response is reassuring.

Adult-Supported Learning

Adults play a very important role in supporting the learning of infants and toddlers. Although it is good for young children to learn to play independently, they will learn more if they spend time with a supportive adult (Hohmann, 1988). This is particularly true of vulnerable children. It is through play that children learn. Children must actively interact with their environment to learn about it. Infants who receive adult scaffolding during their play are likely to learn more. Adults can help children work through the questions and problems that arise during this learning process. They scaffold learning by talking about and playing with what interests the child, the emerging curriculum. An adult may introduce variations on activities, additional props, and new activities or ideas. The adult guides the child's learning and concentration but does not force it. She helps only when needed. By actively playing with young children, adults can make an ongoing assessment of where they are developmentally, so that future appropriate learning activities can be planned.

There are three kinds of support adults offer infants and toddlers: Environmental support, nonverbal support, and verbal support.

Environmental Support

This involves setting up the space that children use so as to encourage play and use of the materials. This includes such things as providing a variety of materials for children to choose and use as well as making sure there are enough materials to meet each child's needs and enough space for children to use materials. It involves planning an environment that meets and stretches children's understanding of their world.

Adults need to encourage and support independent play and exploration to allow the child to control and master his environment. It is important to allow crawlers and walkers to discover concepts and ideas on their own. This does not mean leaving him unattended but rather that the adult arrange the environment in a developmentally appropriate way and then provide cues and suggestions when necessary. The child remains the "doer." They need many opportunities to participate in child-directed and child-selected play.

Environmental support also includes:

- Avoiding interruptions, if possible. Be sure to give toddlers adequate warnings before routine transitions.
- Providing an appropriate physical and emotional environment for play.
- Encouraging toddlers to help put away toys and materials they are finished with.

- Bringing out a few toys at a time to keep activities novel and to maintain toddler as well as adult interest.

Nonverbal Support

Adults can do many things nonverbally to encourage play. Watching what children do with materials and then imitating and expanding their actions may increase their attention span as well as their skill repertoire. Use materials yourself when you are with crawlers and walkers but don't get so involved that you are no longer paying attention to them. Also avoid making models that children request repeatedly because yours are better than the ones they themselves can produce.

Use your body to express interest. Place yourself at the child's eye level. Sit on the floor if he is sitting there. If he is standing, kneel down to be at his level. If he is sitting in a child-sized chair, then you also sit on a child-sized chair. Listen to what they say and acknowledge their speaking.

- Observe play to determine how children are playing, what toys and materials they are playing with, as well as the level of their development. This way you have a good chance to learn their individual characteristics.
- Show interest in what the children are doing. Let children know and see that you value what they do.
- Be available to assist children when necessary. They sometimes have difficulties playing with peers for lengths of time. An adult should be nearby to help children learn to solve problems.

Children are curious about each other. Therefore, if there are enough props, younger children will imitate older children.

- Accept toddlers' statements and explanations. Sometimes adults tend to discredit toddlers' statements. When a child tells an adult that he is hot, the adult may respond with information that the room is not hot nor is the adult hot. Regardless, the child may actually be hot.
- Remain calm in the face of child "mistakes." Most adults have no problem when a child spills the first glass of milk, but when a he spills a second glass, many are tested, even when it is clear that the spill was accidental.

Verbal Support

There are many things that you can do verbally to support a child's learning and to encourage their language development. Talk with them about what they are doing and ask them questions that relate to their play. Encourage them to answer their own questions by saying "What do *you* think?"

- Acknowledge their actions and choices; responding to their answers and explanations helps crawlers and walkers join words and actions.
- Reframing and repeating a child's language, as well as expanding and extending it, provides the foundation for understanding what is happening as well as language development.
- Referring children to one another for problem solving and additional conversation supports social development and decreases the dependency on adults as the only source of information.
- Conversing with nonverbal children supports their understanding of language. Probably more than other children, those who do not yet have language need good language models. Adults find it more rewarding to talk to toddlers who respond by talking back. Talking with those who do not is extremely important.
- Expand play when appropriate. The adult might make verbal suggestions introducing new ideas or variations on what the child is doing. She can describe for and with them what they are doing and ask open-ended questions. She might add props to the play situation that encourage further play.

Crawlers and walkers benefit from adult support and attention. Those who receive support from adults during their play are likely to learn more (Hohmann, 1988; Whitehead, 1989).

Planning for Multi-Age Groupings

Often individuals who work with infants and toddlers find themselves in the position of needing to plan activities for different ages of children at the same time. For example, in a family day-care home there may be an infant of 6 months, toddlers at 18 and 28 months and two preschoolers 3 and 4 years of age. This can be tricky because older children often enjoy toys with small parts which could be dangerous to infants and toddlers. Here are a few suggestions for working with different ages of children:

- Separate the infant, toddler, and preschool materials. For example, have infant toys (rattles, soft balls, and blocks) on the floor and preschool materials such as crayons and paper up on a table where infants can't reach.

- Have some time during the day when the older children can help the younger ones. For example, an older preschooler may enjoy building a block tower which a toddler knocks down again and again. Don't overdo the helping role. Make sure that older children have time to play, experiment, and explore on their own with activities appropriate to their age.

- Plan some activities for the older children while allowing the younger children a choice about participating. Support their participatation in an age-appropriate way. For example, encourage preschoolers to move to the musical directions on a record while you support crawlers and walkers just moving their bodies to the music but without following the directions in the song. If an infant is awake, you may hold her and move her to the music.

- If older children wake up early from a nap, take advantage of the opportunity to play a game with them, talk, cuddle, or do an activity of their choice which is more difficult to do when both infants and toddlers are awake.

- While feeding an infant, tell riddles or play a guessing game with older children.

- When teaching multi-age groups that include toddlers, it is important to adjust your expectations to their developmental level.

- Don't expect toddlers to sit for a long time in a group situation. If you are doing a long activity, allow toddlers to come and go as they please.

- When a disruptive behavior cannot be prevented, anticipate when it will happen. If a toddler typically has a difficult time leaving her parents, plan to have an adult available who can give the toddler undivided attention to help this transition go more smoothly.

- Remember age-appropriate expectations. Different strategies are effective with different ages of children. Crawlers and walkers are more easily distracted than older children.

- Match children's developmental level in an age-appropriate way. Even if a toddler is functioning at a much younger level, try to find toys and materials appropriate for him, not a young infant.

- Redirect children to more appropriate activities when possible. This may be difficult with a persistent toddler who is fascinated by a particular object and can't be distracted. You might find a special time when you can give this child your full attention and let him touch the delicate object with your close supervision. This will often decrease rather than increase the level of stress you are comfortable with. Try not to go much beyond that level.

- Sometimes allow children the option of not participating. They will often watch for a while and then join you when they are ready. Everyone, including children, needs to have control over their environment and letting them choose when they will participate is one way of doing this. Watch, on the other hand, for a child who doesn't want to participate. Find ways of regularly including this child.

■ A well-managed setting is not always quiet and neat. Decide what levels of noise and clutter you can tolerate and make decisions that will maintain those levels.

Communicating with Parents

Communicating with parents remains an important area. With crawlers and walkers, parental concern begins to move from concerns about biological functions to areas of social, emotional, and cognitive development. Although parents of toddlers will want to know generally about sleeping and eating, they are often more concerned about social and emotional aspects of their toddler's day. Because children are so variable, knowing whether or not theirs had a "good" or "bad" day is important for parents. The following information is useful as a guide for informal regular communications.

■ Parents need information about the daily experiences of children.
■ Develop a consistent system of recording information to give parents on a daily basis. This may be a message board, a notebook that travels with the child, or any system that works for you.
■ Parents want to know that you accept and like their child in all of his quick shifting moods. It is imperative that you show these feelings to both the child and the parents, even on "bad" days.
■ Parents need to hear information from you about their child and his successes on a regular basis, no matter how small the accomplishments may seem.

Sometimes informal parent communication provides the impetus for a closer look at the match between the child and the program, including comments such as "Jason seems to be bored with school right now" or "Shaleen used to be eager to go to school and now she seems reluctant to go." Although problems might not be related to the program, that is one alternative that should be considered.

Parent contacts range from the informal greetings and exchanges at arrival and departure to regularly scheduled and specialized conferences. Sometimes important information can be communicated in a matter of moments. However, that does not obviate the need for regularly scheduled conferences to sit back and look carefully at each toddler, how he is growing and developing, and how the programming is adapting to these changes.

Summary

As young children become mobile, planning must be adapted to both support the emerging mobility and to take into account the fact that they can now make more active choices regarding the activities they want to engage in and how long they chose the stay. Planning is a combination of offering choices and planning specific activities for individual children. Play is the work of childhood. At 8 months, infants need adults to support their play; but by 18 months, toddlers can play side by side. Adults support the young toddler's learning in a variety of ways. They arrange the environment so that it is developmentally appropriate and conducive to learning, and they support this learning through both their verbal comments and their nonverbal behavior.

Transitions and routine care are taking up less time and children have more time to engage in play activities. With increased mobility, two areas take on new importance: safety and discipline. Environments need to be evaluated in light of this mobility and sensitive adults need to set limits to keep young toddlers safe. As children get older, they may move from one setting to another. This transition needs to be well planned and gradual to allow the child, parents, and teachers time to adjust. Often children this age are in multi-age groupings which pose some challenges to program planning. The adults in the child's environment are still responsible for exchanging information about the child and planning for continuity in his life. With increasing age, planning becomes less individualized and more oriented to groups of two or three children. This also reflects the growth in social and emotional development.

Application Activities

1. Develop a transition plan for a child moving from an infant to a toddler program at 18 months. Write an information sheet for the parents about this transitioning process and how you plan for it.

2. Visit a child-care setting and make a videotape that depicts a day in that center for a walker and crawler.

3. Talk with a parent of a child who has become a crawler or walker and ask them how they "child proofed" their home to accommodate this. Ask them what they forgot and what they did not expect in the process

Chapter 17

Activities for Crawlers and Walkers: 8 to 18 Months

In just 8 months infants make tremendous strides in growth and development and what they learn about their world. Infants are now sitting and moving beings who have a definite personality and are ready to make some demands on the world around them in a variety of ways. Many of them have been in the care of adults other than their parents for several months, others will be entering into care for the first time.

As the infant moves into toddlerhood, he learns to move around at will, understands much of what is said to him, and can vehemently say "NO" when he does not like what is happening. Crawlers and walkers can now choose what they want to do (and get there); planning and activities must change to meet these abilities.

Despite his skills, the toddler is fragile. He can look as competent as many preschool children one minute and in the next fall apart and cling and cry like an infant. He is curious about his world but he needs to be able to satisfy this curiosity in a safe environment with caring adults. Crawlers and walkers are some of the most satisfying and frustrating children to work with. As they learn about themselves they are teaching us about ourselves as well.

Activities for Crawlers and Walkers

Infants are now actively playing with toys and other materials. Although they have more skills, they still need to practice the ones that are developing. So a variety of similar toys and activities that have many variations are useful. Infants and young toddlers need sturdy toys. They will hold, shake, bat, kick, bang,

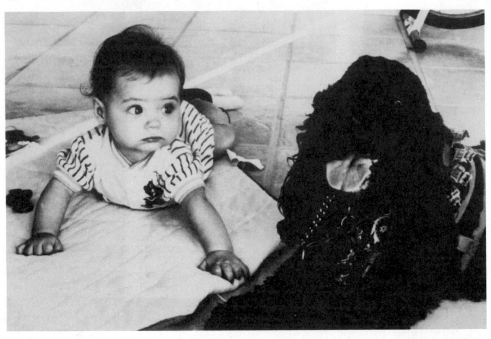

Sometimes things that move, such as dogs, are both intriguing and a little scary.

drop, throw, as well as bite and taste their toys. Being able to sit steadily frees the hands, and with increasing fine-motor skills infants need toys to grasp and hold. As they become more mobile they need toys that move.

Select toys and activities that stimulate the infant and young toddler's imagination and help to develop skills. Choose some toys and activities that can be used independently. It is important to reexamine toys to make sure they are safe. The concern is no longer that small parts might accidentally fall off, but rather, that they can be pulled, dropped, or chewed off. The ability and interest of the infant and young toddler in putting objects in her mouth causes some safety concerns. As tiny objects can easily become lodged in the throat and cause choking, get in the habit of keeping small objects away from young children. Increased, but unstable, mobility adds new safety considerations.

■ **Sensorimotor**

VARIATIONS ON ROLLING

Purpose   To improve sensorimotor integration and large-motor coordination

Materials   Beach towel, ball

Procedure   Have the children participate in various types of rolling activities on a rug or grass. Ask them to:

- Log roll—hands extended over the head, feet together
- Ball roll—hands extended over the head, feet clasping ball

- Torpedo roll—hands at sides of body
- Windmill roll—one hand above head, one at side
- Towel roll—start at one end of a beach towel and roll up into it, then reverse and roll out.
- Circle roll—roll in circles while someone holds their ankles
- Down hill roll—roll down a hill or incline

Easier   Use the above rolls, support the child's attempts and keep the distance short.

Harder   Encourage the children to think about the different rolling experiences and how each feels. Talk with children about when rolling might be a useful way to move. Have children think up new variations.

Comment   Rolling is a good energy release as well as a means to strengthen large muscles. These rolls are good for rainy days or as outdoor activities on the grass. Be sure to clear the area of rocks or other potentially harmful objects.

■ **Sensorimotor**

VARIATIONS ON PUSH AND PULL

Purpose   To improve sensorimotor integration and motor planning

Materials   Variety of push and pull toys

Procedure   First allow the infant to explore the toy and then roll the toy slightly out of his reach. Encourage him to crawl after the toy. As he reaches it, push it a little farther, then encourage him to push it rather than retrieve it. (Don't do this to the point where he is frustrated.) When the child understands about pushing toys, introduce toys that can be pulled as well.

Easier   Help push the toy in front of the infant. Move it slowly so he can crawl after it. Choose toys that move slowly.

Harder   Choose a toy that moves quickly with a small push, like a ball, and encourage the infant to follow after it as quickly as he can. When the child is comfortable using pull toys, encourage to child to take the toy to a specific location.

Comment   Use push toys before pull toys. They are easier. Pull toys are a challenge to the beginning walker as the child must concentrate on holding on to the toy, know where the toy is relative to where he is, and walk at the same time.

■ **Sensorimotor**

VARIATIONS ON WALKING

Purpose   To improve sensorimotor integration and motor planning

Materials   None

Procedure　Have children participate in various types of walks.

- Barefoot walk: Children walk on mud, sand, smooth rocks, and concrete surfaces and finally through a tray of water and talk about how each feels and the sensations involved. Inside use carpet squares, bathmats, woven doormats, foam pads, and so on.
- Walking a line: Children walk a line forward and then backward, keeping each foot on the line. Have children walk pigeon-toed, turning feet out as far as possible, and crossing the front foot over the line each time.
- Walking sideways: Children walk to the right one step at a time, bringing their left foot over to touch their right foot. Reverse when moving to the left. If the children are in a circle or two circles, the activity requires less space and can be done in the classroom. As a long line it can be more like "follow the leader."
- Ostrich: Children bend forward at waist, grasp ankles, and walk forward while keeping knees stiff and stretching neck in and out.
- Duck: Children do a deep knee bend and place hands behind their back; they walk forward one foot at a time, but remain in bent-knee position.

Easier　Use the above walks, accept the child's attempt, and keep the distance short.

Harder　Talk with the toddlers and get their ideas for variations. Have them invent their own walk and name it after them: the "Ginger walk." Encourage others to imitate this walk while you point out the salient features. Talk about how each walk feels to them; that is, could they do the walk for a long or short time and was it hard to keep their balance?

Comment　These are good rainy-day activities and fun ways of moving from a group once the children know the names of the different walks. Don't use these variations until children are confident walkers.

■ **Sensorimotor**

VARIATIONS ON CREEPING AND CRAWLING

Purpose　To improve sensorimotor integration, large-motor coordination, and motor planning

Materials　Record, cassette or compact disc player; materials for an obstacle course, such as yarn, boxes, barrels, boards, chairs, hula hoops

Procedure　Have the children participate in various types of creeping and crawling activities. Play music to set the pace and help children keep a rhythm. Have the toddlers:

- Turtle creep—On hands and knees with a small blanket on top of the child (the blanket looks like a shell) talk to the children about turtles and the purpose of the shell.

- Texture creep—Have them creep on a path of different textures (carpet squares, welcome mats, bubble packing, and so on) and talk about how the different textures feel. Have children do this activity outside.
- Snake crawl—Slither with stomach on floor using only arms to pull.
- Obstacle course—Crawl through a course made of boxes or chairs, barrels, boards, and so on.
- Tape trail—Crawl or creep around the room following a tape trail.

Easier   Make the distance shorter and accept any kind of on-the-floor loco-motion.

Harder   Encourage the children to think about the different crawling experiences and what each feels like. Discuss with children when crawling or creeping might be a useful way to move. Have children participate in thinking up variations.

Comment   Creeping and crawling are skills toddlers have probably mastered so variations add interest.

Note: When creeping or crawling outside, clear the area of harmful objects.

■ **Sensorimotor**

DUMP AND FILL

Purpose   To improve sensorimotor integration and eye-hand coordination

Materials   Dish pans, rice, dry cereal, beans, coffee (beans or ground), plastic measuring cups, measuring spoons

Procedure   Have the child sit on the floor in the middle of a plastic tablecloth. Put about 2 inches of rice, dry cereal, or beans in a dish pan and add a variety of cups and spoons. Place the dish pan in front of the infant and encourage him to fill up the containers and dump them.

Easier   Help the child explore the media itself first. If necessary, place his hands in the container and help him explore the media.

Harder   Have the infant dump from one container into another container.

Comment   This is a precursor to pouring liquids and is a lot less messy. It has the potential for simple exploration as well as being related to concepts about measurement and relative size.

Note: With children this age all materials used in "dump and fill" should be edible. They will be eaten.

■ **Discovery**

CARDBOARD BLOCKS

Purpose   To improve sensorimotor integration and math concepts

Materials   Cardboard blocks or clean cardboard milk or juice containers of various sizes; exacto knife or scissors

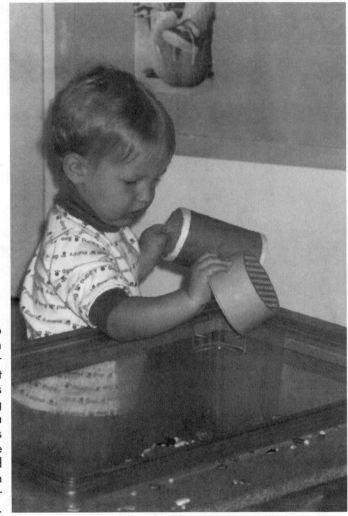

Variations on dump and fill help children develop finger strength and wrist rotation as well as providing experience with a variety of materials and practicing the eye-hand coordination necessary for pouring liquids.

To Make   Cut off top portion of open container where crease is located. Push together open ends of same-sized containers to make block. Use half-pint, pint, and quart containers to make different-sized blocks. Cut some quart and half-gallon containers so that they are shorter; this will result in blocks that are cubes instead of rectangles. These can be covered with contact paper or used as they are.

Procedure   Sit on the floor with the child and begin stacking blocks. Give the child a block and encourage him to join you.

Easier   Use only a few large blocks. Stack the blocks and let the child knock down the blocks you've stacked. Then encourage her to put one

Figure 17.1 | Cardboard Blocks

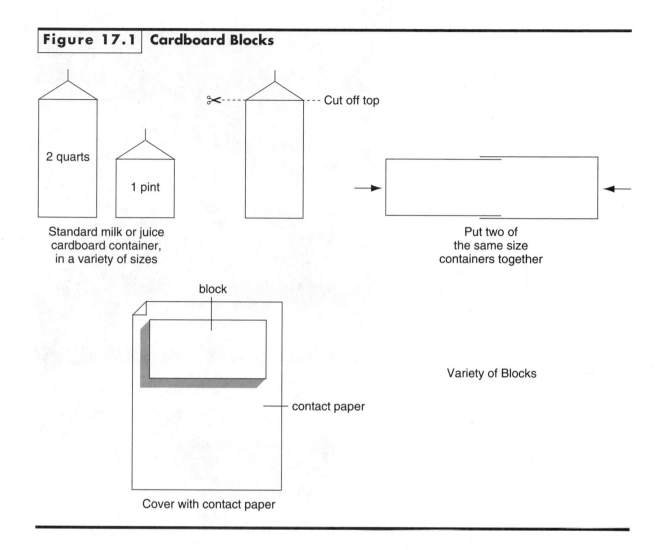

2 quarts

1 pint

Standard milk or juice
cardboard container,
in a variety of sizes

Cut off top

Put two of
the same size
containers together

block

contact paper

Variety of Blocks

Cover with contact paper

block on top of another. Praise any of the child's beginning attempts whether they are successful or not.

Harder   Let the child do most of the building. Provide other materials to extend the child's block play, such as cars or toy people. Begin to build simple structures such as roads, and so on. This can be done easily by stacking blocks side-by-side and "driving" a car over them. Say, "Look! I made a road!"

Comment   Block play has the potential for building both mathematical and creative problem-solving skills for toddlers. At this age, large light blocks are preferable.

Toddlers need light blocks so if they fall the children are not hurt.

■ Discovery

VARIATIONS ON PEEK-A-BOO

Purpose   To develop object permanence

Materials   Small blanket or piece of furniture (chair or couch)

Procedure   Using your voice, get the infant's attention, make eye contact, then

- Hide behind the blanket or furniture. Reappear and say "Peek-a-boo, I see you."
- Put a book between you and the infant to hide your face and then peek around the corners of the book.
- Put a handkerchief over your face and then pull it off saying "Peek-a-boo."

- Put a handkerchief over the infant's face and then pull it off saying "I see you."
- Put your hands over your face to cover it and then move them and say "Peek-a-boo."

Talk to the infant, establish eye contact and then hide again.

Easier   Infants who have not developed object permanence (this usually begins about 8 months) may not see the purpose of the game. Wait a few weeks and play it again. Talk to the child while you are hiding.

Harder   Stay hidden longer or appear from a different spot than you disappeared. (If you hid behind the right side of the chair appear on the left side.)

Comments   Many of the games which adults have played with infants for years, such as "Peek-a-boo," play an important role in healthy child development. "Peek-a-boo" helps infants learn that what they can't see still exists (object permanence). Because the game is similar every time, infants develop the ability to predict what will happen as they play.

■ **Discovery**

HIDE IT

Purpose   To encourage object permanence, tactile perception, and observational skills

Materials   Styrofoam packing material, cardboard box, small objects

Procedure   Place packing material in a large cardboard box and hide a few objects (such as a spoon, ball, cup, or other objects) in the Styrofoam "snow." Have the children try to find the hidden objects.

Easier   Use larger objects which are partially visible and less Styrofoam.
Harder   Make the objects smaller or use more packing material.

Comment   Children are curious about hidden objects and this helps to develop their discrimination of objects through touch. Play other hiding games such as hiding a small object in your hand and switching it back and forth and then having the child choose the hand it is in.

Note: Be sure packing material used is too large to swallow.

■ **Language Arts**

NURSERY RHYMES

Purpose   To increase expressive language and listening skills

Materials   Books with simple nursery rhymes such as *I'm a little teapot; This little piggy; Baa, baa, black sheep; Hickory, dickory dock*

Procedure   Read, chant, or sing nursery rhymes as you turn the pages of the book with a child or small group of children. Plan to use the books frequently so children can learn the rhymes.

Easier   Say, chant or sing nursery rhymes during different times of day with one child.

Harder   Encourage the children to join you in saying the rhymes or parts of rhymes.

Comment   Children often share an adult's enthusiasm and actions as they read. Share other nursery rhyme books. Play a tape or record of nursery rhymes for children.

■ **Language Arts**

PUPPETS

Purpose   To increase expressive language and pretend play

Materials   Easy-to-use animal or people puppets such as sock puppets

Procedure   Encourage the child to put the puppet on her hand and then use the puppets to talk to you or another child. Help children find ways to play together by suggesting simple roles they can take or ways of interacting with their puppets that will prolong the play. They may need your active support for play to continue.

Easier   Play with one child with a puppet where you take the lead and the child responds to your initiations.

Harder   Encourage two children to play together with different but related puppets. For example, two animal puppets, such as a turtle and a fish.

Comment   Sometimes toddlers who are reluctant to talk are more willing to talk and carry on conversations using puppets. Be sure to find ways of including reluctant talkers in puppet play. If you have a multi-age grouping, encourage older children to use puppets with younger children. Talking with puppets may encourage peer interaction as well as development of language skills.

■ **Creative Arts**

DOING IT SONG

Purpose   To encourage creative movements and adaptive skills

Materials   None

Procedure   Talk to the children about what they do during the day. Then tell them that you are going to make up a song about what they do. Encourage them to decide on motions to go with the words. If this is taking a long time, suggest appropriate movements to go with the verse. Try to get several related concepts.

Ask them what happens first in the morning. (Have a sequence that will work in your mind before you start, and only do as many verses as there is interest.) Sing to the tune of "Here We Go Round the Mulberry Bush."

This is the way we wash our hands, wash our hands, wash our hands.

This is the way we wash our hands so early in the morning

Morning

Get out of bed	Wash our hands
Brush our teeth	Comb our hair
Put on our clothes	Eat our breakfast
Come to school	

Substitute an activity theme such as cleaning the house

Sweep the floor	Vacuum the rug
Make our beds	Wipe the table

Another variation is to ask children what they like to play with and incorporate their name into the song.

This is the way Juan plays with the ball, plays with the ball, plays with the ball,

This is the way Juan plays with the ball, and plays with all his friends.

Easier   Get less input from the children and sing fewer stanzas.

Harder   Encourage the children to participate more actively in thinking up the motions that go with the song and what you will sing about.

Comment   Accept the motions that the children choose whether or not they are related to the words. It is unlikely that the children will imitate them accurately anyway. After children have participated in an experience like this, they become more active in offering suggestions.

■ **Creative Arts**

PUDDING FINGER PAINT

Purpose   To encourage creativity and increase body awareness

Materials   Instant pudding mix, milk, bowl, whip, wooden spoon

To Make   Mix the pudding mix and milk together for 2 minutes and then let stand for 5 minutes. If it is too thick add more milk.

Procedure   Place a small amount of the pudding on the tray of a high chair or on a table in front of the toddler. Encourage him to explore the pudding and play with it as he would finger paint. You may need to demonstrate.

Easier   Gently help toddlers feel the pudding and move it around with the fingers of one hand. Talk about how it feels. Encourage (but don't push) greater involvement.

Harder   Encourage the child to make more expansive movements and to use both hands. Talk about how different it looks when he uses a finger versus the palm of his hand.

Comment   If they eat the pudding, there is no problem. This is a very messy activity. Be prepared with clean-up close by. Be sure to show them how they look in a mirror before the clean up process begins.

■ **Creative Arts**

SCRIBBLING

Purpose   To encourage creativity and learn cause-and-effect relationships

Materials   Thick chalk, white paper, tape, sponge, water

Procedure   Tape the paper to the table and let the toddler experiment with different colors of chalk and their effect on the paper. Then wet a portion of the paper or another sheet with the sponge and let them use the chalk again. Talk with them about the differences.

Easier   Use either wet or dry paper but not both.
Harder   Encourage children to compare the effects of the chalk on wet and dry paper both from a sensorimotor perspective as well as a visual perspective.

Comment   Many children may have experience using crayons at home, but rarely chalk. This may hold interest for children. Do however, let them scribble with crayons as well and use large chalk on the sidewalk.

■ **Social Awareness**

MY BOOK ABOUT ME

Purpose   To increase social awareness and self-concept

Materials   Sandwich-size plastic bags that zip closed; photographs of the infant; markers; construction paper or poster board; paste

To Make   Cut construction paper or poster board into 5 1/2-inch-by-6-inch pieces so that each fits inside the plastic bag. Paste the photographs of the infant doing a variety of activities on both sides of the construction paper and put each page in a separate bag. Make a beginning page to identify the infant's book. Put holes through the pages (and bags) and fasten them together with yarn. Photographs can also be laminated or covered with clear contact paper.

Procedure   With the infant on your lap look through the book with him and talk about each picture and what he is doing and how wonderful he is.

Easier   Keep the book short and if possible have the photographs of him alone doing everyday things (eating, sleeping, playing, and so on).

Harder   Have more photographs in the book with a wider range of events, or make several shorter, more specific books, such as "Shalini at Home," "Shalini at School," "Shalini Playing with her Friends."

Comment Infants enjoy looking at these books. You can take photographs of the children at school or ask parents to send in pictures, whichever seems most appropriate.

■ **Social Awareness**

MY BABY

Purpose   To increase social awareness and prosocial skills

Materials   Multi-ethnic male and female dolls

Procedure   Encourage the children to play with and care for the dolls. Help children notice the differences in the ways the dolls look. Talk about the different children in the class and how they differ. Encourage children to carry, cuddle, bottle-feed, sing to, or rock the dolls. When the toddlers are ready, introduce new ways of playing with the doll in an appropriate way. Encourage two toddlers to play together and talk about what each is doing with his doll and why. Encourage them to think about what the baby might want or need.

Easier   Encourage exploration of the doll. Help the child to gently feel the doll's hair, eyes, clothing, and to move body parts. Name body and clothing parts for the child.

Harder   See if the child can imitate more difficult skills, such as pretend feeding with a spoon or combing the doll's "hair." Help the child use his imagination with the doll: Have a tea party, take the doll for a walk in a wagon, wash the baby in a small tub, then dry the doll off, and so on. Help the child develop self-help skills by practicing undressing and dressing not only himself, but also a doll. Talk about the ways in which the dolls are the same and different in both how they look and their need for care.

Comment Children may need to be taught caregiving skills. They are often more willing to practice self-help skills in other situations. Toddlers are struggling to develop their own identity, independence, and self-concept. It is useful for them to explore different roles with the dolls and to practice prosocial behavior.

■ **Social Awareness**

CUPS AND SPOONS

Purpose   To improve self-feeding skills

Materials   Variety of plastic and tin cups with handles, plastic spoons

Procedure   Place infant in highchair and place a cup and spoon on the tray. Encourage the infant to explore each item. Demonstrate how you can use the spoon to hit the cup or to stir, and then give the items back to the infant. Encourage the infant to pick up the cup with the handle and pretend to drink from it or eat with the spoon. When you repeat this activity, use a slightly different cup, perhaps one with a weighted bottom.

Easier   Introduce the cup and spoon separately before pairing them.

Harder   Give the infant several different cups and spoons to play with at the same time.

Comment It is useful for infants to have had experience playing with and exploring the properties of a cup and spoon before they are expected to use them.

■ Social Awareness

GELATIN

Purpose To improve self-feeding skills and creativity

Materials Four envelopes of unflavored gelatin, 3 packages (3 oz. each) flavored gelatin, 4 cups boiling water, and a 13-inch-by-9-inch baking pan

To Make   In large bowl, combine unflavored gelatin and flavored gelatin; add boiling water and stir until gelatin is completely dissolved. Pour into large shallow baking pan (for example, 13 inch by 9 inch) and chill until firm. Cut into squares to serve. Makes about 100 1-inch squares.

Procedure Give the infant several cubes of the gelatin and allow him to both explore the properties of the gelatin and also encourage him to eat it.

Easier   Feed the infant the gelatin using a spoon as well as allowing him to explore it.

Harder   Make different-sized cubes, encourage the infant to use a spoon to try to cut the gelatin and also feed himself.

Comment This provides an interesting texture for infants and another opportunity for self-feeding. Be sure to serve pudding as well. It has a consistency thick enough that they can learn to control it with a spoon and thin enough that it is not finger food.

■ Social Awareness

HAND LOTION

Purpose To increase body awareness and sensorimotor integration

Materials Hand lotion in a push-lever dispenser

Procedure Show the toddler the bottle of hand lotion. If he doesn't understand how it works, show him that you need to press the top of the dispenser lever for the lotion to come out. Have him press the lever with one hand and hold his other hand where the lotion comes out. When the lotion is on his hands, encourage him to rub the front and back of them and to get it on all his fingers and even the little areas between his fingers.

Easier   Have the toddler hold his hands where the lotion comes out while you push the lever on the lotion bottle. Then help him rub the lotion in.

Harder   Have one child help another dispense the lotion.

Comment   You can do a similar activity using liquid soap and hand washing.

Note: Be sure they don't eat the lotion or soap.

■ **Social Awareness**

DRESSING BOOK

Purpose   To increase self-help skills and expressive language

Materials   Cardboard picture book about dressing, such as *My clothes* by Sian Tucker

Procedure   Read the book while the child is sitting on your lap or near you. Name and point to the articles of clothing. Ask the child to point to the picture as you name each article and then point to the same article on himself. Discuss how the colors and styles he is wearing are different from those in the book. Comment on the similarities and differences.

Easier   Name the articles of clothing in the book and point to these same items on the child himself.

Harder   Ask the toddler to name the article of clothing shown in the picture and then find that piece of clothing on himself if he is wearing that article of clothing. Then ask him to show you where each part goes. For instance, "Where do the shoes go? Yes, that's right! Shoes go on your feet!"

Comment   Encourage the children to help undress and dress themselves as much as they are able during daily activities. Wait for toddlers to push their arms and legs through their sleeves and pant legs. Encourage them to pull up socks and put on shoes.

Summary

Activities for crawlers and walkers need to stimulate their emerging motor skills and growing curiosity while at the same time supporting their fragile emotional growth. With the ability to move, activities take on a different form—crawlers and walkers can choose what they want to play with if activities are available on the floor or on low shelves that they can reach. Their mobility also brings in new concerns about safety.

Crawlers and walkers need many opportunities to consolidate motor skills and for one-to-one interaction with adults. They are just reaching the end of the sensorimotor period and can be expected to burst into language in the following months.

Application Activities

1. You have a birthday present to buy for an infant's first birthday. His family has few resources. So you want to be sure the toy is both sturdy and has the potential for being played with for a long time. What will you buy and why?

2. Friends are visiting with a 9-month-old and are playing developmentally *inappropriate* games with him. Ones that you might expect an 18-month-old child to do. How would you talk with them about this and what activities and observations would you share with them that are developmentally appropriate?

3. Visit a child-care setting and observe the infants who are 6 to 12 months. Describe the number of activities they have available, the types of activities they use, and how long infants stay at activities. Discuss with providers how they choose activities for each infant and what type of planning they do.

4. Fifteen-month-old Samuel has just mastered walking independently. The problem is that he keeps toddling toward an unsafe area in the classroom and there is concern for his safety. Discuss why he might be doing this. Give two or three suggestions on how to use materials and methods to deal with this situation.

Chapter 18

Planning Programs for Toddlers and Twos: 18 to 36 Months

The changes that occur between 18 and 36 months are dramatic. Toddlers move from tentative walking to running, climbing, jumping, and twirling around. They learn to throw and sometimes catch a ball, to pick up small objects with their fingers, to scribble, and to feed themselves. They learn to dress themselves in easy-to-put-on-and-take-off clothing and most learn to use the toilet.

Toddlers are also beginning to talk. They use two-word phrases, and finally full sentences. By their second year, most children are capable of holding conversations with adults. With the advent of language skills, their play becomes richer and more imaginative. They begin to pretend with toys and materials and imitate the adults in their world, often playing "mommy" or "daddy."

Toddlers begin to understand themselves as separate individuals with rights and privileges. However, they are only beginning to see that others have these same rights. They are more aware of their own feelings than the feelings of others. This is the stage of increasing independence and possessiveness. You'll hear exclamations such as "mine!" "me do it", and "no!" as children try to assert control over their environment. They notice other children in their world and struggle with the building of social play skills, sometimes eager to share toys with another child and sometimes hoarding all toys for themselves.

Toddlers are emotional beings. They are learning to identify, label, and demonstrate their feelings. They display a range of emotions, from pure delight to utter frustration and sadness, from open curiosity and gregariousness to extreme shyness, from happy cooperation to obstinate noncompliance, and from tender loving to hurtful anger.

Physical development has slowed down but language, cognitive, social, and emotional development are in full swing. It is a period of rapid changes and amazing growth. Toddlers need adults who can accept the inconsistencies in their behavior with loving care and serenity.

Toddlers and twos are challenging to adults in very different ways from infants. Some adults feel very comfortable working with toddlers. For these adults it is like being able to watch a person unfold and develop with all of the trials and tribulations that are inherent in the process. Others prefer to work with infants; they like the dependency and the caring of this age more than the budding autonomy of toddlerhood.

Some characteristics of toddlers that make them challenging for adults to deal with:

- Toddlers have a high need to practice their emerging independence. This is often characterized by the word "No!"
- Toddlers show intense emotional swings for no apparent reason.
- Toddlers are messy. They lack adult coordination so they are often clumsy, spill things, and knock things over. They learn by doing.
- Toddlers are active, they appear to be in constant motion, and they don't slow down.
- Toddlers are egocentric. They can only understand their own perspective. This is different than being selfish.
- Toddlers have limited language skills. They can't put their feelings into words.
- Toddlers also have limited knowledge. Adults may make requests of them that are outside their range of knowledge. An adult may ask a toddler to handle a pet gently, and when he handles the pet roughly the adult may decide that he was not responding to the request. In reality he may not know what gentle means and an adult may have to show him how to act gently.
- Toddlers periodically have separation anxiety as their increasing knowledge of object permanence and long-term memory increases. They know their parents exist when they cannot be seen and they miss them.
- Toddlers learn about their world by the grabbing, hitting, biting, and pushing of both animate and inanimate objects. These are *normal* behaviors for toddlers, but they are not pleasant or acceptable behaviors.
- Toddlers have a very limited understanding of time. This makes it difficult for them to wait for things and also difficult to delay gratification. Asking a toddler to wait 10 minutes for lunch does not mean much to him as he has no concept of 10 minutes.

These characteristics make toddlers a particularly challenging group to work with. They have mobility but lack many of the "common sense" attributes that adults typically assume goes with it.

Developmentally Appropriate Practice for Toddlers and Twos

Being aware of your feelings about toddlers and twos is the first step in program planning. It influences how you plan and the role that children and adults play in your program. A next step is to reexamine your philosophy to incorporate toddlers and twos and to compare your feelings with what national "experts" in the field consider important variables. The following guidelines have been adapted from the National Association for the Education of Young Children (Bredekamp, 1987).

- *Program planning should be grounded in developmental theory and designed to teach the whole child. Programming should reflect what we know about child development, learning theory, and family studies.*

Decide on your theoretical approach to teaching and how you will balance and integrate the different theories in your planning. How much does learning unfold through the natural maturation process? And how much is learning dependent on interactions with the environment, paired with the rewards or positive reinforcement that the child receives? The toddler is an active learner who gains knowledge through his action on objects. Toddlers also learn through watching and imitating. Adults and others are models for them and provide scaffolding for learning. Materials influence the toddler's learning so be sure they are not only safe but leave room for his imagination. A toddler's family culture and ethnicity also influences his learning and should be accounted for in program planning.

- *Learning needs to be relevant, meaningful, and contextual.*

Toddlers do not learn in a vacuum. If it is not relevant to them, they are not likely to attend to it. How do you make important concepts relevant to toddlers? Many care providers use themes that are familiar to young children to create a context conducive to learning. By interacting with activities that relate to a theme children develop connections that make learning more meaningful. Program planning often emerges from the child himself as he shows adults what interests him and they respond to this interest.

- *Program planning needs to be realistic, developmentally and age appropriate, reflective of the needs, interests, and abilities of the children being taught.*

Urban programs should be different from rural programs because the interests and knowledge base of young children in these areas are different. When children with disabilities are included, especially if they have fewer skills than others, it is important that the materials they use be both individually and age appropriate. If a child with a disability is 30 months old and his skills are at a 9 month level, the materials he uses should be different from those you would use with a younger child. When children are very young this is a relatively easy accommodation.

Program Areas Must Have Age and Subject Matter Integrity

Good programs for infants, toddlers, and twos are distinctly different from good preschool programs. Caregiving is a major part of the curriculum and the emphasis is on support, consistency, and stability in the environment rather than exciting activities. Relationships are emphasized and active exploration encouraged.

■ *Toddlers have a small repertoire of behaviors but they are continually learning.*

Planning cannot be static. Activities that are appropriate for a young toddler may no longer be appropriate when the same toddler is two and a half. Planning for toddlers centers around the house, grocery store, senses, and so forth.

■ *Programming moves from what children know to the acquisition and consolidation of new knowledge.*

Toddlers work from what they know to what is new and different. They need a broad base of real experiences with real activities before they can role-play and "pretend." This means that they need field trips to the apple orchard and apples to eat. This may be followed up by looking at a picture of an apple in a book and talking about the trip. Toddlers are probably too young to make applesauce and produce a story about their experience as preschoolers might.

■ *Children are active learners who can learn from errors as well as successes.*

Toddlers want to do it themselves. It is rarely useful to them to be told that something is too big to fit. They need to try it themselves. They learn from what does

Learning to take turns and share is difficult for toddlers. They need supportive adults who empathize with their distress while supporting the importance of these skills.

not work as well as from what does. They need to be given a variety of materials as well as variations of the same materials to test out their learning.

- *Programming emphasizes the importance of social interaction.*

Learning is a social experience. This experience varies from observation of another child to the verbal and nonverbal scaffolding of an adult. Social interaction requires toddlers to acknowledge other children and their wants and needs. Programming should include learning about sharing and taking turns and responding empathetically to those troubled.

- *Programs need to be designed to support children's independence and develop competence.*

Toddlers are trying to be their own person. They need to view themselves as competent beings who have some control over their world. Adults need to support this by helping toddlers learn adaptive skills relating to dressing, eating, and toileting, as well as other areas. Toddlers have preferences and, at least some of the time, these need to be acknowledged.

- *Programs need to be safe for children.*

The environment for toddlers needs to be safe both inside and outside so injuries are prevented. Health precautions, such as judicious hand washing, need to be conscientiously followed so that infections are not spread. Toddlers also need to be psychologically safe in a supportive environment.

- *Programming needs to be flexible.*

Although there should always be a written plan for the day and week, the plan should be flexible to accommodate toddlers. The sequence of events should remain constant but the exact timing of them often reflects the day.

Setting Up the Learning Environment for Toddlers and Twos

Do you believe in the "terrible twos?" Do you think that toddlers need to learn to obey adults? Do you believe it is easier to dress toddlers than to wait for them to dress themselves? Do you think that toddlers learn by adults telling them what they need to know? Do you believe toddlers work best in groups? Do you think that all toddlers are pretty much the same? Do you believe that toddlers are really just little preschool children who need to grow up? Your answers to these questions will influence your expectations for toddlers and how you structure the learning environment. You need to make decisions about *how* children learn, *when* learning takes place, and *what* is to be learned.

　　Planning for toddlers and twos is different than planning for infants or even crawlers and walkers. Although developmentally based, planning for toddlers and twos is typically activity related and organized along traditional subject lines. A good toddler curriculum provides toddlers with choices of activities. Toddlers play with what interests them at any given moment and might reject a particular activity an adult has in mind. If given choices, the toddler can choose the toys or materials she wants to play with from the preselected, developmentally appropriate activities the adult has provided. This is most easily accomplished by having low open shelves with safe toys that children can use. Choices also provide toddlers with the opportunity to assert their independence and autonomy. Choosing for oneself builds self-esteem.

Good toddler planning provides activities that are self-paced and open-ended. A toddler is finished playing when he wants to leave an area. Forcing or coaxing a 2-year-old to "finish" his art project only causes frustration for the adult and the toddler. The adult should accept the individual differences in children's interests and attention spans. Some toddlers will paint for 20 minutes, others for 20 seconds. Even the same child might paint for a long time one day and not show any interest in painting the next.

Good planning provides toddlers opportunities to learn through sensory, creative, physical, and problem-solving activities. Activities are the building blocks of planning. As you think about the activities, think about areas of development and how these can be incorporated into your plan in a developmentally appropriate way. One way to do this is to label the different areas such as Language Arts and then break these areas down into smaller components such as speaking, listening, reading, and writing. Then, think about your expectations for toddlers in all of these areas. Space should be allocated for sand and water play, easel painting, creative art, playdough, simple dramatic play, books, blocks, music, language, and manipulative activities. There should be enough materials for children to use without causing undue frustrations; that is, there should be at least duplicates of some toys and enough of other materials so that sharing isn't a problem.

Toddler activities are designed for children who can get to places and can choose what they want to do; use variations for making activities more difficult. The following characteristics would indicate a toddler classroom with good planning and high-quality care:

- Warm, personal contact with adults (verbal and nonverbal) who are active, enthusiastic, and enjoy playing with toddlers

- Activities that are mostly self-directed and a few that are teacher-directed

- A comprehensive program that includes developmentally appropriate activities that meet the interests of individual children as well as the group. Planning includes physical, emotional, social, language, creative, and cognitive areas of development

- A regular and stable schedule that allows for flexibility in meeting the needs of toddlers, including planned times for quiet and active periods

- Consistent rules and discipline techniques that preserve self-esteem

- Plenty of opportunities to play alone, near peers, and with adults

- A safe classroom environment that encourages active play

- Toddlers do things fast; they get hungry fast, angry fast, or tired fast. However, they also bounce back fast. They are not good at waiting, so keep these times to a minimum, and try to respond *fast*.

- Expect toddlers to alternate between dependence and independence. They may be clingy one minute and saying "I want to do it myself" the next. As children try out their independence, it is normal for them to want a cuddly spot to come back to.
- Offer limited choices whenever possible, and then follow through on allowing the toddler to have his choice. For example, "Do you want to go to the bathroom alone or with me?" However, before you offer a choice, be sure that you are willing to live with whatever option the child chooses. (That is, don't simply ask if the child wants to go to the bathroom when it is obvious that he needs to go.)

Content and Process

The issue of whether content or process is most important has been debated for years. The overall conclusion is that they are both necessary and important. In reality, content and process support each other. However, with toddlers the emphasis is mostly on process. If toddlers are going to scribble (process), they need something to scribble about (content). Relevant content that is integrated across a broad range of activities through appropriate themes supports learning. However, a heavy emphasis on content learned through drill and practice is especially inappropriate with very young children.

Child-Initiated and Teacher-Initiated Instruction

The proportion of time allocated to teacher-directed versus child-directed tasks is another area of concern. Toddlers increase their knowledge by acting upon the environment and by reacting and organizing the feedback they receive. They want to know about what interests them at the moment they are interested and this interest may be fleeting. They can learn from adults, but in small doses. Obviously there is a relationship between content and teacher-initiated instruction and process and child-initiated instruction.

Inclusion and Segregation

Inclusion of infants and toddlers with disabilities in regular early care and education settings has a legislative base. However, you need to look at your personal feelings about inclusion. Some feel that *all* children should be included; others feel that only infants and toddlers with mild to moderate disabilities should be in regular early care and education settings. Who do you believe should be included? Once you are clear about your feelings, you can then go to the next stage and look at how such children will be included and the supports necessary for inclusion, if any.

Time Allocation

Think about your day with toddlers, whether it is a half day or a full day. The first broad plans you develop divide the day into segments that have particular purposes. Toddlers and twos, like infants, have a significant amount of time devoted to routines like diapering and toileting, sleeping, and eating. The decisions you make about how you allocate the remainder of the time reflect your philosophy. Look at the length of group times. Are they appropriate for the age/developmental level of the toddlers? Remember that for young toddlers, 3 to 5 minutes is a long time, and for twos, 10 minutes may seem like forever. Most of the time that toddlers are in care should be allocated to support free choices in their activities.

Number of Activities

How many activities are available for toddlers to choose from? Toddlers need choices but not so many that they are overwhelmed. Are all the children participating in art at the same time and making the same project or are some at the easel, some working with playdough, some building with blocks, while others are in the housekeeping play area and still others are at the water table? Toddlers need practice making decisions and choices about what interests them and how long they stay. It is inappropriate to require them to stay a specific amount of time at an activity or to all participate in the same activity with identical outcomes.

Balance of Activities

Look at your activities to see the balance between active and quiet times, and teacher-directed and child-directed activities. Do these match your philosophy? That is, if you believe that toddlers need choices, can they choose among five or so different activities and in a 2-hour span can toddlers make their own choices for at least 75 percent of the time? Look at the complexity of the activities you offer to be sure that toddlers who are gifted as well as those who learn more slowly still have choices.

Theme-Based Planning for Toddlers and Twos

Themes for toddlers are simpler than for older children. They often revolve around the senses. Because toddlers are so present-time and process oriented, adults often do not think about long-range planning or the development of connections among activities (LeeKeenan & Edwards, 1992). However, the thematic approach for toddlers is getting increasing attention. The topics chosen should be interesting, have the potential for varied activities, and have cognitive integrity (LeeKeenan & Edwards, 1992). Themes can be simple but they should support contextual learning for toddlers. Share information about themes with parents so they can follow up on activities at home to support and expand what toddlers are learning.

Start with the toddler at the center. After all, he is the focus and his characteristics will influence all of the choices you make. First choose a theme to help you

---

Figure 18.1	**Developing a Theme**

It is useful to visually remind yourself of all of the planning areas with a chart such as this. It also helps to focus on the child himself as the center of all planning.

Theme (Idea)

Language Arts
Speaking
Listening
Reading
Writing

Discovery
Mathematics
Science

TODDLER

Sensorimotor
Large Motor
Small Motor
Sensorimotor Integration

Creative Arts
Art
Music
Creative Movement
Dramatic Play

Social Awareness
Social Studies
Health and Safety
Self-Help
Inclusion

---

organize your ideas, then choose activities that support the theme. Themes for toddlers are simple, concrete, and reflect their experiences in the world. Such themes would include food, my body, my senses, at home, on the farm (if they know about farms), and so on. They are too young for dinosaurs, colors, and the sea shore unless they happen to live there. Graphically, the planning process looks something like Figures 18.1 and 18.2.

Developmentally Appropriate Planning for Toddlers and Twos

It is important to include at least one activity from each of the planning areas each day. Because toddlers need choices, it is even better to include more than one if you can support this. Some themes favor one area over another, so be sure to vary your themes enough to have a well-rounded program.

Language Arts

Toddlers need opportunities to both talk to adults and to listen to adults talking to them. They need exposure to reading and writing readiness activities. In addition to the naturally occurring occasions when language is used, there need to be special times during the day when language arts activities are highlighted. Although the four main aspects of language arts (speaking, listening, reading,

Figure 18.2	Thematic Plan: Food

Having a theme makes it easier to decide how to focus planning areas and to integrate information in a way that provides a holistic experience for toddlers and twos with built-in variation and repetition.

Theme: Food

Language Arts

Name fruits and vegetables
Books about food
Record: Raffi—"The Corner Grocery Store"
Finger Play: Way up High in an Apple Tree

Discovery

Make applesauce
Compare whole fruits/
  vegetables with cut-up
  ones

TODDLER

Sensorimotor

Place laminated pictures of food in a tub
Feel and discuss texture of plush/
  plastic fruits and vegetables
Fruit and vegetable puzzles

Creative Arts

Set up dramatic play area as a kitchen
Provide dishes, utensils, basin, water, etc.
  and fruits and vegetables
Make Kool Aid playdough
Fingerpaint with pudding

Social Awareness

Introduce some ethnic food
Talk about what toddlers had for breakfast
Have cut up fruits and vegetables for snack

Potential field trips: Grocery store, orchard or farm (depending on the season), or garden

Vocabulary Words

fruit	milk	grape	lettuce	peel
food	lemon	melon	bread	cut
cookie	pour	potato	juice	core
apple	cracker	peas	vegetable	seeds
orange	cookie	corn	wash	color words
eat	banana	tomatoes	kiwi	eggplant

and writing) can be differentiated, overall program planning would treat them as interrelated and interdependent.

Speaking

Toddlers understand the meaning of many words before they are able to actually speak them. Helping toddlers build an expressive vocabulary is an important goal. Toddler conversations are not the same as adult conversations, so you will need to continue to rely on situational cues for the meanings of toddlers' words. Different toddlers develop language skills at different rates. Some are early talkers and some aren't. Almost all toddlers have problems pronouncing certain sounds or words. Developmentally, children cannot physically make all the sounds necessary for the English language until about age 6 or 7.

Toddlers not only need experience talking, they need experiences to talk about. Offer toddlers a wide range of experiences and talk with them during and following these experiences. Experiences as simple as a stroll around the block, a trip to the grocery store, or looking at and touching a visiting pet, are very important. Point out the flowers you pass on your walk, name different fruits as you place them in the grocery cart, and label the kitten's fur as "fluffy" while the children pet her.

Some ways of supporting language development are:

- Model good language skills when you talk with children.
- If a toddler mispronounces a word, repeat the word correctly in your next sentence. For example, if she says, "Here's a poon," you might say "Oh, you found the *spoon.*"
- When giving toddlers a choice, encourage them to tell you which one they want or to describe what they want, not to just say "yes" or "no."
- Keep sentences simple, but refrain from using the "motherese" that adults use with infants.
- Listen to what toddlers say. Having someone listen encourages their talking.
- Provide materials that encourage talking: toy telephones, puppets, cardboard books.
- Encourage toddlers to label their own body parts and to point to and then name these parts on dolls. Talk with children about the function of these parts.
- Toddlers learn best from concrete experiences. They learn more about the concept of "apple" when they can see, touch, taste, and smell a real apple. However, they need an adult to support their apple experience with language telling them the apple is red, it is crunchy to bite, and it tastes tart.
- Expand concrete experiences by using a variety of objects (if the objects are apples use Granny Smith, Golden Delicious, and Macintosh apples). Be sure to label the apples and their characteristics (color, taste, and shape). But don't expect them to remember the labels. Allow toddlers to see, touch, smell, and eat the apples.
- Field trips offer many opportunities for toddlers to have first-hand experiences with objects.
- Say or read nursery rhymes, use simple fingerplays, and play easy rhyming games.

Expansion and extension are two techniques that encourage toddlers to use more complex language structures. Expansion is the process of extracting the meaning of a toddler's utterance and putting it into a more complex form. For a toddler using telegraphic speech such as "Me go," the expansion might be "Where do you want to go?" or "Are you ready to go now?" The objective is to provide a language model, not just an answer that says "OK".

Extension involves putting the toddler's statement in a broader context; that is, extending the meaning of the phrase. If the toddler says "Me go out," you might respond, "If you want to go outside you need to get your coat on." Using these techniques is particularly effective as the toddler has initiated the "conversation" and is prepared to listen to the response as it is meaningful to him.

Listening

We rarely think about listening as a skill. It is obvious that children learn to speak and must be taught to read and write, but we often think that children come already knowing how to listen. Listening is a complex component of learning. It involves hearing and processing that allows for auditory identification and discrimination of sounds. Then what is heard must be stored in either short- or long-term memory. As with speaking, toddlers are most likely to develop good listening skills if you are a good model. When you are listening to a toddler, LISTEN. If you always repeat what you say, toddlers learn NOT to listen the first time around.

Despite the need to prepare toddlers to listen, an adult's immediate goal is often to have toddlers be quiet so she can speak. Additionally, we rarely think of the skills involved in listening. One of the questions we as adults must consider is "How much of what we say do toddlers find worth listening to?" Would we be willing to sit spellbound for several hours each day listening to boring information? For toddlers to practice good listening skills, they need something stimulating to listen to that lasts for a very short period of time.

Just as with other areas, it is helpful to develop guidelines for listening.

- Use a signal to focus toddlers' attention on listening, such as a chord played on the piano, a particular fingerplay, or flicking the lights.
- Develop simple rules about listening to others, taking turns speaking, not interrupting others, raising your hand before speaking in group time, and so on.
- You might have some speaking rules that relate to listening, such as talking loud enough to be heard and speaking clearly. You can't expect toddlers to listen when it is not possible to hear.
- Fingerplays can help prepare toddlers for listening by zipping their mouths closed, or having them "put on their listening cap."
- It is helpful to rephrase what you say to a toddler if he appears not to understand. Requesting a child to "Tell me in different words," is useful if you don't understand what a toddler is saying to you. This way both you and the child have a second chance to process the information.

Good listening skills allow toddlers to receive more useful information from their environment.

Reading

Programs specifically aimed at helping toddlers become good readers are controversial. Indeed, programs for toddlers which use an academic approach, such as letter and word flash cards, have been criticized for placing undue pressures on them and not letting them "be children" and learning through play experiences. It is, however, very appropriate to work with toddlers to set the stage for reading.

Have a daily time for reading aloud. Young toddlers enjoy sitting on your lap in a rocking chair as you slowly turn the pages in a book and name pictures on

Toddlers particularly enjoy "class" books where each child has a page about her family. This is a way of sharing information and also a support for children who miss their families.

the pages. The close physical contact provided here is often as important as the book itself. Independently, toddlers may chew on books, attempt to turn the pages, screech and slap pages, or carry books with them as they toddle about. Even such playful manipulations of books provide positive early experiences which enhance learning language. Twos can enjoy books in small groups of two or three.

- Encourage toddlers to talk about the pictures in their books.
- If there are words, they should be simple and brief.
- Expect toddlers to bring their favorite book to you to be looked at or read again and again. They like the repetition and the predictability this brings as they are trying to master their environment.
- Interpret illustrations that lend themselves to a game of hide and seek; that is, familiar objects that are repeated on several pages (a mouse hiding on each page that must be discovered) intrigue older toddlers.
- Twos enjoy simple stories about "calamities," such as making a mess, breaking something, or getting dirty.
- During or after reading a story, ask toddlers what they think about the story. Be aware that toddlers might have some unusual ideas!
- Books that can be manipulated, such as "touch-me" books, dress-up books with zippers, scratch-and-sniff books, and squeeze-and-squeak books add variety.

Writing

In the area of writing, the major objectives are to introduce toddlers to the concept of a written language, and for them to understand that there is a connection between written and spoken language. There is no expectation that children this age will write. However, they can learn from an early age that writing is different from creative media.

- Provide writing materials for toddlers such as large crayons and markers. They love coloring and drawing on blank paper.
- Introduce words informally as you write the toddler's name on his paper (Say something like, "This says Inti" each time you write his name).
- As children begin to label their drawings, for instance calling their scribbles a "ball," write the label on the paper, whether or not it looks anything like what they say it is. This will help toddlers make the connection between spoken and written words.

Discovery

Toddlers need to learn about the world they live in. They need many real-life experiences to serve as a foundation for scientific and logical mathematical reasoning. For toddlers to discover these relationships and ideas they need to be actively engaged with their environment. They must have a variety of experiences from which they can abstract ideas. Most things fascinate toddlers and twos—from rain to how the toilet flushes, and the garbage truck to the bug that crawled in. All of these present learning opportunities.

Mathematics

There is no expectation that toddlers will learn complex math skills, but rather, that they will be aware of numbers and the concept of counting. With increasing age, toddlers can make size distinctions between what is big and little, so they can put large pegs in pegboards as adults count them. They can sing counting songs. They may be able to "count" but it is unlikely that they will truly have number concepts at this age. They have some understanding of different shapes and can do simple (3 piece) form boards and puzzles.

Blocks. Blocks are one of the most versatile materials to help young children understand mathematical concepts. Blocks can be used in a variety of ways by children of varying ages. Infants may enjoy reaching for and grasping blocks, young toddlers will like knocking down the towers you build, and older toddlers and twos will enjoy building their own constructions. Both unit blocks and cardboard blocks are useful for toddlers.

- Toddlers learn about cause-and-effect relationships by knocking down block towers. They come to understand that when they hit the tower with their hand, the tower falls and makes a loud sound. They may want you to build towers over and over again as they test to see if the same thing happens each time.

- Twos may enjoy matching blocks to help them gain concepts of shape and size. Give the toddler two blocks of vastly different sizes and have two blocks that match the child's for yourself. Hold up one block and say, "Show me one just like this." As the child is successful, gradually make the task more difficult by using blocks which are closer to each other in size.

- Support toddlers in finding answers to their own problems as much as possible. Let them figure out why their building fell over and how to prevent it happening again. You might ask a good question that gets them thinking on the right track.

- Sometimes simple open-ended statements such as, "I wonder why that happened", to give toddlers the opportunity to think and respond without putting them on the spot.

- Blocks can be used to encourage pretend play with twos. Start initially by using one block to represent an object such as a car or a telephone receiver. Push the "block car" across the floor and say "beep-beep." You can gradually support twos in building more complex structures. You can also provide accessories, such as cars, animals, or people, to extend the play.

- Store blocks in groups by size and shape on a low open shelf. This will give toddlers a chance to practice shape and size sorting as they help clean up.

Science

Science for toddlers involves investigating the world they live in. The process of finding answers is more important than the answers themselves. It is the basis for a way of thinking. For children this age, science is informal, nondirected, free investigation by the toddler. The adult's role is to plan an intriguing environment that invites exploration.

Some adults may think the idea of planning science activities for toddlers is a little farfetched. But science activities are easy to plan and carry out. Science for toddlers includes experiences learning about how plants grow, how animals grow and change, how our own bodies grow and develop, different kinds of weather, foods we eat, how colors mix, and the properties of water.

- Explore the outdoors with toddlers during different seasons or weather conditions. Being outside regularly helps children learn about nature and the environment in which they live. It provides both freedom and a challenge to understand nature.

- Take simple field trips to a park or wooded area to learn about new plant growth, rocks, old plants or trees, possibly even about animals such as rabbits or squirrels, and definitely about insects and spiders. Continue outdoor science experiences inside.

- Let the toddlers plant seeds in individual cups (beans are easy to handle and grow fast) and watch the changes that occur as the plants grow. Or let them help plant a garden patch in the play yard.

- Catch insects or spiders and let toddlers watch them for a day or two. Then have a "born free" time to return the insect to its natural habitat.

- Purchase an ant farm. Toddlers are fascinated by the busy nature of ants.
- Bring back different rocks and set them around your garden or play area. Encourage the toddlers to feel the different textures and talk about the different colors and weights of the rocks. (Also be sure there are rules about not throwing rocks.)
- Schedule a field trip to pick up litter in your neighborhood or surrounding area. It's a good lifetime learning experience and also good exercise. Be sure to have the children wear rubber gloves when they are picking up the litter.
- Use a portable, cordless hand-mixer for cooking/baking with toddlers. You can mix anywhere (low table, on the floor on a tray, outside, and so on) and not have to worry about a cord. Plus there's only one beater to worry about! If the batter isn't too thick, have toddlers take turns mixing with a wooden spoon. Remember, however, that taking turns is not their strength.

Sensorimotor Activities

Children learn about their world through their senses. Infants and young toddlers often use their mouth to learn about their environment. As children get older, they more frequently use their hands. One of the areas of greatest concentration of sensory (tactile or touch) receptors on the human body is the hands. These sensory receptors give the child a great deal of information about his world and how to interact with it. For example, if something is solid and smooth (a firm hug or a smooth toy), the child generally gets a pleasurable feeling. Some sensations, such as light touch (fingerpaint or tickling) may feel uncomfortable and the child may avoid them.

Many sensory experiences can come from everyday activities, such as having the toddler play on different play surfaces (grass, linoleum, carpet, quilt) and giving him different-textured objects with which to play. Messy play activities provide much tactile sensory stimulation, and thus are recommended as a regular part of a toddler's activities. Mud, finger paint, sand, water and playdough are a few examples of sensory play materials that provide tactile experiences important for the overall development of each child.

Large Motor

Toddlers need space and objects to push, pull, carry, and lift. This develops strength in the trunk area. They need safe places to slide and swing. Turn on the music and encourage toddlers to dance either alone or together. This is not ballet, this is moving! Use records that encourage children to exercise, especially when you cannot go outside.

Outside is the ideal place to practice large-motor skills. Many people think that it is a good idea to take young children outside to play even when it is cold. There is more space for active gross-motor play and a different place to play helps keep a toddler's interest. A variety of outside play activities will keep up not only the children's interest and learning, but also your own. It is also a way to purposefully use up some of that exuberant toddler energy. Except for playing in the snow, cold-weather toddler activities are similar to what you might plan for warmer weather.

- Play a game of "chase" with toddlers outside. Play with them as they run off and you slowly chase after them. If they get away, they will probably giggle a lot and end up feeling quite successful. For variation have them chase and "catch" the adult.
- Take walks in the neighborhood; talk about seasonal changes.
- Encourage toddlers to play in the snow. Help toddlers collect some clean snow in a large bowl or saucepan and bring it inside. Let them feel, poke, mold, and watch it slowly melt. Place bowls of snow on highchair trays, on a plastic-covered table, or on an old shower curtain on the floor. If it is clean, let them taste it. You can also mix Kool Aid crystals with it and let them try that.

Sensorimotor Integration

All the various sensory experiences contribute to the way in which the child interacts with his world. Providing sensory experiences contributes to the development of fine-motor skills of toddlers (such as picking up and placing toys and objects) as well as twos (including mastering puzzles, scribbling, and interlocking toys).

- Toddlers enjoy playing in a container of water, a wading pool for several children, or a dish pan for one child. Add a few inches of water and plastic cups and a tablespoon, or a few floating and sinking items such as a cork, a stone, styrofoam pieces, a clothespin, and so on.
- Toddlers also enjoy painting with water. On a warm day, fill a couple of buckets with water and add a couple of old paintbrushes. The children can harmlessly "paint" outside walls, sidewalks, fences, and so on.
- Toddlers enjoy sand play. You can use the same container for sand play that you use for water play. Add cups, spoons, cars, and wooden or plastic people. You can add a little water to the sand to keep the dust down, and it also makes it firm to mold. Watch that toddlers don't eat the sand.
- Good old-fashioned mud play is a dirty but interesting sensory experience. If you have a corner where there is dirt to dig, add some water to make mud. On warm days, strip toddlers down to diapers or shorts and let them play. Mud washes off easily with soap and water! Be sure to use sun block before they go outside.
- Playdough is always good to have on hand. Whatever the children's ages and skill levels, they can squash, roll, pat, pinch, or shape playdough. Add cookie cutters and popsicle sticks (children use these to cut). Playdough is available commercially or you can make it yourself from one of the many different recipes (see Chapter 19, Variations on Playdough). If you make it yourself, it is not a problem if children taste it, and they can even participate in making it.

Small Motor

Small- or fine-motor development involves the toddler's ability to use the small muscles of the arms, hands, and fingers for reaching, grasping, and manipulating objects. With toddlers a real emphasis in the small-motor area is adaptive or self-help skills such as dressing and undressing, toileting, washing and drying hands, and even cleaning up. The ability to care for oneself is an important building block in developing independence and self-esteem.

Muscle and joint stability is a prerequisite for fine-motor control. It is difficult for toddlers to perform fine-motor tasks such as buttoning without the necessary trunk stability. Developmentally, children need to progress through early patterns of grasping (whole hand) to voluntarily releasing before "tools" are useful. Developing strength in the whole-hand grasp is done through such activities as hanging from bars and tree limbs and tug of war.

Fine grasp involves the use of the fingers independently and the ability to use the thumb and index finger together to pick up small objects. Experiences with finger foods, large crayons, and large wooden beads facilitate the development of these skills. Toddlers need to develop motor-planning skills to precisely pick up and release these objects when finished.

- Give toddlers practice with dressing skills such as zipping and buttoning. Use dolls, books, or dressing frames designed for this purpose. Start with big buttons and zippers.

- Encourage toddlers to dress up in oversized clothes that are easy to take on and off.

Creative Arts

Creativity is a process of thinking, acting, or making something that is new or different. It does not mean that the person has to be the first to produce or do something, but rather that it is a new experience for the particular person. For example, finger painting is not new, but it can be a creative experience for a young toddler as he explores the texture and qualities of finger paint. And it can be a creative experience for an older toddler as she experiments with new ways to apply the paint to the paper. These toddlers will deal with fingerpaint very differently, but each can use it in a creative capacity.

Creativity helps to develop a good self-concept. It encourages children to think, to express their own ideas, and to find alternative solutions to problems. It supports children in learning to take risks to develop new skills. Support toddler creativity in your programming.

Creative experiences are usually unstructured opportunities for exploration. They are typically process oriented at this age. So they present the opportunity for learning about oneself as well as the materials involved. Toddlers need to be supported and admired for their creative activities. By objective standards, the products are rarely good; the importance, however, lies in developing a creative style of thinking. Toddlers need the opportunity to freely explore graphic media, move to music and learn simple songs, and play through familiar roles.

Art

Toddlers progress through several predictable developmental stages as they interact with art materials. By about 2½, toddlers begin more refined scribbling that includes repetitive patterns and circles. At some point, children discover the connection between their movements and the marks on the paper. They are now in control. The product may not look different, but the experience is different for the toddler. Control is motivating. It is also generalized. If they know they made a mark on the page, they also know their finger made the hole in the dough. Art now becomes a different experience for children. Although children differ, this usually happens around age 3. Finally, about 3 years, they begin to name their scribbles, even though they may not look like anything to others. By 3, children have the fine-motor skills and eye-hand coordination for more purposeful drawing.

Art for toddlers is messy, fun, free exploration with different materials. It's putting paint on paper, at the easel, or table. It's watching paint drip from a squeeze bottle. It's finger/hand painting. It's squishing paint-filled sponges in one's hands. It's rolling and pounding playdough. It's gluing scraps of paper, cloth or macaroni on paper. It's coloring/scribbling with crayons, chalk or water-based markers.

Art is not a toddler watching the teacher glue precut pictures onto a piece of paper. It's not making something look exactly like everyone else's or the teacher's. It is not crayoning within the lines of a coloring book or ditto. And it's not a one adult-one child activity. Art isn't the nice picture the child takes home for mom and dad; it's the experience the child has in making the product, whatever it looks like. There may not even be a product!

Through interacting with art materials and participating in art activities toddlers:

- Learn how to create something from "raw" materials
- Explore materials with their senses
- Learn different ways to express thoughts and ideas
- Learn to make decisions
- Develop the ability to share materials and appreciate others' work
- Can develop a positive self-concept
- Develop and refine fine-motor and cognitive skills.

Because art for toddlers is messy, it is important to plan for that aspect. Plan to set out a large oil-cloth tablecloth on the floor or cover a child-sized table with newspaper. Protect children's clothes with an art smock (old adult-sized shirts work fine).

The adult role is to ask toddlers to describe what they are making, or the adult can give a verbal description of what the child is doing, if she is too young to talk. It is rarely wise to ask what something "is." Comments should support the process, not the end product.

- Provide opportunities to paint, draw, glue, color, or mold dough each day. Do *not* provide a model for toddlers to copy.

- Keep art activities for creative arts; teach colors or match them at other times.

- Show interest in what toddlers are doing and display all original art work regardless of quality.

- Play with children to encourage their participation. As you play, model the process, not the product; that is, squeeze the dough, roll it, pound it, break it up into smaller pieces, but don't make a smiley face out of it.

- Use your language to support creative thinking. Instead of "What did you make?", say "Tell me about your picture." Instead of giving a direct answer to every question, occasionally ask "What do you think might happen?" Ask *why* and *how* questions, "Why do you think that happened?" or "How did you make that?"

- Give toddlers a variety of materials to explore (for example, if gluing, give toddlers torn paper, macaroni, wood chips, beans, and so on).

Art for toddlers is messy.

- Use variations of a single media. Have toddlers paint using large brushes, rollers, sponges, deodorant bottles filled with paint, and so on. Vary texture by adding sand to tempera paint. Paint on a table or easel.

- Have toddlers fingerpaint with shaving cream and dry tempera paint or pudding. Do this directly on a table and then have them help clean up (Be sure to plan enough time for the clean-up and have enough adult supervision). Because of the probability of it going into their mouth, consider how edible the fingerpaint is.

- Make playdough using a variety of different recipes that influence the consistency and texture of the dough (an edible variety is recommended). For twos add props such as cookie cutters and popsicle sticks.

Music

Toddlers respond to the mood of music. Quiet singing and rocking sets the tone for sleep whereas a fast drum beat encourages movement. Toddlers can use tools to produce sound. They can hit a xylophone with a mallet or a piano with their fingers. The toddler experiments with sound by hitting different instruments with different objects to discover different sounds. By about 18 months toddlers enjoy music and dancing. By 2 years they can learn simple songs and want to sing them again and again. They like simple songs and nursery rhymes that you can sing or chant together. Young children enjoy and learn from a variety of musical experiences. They learn new words, develop memory skills as they recall songs or parts of songs, and develop a sense of rhythm as they sing and listen to music.

- Use musical cues as a signaling system to let toddlers know it is time to move to another activity.

- Play prerecorded music at a variety of times throughout the day. Children's songs will be enjoyed, but classical or popular tunes may be appreciated as well. Fit the music to the activity. Play quiet, relaxing music at nap time, and louder, bouncier music on a rainy day for dancing when toddlers can't go outside.

- Help toddlers make simple instruments which they can "play" while you sing or play prerecorded music. Oatmeal boxes can be painted or covered with construction paper and decorated to make a drum. Shakers can be made from a number of scrap materials including "L'eggs eggs" or empty film containers which can be filled with dried beans and securely fastened with heavy tape. Even the youngest toddlers enjoy pounding on a drum or shaking a shaker.

- Use finger plays to teach toddlers language skills, including listening, remembering, sequencing, and saying words to songs, as well as to increase sensorimotor integration.

- Use music to teach toddlers social skills. Since they usually participate in songs and finger plays with at least one other child, they learn to pay attention to something that interests them and to imitate actions of adults and other children.

Creative Movement

As movement comes more under the toddlers' control, they begin to experiment. About age 2 they like songs with motions and moving to music. They do, however, need frequent breaks; they are not up to prolonged periods of strenuous movement. While movements are still being mastered, toddlers are not as free to be creative.

Creative movement is a personal statement about one's inner self. This is what differentiates it from functional movement which usually has a practical purpose. Because it is a personal statement, there is no right or wrong way to move. It is important not to judge movement as being silly or awkward. All movements should be seen as equally appropriate for boys and girls. Avoid demonstrating movements, as the toddlers may decide that they must do what you do and then it is no longer creative movement. Music is often used to set the tone for movement. Combine music and movement with group games like the "Hokey Pokey" or "Ring around the Rosie" or by singing songs with motions like "If you're happy and you know it." Ask the children for input into movement types of activities.

Dramatic Play

Young toddlers use dramatic play to try out and consolidate adult roles with which they are most familiar. These are usually roles that revolve around the home. Child care, cleaning, and cooking are typical "housekeeping" themes. Toddlers also play through situations that are meaningful to them. One can often learn about the toddlers' feelings by watching and listening to their play. Toddlers as young as 18 months should have dramatic-play experiences. By adding a few props, and perhaps initiating the play, adults can provide toddlers with many rewarding dramatic-play activities. Between 2 and 3, toddlers expand their use of mental representations and symbolic thought. Words become signifiers of objects and events. Toddlers can classify based on function. This allows their play to be more creative. They can "pretend."

Toddlers learn from watching others and then trying activities out on their own. They may show their first signs of pretend play by moving a spoon around a bowl in imitation of daddy cooking or by pretending to feed a doll or a stuffed animal. Encourage these behaviors. If toddlers are not yet doing any pretend play, but show an interest in dolls, stuffed animals, or other possible pretend toys, encourage the toddler to imitate you. Say, "I'm combing" as you pretend to comb the doll's hair, and then say "Now you do it." Help the toddler by gently guiding her hand, if the child doesn't follow through on her own (a physical prompt). Praise any attempts the toddler makes. However, if she doesn't seem interested, she may not yet be at that developmental level and you may need to come back to pretend activities at a later point. Both boys and girls need time to pretend. Boys need chances to feed dolls and cook and girls need chances to push trucks and fire engines as well as having opportunities to practice the more traditional roles. If you show acceptance of boys pretending to cook and girls pretending to drive trucks at a young age, toddlers will grow up with fewer limitations on their future roles.

One way toddlers learn to be social is to imitate or "try on" the actions of adults. That's why their favorite roles are the people they know best. Watching toddlers at pretend play is true pleasure for adults. Sometimes they imitate "mommy," "daddy," or "teacher" more realistically than we'd like. It's interesting to watch, but what do toddlers learn from pretend or dramatic play? Toddlers rarely pretend to be superheroes or "good guys/bad guys" until they are close to 3 years old. Toddlers need to experience events or situations in order to understand them. Since most toddlers experience mommy making dinner or daddy doing the dishes, these events are often the toddler's first dramatic play activities.

Toddlers can learn how to interact with others through dramatic play. Many toddlers have a difficult time playing with peers. With practice and maturation they begin to learn to share, communicate, and negotiate. In dramatic play activities, toddlers have to resolve conflicts over who is going to play mommy (or daddy, big sister, baby), what each role means—just do what they do—and what the general theme behind the play situation is.

Dramatic play activities increase language skills. Toddlers must talk to resolve conflicts constructively in order for play to continue. Dramatic play builds cognitive skills as toddlers learn how different people do things. One child's mother may work outside the home, so part of her "mommy" role includes going to the office and being the boss. Another child's mother may work in a fast food restaurant, so this presents a different role of the working mother. Another child's mother may not work outside the home, so that child's "mommy" role may be different. Through dramatic play, each child gets to learn about different roles that mothers may have.

Dramatic play is also a safe way for children to express negative feelings. It's not uncommon (or harmful) for a toddler who has a new baby brother or sister to hit the baby dolls because "they are bad." Toddlers can release their anger, hurt, or jealousy on inanimate objects rather than hurting the real source of their feelings. Here are some suggestions for encouraging dramatic play with toddlers:

- Set up the dramatic play area as a housekeeping arrangement. Include a play kitchen set (stove/refrigerator), child-sized table and chairs, play dishes and pots, and empty food boxes. (Vary by adding play cleaning supplies or add playdough and turn it into a bakery.) Provide a child-sized broom and dish pan and let toddlers help you when you sweep. Expect that they will spread the dirt around at first rather than gather it together, but, with practice, they will get the idea!

- Put a grocery store in the dramatic play area. Collect lots of empty food containers, paper bags, a cash register, baskets, and shelves for stocking the food. Parents are often willing to bring in empty containers.

- Make the dramatic play area into a shoe store. Collect old pairs of shoes from parents (adult sized). Add shelves for displaying, make a pretend foot-size measure and set up child-sized chairs for children who are customers. Add shoe boxes and bags.

- Try turning the dramatic play area into a nursery. Provide baby dolls, doll clothes, cribs (use cardboard boxes), bottles, blankets, a dish pan and cloth for the baby's bath, empty powder containers, and diapers.

Social Awareness

Toddlers who feel good about themselves can accept themselves as they are. They can also accept others, for social awareness involves the child's growth as a member of a group. To be part of the group, toddlers must learn to share materials, take turns, listen at appropriate times, work independently, and also join the group.

With increasing age, self-awareness grows. Twos can tell you their name, their gender, the members of their family, and their ethnic background. They learn where they live. They also become aware of ways in which they are similar to and different from others. They become aware of their strengths and limitations. They learn about themselves by the way others respond to them.

Social Studies

Toddlers gradually become aware of their near environment, their home and school setting, and then the community in which they live. They do this by taking short field trips, going to the grocery store, and visiting others. They see people who look different than they do. They see adults performing many different tasks. Social studies helps toddlers learn about the complexities of their environment.

One aspect of social awareness for toddlers is learning about their own cultural and ethnic background. Early childhood programs can consciously promote an awareness of the positive aspects and similarities of all individuals regardless of race, ethnicity, gender, or disability. Toddlers need to learn about who they are and who their friends are. They need opportunities to explore similarities and differences with the goal of learning mutual respect and cooperation.

Toddlers don't need multicultural "lessons." They do need the opportunity to interact with friends and adults from different backgrounds, to be exposed to good role models, and to feel good about themselves as human beings. Good programs incorporate many of the following ideas.

- Recognize and treat each toddler as a special person. Acknowledge cultural differences and discuss them as an ongoing normal integrated part of the day. Although not supporting the "holiday curriculum," take advantage of different celebrations to learn about different customs. Invite parents to come and share something special, such as a special food, song, decoration, or even clothing.

- Include books in your library that have pictures of young children of different ethnic backgrounds and depict stories about different cultures.

- Invite parents to share their cultural heritage with the children. This may be through traditional dress or simply a sample of ethnic foods.

- Talk with toddlers about ways in which they are similar to others, as well as about characteristics that make them unique. Celebrate each child's specialness.

- Pair toddlers with a "new friend" to accomplish a task during a small-group activity. This expands friendship patterns and allows you to include all children.

Health and Safety

Health and safety are both matters of concern and areas of study. As toddlers become aware of what it means to be healthy and they develop the knowledge and vocabulary to describe where they hurt, there is less likelihood of undetected illness. When they learn to recognize signs of danger and act appropriately, the environment will be safer for them. Only healthy toddlers who feel safe and secure can participate fully in early childhood programs.

As toddlers learn to label their body parts and become more aware of their body, they can take a more active role in their health care. This is also a time when toddlers are curious about their own bodies and those of others. You may need to discuss "good" touch and "bad" touch. Toddlers need to know that when touch makes them feel uncomfortable they should talk to an adult that they trust. Toddlers can learn health routines early, such as washing their hands before eating and after toileting. They can learn about appropriate clothing for different types of weather and about good nutrition.

- Point out the differences between warm weather and cold weather clothing as children are dressing to go outside or as they come in, to help toddlers learn the relationship between clothing and weather.

- Teach toddlers basic health practices as part of daily routines (such as washing their hands after toileting and before snack).

- Choose healthy snacks for toddlers such as raw vegetables, cut-up or whole fresh fruit, whole-grain bread, rice cakes, yogurt, cheese cubes, or peanut butter spread on bread, apples, bananas, or rice cakes.

- Plan for toddlers to help prepare their snacks occasionally. They are often willing to try new foods that they have helped prepare.

Self-Help

Adaptive or self-help skills for toddlers are a legitimate part of the curriculum and need time allocated for them. Dressing and undressing, toileting, washing, and cleaning up all involve the use of fine-motor skills, sensorimotor integration, and motor planning and sequencing. These skills also support autonomy and self-esteem. While taking off and putting on clothes, especially during the winter, can easily become drudgery, think of ways you can make it a learning experience.

- Analyze tasks and then break tasks down into their component parts. Use backward chaining to teach adaptive skills. That is, if you were teaching a toddler to wash his hands, the FIRST thing you would teach him would be to hang up the towel or throw the paper towel away. Then he would dry his hand and deal with the towel, then turn off the water, and so on. He would get the satisfaction of completing the task successfully without being required to do the entire task from the beginning.

- Putting on coats is difficult for toddlers. Teacher "lore" suggests that the easiest but not most conventional method is as follows:

  1. Place the toddler's coat on the floor with the inside facing up and the collar or hood by the toddler's feet.

2. Have the toddler put both arms partially in the sleeves.

3. Then assist the toddler in flipping the jacket over her head, while her arms stay partially in the sleeves.

4. Slip arms into sleeves the rest of the way, help start the zipper for her if necessary or assist with buttoning and she's ready!

- Routinely involve toddlers in clean-up. When a toddler spills some milk, offer the child a sponge to assist you in wiping it up.
- Build a sense of independence as toddlers become increasingly capable of dressing themselves and capable of other self-help tasks.
- Sneak in cognitive skills during dressing by encouraging toddlers to find their own clothing and match pairs of mittens, boots, and scarf and hat sets.
- Develop language skills as you describe what you or they are doing ("Erin, look how you put your legs in your snowsuit!").
- Help develop social and emotional skills, as you give praise and encouragement with each toddler's effort. This, in turn, will make the toddler feel good about herself.

Taking a few extra minutes to encourage children to help with dressing and undressing and other self-help skills will make the experience more pleasurable and relaxing for all. Thinking about self-help skills in relationship to other areas of development may make you feel more comfortable about it as part of the curriculum for toddlers.

Including Toddlers and Twos with Disabilities

As toddlers become aware of the ways in which they are different from each other, it is the skill of a sensitive teacher that determines the long-term outcome of this awareness. Children look to you as a model. Examine your feelings about including young children with disabilities in your early childhood program. Also check out your feelings about having children from different ethnic and racial backgrounds, and your expectations based on gender, to discover if you have personal values that might make working with some children difficult.

If you pity toddlers with disabilities or are overprotective or condescending toward them, the other children will react the same way. If you celebrate only holidays that a majority of the children share, then those who have different beliefs may feel excluded. If you always choose boys to go to the block area and expect girls to use the dramatic-play area, you are supporting stereotypic gender differences. Awareness is important for *all* children. Toddlers are egocentric. They need support in viewing events from another's perspective.

Adults can successfully facilitate the inclusion of toddlers with disabilities into their programs if they plan to meet the individual needs of all the children in their group. Sometimes special toys or materials will be needed to allow the toddler with a disability the opportunity to learn a new skill. Often, the special toys can be used by other children in the program. By including young children with disabilities in a setting there is potential gain for all children in the classroom. Some suggestions for including toddlers with disabilities are:

- Provide an atmosphere where issues about race, gender, and disability can be freely discussed. Young children are very aware of these differences. Twos learn respect and caring for others who are different from themselves by modeling adults' interactions with the child.

- Support diversity in your classroom through activities, materials, and program planning. Toddlers learn about differences by first-hand experience. If a toddler wears braces, the other children may want to try wearing braces. Under supervision and with the support of a physical therapist who has access to supplies such as crutches, braces, walkers, and wheelchairs, this is a great idea. Toddlers generally dislike blindfolds, so it is probably unwise to simulate a visual impairment. The goal is to have positive, rather than negative, experiences.

- Teach toddlers specific ways of handling situations involving staring or making unkind remarks. Make all toddlers aware of how children who are stared at feel. Teach all children socially acceptable ways of learning about others.

- Teach children specific skills to use in approaching others and entering groups. If other children tease or make unkind remarks about the toddler with a disability, serve as the child's ally. Stop the teasing and explain that words can hurt people's feelings. Give correct information "Camille is not stupid. It just takes her longer to learn new things." Over time, help children build the skills necessary to stand up for themselves.

- Help all toddlers find roles to play and facilitate accommodations and adaptations that allow all children to play together.

- Encourage older children in a multi-age group to help the toddler with a disability as needed. Make sure, however, that this is not a constant responsibility. Also, pair the child with a disability with other, perhaps younger toddlers, so he, too, has the experience of helping.

Including toddlers and twos with disabilities requires more individualized planning. Adults need to plan to meet the needs of all the children in their group as well as the individual needs of a particular child. Typically, these needs are very compatible and need only variations on the general plans. The recommendations for including toddlers with disabilities reflect developmentally appropriate practices for all children this age but may require some adaptation to meet individual toddlers' needs.

Toddlers and Twos with Developmental Delays

Involve toddlers actively in the learning process but expect to repeat this process with variations many times for learning to take place. Have the toddler crawl *under* the table when you are teaching that concept. Point out when he is using an obstacle course that he is *under* the ladder. You may need to use more directive teaching, rather than just assuming the toddler will discover what to do or learn from simply observing others. You may also have to provide more scaffolding for learning to occur.

- Keep a consistent daily schedule so toddlers will know what will happen next. Provide a picture chart to support the schedule.
- Limit choices to two or three activities during free play time or provide some guidance in choosing appropriate activities.
- Limit the potential for distraction, especially during small-group times by seating the child close to you and facing away from busy areas.
- Add cues such as carpet squares to indicate where toddlers should sit.
- Provide safe outlets for the release of excess energy and feelings. Toddlers may need punching bags or silly time when they are encouraged to use up excess energy.
- Sequence tasks from easy to hard and try to match the toddler's developmental level. Use backward chaining where appropriate.
- Be specific about your rules for activities and post these with pictures. Show the toddler the rules as well as telling him.
- Help toddlers organize their activities. For example say, "What will you do first? . . . What comes next?"
- Use a variety of teaching techniques including modeling what you want the toddler to do. Toddlers often learn appropriate behavior by imitating others. Toddlers with developmental delays may have a limited repertoire of behaviors, and modeling can increase this repertoire. You may have to point out the salient features you want the toddler to attend to.
- Help shape a toddler's behavior by breaking an activity down into smaller steps and then leading the toddler through progressively more of the steps, providing many prompts until he can do it all by himself.
- The opposite technique of shaping is fading. As the toddler begins to master a skill, gradually give fewer cues and less information so that she becomes more responsible for doing the skill independently.

Toddlers and Twos with Physical Impairments

Toddlers need materials that encourage the development of large- and small-motor skills. The adult's role is to provide an adequate supply of a variety of materials that encourage all types of movements and reflect a developmental progression for skill building.

- Use adaptive equipment that allows the toddler to participate as normally as possible.
- Use larger versions of manipulative toys.
- Be aware of easily tippable or rolling equipment in the classroom.

- To encourage self-help skills, attach a carry-all or basket to the child's walker or have the child wear a light carry-all around his neck if he is using crutches.
- Encourage the toddler to use her motor skills. Many children shy away from art or manipulative activities because these are difficult for them, but they need the practice.

Toddlers and Twos with Visual Impairments

Help the toddler locate the different areas of the room and help her develop safe ways to get to each (no toys lying around). Keep these areas consistent, and thus encourage independent movement. Providing consistent routines helps children know what to expect and supports their independence.

- Be aware of the toddler's location in the room.

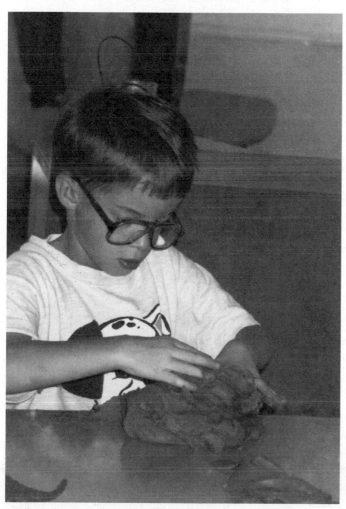

Children with visual impairments need many hands-on experiences with materials.

- Use objects the toddler can feel and pair words with the objects she is feeling. "Chunga, this is a ball. Feel how round it is. Drop it and it bounces back up." Obviously, pictures of objects are not worthwhile for these children.
- Be aware of lighting needs. Some toddlers actually see better in dim settings. If she sees better in some lighting conditions than others, adapt your classroom.
- Use language that is comfortable for you. Don't eliminate the words "see" and "look" from your vocabulary, but describe what you see to the child in the most concrete way you can.

Toddlers and Twos with Hearing Impairments

Parents will decide how they want their toddler to be taught communications skills. Your role is to support this decision. When possible, incorporate the toddler's preferred communication mode into regular activities.

- Remove barriers that may block the child's vision of the classroom, provided such removals don't create runways. Encourage the toddler to look over the choices of what has been set up in the room on any given day before deciding what to do.
- Encourage the toddler to attend to a speaker's face. Look at the child when you talk to her, remind the other children to do the same. "Look at Sofia when you talk to her, it makes it easier for her to understand you."
- Place the toddler in a good visual position during small group time or snack time, probably across from you, and not looking into the sun. Remember to look at the toddler when talking to her.

Toddlers and Twos with Social/Emotional Disorders

An organized, predictable, safe environment will help toddlers to be better organized. A consistent structure provides stability. These children need adult support, warmth, and attention.

- Provide the toddler with many opportunities to run, jump, climb, and swing in a secure environment.
- Develop with the parents a consistent plan for handling disruptions and targeting behaviors to concentrate on.
- Find many opportunities to give positive feedback and help them develop the skills necessary to enter small groups and play with or near other children.

Transitions

Transition is the label given to the time between the end of one event and the beginning of another. This can be the time between activities, the beginning or end of the day, before and after lunch, snacks, and naps, or moving from inside to outside. Transitions are difficult times for toddlers, teachers, and parents. Even at home, the transitions before meals, bedtime, and the like can be stressful. Changes required by transitions cause tension regardless of the physical location. As there are many transitions in a single day, it is important to think of and plan for transitions as a time of learning. Stress created in these transitions can carry over into the next event, so thought must also be given to decreasing the stress.

Why Are Transitions Stressful?

Transitions in general may be more obvious to the adult than to the toddler. As toddlers are just learning about sequences, they may view each event, including the transition as a discrete event unrelated to what went before or to what will follow. A calm but firm response to children is reassuring. Children need to feel secure and know that there are rules and that the adult is in control. The younger the children, the more likely it is that transition periods will take longer. (Compare the time it takes for a 5-year-old versus a 2-year-old to put on boots and a snow suit.) Likewise, the wider the age range of children, the longer the transition. The longer the transition, the more likely it is to be a difficult one. Transitions are difficult for a variety of reasons. Some of these and some possible solutions follow.

Boredom. Transitions often involve waiting. Toddlers who have "nothing to do" will usually find something to do, and it is rarely what you would choose.

Combating boredom. Eliminate as much waiting time as possible. When you can't eliminate it, help toddlers by singing a song with them, do a finger play, tell or read a story. Do not move from an activity until you have the next one prepared; that is, don't have toddlers clean up for lunch until lunch is on the table. Don't wait until all the children are present before starting an activity. Slower toddlers may speed up if they think they are missing something.

Change. Toddlers, like adults, like to change activities when they are finished, not by the clock. They may feel uncertain about what will happen next.

Make changes easier. Be sure to warn toddlers about upcoming changes. "In five minutes it will be clean up time." Follow a schedule. Toddlers cannot tell time, so it is not important whether you allow activities to run a little longer or shorter, but rather that you follow the same sequence of events. Encourage toddlers to think about what will happen next.

Rules. Toddlers may feel uncertain about the "rules" or expectations for them during transition times.

Make rules easier to follow. Help toddlers understand exactly what you expect of them during transition times. To aid cleaning up, for example, you could have a picture or outline of an item on the shelf where it belongs if it is important that it be returned to the right place. Expect some testing behavior at transition time.

Control. Toddlers are trying to gain control over their world and exert their independence and autonomy.

Give toddlers some control. It often helps transitions to give toddlers control of some decisions. Be sure they are choices you are willing to live with. A toddler can decide which book she wants to look at during naptime, not whether or not she will nap.

Separation. Many transitions involve separation, whether from a parent, caregiver, sibling, playmate, or the place itself.

Make separation easier. If a toddler is having a difficult time separating from his parents, talk with them about the issue and jointly develop a plan. A picture schedule is particularly helpful for toddlers who are having problems adjusting to care, as they can see that the final picture is a parent picking them up.

Emerging Skills. Transitions require toddlers to use skills that are new to them such as dressing and undressing, toileting, and self-feeding in a relatively short time frame.

Allow time for practicing emerging skills. Part of the transition process is learning adaptive behavior or self-help skills. Rushing transitions puts pressure on toddlers who are mastering these emerging skills. This often results in toddlers who resist what you want. Additional time is an asset to a toddler who is striving for competence. Try dismissing these slower toddlers first to give them more time, or plan an activity following the transition that is easy for toddlers to join when they are ready.

Lack of Planning. Transitions are an important part of the day and need to have a purpose as well as advanced planning to make them work.

Plan for transitions. Transitions are an opportunity for learning as well as a necessary part of the day. Help increase body awareness by having "toddlers with long hair" or "toddlers with brown eyes" or "toddlers with sneakers" and so on leave first. Be creative. Have toddlers pretend they are cleaning up for a party, or as they move between activities have them jump like kangaroos, move as softly as the wind, march, tiptoe, and so on.

Testing Limits During Transitions

Occasionally all adults get involved in a situation when a toddler is testing the rules. Let's suppose a toddler gets upset because it is time to clean up the toys and he is not finished playing. He cries, throws toys, and refuses to clean up. The adult, after trying to deal with his behavior for several minutes, becomes angry and tries to force the child to comply. What develops is a power struggle, someone wins and someone loses after a fairly lengthy dispute. Everyone loses because time and energy was wasted on a potentially preventable situation.

Given an opportunity to do it again what would you change? Two or three minutes before clean-up time give the toddler a warning that he will need to finish soon and alert him to what is coming next. Then, at clean-up time, give the toddler a choice of what he wants to put away, "You can put the blocks on the shelf or help me put the paints away." If the toddler ignores you, repeat your direction and walk away to start clean up. Generally, the toddler will begin to clean up or leave the area. If he leaves the area, stop him and put something in his hand that needs to be put away and say, "Thanks for helping to clean up, that goes on the shelf. We need to get ready for snack now." Positive directions, that is, telling children what to do, almost always work.

One key for handling toddler outbursts is to remain calm and in control. If the adult is thinking and planning ahead rather than reacting emotionally, tantrum situations will be less likely to occur, or at least, be of lesser intensity. A second key is to have realistic expectations. Toddlers' clean-up will be haphazard and rushed. Remember it's the effort that counts and effort should be praised.

Clean-Up Time

Make the clean-up of toys a normal part of your routine. Toddlers can be involved in the clean-up process. Set low expectations at first (such as having a young toddler put two blocks in the box) and raise them as the toddler becomes more able. Having a particular song that signals clean-up time is useful. It can be a record or a song you sing each day. This lets toddlers know what is happening. The song can be a simple tune you have made up or you can put new words to a familiar tune.

Two frequently used simple songs are

This is the way we pick up our toys, pick up our toys, pick up our toys
This is the way we pick up our toys, so early in the morning.
(sung to the tune of "Here we go 'round the Mulberry Bush").

or

It's time to put our toys away, toys away, toys away;
It's time to put our toys away, for another day.
(sung to the tune of "Mary Had a Little Lamb")

For variation, substitute the name of the toy a child is putting away, substitute a child's name, the name of the setting, or name what will happen next.

This is the way Jack picks up the blocks, picks up the blocks, picks up the blocks
This is the way Jamelia picks up the blocks, and they put them all away.

Choosing Toys, Materials, and Equipment

Toddlers need a variety of toys that are safe and durable. Toys can be anything from dolls and dump trucks to pots, pans, and wooden spoons. Toddlers invent uses and play around the props they are given. When choosing play materials consider these aspects:

- **Authenticity.** For toddlers realism is important. Does the toy look like what it is supposed to be? For truck play, a small wooden truck is more realistic than a wooden block although both can be used similarly. The younger the child, the more realistic the toys need to be.

- **Degree of structure.** Toddlers' ideas are concrete and certain materials can create concrete structures. Certain toys suggest certain play. Examples of structured toys would be cars and play dishes; unstructured materials would be playdough and blocks.
- **Interactiveness.** Does the material encourage children's participation? Materials that encourage interaction support play and learning. Toys that move, make sounds, and change in a child's hands encourage participation from the child.
- **Complexity.** Consider the complexity of a toy. How many different uses does a toy have? A simple toy such as a ball is functionally complex because children can do so many things with it. People are the most functionally complex playthings; therefore, adult-child or child-child interactions increase the complexity of any type of play.
- **Plasticity.** Can the toy be used in more than one way by more than one child over a wide span of ages? Blocks are a good investment because children will play with them in different ways as they grow and develop. Infants may use them to practice grasping, mouthing, and bringing objects together. Toddlers may use them as objects to place in and out of containers as they develop spatial relationships and motor control. Later they may be used for stacking and the beginnings of pretend play. Blocks may also encourage more than one child to become involved in the play. Many art materials such as paint, crayons, and playdough fall into this category.
- **Independence.** Will the toy encourage independence or will the child always be dependent on an adult for assistance with the toy? Although play is usually enhanced by an adult playing along, you do not want the play dependent upon the adult.

Discipline or Punishment?

As children become toddlers and twos they increasingly need adult guidance to help them determine the difference between acceptable and unacceptable behavior. This guidance includes using gentle redirection, acknowledging feelings, giving positive feedback, providing appropriate activities, and even giving a child several minutes of private time. There may be times when a toddler still can't get his act together nor explain what's bothering him. It is apparent to all that something is wrong.

Two-year-olds can be difficult as well as charming. They are emotional because one of their developmental tasks is learning how to control the emotions they feel. One can expect that 2-year-olds will have emotional outbursts and be non-compliant at times. How the adult handles these situations will impact on their frequency, duration, and intensity.

Most adults have many questions about when and how to discipline toddlers. When does discipline start? Typically, adults begin to discipline children at the end of the first year when an infant becomes a toddler and is mobile. Most toddlers behave—in their own minds, they don't misbehave; misbehavior is, to some extent, an interpretation by adults. Sometimes adults are prompted to discipline toddlers because of their growing independence and interest in doing things for themselves. Their seemingly constant activity and their hands-on approach to life can lead adults to take measures to try to control toddler behavior (Morrison, 1988).

Many use the words *discipline* and *punishment* as though they were interchangeable. However, each means something slightly different and their use affects children differently. Gartrell (1987) defines *discipline* as behavior which is designed to encourage self-control. That is, discipline involves any actions or words that help someone learn to self-monitor his behavior so that it is appropriate and acceptable in a given situation. The purpose of discipline, then, is to teach a child what to do in a given situation rather than what not to do. Discipline is teaching another person appropriate or acceptable behavior.

Punishment is an action taken by an individual designed to stop another's particular behavior. Punishment is not concerned with teaching appropriate behavior; the only concern is stopping unwanted behavior. Punishment generally involves the infliction of some negative consequence for a behavior that is deemed inappropriate or wrong (Gartrell 1987). Punishment usually succeeds in stopping unwanted behavior, but may have some negative effects. Toddlers may learn when they can "get away" with negative behavior, usually in the absence of the controlling adult, or they may come to fear adults as harsh and uncaring.

Positive discipline, or guidance, is designed to facilitate the development of good self-concepts, prosocial behaviors, and an ability to control one's own behavior (Gartrell, 1987). It is a process approach designed to guide a toddler's behavior rather than a "one-shot" act. Positive discipline involves awareness of children's feelings, developmental level, and the ability to set and keep sensible limits. When a toddler behaves in an unacceptable way, the logical consequences for his behavior are presented in a way that preserves his self-esteem. As toddlers begin to learn that there are consequences for behavior (positive ones for acting appropriately, and negative ones for inappropriate actions), they will begin to learn to act responsibly and control their own behavior. The goal of discipline is to help toddlers learn socially acceptable limits and to develop the internal controls. Discipline involves facilitating children's social development and prosocial skills (Lawton, 1988).

Most toddlers do not intentionally misbehave. Toddlers are just beginning to think logically about the consequences of their behaviors. The toddler who was ripping pages from the book was not doing it to destroy the book, but because ripping the pages was fun and interesting. We, as adults, often ascribe negative intentions to children's behavior and that's why we get angry. We know ripping pages in a book is inappropriate, a toddler does not.

- If you are angry, use your anger constructively. Let toddlers know you are angry and model appropriate ways to handle that anger. It is important for toddlers to learn how to handle anger, too. For example, "Ricardo, it makes me angry when you hurt Brie. You need to go to another activity."

- Tell the toddler what behavior is unacceptable *and* what they can do instead that is more appropriate. "Noel, you may not climb on the fence. I'll walk you to the jungle gym where you may climb."

- Help toddlers learn to solve their problems themselves. Give younger or more inexperienced toddlers the words to say at first, but eventually they will learn how to talk out their problems. "Regan, tell Irma you don't like it when she hits you."

- If a toddler is having a "bad day," give her some space to work out her feelings. Adding playdough or the water table to the day's activities often provides a good outlet.

- If a toddler has a tantrum, allow him to calm down in a safe place. Being out of control is scary, so an adult should be nearby. Tell the toddler, in a soothing voice, that as soon as he is calm, then the two of you will talk about what happened. Do not try to reason with the toddler while he is screaming and thrashing. You might say, "Chad, when you are calm, we will talk about the problem."

- Provide enough interesting activities and smooth transitions to keep toddlers actively involved in constructive play with minimal time wasted in waiting.

- Provide an atmosphere where exploration is encouraged. This often means putting valuables or other "untouchables" out of reach. If you are spending a lot of your time telling toddlers that they can't touch things, exploration behavior (an important way in which toddlers gain information and learn) will be discouraged.

- Arrange your space to go along with your goals for positive behavior management. For example, if you would like to encourage more independence in toddlers, arrange some carefully selected materials on low open shelves which the toddlers can choose from on their own and have duplicates of the most popular toys when possible.

- Help toddlers realize that their actions and words affect others. For example, "Darrein, did you see Orlando's face? He was really angry when you knocked down his blocks."

Teaching toddlers appropriate behavior is an important task for adults. The long-term goal of disciplining is for toddlers to develop control over their social and emotional behavior. Discipline, not punishment, will support the development of self-control in toddlers.

Managing Aggressive Behavior

The principles for positive management of aggressive behavior are similar to all discipline principles for toddlers but focus particularly on aggressive behaviors. Aggressive and antisocial behaviors for toddlers include hitting, biting, throwing objects at others, hurting others, non-sharing, swearing, and name-calling. In general, there is a victim involved as well as a child who is exhibiting these behaviors.

As in all discipline, you first need to consider the individual toddler and his needs, and his chronological age. Positive behavior management is based on respectful treatment of all children. Your consistent modeling of respectful treatment of toddlers is a powerful behavior management tool. Toddlers who feel loved and respected are more likely to cooperate and comply with well thought-out rules.

In order to effectively combat aggressive and antisocial behavior, it is important to know some specific information. Take three days to watch the toddler and plan a strategy. This is difficult because there is an urge to want to do something about it "now." However, what you have been trying has probably not been working, so the usual approach may not be sufficient. You need to ask the following questions about the behavior.

- **Is there a pattern?** First try to see if there is any pattern to the behavior that is causing the problem.

   Time of day. Does it happen when the toddler first arrives? When the toddler is leaving? Before snack or lunch time? During nap time? Or at all times of day?

   Activities or routines. Does it occur during specific activities or routines? If "yes," do some additional thinking about the activities. Are they structured or free choice, group or individual? Are the children sitting or active?

   Place. Is there a particular place where the behavior occurs? Is it outdoors or indoors? Does it occur in a particular area of the room, such as where the blocks are or where dramatic play is set up?

   Cause. What seems to cause or trigger the behavior? What happened immediately before the incident? Did another child take something away from the toddler or did the toddler ask for something to which another child said "no" or an adult said "no?" Was the toddler in an argument with another child or were the children "fighting" or pretend fighting at the onset? Was the toddler tired? Are there changes occurring in the toddler's life? Is there a new sibling, a grandparent visiting, a parent away? A toddler may just need a soft lap to be held and cuddled in, and an understanding smile rather than hearing that she should be a "big girl" and stop throwing the doll.

- **Who is the victim?** Is the victim anyone who happens to be there, or is it usually a particular child or a few certain children? If it seems to be a variety of children, check if they are mostly boys or girls or both. Are they bigger or smaller children? Are they older or younger children? Are they the aggressive children or the shy, more timid children?

- **How does the toddler act after the behavior?** Does the toddler deny the behavior or admit that it was done? Is the toddler upset by the victim's crying (if that is what happens)? Does the toddler get upset if the victim returns the behavior (e.g. bites or hits back)? Does the toddler look to see if an adult is watching before proceeding with the behavior? Does the toddler walk away? Does the toddler apologize and seem concerned about the victim? (Adapted from Deiner, 1993)

If the behavior is really unusual for that particular child, check to see if the toddler is feeling well. Sometimes the only sign of an ear infection, for example, is a negative change in the child's behavior.

The answers to these questions will help develop some strategies for intervention. When you are faced with a situation that you must deal with, it is important to develop a strategy that is followed by all the adults involved. It should be jointly agreed to and consistently followed. The procedure may be something like this:

- Quickly check on the victim; if possible, have another adult do this.

- Tell the aggressive toddler firmly but quietly that you will not tolerate the behavior. (Think through this statement so that you know exactly what you will say ahead of time.) "I will not allow you to hurt other children. You must sit here until I tell you you may get up." (If the child refuses to sit have another adult sit with her and say. "Mrs. Miller will help you sit here.")

- Note the time or set a timer, turn your back on the child, and walk away. Do not talk to the child or make eye contact with the child during this time. If another child approaches the child simply state that "Amber needs to be alone for a few minutes," and lead the other child to another area.

- Choose a time period that is developmentally appropriate for the child. A definition of appropriate is one minute for each year of the child's age (or one minute of removal for a 1-year-old, two minutes for a 2-year-old, and so on). Although this seems like a short time to adults, a toddler's perception is very different. It is far better to keep it short than to have to deal with a second problem relating to the child's noncompliance.

- When the time is up, go to the child and say "You may get up now." Help the toddler find an activity that is of interest. Don't discuss the incident; the toddler is aware of the reasons for being required to sit in the chair. At this point the incident is over and feelings and behavior should go on as if nothing had happened.

Note: Some people refer to this process as "time out." In reality the procedure was used long before the label was attached (Adapted from Essa, 1990; Deiner, 1993).

Summary

Developmentally appropriate practices for toddlers and twos were discussed with particular emphasis on both age and individual appropriateness. Specific concerns about the learning environment included the relationship between content and process, child-initiated and teacher-initiated instruction, and the inclusion of children with disabilities. The programming for toddlers and twos concentrated on how time during the day was allocated, the number of activities toddlers had to choose from, and the balance of these activities.

Toddlers and twos are actively exploring their world and trying to learn about it. In the planning process it is important to include all the content areas in a developmentally appropriate way. Planning for toddlers uses simpler, concrete themes, and provides time for learning self-help skills, as developing independence is an underlying theme of the curriculum.

The role of the adult in the context of the toddlers' push for autonomy and independence was discussed. Questions about the importance of process versus product, the role of play, and the ways in which adults support learning were clarified. Programming itself was detailed and viewed as more similar to the theme planning of preschoolers than the individualization necessary for infants. Adaptations for including toddlers and twos with disabilities were given.

Transitions were singled out as a particularly stressful time for toddlers. The need to evaluate and perhaps modify transitions to be valid learning experiences as well as less stressful was addressed. Guidelines for discipline practices were developed as toddlers are expected to test limits as they explore their environment.

Application Activities

1. Discipline or Punishment? A toddler is looking at a book and begins to rip the pages from the book. Discuss how you would handle this behavior and the rationale behind your decision.

2. Write your personal philosophy for working with children birth to 3.

3. Plan a week in September for a group of 12 toddlers and twos using a thematic plan. Describe how you would modify this plan for this same group if you repeated the week in March (they would be six months older). What would you have expected them to learn and what developmental changes would impact your planning?

4. Describe developmentally appropriate practice and what it means for adults who work with young children birth to 3. Visit a child-care setting and evaluate it against your ideas about developmentally appropriate practice.

Chapter 19

Activities for Toddlers
and Twos: 18 to 36 Months

A year and a half! Movement is taken for granted. However, now toddlers like to move faster whether it is running or riding. Movements are being refined as growth is slowing down. The milestones are no longer as obvious as the "first step" and the "first word." Changes are more subtle and more in the areas of language, social/emotional, and cognitive development. Toddlers are increasingly able to understand what is happening and say what they want. They understand far more about what is happening around them, easily respond to requests, and of course "NO" is still a major part of their vocabulary. Language is blooming. The infant now uses two-word sentences and points to pictures and objects. He wants to be his own person most of the time and with the improvement in his small-motor skills he is able to do many more things for himself.

Emotionally, toddlers and twos are still fragile. They look competent one minute and fall apart the next. Still curious, their knowledge of safety is just beginning to develop. They are increasingly able to do things for themselves and assert their independence and, although they enjoy adult company, they are more interested in peer relationships. Toddlers are increasingly becoming "good company," interesting companions to spend some time with. They now enjoy adult friendship, and, although curious about peers, find these relationship still a bit difficult.

Activities for Toddlers and Twos

Activities for children this age need to be open ended with the opportunity to play alone or with small groups (two or three) who may come and go frequently. They need the opportunity to practice emerging skills as well as plenty of opportunity for mastery of their motor skills. Although their repertoire has expanded, in many instances planning still emphasizes variation on other activities. Many of the activities in this chapter and the previous one can be used by a wide age range of children. The children, however, will use the materials differently. Play-dough is an example of an activity that is used by both groups. One indication of this type of activity is that they are introduced as "Variations on . . .".

■ **Sensorimotor**

OBSTACLE COURSE

Purpose   To improve sensorimotor integration and motor planning

Materials   Barrels, boxes, boards, chairs, hoops, balance beam

Procedure   Set up an obstacle course either inside or outside. The course may be simple or complex, depending on the past experience of the children, but should require a variety of physical skills and should be long enough that several children can participate at the same time. Use obstacles that require children to move over, under, around and through the obstacles. Allow children to explore the course. When they are comfortable, make suggestions for specific actions.

> **Easier**   Keep the course simple and relatively short or allow the children to stop in the middle. Give children a play-by-play description of what they are doing so they begin to associate the activity with words. Use arrows if the course has options and pictures to show how to move through some obstacles.
>
> **Harder**   Give children more complex activities to do such as picking up a bean bag or walking through a hoop while on the balance beam. Add line drawings of the necessary postures to get through a particular obstacle or add music to determine the pace of movement.

Comment   This is a way for children to practice a variety of movements in a sequence. Often children are better at some movements than others and only use those that they can do well; this provides a short period of practice for a variety of moves.

■ **Sensorimotor**

VARIATIONS ON BALANCING

Purpose   To improve sensorimotor integration, motor planning, and the child's body awareness

Materials   Bean bags, books, paper plates, paint brushes, feathers, crayons

Procedure   Have children balance a bean bag on their heads. Encourage them to stand up and sit down, walk fast and slow while balancing it. Then have them balance the bean bags using other body parts: shoulders, elbow, knee, foot. Have them get down on the floor, feet in the air and balance it on the bottom of one foot and then catch it with their hands.

Easier   Give children feedback about their posture and hints about how to move to make balancing easier.

Harder   Encourage children to experiment with balancing a variety of different objects.

Comment These sensorimotor activities require both static and dynamic balance and concentration.

■ **Sensorimotor**

VARIATIONS ON THROWING

Purpose To improve sensorimotor integration, motor planning, and eye-hand coordination

Materials

bean bag	tennis ball	Velcro-covered ping-pong ball
sponges	small rubber ball	rubber rings
horseshoes	whiffle ball	crumpled paper
koosh ball	milk cartons	sponge ball
targets	ping-pong ball	

Procedure Have the toddlers participate in the various types of throwing activities listed below. Use only one variation in a given day but offer different balls. For example, for the basketball toss have them use a tennis ball, then add a koosh ball and a whiffle ball. Help them verbalize the differences in throwing. Some are easier to do outside whereas others are fine inside.

- Texture ball toss—use a sponge or texture ball (whiffle ball); the children begin with underhand tossing to a person close by. Gradually extend the distance, and graduate to overhand throwing.
- Ring toss—a variation of horseshoes with rubber rings, this game requires a different set of tossing skills.
- Beanbag toss—toss bags through large holes in a target or into empty coffee cans.
- Paper toss—crumple paper into balls and toss them into a wastebasket.
- Tennis ball toss—This game becomes more difficult as the ball bounces; help children to cup hands together to catch the ball if it is low.
- Milk carton toss—use plastic milk bottles or cartons stacked in pyramids. Knock the structure down with a tennis ball.
- Bucket toss—use a bucket or wastebasket for catching balls. First set the bucket on the floor, then raise it on a chair or box.
- Empty box throw—place a bottomless cardboard box on its side on the ground or tape it to the wall. The object is to toss or roll a ball through the box.

- Target toss—use a Velcro-covered ping-pong ball and toss it at a target (with Velcro pieces attached); vary the distance from the target and the size of the target.
- Sponge toss—make a cardboard target with holes of various sizes, or see if they can throw the sponges through suspended hula hoops. On a hot day you might throw wet ones.

Easier   Allow toddlers to add their own variations which may be just exploring the objects and what happens when they throw them. In general, the shorter the distance, the bigger the target, and the larger the ball, the less difficult the task.

Harder   Help children decide which aspects of a particular type of throwing are difficult or easy for them. Discuss which objects are harder to throw and which are easier.

Comment It is the variations that strengthen the sensorimotor component—the need to make adjustments and compensate that makes the learning experience more than just a motor refinement. These activities are good for both indoors and outdoors. Be sure to have toddlers take turns both throwing and retrieving. Always be aware of safety needs.

Note: Discuss with toddlers and twos where it is safe to throw objects and where it is not. Discuss what types of objects should be thrown and what types shouldn't and why.

■ **Sensorimotor**

VARIATIONS ON BALLS

Purpose To improve sensorimotor integration and eye-hand coordination

Materials Variety of balls: small solid rubber ball, under-inflated beach ball, tennis ball, koosh ball, inflated rubber balls of different sizes

Procedure Both inside and outside, have the children participate in various types of ball-related activities with a variety of different balls. Start with the under-inflated beach ball as it is typically the easiest for young children to manage. Have children do the following types of activities:

Roll the ball back and forth sitting with legs in a V-shape.
Roll the ball at a target.
Toss the ball as high as they can.
Toss the ball to another child softly.
Toss the ball into a box or basket.
Kick the ball as far as they can.
Kick the ball at a target.

Easier   Serve as a coach for the child and give pointers, as well as supply and retrieve balls for her.

Harder   Encourage children to take turns so that one kicks or tosses the ball and one chases and then they exchange places.

Comment   Balls and other toys that roll can be used in a variety of ways that make them increasingly complex toys. Provide different sizes of balls, and toys of other textures for rolling. The child can experiment with rolling objects of different weights and sizes. Infants need first-hand experience to discover that balls roll but cubes do not. As toddlers get to be more mobile, it may not occur to them to retrieve toys for themselves and they may need your support doing so until they get the idea. Repeat these activities with different balls. Throwing an under-inflated beach ball and a tennis ball are very different experiences.

■ **Language Arts**

I CAN DO IT

Purpose   To increase language awareness and self-esteem

Materials   Photographs, pictures from magazines, index cards (3 inch by 5 inch), marking pen, ziplocking bags

Procedure   For each child, make a book of things that the child can do. An I-Can-Do-It book has a page for each of a child's major or minor accomplishments that you choose to include. This is most easily done by gluing pictures on paper and inserting pictures (Polaroid are great) in zip-lock bags and then stapling several bags together on their non-ziplocking sides so that pictures can later be removed if desired. Each page has a picture of one accomplishment of the child and a caption. Examples might be "I can stand up by myself now" written under a picture of a toddler standing alone or "I can clap my hands" written on the bottom of a page where the child's two hands are traced. The pictures don't have to be elaborate, but just enough to convey the idea.

Easier   The adult will make the book and read it with the toddler.
Harder   The toddler will take a more active role in making the book and adding to it. Make a larger book that can include some art work samples as well.

Comment   If you add the date to each page this activity can also be a record-keeping system and a method of communicating with families about what children are doing. Often we focus on what children can't do and it is helpful for children to have an opportunity to proudly share their achievements as well. Children can make books about anything that interests them.

■ **Language Arts**

HATS

Purpose   To improve receptive language

Materials   A variety of hats; *Hats* by Debbie Bailey (1993) Annick Press

Procedure   Read the book *Hats* to a small group of toddlers. Show the toddlers a hat and talk about the function of a hat. Have a variety of hats to look at: some for a particular season, and some for a particular purpose. Let the infant play with the hats and talk about the functions and characteristics of the hats. Encourage the infant to try the hats on. Be sure you have a mirror available.

Easier	Read only part of the book. Have fewer hats and concentrate on the experience of playing with the hats rather than the language concepts.
Harder	Talk about the different functions of a variety of hats. Encourage toddlers to "guess" why some hats are made in specific ways.

Comment   One of the difficult aspects of learning a language is the generalization of function and how it relates to labels. It is important that young children have a variety of experiences so they can abstract the quality of "hatness" from the experience. The book can also be read as a follow-up to playing with the hats.

■ **Language Arts**

FLANNEL BOARD STORIES

Purpose   To improve receptive language development and listening skills

Materials   Flannel board, story, flannel board story pieces (trace figures from a coloring book or the story book on pellon and cut them out)

Procedure   Pick a relatively simple story with a few central characters. (Animals work well.) Make felt or Pellon characters. Tell the story and have the children place the pieces on the flannel board as you tell the story. (This may be a new experience for toddlers.)

Easier	Give the child additional directions and support in placing the piece.
Harder	Allow children to play with the flannel board and pieces and make up their own stories.

Comment   These stories are easy to follow and children can participate in the process. This sometimes makes listening easier. Toddlers may be more intrigued with the process than the story so plan to tell it again.

■ **Language Arts**

TAPE IT

Purpose   To improve listening skills and self esteem

Materials   Tape recorder, blank cassette, pictures of the children

Procedure   Over the course of several days, have children talk into the tape recorder for about a minute about what they are doing. When everyone in the class is on tape, have a small-group listening time when the children try to guess who is talking. As children guess a particular child, have the child talk and listen again to the recording.

Easier   Show the children pictures of two or three classmates who might be talking and ask them to choose which one it is.

Harder   Children can try to disguise their voices. Also, children can identify the features in a voice that make it recognizable.

Comment   Be sure to keep a list of the order in which the children speak so that you know for sure who is talking.

■ Discovery

BANANA GRAHAMS

Purpose   To improve cause-and-effect reasoning and sequencing skills

Materials   Bananas, graham crackers, small plastic baggies, rolling pins or cylinder blocks

Procedure   Have toddlers place a graham cracker in the bag and use a roller or hands to crumble the cracker. Help children compare the whole graham crackers with the crumbs and the relationship between how long and how hard they pound or roll the graham cracker with the size of the crumbs. Have toddlers help

| Figure 19.1 | Making Banana Grahams |

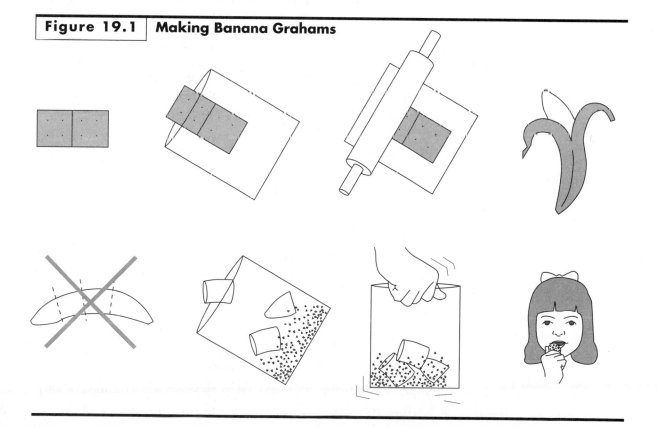

peel the bananas, then an adult can cut the bananas into chunks with a table knife. Toddlers can put several banana pieces in the bag with the graham cracker crumbs, close the bag, and shake. Then, eat the coated banana pieces.

Easier   Have the bananas peeled and cut up and the graham crackers crushed so the children only have to put the bananas in the bag and shake and then eat them.

Harder   Draw a sequence picture of the process and see if children can do the process step by step.

Comment   Children enjoy eating what they have helped to make. The process helps make them more aware of changes in state and effects of actions. Use this for other sequential projects such as making pizza.

■ Discovery

GOOP

Purpose   To improve cause-and-effect reasoning and sensorimotor integration

Materials   Water, cornstarch, bowls, jelly roll trays

Procedure   Start with one box of cornstarch in a 2-quart bowl. Gradually add water (and food coloring, if desired) and stir to make a consistency of thick liquid. Goop will get somewhat solid, then turn to liquid as it is picked up. (Use about equal amounts of cornstarch and water to make goop.) Allow children to experiment with the proportions and observe the results. Put goop in jelly roll trays for children to play with. Help children talk about the different and confusing states of the goop. Encourage them to feel, squeeze, drip, drop, slop, and slide. Play with the goop by itself or add items, such as spoons, scoops and small containers.

Easier   Help children explore the goop. Break off a piece and help them observe that at first it is rough, and then it all runs together. Poke it and watch the hole disappear. Let it run through your fingers and so on.

Harder   Help children experiment with different amounts of water or by adding cornstarch as they play with the goop to see what happens.

Comment   Goop is edible and relatively easy to clean up. Goop requires little strength to manipulate and defies coordination. It is a soothing, yet intriguing medium, even for adults.

■ Discovery

VARIATIONS ON PLAYDOUGH

Purpose   To improve cause-and-effect reasoning and sensorimotor integration

Materials   Bowls, wooden spoons, water, measuring cups and spoons, playdough

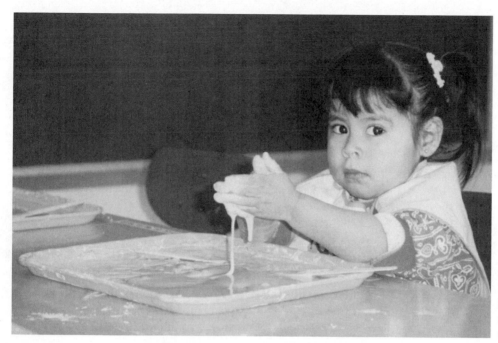

Goop is an intriguing media for toddlers and a relatively clean one as well.

To Make Textured Playdough

Ingredients   Flour, salt, vegetable oil

Mix the following ratios of flour to salt to make playdough

7 parts flour to 1 part salt + water (tbsp or so of vegetable oil)

2 parts flour to 1 part salt + water (tbsp or so of vegetable oil)

Mix flour and salt together. Add vegetable oil and water until it reaches the desired consistency and mix. Have additional flour available if it is too sticky.

To Make Kool-Aid Playdough

Ingredients   Flour, salt, cream of tartar, oil, Kool-Aid

1½ cups flour	¾ cup salt
3 teaspoons cream of tartar	1½ cups warm water
1½ tablespoons oil	Kool-Aid (start with ¼ cup)

Blend all ingredients. Cook over medium heat for 5 to 10 minutes, stirring constantly. It will form a ball. When cool enough to touch, knead until smooth. Store in plastic bag or covered plastic container in refrigerator.

To Make Cinnamon Playdough

Ingredients   Salt, flour, oil, water, cinnamon

Mix together:

½ cup salt	1 cup flour
1 tablespoon oil	½ cup water

Stir with a spoon. Then shake on cinnamon and mix again.

To Make Edible Playdough

Ingredients   Peanut butter, raisins, honey, powdered milk

⅓ cup peanut butter   1 tablespoon honey
raisins   about 2 tablespoons powdered milk
                                        (enough to make dough)

Combine the ingredients in the bowl and have children mix them with the spoon until doughy. Encourage children to push raisins into playdough. Raisins can also be for decorations.

Procedure   Have the children help to make the playdough. Talk with them about how different ingredients affect the playdough. Encourage children to think about the playdough they want to make. After the playdough is finished, have children play with the different varieties and talk about the differences.

Easier   Have children play with the playdough but not participate in making it. When you talk about the differences start with gross discrimination.

Harder   Have children classify the playdough by touch. Talk about uses for the different textures. Have children make other recipes by adding sawdust, sand, and so on. Use small quantities as some of the products might not be appealing.

Comment   When children participate in the process of making the dough, they can begin to understand why the dough feels different. Children often learn more when they can use more than one of their senses. Playdough can help children develop their finger control and can also help develop their sense of touch. Adding a scent to the playdough increases the variety of sensory stimulation offered through the activity and gives children the chance to practice using their senses together. Most children love tasting playdough. Rather than asking them to stop eating the playdough, sometimes use an edible and nutritious playdough which is meant for tasting.

Note: Have children wash hands before starting the activity. Be careful of the children eating some varieties (sawdust).

■ Discovery

OUTDOOR TREASURE BOX

Purpose   To improve identification, classification, and generalization skills

Materials   Shoe box, large crayon

Procedure   Print each child's name on the top of a separate box. Talk with each about the idea of treasures and that the box is a place to keep treasures safe. Take the children on a short walk. Have an adult hand for each child. The walk will vary with the season and part of the country. If it is a spring walk, point out the sights ("Look at the pretty pink flowers on that tree"), sounds ("Listen! Can you hear the birds?"), smells ("Ooh, smell this flower. Do you like the way it smells?"), and textures ("This is called a pussy willow because it feels soft like a

Playdough has the potential for promoting social interaction as well as sensorimotor integration.

kitty.") When children are just learning language, use general names such as "flower" or "bird" to describe what you see. Encourage them to find "treasures," items that they would like to put into their treasure box to take inside and look at more carefully. When you come inside, talk with each toddler about his particular treasures and verbally label them.

Easier   Offer the child an object like a stone or piece of grass to see if the child is interested in keeping those as treasures.

Harder   Help children think about their treasures categorically by color, shape, size or function.

Comment Children like to collect small items and this activity provides the opportunity for a learning experience. Young children learn about their environment through their senses: by seeing, smelling, touching, tasting, and hearing. Give them many first-hand opportunities to learn. With the right clothing, take walks in all seasons, and even in the rain. You can have many different kinds of treasure boxes if this activity happens to be something that works well for the children you teach.

■ **Discovery**

BOXES, BOXES, BOXES

Purpose To improve shape, size, and measurement concepts and sensorimotor integration

Materials Cardboard boxes of varying sizes, a large box (one from an appliance works well)

Procedure   Place small, medium, and large boxes in an open area. Encourage children to climb in and out of the small and medium-size boxes. Some children may even enjoy "hiding" for a short time in larger boxes. Allow children to put toys in the boxes and push and pull toys or other children (in boxes) around the area. Talk about size concepts such as small, medium, and large boxes and the objects that might be placed in each. Use language about spatial relations, *in, out, in front of, behind,* and *beside.* With a larger appliance box children may enjoy having their own private "house." Help them decide where the windows and doors should be placed, decide how to measure the height and area of each and how large they should be.

Easier   Support children's exploration of the boxes both verbally and physically. Place children in boxes if they need help.

Harder   Encourage children to use the boxes in imaginative play, for example, making a train. Help them arrange the boxes in a sequential order by size. See if children can build a tower with the boxes.

Comment   This is a good outdoor activity in nice weather. It increases spatial awareness using the large muscles of the body. Toddlers will enjoy the nondemanding creative aspect.

■ **Creative Arts**

SHAVING CREAM FINGERPAINT

Purpose   To encourage creativity and sensorimotor integration

Procedure   Shake up the shaving cream and spray it directly on a table. Encourage the children to explore the shaving cream and use it as if it were fingerpaint. Point out its characteristic feel and smell. As it tends to break down, be prepared to add more as needed.

Easier   Put a little shaving cream on your fingers and allow the children to touch it before they use it themselves.

Harder   Sprinkle powder tempera paint on the shaving cream to give it some color.

Comment   This is a good activity to have on hand if something else falls through or it rains unexpectedly. Toddlers enjoy the experience, it can be set up in a matter of a few minutes and it is easy to clean up.

■ **Creative Arts**

TORN PAPER PICTURES

Purpose   To encourage creativity and eye-hand coordination

Materials   Construction paper, colored paper scraps, paste, crayons, scissors

Procedure   Show children how to tear paper and use the paste. Encourage them to tear different colors and sizes of paper and then paste the pieces on a piece of construction paper.

Easier   Have the children just tear the paper.
Harder   Encourage children to both cut and tear the paper into shapes. Include different types of paper like aluminum foil, wax paper, wall paper, origami paper, and so on. These paper products will tear differently.

Comment   Tearing is a frustration release and is satisfying for children who have trouble cutting, and one would expect most twos to find cutting difficult, even with adapted scissors.

■ **Creative Arts**

MOOD DANCING

Purpose   To encourage creative movement and sensorimotor integration

Materials   Record, cassette, or compact disc player; music

Procedure   Play music for toddlers to dance to. Use many different types of music, but be sure to choose music that has a definite rhythm and mood. Talk to toddlers about the mood of the music: whether it is fast or slow, happy or sad, light or heavy. If toddlers don't dance, dance with them or pair them with other children who have the idea. Do dance too, to help them interpret the mood. Your modeling will encourage participation.

Easier   Encourage movement of any type regardless of its relationship to the mood of the music.
Harder   Have the children listen for about a minute and talk about the mood, the beat, and the concepts of fast and slow before they begin to dance. Add props such as scarves.

Comment   Moving to music is a life-long skill.

■ **Social Awareness**

BIG PICTURE

Purpose   To encourage social awareness, cooperation, and creativity

Materials   Large sheet of newsprint, water-based markers, large crayons, large chalk, masking tape

Procedure   Cover a table with the paper. Tape it down so it won't move. Be sure that each child has her own space to work in with her own set of markers, crayons and chalk, yet encourage the children to work together and talk.

Easier   Support and accept any marks the child makes on the paper.
Harder   Make the picture part of a theme and have the children scribble something theme related. If the children desire, label the scribble and write what they say about it.

Comment   Leave the paper out for a long enough time so that children can leave the activity and then come back and participate again. Group projects are difficult for children this young but flexible ones such as this one can be a good beginning. Encourage children to look at what others in the group have done. Hang it so children can share it with their families. This can also be done outside on a sidewalk.

■ Social Awareness

CELEBRATIONS

Purpose   To increase awareness of individual differences and cultural diversity

Materials   None (unless supplied by parents)

Procedure   Talk with the children briefly about different holiday celebrations, how families celebrate different holidays and, when they have the same holidays, how families celebrate in different ways. Discuss the feelings, excitement, and expectations that come with celebrations. As occasions arise, invite families to come in and share some aspects of their celebrations. Plan some activities that support the ideas talked about. As food is part of many celebrations, plan to have snacks that support the occasion.

   Easier   Encourage a child to sit with his family as celebrations are discussed.
   Harder   Encourage children to take a more active role in talking about the celebration.

Comment   Whether or not classes have diversity in celebrations, it is important that children learn that people celebrate many different occasions. Be aware of children in your class who do not participate in celebrating particular holidays. Find out from them and their families how they want to share this information with their classmates.

■ Social Awareness

TOOLS

Purpose   To improve adaptive/self-help skills and sensorimotor integration

Materials   Tub with sand or oatmeal, small objects and a variety of "tools" such as:

salad tongs	tablespoon	pie or cake server
spatula	tweezers	sugar tongs
spaghetti spoon	pierced serving spoons	needle nose pliers

Procedure   Place the small objects in the tub with the sand and have the child retrieve the objects using the different tools.

   Easier   Children can first use their hands to find the objects in the sand, then use the spoon, and finally use more complex tools.
   Harder   Have child use more complex tools that require better coordination such as the tongs or tweezers.

Comment Children need practice using tools. Although dealing with the very small objects is challenging for them, young children are fascinated by tiny things.

■ **Social Awareness**

DRESS UP

Purpose To improve adaptive/self-help skills and language concepts

Materials Clothes to dress up in, sized for a 5- or 6-year-old or small adult; accessories: scarves, necklaces, hats, gloves, shoes, belts, pocketbooks, and so on

Procedure Use larger size children's clothing so it will fit over the toddlers' clothes. Ask the child to name the article of clothing that he is wearing or putting on. Encourage him to try to get the clothing on and off himself. The accessories add to the fun and increase the language opportunities. Talk with the children about where they are going and the role they are playing.

Easier Help the children get into the dress-up clothing but see if they can undress themselves. Choose simpler articles of clothing.

Harder Include items with smaller and more complex fasteners and encourage children to do more of the dressing and undressing independently. Encourage children to play together with complementary roles. Help them use accessories.

Comment This activity fosters self-help as well as language development. It also provides a time to practice those skills that are "fun" as opposed to a transition time where there is an emphasis on speed.

Summary

The big change for toddlers and twos is language. With increasing language skills, imaginative play activities are added. Toddlers play what they know so they sometimes need field trips to support this new play. They are struggling with their new skills in independence such as dressing and undressing and need activities to support these emerging skills.

Toddlers and twos are also building social play skills. So activities are designed to allow young children to play beside each other but without high demands for cooperation. As skills emerge, they are unpredictable. Sometimes toddlers willingly share and cooperate; other times this is not possible. Activities for toddlers and twos are more complex and require more mental representation and imagination.

Application Activities

1. Choose a toy and evaluate it. Decide for what ages it is appropriate, what skills it facilitates or encourages, and what types of activities you can do with it.

2. Decide how you could adapt the above toy to use with an infant or toddler with one of the following disabilities: visual, hearing, physical impairment, or a developmental delay.

3. Using some of the activities in this chapter as prototypes, decide on a theme and plan a day for a group of six children 18 to 36 months.

References

Abbott, C. F., & Gold, S. (1991). Conferring with parents when you're concerned that their child needs special services. *Young Children, 46*(4), 10–14.

Abel, E. L., & Sokol, R. J. (1987). Incidence of fetal alcohol syndrome and economic impact of FAS–related anomalies. *Drug and Alcohol Dependence, 19,* 51–70.

Adams, R. J. (1987). An evaluation of color preference in early infancy. *Infant Behavior and Development, 10,* 143–150.

Afriat, C. I., & Coustan, D. R. (1995). Birth. In D. R. Coustan (Ed.), *Human Reproduction: Growth and Development* (pp. 307–326). Boston, MA: Little Brown and Company.

Ahlburg, D., & DeVita, C. (1992). New realities of the American family. *Population Bulletin, 47*(2) Washington, DC: Population Reference Bureau.

Ainsworth, M. D. (1963). The development of infant–mother interaction among the Ganda. In B. M. Foss (Ed.), *Determinants of Infant Behaviour* (Vol. 2). London: Methuen.

Ainsworth, M. D. , Salter, D. & Wittig, B. A. (1967) Attachment and exploratory behavior of one-year-olds in a strange situation. In B. M. Foss (Ed.), *Determinants of infant behavior.* Vol. IV. New York: Wiley.

Ainsworth, M. D. (1969). Object relations, dependency, and attachment: A theoretical review of the infant–mother relationship. *Child Development. 40,* 969–1025.

Ainsworth, M. D. (1973). The development of infant–mother attachment. In B. M. Caldwell & H. N. Ricciuti (Eds.), *Review of child development research* (Vol. 3, pp. 1–94). Chicago, IL: University of Chicago Press.

Alan Guttmacher Institute. (1993). *Facts in brief: Teenage sexual and reproductive behavior.* New York: Author.

Alsdurf, J., & Alsdurf, P. (1989). *Battered into submission.* Illinois: Intervarsity Press.

American Association on Mental Deficiency. (1992) *Mental Retardation: Definition, classification, and systems of supports* (9th ed.). Washington, DC: Author.

American Psychiatric Association. (1994). *Diagnostic and statistical manual of mental disorders* (4th ed.). Washington, DC: Author.

Ammann, A. J. (1994). Human immunodeficiency virus infections/AIDS in children: The next decade. *Pediatrics, 93,* 930–935.

Anand, K. J. S., & Hickey, P. R. (1987). Pain and its effects in the human neonate and fetus. *The New England Journal of Medicine, 317,* 1321–1329.

Anastasiow, N. J., & Harel, S. (1993). *At–risk infants: Interventions, families and research.* Baltimore, MD: Paul H. Brookes.

Anderson, V. (1990). Understanding HIV infection and its medical impact on children and youth. In G. R. Anderson (Ed.), *Courage to care: Responding to the crisis of children with AIDS* (pp. 17–26). Washington, DC: Child Welfare League of America.

Annie E. Casey Foundation. (1994). *Kids count data book: State profiles of child well-being.* Baltimore, MD: Author.

Arulkumaran, S. (1994). Poor progress in labor including augmentation, malpositions and malpresentations. In D. K. James, P. J. Steer, C. P. Weiner, & B. Gonik (Eds.), *High risk pregnancy: Management options* (pp. 1061–1075). London: W. B. Saunders.

Ayers, A. J. (1979). *Sensory integration and the child.* Los Angeles, CA: Western Psychological Services.

Bahrick, L. E., & Pickens, J. N. (1994). Amodal relations: The basis for intermodal perception and learning in infants. In D. J. Lewkowicz & R. Lickliter (Eds.), *The development of intersensory perception: Comparative perspectives* (pp. 205–234). Hillsdale, NJ: Lawrence Erlbaum Associates, Publishers.

Bailey, D. (1988). Considerations in developing family goals. In D. Bailey &. R. Simeonsson (Eds.), *Family assessment in early intervention* (pp. 229–249). Columbus, OH: Charles E. Merrill.

Baillargeon, R. (October, 1994). How do infants learn about the physical world? *Current direction in psychological science,* 133–140.

Balaban, N. (1992) The role of the child care professional in caring for infants, toddlers, and their families. *Young Children, 47*(5), 66–71.

Bale, J. F. Jr. (1990). The neurological complications of AIDS in infants and young children. *Infants and Young Children, 3,* 15–23.

Balfour–Lynn, I. M., & Valman, H. B. (1993). *Practical management of the newborn* (5th ed.). Oxford: Blackwell Scientific Publications.

Bamford, F. N., Bannister, R. P., Benjamin C. M., , Hillier, V. F., Ward, B. S., & Moore, W. M. O. (1990). Sleep in the first year of life. *Developmental Medicine and Child Neurology, 32,* 718–724.

Bandler, R., Grinder, J., & Satir, V. (1976). *Changing with families: A book about further education for being human.* Palo Alto, CA: Science and Behavior Books, Inc.

Bandura, A. (1992). Social cognitive theory. In R. Vasta (Ed.). *Six Theories of Child Development* (pp. 1–60). United Kingdom: Jessica Kingsley Publishers Ltd.

Barclay, L. K. (1985). *Infant development.* Fort Worth, TX: Holt, Rinehart and Winston.

Baron, N. S. (1992). *Growing up with language.* Reading, MA: Addison-Wesley Publishing Company, Inc.

Barron, W. M., & Lindheimer, M. D. (1995). Guidelines for prescribing drugs to pregnant women. In W. M. Barron & M. D. Lindheimer (Eds.), *Medical disorders during pregnancy* (2nd ed., pp. xi–xiii). St. Louis, MO: Mosby.

Barton, M., & Williams, M. (1993). Infant day care. In C. H. Zeanah, Jr. (Ed.), *Handbook of infant mental health* (pp. 445–461). New York: The Guilford Press.

Bassuk, E., & Buckner, J. (1993). Troubling families. *American Behavioral Scientist, 37*(3), 412–421.

Bates, E., Canaioni, L., & Volterra, V. (1975). The acquisition of performatives prior to speech. *Merrill Palmer Quarterly, 21,* 205–226.

Bates, E., Bretherton, I., & Snyder, L. (1988). *From first words to grammar: Individual differences and dissociable mechanisms.* Cambridge, MA: Cambridge University Press.

Bates, E., O'Connell, B., & Shore, C. (1984). First sentences in language and symbolic play. *Developmental Psychology. 20*(5), 872–880.

Batshaw, M. L., & Perret, Y. M. (1992). *Children with handicaps: A medical primer* (3rd ed.). Baltimore, MD: Paul H. Brookes.

Batshaw, M. L., Perret, Y. M., & Reber, M (1992). Autism. In M. L. Batshaw & Y. M. Perret (Eds.), *Children with disabilities: A medical primer* (pp. 407–420). Baltimore, MD: Paul H. Brookes

Baumrind, D. (1971). Current patterns of parental authority. *Developmental Psychology Monograph, 4* (1, Pt.2).

Baumrind, D. (1967). Effects of authoritative parental control on child behavior. *Child Development, 37,* 887–907.

Bayley, N. (1993). *Bayley Scales of Infant Development,* 2nd Ed. New York: Psychological Corporation.

Beckman, P. J., Robinson, C. C., Jackson, B., & Rosenberg, S. A. (1985). Translating developmental findings into teaching strategies for young handicapped children. *Journal of the Division for Early Childhood, 10* (1), 45–52.

Beilin, H. (1992). Piaget's enduring contribution to developmental psychology. *Developmental Psychology, 28,* 191–204.

Bellum, D., Breunig, G. S., Lombardi, J., & Whitebook, M. (1992). On the horizon: New policy initiatives to enhance child care staff compensation. Child Care Employee Project. *Young Children, 47*(5), 39–42.

Belsky, J. (1988). The 'effects' of infant day care reconsidered. *Early Childhood Research Quarterly, 3,* 235–272.

Belsky, J. (1992). Consequences of child care for children's development: A deconstructionist view. In A. Booth (Ed.), *Child care in the 1990s: Trends and consequences* (pp. 83–94). Hillsdale, NJ: Lawrence Erlbaum Associates, Publishers.

Belsky, J., Farduque, L., & Hrncir, E. (1984). Assessing performance, competence and executive capacity in infant play: Relations to home environment and attachment security. *Developmental Psychology, 20,* 406–417.

Belsky, J., & Kelly, J. (1994). *The transition to parenthood.* New York: Delacorte Press.

Belsky, J., & Rovine, M. (1984). Social-network contact, family support, and the transition to parenthood. *Journal of Marriage and the Family, 46,* 455–462.

Belsky, J., & Rovine, M. (1988). Non-maternal care in the first year of life and attachment security. *Child Development, 59,* 157–167.

Bemner, S. (1992). *Assessing young children with special needs: An ecological perspective.* New York: Longman.

Bennett, F. C. (1995). Recent advances in developmental intervention for biologically vulnerable infants. In J. A. Blackman (Ed.), *Treatment options in early intervention. Infants and Young Children Series* (pp. 84–93). Gaithersburg, MD: An Aspen Publication.

Berger, E. H. (1991). *Parents as partners in education: The school and home working together* (3rd ed.). New York: Merrill.

Berger, E. H. (1995). *Parents as partners in education: The school and home working together* (4th ed.). New York: Merrill.

Berk, L. E. (1994). Vygotsky's theory: The importance of make-believe play. *Young Children, 50*(1), 30–39.

Berlin, G., & McAllister, W. (1994). Homeless family shelters and family homelessness. *American Behavioral Scientist, 37*(3), 422–433.

Bernstein, A. C. (1989). *Yours, mine and ours: How families change when remarried parents have a child together.* New York: Scribners.

Bert, C., Greene, R., & Bert, M. (1992). *Fetal alcohol syndrome in adolescents and adults* (pp. 1–16). Miami FL: Independent Native American Development Corporation of Florida.

Bijou, S. W. (1992). Behavior analysis. In R. Vasta (Ed.), *Six Theories of Child Development* (pp. 61–84). United Kingdom: Jessica Kingsley Publishers Ltd.

Bijou, S. W., & Baer, D. M. (1961). *Child development: A systematic and empirical theory* (Vol. 1). Englewood Cliffs, NJ: Prentice-Hall.

Bijou, S. W., & Baer, D. M. (1965). *Child development: Universal stage of infancy* (Vol. 2). Englewood Cliffs, NJ: Prentice-Hall.

Bijou, S. W., & Baer, D. M. (1978). *Behavior analysis of child development.* Englewood Cliffs, NJ: Prentice-Hall.

Billeaud, F. P. (1993). *Communication disorders in infants and toddlers: Assessment and intervention.* Boston: Andover Medical Publishers.

Birch, E., & Held, R. (1983). The development of binocular summation in human infants. *Investigative Ophthalmology and Visual Science, 24,* 1103–1107.

Birch, L., Johnson, S. L., & Fisher, J. A. (1995). Children's eating: The development of food–acceptance patterns. *Young Children, 50*(2), 71–78.

Bird, A. (1989). Cognitive and language development. In C. Semmler (Ed.), *A guide to care and management of very low birth weight infants: A team approach* (pp. 190–215). Tucson, AZ: Therapy Skill Builders.

Bissell, J., Fisher, J., Owens, C., & Polcyn, P. (1988). *Sensory Motor Handbook: A guide for implementing and modifying activities in the classroom.* Torrance, CA: Sensory Integration International.

Bjorklund, G., & Burger, C. (1987). Making conferences work for parents, teachers, and children. *Young Children, 42*(2), 26–31.

Blass, E. M. (1990). Suckling: Determinants, changes, mechanism, and lasting impressions. *Developmental Psychology, 26,* 520–533.

Bloch, H., & Bertenthal, B. I. (1990). Preface. In H. Bloch & B. I. Bertenthal. *Sensory–motor organizations and development in infancy and early childhood* (Series D–Vol. 56, pp. xi–xiv). Dordrecht: Kluwer Academic Publishers.

Bloom, L. (1993). *The transition from infancy to language: Acquiring the power of expression.* New York: Cambridge University Press.

Bluestone, C. D., & Klein, J. O. (1988). *Otitis media in infants and children.* Philadelphia: W. B. Saunders.

Boothe, R. G., Dobson, V., & Teller, D. Y. (1985). Postnatal development of vision in human and nonhuman primates. *Annual Review of Neuroscience, 8,* 495–545.

Bornstein, M. H., & Sigman, M. D. (1986). Continuity in mental development from infancy. *Child Development, 57,* 251–274.

Bornstein, M. & Lamb, M. (1992). *Development in infancy: An introduction.* New York: McGraw-Hill.

Bowdry, C. (1990). Toward a treatment–relevant topology of child abuse families. *Child Welfare. 49*(4), 333–340.

Bower, T. G. R. (1975). Infant perception of the third dimension and object concept development. In E. B. Cohen & P. Salapatek (Eds.), *Infant Perception: From sensation to cognition, Vol. 2: Perception of space, speech and sound.* New York: Academic Press.

Bower, T. G. R., & Patterson, J. G. (1972). Stages in the development of object concept, *Cognition, 1,* 47–55.

Bower, T. G. R., & Wishart, J. G. (1972). The effects of motor skill on object permanence. *Cognition, 1,* 165–172.

Bowlby, J. (1940). The influence of early environment. *International Journal of Psycho-Analysis, 21,* 154–178.

Bowlby, J. (1944). Forty-four juvenile thieves. *International Journal of Psycho-Analysis, 25,* 1– 57.

Bowlby, J. (1952). *Maternal care and mental health* (2nd ed). Geneva: World Health Organization: Monograph Series, N.2.

Bowlby, J. (1958). The nature of the child's tie to his mother. *International Journal of Psychoanalysis, 39,* 350.

Bowlby, J. (1969). *Attachment and loss: Vol. 1. Attachment* (2nd ed.). New York: Basic Books.

Bowlby, J. (1989). The role of attachment in personality development and psychopathology. In S. I. Greenspan & G. H. Pollock (Eds.), *The course of life: Vol. 1 Infancy.* (pp. 229–270), Washington, DC: U.S. Government Printing Office.

Bowman, B. (1992). Child development and its implication for day care. In A. Booth (Ed.), *Child care in the 1990s: Trends and consequences* (pp. 95–100). Hillsdale, NJ: Lawrence Erlbaum Associates, Publishers.

Brandt, P. (1995). Negotiation and problem-solving strategies: Collaboration between families and professionals. In J. A. Blackman (Ed.), *Working with families in early inter-*

vention. Infants and Young Children Series (pp. 94–102). Gaithersburg, MD: An Aspen Publication.

Brazelton, T. B. (1979). Behavioral competence of the newborn infant. *Seminars in Perinatology, 3,* 35–44.

Brazelton, T. B. (1983). *Infants and mothers: Differences in development* (Rev ed). New York: Dell Publishing.

Brazelton, T. B. (1992). *Touchpoints: Your child's emotional and behavioral development.* Reading, MA: Addison-Wesley Publishing Company.

Bredekamp, S. (Ed.). (1987). *Developmentally appropriate practice in early childhood programs serving children from birth through age 8.* Expanded edition. Washington, DC: National Association for the Education of Young Children.

Bredekamp, S. (1993). The relationship between early childhood education and early childhood special education: Healthy marriage or family feud? *Topics in Early Childhood Education, 13,* 258–273.

Bredekamp, S. (1995). What do early childhood professionals need to know and be able to do? *Young Children, 50*(2), 67–69.

Bremner, J. G. (1994). *Infancy* (2nd ed.). Oxford: Blackwell Publishers.

Briere, J. (1992). *Child abuse trauma: Theory and treatment of the lasting effects.* Newbury Park, CA: Sage Publications.

Brigance, A. (1991). *Brigance Diagnostic Inventory of Early Development.* North Billerica, MA: Curriculum Associates, Inc.

Bronfenbrenner, U. (1979). *The ecology of human development.* Cambridge, MA: Harvard University Press.

Bronfenbrenner, U. (1986). Ecology of the family as a context for human development research perspectives. *Developmental Psychology, 22,* 723–742.

Bronfenbrenner, U. (1992). Ecological Systems Theory. In R. Vasta (Ed.), *Six theories of child development: Revised formulations and current issues* (pp. 187–250). London: Jessica Kingsley Publishers, Ltd.

Bronfenbrenner, U. (1993). The ecology of cognitive development: Research models and fugitive findings. In R. H. Wozniak & K. W. Fischer (Eds.), *Development in context: Acting and thinking in specific environments* (pp. 3–44). Hillsdale, NJ: Lawrence Erlbaum Associates.

Brophy, J., & Statham, J. (1994). Measure for measure: Values, quality and evaluation. In P. Moss & A. Pence (Eds.), *Valuing quality in early childhood services: New approaches to defining quality* (pp. 61–75). New York: Teachers College Press.

Brown, J. L. (1964). States in newborn infants. *Merrill-Palmer Quarterly, 10,* 313–327.

Brown, J. W. (1994). Morphogenesis and mental process. *Development and Psychopathology, 6,* 551–563.

Brown, R. (1973). *A first language, the early stages.* Cambridge, MA: Harvard University Press.

Bruder, M. B., Deiner, P. L., & Sachs, S. (1992). Models of integration through early intervention–Child care collaborations. In S. Provence, J. Pawl, & E. Fenichel (Eds.), *The zero to three child care anthology 1984–1992* (pp. 46–51). Arlington, VA: National Center for Clinical Infant Studies.

Bussell, D. A., & Reiss, D. (1993). Genetic influences on family process: The emergence of a new framework for family research. In F. Walsh (Ed.), *Normal Family Processes* (2nd ed), New York: The Guilford Press.

Caldeyro-Barcia, R. (1975). Supine called the worst position for labor and delivery. *Family Practice News, 5,* 11.

Caldeyro-Barcia, R. (1978). The influence of maternal position during the first stage of labor. In P. Simplin & C. Reinke (Eds.), *Kaleidoscope of childbearing: Preparation, birth, and nurturing* (Highlights of the 10th Biennial Convention of the International Childbirth Education Association, Inc.). Seattle, WA: Penny Press.

Camras, L., & Sachs, V. (1991). Social referencing and caretaker expressive behavior in a day care setting. *Infant Behavior and Development, 14,* 27–36.

Carey, S. (1984). Constraints on semantic development. In J. Mehler & R. Fox (Eds.), *Neonate cognition: Beyond the blooming buzzing confusion* (pp. 381–398). Hillsdale, NJ: Lawrence Erlbaum Associates, Publishers.

Carlsson-Paige, N., & Levin, D. E. (1987). *The war play dilemma: Balancing needs and values in the early childhood classroom.* New York: Teachers College Press.

Carnegie Task Force on Meeting the Needs of Young Children. (1994). *Starting Points: Meeting the needs of our youngest children.* New York: Carnegie Corporation of New York.

Carter, B. & McGoldrick, M. (1989). Overview: The changing family life cycle: A framework for family therapy. In B. Carter & M. McGoldrick (Eds.), *The changing family life cycle* (pp. 3–27). Boston, MA: Allyn & Bacon

Carter, B., & McGoldrick, M. (1993). The changing family life cycle. In F. Walsh (Ed.), *Normal family processes* (2nd ed.). New York: The Guilford Press.

Case, R. (1985). *Intellectual development: Birth to adulthood.* New York: Academic Press.

Cashore, W. (1995). Care of the newborn. In D. R. Coustan (Ed.), *Human Reproduction: Growth and Development* (pp. 379–390). Boston, MA: Little Brown and Company.

Cattell, R. B. (1971). *Abilities: Their structure, growth and action.* Boston: Houghton-Mifflin.

Caughy, M. O., DiPietro, J. A., & Strobino, D. M. (1994). Day-care participation as a protective factor in the cognitive development of low-income children. *Child Development, 65*(2), 457–471.

Cawlfield, M. (1992). Velcro time: The language connection. *Young Children, 47* (4), 26–30.

CDA pilot projects: Innovations (1978). Washington, DC: University Research Corporation.

Centers for Disease Control (1991). The HIV/AIDS epidemic: The first 10 years. *Journal of the American Medical Association, 265,* 3228.

Chase–Lansdale, P. L., & Owen, M. T. (1987). Maternal employment in a family context: Effects on infant-mother and infant-father attachments. *Child Development, 58,* 1505–1512.

Chasnoff, I. J. (1991). Cocaine and pregnancy: Clinical and methodological issues. *Clinics in Perinatology, 18*(1), 113–123.

Chess, S. (1983). Basic adaptations required for successful parenting. In V. Sasserath (Ed.), *Minimizing high-risk parenting* (pp. 5–11). Skillman, NJ: Johnson & Johnson.

Chess, S. & Thomas, A. (1990). The New York longitudinal study (NYLS): The young adult periods. *Canadian Journal of Psychiatry, 35,* 557–561.

Chess, S., & Thomas, A. (1977). Temperamental individuality from childhood to adolescence. *Journal of Child Psychiatry, 16,* 218–226.

Children's Defense Fund. (1989). *A vision for America's future.* Washington, DC: Author.

Children's Defense Fund. (1990). *Children 1990: A report card, briefing book and action primer.* Washington, DC: Author.

Children's Defense Fund. (1994a). *The state of America's children yearbook.* Washington, DC: Author.

Children's Defense Fund (1994b). Child poverty highest in three decades. *Children's Defense Fund Reports, 15*(12), 1–2, 12.

Children's Defense Fund. (1995a). *The state of America's children yearbook.* Washington, DC: Author.

Children's Defense Fund. (1995b). *Children in the states.* Washington, DC: Author.

Children's Defense Fund (1995c). Federal program eligibility. *Children's Defense Fund Reports, 16*(5), 9.

Chomsky, N. A. (1957). *Syntactic Structures.* The Hague: Mouton.

Chomsky, N. A. (1959). Review of Verbal behavior by B. F. Skinner. *Language,* 36, 26–58.

Chomsky, N. A. (1965). *Aspects of the theory of syntax.* Cambridge, MA: MIT Press.

Chomsky, N. A. (1968). *Language and mind.* New York: Harcourt, Brace, and World.

Chomsky, N. A. (1985). *Knowledge of language: Its nature, origin, and use.* New York: Praeger.

Cicchetti, D., & Lynch, M. (1993). Toward an ecological/transaction model of community violence and child maltreatment: Consequences for child development. In D. Reiss, J. E. Richters, & M. Radke-Yarrow (Eds.), *Children and violence* (pp. 96–118). New York: Guilford Press.

Cicchetti, D. & Tucker, D. (1994). Development and self-regulatory structures of the mind. *Development and Psychopathology,* 6, 533–549.

Clarke-Stewart, K. A. (1987). Predicting child development from child care forms and features: The Chicago Study. In D. A. Phillips (Ed.), *Quality in child care: What does research tell us?* (pp. 1–19). Washington, DC: National Association for the Education of Young Children.

Clarke-Stewart, K. A. (1989). Infant day care: Maligned or malignant *American Psychologist,* 44, 266–273.

Clarke-Stewart, K. A. (1992a). Consequences of child care for children's development. In A. Booth (Ed.), *Child care in the 1990s: Trends and consequences* (pp. 63–82). Hillsdale, NJ: Lawrence Erlbaum Associates, Publishers.

Clarke-Stewart, K. A. (1992b). Consequences of child care—one more time: A rejoinder. In A. Booth (Ed.), *Child care in the 1990s: Trends and consequences* (pp. 116–124). Hillsdale, NJ: Lawrence Erlbaum Associates, Publishers.

Clarke-Stewart, K. A., & Fein, G. G. (1983). Early childhood programs. In P. H. Mussen, M. Haith & J. Campos (Eds.), *Handbook of child psychology* (Vol 2, pp. 917–1000). New York: Wiley.

Clarke-Stewart, K. A., Gruber, C. P., & Fitzgerald, L. M. (1994). *Children at home and in day care.* Hillsdale, NJ: Lawrence Erlbaum Associates, Publishers.

Cohen, A. (1996, June). Personal communication, Child Care Law Center, San Francisco, CA.

Cohen, J. S., & Westhues, A. (1990). *Well functioning families for adoptive and foster children.* Toronto: University of Toronto Press.

Collins, R., & Coltrane, S. (1995). *Sociology of marriage and the family: Gender, love, and property* (4th ed.). Chicago, IL: Nelson-Hall Publishers.

Coltrane, S. (1990). Birth timing and the division of labor in dual-earner families. *Journal of Family Issues,* 11, 157–181.

Combrinck-Graham, L. (1985). A developmental model for family systems. *Family Process,* 24, 139–150.

Congdon, T. (1994). *Having babies.* New York: Simon & Schuster.

Conger, R. D., Elder, K. J., & Lorenz, F. O. (1992). A family process model of economic hardship and adjustment of early adolescent boys. *Child Development,* 63, 526–541.

Conlon, C. J. (1992). New threats to development: Alcohol, cocaine, and AIDS. In M. L. Batshaw & Y. M. Perret. *Children with disabilities: A medical primer* (3rd ed., pp. 111–136), Baltimore, MD: Paul H. Brooks.

Connor, F. P., Williamson, G. G., & Siepp, J. M. (1978). *Program guide for infants and toddlers with neuromotor and other developmental disabilities.* New York: Teachers College Press.

Consortium for Longitudinal Studies. (1983). *As the twig is bent: Lasting effects of preschool programs.* Hillsdale, NJ: Erlbaum.

Cost, Quality, and Outcomes Study Team. (1995). Cost, quality, and child outcomes in child care centers: Key findings and recommendations. *Young Children,* 50(4), 40–44.

Coustan, D. R. (1995). Obstetric complications. In D. R. Coustan (Ed.), *Human Reproduction: Growth and Development* (pp. 431–455). Boston, MA: Little Brown and Company.

Crockenberg, S., Lyons–Ruth, K., & Dickenstein, S. (1993). The family context of infant mental health: II. Infant development in multiple family relationships. In C. H. Zeanah, Jr. (Ed.), *Handbook of infant mental health* (pp. 38–55). New York: The Guilford Press.

Cross, T. L., Bazron, B. J., Dennis, K. W., & Isaacs, M. R. (1989). *Towards a culturally competent system of care: A monograph on effective services for minority children who are severely emotionally disturbed.* Washington, DC: Child and Adolescent Service System Program (CASSP) Technical Assistance Center, Georgetown University Child Development Center.

Crowther, C. A. (1994). Multiple pregnancy including delivery. In D. K. James, P. J. Steer, C. P. Weiner, & B. Gonik (Eds.), *High risk pregnancy: Management options* (pp. 137–149). London: W. B. Saunders.

Cummings, E. M., Hennessy, K., Rabideau, G., & Cicchetti, D. (1994). Responses of physically abused children to different forms of interadult anger, *Child Development. 65*(3), 815–828.

Cunningham, F., MacDonald, P. C., & Grant, N, F. (1989). *Williams Obstetrics* (18th ed.). Norwalk, CN: Appleton & Lange.

Curet, L. B. (1995). Diagnosis and management of drug abuse during pregnancy. In D. R. Coustan (Ed.), *Human Reproduction: Growth and Development* (pp. 137–159). Boston, MA: Little Brown and Company.

Daniel, J. E. (1993). Infants to toddlers: Qualities of effective transitions. *Young Children, 48*(6), 16–21.

Daniel, J. E. (1995). Advancing the care and education paradigm: A case for developmentalists. *Young Children, 50*(2), 2.

Daro, D., & McCurdy, K. (1990). *Current trends in child abuse reporting and fatalities: The results of the 1990 annual fifty-state survey.* Chicago, IL: National Committee for the Prevention of Child Abuse.

Davis-Floyd, R.E. (1992). *Birth as an American rite of passage.* Berkeley and Los Angeles, CA: University of California Press.

Day, N. L., & Richardson, G. A. (1991). Prenatal marijuana use: Epidemiology, methodological issues, and infant outcome. *Clinics in Perinatology, 18*(1), 77–91.

DeCasper, A. J., & Fifer, W. P. (1980). Of human bonding: Newborns prefer their mothers' voices. *Science, 208,* 1174–1176.

DeCasper, A. J., & Prescott, P. A. (1984). Human newborn's perception of male voices: Preferences, discrimination, and reinforcing value. *Developmental Psychobiology, 17,* 481–191.

DeCasper, A. J., & Spense, M. J. (1986). Prenatal maternal speech influences newborns' perception of speech sound. *Infant Behavior and Development, 9,* 133–150.

Deiner, P. L. (1992). Family day care and children with disabilities. In D. L. Peters & A. R. Pence (Eds.), *Family day care: Current research for informed public policy* (pp.129–145). New York: Teachers College Press.

Deiner, P. L. (1993). *Resources for teaching young children with diverse abilities: Birth through eight* (2nd ed). Fort Worth, TX: Harcourt Brace College Publishers.

Deiner, P. L., & Whitehead, L. C. (1988). *Levels of respite care as a family support system. Topics in Early Childhood Special Education, 8,* 51–61.

Demo, D., & Acock, A. (1991). The impact of divorce on children. In A. Booth (Ed.), *Contemporary families: Looking forward, looking back* (pp. 162–191). Minneapolis, MN: National Council on Family Relations.

Denk–Glass, R., Laber, S., & Brewer, K. (1982). Middle ear disease in young children. *Young Children, 37*(6), 51–53.

Dennen, P. C. (1994). Forceps deliveries. In D. K. James, P. J. Steer, C. P. Weiner, & B. Gonik (Eds.), *High risk pregnancy: Management options* (pp. 1140–1144). London: W. B. Saunders.

Dennis, W. (1935). The effect of restricted practice upon the reaching, sitting, and standing of two infants. *Journal of Genetic Psychology, 47,* 17–32.

Dennis, W. (1938). Infant development under conditions of restricted practice and of minimum social stimulation: A preliminary report. *Journal of Genetic Psychology, 53,* 149–158.

Dennis, W. (1941). Infant development under conditions of restricted practice and of minimal social stimulation. *Genetic Psychology Monographs, 23,* 143–191.

Dennis, W., & Dennis, M. G. (1940). The effect of cradling practices upon the onset of walking in Hopi children. *Journal of Genetic Psychology, 56,* 77–86.

Diaz, A. G., Schwarcz, R. F., & Caldeyro–Barcia, R. (1980). Vertical position during the course of the first stage of labor and neonatal outcome. *European Journal of Obstetrics and Gynecological Reproductive Biology, 11,* 1–7.

Dick–Read, G. (1959). *Childbirth without fear: The principles and practices of natural childbirth.* New York: Harper and Row.

Dickinson, J. E. (1994). Cesarean section. In D. K. James, P. J. Steer, C. P. Weiner, & B. Gonik (Eds.), *High risk pregnancy: Management options* (pp. 1153–1166). London: W. B. Saunders.

Division for Early Childhood, Council for Exceptional Children, National Association for the Education of Young Children, & Association of Teacher Educators. (1995). Personnel standards for early education and early intervention: Guidelines for licensure in early childhood special education. *Communicator 21*(3), 1–16.

Donn, S. M. (Ed.). (1992). *The Michigan manual: A guide to neonatal intensive care.* Mount Kisco, NY: Futura Publishing Company, Inc.

Drell, M., Siegel, C., & Gaensbauer, T. (1993). Post–traumatic stress disorder. In C. H. Zeanah (Ed.), *Handbook of infant mental health* (pp. 291–304). New York: Guilford Press.

Driscoll, M. P. (1994). *Psychology of learning for instruction.* Boston: Allyn and Bacon.

Dumtschin, J. U. (1988). Recognize language development and delay in early childhood. *Young Children, 43*(3), 16–24.

Dunn, J., & McGuire, S. (1994). Young children's nonshared experiences: A summary of studies in Cambridge and Colorado. In E. M. Hetherington, D. Reiss, & R. Plomin (Eds.), *Separate social worlds of siblings: The impact of nonshared environment on development.* Hilllsdale, NJ: Lawrence Erlbaum Associates.

Dunst, C. J., Brooks, P. H., & Doxsey, P. A. (1982). Characteristics of hiding places and the transition to stage IV performance in object permanence tasks. *Developmental Psychology, 18,* 671–681.

Duvall, E. (1977). *Marriage and family development* (5th ed.), Philadelphia: Lippincott.

Edme, R. N., Bingham, R. D., & Harmon, R. J. (1993). Classification and the Diagnostic Process in Infancy. In C. H. Zeanah, Jr. (Ed.), *Handbook of Infant Mental Health* (pp. 225–235). New York: The Guilford Press.

Edme, R. N., & Buchsbaum, H. K. (1989). Towards a psychoanalytic theory of affect: II. Emotional development and signaling in infancy. In S. I. Greenspan & G. H. Pollock (Eds.), *The course of life: Vol. 1 Infancy* (pp. 193–227). Washington, DC: U.S. Government Printing Office.

Eheart, B. K., & Leavitt, R. L. (1985). Supporting toddler play. *Young Children, 40*(3), 18–22.

Einbinder, S. D. (1994). A statistical profile of children living in poverty: Children under three and children under six, 1990. Unpublished document from the National Center for Children in Poverty. New York: Columbia University, School of Public

Health, 1992. Cited in The report of the Carnegie Task Force on Meeting the Needs of Young Children. *Starting Points: Meeting the needs of our youngest children.* New York: Carnegie Corporation of New York.

Emery, R. E. (1988). *Marriage, divorce, and children's adjustment.* Newbury Park, CA: Sage.

Engen, T. (1986). The acquisition of ordour hedonics. In S. V. Toller & G. H. Dodd (Eds.), *Perfumery: The psychology and biology of fragrance* (pp. 79–93). London: Chapman & Hall.

England, M. A. (1990). *A color atlas of life before birth: Normal fetal development.* London: Wolfe Medical Publications Ltd.

Entwisle, D. R., & Doering, S. G. (1981). *The first birth: A family turning point.* Baltimore, MD: The Johns Hopkins University Press.

Epstein, J. L. (1987). Parent involvement: What research says to administrators. *Education and Urban Society, 19*(2), 119–136.

Erikson, E. H. (1989). Elements of a psychoanalytic theory of psychosocial development. In S. I. Greenspan & G. H. Pollock (Eds.), *The course of life: Vol. 1 Infancy.* (pp. 15–84). Washington, DC: U.S. Government Printing Office.

Essa, E. (1990). *A practical guide to solving preschool behavior problems.* (2nd ed.). Albany, NY: Delmar.

Evans, A. T., & Gillogley, K. (1991). Drug use in pregnancy: Obstetric perspectives. *Clinics in Perinatology, 18*(1), 23–32.

Eysneck, M. W. (1986). The theory of intelligence and the psychophysiology of cognition. In R. J. Sternberg (Ed.), *Advances in the Psychology of Human intelligence* (Vol 3). Hillsdale, NJ: Erlbaum.

Faller, K. (1989). Why sexual abuse? An exploration of the intergenerational hypothesis. *Child Abuse and Neglect, 13,* 543–548.

Family Resource Service. (1993). *Helping your child into positive sleep patterns.* The Partnership Group (1–800–847–5437).

Fantz, R. L. (1963). Pattern vision in newborn infants. *Science, 140,* 296–297.

Feeney, S., & Kipnis, K. (1991). NAEYC Code of Ethical conduct and statement of commitment. In L. G. Katz & E. H. Ward (Eds.), *Ethical behavior in early childhood education* (Expanded Edition) (pp. 27–37). Washington, DC: National Association for the Education of Young Children.

Feinman, S. (1992). In the broad valley: An integrative look at social referencing. In S. Fineman (Ed.), *Social referencing and the social construction of reality in infancy* (pp. 3–14). New York: Plenum Press.

Feinman, S., & Lewis, M. (1991). Influence lost, influence gained. In M. Lewis & S. Feinman (Eds.). *Social influences and socialization in infancy* (pp. 1–22). New York: Plenum Press.

Feiring, C., & Lewis, M. (1982). Early mother-child interaction: Families with only and first born children. In G. L. Fox (Ed.), *The childbearing decision: Fertility attitudes and behavior.* Berkeley, CA: Sage.

Feldman, D. H. (1994). Introduction to the Second Edition. In. D. H. Feldman (Ed.), *Beyond universals in cognitive development* (2nd ed., pp. 1–15). Norwood, NJ: Ablex Publishing Corporation.

Feldman, D. H., & Snyder, S. S. (1994). Universal to Unique—Mapping the development terrain. In D. H. Feldman (Ed.), *Beyond universals in cognitive development.*(2nd ed., pp. 15–38). Norwood, NJ: Ablex Publishing Corporation.

Fenson, L., & Ramsey, D. S. (1980). Decentration and integration of the child's play in the second year. *Child Development, 51,* 171–178.

Fetters, L. (1984). Motor Development. In M. J. Hanson (Ed.), *Atypical infant development* (pp. 313–358). Baltimore MD: University Park Press.

Fewell, R. (1986). *Families of handicapped children: Needs and supports across the life span.* Austin, TX: PRO-ED.

Field, T. (1982). Affective displays of high-risk infants during early interactions. In T. Field & A. Fogel (Eds.), *Emotion and early interaction* (pp. 101–125). Hillsdale, NJ: Erlbaum.

Fifer, W. P., & Moon, C. (1989). Psychobiology of newborn auditory preferences. *Seminars in Perinatology, 13,* 393–402.

Finkelhor, D., & Dziuba-Leatherman, J. (1994). Victimization of children. *American Psychologist,* 173–183.

Finkelhor, D. (1995). The victimization of children: A developmental perspective. *American Journal of Orthopsychiatry, 65*(2), 177–193.

Fishbane, R. H. (1993). *Annual report of the domestic violence coordinating council.* Delaware: Domestic Violence Coordinating Council.

Flaim, P. O. (1986). Work schedules of Americans: An overview of new findings. *Monthly Labor Review, 109*(11), 3–6.

Flavell, J. H. (1963). *The developmental psychology of Jean Piaget.* Princeton, NJ: Van Nostrand.

Flavell, J. H. (1971). Stage related properties of cognitive development. *Cognitive Psychology, 2,* 421–453.

Flavell, J. H. (1985). *Cognitive Development* (2nd ed.). Englewood Cliffs, NJ: Prentice-Hall.

Flynn, A. M., Kelly, J., Hollins, G., & Lynch, P. F. (1978). Ambulation in labor. *British Medical Journal, 5,* 591–593.

Ford, S. A. (1993). The facilitator's role in children's play. *Young Children, 48*(6), 66–69.

Fraiberg, S. (1965). *The magic years.* New York: Scribner.

Frankenburg, W. K. (1986). *Revised Denver Prescreening Developmental Questionnaire.* Denver: Denver Developmental Materials.

Frankenburg, W. K. , & Dodds, J. B. (1990). *Denver Developmental Screening Test II.* Denver, CO: Denver Developmental Materials.

Freud, S. (1940). *An outline of psychoanalysis.* New York: Norton.

Friedman, D. F. (1986, March-April). Child care for employee's kids. *Harvard Business Review,* 28–34.

Friedrich, W., Beilke, R. L., & Urquiza, A. J. (1988). Behavior problems in young sexually abused boys. *Journal of Interpersonal Violence, 2,* 391–402.

Fromkin, V., & Rodman, R. (1974). *An introduction to language.* New York: Holt, Rinehart and Winston.

Furman, R. A. (1995). Helping children cope with stress and deal with feelings. *Young Children, 50*(2), 33–41.

Furstenberg, F. F., Jr. (1988). Child care after divorce and remarriage. In E. M. Hetherington & J. D. Arasteh (Eds.), *Impact of divorce, single parenting and stepparenting on children* (pp. 245–261). Hillsdale, NJ: Erlbaum.

Furstenberg, F. F. Jr., & Cherlin, A. (1991). *Divided Families.* Cambridge, MA: Harvard University Press.

Furuno, S., O'Reilly, K., Hosaka, C., Inatsuku, T., & Zeisloft–Falbey, B. (1987). *The Hawaii early learning profile.* Palo Alto, CA: VORT Corporation.

Furuno, S., O'Reilly, K., Inatsuka, T., Hosaka, C., Allman, T., & Ziesloft-Falbey, B. (1991). *HELP Chart: Gross motor, fine motor.* Palo Alto, CA: VORT Corporation.

Galinsky, E. (1988). Parents and teachers-caregivers: Sources of tension, sources of support. *Young Children, 43*(3), 4–12.

Galinsky, E., & Friedman, D. F. (1993). *Education before school: Investing in Quality Child Care.* New York: Scholastic Inc.

Galinsky, E., Howes, C., & Kontos, S. (1994). *The Family Child Care Training Study.* New York: Families and Work Institute.

Galinsky, E., Howes, C., Kontos, S., & Shinn, M. (1994). The study of children in family child care and relative care—Key findings and policy recommendations. *Young Children, 50*(1), 58–61.

Garbarino, J. (1990) Future directions. In R. T. Ammerman and M. Hersen (Eds.), *Children at risk: An evaluation of factors contributing to child abuse and neglect.* (pp. 291–298). New York: Plenum Press.

Garber, H. L., Hodge, J. D., Rynders, J., Dever, R., & Velu, R. (1991). The Milwaukee Project: Setting the record straight. *American Journal on Mental Retardation, 95*(5), 493–525.

Garcia, E. (1983). Becoming bilingual during early childhood. *International Journal of Behavioral Development, 6,* 375–404.

Gartrell, D. (1987). Punishment or guidance? *Young Children, 42*(3), 55–61.

Gelman, R. (1979). Preschool thought. *American Psychologist, 34,* 900–905.

Genishi, C. (1992). *Ways of assessing children and curriculum: Stories of early childhood practice.*

George, G., & Main, M. (1979). Social interactions of young abused children: Approach, avoidance, and aggression. *Child Development, 50,* 306–318.

Gesell, A. L. (1928). *Infancy and human growth.* New York: Macmillian.

Gesell, A. L. (1934). *An atlas of infant behavior.* New Haven, CN: Yale University Press.

Gesell, A. L. & Thompson, H. (1929). Learning and growth in identical infant twins. *Genetic Psychological Monographs, 6,* 1– 23.

Gestwicki, C. (1992). *Home, school and community relations.* Albany, NY: Delmar Publishers Inc.

Gibbs, E. D., & Teti, D. M. (1990). *Interdisciplinary assessment of infants: A guide for early intervention professionals.* Baltimore, MD: Paul H. Brookes.

Gibson, E. J. (1969). *Principles of perceptual learning and development.* New York: Appleton-Century-Crofts.

Gibson, E. J., & Walk, R. D. (1960). The "visual cliff." *Scientific American, 202,* 64–71.

Gibson, E. J., & Walker, A. (1984). Development of knowledge of visual-tactual affordances of substance. *Child Development, 55,* 453–460.

Gilbert, E. S., & Harmon, J. S. (1993). *Manual of high risk pregnancy and delivery.* St. Louis, MO: Mosby.

Gilkerson, L., Gorski, P., & Panitz, P. (1992). Hospital-based intervention for preterm infants and their families. In S. J. Meisels & J. P. Shonkoff (Eds.), *Handbook of Early Childhood Intervention* (pp. 445–468). Cambridge, MA: Cambridge University Press.

Giovangrandi, Y., Weiner, C. P., Smoleniec, J., & Brettes, J. P. (1994). Fetal infection. In D. K. James, P. J. Steer, C. P. Weiner, & B. Gonik (Eds.), *High risk pregnancy: Management options* (pp. 841–870). London: W. B. Saunders.

Gladding, S. T. (1995). *Family therapy: History, theory, and practice.* Englewood Cliffs, NJ: Prentice-Hall, Inc.

Gleason, J. B. (1987). Sex differences in parent-child interaction. In S. Stede & C. Tanz (Eds.), *Language, gender, and sex in contemporary perspective.* Cambridge, England: Cambridge University Press.

Glick, P. C., & Lin, S. (1986). Recent changes in divorce and remarriage. *Journal of Marriage and the Family, 48,* 737–747.

Goelman, H., & Pence, A. R. (1987). Some aspects of the relationships between family structure and child language development in three types of day care. In D. L. Peters & S. Kontos (Eds.), *Continuity and discontinuity of experience in child care* (pp. 129–146). Norwood, NJ: Ablex.

Goldman-Eisler, F. (1951). The problem of "orality" and it origin in early childhood. *Journal of Mental Science, 97,* 765–782.

Goldstein, S. (January, 1992). Young children at risk: The early signs of attention-deficit hyperactivity disorder. *CH.A.D.D.er Box, 5,* 7.

Gondolf, E. (1988). *Battered women as survivors*. Lexington, KY: Lexington Books.

Gottschall, S. (1989). Understanding and accepting separation feelings. *Young Children, 44*(6), 11–16.

Gottwald, S., Goldbach. P., & Isack, A. (1985). Stuttering: Prevention and detection. *Young Children, 40*(7), 9–14.

Gowen, J. W. (1995). The early development of symbolic play. *Young Children, 50*(3), 75–84.

Gratch, G., Appel, K. J., Evans, W. F., LeCompte, G. K., & Wright, N. A. (1974). Piaget's stage IV object concept error: Evidence of forgetting or object conception. *Child Development, 45,* 71–77.

Gratch, G., & Schatz, J. A. (1987). Cognitive development: The relevance of Piaget's infancy books. In J. D. Osofsky (Ed.), *Handbook of infant development* (pp. 204–237). New York: John Wiley & Sons, Inc.

Gravett, M. G., & Sampson, J. E. (1994). Other infectious conditions. In D. K. James, P. J. Steer, C. P. Weiner, & B. Gonik (Eds.), *High risk pregnancy: Management options* (pp. 509–550). London: W. B. Saunders.

Gray, H. (1973). *Anatomy of the Human Body* (29th ed.), C. M. Gross (Ed.), Philadelphia: Lea & Febiger.

Greenspan, S. I., & Greenspan, N. T. (1985). *First feelings: Milestones in the emotional development of your baby and child*. New York: Viking.

Greer, D., Potts, R., Wright, J., & Huston, A. (1982). The effects of television commercial form and commercial placement on children's social behavior and attention. *Child Development, 53,* 611–619

Griswold, R. L. (1993). *Fatherhood in America: A history*. New York: Basic Books.

Groves, B., Zuckerman, B., Marans, S., & Cohen, D. (1993). Silent victims: Children who witness violence. *Journal of the American Medical Association, 269,* 262–264.

Grunwald, L. (1993). The amazing minds of infants. Reprinted in Annual Editions: *Child Growth and Development 96/97* (pp. 38–43). Guilford, CT: Dushkin Publishing Group.

Guralnick, M. J. (1990). Social competence and early intervention. *Journal of Early Intervention, 14*(1), 3–14.

Gwiazda, J., Brill, S., Mohindra, I., & Held, R. (1980). Preferential looking of infants from 2 to 58 weeks of age. *American Journal of Optometry and Physiological Optics, 57,* 428–432.

Gyco, P. G., & Beckerman, R. C. (1990). Sudden infant death syndrome. *Current Problems in Pediatrics, 20,* 297–346.

Haith, M. M. (1980). *Rules that infants look by*. Hillsdale, NJ: Lawrence Erlbaum.

Haith, M. M., Bergman, T., & Moore, M. J. (1977). Eye contact and face scanning in early infancy. *Science, 198,* 853 –855.

Hallahan, D., & Kauffman, J. (1992). *Exceptional Children: Introduction to Special Education* (5th ed.). Englewood Cliffs, NJ: Prentice-Hall.

Halpern, R. (1990). Poverty and early childhood parenting. *American Journal of Orthopsychiatry, 60* (1), 6–16.

Hanson, M. J. (Ed.). (1984). *Atypical infant development*. Baltimore, MD: University Park Press.

Hanson, M. J. (1992). Ethnic, cultural and language diversity in intervention settings. In E. W. Lynch & M. J. Hanson (Eds.), *Developing cross-cultural competence: A guide for working with young children and their families* (pp. 3–18). Baltimore, MD: Paul H. Brookes.

Hanson, M. J., Lynch, E. W., & Wayman, K. I. (1990). Honoring the cultural diversity of families when gathering data. *Topics in Early Childhood Special Education, 10*(1), 112–131.

Hanson, S. M. H. (1988). Divorced fathers with custody. In P. Bronstein & C. P. Cowen (Eds.), *Fatherhood today: Men's changing roles in the family*. New York: Wiley.

Hardy, J. B., & Zabin, L. S. (1991). *Adolescent pregnancy in an urban environment: Issues, programs, and evaluation*. Washington, D.C.: The Urban Institute Press.

Harel, S., & Anastasiow, N. J. (Eds.). (1985). *The at-risk infant*. Baltimore, MD: Paul H. Brookes Publishing Co., Inc.

Harkin, T. (1991). Another point of cure. *The Journal of the American Medical Association, 269*, 1692–1693.

Harman, C. (1994). The routine 18–20 week ultrasound scan. In D. K. James, P. J. Steer, C. P. Weiner, & B. Gonik (Eds.), *High risk pregnancy: Management options* (pp. 661–692). London: W. B. Saunders.

Harms, T., & Clifford, R. M. (1980). *Early Childhood Environmental Rating Scale*. New York: Teachers College Press.

Harms, T., & Clifford, R. M. (1984). *Family Day Care Rating Scale*. New York: Teachers College Press.

Harms, T., & Clifford, R. M. (1989). *Infant/Toddler Environmental Rating Scale*. New York: Teachers College Press.

Harris, P. (1983). Infant cognition. In M. Harth & J. Campos (Eds.), *Handbook of child psychology: Vol. 2. Infancy and developmental psychology* (pp. 689–782). New York: Wiley.

Hay, D. F., Nash, A., & Pederson, F. (1983). Interaction between six-month-old peers. *Child Development, 54*, 557–562.

Hayes, C. D. (Ed.). (1987). *Risking the future: Adolescent sexuality, pregnancy, and childbearing*. Washington, DC: National Research Council.

Haynes, H., White, B. L., & Held, R. (1965). Visual accommodation in human infants. *Science, 148*, 528–530.

Hedrick, D., Prather, E., & Tobin, A. (1984). *Sequenced inventory of communication development–revised*. Seattle, WA: University of Washington Press.

Held, R. (1985). Binocular vision. In J. Mehler & R. Fox (Eds.), *Neonate cognition: Beyond the blooming buzzing confusion* (pp. 37–44). Hillsdale, NJ: Lawrence Erlbaum Associates, Publishers.

Hepper, P. G. (1992). Fetal psychology: An embryonic science. In J. Nijhuis (Ed.), *Fetal behavior: Developmental and perinatal aspects*. Oxford: Oxford University Press.

Hepper, P. G., & Shahidullah, S. (1992). Habituation in normal and Down syndrome fetuses. *Quarterly Journal of Experimental Psychology*. Special Issue: Comparative studies of prenatal learning and behavior. Vol. 44B (3–4), 305–317.

Hepper, P. G., White, R., & Shahidullah, S. (1991). The development of fetal responsiveness to external auditory stimulation. *British Psychological Society Abstracts, 30*.

Hetherington, E. M. (1989). Coping with family transitions: Winners, losers, and survivors. *Child Development, 60*, 1–14.

Hetherington, E. M., Cox, M., & Cox, R. (1982). Effects of divorce on parents and children. In M. Lamb (Ed.), *Nontraditional families: Parenting and child development*. Hillsdale, NJ: Lawrence Erlbaum Associates.

Hetherington, E. M., Law, T. C., & O'Connor, T. G. (1993). Divorce: Challenges, changes, and new chances. In F. Walsh (Ed.) *Normal family processes* (2nd ed, pp. 208–234). New York: The Guilford Press.

Hetherington, E. M., & Tryon, A. S. (1989). His and her divorces. *The Family Therapy Networker, 13*(6), 58–61.

Heyne, E. (1989). Low birth weight infant follow-up at children's medical center, Dallas. In C. Semmler (Ed.), *A guide to care and management of very low birth weight infants: A team approach* (pp. 124–135). Tucson, AZ: Therapy Skill Builders.

Hilgard, H. R. (1932). Learning and maturation in preschool children. *Journal of Genetic Psychology, 41*, 31–56.

Hill, P. M., & McCune–Nicholich, L. (1981). Pretend play and patterns of cognition in Down syndrome children. *Child Development, 52,* 611–617.

Hitz, R. & Driscoll, A. (1988). Praise or encouragement? New insights into praise: Implications for early childhood teachers. *Young Children, 43*(5), 6–13.

Hochschild, A. (1989). *The second shift: Working parents and the revolution at home.* New York: Viking.

Hoegerman, G., & Schnoll, S. (1991). Narcotic use in pregnancy. *Clinics in Perinatology, 18*(1), 51–76.

Hofferth, S. L. (1992). The demand for and supply of child care in the 1990s. In A. Booth (Ed.), *Child care in the 1990s: Trends and consequences* (pp. 3–25). Hillsdale, NJ: Lawrence Erlbaum Associates, Publishers

Hofferth, S. L., Brayfield, S., Deich, S., & Holcomb, P. (1991). *The National Child Care Survey 1990.* Washington, DC: The Urban Institute.

Hoffman, H., Damus, K., Hillman, L., & Krongrad, E. (1988). Risk factors for SIDS. In P. Schwartz, D. Southall, & M. Valdes-Dapena (Eds.), *Sudden infant death syndrome: Cardiac and respiratory mechanisms and interventions* (pp. 13–31). New York: Annals of the New York Academy of Science.

Hoffman, M. L. (1970). Moral Development. In P. H. Mussen (Ed.), *Carmichael's manual of child psychology* (Vol. II, pp. 261–360). New York: John Wiley & Sons, Inc.

Hoffman, M. L. (1981). Is altruism part of human nature? *Journal of Personality and Social Psychology, 40,* 121–137.

Hoffman, S. D., & Duncan, G. J. (1988). What are the economic consequences of divorce? *Demography, 25*(4), 641–645.

Hohmann, M. (Spring/Summer 1988). Children get along fine without adults . . . Or do they? *High Scope Resource.* Ypsilanti, MI: The High/Scope Press.

Holzgreve, W., & Miny, P. (1994). Chorionic villus sampling and placental biopsy. In D. K. James, P. J. Steer, C. P. Weiner, & B. Gonik (Eds.), *High risk pregnancy: Management options* (pp. 635–642). London: W. B. Saunders.

Honig, A. S. (1979). *Parent involvement in early childhood education.* Washington, DC: National Association for the Education of Young Children.

Honig, A. S. (1982a). Infant–mother communication. *Young Children, 37*(3), 52–62.

Honig, A. S. (1982b). Language environments for young children. *Young Children, 38,* 56–67.

Honig, A. S. (1983). Evaluation of infant/toddler intervention programs. In B. Spodek (Ed.), *Studies in educational evaluation* (Vol 8, pp. 305–316). London: Pergamon.

Honig, A. S. (1986). Stress and coping in children. In J. B. McCracken (Ed.), *Reducing stress in young children's lives* (pp. 142–167). Washington, DC: National Association for the Education of Young Children.

Honig, A. S. (1986). Stress and coping in children (Part 2): Interpersonal family relationships. *Young Children, 41*(5), 47–59.

Honig, A. S. (1987). The shy child. *Young Children, 42*(4), 54–64.

Honig, A. S. (1989). Quality infant/toddler care giving: Are there magic recipes? *Young Children, 44*(4), 4–10.

Honig, A. S. (1993). Mental health for babies: What do theory and research teach us? *Young Children, 48*(3), 69–76.

Honig, A. S., & Wittmer, D. S. (1996). Helping children become more prosocial: Ideas for classrooms, families, schools, and communities. *Young Children, 51,* 2, 62–70.

Horney, K. (1937). *The neurotic personality of our time.* New York: Norton.

Horney, K. (1945). *Our inner conflicts.* New York: Norton.

Horowitz, F. D. (1992). The challenge facing infant research in the next decade. In G. J. Suci & S. S. Robertson (Eds.), *Future directions in infant development research* (pp. 89–103). New York: Springer Verlag.

Hostetler, L., & Klugman, E. (1982). Early childhood job titles: One step toward professional status. *Young Children, 37*(3), 13–22.

Howe, M. C., & Briggs, A. K. (1989). Ecological systems model for occupational therapy. In
B. H. Hanft (Ed.), *Family-centered care: An early intervention resource manual* (pp. 1–39
to 1–45). Rockville, MD: The American Occupational Therapy Association, Inc.

Howes, C., & Olenick, M. (1986). Family and child care influences on toddler's compliance. *Child Development, 57,* 202–216.

Howes, C. (1992). *The collaborative construction of pretend: Social pretend play functions.*
Albany: State University of New York Press.

Howes, C., & Farber, J. (1987). Toddlers' responses to the distress of their peers. *Journal of
Applied Developmental Psychology, 8,* 441–452.

Howes, C., Rodning, C., Gulluzo, D., & Meyers, L. (1988). Attachment and child care: Relations with mother and caregiver. *Early Childhood Research Quarterly, 3,* 403–416.

Howes, C., Smith, E., & Galinsky, E. (1994). *The Florida Child Care Quality Improvement
Study.* New York: Families and Work Institute.

Howes, C., Unger, O., & Seidner, L. B. (1989). Social and pretend play in toddlers: Parallels
with social play and solitary pretend. *Child Development, 60,* 77–84.

Hrncir, E. J. & Eisenhart, C. E. (1991). Use with caution: The "at–risk" label. *Young Children,
46*(2), 23–27.

Hughes, F. P., Elicker, J., & Veen, L. C. (1995). A program of play for infants and their caregivers. *Young Children, 50*(2), 52–58.

Hussey, B. (1987). *My special signals: A guide to parents of premature infants.* Chapel Hill, NC:
North Carolina Memorial Hospital.

Huston, A. (1983). Sex typing. In E. M. Heatherington (Ed.), *Handbook of child psychology:
Vol. 4. Socialization, personality, and social development* (pp. 387–467). New York:
Wiley.

Huston, A., Donnerstein, E., Fairchild, H., Feshbach, N., Katz, P., Murray, J., Rubinstein,
E., & Wilcox, B. (1992). *Big world, small screen.* Lincoln, NE: University of Nebraska
Press.

Huston, A., Watkins, B., & Kunkel, D. (1989). Public policy and children's television. *American Psychologist, 44,* 424–433.

Hyson, M. C. (1994). *The emotional development of young children: Building an emotion-centered
curriculum.* New York: Teachers College Press.

Hyson, M. C., & Van Triest, K. (1987). The shy child. *Eric Digests.* Urbana, IL: ERIC Clearinghouse on Elementary and Early Childhood Education.

Hyson, M. C., Whitehead, L. C., & Prudhoe, C. M. (1988). Influences on attitudes toward
physical affection between adults and children. *Early Childhood Research Quarterly, 3,*
55–75.

Infant Health and Development Program. (1990). Enhancing the outcomes of low-birth-
weight, premature infants: A multisite, randomized trial. *Journal of American Medical
Association, 263,* 3035–3042.

Ingrassia, M., & Beck, M. (1994, July). Patterns of Abuse. *Newsweek,* 26–33.

Izard, C. E. (1991). *The psychology of emotions.* New York: Plenum.

Izard, C. E., & Hyson, M. C. (1986). Shyness as a discrete emotion. In W. H. Jones (Ed.),
Shyness. New York: Plenum.

Izard, C. E., & Malatesta, C. Z. (1987). Perspectives on emotional development I: Differential emotions theory of early emotional development. In J. D. Osofsky (Ed.), *Handbook of infant development* (2nd ed., pp. 494–554). New York: John Wiley & Sons, Inc.

Jacobson, J., Jacobson, S., Padgett, R., Brumitt, G., & Billings, R. (1992). Effects of prenatal
PCB exposure on cognitive processing efficiency and sustained attention. *Developmental Psychology, 28,* 297–306.

Jaffee, P., Wilson, S., & Wolfe, D. (1988). Specific assessment and intervention strategies for children exposed to wife battering: Preliminary empirical investigations. *Canadian Journal of Community Mental Health, 7*, 157–163.

Jalongo, M. R. (1987). Do security blankets belong in preschool? *Young Children, 42*(3), 3–8.

James, D. K. (1994a). Genetic Counseling. In D. K. James, P. J. Steer, C. P. Weiner, & B. Gonik (Eds.), *High risk pregnancy: Management options* (pp. 9–20). London: W. B. Saunders.

James, D. K. (1994b). Counseling about pediatric problems. In D. K. James, P. J. Steer, C. P. Weiner, & B. Gonik (Eds.), *High risk pregnancy: Management options* (pp. 1215–1225). London: W. B. Saunders.

James, W. (1890). *Principles of Psychology* (2 Vols.). New York: Holt.

Johnson, B. H., McGonigel, M. J., & Kaufmann, R. K. (Eds.). (1989). *Guidelines and recommended practices for the individualized family service plan.* Washington, DC: National Early Childhood Technical Assistance System and the Association for the Care of Children's Health.

Johnson, J. E., Christie, J. F., & Yawkey, T. D. (1987). *Play and early childhood development.* Glenview, IL: Scott, Foresman & Co.

Johnson, M. (1991). American Indians and Alaska natives with disabilities. *Indian Nations At Risk Task Force commissioned papers* (pp. 1–42).

Jones, S., & Meisels, S. J. (1987). Training family day care providers to work with special needs children. *Topics in Early Childhood Special Education, 7*, 1–12.

Kagan, R. & Schlosberg, S. (1989). *Families in perpetual crisis.* New York: W. W. Norton & Co.

Kamphaus, R. W., Dresden, J., & Kaufman, A. S, (1993). Clinical and psychometric considerations in the cognitive assessment of preschool children. In J. L. Culbertson & D. J. Willis (Eds.), *Testing young children: A reference guide for developmental, psychoeducational, and psychosocial assessments* (pp. 55–72). Austin, TX: Pro-ed.

Karmel, M. (1965). *Thank you, Dr. Lamaze.* New York: Dolphin Books.

Karmerman, S. B., & Kahn, A. J. (1988). *Mothers alone: Strategies for a time of change.* Dover, MA: Auburn House Pub. Co.

Katz, L. G. (1991). Ethical issues in working with young children. In L. G. Katz & E. H. Ward (Eds.), *Ethical behavior in early childhood education* (Expanded Edition) (pp. 1–16). Washington, DC: National Association for the Education of Young Children.

Keith, D. V. (1989). The family's own system: The symbolic context of health. In L. Combrinck-Graham (Ed.), *Children in family contexts: Perspectives on treatment* (pp. 327–346). New York: The Guilford Press.

Kendall–Tackett, K. A., Williams, L. M., & Finkelhor, D. (1993). Impact of sexual abuse on children: A review and synthesis of recent empirical studies. *Psychological Bulletin, 113*(1), 164–180.

Kenny, T. J., & Culbertson, J. L. (1993). Developmental screening for preschoolers. In J. L. Culbertson & D. J. Willis (Eds.), *Testing young children: A reference guide for developmental, psychoeducational, and psychosocial assessment* (pp. 73–100). Austin, TX: Pro-ed.

Kessen, W. (1965). *The child.* New York: Wiley.

Ketterlinus, R. D., Lamb, M. E. , & Nitz, K. (1991). Developmental and ecological sources of stress among adolescent parents. *Family Relations, 40*, 435–441.

Kilbride, J. E., & Kilbride, P. L. (1979). Sitting and smiling behavior of Baganda infants. *Journal of Cross-Cultural Psychology, 6*, 88–107.

Kitson, G., & Sussman, M. (1982). Marital complaints, demographic characteristics, and symptoms of mental distress in divorce. *Journal of Marriage and the Family, 44*, 87–101.

Klass, C. S. (1987). Childrearing interactions within developmental home- or center-based early education. *Young Children, 42*(3), 9–13, 67–70.

Klein, A. G. (1992). *The debate over child care 1969–1990: A sociohistorical analysis.* Albany, NY: State University of New York Press.

Klein, T. , Bittel, C., & Molnar, J. (1993). No place to call home: Supporting the needs of homeless children in the early childhood classroom. *Young Children, 48*(6), 22– 31.

Knobloch, H., & Pasamanick, B. (1974). *Gesell and Amatruda's Developmental Diagnosis* (3rd ed.). New York: Harper & Row.

Konje, J. C., & Walley, R. J. (1994). Bleeding late in pregnancy. In D. K. James, P. J. Steer, C. P. Weiner, & B. Gonik (Eds.), *High risk pregnancy: Management options* (pp. 119–136). London: W. B. Saunders.

Kontos, S. (1984). Congruence of parent and early childhood staff perceptions of parenting. *Parenting Studies, 1*(1), 5–10.

Kontos, S. (1992). Family day care: The "other" form of care. In B. Spodek, & O. N. Saracho (Eds.), *Issues in child care* (pp. 107–124). New York: Teachers College Press.

Kontos, S., Howes, C., Shinn, M., & Galinsky, E. (1995). *Quality in family child care and relative care.* New York: Teachers College Press.

Kontos, S., & Wells, W. (1986). Attitudes of caregivers and the day care experiences of families. *Early Childhood Research Quarterly, 1*, 47–67.

Korner, A. F. (1972). State as variable, obstacle and as mediator of stimulation in infant research. *Merrill–Palmer Quarterly, 18*, 77–94.

Krajicek, M. J. (1991). *Handbook for the care of infants and toddlers with disabilities and chronic conditions.* Lawrence, KS: Learner Managed Designs.

Krashen, S. D., Scarella, R. C., Long, M. H. (Eds.), (1982). *Child-adult differences in second language acquisition.* Rowley, MA: Newbury House Publishers.

Kryden-Coe, J. H., Salamon, L. M., & Molnar, J. M. (Ed.). (1991). *Homeless children and youth: A new American dilemma.* (pp. 19–24). New Brunswick, NJ: Transaction Publishers.

Kuebli, J. (1994). Young children's understanding of everyday emotions. *Young Children, 49*(3), 36–47.

Kuebli, J., & Fivush, R. (1992). Gender differences in parent-child conversations about past emotions. *Sex Roles, 27*(11/12), 683–698.

Lally, J. R., Provence, S., Szanton, E., & Weissbourd, B. (1987). Developmentally appropriate care for children from birth to age 3. In S. Bredekamp (Ed.), *Developmentally appropriate practice in early childhood programs serving children from birth through age 8.* (pp. 17–46). Washington, DC: National Association for the Education of Young Children.

Lamaze, F. (1956). *Painless childbirth: The Lamaze method.* New York: Pocket Books.

Lamb, M. E. (1976). Twelve month olds and their parents: Interaction in a laboratory playroom. *Developmental Psychology, 13*, 639–649.

Lamb, M. E. (1977). The development of parental preferences in the first two years of life. *Sex Roles, 3*, 495–497.

Lamb, M. E. (1986). The changing roles of fathers. In M. E. Lamb (Ed.), *The father's role: Applied perspectives* (pp. 3–28). New York: John Wiley & Sons.

Lamb, M. E., & Oppenheim, D. (1989). Fatherhood and father-child relationships. In S. Cath, A. Gurwitt, & L. Gunsberg (Eds.), *Fathers and their families.* (pp. 1–26). Hillsdale, NJ: Erlbaum.

Lamb, M. E., Pleck, J. H., & Levine, J. A. (1987). Effects of increased paternal involvement on fathers and mothers. In C. Lewis & M. O'Brien (Eds.), *Researching fatherhood* (pp. 109–125). London: Sage.

Landon, M. B., & Gabbe, S. G. (1994). Diabetes Mellitus. In D. K. James, P. J. Steer, C. P. Weiner, & B. Gonik (Eds.), *High risk pregnancy: Management options* (pp. 277–298). London: W. B. Saunders.

Langley, M. B. (1985). Selecting, adapting, and applying toys as learning tools for handi-capped children. *Topics in Early Childhood Special Education, 5*(3), 101–118.

Langsted, O. (1994). Looking at quality from the child's perspective. In P. Moss & A. Pence (Eds.), *Valuing quality in early childhood services: New approaches to defining quality* (pp. 28–42). New York: Teachers College Press.

Larner, M., & Phillips, D. (1994). Defining and valuing quality as a parent. In P. Moss & A. Pence (Eds.), *Valuing quality in early childhood services: New approaches to defining quality* (pp. 43–60). New York: Teachers College Press.

Lawton, J. T. (1988). *Introduction to child care and early childhood education.* Boston: Scott, Foresman & Co.

Leboyer, F. (1975). *Birth without violence.* New York: Knopf.

Lee, J., & Nisivoccia, D. (1989). *Walk a mile in my shoes.* Washington, DC: Child Welfare League of America.

LeeKeenan, D., & Edwards, C. P. (1992). Using the project approach with toddlers. *Young Children, 47*(4), 31–35.

LeMay, D., Griffin, P., & Sanford, A. (1978). *Learning Accomplishment Profile–Diagnostic Edition.* Lewisville, NC: Kaplan School Supply Corporation.

Lenneberg, E. (1967). *The biological foundation of language.* New York: Wiley.

Lester, B., Zacharaial Boukydis, C. F., Garcia-Coll, C. Hole, W., & Peucker, M. (1992). Infan-tile colic: Acoustic cry characteristics, maternal perception of cry, and temperament. *Infant Behavior and Development, 15,* 15–26.

Levin, D. E., & Carlsson–Paige, N. (1994). Developmentally appropriate television: Putting children first. *Young Children, 49*(5), 38–44.

Lewis, M. (1987). Social development in infancy and early childhood. In J. D. Osofsky (Ed.). *Handbook of infant development* (2nd ed., pp. 419–493). New York: John Wiley & Sons, Inc.

Lewis, M. (1992). *Shame: The exposed self.* New York: The Free Press.

Lewkowicz, D. A. (1991). Development of intersensory functions in human infancy: Auditory/visual interactions. In M. J. Weiss & P. R. Zelazo (Eds.), *Newborn atten-tion: Biological constraints and the influence of experience* (pp. 308–338). Norwood, NJ: Ablex.

Lewkowicz, D. A. (1994). Development of intersensory perception in human infants. In D. J. Lewkowicz & R. Lickliter (Eds.), *The development of intersensory perception: Com-parative perspectives* (pp. 165–204). Hillsdale, NJ: Lawrence Erlbaum Associates, Pub-lishers.

Liddell, H. S., & Fisher, P. R. (1985). The birthing chair in the second stage of labor. *Aus-tralia–New Zealand Journal of Obstetrics and Gynaecology, 25,* 65–68.

Lipsitt, L. P. (1986). Learning in infancy: Cognitive development in babies. *The Journal of Pediatrics, 109,* 172–182.

Lipsitt, L. P., & Behl, G. (1990). Taste-mediated differences in the sucking behavior of human newborns. In E. D. Capaldi & T. L. Powley (Eds.), *Taste, experience, and feed-ing* (pp. 75–93). Washington, DC: American Psychological Association.

Lipsitt, L. P., & Kaye, H. (1965). Change in neonatal response to optimizing and non-optimizing sucking stimulation. *Psychonomic Science, 2,* 221–222.

Lobel, T. & Menashin, J. (1993). Relations of conceptions of gender-role transgressions and gender constancy to gender-typed toy preferences. *Developmental Psychology, 29,* 150–155.

Lorenz, K. Z. (1965). *Evolution and the modification of behavior.* Chicago: University of Chicago Press.

Lund, N. J., & Duchan, J. F. (1993). *Assessing children's language in naturalistic contexts.* (3rd ed.). Englewood Cliffs, NJ: Prentice-Hall.

Lupe, P. J., & Gross, T. L. (1986). Maternal upright posture and mobility in labor: A review. *Obstetrics and Gynecology, 67*, 727–734.

Lyons-Ruth, K., & Zeanah, Jr., C. H. (1993). The family context of infant mental health: I. Affective development in the primary caregiving relationship. In C. H. Zeanah, Jr. (Ed.), *Handbook of infant mental health.* (pp. 15–37). New York: The Guilford Press.

Lynch, E. W., & Hanson, M. J. (Eds.). (1992). *Developing cross-cultural competence: A guide for working with young children and their families.* Baltimore, MD: Paul H. Brookes Publishing Co., Inc.

MacDonald, K. (1985). Early experience, relative plasticity, and social development. *Developmental Review, 5*, 99–121.

MacFarlane, J. A. (1975). *Olfaction in the development of social preferences in the human neonate.* Amsterdam: Elsevier.

Machado, J. M. (1990). *Early childhood experiences in language arts.* Albany, NY: Delmar Publishers Inc.

Main, M., & Solomon, J. (1990). Procedures for identifying infants as disorganized/disoriented during the Ainsworth Strange Situation. In M. Greenberg, D. Cicchetti, & E. M. Cummings (Eds.), *Attachment in the preschool years: Theory, research and intervention* (pp. 121 –160). Chicago: University of Chicago Press.

Maluccio, A. N., Kreiger, R., & Pine, B. A. (1990). *Preparing adolescents for life after foster care.* Washington, DC: Child Welfare League of America.

Maresh, M., & Neales, K. (1994). High dependency care of the obstetric patient. In D. K. James, P. J. Steer, C. P. Weiner, & B. Gonik (Eds.), *High risk pregnancy: Management options* (pp. 1227–1257). London: W. B. Saunders.

Marotz, L. R., Cross, M. Z., & Rush, J. M. (1993). *Health, safety and nutrition for the young child.* Albany, NY: Delmar Publishers, Inc.

Marsiglio, W. (1991). Paternal engagement activities with minor children. *Journal of Marriage and the Family, 53*, 973–986.

Marsiglio, W. (1995). Fatherhood scholarship: An overview and agenda for the future. In W. Marsiglio (Ed.). *Fatherhood: Contemporary theory, research and social policy.* Thousand Oaks, CA: Sage Publications.

Marzek, P. J. (1993). Maltreatment and infant development. In C. H. Zeanah, Jr. (Ed.), *Handbook of Infant Mental Health* (pp. 159–170). New York: The Guilford Press.

Mason, E., & Lee, R. V. (1995). Drug abuse. In W. M. Barron & M. D. Lindheimer (Eds.), *Medical disorders during pregnancy* (2nd ed., pp. 465–486). St. Louis, MO: Mosby.

Maurer, D., & Maurer, C. (1988). *The world of the newborn.* New York: Basic Books, Inc.

McAdoo, J. L. (1986). A black perspective on the father's role in child development. *Marriage and Family Review, 9*(3/4), 117–133.

McColl, R. & Carriger, M. (1993). A meta-analysis of infant habituation and recognition memory performance as indicators of later IQ. *Child Development, 64*, 57–79.

McCormick, L., & Feeney, S. (1995). Modifying and expanding activities for children with disabilities. *Young Children, 50*(4), 10 –17.

McCormick, M. C. (1989). Long term follow-up of infants discharged from neonatal intensive care units. *Journal of the American Medical Association*, 1767–1771.

McCubbin, H., & Dahl, B. B. (1985). *Marriage and family: Individuals and life cycles.* New York: Macmillian Publishing Company.

McGoldrick, M. (1993). Ethnicity, cultural diversity, and normality. In F. Walsh (Ed.), *Normal family processes.* (2nd. ed., pp. 331–360). New York: The Guilford Press.

McGoldrick, M., Heiman, M., & Carter, B. (1993). The changing family life cycle: A perspective on normalcy. In F. Walsh (Ed.), *Normal family processes* (2nd ed., pp. 405–443). New York: The Guilford Press.

McGraw, M. B. (1935). *Growth: A study of Johnny and Jimmy.* New York: Appleton-Century.

McGraw, M. B. (1943). *The neuromuscular maturation of the human infant.* New York: Columbia University Press.

McKenna, J. (1990). Evolution and sudden infant death syndrome: Infant responsivity to parental contact. *Human Nature, I,* 145–177.

McLean, L. K. S. (1990). Communication development in the first two years of life: A transactional process. *Zero to Three,* 13–19.

Mcleod, J. D., & Shanahan, M. J. (1993). Poverty, parenting, and children's mental health. *American Sociological Review, 58,* 351–366.

Meadows, S. (1993). *The child as thinker: The development and acquisition of cognition in children.* London: Routledge.

Meddin, B., & Rosen, A. (1986). Child abuse and neglect: Prevention and reporting. *Young Children, 41*(4), 26–30.

Mehler, J. (1985). Introduction: Some reflections on initial state research. In J. Mehler & R. Fox (Eds.), *Neonate cognition: Beyond the blooming buzzing confusion* (pp. 1–6). Hillsdale, NJ: Lawrence Erlbaum Associates, Publishers.

Mehler, J., & Dupoux, E. (1994). *What infants know: The new cognitive science of early development* (P. Southgate, Trans.). Cambridge, MA: Blackwell.

Mercer, R. (1990). *Parents at risk.* New York: Springer Publishing Co., Inc.

Miedzian, M. (1991). *Boys will be boys: Breaking the link between masculinity and violence.* New York: Doubleday.

Miller, W. A. (1990). Prenatal genetic diagnosis. In S. M. Pueschel & J. A, Mulick (Eds.), *Prevention of Developmental Disabilities* (pp. 123–141). Baltimore, MD: Paul H. Brookes Publishing Co.

Miller, S., Nunnally, E. W., & Wackmen, D. B. (1975). *Alive and aware: How to improve your relationships through better communications.* Minneapolis, MN: Interpersonal Communications Programs.

Mollick, L., & Etra, K. (1981). Poor learning ability. . . or poor hearing? *Teacher.* Reprinted in *Annual Editions, Educating Exceptional Children.* (1992). (pp. 178–179). Guilford, CT: The Dushkin Publishing Group, Inc.

Moore, K. A., & Burt, M. R. (1982). *Private crisis, public cost: Policy perspectives on teenage childbearing.* Washington, DC: Urban Institute.

Morgan, B., (1994). Maternal anesthesia and analgesia in labor. In D. K. James, P. J. Steer, C. P. Weiner, & B. Gonik (Eds.), *High risk pregnancy: Management options* (pp. 1101–1118). London: W. B. Saunders.

Morgan, E. L. (1989). Talking with parents when concerns come up. *Young Children, 44*(2) 52–56.

Morgan, G., Azer, S. L., Costley, J. B., Elliott, K., Genser, A., Goodman, I. F., & McGimsey, B. (1994). Future pursuits: Building early care and education careers. *Young Children 49*(3), 80–83.

Morrell, P., & Norton, W. (1980). Myelin. *Scientific American, 242,* 99–119.

Morris, J. C. (1994). Introverts. *Young Children, 49*(2), 32–33.

Morris, S. L. (1995). Supporting the breast–feeding relationship during child care: Why is it important? *Young Children, (50)*2, 59–62.

Morrison, G. S. (1988). *Education and development of infants, toddlers and preschoolers.* Boston: Scott, Foresman & Co.

Moss, P. (1994). Defining Quality: Values, stakeholders and processes. In P. Moss & A. Pence (Eds.), *Valuing quality in early childhood services: New approaches to defining quality* (pp. 1–9). New York: Teachers College Press.

Mrazek, P. (1993). Maltreatment and infant development. In C. H. Zeanah (Ed.), *Handbook of Infant Mental Health* (pp. 159–170). New York: The Guilford Press.

Mulroy, E. (1988). *Women as single parents: Confronting institutional barriers in the courts, the workplace, and the housing market.* Dover, MA: Auburn House Pub. Co.

Nath, P. S., Borkowski, J. G., & Schellenbach, C. J. (1991). Understanding adolescent parenting: The dimensions and functions of social support. *Family Relations, 40,* 11–420.

National Association for the Education of Young Children. (1985). Turnover in family day care. Child Care Information Service, *Young Children, 40*(5), 40–41.

National Association for the Education of Young Children. (1992). NAEYC Governing board reaffirms commitment to addressing inadequate compensation in early childhood programs. *Young Children, 47*(5), 43–44.

National Association for the Education of Young Children. (1994). NAEYC position statement: A conceptual framework for early childhood professional development, *Young Children, 49*(3), 68–77.

National Association for the Education of Young Children. (1995a). *Guidelines for preparation of early childhood professionals: Associate, baccalaureate, and advanced levels: Position State of the National Association for the Education of Young Children.* Washington, DC: Author.

National Association for the Education of Young Children. (1995b). Welfare reform—Preparing for the debate. *Young Children, 50*(2), 63–66.

National Association for the Education of Young Children. (1995c). Reaffirming a national commitment to children. *Young Children, 50*(3), 61–63.

National Association for the Education of Young Children. (1996). The national television violence study: Key findings and recommendations. *Young Children, 51*(3), 54–55.

National Center for Children in Poverty. (1995, Winter/Spring). Number of poor children under six increased from 5 to 6 million 1987–1992. *News and Issues 5*(1) 1–2.

National Center for Clinical Infant Programs. (1991). *Diagnostic classification study manual.* Arlington, VA: Author.

National Center for Education in Maternal and Child Health. (1991). *Understanding DNA testing: A basic guide for families.* Washington, DC: U.S. Department of Health and Human Services.

National Household Survey profile of preschool children's care and early education program participation, National Center for Education Statistics, (1993). Washington, DC: U.S. Department of Education, Office of Educational Research and Improvement, National Center for Education Statistics.

National Center for Health Statistics. (1976). *Monthly vital statistics report: Health examination survey data. 25,* 3 (supplement), 1–22.

National Coalition Against Domestic Violence (1994). Pamphlet Materials.

National Committee to Prevent Child Abuse (1993). *Current trends in child abuse reporting and fatalities: The results of the 1993 annual fifty state survey.* Chicago, IL: Author.

Neisworth, J., & Bagnato, S. (1987). *The young exceptional child: Early development and education.* New York: Macmillan Publishing Company.

Nelson, K. (1973). Structure and strategy in learning to talk. *Monographs of the Society for Research in Child Development, 38,* Serial No. 149.

Nelson, L. B., Calhoun, J. H., & Harley, R. D. (1991). *Pediatric ophthalmology (3rd ed.). Philadelphia: W. B. Saunders.*

Neugebauer, R. (1992). Child care 2000: Five trends shaping the future for early childhood centers. In B. Spodek, & O. N. Saracho (Eds.), *Issues in child care* (pp. 1–8). New York: Teachers College Press.

Newborg, J., Stock, J., Wnek, L., Guidubaldi, J., & Svinicki, J. (1984). *Battelle Developmental Inventory.* Allen, TX: DLM Teaching Resources.

Noonan, M. J., & McCormick, L. (1993). *Early intervention in natural environments: Methods and Procedures.* Pacific Grove, CA: Brooks/Cole Publishing Co.

Nugent, J. K. (1994). Cross-cultural studies of child development: Implications for clinicians. *Zero to Three 15*(2), 1–8.

Olson, D., McCubbin, H., Barnes, H., Larsen, S., Muxen, M., Wilson, M. (1983). *Families: What makes them work.* Beverly Hills, CA: Sage.

Olson, D., Portner, J., & Levee, Y. (1985). *FACES III.* Family Social Science, St. Paul, MN: University of Minnesota.

Olson, R. A., Huszti, H. C., Mason, P. J., & Seibert, J. M. (1989). Pediatric AIDS/HIV infection: An emerging challenge to pediatric psychology. *Journal of Pediatric Psychology, 14,* 1–21.

Osgood, C. E. (1968). Toward a wedding of insufficiencies. In T. R. Dixon & D. L. Horton (Eds.), *Verbal behavior and general behavior theory.* (pp. 27–56) Englewood Cliffs, NJ: Prentice-Hall, 262

Osofsky, J. D. (1993/1994). Introduction. In J. D. Osofsky & E. Fenichel (Eds.), Hurt, healing, hope: Caring for infants and toddlers in violent environments. *Zero to Three, 14*(3) 3–6.

Osofsky, J. D., (1993). *Violence in the lives of young children.* Position paper for the Carnegie Corporation Task Force on Meeting the Needs of Young Children. New York: Carnegie Corporation.

Osofsky, J. D., & Jackson, B. R. (1993/1994) Parenting in violent environments. In J. D. Osofsky & E. Fenichel (Eds.) Hurt, healing, hope: Caring for infants and toddlers in violent environments. *Zero to Three, 14*(3) 8–12.

Palfrey, J. S., Singer, J. D., Walker, D. K., & Butler, J. A. (1987). Early identification of children's special needs: A study in five metropolitan communities. *Journal of Pediatrics,* 651–659.

Palkovitz, R. (1982). Fathers' birth attendance, early extended contact and father–infant interaction at five months postpartum. *Birth: Issues in Perinatal Care, 9,* 173–177.

Palkovitz, R (1992). Changes in father–infant bonding beliefs across couple's first transition to parenthood. *Maternal Child Nursing Journal, 4,* 141– 154.

Palkovitz, R. (in press). The recovery of fatherhood? In A. Carr & M S. Lan Leeuwen (Eds.), *Religion, feminism and the family.* New York: John Knox/Westminister Press.

Parten, M. B. (1932). Social participation among preschool children. *Journal of Abnormal Psychology, 27,* 243–269.

Pastorek II, J. G. (1994). Viral Diseases. In D. K. James, P. J. Steer, C. P. Weiner, & B. Gonik (Eds.), *High risk pregnancy: Management options* (pp. 481–508). London: W. B. Saunders.

Pawl, J. H. (1992). Infants in day care: Reflections on experiences, expectations and relationships. In S. Provence, J. Pawl & E. Fenichel (Eds.), *The zero to three child care anthology 1984–1992* (pp. 7–13). Arlington, VA: National Center for Clinical Infant Studies.

Penn, Z. H., & Steer, P. J. (1994). Breech presentation. In D. K. James, P. J. Steer, C. P. Weiner, & B. Gonik (Eds.), *High risk pregnancy: Management options* (pp. 173–199). London: W. B. Saunders.

Peters, D. L., & Kontos, S. (1987). Continuity and discontinuity of experience: An intervention perspective. In D. L. Peters & S. Kontos (Eds.), *Continuity and discontinuity of experience in child care.* Norwood, NJ: Ablex Publishing Corporation.

Peterson, N. L. (1987). *Early intervention for handicapped and at–risk children: An introduction to early childhood special education.* Denver, CO: Love Publishing Co.

Petite, L. A., & Marentelle, P. (1991, March). Babbling in the manual mode: Evidence of ontogeny of language. *Science, 251,* 2493–2495.

Phillips, C. B. (1990). The child development associate program: Entering a new era. *Young Children, 45*(3), 24–26.

Phillips, D., & Howes, C. (1987). Indicators of quality in child care: Review of research. In *Quality in child care: What does the research tell us?* Washington, DC: National Association for the Education of Young Children.

Piaget, J. (1952/1936). *The origins of intelligence.* New York: Basic.

Piaget, J. (1954/1937). *The construction of reality in the child.* New York: Basic.

Piaget, J. (1962/1945). *Play, dreams and imitation in childhood.* New York: Norton.

Piaget, J. (1963/1952). *The origins of intelligence in children.* New York: Norton.

Piaget, J. (1970). Piaget's theory. In P. H. Mussen (Ed.), *Carmichael's manual of child psychology, Vol. 1.* (3rd ed., pp. 703–732). New York: John Wiley.

Pick, H. L. (1989). Motor development: The control of action. *Developmental Psychology, 25,* 867–870.

Pietrantoni, M., & Knuppel, R. A. (1991). Alcohol use in pregnancy. *Clinics in Perinatology, 18(1),* 93–111.

Pinneau, S. R. (1950). A critique on the articles by Margaret Ribble. *Child Development, 21,* 203–228.

Piotrkowski, C. S., & Hughes, D. (1993). Dual-earner families in context: Managing family and work systems. In F. Walsh (Ed.), *Normal family processes* (2nd ed., pp. 185 –207). New York: The Guilford Press.

Poisson, S. S., & DeGangi, G. A. (1992). *Emotional and sensory processing problems: Assessment and treatment approaches for young children and their families.* Rockville, MD: Reginald S. Lourie Center for Infants and Young Children.

Pope, S. K., Whiteside, L., Brooks-Gunn, J., Kelleher, K. J., Rickert, V. I., Bradley, R. H., & Casey, P. H. (1993). Low-birth-weight infants born to adolescent mothers: Effects of coresidency with grandmother on child development. *Journal of the American Medical Association, 269,* 1396–1400.

Population Reference Bureau for the Center for the Study of Social Policy. (1992). *The challenge of change: What the 1990 census tells us about children.* Washington, DC: Center for the Study of Social Policy.

Porter, R. H. (1991). Mutual mother–infant recognition in humans. In P. G. Hepper (Ed.), *Kin recognition* (pp. 413–432). Cambridge: Cambridge University Press.

Powell. D. R. (1989). *Families and early childhood programs.* Research monographs of the National Association for the Education of Young Children, Vol. 3 (1–143 entire issue). Washington, DC: NAEYC.

Powell, D. R. (1990). *Parent education and support programs.* ERIC Digest. Urbana, IL: Clearinghouse on Elementary and Early Childhood Education.

Pransky, J. (1991). *Prevention: The critical need.* Springfield, MO: Burrell Foundation.

Prechtl, H. F. R. (1965). Problems of behavioral studies in the newborn infant. In D. S. Lehrman, R. A. Hinde, & E. Shaw (Eds.), *Advances in the study of behavior* (pp. 75–96). New York: Academic Press.

Prechtl, H. F. R., & Beintema, D. H. (1964). The neurological examination of the full–term newborn infant. *Clinics in Developmental Pediatrics* (No. 12). London: Spastics Society with Heinemann.

Provence, S. (1992). Choosing child care for infants and toddlers: Look first at the caregiver. In S. Provence, J. Pawl, & E. Fenichel (Eds.), *The zero to three child care anthology 1984–1992* (pp. 14–16). Arlington, VA: National Center for Clinical Infant Studies.

Public Health Service Expert Panel on the Content of Prenatal Care. (1989). *Caring for Our Future: The Content of Prenatal Care.* Washington, DC: Public Health Service.

Pueschel, S. M., Scola, P. S., & McConnel, K. S. (1990). Infections during pregnancy. In S. M. Pueschel & J. A, Mulick (Eds.), *Prevention of Developmental Disabilities* (pp. 101–122). Baltimore, MD: Paul H. Brookes Publishing Co.

Putnam, F. W. (1991). Dissociative disorders in children and adolescents: A developmental perspective. *Psychiatric Clinics of North America, 14,* 519–531.

Putnam, F. W., & Trickett, P. K. (1993). Child sexual abuse: A model of chronic trauma. In D. Reiss, J. E. Richters, & M. Radke-Yarrow (Eds.), *Children and violence* (pp. 96–118). New York: The Guilford Press.

Ralabate, P. (1987). What teachers should know about middle ear dysfunction. *NEA Today,* 10.

Ramey, C. T., Brandt, D. M., Wasik, B. H., Sparling, J. J., Fendt, K. H., & LaVange, L. M. (1992). The Infant Health Development Program for low birth weight, premature infants: Program elements, family participation, and child intelligence. *Pediatrics, 89,* 4545–465.

Ramsey, P. A., & Fisk, N. M. (1994). Amniocentesis. In D. K. James, P. J. Steer, C. P. Weiner, & B. Gonik (Eds.), *High risk pregnancy: Management options* (pp. 735–744). London: W. B. Saunders.

Reinsberg, J. (1995). Reflections on quality infant care. *Young Children, 50*(6), 23–25.

Research and Policy Committee of the Committee for Economic Development. (1987). *Children in need: Investment strategies for the educationally disadvantaged.* New York: Committee for Economic Development.

Research and Policy Committee of the Committee for Economic Development. (1993). *Why child care matters: Preparing young children for a more productive America.* New York: Committee for Economic Development.

Ribble, M. A. (1944). Infantile experience in relation to personality development. In J. McV. Hunt (Ed.), *Personality and the behavior disorders* (pp. 621–651). New York: Ronald Press.

Ricciuti, H. N. (1992). Current and future directions in infant development research: Brief overview. In G. J. Suci & S. S. Robertson (Eds.), *Future Directions in Infant Development Research* (pp. 105–117). New York: Springer Verlag.

Rindfuss, R. R. & Bumpass, L. L. (1977). Fertility during marriage disruption. *Journal of Marriage and the Family, 39,* 517–528.

Riordan, J., & Auerbach, K. G. (1993). *Breast-feeding and human lactation.* Boston, MA: Jones and Bartlett Publishers, Inc.

Roberts, E. (1944). Thumb and finger sucking in relation to feeding in early infancy. *American Journal of Diseases of Children, 68,* 7–8.

Roberts, J. C., Mendez–Bauer, C., & Woodell, D. A. (1983). The effects of maternal position on uterine contractility and efficiency. *Birth, 10*(4), 243–249.

Rogers, C., & Morris, S. (1986). Reducing sugar in children's diets: Why? How? *Young Children, 41*(5), 11–19.

Rogoff, B. (1991). The joint socialization of development by young children and adults. In M. Lewis & S. Feinman (Eds.), *Social influences and socialization in infancy* (pp. 253–280). New York: Plenum Press.

Rose, S. A., Gottfried, A. W., & Bridger, W. H. (1981). Cross model transfer in 6–month–old infants. *Developmental Psychology, 25,* 871–884.

Rosenblith, J. F. (1992). *In the beginning: Development from conception to age two.* (2nd ed.). Newbury Park, CA: Sage Publications.

Ross, G., Lipper, E. G., & Auld, P. (1990). Social competence and behavior problems in premature children at school age. *Pediatrics, 86,* 391–397.

Rossetti, L. M. (1986). *High risk infants: Identification, assessment, and intervention.* London: Taylor & Francis.

Rounds, K. A., Weil, M., & Bishop, K. K. (1994). Practice with culturally diverse families of young children with disabilities. *Families in Society: The Journal of Contemporary Human Services, 38,* 3–12.

Rubin, K. H., & Howe, N. (1985). Toy and play behaviors: An overview. *Topics in Early Childhood Special Education, 5*(3), 1– 9.

Rutter, M. (1979). Protective factors in children's responses to stress and disadvantage. In M. W. Kent & J. A. Rolf (Eds.), *Primary prevention of psychopathology: Vol 3. Social competence in children.* Hanover, NH: University Press of New England.

Rutter, M. (1988). The role of cognition in child development and disorder. *Annual Progress in Child Psychiatry and Child Development, 21,* 77–101.

Salapatek, P. (1975). Pattern perception in early infancy. In L. B. Cohen & P. Salapatek (Eds.), *Infant perception from sensation to cognition: Basic visual processes.* New York: Academic Press.

Sameroff, A. J. (1993). Models of development and developmental risk. In C. H. Zeanah, Jr. (Ed.), *Handbook of infant mental health* (pp. 3–13). New York: The Guilford Press.

Sandler, D., Everson, R., Wilcox, B., & Browder, J. (1985). Cancer risk in adulthood from early life exposure to parents' smoking. *American Journal of Public Health, 75,* 487–492.

Schmitt, B. D., & Krugman, R. D. (1992). Abuse and neglect of children. In R. E. Behrman (Ed.), *Nelson Textbook of Pediatrics* (14th ed., pp. 78–83). Philadelphia: W. B. Saunders.

Schneider, J. W., & Chasnoff, I. J. (1987). Cocaine abuse during pregnancy: Its effects on infant motor development—A clinical perspective. *Top Acute Care Trauma Rehabilitation, 2*(1), 59–69.

Schubert, P. J., & Savage, B. (1994). Smoking, alcohol and drug abuse. In D. K. James, P. J. Steer, C. P. Weiner, & B. Gonik (Eds.), *High risk pregnancy: Management options* (pp. 783–801). London: W. B. Saunders.

Scott, K. G., Field, T., & Robertson, E. G. (1981). *Teenage parents and their offspring.* New York: Grune & Stratton, Inc.

Sears, R. R., Maccoby, E. E. & Levin, H. (1957). *Patterns of child rearing.* Evanston, IL: Row, Peterson.

Sears, R. R., Whiting, J., Nowlis, V., & Sears, P. (1953). Some child rearing antecedents of aggression and dependency in young children. *Genetic Psychological Monographs, 47,* 135–234.

Sedlak, A. J. (1991). *National incidence and prevalence of child abuse and neglect: 1988–Revised report.* Rockville, MD: Westat, Inc.

Seefeldt, C. (1985, November/December). Parent involvement: Support or stress. *Childhood Education,* 98–102.

Segal, J., & Segal, Z. (1992). Living with an autistic child. *Parents, 67,* 88–93.

Seitz, V., Rosenbaum, L. K., & Apfel, N. H. (1985). Effects of family support intervention: A ten year follow–up. *Child Development, 56*(2), 528–539.

Semmler, C. (1989a). Introduction. In C. Semmler (Ed.), *A guide to care and management of very low birth weight infants: A team approach* (pp. 1–7). Tucson, AZ: Therapy Skill Builders.

Semmler, C. (1989b). Intracranial hemorrhage. In C. Semmler (Ed.), *A guide to care and management of very low birth weight infants: A team approach* (pp. 77–98). Tucson, AZ: Therapy Skill Builders.

Shea, T. M., & Bauer, A. M. (1991). *Parents and teachers of children with exceptionalities: A handbook for collaboration* (2nd ed.). Boston, MA: Allyn and Bacon.

Shelov, S. P. (Ed.). (1993). *Caring for your baby and young child: Birth to age 5.* New York: Bantam Books.

Shirk, S. R. (1988). The interpersonal legacy of physical abuse of children. In M. B. Straus (Ed.), *Abuse and victimization across the life span* (pp. 57–81). Baltimore, MD: Johns Hopkins University Press.

Shirley, M. M. (1931). *The first two years. A study of twenty–five babies. Vol I. Postural and loco-motor development.* Minneapolis: University of Minnesota Press.

Shirley, M. M. (1933). *The first two years. A study of twenty–five babies. Vol II. Intellectual development.* Minneapolis: University of Minnesota Press.

Shuster, C. K., Finn-Stevenson, M., & Ward, P. (1992). Family day care support systems: An emerging infrastructure. *Young Children, 47*(5), 29–35.

Silverstein, C. (Ed.) (1991). *Gays, lesbians, and their therapists: Studies in psychotherapy.* New York: W. W. Norton & Company.

Simon, H. A. (1981). *The sciences of the artificial.* (2nd ed, revised and enlarged), Cambridge, MA: MIT Press.

Sinclair, H., Stambak, M., Lexine, I., Rayne, S., & Verba, M. (1989). *Infants and objects: The creativity of cognitive development.* San Diego, CA: Academic Press, Inc.

Skinner, B. F. (1969). *Contingencies of reinforcement: A theoretical analysis.* Englewood Cliffs, NJ: Prentice-Hall.

Smilansky, S. (1968). *The effects of socio-dramatic play on disadvantaged preschool children.* New York: Wiley.

Smilansky, S., & Shefatya, L. (1990). *Facilitating play: A medium for promoting cognitive, socio-emotional, and academic development in young children.* Gaithersburg, MD: Psychosocial & Educational Publications.

Smith, B. (1995). DEC issues early childhood special education personnel standards. *Communicator, 21*(3), 3.

Smith, J. K. (1990). Questions of measurement in early childhood. In E. D. Gibbs & D. M. Teti (Eds.), *Interdisciplinary assessment of infants: A guide for early intervention professionals* (pp. 3–14). Baltimore, MD: Paul H. Brookes Publishing Co.

Soderman, A. (1985). Dealing with difficult young children: Strategies of teachers and parents. *Young Children, 40*(5), 15–20.

Solter, A. (1992). Understanding tears and tantrums. *Young Children, 47*(4), 64–68.

Soto, L. D. (1991). Understanding bilingual/bicultural young children. *Young Children, 46,* 2, 30–36.

Sparrow, S., Balla, D., & Cicchetti, D. (1984). *The Vineland Adaptive Behavior Scales.* Circle Pines, MN: American Guidance Service.

Spelke, E. S. (1991). Physical knowledge in infancy: Reflections on Piaget's theory. In S. Carey & R. Gelman (Eds.) *The epigenesis of mind: Essays on biology and cognition.* Hillsdale, NJ: Erlbaum.

Spelke, E. S. , Breinlinger, K., Macomber, J., & Jacobson, K. (1992). Origins of knowledge. *Psychological Review, 99,* 605–632.

Spitz, R. A. (1945). Hospitalism: An inquiry into the genesis of psychiatric conditions in early childhood. *The Psychoanalytic Study of the Child, 1,* 53–74.

Spitz, R. A. (1946). Hospitalism: A follow-up report on investigation described in volume I. *The Psychoanalytic Study of the Child, 2,* 113–117.

Spodek, B., & Saracho, O. N. (1992). Child Care: A look to the future. In B. Spodek, & O. N. Saracho (Eds.), *Issues in child care* (pp. 187–198). New York: Teachers College Press.

Spodek, B., Saracho, O. N., & Peters, D. L. (1988). Professionalism, semiprofessionalism and craftsmanship. In B. Spodek, O. Saracho & D. L. Peters (Eds.), *Professionalism and the early childhood practitioner* (pp. 3–9). New York: Teachers College Press.

Spohr, H., Williams, J., & Steinhausen, H. (1993, April, 10). Prenatal alcohol exposure and long-term developmental consequences. *The Lancet,* 907–910.

Stark, E., & Flitcraft, A. H. (1991). Abuse and neglect of children. In M. L. Rosenberg & M. A. Fenley (Eds.), *Violence in America* (pp. 123–157). New York: Oxford.

Stark, R. (1986). Prespeech segmental feature development. In P. Fletcher & M. Garman (Eds.), *Language Acquisition*, (2nd ed. pp. 149–173). New York: Cambridge University Press.

Starrels, M. E. (1994). Gender differences in parent–child relations. *Journal of Family Issues, 15*, 148–165.

Steer, P. J., & Danielian, P. J. (1994). Fetal distress in labor. In D. K. James, P. J. Steer, C. P. Weiner, & B. Gonik (Eds.), *High risk pregnancy: Management options* (pp. 1077–1100). London: W. B. Saunders.

Steinberg, L., & Meyer, R. (1995). *Childhood.* New York: McGraw-Hill, Inc.

Stenchever, M. A., & Sorenson, T. (1993). *Management of the patient in labor.* St. Louis, MI: Mosby.

Still, D. K. (1994a). Postpartum hemorrhage and other problems of the third stage. In D. K. James, P. J. Steer, C. P. Weiner, & B. Gonik (Eds.), *High risk pregnancy: Management options* (pp. 1167–1181). London: W. B. Saunders.

Still, D. K. (1994b). Puerperal problems. In D. K. James, P. J. Steer, C. P. Weiner & B. Gonik (Eds.), *High risk pregnancy: Management options* (pp. 1183–1191). London: W. B. Saunders.

Straus, M. A., Gelles, R., & Steinmetz, S. K. (1980). *Behind closed doors: Violence in the American family.* Garden City, NY: Anchor Press.

Streri, A., & Molina, M. (1994). Constraints on intermodal transfer between touch and vision in infancy. In D. J. Lewkowicz & R. Lickliter (Eds.). *The development of intersensory perception: Comparative perspectives* (pp. 285–308). Hillsdale, NJ: Lawrence Erlbaum Associates, Publishers.

Streri, A., Molina, M., & Rameix, E. (1993). Specific and amodal mechanisms of object perception and exploration in infancy: The case of touch. *Cognition, 67*, 251–279.

St. James-Roberts, I., & Halil, T. (1991). Infant crying patterns in the first year. *Journal of Child Psychology and Psychiatry, 32*, 951–968.

Svigos, J. M., Robinson, J. S., & Vigneswaran, R. (1994). Premature rupture of the membranes. In D. K. James, P. J. Steer, C. P. Weiner, & B. Gonik (Eds.), *High risk pregnancy: Management options* (pp. 163–172). London: W. B. Saunders.

Tager–Flusberg, H. (1994). Language development. In M. Rutter & D. H. Hay (Eds.), *Development through life: A handbook for clinicians* (pp. 212–238). London: Blackwell Scientific Publications.

Task Force for Prevention of Developmental Handicaps—1991 update. (1991). *Florida's children: Their future is in our hands. Preventing and minimizing disabilities: A focus on the first 60 months of life.* Tallahassee, FL: Developmental Disabilities Planning Council.

Teti, D. M., & Gibbs, E. D. (1990). Infant assessment: Historical antecedents and contemporary issues. In E. D. Gibbs & D. M. Teti (Eds.), *Interdisciplinary assessment of infants: A guide for early intervention professionals* (pp. 3–14). Baltimore, MD: Paul H. Brookes Publishing Co.

Thal, D., & Bates, E. (1990). Continuity and Variation in Early Language Development. In J. Colombo & J. Fegen (Eds.), *Individual differences in infancy: Reliability, stability, prediction.* Hillsdale, NJ: Lawrence Erlbaum Associates, Publishers.

Thal, D., Tobias, S., & Morrison, D. (1991). Language and gesture in late talkers: A 1-year follow-up. *Journal of Speech and Hearing Research, 34*(3) 604–612.

Thatcher, R. W. (1994). Psychopathology of early frontal lobe damage: Dependence on cycles of development. *Development and Psychopathology, 6*, 565–596.

Theilheimer, R. (1994). Not telling young parents how to raise their children: Dilemmas of caregivers and parent group leaders at a program for out-of-school youth and their babies. *Zero to Three, 14*(4), 1–6.

Thomas, A., Chess, S., & Birch, C. (1968). *Temperament and behavior disorders in children.* New York: New York University Press.

Thompson, W. R., & Grusec, J. E. (1970). Studies of early experience. In P. H. Mussen (Ed.), *Carmichael's manual of child psychology* (3rd ed., pp. 565–654). New York: John Wiley & Sons, Inc.

Thompson, T., & Hupp, S. (Eds.). (1992). *Saving children at risk.* Newbury Park: Sage Publications, Inc.

Tirosh, E., & Scher, A. (1993). Neonatal behavior: Physiological, temperamental, and developmental correlates in infancy. In N. J. Anastasiow & S. Harel (Eds.), *At–risk infants: Interventions, families and research* (pp. 137–144). Baltimore, MD: Paul H. Brookes.

Trad, P. V. (1994). Previewing as a remedy for interpersonal failure in the parent–infant dyad. *Infants and Young Children, 7*(1), 1–13.

Trawick-Smith, J. (1991). The significance of toddler pretend play in child care. *Early Child Development and Care, 68, 11–18.*

Trawick-Smith, J., & Lambert, L. (1995). The unique challenges of the family child care provider: Implications for professional development. *Young Children, 50*(3), 25–32.

Trickett, P. K., & Kucznski, L. (1986). Children's misbehaviors and parental discipline strategies in abusive and nonabusive families. *Developmental Psychology, 22*(1), 115–123.

Turnbull, A. P., & Turnbull, H. R. (1990). *Families, professions, and exceptionality: A special partnership.* Columbus, OH: Merrill Publishing Company.

Turner, G. (1994). Prepregnancy education. In D. K. James, P. J. Steer, C. P. Weiner, & B. Gonik (Eds.), *High risk pregnancy: Management options* (pp. 1–8). London: W. B. Saunders.

U.S. Bureau of the Census (1990). *Current population reports.* P–20, No. 454. Washington, DC: Author.

U.S. Bureau of the Census. (1991). *Statistical Abstracts of the United States.* Washington, DC: Author.

U.S. Bureau of the Census. (1991). Child support and alimony: 1989. *Current Population Reports, Series P–60, No. 173.* Washington, DC: U.S. Government Printing Office.

U.S. Bureau of the Census. (1992). Marriage, divorce, and remarriage in the 1990s. *Current Population Reports P–23, No. 180.* Washington, DC: U.S. Government Printing Office.

U.S. Bureau of the Census. (1992). Studies in the distribution of income. *Current Population Reports, Series P–60, No. 183.* Washington, DC: U.S. Government Printing Office.

U. S. Bureau of the Census, *Statistical Abstracts of the United States: 1995* (115th edition). Washington, DC: Author.

U.S. Department of Health, Education, and Welfare. (1972). *Day care: Serving children with special needs.* (DHEW Publication No. (OCD) 73-1063). Washington, DC: Office of Child Development.

U.S. Department of Health and Human Services, Public Health Service, National Institutes of Health. (1995). *The human genome project: From maps to medicine.* National Center for Human Genome Research, Bethesda MD: NIH Publication No. 95-3897.

U. S. Department of Health and Human Services (1992). Maternal drug abuse and drug exposed children: Understanding the problem, DHHS publication No. (ADM) 92–1949.

U.S. General Accounting Office. (1994). *Child care: Working poor and welfare recipients face service gaps.* Washington, DC: Author.

VanRy, M. (1993). *Homeless Families: Causes, effects and recommendations.* New York: Garland.

van der Boon, D. (1990). Preventive intervention and the quality of mother-infant interaction and infant exploration in irritable infants. In W. Koops, et al. (Eds.), *Developmental psychology behind the dikes* (pp. 249–270). Amsterdam: Eburon.

VanTuinen, I., & Wolfe, S. M. (1992). *Unnecessary cesarean sections: Halting a national epidemic.* Public Citizen's Health Research Group.

Violence Study Group. (1993/1994). Call for violence prevention and intervention on behalf of very young children. In J. D. Osofsky & E. Fenichel (Eds.), Hurt, healing, hope: Caring for infants and toddlers in violent environments. *Zero to Three, 14*(3), 38–41.

Visher, E. B., & Visher, J. S. (1993). Remarriage families and stepparenting. In F. Walsh (Ed.), *Normal family processes* (2nd ed., pp. 235 –253). New York: The Guilford Press.

Volling, B., & Belsky, J. (1992). The contribution of mother-child and father-child relationships to the quality of sibling relationships. *Child Development, 63,* 1209–1222.

von Bertalanffy, L. (1950). An outline of general system theory. *British Journal of the Philosophy of Science, 1,* 134–165.

Vygotsky, L. S. (1962). *Thought and language.* Boston, MA: MIT Press.

Vygotsky, L. S. (1986/1934). *Thought and language.* Cambridge, MA: MIT Press.

Vygotsky, L. S. (1978/1933). *Mind in society: The development of higher psychological processes.* Cambridge, MA: Harvard University Press.

Vygotsky, L. S (1987/1934). Thinking and speech. In R. Rieber & A. S. Carton (Eds.), *The collected works of L. S. Vygotsky: Vol. 1. Problems of general psychology* (N. Minick, Trans.; pp. 37–285). New York: Plenum.

Wallerstein, J. S., & Blakeslee, S. (1989). *Second changes: Men, women, and children. A decade after divorce.* New York: Trenor and Fields.

Wallis, C. (1985, February 4). Chlamydia: The silent epidemic. *Time,* p. 67.

Walsh, F. (1989). Reconsidering gender in the marital quid pro quo. In M. McGoldrick, C. Anderson, & F. Walsh (Eds.), *Women in families* (pp. 267–285). New York: Norton.

Warren, K. (1985). Alcohol-related birth defects: Current trends in research. *Alcohol World: Health and Research, 10*(1), 4–5.

Warren, M. P. (1989). The auditory brainstem response in pediatrics. *Otolaryngologic Clinics of North America, 22,* 473–500.

Watson, J. B. (1924). *Behaviorism.* New York: Norton.

Watson, J. B. (1928). *Psychological care of the infant and child.* New York: Norton.

Watson, R. R. (Ed.), (1995). *Substance abuse during pregnancy and childhood: Drug and alcohol abuse reviews: Vol 8.* (pp. 1–11). Totowa, NJ: Humana Press.

Weil, J. L. (1992). *Early deprivation of empathic care.* Madison, CN: Internal Universities Press.

Weiner, C. P. (1994). Fetal hemolytic disease. In D. K. James, P. J. Steer, C. P. Weiner, & B. Gonik (Eds.), *High risk pregnancy: Management options* (pp. 783–801). London: W. B. Saunders.

Wheeler, C. (1995). Labor: Normal and dysfunctional. In D. R. Coustan (Ed.), *Human Reproduction: Growth and Development* (pp. 291–306). Boston, MA: Little Brown and Company.

Whitebook, M., Howes, C., & Phillips, D. (1990). *Who cares? Child care teachers and the quality of care in America.* Final report of the national child care staffing study. Oakland, CA: Child Care Employee Project.

Whitehead, L. C. (1989). Cohesion and communication between families and day care: A proposed model. *Child and Youth Care Quarterly, 17,* 255–267.

Whitehead, L. C. (1989) Adult supported learning. In P. L. Deiner, L. C. Whitehead, & C. M. Prudhoe (Eds.), *Information sheets for day care providers and families of children with special needs.* Technical Assistance Manual prepared for the DOE, HCEEP (Grant #G008630267) and the Delaware Department of Public Instruction (Grant # 88-02-23-02).

Whiteside, M. F. (1989). Remarried Systems. In L. Combrinck–Graham (Ed.), *Children in family contexts: Perspectives on treatment* (pp. 135–160). New York: The Guilford Press.

Widerstrom, A. H., Mowder, B. A., & Sandall, S. R. (1991). *At-risk and handicapped newborns and infants: Development, assessment, and intervention.* Englewood Cliffs, NJ: Prentice-Hall.

Wildschut, H. I. (1994). Maternal weight and weight gain. In D. K. James, P. J. Steer, C. P. Weiner, & B. Gonik (Eds.), *High risk pregnancy: Management options* (pp. 67–74). London: W. B. Saunders.

Willer, B. (1991). *The demand and supply of child care in 1990.* Washington, DC: National Association for the Education of Young Children.

Williams, L. B., & Pratt, W. F. (1990). Wanted and unwanted childbearing in the United States: 1973–1988. *Data from the National Survey of Family Growth. Advance Data from Vital and Health Statistics.* No. 189. Hyattsville, MD: National Center for Health Statistics.

Williamson, R. A. (1994). Abnormalities of alpha-fetoprotein and other biochemical tests. In D. K. James, P. J. Steer, C. P. Weiner, & B. Gonik (Eds.), *High risk pregnancy: Management options* (pp. 643–660). London: W. B. Saunders.

Wilson, L. C. (1990). *Infants and toddlers: Curriculum and teaching* (2nd ed.). Albany, NY: Delmar Publishers Inc.

Winkleby, M. A., & Boyce, T. (1994). Health-related risk factors of homeless families and single adults. *Journal of Community Health, 19*(1), 7–18.

Wittmer, D. S. & Honig, A. S. (1994). Encouraging positive social development in young children. *Young Children, 49*(5), 4–12.

Wolery, M., Holcombe, A., Venn, M. L., Brookfield, J., Huffman, K., Schroeder, C., Martin, C. G., & Fleming, L. A. (1993). Mainstreaming in early childhood programs: Current status and relevant issues, *Young Children, 49(1), 78–84.*

Wolfe, D., & Mosk, M. (1983). Behavioral comparisons of children from abusive and distressed families. *Journal of Consulting and Clinical Psychology, 51,* 702–708.

Wolff, P. H. (1966). The causes, controls, and organization of behavior in the neonate. *Psychological Issues, 5,* (Whole No. 7).

Worobey, J., & Brazelton, T. B. (1990). Newborn assessment and support for parenting: The neonatal behavioral assessment scale. In E. D. Gibbs & D. M. Teti (Eds.), *Interdisciplinary assessment of infants: A guide for early intervention professionals.* Baltimore, MD. Paul H. Brookes.

Yonas, A., & Granrud, C. E. (1985). Development of visual space perception. In J. Mehler & R. Fox (Eds.), *Neonate cognition: Beyond the blooming buzzing confusion* (pp. 45–68). Hillsdale, NJ: Lawrence Erlbaum Associates, Publishers.

Yonas, A., & Owsley C. (1987). Development of visual space perception. In P. Salapatek & L. B. Cohen (Eds.), *Handbook of infant perception.* New York: Academic Press.

Zahn-Waxler, C. (1995). Introduction to special section: Parental depression and distress: Implications for development in infancy, childhood, and adolescence. *Developmental Psychology, 31*(3), 347–348.

Zambone, A. M. (1995). Serving the young child with visual impairments: An overview of disability impact and intervention needs. In J. A. Blackman (Ed.), *Treatment options in early intervention. Infants and Young Children Series* (pp. 51–67). Gaithersburg, MD: An Aspen Publication.

Zilbach, J. J. (1986). *Young children in family therapy.* New York: Brunner/Mazel.

Zilbach, J. J. (1989). The family life cycle: A framework for understanding children in family therapy. In L. Combrinck–Graham (Ed.), *Children in family contexts: Perspectives on treatment* (pp. 46–66). New York: The Guilford Press.

Zimmerman, I., Steiner, V., & Evatt, R. (1979). *Preschool language scale.* Columbus OH: Chas. E. Merrill.

Zuravin, S. J. (1987). Unplanned pregnancies, family planning problems and child maltreatment. *Family Relations, 36,* 36–139.

Author Index

Subject Index